OXFORD STUDIES IN EUROPEAN LAW

Series Editors

PAUL CRAIG

Professor of English Law at St John's College, Oxford

GRÁINNE DE BÚRCA

Professor of Law at New York University School of Law

National Parliaments After the Lisbon Treaty and the Euro Crisis

OXFORD STUDIES IN EUROPEAN LAW

Series Editors: Paul Craig, Professor of English Law at St John's College, Oxford and

Gráinne de Búrca, Professor of Law at New York University School of Law

The aim of this series is to publish important and original research on EU law. The focus is on scholarly monographs, with a particular emphasis on those which are interdisciplinary in nature. Edited collections of essays will also be included where they are appropriate. The series is wide in scope and aims to cover studies of particular areas of substantive and of institutional law, historical works, theoretical studies, and analyses of current debates, as well as questions of perennial interest such as the relationship between national and EU law and the novel forms of governance emerging in and beyond Europe. The fact that many of the works are interdisciplinary will make the series of interest to all those concerned with the governance and operation of the EU.

Other titles in this series

Environmental Integration in Competition and Free-Movement Laws
Julian Nowag

EU Agencies
Legal and Political Limits to the Transformation of the EU Administration
Merijn Chamon

Coherence in EU Competition Law
Wolf Sauter

Foreign Policy Objectives in European Constitutional Law
Joris Larik

Economic Governance in Europe
Comparative Paradoxes and Constitutional Challenges
Federico Fabbrini

Private Regulation and the Internal Market
Sports, Legal Services, and Standard Setting in EU Economic Law
Mislav Mataija

The EU Deep Trade Agenda
Law and Policy
Billy A. Melo Araujo

The Human Rights of Migrants and Refugees in European Law
Cathryn Costello

An Ever More Powerful Court?
The Political Constraints of Legal Integration in the European Union
Dorte Sindbjerg Martinsen

The Concept of State Aid under EU Law
From internal market to competition and beyond
Juan Jorge Piernas López

Justice in the EU
The Emergence of Transnational Solidarity
Floris de Witte

The Euro Area Crisis in Constitutional Perspective
Alicia Hinarejos

The European Fundamental Freedoms
A Contextual Approach
Pedro Caro de Sousa

National Parliaments After the Lisbon Treaty and the Euro Crisis

Resilience or Resignation?

Edited by
DAVOR JANČIĆ
Lecturer in Law, Queen Mary University of London

OXFORD
UNIVERSITY PRESS

OXFORD
UNIVERSITY PRESS

Great Clarendon Street, Oxford, OX2 6DP,
United Kingdom

Oxford University Press is a department of the University of Oxford.
It furthers the University's objective of excellence in research, scholarship,
and education by publishing worldwide. Oxford is a registered trade mark of
Oxford University Press in the UK and in certain other countries

First Edition published in 2017

Impression: 1

Published in the United States of America by Oxford University Press
198 Madison Avenue, New York, NY 10016, United States of America

British Library Cataloguing in Publication Data
Data available

Library of Congress Control Number: 2017930568

ISBN 978–0–19–879162–1

Printed and bound by
CPI Group (UK) Ltd, Croydon, CR0 4YY

Preface

At a time when the position, legitimacy and even the continued existence of the European Union has been seriously questioned, and the EU confronts a range of daunting challenges, a book which examines the role of national parliaments is to be welcomed. After all, one of the reasons often suggested for the lack of popular support for the EU is the remoteness of the Brussels institutions from national political institutions and from daily life in the member states. More substantial involvement by national parliaments in the workings of the EU has often been proposed as one possible avenue for addressing the EU's democratic legitimacy deficit, enhancing its domestic connectedness and improving the representative nature of its decision-making.

This book adds to the burgeoning literature on national parliaments by focusing on the changed role of national parliaments within the EU after the coming into force of the Lisbon Treaty. The book gives particular attention to the question of how national parliaments have responded to the increased centralization and intergovernmentalism of the EU's functioning in the wake of the Euro crisis.

The editor and contributors have taken the view that ex-ante involvement by national parliaments in EU law and policy making is more significant than ex-post involvement, and the various chapters in the book emphasize the importance of the representative function of national parliaments, as well as their capacity to express aspects of national identity.

The different sections of the book contain a range of detailed and interesting contributions dealing with topics including the contribution of national parliamentary activity to the democratic legitimacy of the EU, the various ways in which the financial crisis and the EU's response to it have affected national parliaments, the subsidiarity mechanism and the range of ways in which national parliaments interact and cooperate with one another across the EU. The contributors include academics from various disciplinary backgrounds and policy-makers with insights into different aspects of the functioning of national parliaments.

This is a timely and welcome book which should be of interest to all students and scholars of the law and politics of the European Union.

Gráinne de Búrca
Paul Craig

Acknowledgements

The role of national parliaments in the European Union is one of the most topical institutional issues of European integration and democracy. This is because, despite recurring amendments of the EU founding treaties and incremental Europeanization of national parliaments in terms of adapting to the exigencies of EU policy-making, their role remains in the constitutional shadow of executive actors and courts. Taking them out of this shadow by incorporating them into the EU's institutional spectrum in a way that creates a stronger linkage between the citizens and EU decision-making processes remains a puzzle and an object of disagreement in both academia and political practice.

This raises important theoretical questions related to the concepts of constitutionalism and democratic legitimacy. The outbreak of the sovereign debt crisis in the Eurozone has engendered a new context in which parliaments have had to calibrate their functions afresh. A rapidly developing network of relations between national parliaments themselves, as well as between them and the European Parliament and the European Commission has been a constantly evolving dynamic of EU development. This edited volume addresses these three issues in greater depth in a manner that will appeal to both scholars and policy-makers.

The book is based on the LSE and British Academy conference that the editor organized together with Prof. Damian Chalmers on 10 April 2015 at the LSE Department of Law. The event took stock of the evolution of the functions of national parliaments in the contemporary EU. The conference was funded by the British Academy's Newton International Fellowship scheme in cooperation with the LSE and marked the completion of the editor's two-year post-doctoral tenure at the LSE.

I am therefore indebted to the British Academy, the LSE Law Department, and Prof. Chalmers personally, for their generous financial, academic, and logistical support in organizing this conference, without which this book would not have been possible. I would also like to thank the speakers at the conference, who have contributed chapters to this book, and to all the participants. Their diverse disciplinary background and inquisitive minds have enriched the debate and greatly helped to develop ideas for the contents of the book. Despite being an EU law volume, legal scholars have joined forces with political scientists to provide interdisciplinary insights into a topic that is inevitably of appeal to both disciplines.

I am also very grateful to the TMC Asser Instituut from The Hague for their institutional support and for creating a congenial atmosphere in which I was able to work on this book.

Perhaps most of all, I am thankful to all the contributors for their cooperation, effort, and commitment and for putting up with my numerous comments and requests in the process of producing this volume. I hope our collaboration will yield new knowledge, provoke further research projects, and solidify our contribution to analyzing and strengthening EU democracy in this turbulent period of European integration.

The manuscript was sent to production on 28 August 2016.

London, 12 September 2016
Dr Davor Jančić
Lecturer in Law, Queen Mary University of London

Contents

List of Abbreviations

ACTA	Anti-Counterfeiting Trade Agreement
AFCO	Committee on Constitutional Affairs (in the European Parliament)
AFET	Committee on Foreign Affairs (in the European Parliament)
AMR	Alert Mechanism Report
BL	Basic Law
BVerfG	Bundesverfassungsgericht (German Federal Constitutional Court)
BZÖ	Bündnis Zukunft Österreich (Alliance for the Future of Austria)
CAP	Common Agricultural Policy
CBO	Congressional Budget Office
CDU/CSU	Christlich Demokratische Union Deutschlands/Christlich Soziale Union (Christian Democrats)
CETA	Comprehensive Economic and Trade Agreement (EU-Canada)
CFSP	Common Foreign and Security Policy
CJEU	Court of Justice of the European Union
CODACC	Conference of Defence Affairs Committee Chairpersons
CoE	Council of Europe
COFACC	Conference of Foreign Affairs Committee Chairpersons
COSAC	Conference of Parliamentary Committees for Union Affairs of Parliaments of the European Union
CSDP	Common Security and Defence Policy
DATA	Digital Accountability and Transparency Act
DROI	Sub-Committee on Human Rights (in the European Parliament)
EAC	European Affairs Committee
ECA	European Communities Act
ECB	European Central Bank
ECI	European Citizens' Initiative
ECJ	European Court of Justice
ECON	Committee on Economic and Monetary Affairs (in the European Parliament)
EDA	European Defence Agency
EEAS	European External Action Service
EELV	Europe Ecologie – Les Verts (Europe Ecology – The Greens)
EFSF	European Financial Stability Facility
EIDHR	European Instrument for Democracy and Human Rights
EMU	Economic and Monetary Union
EP	European Parliament
ESC	European Scrutiny Committee
ESCB	European System of Central Banks
ESM	European Stability Mechanism
ESRB	European Systemic Risks Board
EU	European Union
EUC	European Union Committee
EWM	early warning mechanism (synonymous with 'early warning system')
EWS	early warning system (synonymous with 'early warning mechanism')
FDP	Freie Demokratische Partei Deutschlands (Free Democratic Party)
Fed	Federal Reserve System (US)
FPÖ	Freiheitliche Partei Österreichs (Freedom Party)
FTAs	free trade agreements

GDP	gross domestic product
GDR	Gauche Démocrate et Républicaine (Democratic and Republican Left)
GFCC	German Federal Constitutional Court
GG	Grundgesetz (German Basic Law)
HR/VP	High Representative of the Union for Foreign Affairs and Security Policy
ICMs	Interparliamentary Committee Meetings
IIAs	interinstitutional agreements
ILK	Interkantonale Legislativkonferenz (Intercantonal Legislative Conference)
IMF	International Monetary Fund
INTA	Committee in International Trade (in the European Parliament)
IPCs	Interparliamentary Conferences
IPK	Interparlamentarische Konferenz der Nordwestschweiz (The Interparliamentary Conference of Northwestern Switzerland)
JCM	Joint Committee Meeting
JHA	Justice and Home Affairs
JPM	Joint Parliamentary Meeting
JPSG	Joint Parliamentary Scrutiny Group
LIBE	Committee on Civil Liberties, Justice and Home Affairs (in the European Parliament)
LTROs	long-term refinancing operations
MEPs	Members of the European Parliament
MPs	Members of Parliament
NAPs	National Action Plans
NCBs	national central banks
NCSL	National Conference of State Legislatures
NHRI	national human rights institutions
NKK	Nationale Konferenz der Kantonsparlamente (National Conference of Cantonal Parliaments)
NPRs	national parliamentary representatives
NPs	national parliaments
OMC	Open Method of Coordination
OMT	Outright Monetary Transactions
ÖVP	Österreichische Volkspartei (Austrian People's Party)
PIREDEU	Providing an Infrastructure for Research on Electoral Democracy in the European Union
PMBs	Private Members' Bills
PPERA	Political Parties, Elections and Referendums Act
PREA	Prison Rape Elimination Act
PSC	Political and Security Committee
QE	Quantitative Easing
RQMV	Reverse Qualified Majority Voting
SEA	Single European Act
SECG Conference	Interparliamentary Conference on Stability, Economic Coordination and Governance in the European Union
SEDE	Sub-Committee on Security and Defence (in the European Parliament)
SNP	Scottish National Party
SPD	Sozialdemokratische Partei Deutschlands (Social Democratic Party of Germany)
SPÖ	Sozialdemokratische Partei Österreichs (Social Democratic Party of Austria)

SRC	Socialiste, Républicain, Citoyen et divers gauche (political group of Socialists, Republicans and Citizens in France)
SSM	Single Supervisory Mechanism
TESM	Treaty establishing the European Stability Mechanism
TEU	Treaty on European Union
TFEU	Treaty on the Functioning of the European Union
TLTROs	targeted longer-term refinancing operations
TSCG	Treaty on Stability, Coordination and Governance in the Economic and Monetary Union (Fiscal Compact)
TTIP	Transatlantic Trade and Investment Partnership
UDI	L'Union des Démocrates et Independents (Union of Democrats and Independents)
UK	United Kingdom
UKIP	UK Independence Party
UMP	Union pour un Mouvement Populaire (Union for a Popular Movement)
UMRA	Unfunded Mandates Reform Act
US	United States
VAT	value added tax
VP	Vice President
WEU	Western European Union

List of Contributors

Leonard Besselink is Professor of Constitutional Law at the Faculty of Law, University of Amsterdam.

Gavin Barrett is Jean Monnet Professor of European Constitutional and Economic Law and a Professor at Sutherland School of Law, University College Dublin.

Karolina Borońska-Hryniewiecka is Head of European Union Programme at the Polish Institute of International Affairs (PISM) and an Assistant Professor of Political Science at the Institute of Political Science, University of Wrocław.

Ian Cooper is a Jean Monnet Fellow at the Robert Schuman Centre for Advanced Studies, European University Institute.

Cristina Fasone is an Assistant Professor of Comparative Public Law at the Department of Political Science, LUISS Guido Carli University.

Diane Fromage is an Assistant Professor in EU Law at the School of Law, Utrecht University.

Katarzyna Granat is Marie Curie Fellow and Junior Research Fellow at Durham Law School, Durham University.

Davor Jančić is a Lecturer in Law at the Department of Law, Queen Mary University of London.

Peter Lindseth is Olimpiad S Ioffe Professor of International and Comparative Law at the School of Law, University of Connecticut.

Nicola Lupo is Professor of Public Law at the Department of Political Science, LUISS Guido Carli University.

Aleksandra Maatsch is the Chair of European and Multilevel Politics (Interim), University of Cologne.

Ingolf Pernice is Professor of Public and European and International Law and Director of the Walter Hallstein Institute for European Constitutional Law, Humboldt-Universität zu Berlin.

Kolja Raube is a Senior Researcher at the Leuven Centre for Global Governance Studies, University of Leuven.

Julie Smith (Baroness Smith of Newnham) is a Member of the House of Lords and Director of the European Centre at POLIS, University of Cambridge.

Frank Wendler is a DAAD Visiting Assistant Professor at the Department of Political Science at the Jackson School of International Studies, University of Washington.

Jan Wouters is Jean Monnet Chair *ad personam* in EU and Global Governance and Director of the Leuven Centre for Global Governance Studies, University of Leuven.

List of Contributors

1

The Legacy of an Evolving Polity

Democracy, National Identity, and the Good Functioning of the EU

Davor Jančić

1. Theme, Objectives, and State of the Art

This book analyses the latest phase of the evolution of the role of national parliaments (NPs) in the EU as shaped by two key factors: the entry into force of the Lisbon Treaty[1] and the outbreak and management of the sovereign debt crisis in the Eurozone.[2] These two ground-breaking events carry important repercussions for NPs,[3] both in terms of their traditional constitutional functions and in terms of the newly emerging functions that they are seeking to assume at a time of exceptional turbulence across Europe.[4]

The overarching research question posed in this volume is whether NPs exhibit resilience or resignation in these changed politico-legal and socio-economic circumstances in the Union. Resilience is understood as a set of successful individual and collective efforts of NPs to increase their presence and power in the EU, while resignation signifies the lack thereof. This simple dichotomy between resilience and resignation is chosen to facilitate capturing and evaluating the main trends that underlie the development of the NPs' European role. This dichotomy is used not only to expound the factual constitutionalization of that role, but, where relevant, also as an instrument for a normative appraisal of the constitutional thought about this process.

There is, however, no scarcity of accounts on this topic. In internal EU affairs, the literature typically observes their role as a matter of subsidiarity monitoring[5] and as a

[1] Paul Craig, 'The Treaty of Lisbon: Process, Architecture and Substance' (2008) 33 EL Rev 137, 149ff; Philipp Kiiver, 'European Treaty Reform and the National Parliaments: Towards a New Assessment of Parliament-friendly Treaty Provisions' in Jan Wouters, Luc Verheij, and Philipp Kiiver (eds), *European Constitutionalism beyond Lisbon* (Intersentia 2009); Alain Delcamp, 'Les parlements nationaux et l'Union européenne: de la reconnaissance à l'engagement' (2011) 544 Revue du Marché Commun et de l'Union Européenne 7.

[2] Alicia Hinarejos, *The Eurozone Crisis in Constitutional Perspective* (Oxford University Press 2015); Kaarlo Tuori and Klaus Tuori, *The Eurozone Crisis: A Constitutional Analysis* (Cambridge University Press 2014); Giandomenico Majone, *Rethinking the Union of Europe Post-crisis: Has Integration Gone Too Far?* (Cambridge University Press 2014) ch 6.

[3] Katrin Auel and Thomas Christiansen, 'After Lisbon: National Parliaments in the European Union' (2015) 38 WEP 261, 277.

[4] Tapio Raunio, 'The Role of National Legislatures in EU Politics' in Olaf Cramme and Sarah Hobolt (eds), *Democratic Politics in a European Union under Stress* (Oxford University Press 2014).

[5] See most recently: Anna Jonsson Cornell and Marco Goldoni (eds), *National and Regional Parliaments in the EU-Legislative Procedure Post-Lisbon: The Impact of the Early Warning Mechanism* (Hart Publishing 2017); Philipp Kiiver, *The Early Warning System for the Principle of Subsidiarity: Constitutional Theory and Empirical Reality* (Routledge 2012).

The Legacy of an Evolving Polity: Democracy, National Identity, and the Good Functioning of the EU. First Edition. Davor Jančić. Published 2017 by Oxford University Press

matter of Europeanization.[6] In external EU affairs, the academic debate views NPs as vehicles for democratizing EU foreign policy broadly conceived. These three strands of scholarly endeavour are inspired by the quest for a solution to the infamous EU democratic deficit.[7] Yet each of them exhibits certain limitations thus laying bare further research needs. The first strand by and large agrees that subsidiarity only enables parliaments to provide limited input in EU decision-making. There are hence strong arguments in favour of reforming this mechanism, affording NPs greater leeway to render political judgments on EU policy, and enhancing their agenda-setting competence.[8] The second literature strand, which began in the mid-1990s, has spurred an unabated discussion both on the domestic adaptation of the parliamentary scrutiny arrangements to the exigencies of European integration and on the changing morphology of executive-legislative relations. Their conclusion is that most parliaments have improved their standing in EU affairs, but that the ever-evolving Union requires constant reform. The third strand almost infallibly concentrates on the NPs' control over the areas of Common Foreign and Security Policy (CFSP) and Common Security and Defence Policy (CSDP),[9] while virtually no attention has been paid to their involvement in other areas of EU external action, such as trade, development, and human rights.

The existing literature thus provides an invaluable basis for this volume, whose objective is to take the discussion forward by filling some of the said gaps and to offer novel insights by raising foundational theoretical questions of EU constitutionalism, separation of powers, and democratic legitimacy from evolutional, context-driven, and path-dependent perspectives. To do so, the book rests on the premise that the 'gatekeeping'[10] and 'networking'[11] functions of NPs are becoming increasingly important yet multifaceted concepts. This book unpacks them through the lens of the burgeoning array of parliamentary processes, actors, and factors brought about by the Lisbon Treaty and the euro crisis. In particular, the contributions to the volume examine: how NPs envision their constitutional purposefulness in the wake of these two events; how they have responded to the challenges flowing from the crisis-sponsored centralization and intergovernmentalization of EU policy-making; how this has affected the relations between NPs, governments, courts, and EU institutions; and whether new parliamentary initiatives are suited to reinforcing the EU's democratic fundament. Through an analysis of NPs in the EU, the volume also speaks to the more encompassing questions

[6] See the most recent among a long line of works on this: Claudia Hefftler and others (eds), *The Palgrave Handbook of National Parliaments and the European Union* (Palgrave 2015); Gavin Barrett (ed.), *National Parliaments and the European Union: The Constitutional Challenge for the Oireachtas and Other Member State Legislatures* (Clarus Press 2008); John O'Brennan and Tapio Raunio (eds), *National Parliaments within the Enlarged European Union: From Victims of Integration to Competitive Actors?* (Routledge 2007).

[7] Stephen C Sieberson, 'The Treaty of Lisbon and Its Impact on the European Union's Democratic Deficit' (2008) 14 Colum J Eur L 445.

[8] See a set of main challenges in Cristina Fasone, Diane Fromage, and Zoe Lefkofridi (eds), 'Parliaments, Public Opinion and Parliamentary Elections in Europe', EUI Working Paper MWP 2015/18.

[9] Ariella Huff, 'Executive Privilege Reaffirmed? Parliamentary Scrutiny of the CFSP and CSDP' (2015) 38 WEP 396; Anna Herranz-Surrallés, 'The EU's Multilevel Parliamentary (Battle)Field: Interparliamentary Cooperation and Conflict in Foreign and Security Policy' (2014) 37 WEP 957.

[10] Tapio Raunio, 'The Gatekeepers of European Integration? The Functions of National Parliaments in the EU Political System' (2011) 33 J Eur Integration 303.

[11] Carina Sprungk, 'A New Type of Representative Democracy? Reconsidering the Role of National Parliaments in the European Union' (2013) 35 J Eur Integration 547.

of authority in EU law and competence delimitation between the EU and the Member States.[12]

However, some choices had to be made given that the volume does not pretend to cover all areas of relevance to the European role of NPs. Two significant areas are excluded. The first is the role of regional parliaments. This is omitted chiefly because decisions taken at the regional level are less likely to have a direct impact on a given Member State and the EU as a whole, even though it is acknowledged that sub-national parliamentary bodies contribute to the formation and enrichment of national identity.[13] The second is the transposition of directives into domestic legal orders.[14] Although this is an important area where parliaments may perform a legislative role in the context of the EU, the volume adheres to the thesis that *ex ante* involvement is more conducive to exerting influence and rectifying the democratic deficit. The volume nonetheless espouses the view that the existence of parliamentary rights does not equate with influence,[15] and it refrains from measuring influence as this is virtually impossible owing to the intervention of a vast multitude of very elusive parameters, which are well documented in political science.[16]

To grasp the political and discursive contexts in which the continuous delegation of powers from the Member States and their parliaments to the EU unravelled—one is advised to take a brief look back at the history. This is the topic of the next section. The section after that explicates why the Lisbon Treaty and the euro crisis have been fundamental to NPs' positioning on the EU's constitutional map. On that basis, the notions of 'national identity' and 'good functioning of the EU' are decomposed and reconstructed as core determinants of the permanence of NPs in European public law. It will be argued that the manner in which NPs shape these two notions constitutes the linchpin of the discursive component of EU democracy, which has been at the heart of the problem of the Union's legitimacy for decades. This will enable one to understand why EU-related activity of parliaments has grown, despite the modesty in their formal powers. The chapter ends by outlining the structure of the book.

2. National Parliaments in European Integration: Roots and Inspiration

The European Coal and Steel Community of 1951 began with a toothless Common Assembly with merely supervisory powers. The Assembly was composed of national parliamentarians and endowed with the task of counterbalancing the European Commission's predecessor, the High Authority.[17] In fact, the Assembly only surfaced

[12] Stephen Weatherill, 'Using National Parliaments to Improve Scrutiny of the Limits of EU Action' (2003) 28 EL Rev 909.

[13] Karolina Borońska-Hryniewiecka, 'Differential Europeanization? Explaining the Impact of the Early Warning System on Subnational Parliaments in Europe' Eur Pol Sci Rev (forthcoming); Anna-Lena Högenauer, 'The Impact of the Lisbon Reform Treaty on Regional Engagement in EU Policy-making—Continuity or Change?' (2008) 10 Eur J L Reform 535, 537; Philipp Kiiver (ed), *National and Regional Parliaments in the European Constitutional Order* (Europa Law Publishing 2006).

[14] Carina Sprungk, 'Legislative Transposition of Directives: Exploring the Other Role of National Parliaments in the European Union' (2013) 51 JCMS 298.

[15] Katrin Auel, 'Democratic Accountability and National Parliaments: Redefining the Impact of Parliamentary Scrutiny in EU Affairs' (2007) 13 ELJ 487.

[16] This is why political science literature usually focuses on 'strength' rather than 'influence' of NPs.

[17] Berthold Rittberger, 'Building Europe's Parliament: Democratic Representation beyond the Nation State' (Oxford University Press 2005) 73 ff.

at a later stage of the Schuman Plan negotiations, which led to the creation of this first, and often forgotten, Community. The rationale for the 'founding Six' to include a representative body with some electoral credentials as a check on the supranational executive is ever so important, because it was rooted in exactly the same concern that underlies the increasing popular scepticism towards the EU of today.[18] That concern is the democratic legitimacy of and accountability for the 'new' and 'unknown' ways and means of life and the preservation of the 'old' and 'well-known' ones.[19]

Nowhere was this kind of concern more tangible than in Britain, where there was bipartisan consensus against the experimental pooling of competences beyond the nation state.[20] This consensus was based less on an economic calculus than on the perceived necessity to protect economic freedom, political autonomy, and a sense of national pride. In the *European Unity* pamphlet, which the then governing Labour Party published in 1950, Foreign Secretary Ernest Bevan claimed that the UK is 'in every respect except distance … closer to our kinsmen in Australia and New Zealand on the far side of the world, than … to Europe', and especially in terms of language, origins, social habits, institutions, political outlook, and economic interest.[21] His party colleague, Chancellor of the Exchequer Stafford Cripps, argued in the House of Commons that 'participation in a political federation, limited to Western Europe, is not compatible either with our Commonwealth ties, our obligations as a member of the wider Atlantic community, or as a world power'.[22] Harold Adams MP (Lab) thought that this would 'destroy the future greatness' of the UK,[23] while Julian Amery MP (Con), although being in favour of Britain's approximation with continental Europe, stated that: 'it is not a bad thing for ministers to think that the British people are superior to anyone else—I confess I rather share that view myself'.[24] Even Winston Churchill, who in 1946 in Zurich famously called for the creation of a United States of Europe, did not envisage the UK being a member of it but merely its 'friend and sponsor' alongside the United States, because Britain had 'its own Commonwealth'.[25] In Parliament, Churchill found supranationalism to be a repulsive notion, because, as he stressed, he would be unhesitatingly opposed to a 'supranational authority which has the power to tell Great Britain not to cut any more coal or make any more steel, but to grow tomatoes instead'.[26]

[18] The Eurobarometer survey of July 2016 shows that: (a) the number of the EU citizens interviewed who feel that their voice does not count in the EU has risen to 55 per cent, while those believing it does has declined to 38 per cent; (b) by far the most important concerns are immigration (48 per cent, down by 10 per cent) and terrorism (39 per cent, up by 14 per cent); (c) 55 per cent support the euro and the Economic and Monetary Union (EMU), while 38 per cent do not; (d) 66 per cent feel like a citizen of the EU (up by 2 per cent), while 33 per cent do not (down by 1 per cent); (e) 72 per cent have a positive or neutral image of the EU, while 27 per cent have a negative image of it (1 per cent do not know). Finally, a declining majority of EU citizens are optimistic about the EU's future: 50 per cent (down by 3 per cent) against 41 per cent (up by 3 per cent) of those who are pessimistic. See Standard Eurobarometer 85, 'Public Opinion in the European Union—First Results' http://ec.europa.eu/COMMFrontOffice/PublicOpinion/index.cfm/ResultDoc/download/DocumentKy/70150 (last accessed 13 October 2016).

[19] Habermas has described subsidiarity as a way to 'protect national ways of life'. Jürgen Habermas, 'Democracy in Europe: Why the Development of the EU into a Transnational Democracy Is Necessary and How It Is Possible' (2015) 21 ELJ 546, 555.

[20] See more on the UK Parliament's European role in the chapter by Julie Smith in this volume.

[21] Edmund Dell, *The Schuman Plan and the British Abdication of Leadership in Europe* (Oxford University Press 1995) 199.

[22] HC Deb 26 June 1950, vol 476, col 1948.

[23] ibid, col 2028.

[24] ibid, col 2020.

[25] The Churchill Society, Zurich Speech of 19 September 1946 http://www.churchill-society-london.org.uk/astonish.html (last accessed 13 October 2016).

[26] HC Deb 27 June 1950, vol 476, col 2147.

Over sixty-five years on, the rhetoric principally reliant on sovereigntist imagery is more alive than ever. If the Commons debates held in the early 1950s sound familiar, this is because very similar arguments were the cornerstone of the 'Leave' campaign in the UK's referendum on EU membership that took place on 23 June 2016. Briefly, the surrender of sovereignty was and, whatever is left of it, remains at stake.[27] The parliament was and remains the political marketplace, where views and visions of the goals and manner of coexistence and joint action are exchanged.[28] Talking shops, you might think. But talking shops confront 'demand' with 'supply', so that the two can be weighed out and a decision taken on how to satisfy one's needs or, rather, those of an entire polity. This is the value that NPs add to 'Europe'.

However, the restricted scope of the Common Assembly's competences—captured by the right to censure the High Authority at its single annual meeting—was not its only woe. More chronically, its meaningfulness was undercut by the 'lack of supranational identification among the Community's population'.[29] Therein lies a perennial conundrum that consecutive Treaties have sought to address with more or less success. The undying puzzle is how to strike a *balance* between collective action through various forms and levels of integration and the relinquishment of the methods of taking the same action individually—all of this in a way that is *acceptable* to Europe's different nations. Each of these nations has its own individual historical, cultural, and socio-economic interests, affinities, and biases, which are in the first place expressed in their NPs.[30]

Jean Monnet himself very relevantly underlined that no matter the path of integration—whether through a variant of federalism or intergovernmentalism—the domestic embedding of the pursuit of integration is of critical importance. On leaving the presidency of the High Authority, Monnet delivered a farewell speech in the Common Assembly saying that: 'the decision to transfer new powers to the European institutions belongs entirely to the [national] parliaments and governments. The impulse must, therefore, come from without'.[31] Although external, NPs were therefore the formative spark *sine qua non* of European unification. This is why European integration has been a fundamentally political process from its very inception and NPs have been the bedrock of it.

Soon, the dual mandate of national parliamentarians, which had been foreseen as a temporary solution, proved unworkable owing to absenteeism and the lack of powers. The first direct election of the European Parliament (EP) in 1979 inaugurated a new era in the democratization of the Communities. The structural linkage with NPs was severed and two separate channels of parliamentary representation were born: one operating directly at the Community level through the EP and one indirectly at the national level through NPs. Their mutual relationship has formally developed as one of amity, while informally the EP and NPs have gone through numerous patches of rivalry and

[27] Raymond Vernon, 'The Schuman Plan: Sovereign Powers of the European Coal and Steel Community' (1953) 47 AJIL 183, 188.

[28] See similarly Sonja Puntscher Riekmann, 'Constitutionalism and Representation: European Parliamentarism in the Treaty of Lisbon' in Petra Dobner and Martin Loughlin (eds), *The Twilight of Constitutionalism* (Oxford University Press 2010) 120, 133.

[29] Gerhard Bebr, 'The European Coal and Steel Community: A Political and Legal Innovation' (1953) 63 Yale LJ 1, 38.

[30] Giandomenico Majone, *Europe as the Would-be World Power: The EU at Fifty* (Cambridge University Press 2009) 156.

[31] Walter Yondorf, 'Monnet and the Action Committee: The Formative Period of the European Communities' (1965) 19 Int'l Org 885, 889.

institutional jealousy.[32] The reason for this is that they have the same principal—first the peoples of the Member States, later EU citizens. Either way, the absence of a single European *demos* and the consequent conceptualization of the EU as a system of *demoicracy* meant that the public sphere was dispersed across individual countries, causing sentiments to be nurtured nationally rather than on an EU-wide scale. Integration thus presupposes mutual recognition and not a merger of the many European identities.[33]

Within the separate public spheres and apart from the media, NPs and political parties have played a notable part in the creation of the public opinion on the EU and in performing scrutiny and control over the EU policy of their executive, thereby ensuring the plurality and complementarity of the avenues for bringing EU governance closer to the citizen.[34] Compared to the EP, NPs' competences in the spheres of democratic legitimacy and accountability have thus rightly been assessed as unmatched.[35] Although NPs were mentioned in a declaration appended to the Maastricht Treaty, the Lisbon Treaty was the first one to grant them an explicit place in the Treaty texts.

3. The Lisbon Incentive

The Lisbon Treaty merits credit for empowering the EP and for recognizing that NPs of the EU Member States do have a role in the European integration process beyond merely authorizing it. However, NPs' powers remain circumscribed by the understandable unwillingness to usurp the EU institutional balance and by the centrality of their functions at the domestic level.

The key post-Lisbon prerogatives of NPs are to receive information on draft EU legislation and third-country applications for EU membership, to police the principle of subsidiarity, to monitor Europol's and Eurojust's activities, to participate in the revision of the Treaties, and to build tighter relations with the EP. As Table 1.1 shows, these rights refer to both primary and secondary EU law and can be divided into active and passive ones. Despite this, it has rightly been emphasized that NPs have not been recentred in EU law-making.[36] In fact, some have suggested that the EU's democratic deficit resides primarily at the national level,[37] which highlights the weakness of NPs. However, this also speaks of their essentiality because if NPs did not matter, they would not be able to affect the quality of EU democracy.[38] There is much historical and empirical evidence that shows that the EP was largely devised as a compensation for the diminution of the powers of domestic parliamentary institutions.[39] The Dutch

[32] Karlheinz Neunreither, 'The European Parliament and National Parliaments: Conflict or Cooperation?' (2005) 11 J Legis Stud 466. See more comprehensively Lucile Debras, *Les relations entre le Parlement européen et les parlements nationaux depuis 1979: étude comparative des cas allemand, belge et français* (2008) PhD dissertation, Université de la Sorbonne Nouvelle–Paris III.

[33] Kalypso Nicolaïdis, 'The Idea of European Demoicracy' in Julie Dickson and Pavlos Elefteriadis (eds), *Philosophical Foundations of European Union Law* (Oxford University Press 2012) 248, 267.

[34] Kalypso Nicolaïdis, 'European Demoicracy and Its Crisis' (2013) 51 JCMS 351, 363–64.

[35] Kaarlo Tuori, *European Constitutionalism* (Cambridge University Press 2015) 330.

[36] Adam Cygan, 'The Parliamentarisation of EU Decision-making? The Impact of the Treaty of Lisbon on National Parliaments' (2011) 36 EL Rev 480.

[37] Francis Cheneval and Frank Schimmelfennig, 'The Case for Demoicracy in the European Union' (2013) 51 JCMS 334, 347.

[38] See the 'grassroots' approach to NPs in Olaf Tans, Carla Zoethout, and Jit Peters (eds), *National Parliaments and European* Demoicracy*: A Bottom-up Approach to European Constitutionalism* (Europa Law Publishing 2008).

[39] Berthold Rittberger, 'The Creation and Empowerment of the European Parliament' (2003) 41 JCMS 203, 218.

Table 1.1 Exhaustive list of the rights of national parliaments under the Lisbon Treaty

Type		Substance	Article
Primary EU Law	**Active**	1. participation in a Convention for ordinary Treaty amendment	48(3)(1) TEU
		2. opposition within 6 months to European Council proposals for simplified Treaty amendment, ie, the two general bridging clauses authorising the Council, without ratification by the Member States, to act by qualified majority instead of by unanimity or in accordance with the ordinary legislative procedure instead of in accordance with the special legislative procedure	48(7)(3) TEU
	Passive	1. notification of proposals for ordinary Treaty amendment	48(2) TEU
		2. notification 6 months in advance of European Council's initiatives for simplified Treaty amendment	6 Prot. NPs
		3. notification of third-country applications for EU membership	49(1) TEU
Secondary EU Law	**Active**	1. subsidiarity monitoring: - in general - in the field of judicial cooperation in criminal matters and in police cooperation	5(3)(2) TEU69 TFEU
		2. sending within 8 weeks reasoned opinions to EU institutions on the compliance with subsidiarity of draft legislative acts	3 Prot. NPs +6 Prot. Subs.
		3. bringing actions before the Court of Justice for infringements of subsidiarity by EU legislative acts	8 Prot. Subs.
		4. opposition within 6 months to the use of the special bridging clause in cross-border family law	81(3)(3) TFEU
		5. evaluation of Eurojust's activities	85(1)(3) TFEU
		6. scrutiny of Europol's activities	88(2)(2) TFEU
		7. participation in COSAC	10 Prot. NPs
	Passive	1. receipt directly from the Commission of draft legislative acts, amended drafts, consultation documents (Green and White Papers and communications), annual legislative programmes and other instruments of legislative planning or policy (or from the EP and Council in case of non-Commission drafts)	1&2 Prot. NPs + 4 Prot. Subs.

(Continued)

Table 1.1 Continued

Type	Substance	Article
	2. receipt of detailed statements on subsidiarity and proportionality that accompany draft legislative acts, with information on the financial impact, implications of directives for implementation, qualitative and quantitative indicators, financial or administrative burden	5 Prot. Subs.
	3. assurance that no agreement may be reached in the Council on a draft legislative act during the 8 weeks between receiving a draft legislative act and its being placed on the Council's agenda for decision as well as during 10 days between its placing on the Council's agenda and the Council's decision (both periods can be overridden in cases of urgency, which needs to be duly explained)	4 Prot. NPs
	4. receipt directly from the Council of the agendas and outcomes of its meetings and minutes of meetings where draft legislative acts were deliberated	5 Prot. NPs
	5. receipt of the Commission's annual reports on the application of the subsidiarity principle	9 Prot. Subs.
	6. receipt of annual reports of the Court of Auditors	7 Prot. NPs
	7. information on the content and results of evaluations of the implementation by the Member States' authorities of Union policies in the Area of Freedom, Security and Justice	70 TFEU
	8. information on the proceedings of a Council standing committee charged with coordinating operational cooperation between Member States' authorities competent for internal security	71 TFEU
	9. attention drawn to the recourse to the flexibility clause	352(2) TFEU

ratification of the Lisbon Treaty demonstrates this 'compensatory' reasoning rather well, because, except for a limited number of cases, the requirement of parliamentary consent to the government's position on draft EU decisions in the area of freedom, security, and justice was abolished because the EP had acquired those powers.[40]

The Lisbon Treaty furthermore enshrines the principle that the EU is based on *representative democracy*.[41] In this respect, the domestic constitutional link between NPs and their executive is all but symbolic. Quite on the contrary, in addition to the EP, this link is vital because it establishes the structural, albeit indirect and still evolving, relationship of democratic accountability between NPs and the Council and the European Council, which are composed of representatives of national governments and heads of state.[42] This is a fundamental linkage that ensures that EU decisions are taken 'as openly and as closely as possible to the citizen'.[43] Yet the Lisbon Treaty supplements the parliamentary means of legitimization with two methods of participatory democracy—stakeholder consultations and the European Citizens' Initiative.[44]

While these mechanisms seek to improve the citizens' input in EU policy-making, their democratic potential has been questioned on the grounds that they favour the representation of the interests of business and industry organizations, that their political representativeness is dubious and requires extensive civil society mediation, and that the registration and admissibility requirements that may apply are rather restrictive.[45] On top of this, domestic law infuses European integration with episodes of direct democracy through referenda, which can refer to treaty ratification, EU membership, or participation in certain policy fields.[46] Hence, NPs operate in a maze of institutional frameworks for enhancing the democratic character of EU decision-making.

However, the role of NPs in the EU is much wider than that which the Treaties prescribe. Besides the 'Lisbon' rights, parliaments have crucial *representative* functions. These are fulfilled not only through subsidiarity review but also through mediating political conflicts over the nature, objectives, and direction of European integration.[47] Acting as 'access points for voices and perspectives beyond those represented by governments',[48] parliaments are indispensable to informing the debate within their electorates of the desired 'depth' of integration, manner of attaining it, as well as, ultimately,

[40] Leonard Besselink and Brecht van Mourik, 'The Roles of the National Parliament and the European Parliament in EU Decision-making: The Approval of the Lisbon Treaty in the Netherlands' (2009) 15 EPL 307, 314.

[41] TEU, art 10(1).

[42] ibid art 10(2), second sentence. See more broadly Mark Bovens and Deirdre Curtin, 'An Unholy Trinity of EU Presidents? Political Accountability of EU Executive Power' in Damian Chalmers, Markus Jachtenfuchs, and Christian Joerges (eds), *The End of the Eurocrats' Dream: Adjusting to European Diversity* (Cambridge University Press 2016).

[43] TEU, art 10(3).

[44] ibid art 11.

[45] See these arguments fleshed out in Acar Kutay, 'Limits of Participatory Democracy in European Governance' (2015) 21 ELJ 803; Christian Marxsen, 'Open Stakeholder Consultations at the European Level—Voice of the Citizens?' (2015) 21 ELJ 257; James Organ, 'Decommissioning Direct Democracy? A Critical Analysis of Commission Decision-making on the Legal Admissibility of European Citizens Initiative Proposals' (2014) 10 EuConst 422.

[46] Fernando Mendez, Mario Mendez, and Vasiliki Triga, *Referendums and the European Union: A Comparative Inquiry* (Cambridge University Press 2014).

[47] See a critique of this in Gareth Davies, 'Democracy and Legitimacy in the Shadow of Purposive Competence' (2015) 21 ELJ 2. See more on the EU's mediated legitimacy in the chapter by Peter Lindseth in this volume.

[48] Damian Chalmers, 'The Democratic Ambiguity of EU Law-making and Its Enemies' in Anthony Arnull and Damian Chalmers (eds), *The Oxford Handbook of European Union Law* (Oxford University Press 2015).

whether to propel, unravel, or even discontinue the EU project.[49] Only in this way can domestic legislatures substantively reclaim some of the prerogatives conferred on the Union and help internalize the authority of EU law. Only in this way can a pan-European conversation, involving both the EP and NPs, be had on the desirability of an 'ever closer union among the peoples of Europe'.[50] Whether or not this is accompanied by binding rights of pronouncement,[51] public debate and the expression of the political will of the Union's constituent nations can generate critical mass that can produce important political effects in the EU, such as a change in the approach to law-making towards a more inclusive and citizen-sensitive process. The basis for this is the NPs' vote of approval of the EU Treaties, which gave the latter 'origin-based constitutional legitimacy'.[52] These considerations warrant the call for weaving parliaments into the EU's 'cooperative constitutionalism' dominated by the dialogue between domestic and EU courts.[53] This is why the debate on the NPs' European calling has been incessant.

The Lisbon Treaty touches on the essence of the NPs' place in the EU's multilevel constitution in the parts where it addresses 'national identity' and the 'good functioning of the Union'. These two notions, examined in turn below, entrench the precedence of identity over integration and underscore the intrinsically polemical nature of the EU's future progress.

3.1 National Identity as Democratic Identity

The Lisbon Treaty enjoins the EU to respect the Member States' national identities, which are inherent in their fundamental political and constitutional structures.[54] As the previous section has demonstrated, the question of identity has pervaded the process of European integration since its onset. Confining NPs to being subsidiarity overseers, called upon to comment on whether the EU should exercise the competence it shares with the Member States, thus appears rather apolitical and prohibitive of the citizens' and their representatives' inner *homo politicus*. National identity, however, has many dimensions. For the analysis of NPs, key among them is constitutional identity.

The constitutional guise of national identity refers to norms of a constitutional character, whether written in a constitutional document or not, that are of an overriding importance. Since the EU constitutional order builds on those of its Member States and is therefore a *Verfassungsverbund*,[55] the values inspiring national constitutions inform the European integration process writ large. This is important because NPs have a significant role in shaping these values. Indeed, values underpinning national constitutional orders are a product of political consensus and are defended and disputed in parliaments. The latter take part in the creation, affirmation, protection, and moulding of national identity, which stems from the common historical heritage and interests particular to a given political community. No other body in the EU is so

[49] See contra András Jakab, *European Constitutional Language* (Cambridge University Press 2016) 198.

[50] TEU, art 1(2).

[51] See a discussion of this in the concluding chapter to this volume by Davor Jančić.

[52] Tuori, *European Constitutionalism* (n 35) 33.

[53] Anneli Albi, 'Supremacy of EC Law in the New Member States: Bringing Parliaments Into the Equation of "Co-operative Constitutionalism"' (2007) 3 EuConst 25, 66.

[54] TEU, art 4(2). See analyses in Armin von Bogdandy and Stephan Schill, 'Overcoming Absolute Primacy: Respect for National Identity Under the Lisbon Treaty' (2011) 48 CML Rev 1417; Leonard Besselink, 'National and Constitutional Identity Before and After Lisbon' (2010) 6 Utrecht L Rev 36.

[55] Ingolf Pernice, 'The Treaty of Lisbon: Multilevel Constitutionalism in Action' (2009) 15 Colum J Eur L 349, 352.

directly involved in these domestic processes, which are of primary concern to the citizens and which define the EU's own constitutional fibre.[56] It has therefore rightly been posited that constitutional identity is a more effective check on the exercise of EU competences than subsidiarity: it ensures the diversity of domestic approaches to regulation and upholds substance-oriented review of EU action rather than that focused on procedure.[57]

National constitutional values have been the object of judicial dialogue between domestic and EU courts about the limits of EU competences and about the necessity to shield national legal orders from unwanted effects of EU law.[58] It is argued here that constitutional identity is not only the province of adjudication but also of legislation and politicization through NPs. Several examples shed more light on the institutional and substantive aspects of this argument.

In *institutional* terms, one of the strongest and most orthodox protections of constitutional identity qua 'parliamentary identity' is performed by Germany.[59] Besides ultra vires review, the German Federal Constitutional Court (*Bundesverfassungsgericht—BVerfG*) applies 'identity review' (*Identitätskontrolle*) to check that EU law does not encroach on the non-amendable parts of the Basic Law (*Grundgesetz*).[60] These include fundamental rights, the rule of law, social state, federalism, and, crucially, the principle of democracy.[61] Insistence on democracy refers to the participation in EU affairs of the *Bundestag* acting as constituted power, one existing within the margins of the Basic Law. However, it is important to note that, because of Germany's national socialist past, preoccupation about the maintenance of democracy goes beyond majority rule itself. Encapsulated by the concept of militant democracy (*streitbare Demokratie*) is precisely the idea that even elected representatives may not abolish the state's liberal democratic order.[62] This is because such an order is the domain of constituent power and not that of constituted power—a matter of *Verfassungsidentität* and not of the *Identität der Verfassung*.[63] All organs of constitutional power thus enjoy wide powers to shield this original claim to democracy from any threats of subversion in the direction of what led to the adoption of the Enabling Act of 1933 and the subsequent instalment of a totalitarian regime.

Further aspects of the parliamentary dimension of constitutional identity relate to the core tenets of constitutional structuring: the nature of the electoral system, the composition and competences of constitutional organs, the legislative process, the rules of executive accountability, and internal proceedings of the domestic representative body.

[56] See similarly Elke Cloots, *National Identity in EU Law* (Oxford University Press 2015) 145.

[57] François-Xavier Millet, 'The Respect for National Constitutional Identity in the European Legal Space: An Approach to Federalism as Constitutionalism' in Loïc Azoulai (ed), *The Question of Competence in the European Union* (Oxford University Press 2014) 253, 262.

[58] Theodore Konstadinides, 'Dealing with Parallel Universes: Antinomies of Sovereignty and the Protection of National Identity in European Judicial Discourse' (2015) 34 YEL 127; Alejandro Saiz Arnaiz and Carina Alcoberro Llivina (eds), *National Constitutional Identity and European Integration* (Intersentia 2013).

[59] See more on the role of the German Federal Constitutional Court in this regard in the chapter by Ingolf Pernice in this volume.

[60] Basic Law, art 79(3) (so-called 'eternity clause' or *Ewigkeitsklausel*).

[61] ibid art 38. See Davor Jančić, 'Caveats from Karlsruhe and Berlin: Whither Democracy After Lisbon?' (2010) 16 Colum J Eur L 337.

[62] See a further discussion in Jan-Werner Müller, 'Militant Democracy' in Michel Rosenfeld and András Sajó (eds), *The Oxford Handbook of Comparative Constitutional Law* (Oxford University Press 2012).

[63] Monica Claes and Jan-Herman Reestman, 'The Protection of National Constitutional Identity and the Limits of European Integration at the Occasion of the *Gauweiler* Case' (2015) 16 German LJ 917, 920.

Member States are thus free to organize the operation of their legislatures and decide how parliamentarians are elected or, in the case of the British House of Lords, whether they need to be elected in the first place. For instance, it is the UK's first-past-the-post system that allows a political party, in this case UKIP, to win some 3.8 million votes and gain just one Member of Parliament (MP), while the EU's proportional electoral system allows the same party to be the most represented British party at the EU level with twenty-four Members of the European Parliament (MEPs). The same applies to France, where *Front National* has only two MPs in the *Assemblée nationale* but no less twenty-three MEPs at the EU level.

That electoral autonomy is constitutionally sensitive is attested by the EP's proposal for a reform of EU electoral law, which is mandated by the Lisbon Treaty.[64] This elicited six reasoned opinions within the early warning mechanism and seven opinions within the political dialogue.[65] Besides the Dutch, Swedish, and Luxembourgish parliamentary chambers, both Houses of the UK Parliament objected too. Apart from procedural shortcomings related to the lack of a detailed statement corroborating the proposal, the Commons and the Lords also invoked constitutional identity concerns.[66] These challenged the obligations to render regional parliamentarians ineligible for EP elections, to ensure gender equality of electoral candidates, to agree common deadlines for candidate lists, to accept a mandatory 3–5 per cent threshold for gaining a seat in the EP, and to extend the right to vote to EU citizens living beyond EU borders.[67] Such constitutional specificities hence have a strong impact on the structure of democratic representation. By implication, this parliamentary identity has significant repercussions for both domestic and EU policy-making.

In *substantive* terms, the UK's 2016 referendum on EU membership provides a powerful illustration.[68] A wide-ranging London School of Economics survey of the potential impact of a 'Brexit' concludes that concerns about the EU's democracy and accountability is reinforced by 'a sense of our [British] identity being threatened'.[69] Close to a half of some 3,000 UK citizens interviewed between July and November 2015 felt that the EU is 'undermining Britain's distinctive identity'.[70] Public opinion on this issue is crucially shaped by parliamentarians and political parties. Furthermore, the so-called 'emergency brake' that was foreseen in the now defunct UK–EU settlement of February 2016 aimed to enable Britain to restrict EU migrants' access to in-work benefits.[71] But this would only have been permissible if an inflow of workers

[64] According to TFEU, art 223(1), the EP 'shall draw up a proposal to lay down the provisions necessary for the election of its Members by direct universal suffrage in accordance with a uniform procedure in all Member States or in accordance with principles common to all Member States'.

[65] IPEX data http://www.ipex.eu/IPEXL-WEB/dossier/document/PE20152035.do#dossier-APP20150907 (last accessed 13 October 2016).

[66] See other examples of subsidiarity violations in Pietro Faraguna, 'A Living Constitutional Identity: The Contribution of Non-judicial Actors', (2015) Jean Monnet Working Paper No 10/15, 67 ff.

[67] See House of Lords, EU Committee, HL Paper 87 'Subsidiarity Assessment: Reform of the Electoral Law of the EU', 7th Report of Session 2015–16 of 27 January 2016; House of Commons, European Scrutiny Committee, HC 342-xviii 'Reform of the Electoral Law of the EU', 19th Report of Session 2015–16 of 13 January 2016.

[68] Patrick Birkinshaw and Andrea Biondi, *Britain Alone! The Implications and Consequences of United Kingdom Exit From the EU* (Kluwer Law International 2016).

[69] LSE Commission on the Future of Britain in Europe, 'Overview and Summary of Reports', 7 June 2016, 14.

[70] John Curtice, 'A Question of Culture or Economics? Public Attitudes to the European Union in Britain' (2016) 87 Pol Quarterly 209, 214.

[71] European Council, 'A New Settlement for the United Kingdom Within the European Union', Annex I ('Decision of the Heads of State or Government, meeting within the European Council,

into the UK existed 'on a scale that affects essential aspects of its social security system, including the primary purpose of its in-work benefits system, or which leads to difficulties which are serious and liable to persist in its employment market or are putting an excessive pressure on the proper functioning of its public services'. Determining whether these conditions have been fulfilled is highly politically salient and occupies parliamentary agendas through both legislation and deliberation. It would be hard for EU institutions to decide for the UK what the purpose of the British social assistance system is and whether British public services are overly strained. Because this is a matter of constitutional identity, where deference to UK institutions would be appropriate, the said settlement included a declaration that the EU considered these conditions to have been met.[72]

Finally, apart from constitutional identity, national identity also encompasses economic and cultural identity. In the area of economic policy, even in the post-crisis period, the continuing non-hierarchical allocation of competences between the Member States and the Union, which has the ingredients of pluralist governance, has been viewed as a means of reconciling 'economic efficiency with respect for national identity and democracy'.[73] The impact of economic governance on NPs is further elaborated below in the section on the euro crisis.

When it comes to culture, some of the Slovakian Parliament's pronouncements are exemplary. In preparations for the country's EU accession, the National Council (*Národná Rada*) adopted a declaration where, although affirming 'the identity of the Slovak Republic as a country belonging to the history, culture and values of the European civilisation', parliamentarians warned of the risks of relativizing these values and called for national sovereignty to be respected in cultural and ethical issues.[74] For that reason, they specifically requested that decisions in the fields related to the protection of life and human dignity, family and marriage, health, and education remain the exclusive competence of the Member States. The ongoing refugee crisis gave rise to another parliamentary statement invoking various dimensions of national identity. On the one hand, the *Rada* rejected the mandatory quotas foreseen in the EU's migrant resettlement and relocation programmes and insisted on voluntary contributions by the Member States. On the other hand, Slovak parliamentarians noted that any such measures needed to 'take into account cultural, historical and socio-economic characteristics of the individual Member States'.[75]

Expressions of the many facets of national identity are therefore part and parcel of parliamentary involvement in EU affairs. Because they are to a significant extent articulated and contested in NPs by members of various political affiliations, national identity can be viewed as contributing to the EU's own 'democratic identity'. However, it remains to be seen whether this merely serves to channel nationalist tendencies against the achievement of common EU goals, or whether it may foster a more

concerning a new settlement for the United Kingdom within the European Union', Section D on Social Benefits and Free Movement), [2016] OJ C 69I/1.

[72] See a further analysis in Eiko Thielemann and Daniel Schade, 'Buying into Myths: Free Movement of People and Immigration' (2016) 87 Pol Quarterly 139.

[73] Roland Bieber, 'The Allocation of Economic Policy Competences in the European Union' in Loïc Azoulai (ed), *The Question of Competence in the European Union* (Oxford University Press 2014) 86, 100.

[74] Declaration on the sovereignty of EU Member States and candidate countries in cultural and ethical issues, Order No 1853 of 30 January 2002.

[75] Declaration on tackling the migration challenges currently facing the European Union, Order No 1837 of 24 June 2015.

inclusive approach towards 'constitutional patriotism' (*Verfassungspatriotismus*) by feeding domestic anxieties into the EU's soul-searching process, in which transnational political allegiance is owed to the values of a pluralistic EU constitution.[76]

3.2 Good Functioning of the EU as the Normative Battleground for Political Contestation

In a rather indeterminate manner, the Lisbon Treaty states that NPs 'contribute actively to the good functioning of the Union'.[77] This spells out their transversal role in the EU and provides a general framework for the fulfilment of all the other European roles that domestic legislatures perform (see Table 1.1). Some year and a half before the signing of the Lisbon Treaty, the Commission explained that NPs should be 'more closely involved with the development and execution of European policy', because that can help the latter to be 'more attuned to diverse circumstances and more effectively implemented'.[78] This, therefore, ties in with the reasoning behind understanding national identity as democratic identity. Indeed, the overwhelming public opinion across Europe is that the EU cannot function well unless democratic requirements are satisfied. However, the heart of the problem of EU democracy is exactly that there is not one single view of what these requirements are, how they should be agreed, and when one should consider that the Union functions well and when it functions badly.

The notion of 'good functioning' is politically phenomenally divisive and polarizing. If there is an event that demonstrates this convincingly, it is the sovereign debt crisis, where European leaders collided as to whether to resort to bail-outs or whether to let certain Member States default on their financial obligations and, thus, whether to keep the political geography of the Eurozone intact or whether to consider unwinding it. The pinnacle of it was the so-called 'Grexit' debate,[79] in which some NPs were vocal participants. The Grand Committee of the Finnish Parliament (*Eduskunta*), which scrutinizes EU affairs, issued a mandate to the government in July 2015 demanding the rejection of a third bail-out programme for Greece, with the second largest parliamentary party—the eurosceptic Finns Party—threatening to bring the government down.[80]

While this shows parliamentary influence, domestic party politics and the political pressures of avoiding a Eurozone crash may weaken it. This is what happened in Finland, where for these exact two reasons the Grand Committee withdrew its opposition and the Finns eventually unanimously voted in favour of the bail-out.[81] Less than a year on, in April 2015, the *Eduskunta* held a debate on exit from the euro ('Fixit'), which Paavo Väyrynen, a Finnish MEP and former government minister, initiated

[76] See to this effect Clarissa Rile Hayward, 'Democracy's Identity Problem: Is "Constitutional Patriotism" an Answer' (2007) 14 Constellations 182; Jan-Werner Müller and Kim Lane Scheppele (eds), Symposium 'Constitutional Patriotism' (2008) 6 ICON.

[77] TEU, art 12.

[78] European Commission, Communication 'A Citizens' Agenda—Delivering Results for Europe', COM(2006) 211 of 10 May 2006.

[79] Jennifer Rankin, 'Eurozone Crisis: Which Countries Are For or Against Grexit' *Guardian* (12 July 2015) http://gu.com/p/4at9h/stw (last accessed 13 October 2016).

[80] 'Finnish Parliament in Favour of "Grexit": Report' *Business Insider* (11 July 2015) http://www.businessinsider.com/afp-finnish-parliament-in-favour-of-grexit-report-2015-7 (last accessed 13 October 2016).

[81] 'Soini Defends U-turn as Finland Accepts Third Bailout for Greece' *Yle Uutiset* (Finnish public broadcaster) (13 August 2015) http://yle.fi/uutiset/8226493 (last accessed 13 October 2016).

by means of a petition signed by 53,000 citizens.[82] As a result of the euro crisis, the Finnish Parliament underwent a 'major domestic politicisation of Europe'.[83] All of this highlights that, although their powers at the EU level remain constrained, NPs form a part of the wider public discourse on the future functioning of the Union.

What constitutes 'good' and what 'bad' functioning is a matter of political judgment based on a normative assessment of the competing political interests and preferences. As such, the EU's functioning, the Treaties state, refers primarily to subsidiarity monitoring. Yet, because NPs were the ones to validate the delegation of a portion of national competences to the EU level, they are also the ones to enjoy the authority to verify the continued existence of the domestic consensus on integration in a given policy field or in a certain direction. This can be carried out through parliamentary debates on, and periodic appraisals of, the balance of competences between the EU and the Member States, of the sort trialled by the UK Government in 2015.[84] This 'conferral review' by NPs falls outside of the margins of the Treaties, but it represents a way to relegitimize the European integration process regardless of the constraints posed by the Treaties.[85] However, these very constraints, which keep NPs on the sidelines, may prove to be their strength, because they are not directly implicated in the workings of the EU policy-making machinery, thus avoiding the risks associated with *dédoublement fonctionnel*,[86] which forces their governments at the same time to make EU decisions in pursuit of the common good and stand up for the national interest. Parliaments, for their part, shape the EU common good indirectly by politicizing the means of achieving it. This means that conferral is not a mathematical formula, but one that hinges on the weighing out of the benefits of integration against those of non-integration. This is significant because such a balancing exercise involves matters such as trust, the feeling of belonging, and identity, which are not rational categories.

It is argued here that this kind of scrutiny of EU affairs enables domestic constituents to contrast different conceptions of the 'good life' and evaluate the extant deficit in 'democratic justice', which is caused by the discrepancy between the 'easy' supranationalization of the market and the capital and the 'uneasy' transcendence of social democracy beyond the state.[87] The EP's action, in turn, is focused on aggregating 'transnational' commonalities and is thus farther away from the 'local' centres of gravity that make up the polycentric EU. The EP and NPs therefore act in complementary ways. Accordingly, NPs are commonly seen as bridges for the democratic contestation of the choices driving EU progress and for the shaping of a sense of citizenship

[82] Jussi Rosendahl, 'Finnish Parliament, Pressured by Weak Economy, Debates Euro Exit' *Reuters* (28 April 2016) http://www.reuters.com/article/us-eurozone-finland-exit-idUSKCN0XP2FP (last accessed 15 November 2016); 'Finnish MPs to Debate Euro Exit after "Fixit" Petition' *EUbusiness* (10 March 2016) http://www.eubusiness.com/news-eu/finland-economy.16wz (last accessed 13 October 2016).

[83] Tapio Raunio, 'The Politicization of EU Affairs in the Finnish Eduskunta: Conflicting Logics of Appropriateness, Party Strategy or Sheer Frustration?' (2016) 14 Comp Eur Pol 232, 233.

[84] House of Lords, EU Committee, HL Paper 140 'The Review of the Balance of Competences between the UK and the EU', 12th Report of Session 2014–15 of 25 March 2015.

[85] Davor Jančić, 'The Game of Cards: National Parliaments in the EU and the Future of the Early Warning Mechanism and the Political Dialogue' (2015) 52 CML Rev 939, 953 ff.

[86] Leonard Besselink, 'National Parliaments in the EU's Composite Constitution: A Plea for a Shift in Paradigm' in Philipp Kiiver (ed), *National and Regional Parliaments in the European Constitutional Order* (Europa Law Publishing 2006) 117, 125.

[87] See on these concepts Michael Wilkinson, 'Politicising Europe's Justice Deficit: Some Preliminaries' in Dimitry Kochenov, Gráinne de Búrca, and Andrew Williams (eds), *Europe's Justice Deficit* (Hart Publishing 2015); Floris de Witte, *Justice in the EU: The Emergence of Transnational Solidarity* (Oxford University Press 2015) 23.

and political community across the EU.[88] Since, for better or worse, a portion of the European political process occurs at the national level, NPs are inevitably integral to the plea to bolster the 'political' dimension of European integration and combat the institutionalized stifling of political conflict at the EU level. Ultimately, parliaments have a role in addressing the perception of the EU as an authoritarian liberal conglomerate beyond merely throwing a spanner in the works of EU institutions through subsidiarity objections.

For this to materalize, it has been proposed that a predetermined number of national parliamentarians should become members of a reformed Council.[89] Another suggestion has been to allow individual Member States to opt out from ordinary EU legislation, which would incite NPs and political parties to debate European policy options.[90] More modest models of direct national parliamentary entanglement in EU-level politicization are presently developing through the political dialogue with the Commission (the Barroso Initiative),[91] extensive cross-level interparliamentary cooperation,[92] and the 'green card' project.[93] The latter seeks to give legislatures a say in the EU policy-formulation process and corresponds to the 'Parliamentary Legislative Initiative' proposal.[94] These arrangements seek to overcome obstructive participation of NPs in EU decision-making and reconfigure it towards more constructive involvement.

Certainly, NPs are not a panacea for the EU's democracy ills. They suffer from numerous fallacies themselves. Governments typically determine their agendas, draft laws, dominate parliamentary majorities, and are often able to evade accountability and the ultimate punishment of ouster. However, NPs are long-standing institutional resources for mediating ideological approaches to societal commitments to collective goods and they are therefore a valuable democratic asset for both the citizens, the Member States, and the EU. This is what qualifies them as candidates for reinforcing EU legitimacy. Absent a full federalization of the EU through the creation of a political union, preconditions for which are largely lacking, NPs are highly likely to remain on the drawing board of European institutional reform. All of these 'Lisbon' incentives go hand in hand with those engendered by the euro crisis.

4. The Crisis Incentive

The Economic and Monetary Union (EMU) combines centralized monetary authority with decentralized economic policy. With respect to the latter, the sovereign debt

[88] Damian Chalmers, 'Losing Citizenship and Democratic Authority in Europe' *openDemocracy* (25 March 2016) https://www.opendemocracy.net/brexitdivisions/damian-chalmers/losing-citizenship-and-democratic-authority-in-europe (last accessed 13 October 2016).

[89] Mark Dawson and Floris de Witte, 'From Balance to Conflict: A New Constitution for the EU' (2016) 22 ELJ 204, 217. See a variation of this proposal in Gerhard van der Schyff and Gert-Jan Leenknegt, 'The Case for a European Senate. A Model for the Representation of National Parliaments in the European Union' (2007) 62 Zeitschrift für öffentliches Recht 237.

[90] Fritz W Scharpf, 'After the Crash: A Perspective on Multilevel European Democracy' (2015) 21 ELJ 385, 402.

[91] See Jančić (n 85). See also Davor Jančić, 'The Barroso Initiative: Window Dressing or Democracy Boost?' (2012) 8 Utrecht L Rev 78.

[92] Nicola Lupo and Cristina Fasone (eds), *Interparliamentary Cooperation in the Composite European Constitution* (Hart Publishing 2016). See more in the chapter by Ian Cooper in this volume.

[93] See more in the chapter by Karolina Borońska-Hryniewiecka in this volume.

[94] Sandra Kröger and Richard Bellamy, 'Beyond a Constraining Dissensus: The Role of National Parliaments in Domesticating and Normalising the Politicization of European Integration' (2016) 14 Comp Eur Pol 131, 146.

crisis in the Eurozone, hence dubbed the 'euro crisis', has led to the EU's incursion, by means of both EU law proper and EU-related international law, into the fiscal area commonly considered the core of national sovereignty. Through the adoption of the Six Pack (November 2011), the Two Pack (May 2013), the European Stability Mechanism (ESM) Treaty (February 2012), the Treaty on Stability, Coordination and Governance in the Economic and Monetary Union called the Fiscal Compact (March 2012), and unconventional monetary policy decisions of the European Central Bank (ECB), such as the Outright Monetary Transactions (OMT) programme and quantitative easing, EU institutions—above all the Commission, the European Council, the Council, and the ECB—have been de jure empowered.[95] Moreover, one witnesses the de facto strengthening of the Eurogroup and the nascence of Eurozone summitry in 2008. The cumulative normative outcome of this policy mix is the nominal subjugation of NPs' fiscal authority,[96] and an even tighter and closer EU coordination of the economic policies of the Member States.[97] This is accomplished through preventive and corrective means.

On the *preventive* side, the EU relies on broad economic policy guidelines and multilateral surveillance to ensure that the Member States' budget deficit does not exceed 3 per cent and their public debt 60 per cent of the gross domestic product (GDP).[98] These two Treaty tools are further supplemented by procedures foreseen in a set of secondary EU legislation of the substantially expanded but thus far variably successful Stability and Growth Pact (adopted in 1997 and amended in 2005 and 2011). These procedures entitle the EU to monitor draft national budgets through the so-called 'European Semester'. To enable this, the Commission drafts annual growth surveys and the European Council adopts economic policy priorities. On this basis, euro area Member States prepare and submit stability programmes and non-euro area Member States convergence programmes, while both send national reform programmes. After that, the Council adopts country-specific recommendations, which the Member States take into account in drafting their annual budgets. Embedded within the European Semester is the macroeconomic imbalances procedure. This begins with the adoption by the Commission of alert mechanism reports and in-depth reviews, which are then incorporated into the said country-specific recommendations. Further to this, the Fiscal Compact demands the enactment of permanent and binding national provisions setting the maximum ceiling of structural deficit at 0.5 per cent of GDP (the so-called 'debt brake' or 'golden rule').[99]

On the *corrective* side, the EU uses two procedures to enforce the elimination of fiscal deviations. The first one is the excessive deficit procedure, which applies to both deficit and debt targets. It entails the issuance of Council recommendations and

[95] Kenneth Armstrong, 'The New Governance of EU Fiscal Discipline' (2013) 38 EL Rev 601. See on the European Council's crisis role in Sergio Fabrini and Uwe Puetter (eds), Special Issue 'Integration without Supranationalisation: The Central Role of the European Council in Post-Lisbon EU Politics' (2016) 38 J Eur Integration 481.

[96] Alexander Somek, 'Delegation and Authority: Authoritarian Liberalism Today' (2015) 21 ELJ 340, 343–45.

[97] See an excellent overview in Rosa M Lastra and Jean-Victor Louis, 'European Economic and Monetary Union: History, Trends, and Prospects' (2013) 32 YEL 57.

[98] TFEU, arts 120–26. These are general reference values, regarding which there is some flexibility where positive national economic trends suggest sufficient convergence towards these values.

[99] Fiscal Compact, art 3(b). See Lastra and Louis (n 97) 125. See also Paul Craig, 'The Stability, Coordination and Governance Treaty: Principle, Politics and Pragmatism' (2012) 37 EL Rev 231; Maurice Adams, Federico Fabbrini, and Pierre Larouche (eds), *The Constitutionalization of European Budgetary Constraints* (Hart Publishing 2014).

notices and the preparation by the Member State concerned of an economic partnership programme laying out policies and structural reforms for a durable correction of the excessive deficit.[100] The second procedure is the excessive imbalance procedure. The system of sanctions for non-compliance has been reformed and ranges from non-interest-bearing deposits to interest-bearing deposits and fines, which henceforth can also be handed down for the manipulation of statistical data on debts and deficits.[101] The purpose of these programmes and procedures is to enable the Commission, acting as appropriate in partnership with the Council and the European Council, to oversee and compel the observance of EU fiscal rules through the adjustment of national macroeconomic plans and thereby to maintain the health of the overall EMU.

The euro crisis has precipitated sizeable excesses in sovereign debt, causing bail-outs to be agreed for Greece, Portugal, Ireland, Spain, and Cyprus (partial bail-in). This was carried out through loans by other EU Member States, bilaterally or through the ESM, acting in cooperation with the International Monetary Fund (IMF). Greece's debt reached catastrophic proportions peaking at 180 per cent of GDP in 2014,[102] bringing the country to the brink of exit from the Eurozone.[103] Worse still, in late June 2015, Greece infamously became the first developed country in history to default on its loan repayment to the IMF.[104] In return for loans, strict conditionality was imposed in the form of memoranda of understanding, which required bail-out recipient states to pass debt-reducing measures in areas as diverse and sensitive as taxation, the labour market, pensions, social welfare, healthcare, public procurement, and the regulation of energy, transport, and water industries.[105] These austerity reforms hence cut deeply into the domestic fiscal autonomy and sharply restrict the room for discretionary legislative action and political control by NPs.[106] This is a justified corollary of the violations of EMU rules, argues a former judge of the *BVerfG*, adding that '[n]o parliament in the capitals of Europe can burden other states with debt without doing harm to the principle of democracy'.[107] Most of the academic comment, however, has been critical of austerity

[100] Regulation (EU) No 473/2013 of the European Parliament and of the Council of 21 May 2013 on common provisions for monitoring and assessing draft budgetary plans and ensuring the correction of excessive deficit of the Member States in the euro area (part of the Two Pack), art 9. See also TSCG, art 5.

[101] Regulation (EU) No 1173/2011 of the European Parliament and of the Council of 16 November 2011 on the effective enforcement of budgetary surveillance in the euro area, arts 4–8; and Regulation (EU) No 1174/2011 of the European Parliament and of the Council of 16 November 2011 on enforcement measures to correct excessive macroeconomic imbalances in the euro area (both part of the Six Pack).

[102] Eurostat data http://ec.europa.eu/eurostat/tgm/table.do?tab=table&init=1&language=en&pcode=teina225&plugin=1 (last accessed 13 October 2016).

[103] See possible ways out in Mark Hallerberg, 'Fiscal Federalism Reforms in the European Union and the Greek Crisis' (2011) 12 Eur Union Pol 127.

[104] Ian Talley, 'Greek Default Deals Blow to IMF' *Wall Street Journal* (30 June 2015) http://www.wsj.com/articles/greek-default-deals-blow-to-imf-1435704271 (last accessed 13 October 2016).

[105] See the Memorandum of Understanding between the European Commission, acting on behalf of the European Stability Mechanism, the Hellenic Republic, and the Bank of Greece, 19 August 2015 http://ec.europa.eu/economy_finance/assistance_eu_ms/greek_loan_facility/pdf/01_mou_20150811_en.pdf (last accessed 13 October 2016). See further Georgios Karyotis and Roman Gerodimos (eds), *The Politics of Extreme Austerity: Greece in the Eurozone Crisis* (Palgrave 2015).

[106] Fritz W Scharpf, 'Monetary Union, Fiscal Crisis and the Disabling of Democratic Accountability' in Armin Schäfer and Wolfgang Streeck (eds), *Politics in the Age of Austerity* (Polity Press 2013); Mark Dawson, 'The Legal and Political Accountability Structure of "Post-crisis" EU Economic Governance' (2015) 53 JCMS 976.

[107] Udo di Fabio, 'Karlsruhe Makes a Referral' (2014) 15 German LJ 107, 109.

politics, casting it as a 'travesty of democracy' with serious implications for the very idea of justice in Europe.[108]

The EU's brand of fiscal federalism therefore poses formidable constitutional challenges.[109] Facing little leeway to reject external emergency lending, NPs have reacted in other ways, mainly by increasing scrutiny and debate over the EU-derived segments of the national budgetary process.[110] Citizens themselves (70 per cent in 2015) support even greater EU coordination of domestic economic and budgetary policies.[111] NPs may indeed be the vessels for reconciling the distributional and democratic asymmetries generated by the crisis,[112] which call for a binary choice between further unity or fragmentation and dismantlement.[113]

5. Structure, Contents, and Relevance of the Book

The developments and considerations charted above require a reorientation of the focus of scholarly analysis of NPs towards an assessment of the constitutional, institutional, and functional implications of the Lisbon Treaty and the euro crisis for the structure and operation of EU democracy.[114] This volume recognizes this and studies the impact of EU law and politics both on the legislative and controlling competences of NPs as well as on their budgetary power and representative functions. It probes the parliamentary, executive, judicial, and party political reactions to the post-Lisbon constitutional settlement, which is changing in light of the post-crisis redistribution of power and wealth within the EU and which thus directly impinges on the citizens' welfare.[115] The volume unveils parliaments' strategy and positioning on contemporary

[108] Sionaidh Douglas-Scott, 'Rethinking Justice for the EU' in Miguel Maduro, Kaarlo Tuori, and Suvi Sankari (eds), *Transnational Law: Rethinking European Law and Legal Thinking* (Cambridge University Press 2014) 206, 214.

[109] Alicia Hinarejos, 'Fiscal Federalism in the European Union: Evolution and Future Choices for EMU' (2013) 50 CML Rev 1621; Sergio Fabbrini, *Which European Union? Europe After the Euro Crisis* (Cambridge University Press 2015); Federico Fabbrini, *Economic Governance in Europe. Comparative Paradoxes and Constitutional Challenges* (Oxford University Press 2016); Pavlos Eleftheriadis, 'Democracy in the Eurozone' in Wolf-Georg Ringe and Peter M Huber (eds), *Legal Challenges in the Global Financial Crisis: Bail-outs, the Euro and Regulation* (Hart Publishing 2014).

[110] Davor Jančić, 'National Parliaments and EU Fiscal Integration' (2016) 22 ELJ 225; Aleksandra Maatsch, *Parliaments and the Economic Governance of the European Union: Talking Shops or Deliberative Bodies* (Routledge 2016).

[111] Valentin Kreilinger, 'National Parliaments, Surveillance Mechanisms and Ownership in the Euro Area', Jacques Delors Institute, Studies and Reports No 110, March 2016, 54.

[112] Sergio Fabbrini, 'From Consensus to Domination: The Intergovernmental Union in a Crisis Situation' (2016) J Eur Integration 587.

[113] See to this end Kalypso Nicolaïdis and Max Watson, 'Sharing the Eurocrats' Dream: A Demoicratic Approach to EMU Governance in the Post-crisis Era' in Damian Chalmers, Markus Jachtenfuchs, and Christian Joerges (eds), *The End of the Eurocrats' Dream: Adjusting to European Diversity* (Cambridge University Press 2016).

[114] See eg Deirdre Curtin, 'Democratic Accountability of EU Executive Power: A Reform Agenda for Parliaments' in Federico Fabbrini, Ernst Hirsch Ballin, and Han Somsen (eds), *What Form of Government for the European Union and the Eurozone?* (Hart Publishing 2015); Ton van den Brink, 'National Parliaments and EU Economic Governance. In Search of New Ways to Enhance Democratic Legitimacy' in Flora Goudappel and Ernst Hirsch Ballin (eds), *Democracy and Rule of Law in the European Union* (T.M.C. Asser Press/Springer 2016); Pieter de Wilde and Tapio Raunio, 'Redirecting National Parliaments: Setting Priorities for Involvement in EU Affairs' Comparative Eur Pol (forthcoming); Katjana Gattermann, Anna-Lena Högenauer, and Ariella Huff, 'Research Note: Studying a New Phase of Europeanisation of National Parliaments' (2016) 15 Eur Pol Sci 89.

[115] Damian Chalmers, 'The European Redistributive State and a European Law of Struggle' (2012) 18 ELJ 667.

EU affairs. These seem to go in the direction of increased deliberation, politicization, and informal 'soft law' engagement in an attempt to resist their estrangement from 'Europe', reconnect with the citizens, and shore up the Union's legitimating capacity.[116] Saliently, these issues inform the EU policy debate set out by the Five Presidents' Report published in June 2015.[117] In setting out the steps necessary for the completion of the EMU, this document affirms the necessity of heightened parliamentary control and consultation in a renewed European Semester process of budgetary coordination. The rest of this book is divided into three parts. *Part I* focuses on the relationship between NPs and the concepts of EU *constitutionalism and democratic legitimacy*. The discussion begins with a reflective essay (Leonard Besselink) on the constitutional permeability of the EU legal order and on the relative value of foundational democratic claims made in favour of parliaments and in favour of the 'people'. This is followed by an account (Peter Lindseth) of the historical evolution of the EU as a system of mediated legitimacy, in which NPs are relied upon to address the democratic disconnect rooted in the separation of power from legitimacy in EU governance. Yet, such mediation is to a great extent contingent on the relationship between NPs and courts (Cristina Fasone and Nicola Lupo), which are influential in determining the level of constitutional protection that the former enjoy in EU affairs. The actual practice of national parliamentary involvement in European matters beyond the scrutiny of draft EU proposals is demonstrated with the case study of the UK Parliament (Julie Smith) through an insight into the roles of the House of Commons and the House of Lords in the legislative and political preparations for the EU membership referendum that the UK held on 23 June 2016. The next contribution (Gavin Barrett) elucidates a somewhat obscure aspect of national parliamentary scrutiny—that of comitology and the open method of coordination.[118]

Part II is devoted to the effect of the *euro crisis* on NPs and party politics. The analysis starts with a critical overview (Ingolf Pernice) of the role of NPs after the financial crisis, with a focus on the German Federal Constitutional Court's pronouncements on the OMT programme in its first preliminary ruling reference to the ECJ and on the follow-up judgments by the two courts. Linking to this is an inquiry (Davor Jančić) into the projected deepening of the EMU and the question of the accountability of an ever more influential ECB. After this, the domestic accountability of national governments for their action in the European Council and the Council is examined (Diane Fromage) with a view to showing the changing nature of political control in EU affairs. The following two chapters take an empirical perspective and examine the effect of the euro crisis on the actual behaviour of parliaments and political parties in political practice. This is carried out by means of comparative assessments, on the one hand of the parliamentary votes authorizing bail-out packages and the establishment of the ESM (Frank Wendler) and, on the other, of the NPs' responsiveness to compliance requirements imposed within the European Semester (Aleksandra Maatsch).

Part III concentrates on *interinstitutional relations* and examines interactions developing between NPs themselves, as well as between NPs and EU institutions. This Part

[116] Katrin Auel and Oliver Höing, 'National Parliaments and the Eurozone Crisis: Taking Ownership in Difficult Times?' (2015) 38 WEP 375.

[117] European Commission (Jean-Claude Juncker in close cooperation with Donald Tusk, Jeroen Dijsselbloem, Mario Draghi, and Martin Schulz), 'Completing Europe's Economic and Monetary Union', 22 June 2015 https://ec.europa.eu/priorities/sites/beta-political/files/5-presidents-report_en.pdf (last accessed 15 November 2016).

[118] See also Rik de Ruiter, 'EU Soft Law and the Functioning of Representative Democracy: The Use of Methods of Open Co-ordination by Dutch and British Parliamentarians' (2010) 17 JEPP 874.

sets out with a conceptualization of the increasingly discernible patterns of collective action of NPs at the EU level that have been emerging after the Lisbon Treaty in the form of an intricate web of policy-specific interparliamentary relations (Ian Cooper). The 'green card' initiative is then analyzed (Karolina Borońska-Hryniewiecka) as a nascent and informal, non-Treaty project proposed to the Commission by NPs themselves in search of a more creative role in initiating or repealing EU legislation. These insights are complemented by valuable lessons drawn from outside the EU through a study of non-EU federal regimes: the cooperation between State legislatures in the United States and between cantonal parliaments in Switzerland (Katarzyna Granat). Remaining in the sphere of foreign affairs, the next contribution (Kolja Raube and Jan Wouters) investigates the involvement of national and European parliaments in EU external relations not only in the traditional areas of CFSP and CSDP, but also in the less studied fields of trade, development, and human rights.

The closing contribution (Davor Jančić) sums up the findings of the chapters on the resilience or resignation of NPs as an institutional device for the democratization of the EU. It also reflects on the NPs' third 'yellow card', issued in May 2016 against the proposed revision of the Directive on the Posting of Workers as the latest development in the evolution of the early warning mechanism of subsidiarity monitoring. Finally, avenues are discussed as to how to move forward in search of a European role of domestic legislatures.

PART I

EUROPEAN CONSTITUTIONALISM AND DEMOCRATIC LEGITIMACY

2

EU Constitutionalism and National Parliaments

Insiders or Outsiders?

*Leonard Besselink**

In this chapter, I reflect on the ways in which the national parliaments (NPs) of the Member States relate to the European Union (EU). In certain respects, they seem to be outside the EU legal order, but both in practice and legally they are at the same time part of the European legal order. I engage in this reflection starting with an abstract consideration of the issue of whether NPs are insiders or outsiders. Next, I reflect on the question of the way in which the euro crisis and the recent direct calls to the people in the form of referenda affect the legitimating role of parliaments in the EU.

1. In or Out?

We start with some basic questions. What is 'inside'? What is 'outside'? And inside what, or outside what? Simple as they may seem, these questions are fundamental. We can picture the sequence of these questions as follows. Graphically, this would seem to be the 'outsider' position:

Figure 1

* This chapter elaborates some initial thoughts developed in Section V of 'The Place of National Parliaments Within the European Constitutional Order' in Cristina Fasone and Nicola Lupo (eds), *Interparliamentary Cooperation in the Composite European Constitution* (Hart Publishing 2016) 23–38, at 34–37.

EU Constitutionalism and National Parliaments: Insiders or Outsiders? First Edition. Leonard Besselink.

And this is the 'insider' position:

Figure 2

This, however, would not reflect the real situation as to the relation between the EU and the NPs of the Member States.

The 'outsider' position sketched above suggests that Member State parliaments and the EU are juxtaposed, stand side by side, the one not really touching upon the other. That has never really been the case, since originally NPs appointed the members of the European Parliament (EP), which was then called 'Assembly'. Moreover, within Member States, NPs have in one way or another always kept themselves busy with at least certain types of European activity, such as agriculture (Common Agricultural Policy (CAP)) and finance (VAT) already long before direct elections.[1] For that matter, they did so also with regard to and within parallel European organizations that have from the beginning maintained a relationship with the project of integration: notably, the Western European Union and the Council of Europe.

The 'insider' picture could also be a misrepresentation, in as much as NPs are not locked into the EU institutional frame in the exclusive way that this picture would suggest. Two different, somewhat more abstract pictures would pose the question whether NPs are insiders or outsiders more correctly:

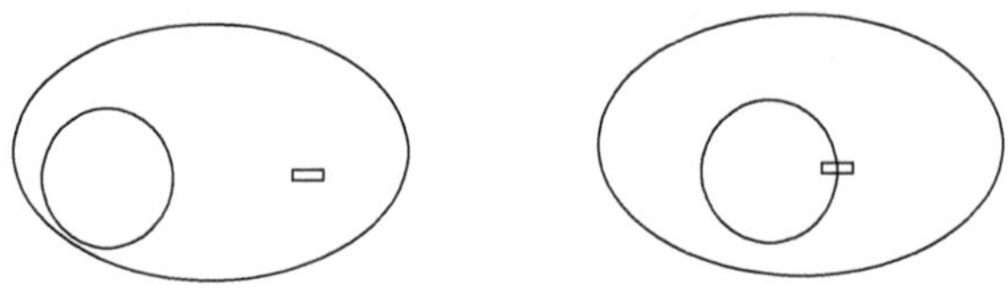

Figure 3

In these two representations, the larger circles represent the encompassing European political and constitutional order, the EU is symbolized by the smaller circles, and NPs by the small rectangle. The pictures articulate in two different ways the manner in which NPs, as integral parts of a wider European political order, relate to the EU: as outsiders or, alternatively, as at least partially participating within the EU.

From the legal point of view of EU law, the latter seems the better representation. This is the case at least since the EU Treaty recognized that NPs 'contribute actively to the good functioning of the European Union',[2] granting them a competence of their

[1] See the early involvement of NPs in European affairs in Michael Niblock, *The EEC: National Parliaments in Community Decision-making* (Chatham House 1971).

[2] TEU, art 12.

own. National parliaments each act within the EU framework independently from governments, or at least are constitutionally mandated to do so in terms of EU law.[3] A whole range of provisions in primary EU law give NPs a role to play.[4] Moreover, even without an explicit legal basis, they participate in the 'political dialogue' that the former Commission President José Barroso started.[5] National parliaments act not only as Member State representatives, therefore, but also as Union actors, most evidently in the framework of subsidiarity review (the 'early warning system'),[6] which goes as far as granting them the power to bring a case to the Court of Justice of the European Union (CJEU).[7]

But the notion of 'national parliaments' in all these provisions is *not* an autonomous EU concept. Their role within the framework of the EU does not enclose them in any exclusive manner within the bounds of EU law. They are set up, empowered, and regulated by national constitutions. Even the matter of who determines and issues the 'two votes' that each parliament is given in the context of subsidiarity review under Article 7 of Protocol No 2 is exclusively governed by national law.

We can conclude, therefore, that insofar as EU law empowers them to act within the EU framework, national parliaments, as *EU actors within the EU legal order*, are:

- governed *heteronomously* by the constitutive rules of national constitutional law
- attributed with *certain* powers under EU law as regards their proper function within the EU legal order and
- regulated *equally* by EU law and national law as regards the use of their EU-related powers.

Hence, from the *national constitutional perspective*, NPs are constituted *autonomously* by national constitutional law, and when acting within the legal framework provided by EU law, they are heteronomously attributed certain powers in the EU decision-making structure that are regulated by EU law, without erasing their powers and the regulation of their exercise under national law when acting in the EU context.[8]

2. Foundational and Ordinary Political Legitimacy: The Legitimating Role of National Parliaments

How does this state of affairs contribute to the parliamentary democratic legitimacy of the Union in its present state?

[3] This is no different when we look at the language of art 8 of Protocol No 2, which speaks of subsidiarity complaints being 'brought in accordance with the rules laid down in Article 263 of the Treaty on the Functioning of the European Union by Member States, or notified by them in accordance with their legal order on behalf of their national Parliament or a chamber thereof'. The 'Member States', ie as represented by their governments, bring cases merely as messengers of the parliaments that—under the Protocol—determine whether a case alleging infringement of subsidiarity is brought. No parliament has brought such a case as yet.

[4] TEU, arts 5(3), 10(2), 12, 48, and 49; TFEU, arts 69, 70, 71, 81 (family law), 85 (Eurojust), 88 (Europol), and 352(3); Protocols Nos 1 and 2; Protocol No 36, art 2(2)(b), as well as Fiscal Compact, art 13.

[5] Davor Jančić, 'The Barroso Initiative: Window Dressing or Democracy Boost?' (2012) 8 Utrecht L Rev 78.

[6] Anna Jonsson Cornell and Marco Goldoni (eds), *National and Regional Parliaments in the EU-Legislative Procedure Post-Lisbon: The Impact of the Early Warning Mechanism* (Hart Publishing 2016).

[7] Protocol No 2, arts 6, 7, and 8. See further on the relationship between courts and NPs in the chapter by Cristina Fasone and Nicola Lupo in this volume.

[8] See other constitutional aspects of national identity in the introductory chapter to this volume.

A first distinction could be made between foundational legitimacy and legitimacy in the day-to-day political operation of the Union. With 'foundation legitimacy', I refer to the legitimacy deriving from NPs' involvement when becoming a Member State of the Union and whenever a step is taken towards further integration that makes a fundamental change to the Union's powers under primary law. In this respect, parliaments have an enabling or preventing power.[9]

This foundational legitimacy is to be distinguished from the legitimating function of national parliamentary review as regards day-to-day EU decision-making by the Union's institutions under the powers that have been conferred upon them. This comprises NPs' scrutiny of EU decision-making,[10] mandating their executives,[11] triggering scrutiny reserves,[12] and, in appropriate cases that are determined primarily by national constitutional law, approving or vetoing certain EU decisions.[13] All this is *aimed at* EU decision-making, and has its effects in the EU institutions, mainly the Council.

These effects can, for instance, be observed when national parliamentary scrutiny requires a Member State representative in the Council to make a reservation pending the completion of such scrutiny,[14] or, even more visibly, when scrutiny results in a negative rather than a positive vote that is instigated by a parliament's power of influence over the national executive rather than by the national executive itself (be it based on a legal veto, mandating power, or ordinary political influence). Yet, such influence takes shape and is mainly performed within the national context of parliamentary activity. This may seem paradoxical because the activity takes shape in the national context, but the results play out in the EU context. Note that in the vast majority of cases they play out *invisibly*, inasmuch as scrutiny, mandating, and parliamentary votes on draft EU decisions lead to a positive outcome: they approve of the EU decision, thus providing it with a degree of parliamentary democratic legitimacy. That this may in a sense not be very noticeable does not in itself diminish the legitimating role of NPs, although that invisibility might foster the idea in the general public that EU decisions

[9] See TEU, arts 48 and 49; TFEU, arts 69, 70, 71, 81, 85, 88, and 352(3).

[10] This was a prominent practice by the House of Lords and the House of Commons since the UK accession, which was taken over around the same time by other parliaments. See more on the UK Parliament in the chapter by Julie Smith in this volume.

[11] Typical for the Danish Parliament since the cabinet crises that were triggered by Community law decisions in the fields of agriculture and fisheries shortly after Denmark's EU accession.

[12] Now a common feature for virtually all NPs, although it is up to national governments to invoke those reserves in the Council.

[13] Historically, the first parliament to claim a veto right as to the position to be taken by the representative in the Council was the Netherlands. This was performed through the *Berg* Resolution of the Netherlands Lower House of 11 January 1967. See Leonard Besselink and Brecht van Mourik, 'The Parliamentary Legitimacy of the European Union: The Role of the States General in the European Union' (2012) 8 Utrecht L Rev 28. In the Netherlands, a further parliamentary veto right was enacted concerning binding decisions in the field of justice and home affairs in which the EP had no role to play. This was done by means of the Act approving the Maastricht Treaty and subsequent amendment Treaties, but most of the veto rights were withdrawn in the Act approving the Lisbon Treaty. In the UK, parliamentary approval requirements, thus creating veto rights, have been created for the UK in the European Union Act 2011 and its 'shopping list' of parliamentary approvals and referenda. In Germany, such approval rights were enacted with regard to the financial and monetary instruments of the European Financial Stability Facility and the European Stability Mechanism in the *Integrationsverantwortungsgesetz*, and the *Gesetz über die Zusammenarbeit von Bundesregierung und Deutschem Bundestag in Angelegenheiten der Europäischen Union.* See Leonard Besselink and others, Study for the European Parliament, DG for Internal Policies, Policy Department C: Citizens' Rights and Constitutional Affairs, 'National Constitutional Avenues for Further EU Integration', March 2014, available at http://www.europarl.europa.eu/RegData/etudes/etudes/join/2014/493046/IPOL-JURI_ET%282014%29493046_EN.pdf (last accessed 10 October 2016).

[14] Katrin Auel, Olivier Rozenberg, and Anja Thomas, 'Lost in Transaction? Parliamentary Reserves in EU Bargains', OPAL Online Paper No 10/2012.

are taken beyond any kind of national oversight. Facing internal criticism, politicians too often find it easier to ride the bandwagon of the national 'right' and the European 'wrong' than acknowledging that they themselves have gone along with and often also endorsed those same EU decisions.

The visibility of the legitimating role of NPs is somewhat clearer as regards subsidiarity scrutiny and the political dialogue with the Commission, since this is indeed largely (although of course not exclusively) shaped in the institutional context of the EU.[15] But here the ultimate impact is rarely direct. This indirectness—apart from institutional short-sightedness of a very restrictive and the Commission's overly legalistic approach to the principle of subsidiarity—is to a great extent due to the early stage at which this national parliamentary influence occurs. Apart from the role of the Council in the 'orange card' procedure,[16] it is only in the subsequent parliamentary scrutiny that any early parliamentary hesitations or objections—if these were not already shared by the relevant parliament's executive—could become effective and result in a negative vote on the part of the relevant member of the Council. Streamlining subsidiarity and subsequent scrutiny is thus of the greatest practical relevance for rendering parliamentary influence on EU decision-making effective.

To sum up, with regard to EU instruments given to NPs, domestic parliamentary action takes place within an EU framework, but the results are to a large extent dependent on subsequent scrutiny in the national parliamentary arena, which may or may not result in a negative vote cast in the Council. These somewhat paradoxical ways in which national and EU law are entwined, illustrate nicely that it is not really possible to say that NPs are simply insiders or outsiders vis-à-vis the EU, even when they are active. The boundaries, if there are any, are essentially fuzzy and blurred.

3. Day-to-day Political Legitimacy: the Sanctioning Powers of the European Parliament and National Parliaments

A differentiation between the legitimating functions can be observed when we compare NPs and the EP. The EP does indeed provide direct parliamentary legitimacy basis for the political day-to-day functioning of the Commission and for the adoption of legislation for which codecision (now ordinary legislative procedure) is required. It has powers of sanction towards the Commission that go well beyond the letter of the Treaties. Contrary to what Article 17 TEU suggests, not only does a newly established Commission collectively require a vote of confidence of the EP, but *individual* candidates for the new Commission after EP elections also need such confidence. This was the case with the investiture of the first Barroso Commission in 2005 when Buttiglione was rejected as a candidate for the post of Commissioner, and this was confirmed in the subsequent practice.[17] Moreover, the

[15] This also has a certain transnational component inasmuch as there are sometimes 'horizontal' processes of communication and coordination, such as through the EU Interparliamentary Exchange platform (IPEX). These are used to achieve certain results in the early warning mechanism of subsidiarity review. A good example of it is the third yellow card, raised against the Commission's proposal for the revision of the Posting of Workers Directive, which was the result of a coordinated effort of the newer Member States from Central and Eastern Europe and Denmark.

[16] Protocol No 2, art 7(3)(a) and (b).

[17] Thomas Beukers, 'The Barroso Drama. Enhancing Parliamentary Control over the European Commission and the Member States: Constitutional Development Through Practice' (2006) 2 EuConst 21.

2015 elections of the EP and practice of indicating *Spitzenkandidaten* has meant a shift away from the letter of Article 17 TEU as regards the power of the European Council freely to designate the president of the new Commission towards following the preference of the Parliament, as was done that year by designating the candidate of the winning European party—Jean-Claude Juncker.[18] This trajectory of the democratic powers of the Parliament over the Commission—and actually already as regards its powers of the purse strings decades ago—follows closely that of the development of the parliamentary system of government in many of the Member States.

In this regard, NPs lack the power of sanction: they cannot vote out the Commission (as the EP can); nor can they vote out the Council as a collective body (which the EP cannot either). But constitutionally they do have a firm grip over the individual members of the Council, which the EP does not have. This is hardly ever commented on in EU law textbooks, but Article 10 TEU is quite right in saying that the Council is legitimated by NPs insofar as:

> Citizens are directly represented at Union level in the European Parliament. Member States are represented in the European Council by their Heads of State or Government and in the Council by their governments, themselves democratically accountable either to their national Parliaments, or to their citizens.

European politics has indeed played a role within many other Member States on a variety of cases that were specific to that Member State. It is no accident that in several Member States parliamentary debates take place after and before meetings of the European Council.[19] This is the opportunity for parliaments to sanction the governments in the countries with parliamentary systems, while in France this is done more intermittently at presidential elections. In fact, it may be good to remind ourselves that parliamentary scrutiny in Denmark, for instance, was triggered by and took form immediately after the national political upheaval over the EC Council decisions concerning pork prices and herring quota shortly after the accession of Denmark.[20]

[18] For different perspectives on this innovative aspect of EU politics see Marco Goldoni, 'Politicising EU Lawmaking? The Spitzenkandidaten Experiment as a Cautionary Tale' (2016) 22 ELJ 279; Thomas Christiansen, 'After the Spitzenkandidaten: Fundamental Change in the EU's Political System?' (2016) 39 WEP 992; Desmond Dinan, 'Governance and Institutions: The Year of the Spitzenkandidaten' (2015) 53 JCMS 93; Sara B Hobolt, 'A Vote for the President? The Role of Spitzenkandidaten in the 2014 European Parliament Elections' (2014) 21 JEPP 1528.

[19] See more in Roger J Goebel, 'The European Council After the Treaty of Lisbon' (2011) 34 Fordham Int'l LJ 1251; Wolfgang Wessels and others, Study for the European Parliament, DG for Internal Policies, Policy Department C: Citizens' Rights and Constitutional Affairs, 'Democratic Control in the Member States of the European Council and the Euro Zone Summits', January 2013, available at http://www.europarl.europa.eu/RegData/etudes/etudes/join/2013/474392/IPOL-AFCO_ET(2013)474392_EN.pdf (last accessed 10 October 2016).

[20] The 'bacon crisis' contributed to the early dissolution of parliament in November 1973. Helle Krunke, 'Developments in National Parliaments' Involvement in Ordinary Foreign Policy and European Policy–Denmark' (2007) 13 EPL 335, 339–41. On the present functioning of the mandating system of the Danish Parliament, see Mette Buskjaer Christensen, 'The Danish Folketing and EU Affairs: Is the Danish Model of Parliamentary Scrutiny Still Best Practice?' in Claudia Hefftler and others (eds), *The Palgrave Handbook of National Parliaments and the European Union* (Palgrave Macmillan 2015).

4. The Foundational Legitimating Power Resides in National Parliaments

Contrary to much of the anti-EU populist rhetoric, it is quite clear that from a foundational perspective NPs have retained their role as sovereign gatekeepers. It was NPs which were to decide the foundation, the accession, and amendment of the EU Treaties. They are the Masters of the Treaties insofar as they determine, as a matter of principle, the constitutional outlines of the Union, both in its constitutive aspect, the institutions constituted, and as regards these institutions' empowerment at the moment of approval of the Treaties and their amendments.

In this regard, the EP is not quite the NPs' match. The EP can propose amendments to the Treaty and must be heard on proposed amendments by the European Council,[21] but it has neither the monopoly to initiate Treaty amendments nor any decisive powers. Only under the procedure to switch from unanimity to qualified majority and from the special legislative procedure to the ordinary legislative procedure, do relevant decisions require the 'consent' of the EP.[22] So, the EP provides less democratic legitimacy to *constitutive* acts than NPs do. Because they do so together but also severally, one can say that they do that not only by acting as the European Masters of the Treaties but also as autonomous bodies. They are indeed both European actors as well as sovereign gatekeepers.

5. The Crises of European Integration: Parliaments on the Brink of European Disintegration

When we look at the legitimating role of NPs in the functioning of the EU, the Union is much as Andrew Shonfield famously depicted it in 1972: it is not supranational in the simple, old-fashioned sense of standing above the Member States; 'bits and pieces' of Member States are themselves part of the Union. The resulting Europe of bits and pieces together looks more like a bag of marbles than a melting pot.[23] And indeed, the prevailing compilation of difficulties facing the Union may make one wonder whether the bits and pieces will hold together and whether the marbles will spill away in all different directions.

The crises that Europe faces comprise the complex of the banking, public finance, and monetary crises and the complex of the migration crisis and related xenophobic populism. The latter translates into a revival of the rhetoric of sovereigntism and a call for EU exit referenda well beyond the UK, a call that echoes the populist reproach of the very undemocratic nature of the Union.

[21] TEU, art 48(2)–(3). See more in Cesare Pinelli, 'The Convention Method' in Nicola Lupo and Cristina Fasone (eds), *Interparliamentary Cooperation in the Composite European Constitution* (Hart Publishing 2016).

[22] TEU, art 48(7). See more in Katarzyna Granat, 'Interparliamentary Cooperation and the Simplified Revision Procedures' in Nicola Lupo and Cristina Fasone (eds), *Interparliamentary Cooperation in the Composite European Constitution* (Hart Publishing 2016).

[23] Andrew Shonfield, *Europe: Journey to an Unknown Destination* (Penguin Books 1973) 17. This was originally broadcast by the BBC in 1972 in the form of lectures, available at https://soundcloud.com/bbcreithlectures/rla-andrew-shonfield-europe (last accessed 10 October 2016) at 15':10"–16':55".

6. The Impact of the Euro Crisis

Let us first say something about the euro crisis and the role of parliaments. Parliaments' functions have been touched to their core by the perceived necessity to have a coordinated approach to fiscal matters that affect the prime amongst parliamentary powers: the power of the purse strings. The previously existing EU rules of the Stability and Growth Pact were complemented first with a so-called 'Six Pack' of five Regulations and a Directive (2011), then with the 'Two Pack' of Regulations introducing coordination, supervision, and surveillance of the national fiscal situations (2013). In addition, rescuing funds in the form of the European Financial Stability Facility and the European Stability Mechanism were set up formally outside the EU law framework and the so-called 'Fiscal Compact', ie the Treaty on Stability, Coordination and Governance in the Economic and Monetary Union (2012), was concluded containing an obligation to introduce a 'balanced budget' rule in the national constitutional orders.[24] These measures have together given a strong supervisory role to the Commission over core areas of national parliamentary powers.[25] Thus, an interstate agreement such as the Fiscal Compact, a treaty under public international law that would in EU jargon be considered 'intergovernmental', creates significant powers for supranational EU institutions, even for the Court of Justice for that matter.[26]

This is not to say that NPs' role adumbrated by Articles 10 and 12 TEU is totally ignored. The Fiscal Compact has required the introduction of independent national budgetary authorities to supervise national compliance, while these are supposed to 'fully respect the prerogatives of national Parliaments'. True to the composite nature of democracy in the context of integration within the Union, the Fiscal Compact also provides for the setting up of an inter-parliamentary conference of European and NPs' committee representatives, the so-called 'Article 13 Conference'.[27] The Fiscal Compact suggests that this is as 'provided for in Title II of Protocol (No 1) on the role of national Parliaments in the European Union', but of course this Protocol does not provide for such conferences, which strictly speaking are outside the EU treaty framework.

Again, the conclusion must be that the Fiscal Compact adds to the 'composite' nature of the Union and the parliaments' role within it.[28] On balance, on the one hand, parliaments have a role to play; but, on the other hand, the Fiscal Compact changes NPs' role altogether as compared to the days when Member States were autonomous in budgetary matters.[29]

7. Referenda on Membership, Association, and Exit

It is true to say that the EU is not founded on a direct foundational act of the peoples of the Member States establishing the Union or acceding to the Union. Nevertheless,

[24] See further Leonard Besselink and Jan Herman Reestman, 'The Fiscal Compact and the European Constitutions: "Europe Speaking German"' (2012) 8 EuConst 1 (Editorial).

[25] Michael W Bauer and Stefan Becker, 'The Unexpected Winner of the Crisis: The European Commission's Strengthened Role in Economic Governance' (2014) 36 J Eur Integration 213.

[26] Fiscal Compact, art 8.

[27] See more on this in the chapter by Ian Cooper in this volume.

[28] Leonard Besselink, *A Composite European Constitution* (Europa Law Publishing 2007). See another interpretation of 'compositeness' in Philipp Kiiver, 'The Composite Case for National Parliaments in the European Union: Who Profits from Enhanced Involvement?' (2006) 2 EuConst 227.

[29] See further Davor Jančić, 'National Parliaments and EU Fiscal Integration' (2016) 22 ELJ 225.

we must note that in nineteen out of the twenty-eight Member States there have been popular referenda—mostly with a positive outcome. These concerned becoming or remaining a member of the EU or Treaty amendments (notably, but not exclusively, the Maastricht and Lisbon Treaties and the Treaty establishing a Constitution for Europe).[30]

If we then connect Article 10(1) TEU with foundational legitimacy as defined in this chapter, this Article does not quite represent the reality either,[31] given that it stipulates that 'the functioning of the Union shall be founded on representative democracy'. This is because for two-thirds of the Member States, the Union is founded on an act of direct democracy. However, as long as a third of the Member State populations have not at any time had the chance to participate in such referenda, the ones held are insufficient to conclude that together they make for a popular constitutive, foundational act of the Union.

Pressure exists in various Member States towards direct legitimation in the form of calls for referenda.[32] Unlike the days of the abortive Treaty establishing a Constitution for Europe, referenda do seem to be sought as a method to imbue the Union with legitimacy, but are to the contrary motivated by questioning the popular support for the process that has led Member States to integrate in the Union in order to cope with problems that were considered could not adequately be resolved or governed by individual European states in isolation.[33] The EU is put to the test.

This was the case with the consultative and corrective[34] referendum in the Netherlands on 6 April 2016. A private initiative of anti-EU activists managed to collect 300,000 signatures to have a referendum on the Act approving the Association Agreement with Ukraine. This was carried out just months after the passage of the new Consultative Referendum Act 2014, which enabled a corrective consultative referendum to be held after the adoption of acts of parliament and prior to their entry into force.[35]

The promoters of the referendum acknowledged that the Act approving Ukraine's association might not be the best target for an EU referendum, but they considered it the only feasible manner to have the European project put before the people. In the referendum, 61 per cent of voters voted against the Act, with a turnout of 32 per cent—the 'no' vote thus comprising less than 20 per cent of the electorate. This percentage is slightly lower in proportion to the members of parliament who voted against the approval of the Association Agreement in the Lower House (*Tweede Kamer*).

Under the present legislation, the outcome of the referendum is valid if 30 per cent of voters turn out. The outcome is not binding, but it appears politically difficult to ignore

[30] For the calculation I used the following website of the Danish Parliament that provides data on all EU referenda: http://english.eu.dk/en/faq/faq/referendums (last accessed 10 October 2016). See a more analytical overview in Matt Qvortrup, 'Referendums on Membership and European Integration 1972–2015' (2016) 87 Pol Quarterly 61.

[31] This would require the reader to trivialize the words 'the *functioning of* the Union' as if it reads 'The Union shall be founded on representative democracy'.

[32] Fernando Mendez, Mario Mendez, and Vasiliki Triga, *Referendums and the European Union: A Comparative Inquiry* (Cambridge University Press 2014).

[33] See more on the reasons behind governments' voluntary promises to hold EU referenda in Kai Oppermann, 'The Politics of Discretionary Government Commitments to European Integration Referendums' (2013) 20 JEPP 684.

[34] The referendum outcome was not legally binding and therefore *consultative*; it was *corrective* in the sense that it could only be triggered after the adoption of an Act, with a view to assessing the approval or rejection of it by the electorate. This is the only possibility for holding a referendum under the present constitutional rules and legislation in the Netherlands.

[35] Act of 30 September 2014 on the consultative referendum [*Wet van 30 september 2014, houdende regels inzake het raadgevend referendum (Wet raadgevend referendum)*].

the clear majority of the vote, even if the 'no' vote represents only such a small minority of the electorate. Legally, the result is not binding, but the national government must reconsider its position. Prime Minister Mark Rutte announced that the Association Agreement would not be ratified 'unconditionally', and has sought a Decision by the European Council to take away a number of concerns the government understands the referendum outcome to mean. At the time of writing, the European Council has adopted the desired Decision, but it is uncertain whether the Dutch Parliament will find this sufficient.[36]

On 23 June 2016, the UK electorate voted by a narrow majority of those who voted (51.9 per cent against 48.1 per cent) to leave the EU.[37] Just as in the Dutch case, this majority did not constitute a majority of the electorate, with the 'Leave' votes constituting less than 38 per cent of the electorate. Contrary to the referendum in the Netherlands, however, the British referendum was not corrective, but must be considered abrogative, in as much as it aims to bring to an end the legal and constitutional situation as it applied generally thus far. So, unlike corrective referenda that are held to enable the electorate to prevent a certain act of a legislature to enter into force, the electorate thus being a popular corrective of an explicit and concrete parliamentary majority on a precise piece of legislation—in an abrogative referendum a matter on which parliament has not taken a specific position is left to the popular will to decide. Hence, the relation between an electorate voting in parliamentary elections and that voting in a referendum cannot easily be established.

For assessing the referendum's representative legitimacy, the turnout is not decisive, at any rate in its relation to the electorate represented in parliament. Moreover, the British referendum did not have any threshold, so it could not create a dilemma for the 'Remain' voters as to whether they would contribute to reaching the threshold by voting and thus to the validity of the outcome (as was a massive dilemma in the Netherlands Ukraine referendum that dominated the news and media on the day of the vote). Therefore, however narrow the margin, the results in the UK can be considered both representative and legitimate in terms of numbers and voters.

There is uncertainty, however, as to how long the outcomes of popular referenda hold their legitimating authority. The British referendum of 1975 had evidently reached its 'use by' date in June 2016. So who knows whether in forty years there might be another referendum on UK accession to the Union—if the UK and the EU still exist then.

8. Conclusion: National Parliaments Within the EU

Where does this leave the NPs of the Member States that are inside the EU and intend to remain so?[38] Should we divert our attention to the people rather than to its parliamentary representation?

[36] The Decision sets out the common understanding of the Parties to the Association Agreement that Ukraine is not a candidate Member State, that the Agreement does not provide for collective security guarantees, free movement of workers, or Member State obligations to provide bilateral financial support to Ukraine, while the combat of corruption in Ukraine and cooperation to strengthen the rule of law is aimed at strengthening the judiciary's independence, and Ukraine's compliance with the EU's fundamental values is subject to monitoring and sanctions. See European Council conclusions on Ukraine (15 December 2016), Annex I.

[37] The electorate counted 46,500,001 voters. The turnout was 72.2 per cent with 'Remain' receiving 16,141,241 votes (48.1 per cent of the votes cast) and 'Leave' 17,410,742 votes (51.9 per cent of the votes cast). See the official results at http://www.electoralcommission.org.uk/find-information-by-subject/elections-and-referendums/upcoming-elections-and-referendums/eu-referendum/electorate-and-count-information (last accessed 10 October 2016).

[38] At this stage, an equally interesting and speculative question is that of the extent to which the British Parliament and the devolved parliaments of Scotland and Wales will act as participants that

There are certainly indications that some of the social determinants of representative politics in Europe that affect representative democracy have eroded.[39] In many ways, one could say that in terms of constitutional history the 'long' 19th century (from the French Revolution to the First World War) was about democracy in an institutional sense, revolving around the powers of governments versus parliaments, which resulted in the adoption of the general franchise and in the establishment of some form of parliamentary government in practically all European states. The 20th century, at any rate since the end of the Second World War, became the century of individual constitutional rights. In the early 21st century, individualism drives to further extremes under the influence of technological change. What are paradoxically called 'social media' are extremely individualist media, to which anyone can have active access—and a 'public' can too, provided one's messages are short and easy to understand.

Politics is deeply affected by this. Aggregation of political action through organized social movements in the form of political parties has become more difficult as these are no longer the main channels of political opinion formation leading to political action. Fragmentation may sooner or later spill over to the institutions of politics and actually make the polity, as we have known its development since the end of the Middle Ages, a less self-evident form of living in pursuit of happiness.

In many ways, political and institutional fragmentation is not only *inwards* from state and government to individual citizens; it institutionally extends *outwards* as well. Parliaments are no longer institutions that operate within the confines of single states only. They are 'genetically' state institutions, constituted in accordance with the historical preferences and developments of the state involved, and at the same time actors in the surrounding world, most specifically and practically regulated in the EU context.

As long as the Union has been neither legitimated nor delegitimated by referenda, there is a crucial role for NPs. They provide day-to-day democratic legitimacy, including a sanctioning power as regards Member State representatives in the Council. They provide such legitimacy also for EU decision-making in general to the extent of their scrutinizing activity in parallel to the legitimating function of the EP.

There is still much reason to divert attention away from popular and populist politics towards the democratic legitimating function of parliaments, although there may well be space to make their role more visible and transparent[40] in the complex order of the Union as a political entity that aims at the common good in an era of globalization.[41]

are more 'inside' or more 'outside' the EU—and what the difference would be once an agreement has been struck with the EU on the terms of 'Brexit'. At any rate, notwithstanding pledges to fulfil EU legal obligations and the unaltered national constitutional rules, Westminster must be considered to be more outside it than was the case before the June 2016 EU membership referendum.

[39] See a brief analysis of the case of the Netherlands in Leonard Besselink and Monica Claes, 'The Netherlands' in Anneli Albi (ed), *National Constitutions in European and Global Governance: Democracy, Rights, the Rule of Law* (Springer 2017, forthcoming). See more on the present-day understanding of popular sovereignty from a Canadian background in Simone Chambers, 'Democracy, Popular Sovereignty, and Constitutional Legitimacy' (2004) 11 Constellations 153.

[40] One particularly important improvement would be in the area of scrutiny of the principle of conferral, similar to scrutiny of subsidiarity. See Davor Jančić, 'The Game of Cards: National Parliaments in the EU and the Future of the Early Warning Mechanism and the Political Dialogue' (2015) 52 CML Rev 939.

[41] See further discussions in Robert O Keohane, 'Nominal Democracy? Prospects for Democratic Global Governance' (2015) 13 ICON 343; Wojciech Sadurski, 'Supranational Public Reason: On Legitimacy of Supranational Norm-producing Authorities' (2015) 4 Glob Con 396.

3

National Parliaments and Mediated Legitimacy in the EU

Theory and History

Peter L Lindseth

1. The Theory Introduced

Legitimacy is a protean concept in law and politics. In general terms, legitimacy refers to the manner in which social and political actors experience a system of governance as worthy of their acceptance, loyalty, and respect. In this way, legitimacy can provide a degree of stability and durability to forms of social organization and rule. But how actors in fact experience a system may well shift not only by social or political context but also over time. Moreover, although these shifts may at times appear obvious, they are often perceptible only in the slow evolution of the system itself. Legitimacy thus presents an analytical challenge to anyone interested in the relationship between legal and political change and their socio-political, socio-cultural underpinnings.

Consider, for example, the changing nature of the legitimacy of a 'constitutional' legislature (say, a national parliament) as opposed to a merely 'administrative' body (say, an executive department or, in more recent times, an independent agency). In modern governance, both types of institutions are generally experienced as legitimate producers of rules of general and prospective application, albeit in different contexts and under different constraints. The rules produced by administrative bodies are, legally at least, generally experienced as inferior to, indeed even dependent upon, the rules produced by legislatures. For lawyers, this is a straightforward question of the hierarchy of norms. But behind that sense of normative hierarchy is in fact a complex socio-historical phenomenon of legitimacy that is anything but straightforward. The rules produced by administrative bodies—'regulations', 'ordinances', 'statutory instruments', as the case may be—may in the lawyer's mind be self-evidently subordinate to 'legislation'. But we also know that, as an historical matter, the realm of administrative power has greatly expanded over the course of the twentieth century (particularly after 1945), in a way that has significantly altered, and perhaps even diminished, the role of national parliaments.[1] What do these broader socio-political shifts suggest about the differential legitimacy of rule-making in these different types of bodies?

This question is crucial to understanding the role of national parliaments (NPs) in EU governance. The emergence of the EU over the last six and a half decades presents

[1] See generally Peter L Lindseth, *Power and Legitimacy: Reconciling Europe and the Nation-State* (Oxford University Press 2010) ch 2. See also Peter L Lindseth, 'The Paradox of Parliamentary Supremacy: Delegation, Democracy, and Dictatorship in Germany and France, 1920s–1950s' (2004) 113 Yale LJ 1341.

National Parliaments and Mediated Legitimacy in the EU: Theory and History. First Edition. Peter L Lindseth 2017.

a fascinating case study in legal and political change in which varying conceptions of legitimacy have played a crucial role. The aim of this chapter is to explore how those conceptions have manifested themselves in the context of the evolving role of NPs in EU public law. To this end, we must confront the variable nature of legitimacy in more theoretical depth. That is the objective of section 1, culminating in a discussion of what this chapter calls *mediated legitimacy* in modern administrative governance. Section 2 then explores how the theory of mediated legitimacy might illuminate the historical evolution of national parliamentary scrutiny in EU affairs. The conclusion to the chapter reflects on the broader question of 'resilience' and 'resignation' of NPs in the process of European integration going forward.

1.1 The Many Faces of Legitimacy in Modern Governance

Let us begin with a schematic overview of the possible types of legitimacy of administratively produced norms as a way of exploring the variable character of legitimacy in modern governance more generally.

First, administratively produced norms are generally experienced as at least *legally* legitimate when they are understood to remain within the substantive and procedural constraints of the enabling legislation and the constitution. Furthermore, they are often experienced as *technocratically* legitimate when they are seen as the product of administrative expertise derived from informed evidence gathering and reason-giving (by contrast, norms produced by constitutional legislatures are not, generally speaking, subject to the same expertise-based constraints). Additionally, administrative rules are experienced as *functionally* legitimate in the face of the perceived incapacity of constitutional legislatures to produce norms of the scope and depth needed to address 'modern problems'—a claim often used to justify delegations of normative and regulatory power to supposedly more capable administrative actors.[2] This functional necessity is also often at the heart of the willingness to confer normative *autonomy and independence* on administrative bodies, at least when the technocratic justification combined with the desire for insulation from 'politics' is also strong (factors felt acutely but not exclusively in the realm of central banking, for example).[3]

Despite the force of these alternative claims of administrative legitimacy—legal, technocratic, and functional—they have arguably not been sufficient to give legitimacy to administrative rule-making along one final dimension: democracy. We live, or at least hope we still live, in an age where democracy is the ultimate legitimating baseline of modern governance. Administrative norms are generally not experienced as *democratically* legitimate in themselves, particularly if they are produced with some measure of autonomy and independence from hierarchical political control. Moreover, even if

[2] For classic statements of this type of functional legitimacy see James Landis, *The Administrative Process* (Yale University Press, Oxford University Press 1938); John Willis, 'Three Approaches to Administrative Law: The Judicial, the Conceptual, and the Functional' (1935) 1 U Toronto LJ 53. For more recent discussions see Martin Loughlin, 'The Functionalist Style in Public Law' (2005) 55 U Toronto LJ 361; Peter L Lindseth, 'Transatlantic Functionalism: New Deal Models and European Integration' (2015) 2 Critical Analysis of Law 83.

[3] See eg *Brunner v European Union Treaty* (the German Maastricht Decision), 12 October 1993, BVerfGE 89, 155, [1994] 1 CMLR 57, 33 ILM 388 [1994], specifically at 439 (rationalizing transfer of control over monetary policy to the European Central Bank 'in order to ensure that currency is not vulnerable to pressure groups or to holders of public office seeking re-election').

not legally mandated (as with independent agencies), such autonomy is in some sense unavoidable, simply by virtue of bureaucratic density and complexity.[4] Lacking democratic and constitutional legitimacy of their own, administratively produced norms are normally seen as at best *derivative* of the legitimacy of democratic and constitutional institutions that reside elsewhere in the system.

The national legislature is the presumptive source of such legitimacy, a privileged role often inscribed in the constitution itself. Over the course of the twentieth century, however, increasingly plebiscitarian 'chief executives' (heads of state or government) became a competing source in many systems, particularly in providing hierarchical oversight or control within the burgeoning administrative sphere. Nonetheless, nearly all constitutional systems continue to reserve at least one core normative domain to the legislature: the power to define the precise circumstances of compulsory societal mobilization, whether human (defence or policing) or fiscal (taxing, spending, and borrowing).[5] In this crucial domain, robust democratic and constitutional legitimacy via the historically 'constituted' legislature continues to be experienced as essential; mere administrative or even plebiscitarian executive legitimacy would not be enough. Courts and court-like bodies, like the French *Conseil d'Etat*, also play an important democratizing role here, by policing the constitutional boundary between democratic politics (legislative and executive) and the realm of administrative actors, while also defending individual rights.

The struggle to define a workable boundary between democratic politics and administrative power was in fact central to the evolution of public law in the North Atlantic world over the course of the twentieth century.[6] The great achievement of post-war governance was to develop an institutional and legal formula that, on the national level at least, could help to reconcile the growth of administrative governance with a historically recognizable, if evolving, sense of democratic self-government grounded in the classic *trias politica*. Legislatures, the political summit of the executive, as well as courts and court-like review bodies each played a crucial role in legitimizing the output of the administrative sphere in democratic terms. The term of art that my work has used to refer to this legal-historical reconciliation is the *post-war constitutional settlement of administrative governance*.[7]

The essence of that settlement was this: even as functional and technocratic demands continued to impel ever greater delegations of normative power to administrative bodies, '[t]he branches of government that enjoyed constitutional legitimacy inherited from the past—whether democratic (ie executive or legislative) or judicial—became conduits through which the legitimacy of the new forms of administrative governance could be *mediated*'.[8] How did mediated legitimacy work? Not necessarily through direct control, particularly where claims or simply the realities of administrative autonomy have been strong. In fact, autonomy is often the very

[4] Peter L Lindseth, 'Agents Without Principals? Delegation in an Age of Diffuse and Fragmented Governance' in Fabrizio Cafaggi (ed), *Reframing Self-regulation in European Private Law* (Kluwer Law International 2006).

[5] Peter L Lindseth, 'Between the "Real" and the "Right": Explorations Along the Institutional-Constitutional Frontier' in Maurice Adams, Ernst Hirsch Ballinf, and Anne Meuwese (eds), *Constitutionalism and the Rule of Law: Bridging Idealism and Realism* (Cambridge University Press, forthcoming) http://papers.ssrn.com/sol3/papers.cfm?abstract_id=2716185 (last accessed 12 October 2016).

[6] See generally Lindseth, 'The Paradox of Parliamentary Supremacy' (n 1).

[7] Lindseth, *Power and Legitimacy* (n 1).

[8] Lindseth, 'The Paradox of Parliamentary Supremacy' (n 1) 1415.

purpose of delegation, if not also its inevitable side-effect, given the diffusion and fragmentation of normative power in modern governance.[9] We must thus dispense with an idealized understanding of a 'Westphalian' principal with unbridled control over administrative agents or power to direct regulatory outcomes within a particular territory. This is an ahistoric reading of state sovereignty if ever there was one,[10] as well as a caricature of the principal-agent relationship that is far from the actual historical reality, not just supranationally but also nationally. Instead, mediated legitimacy in modern administrative governance is more often accomplished through looser forms of supervision, coordination, or what an American administrative lawyer would call 'oversight'.[11]

Mediated legitimacy and associated forms of oversight have been deeply bound up with the changing nature of public law under the post-war constitutional settlement. Public law has become less a system of rules demarcating seemingly clear lines between 'valid' and 'invalid' exercises of authority, as classical understandings of the *Rechtsstaat, l'Etat de droit*, or the Rule of Law might have demanded.[12] Instead, public law has evolved toward something more focused on 'the allocation of burdens of reason-giving',[13] or, as European scholars are increasingly calling it, 'accountability'. As Benz, Harlow, and Papadopoulos put it, accountability is 'a process of communication in which information is transferred and reasons for policies discussed', which in turn serves as 'a significant institutional element of effective and legitimate organisations ... accepted by every discipline as an essential aspect of principal–agent theory'.[14]

Such accountability mechanisms may be understood as a system of 'resistance norms', operating 'as a "soft limit" which may be more or less yielding depending on the circumstances', to borrow a powerful distinction first advanced by Ernest Young.[15] Rarely do these norms prevent the exercise of delegated authority outright; rather, they serve to raise the costs to the agent of using that power,[16] while having the added benefit of simultaneously reducing the information costs to the principal, thus enabling more effective oversight. In this way, oversight serves to maintain a legitimating connection between the burgeoning, often autonomous realm of administrative governance and the 'paradigmatic function' of the historical institutions of constitutional government—legislative, executive, and judicial—that we inherit from the past.[17]

[9] Lindseth, 'Agents Without Principals? Delegation in an Age of Diffuse and Fragmented Governance' (n 4).

[10] James J Sheehan, 'Presidential Address: The Problem of Sovereignty in European History' (2006) 111 Am Hist Rev 1.

[11] See eg Peter L Strauss, 'Foreword: Overseer, or "the Decider"? The President in Administrative Law' (2007) 75 Geo Wash L Rev 696.

[12] cf Ernest A Young, 'Constitutional Avoidance, Resistance Norms, and the Preservation of Judicial Review' (2000) 78 Texas L Rev 1549, 1594.

[13] Alexander Somek, 'Dogmatischer Pragmatismus. Die Normativitätskrise der Europäischen Union' in Stefan Hammer and others (eds), *Demokratie und sozialer Rechtsstaat in Europa. Festschrift für Theo Öhlinger* (WUV-Universitätsverlag 2004) 58.

[14] Arthur Benz, Carol Harlow, and Yannis Papadopoulos, 'Introduction' (2007) 13 ELJ [Special Issue: Accountability in EU Multilevel Governance] 441, 445.

[15] Young (n 12) 1504.

[16] cf Matthew C Stephenson, 'A Costly Signaling Theory of "Hard Look" Judicial Review' (2006) 58 Admin L Rev 753; Matthew C Stephenson, 'The Price of Public Action: Constitutional Doctrine and the Judicial Manipulation of Legislative Enactment Costs' (2008) 118 Yale LJ 2.

[17] Peter L Strauss, 'Formal and Functional Approaches to Separation-of-Powers Questions—A Foolish Inconsistency?' (1987) 72 Cornell L Rev 488, 493.

1.2 Building on the Post-war Constitutional Settlement: Mediated Legitimacy in EU Governance

At this point, the reader may want to press the question: what do these various forms of legitimacy in modern administrative governance—most importantly mediated legitimacy—have to do with the evolving role of NPs in EU affairs?

The answer is simple, even if the theoretical argument is ultimately complex. As my work has argued elsewhere in much greater detail, the legitimacy of EU governance as a whole remains primarily 'administrative, not constitutional'.[18] The EU's legitimacy, in other words, is not autonomously democratic and constitutional in its own right, at least not in a socio-historical sense, but rather derivative. This is not to deny that European integration involves 'politics' or has profound 'constitutional' implications for its Member States or citizens (so too did the expansion of administrative power on the national level over the course of the twentieth century, by the way). The 'administrative, not constitutional' label is meant only to stress that the legitimacy of EU rule-making, enforcement, and adjudication comes closer to the sort of administrative legitimacy that is mediated through national executives, national courts, and national parliaments than is commonly supposed.

The strongest indicator of the EU's lack of autonomous democratic and constitutional legitimacy is so fundamental that it is puzzling why EU legal scholarship so often ignores it. I am referring to the unwillingness of Europeans to grant EU institutions *any macroeconomically or geopolitically significant powers of compulsory mobilization of fiscal or human resources*. This, as noted above, remains the core attribute of national parliaments even in the era of administrative governance and is also the strongest indicator of their privileged position as sources of democratic and constitutional legitimacy in modern governance.[19] The EU's autonomous fiscal resources are limited to a supranational budget amounting to roughly 1 per cent of the aggregated Member States' GDPs, only a limited portion of which actually derives from the EU's 'own resources'. The EU's capacity to mobilize human resources for defence or policing is even more limited, restricted to border-control support through Frontex and coordination through Europol and the European Defence Agency (EDA). All other mobilization of fiscal and human resources in the EU ultimately depends on the more robust democratic and constitutional legitimacy of national parliaments, a limitation that has had a real impact on EU capacities in the face of various recent crises—the Eurozone, refugees, and terrorism.[20] Without such legitimacy, the EU becomes a primarily normative, regulatory entity—a powerful one to be sure, but nonetheless one whose authority depends almost entirely on the Member States to mobilize the resources needed to enforce its norms.

The EU's normative power, like all power of an ultimately administrative character, finds its legitimacy primarily in legal, technocratic, and functional claims. The EU benefits in particular from the need to coordinate a range of regulatory policies across multiple Member States. This coordination demands delegation from the national to the supranational level in order to produce rules to further the policy goals of integration among the Member States themselves—what Fritz Scharpf effectively alluded to when he famously spoke of the EU's 'output legitimacy'.[21] In this way, the EU's

[18] Lindseth, *Power and Legitimacy* (n 1).

[19] See n 5 and accompanying text.

[20] See nn 98–102 and accompanying text.

[21] See generally Fritz W Scharpf, *Governing in Europe: Effective and Democratic?* (Oxford University Press 1999).

supranational system of governance exists as a kind of hyper-powerful agency exercising delegated normative and regulatory power conferred upon it by multiple national constitutional principals. These principals have for sound functional reasons committed themselves to the surveillance of 'pre-commitment' agents at the EU level—eg the Commission, the European Court of Justice (ECJ, now the Court of Justice of the European Union (CJEU)), and the European Central Bank (ECB)—in order to make integration a functioning reality and not just a legal fiction.[22]

In pursuing its mandate, the EU possesses a degree of electoral legitimacy through the European Parliament (EP), as well as some indirect electoral legitimacy through the Council (Scharpf's 'input legitimacy').[23] The EU's problem, however, is neither inputs nor outputs but *demos*-legitimacy: Europeans have not yet come to experience its regulatory apparatus as the expression of an identity between a population—a historically coherent *demos*—and a set of institutions that is perceived as the *demos*'s 'own', constituted over time for the purposes of self-government.[24] The EU remains primarily derivative of national *demoi*. This sort of historically constructed identity between ruling institutions and the ruled is the ultimate foundation of democratic and constitutional legitimacy in modern governance, one that makes true solidarity (not to mention compulsory mobilization) possible on a socio-political scale. Whereas the EU's output legitimacy might create a sense of 'government *for* the people' and its input legitimacy a sense of 'government *by* the people', what the EU lacks is a sense of an identity-based 'government *of* the people'. As Kalypso Nicolaïdis has stressed, the EU is 'a community of projects, not a community of identity'.[25] The EU is thus *demoi*-cratic rather than democratic. Its democratic legitimacy is polycentrically distributed among the Member States.

It is thus unsurprising that the public law of European integration has continually resorted to mechanisms of nationally mediated legitimacy—executive, legislative, and judicial—in order to 'borrow' legitimacy from the national level. National executives were the primary source of this mediated legitimacy for much of integration history, by way of the Council of Ministers and the European Council. However, over the last several decades, national high courts and eventually even NPs have become increasingly important sources as well. Indeed, EU public law has long heavily depended on cooperation of national courts, and this is something they have generally been willing to provide subject to more recent outer limitations designed to protect the democratic character of national government (very much in keeping with the judicial role under the post-war constitutional settlement).[26] As for NPs, establishing forms of mediated legitimacy—in the sense of information flows and oversight—have arguably been the principal motivation behind national parliamentary scrutiny mechanisms in the EU context, as the history in section 2 will suggest. These mechanisms target not merely the actions of national executives operating at the EU level but also the supranational

[22] This is in keeping with the role of delegation on the national level. On the relationship between national and supranational forms of delegation as pre-commitment mechanisms see Giandomenico Majone, 'Europe's "Democratic Deficit": The Question of Standards' (1998) 4 ELJ 5.

[23] Scharpf (n 21).

[24] For an eloquent statement of this understanding of the EU, see Matteo Renzi's 'Programme of Activities of the Italian Presidency' before the EP (2 July 2014) http://www.europarl.europa.eu/sides/getDoc.do?pubRef=-//EP//TEXT+CRE+20140702+ITEMS+DOC+XML+V0//EN&language=EN#creitem13 (last accessed 12 October 2016). For more elaboration of the point, see Peter L Lindseth, 'Of the People: Democracy, the Eurozone, and Lincoln's Threshold Criterion' [2012] Berlin Journal 4.

[25] Kalypso Nicolaïdis, 'We, the Peoples of Europe …' (2004) 83 Foreign Aff 97, 102.

[26] For a review of some of the leading cases, see Lindseth, *Power and Legitimacy* (n 1) ch 4.

regulatory output of EU institutions themselves, through the so-called early warning mechanism (EWM) established in the Treaty of Lisbon.

1.3 National Parliaments as Instruments of Mediated Legitimacy: Addressing the Democratic Disconnect in the EU

Once we look at NPs as instruments of mediated legitimacy in EU policy-making, we begin to appreciate how NPs have proven to be both 'resilient' and 'resigned' in the process of European integration, a topic this chapter takes up in greater detail in the conclusion.

On the one hand, NPs have been resigned in the face of functional demands for delegation and autonomy in EU affairs. NPs simply lack the time, expertise, or capacity to develop the range of regulatory norms that such governance demands, particularly where integration requires multilateral cooperation and coordination across national borders. Certain supranational agents—the Commission, the EP, the CJEU, and the ECB, as well as the institutions in which national executives play a key role (the Council and the European Council)—are all necessary to achieve goals that NPs are functionally incapable of achieving on their own. Tempered somewhat by the electoral legitimacy of the EP (which should not be confused with *demos*-legitimacy),[27] these supranational bodies are ultimately manifestations of the technocratic, juristocratic, and executive orientation of EU governance, building on similar dimensions of governance under the post-war constitutional settlement on the national level.

Despite this inevitable degree of resignation, NPs have lately also proven to be quite resilient, indeed assertive, in providing mediated legitimacy to EU governance. Just as in the administrative state, the expansion of supranational regulatory power has demanded some degree of mediated legitimacy through national parliamentary scrutiny, even as national executive oversight has remained the predominant source of legitimation. Although the EWM is the most prominent manifestation of this reassertion of parliamentary prerogatives in EU public law, the role of NPs as a source of mediated legitimacy has historical roots stretching at least back to the 1970s if not before, as we shall see below in section 2.

The purpose of these national parliamentary scrutiny mechanisms, this chapter suggests, is to address not the 'democratic deficit' but the 'democratic disconnect' at the heart of the integration process. My insistence on this alternative conceptual vocabulary is deliberate. The 'deficit' view implies that the legitimacy challenge is simply one of institutional engineering: how to ensure broader powers for the elected EP (or perhaps for the electorate itself through the European Citizens' Initiative) in order to make up for the legitimacy shortfall that prevents the EU from becoming an autonomous level of democratic and constitutional governance in a quasi-federal system. The 'disconnect' view, by contrast, stresses the dynamic at the heart of the EU's ultimately 'administrative, not constitutional' character: the separation of regulatory *power* from democratic *legitimacy* in EU governance. The challenge facing the EU is not one of fixing a 'deficit' but overcoming, in a more socio-political way, the 'disconnect' between the EU's regulatory power and its sources of democratic legitimacy at the national

[27] cf JHH Weiler, 'The Political and Legal Culture of European Integration: An Exploratory Essay' (2011) 9 ICON 678, 679 ('The manifestations of the so-called democracy deficit are persistent, and no endless repetition of the powers of the European Parliament will remove them'); see also Peter L Lindseth, *Disequilibrium and Disconnect: On Weiler's (Still Robust) Theory of European Transformation* (9 May 2013) U Conn School of Law Working Papers No 2013/01.

level.[28] The 'disconnect' view derives from an empirically based historical recognition that, at this point in Europe's development, such democratic and constitutional legitimacy at the EU level is lacking.[29] Consequently, European elites cannot easily engineer that legitimacy into existence, as the 'deficit' claim implies, at least in the short or intermediate term.

Caution over the capacity of institutional engineering, however, is also the reason why we should not be excessively sanguine about the capacity of mediated legitimacy to support democratically the full scope of EU regulatory power—whether via NPs under the EWM or otherwise. By design, EU institutions exercise their power with extraordinary autonomy from the control of any single Member State, and rightfully so from the perspective of enforcing national 'pre-commitments' to the goals of integration.[30] The problem is that, given the multiplicity of constitutional principals at the national level, the EU's technocratic agents in Brussels and Frankfurt, as well as its juristocratic agents in Luxembourg, are more entrenched than are pre-commitment bodies in purely national forms of administrative governance. The fact of multiple national constitutional principals—and therefore of even more 'veto players'[31]—means that the political coordination needed to reverse supranational action is vastly more challenging and transnational in the EU. This supranational entrenchment can give rise to a seeming *principal-agent inversion* in which supranational bodies appear to take on the character of principals in the integration process, supervising the conduct of Member States as their agents.[32]

Viewed exclusively from a functionalist perspective—which is arguably the true foundation of supranational 'constitutionalism' in the EU, such as it is[33]—this inversion is perhaps uncontroversial. Viewed from the broader perspective of democratic and constitutional legitimacy at the national level, it becomes the source of resentment and backlash. Hence the ongoing process of contestation—a kind of tug-of-war—that has pitted the functional necessity of EU power against national prerogatives derived from the Member States' superior democratic and constitutional legitimacy. This tug-of-war has deeply shaped the legal and political history of European integration and it helps to explain historical evolution of national parliamentary scrutiny in EU affairs. It is to that topic we now turn.

2. Reading the History in Light of the Theory

As the discussion in section 1 suggests, in order to understand the evolution of the involvement of NPs in EU affairs, one must follow two strands of development, one national and one supranational, even as these histories are in fact intertwined.[34] The discussion in section 2 will initially bracket the development of parliamentary scrutiny mechanisms on the national level, which started embryonically in the 1950s and 1960s

[28] See generally Peter L Lindseth, 'Delegation Is Dead, Long Live Delegation: Managing the Democratic Disconnect in the European Market-Polity' in Christian Joerges and Renaud Dehousse (eds), *Good Governance in Europe's Integrated Market* (Oxford University Press 2002).

[29] cf Neil Fligstein, *Euroclash: The EU, European Identity, and the Future of Europe* (Oxford University Press 2008).

[30] See n 22 and accompanying text.

[31] George Tsebelis, *Veto Players: How Political Institutions Work* (Princeton University Press 2002).

[32] This inversion is detailed in Lindseth, *Power and Legitimacy* (n 1) 254–56.

[33] Turkuler Isiksel, *Europe's Functional Constitution: A Theory of Constitutionalism Beyond the State* (Oxford University Press 2016).

[34] The discussion in section 2 draws from Lindseth, *Power and Legitimacy* (n 1) ch 5.

and gained a bit more traction with the accession of Denmark and the UK in the 1970s. The discussion will instead begin in a somewhat unorthodox fashion—in the middle of the history—by analyzing the pivotal changes occurring in European law in the mid-1980s and early 1990s that accompanied the vast expansion in supranational regulatory power.

The most important developments in that regard were the Single European Act of 1986, the programme to complete the internal market by 1992, as well as the entry into force of the Treaty of Maastricht in 1993, along with the recognition of subsidiarity as a foundational principle in EU public law. One cannot understand why the earlier efforts at developing national parliamentary scrutiny would later culminate in the establishment of an EWM without first appreciating two inter-related phenomena: the increasing penetration of EU norms into national legal orders, as well as the failure of the ECJ to police that penetration under the principle of subsidiarity in any meaningful way.[35] The result of this intermediate history was the political transformation of the EU's legislative process, with the creation of a kind of administrative-procedural code stressing information flows to NPs, on which the development of all subsequent forms of national parliamentary scrutiny—ie mediated legitimacy—would come to depend.

2.1 Subsidiarity and the Expansion of Supranational Regulatory Power

As a commentator noted in the early 1990s, it was 'no coincidence' that the drafters of the EU Treaties would 'put subsidiarity in plain view' after the vast expansion in EU regulatory power over the prior half-decade.[36] And yet, there was still a great deal of scepticism with regard to the legal effects of this principle, most importantly its justiciability by the ECJ. Lord Mackenzie Stuart, the Scottish former President of the ECJ, expressed the conventional view in 1991: 'To decide whether a given action is more appropriate at Community level, necessary at Community level, effective at Community level is essentially a political topic. It is not the sort of question a Court should be asked to decide'.[37]

This judicial scepticism, however, did little to deter the Member States from giving special emphasis to subsidiarity in the 1990s. This was especially the case in those Member States that were arguably the most ambivalent about the direction of integration. For example, following the rejection of the Maastricht Treaty in Denmark in the referendum of June 1992, the Danish parties drafted a 'National Compromise', which inter alia specifically looked to subsidiarity as a way to 'take greater account of different traditions and forms of organization in the individual Member States', linking this with calls for heightened transparency, regulatory simplicity, and national parliamentary scrutiny.[38] This linkage was echoed in the conclusions of the Lisbon

[35] See the relationship between national courts and NPs in the chapter by Cristina Fasone and Nicola Lupo in this volume.

[36] George A Bermann, 'Taking Subsidiarity Seriously: Federalism in the European Community and the United States' (1994) 94 Colum L Rev 331, 345.

[37] Quoted in Stephen Weatherill, 'Competence Creep and Competence Control' (2005) 23 YEL 2004 1, 16.

[38] Danish National Compromise, 'EU Information Centre of the Folketing' (1992) http://www.euo.dk/upload/application/pdf/97ca9e4c/EU%20kompromis.pdf (last accessed 12 October 2016); Helle Krunke, 'Peoples' Vengeances—From Maastricht to Edinburgh: The Danish Solution' (2005) 1 EuConst 339.

European Council meeting soon after the failed Danish referendum, as well as in conclusions of the Birmingham European Council meeting in October 1992 following the shockingly close victory of the 'yes' side in the French referendum of the same year. The Birmingham Declaration, as one observer put it, emphasized 'elements … designed [not merely] to appeal in Denmark, but also to reticent backbenchers in the UK' who had yet to vote on the Maastricht Treaty.[39] These elements would include greater respect for cultural traditions, better information for NPs, and the introduction of procedures to make enforcement of the principle of subsidiarity a reality.

The primary aim of the Danish National Compromise was to specify the four so-called 'exceptions' that Denmark demanded as the basis for a second referendum on the Maastricht Treaty.[40] But in acquiescing to Danish demands, the heads of state and government who reassembled as the European Council at Edinburgh in December 1992 were acutely sensitive not just to the concerns of the electorate in Denmark or backbenchers in the UK. They were also increasingly anxious about public opinion throughout Europe. Thus, the Edinburgh European Council took steps to realize the goals of the Birmingham Declaration by conspicuously adopting a new set of subsidiarity 'guidelines' that were paired with additional 'measures to increase transparency and openness in the decision-making process of the Community'.[41] The following year, the Commission, the Council, and the EP took the Edinburgh guidelines one step further by entering into an interinstitutional agreement 'on procedures for implementing the principle of subsidiarity'.[42] The most important feature of this agreement, for our purposes, was the commitment of the Commission, in exercising its right of legislative initiative, to 'take into account the principle of subsidiarity and show that it has been observed' (section II(1)). More specifically, the Commission agreed that, as part of its explanatory memorandum for any proposal, it would submit 'a justification … under the principle of subsidiarity' (section II(2)).

While the actual content of these commitments remained extremely vague, they nevertheless suggested that the key dimension of subsidiarity was in fact procedural, not substantive or even jurisdictional. Subsidiarity, understood procedurally, directed 'the legislative institutions of the Community to engage in a particular inquiry before concluding that action at the Community rather than Member State level is warranted'.[43] This procedural interpretation of subsidiarity also implied a role for the ECJ, in which this Court would verify 'whether the institutions themselves examined the possibility of alternative remedies at or below the Member State level'.[44] The Court would need to ensure, procedurally, that supranational institutions, particularly the Commission, 'structure[d] their discussion and focus[ed] their debate' specifically on questions of subsidiarity, which then 'should promote a realistic assessment … of the costs and benefits of Community action and inaction alike'.[45]

In the EU context, however, it would not be the Court but rather the Member States that would advance this obligation of reasoned subsidiarity analysis. In several cases before the ECJ in the late 1990s and early 2000s, the Court demonstrated itself to be

[39] Richard Corbett, *The Treaty of Maastricht from Conception to Ratification: A Comprehensive Reference Guide* (Longman Current Affairs 1993) 69.

[40] See generally Krunke (n 38).

[41] Edinburgh European Council (1992) 12–1992 Bulletin of the European Communities 7, 9.

[42] Interinstitutional Agreement of 25 October 1993 between the European Parliament, the Council and the Commission on Procedures for Implementing the Principle of Subsidiarity, 1993 OJ (C 329) 135.

[43] Bermann (n 36) 336. [44] ibid 391. [45] ibid.

singularly disinterested in the procedural dimension of subsidiarity.[46] In the first case, the Court simply inferred, in the absence of any evidence, that the legislation satisfied subsidiarity solely by virtue of the Council's decision to legislate.[47] In the second, the Court relied exclusively on conclusory statements contained in the Directive's recitals, finding somewhat sweepingly that 'the Parliament and the Council did explain why they considered that their action was in conformity with the principle of subsidiarity'.[48] In the third case, the Court found that compliance with subsidiarity could be 'implicit' in the Directive's recitals, without any detailed statement of reasons.[49] As one commentator concluded, once it was 'determined that a competence to establish common rules exists, the political decision to exercise that competence seem[ed] *in practice* immune from judicial supervision'.[50]

The Court's permissive attitude helps to explain why the Member States felt compelled to specify what Europe's supranational judges would not: that in order to satisfy the requirements of subsidiarity, EU institutions would need to assemble an evidentiary record showing why supranational legislation was required in the particular case. The first step was the insertion of the Subsidiarity Protocol into the EC Treaty by virtue of the Treaty of Amsterdam of 1997, at the particular urging of France, Germany, and the United Kingdom. The Amsterdam Subsidiarity Protocol provided, in pertinent part, that '[f]or any proposed Community legislation, the reasons on which it is based shall be stated with a view to justifying its compliance with the principles of subsidiarity and proportionality', stating further that 'the reasons ... must be substantiated by qualitative or, wherever possible, quantitative indicators'. The Protocol further obligated the Commission to 'consult widely before proposing legislation and, wherever appropriate, publish consultation documents' as well as 'to take duly into account' the burdens of the rules it was proposing on 'national governments, local authorities, economic operators and citizens'. The Protocol finally obligated the Commission to issue an annual report to the European Council and the other EU institutions on the application of the principles of subsidiarity and proportionality.

The Amsterdam Subsidiarity Protocol thus established the rudiments of an administrative procedural 'code' for the EU legislative process, one obligating the Commission to consult interests, assess impacts, and report to oversight bodies in a way that would inevitably constrain the Commission's exercise of its right of legislative initiative. Successive European Councils—at Lisbon in March 2000, Stockholm in March 2001, Gothenburg in June 2001, Laeken in December 2001, and Barcelona in March 2002—would call on the Commission to develop 'a strategy for further coordinated

[46] This historical analysis focuses on the following three judgments: Case C-84/94, *United Kingdom v Council* [1996] ECR I-5755 (Working Time Directive); Case C-233/94, *Germany v Parliament and Council* [1997] ECR I-2405 (Deposit-Guarantee Schemes); and Case C-491/01, *R v Secretary of State ex parte BAT and Imperial Tobacco* [2002] ECR I-11543. For a detailed critique of the first two judgments, see Peter L Lindseth, 'Democratic Legitimacy and the Administrative Character of Supranationalism: The Example of the European Community' (1999) 99 Colum L Rev 628, 714–26; for a critique of the third, see Weatherill (n 37) 15–16.

[47] Case C-84/94, *United Kingdom v Council* [1996] ECR I-5755, I-5809, para 47 (Working Time Directive). For a critique, see Lindseth (n 46) 715–16.

[48] Case C-233/94, *Germany v Parliament and Council* [1997] ECR I-2405, I-2453, para 28 (Deposit-Guarantee Schemes). See Lindseth (n 46) 716. One might also note that the Directive satisfied the rather perfunctory general reason-giving obligation under the old Article 190 (TFEU, art 296), at least as it was permissively interpreted by the Court. See Lindseth (n 46) 692–93.

[49] Case C-377/98, *Netherlands v Parliament and Council* [2001] ECR I-07079, para 33 (Biotechnological Inventions).

[50] Weatherill (n 37) 15–16 (emphasis in original), discussing Case C-491/01, *R v Secretary of State ex parte BAT and Imperial Tobacco* [2002] ECR I-11543.

action to simplify the regulatory environment'. The Commission in turn produced its now-famous White Paper on Governance, committing itself to a programme of improving the quality of EU legislation.[51] From 2001 onwards, the Commission progressively introduced a detailed procedural system where each major policy initiative must include a consultation with stakeholders, an analysis of the measure's expected impact, and a justification of action at the EU level in accordance with the principles of subsidiarity and proportionality.

It was against this background that the Convention on the Future of Europe in 2004 developed the basic elements of what would eventually become the EWM in the Treaty of Lisbon.[52] However, the EWM would have been all but impossible to put into effect without developments under national law over the prior three decades, which significantly strengthened national parliamentary scrutiny vis-à-vis national executives in the formulation of their EU policies. In the next section, we take up these national developments, tracing the emergence of the various models of scrutiny from the 1970s to the 2000s, focusing on the two leading competitors, the Danish 'mandating' and the British 'document-based' systems. As we shall see below, these developments were essential to reinforcing the role of mediated legitimacy of NPs in EU affairs, providing the essential foundation upon which the EWM would subsequently build.

2.2 The Institutionalization of National Parliamentary Scrutiny Under National Law

At the inception of European integration in the 1950s, the parliaments of the original six Member States showed relatively little sustained interest in establishing European scrutiny mechanisms. Over the course of the next decade, there were intermittent attempts to create rudimentary parliamentary committees devoted to European affairs, but they were relatively superficial and weak.[53] National parliamentarians understood their function primarily as one of ratifying the Treaties and then allowing the national executive to take the policy-making lead, which was further seen primarily as an aspect of foreign policy.[54] There was little or no political pressure for detailed national parliamentary scrutiny of European policy in the early years of integration, which was not yet perceived as having a major domestic regulatory impact and thus did not yet require mediated legitimacy through NPs.

The entry of Denmark and the UK into the Community in 1973, however, marked a turning point. By the early 1970s, the legal consequences of Community membership—both in terms of its impact specifically on parliamentary prerogatives and more generally on national sovereignty—were much more evident than in the 1950s. The Luxembourg Compromise of 1966 had made clear the foundational importance of the national executives in the Community decision-making process, whereas the creation of the European Council in 1974 further accentuated the role of national chief executives. Over the course of the 1960s and into the early 1970s, the ECJ also issued an array of decisions on the direct effect of Treaty provisions (*Van Gend en Loos*

[51] European Commission, 'European Governance: A White Paper (21 July 2001)', COM(2001) 428, 2001.

[52] See section 2.3.

[53] See Lindseth, *Power and Legitimacy* (n 1) 205–06.

[54] Antonio Cassese, *Parliamentary Foreign Affairs Committees, the National Setting: Essays* (Cedam 1982); Andreas Maurer and Wolfgang Wessels, 'National Parliaments after Amsterdam: From Slow Adapters to National Players?' in Andreas Maurer and Wolfgang Wessels (eds), *National Parliaments on Their Ways to Europe: Losers or Latecomers* (Nomos 2001) 429.

in 1963), the supremacy of Community law (*Costa* in 1964), the direct effect of certain decisions (*Grad* in 1970), as well as the implied powers of the Commission (*ERTA* in 1971). On this basis, the ECJ would soon hold in favour of the direct effect of directives in certain circumstances (*Van Duyn* in 1974). Thus, timing of entry, as well as the greater awareness of what membership entailed, arguably played a role in prompting greater parliamentary scrutiny in Denmark and the UK. Following the Danish and UK models, new Member States would henceforth create, from the moment of accession, a parliamentary scrutiny mechanism that generally included oversight by some form of European Affairs Committee (EAC). However, the relative strength of the British and Danish systems, not to mention their very different forms and methods, must also be explained by examining the political and constitutional contexts of the two countries.

Consider first the British example. The entry of the UK came in the midst of a quite 'passionate debate' over how to 'restor[e] the influence of the Commons' in administrative governance more generally, in the face of the 'widespread agreement that the power of the Executive had grown vis-à-vis Parliament'.[55] Inevitably, this atmosphere influenced the debate over the European Communities Bill in 1972. Two more specific concerns were commonly expressed: first, 'the apparently bureaucratic nature of Community decision-making, with the close interlocking between the Community and the Executives of the Member States'; and, secondly, the general inadequacy of 'British Parliamentary control over *all* delegated legislation', with 'the power of the Executive consequently increasing'.[56] Thus, from the outset, in contrast with the original six Member States, the parliamentary debate in Britain seemed to focus intuitively on the relationship between European integration and administrative governance as it had evolved at the national level over the post-war decades.

After the UK's accession, a dual committee system for parliamentary scrutiny emerged, one for each house, the details of which have evolved but whose basic contours have remained stable ever since. Most importantly, like the scrutiny of domestic statutory instruments, the focus of European scrutiny in the UK was and is on the documents themselves—primarily, but not exclusively, on Commission legislative proposals. Two additional features—the 'scrutiny reserve' and the 'explanatory memorandum'—would define the British document-based system. If the scrutiny committee has referred a European document for further consideration, then the scrutiny reserve prohibits the government from taking action on it at the EU level until national parliamentary scrutiny is complete. The reserve was never meant, however, to be applied inflexibly: from its establishment in 1980, a minister could override a reserve upon a showing of 'special reasons', which the minister in turn must explain to the House concerned in a timely fashion. Reason-giving is also the inspiration behind the 'explanatory memorandum'. Early in the development of the British scrutiny system, parliament demanded that the government must provide a short memorandum on every European document.[57] These memoranda have evolved into rather elaborate statements describing, among other things: the subject matter of the proposal; where ministerial responsibility lies; its legal basis in the Treaties and the applicable voting procedure; its impact on UK law; compliance with the principle of subsidiarity;

55 Michael Ryan and Paul Isaacson, 'Parliament and the European Communities' (1974) 28 Parl Aff 199, 200.

56 Anne Stevens, 'Problems of Parliamentary Control of European Community Policy' (1976) 5 Millenium J Intl Stud 269, 269–70.

57 T St J N Bates, 'European Community Legislation before the House of Commons' (1991) 12 Statute L Rev 109, 118, citing 874 *HC Debs* col 1426.

and regulatory impact and/or risk assessment. The competent minister must sign the memorandum, which thus constitutes 'the Minister's evidence to Parliament'.[58] The memorandum in turn serves as the foundation for all subsequent parliamentary review, whether formally (through referral to Standing Committees, appearance of ministers for questioning, referral to the full House), or through informal processes.[59]

Since the 1970s, however, British critics have been remarkably consistent in their complaints about the inadequacy of the document-based system, invoking the simultaneously developed Danish 'mandating' system as a clearly superior alternative from the standpoint of maintaining parliamentary control.[60] This admiration ignored that 'such an extreme system requires very special political circumstances in order to work'.[61] This also suggests why, although a large number of new EU entrants since the 1990s have opted for some form of the mandating system, none has opted for the Danish variant in its strongest form. The most important peculiarity of Danish politics is the regularity of minority, or weak coalition, governments combined with unusually strong party cohesion and discipline. This leads to a heavy emphasis on consensus politics and inter-party bargaining. Consequently, the Danish EAC sees itself very much as a 'bargaining committee', a forum to discuss the contours of the Danish position on key questions of EU policy and to pound out compromises among the parties.[62] Outright rejection of the government's proposed mandate rarely occurs, because the government usually changes or modifies its proposal on the basis of the discussions in the EAC.

If we are looking for factors leading to the development of EACs in other Member States in the 1970s and 1980s, ECJ judgments again played a role. Most important was the jurisprudence on the potential direct effect of directives (*Van Duyn* in 1974), effectively circumventing the need for national parliamentary transposition in certain circumstances. Previously quiescent NPs, like the French National Assembly, began to agitate against 'directives that are in reality regulations'.[63] At the end of the 1970s, French MPs called on the government to establish some mechanism like those in Denmark and the UK to 'consult with their parliaments before deciding [in the Council] on directives and even regulations'.[64] By statute the following year,[65] the French government authorized the establishment of scrutiny committees in both the National Assembly and the Senate. Thereafter, French parliamentarians

[58] Clerk of the House, 'The European Scrutiny System in the House of Commons: A Short Guide for Members of Parliament by the Staff of the European Scrutiny Committee' (2005) 7 www.parliament.uk/documents/upload/TheEuroScrutinySystemintheHoC.pdf (last accessed 12 October 2016).

[59] On the importance of informal control see Katrin Auel, 'Democratic Accountability and National Parliaments: Redefining the Impact of Parliamentary Scrutiny in EU Affairs' (2007) 13 ELJ 487.

[60] John Fitzmaurice, 'The Danish System of Parliamentary Control over European Community Policy' in Valentine Herman and Rinus van Schendelen (eds), *The European Parliament and the National Parliaments* (Saxon House 1979) 201. See, more recently, Michael Gove MP, Foreword in Lorraine Mullally, Barry Watts, and Neil O'Brien, 'Getting a Grip: Reforming EU Scrutiny at Westminster' (Open Europe 2006) 2 http://www.openeurope.org.uk/scrutiny.pdf (last accessed 17 June 2009), available in summary form at http://archive.openeurope.org.uk/Content/documents/Pdfs/scrutiny.pdf (last accessed 1 November 2016).

[61] See Fitzmaurice (n 60) 202.

[62] Hans Hegeland and Ingvar Mattson, 'To Have a Voice in the Matter: A Comparative Study of the Swedish and Danish European Committees' (1996) 2 J Legis Stud 198, 204.

[63] Jean-Dominique Nuttens and François Sicard, *Assemblées Parlementaires et Organisations Européennes* (La Documentation française 2000) 63, Statement of Jean Foyer, 'Extraits du débat parlementaire du 30 novembre 1978 sur la transposition de la sixième directive sur la TVA'.

[64] ibid.

[65] Loi no 79–564 du 6 juillet 1979, *JO, Lois et Décrets*, 7 July 1979, 1643 (rectificatif, *JO, Lois et Décrets*, 18 July 1979).

would be among the most active in the Community (and later Union) in demanding an increase in the national parliamentary role in European affairs.[66]

It would not be until the decade between the SEA in 1986 and the Treaty of Amsterdam in 1997, however, that formal and often constitutionally grounded rights for national parliamentary scrutiny would see themselves adopted in many Member States. Feeding into these developments was an intensifying debate over Europe's purported 'democratic deficit', a phrase that gained broad currency in the late 1980s as a shorthand for a whole range of complaints, not least executive dominance of the integration process.[67] New provisions added to national constitutions in response to the Treaty of Maastricht—such as Article 88-4 of the French Constitution, or Articles 23 and 45 of the German Basic Law—reflected a new direction in the legal contestation over European governance. By constitutionalizing certain rights to information and scrutiny, these provisions amounted to a legal commitment to an ongoing role for NPs, no matter how limited that role might be in some cases.[68]

In the competition between models of scrutiny over the course of the 1990s and into the 2000s, document-based systems were clearly dominant at the outset, although this would eventually change. In the 1995 and 2004 enlargements, ten out of the thirteen new Member States opted for a mandating system in some form.[69] For many of the Member States from Eastern and Central Europe, mandating systems appeared the best way of reconciling integration's functional demands, including a largely executive and technocratic policy process, with their restored national sovereignty and the democratic legitimacy embodied or expressed in the elected legislature. Even among those NPs opting for document-based systems, procedures varied, most importantly as to the scrutiny reserve. By 2005, a total of five NPs using the document-based system had explicitly established some form of scrutiny reserve, although often entailing relatively brief fixed time periods.[70]

2.3 The Significance of the Early Warning Mechanism: Mediated Legitimacy and National Parliamentary Scrutiny in EU Governance

Over roughly the same time period as parliamentary scrutiny mechanisms were developing at the national level—certainly since the advent of direct election of Members of the European Parliament (MEPs) in 1979—the European Parliament began to assert itself 'as the deepest expression of European democracy and integration'.[71] Given this

[66] French parliamentarians, for example, would be instrumental in the creation of COSAC (the Conference of Community and European Affairs Committees of Parliaments of the European Union) at the end of the 1980s. COSAC Secretariat, 'History of COSAC' (2014) 4–5 http://www.cosac.eu/documents/ (last accessed 12 October 2016).

[67] Berthold Rittberger, *Building Europe's Parliament: Democratic Representation Beyond the Nation-State* (Oxford University Press 2005) 28.

[68] Monica Claes, 'Constitutionalising Europe at Its Source: Europe Provisions in National Constitutions: Evolution and Typology' (2005) 24 YEL 2003 81

[69] COSAC Secretariat, 3rd Bi-annual Report (2005) 14–16; Ann-Cathrine Jungar, 'The Rules of Attraction: Policy Transfer and the Design of Parliamentary EU Scrutiny Mechanisms in New EU Member States' (*European Union Studies Association, 10th Biennial International Conference* 2007) 14–17 http://aei.pitt.edu/7928/01/jungar-a-11h.pdf (last accessed 12 October 2016) (cited with permission).

[70] COSAC Secretariat (n 69) 14–16.

[71] See Joint Statement to the Press by Joseph Daul, on Behalf of the EPP Group, Martin Schulz, on Behalf of the S&D Group, and Guy Verhofstadt, on Behalf of the ALDE Group, 14 July 2009 http://arc.eppgroup.eu/press/showpr.asp?prcontroldoctypeid=1&prcontrolid=8674&prcontentid=15026&prcontentlg=en (last accessed 12 October 2016).

self-image, it is hardly surprising that the EP sought, often successfully, to expand its prerogatives in European governance, not just legislatively but also in the supervision of the Commission and other forms of oversight. Berthold Rittberger has analyzed the political history behind this process and concluded that the EP's expanding powers reflect an effort by political elites, not just MEPs but also members of the Commission and national politicians, to translate a model of 'representative, parliamentary democracy' into workable supranational form.[72] Although Rittberger acknowledges a more recent turn to NPs as an alternative legitimating mechanism, he views this as merely 'a shift in emphasis within the representative, parliamentary model of democracy' applied to the supranational level.[73]

Does the historical record suggest that NPs serve primarily as supplements to the legitimizing function of the EP and as manifestations of the same model of supranational 'representative, parliamentary democracy'? The idea is obviously controversial.[74] European public law has in fact consistently refused to recognize the EP as the ultimate democratic 'principal' in the system of European governance, akin to a democratic parliament on the national level. 'This is why', to borrow the words of former Advocate General Miguel Poiares Maduro, 'the European Parliament does not have the same power as national parliaments in the legislative process'.[75] To acknowledge this reality is not to say that the EP cannot play a significant role in the EU system, for example as a means of supervising the Commission or as a forum for forging compromises among disparate cross-national interests. But from a socio-legal perspective, in light of the position of NPs as the privileged repositories of democratic and constitutional legitimacy, they are also clearly entitled to a role in overseeing the EU legislative and rule-making processes, notably on the basis of subsidiarity.[76]

The strongest evidence of the distinct role of NPs as a source of democratic legitimacy can be found, ironically, in the failure of efforts to incorporate the NPs directly into the supranational legislative apparatus through a so-called 'second chamber'. This may seem paradoxical to some readers, because the very purpose of such proposals was seemingly to *augment* the national parliamentary role in European affairs. The real problem, however, was that such proposals carried with them an unacceptable constitutional quid pro quo—ie the new centralization of specifically 'parliamentary' legitimacy within the EU, consistent with aim of giving supranational institutions a strong legitimacy on par with the 'constituted' bodies of the Member States. This is something that NPs have been unable to accept.

A second chamber of sorts, of course, already existed at the EU level in the form of the Council, as many would note.[77] Article 10(2) TEU, as modified by the Treaty of Lisbon, would eventually make the Council's role in this regard explicit, stating the Member States are represented 'in the Council by their governments, themselves democratically accountable either to their national Parliaments, or to their citizens'. The problem with the Council as a 'second chamber', however, was and is that its source of legitimacy is only indirectly parliamentary and much more squarely executive, even if it exercises legislative functions at the supranational level. This helps to explain why, at

[72] Rittberger (n 67). [73] ibid 200.

[74] See eg Davor Jančić, 'Caveats From Karlsruhe and Berlin: Whither Democracy After Lisbon?' (2010) 16 Colum J Eur L 337.

[75] Case C-411/06, *Commission v Parliament and Council* [2009] ECR I-7585, Opinion of Advocate General Poiares Maduro delivered on 26 March 2009, ECLI:EU:C:2009:189, n 5.

[76] See similarly Davor Jančić, 'The Game of Cards: National Parliaments in the EU and the Future of the Early Warning Mechanism and the Political Dialogue' (2015) 52 CML Rev 939.

[77] See eg Jürgen Habermas, 'Why Europe Needs a Constitution' (2001) 11 New Left Rev 5, 17.

the outset of the process leading to the drafting of the Constitutional Treaty, proposals for a chamber composed of purely national parliamentarians figured prominently in the discussion.[78] Nonetheless, they had little ultimate impact.[79]

In the lead up to the Laeken European Council meeting (2001), the UK House of Lords' Select Committee on European Union issued an extensive report (based in part on submissions from other NPs), that was evocatively entitled *A Second Parliamentary Chamber for Europe: An Unreal Solution to a Real Problem*.[80] In criticizing the idea of a second chamber and calling instead for strengthened national parliamentary scrutiny in EU governance, the report suggested a very different understanding of the EU's democratic legitimacy challenges. That situation, the report argued, was really one of 'disconnection' rather than 'democratic deficit', something that institutional or procedural changes at the EU level could not solve in the absence of deeper transformations in 'public perceptions' and 'political culture' (paras 56–57). The Lords' report thus brings us back to the notion of 'democratic disconnect' described in section 1.[81] The purpose of mediated legitimacy, whether through NPs' scrutiny or otherwise, is not to render the EU autonomously democratic in its own right; rather, it is to overcome the sense of disconnection. Establishing a viable form of national parliamentary scrutiny in EU affairs is another way to 'maintain the connection' between those national institutions possessing strong forms of democratic legitimacy and administrative power in its now supranational guise.[82]

Rather than serving as a 'virtual third chamber',[83] the new EWM would seek to provide an avenue for NPs to scrutinize, but not necessarily control, their supranational 'pre-commitment' agents in the EU legislative process. The relationship between scrutiny and control is, and always has been, an extraordinarily difficult balance to strike in EU governance, precisely because the very purpose of delegating power to supranational pre-commitment agents is to create some measure of decisional autonomy and thus counteract the risk of 'principal drift'.[84] The Commission's reason-giving obligation in response to a 'yellow card' from NPs under the EWM, for example, was designed to build on the Commission's other obligations to 'consult widely' before making a proposal and to issue an initial 'detailed statement' justifying the proposal on subsidiarity grounds, including an analysis of its implications for future national implementing legislation, as well as any potential administrative or financial burdens on the Member States.[85] The more challenging issue at the Convention was whether

[78] Perhaps the most famous of these proposals came from then-German Foreign Minister Joschka Fischer, who sought the establishment of an explicitly federal Europe featuring a 'Senate' of national parliamentarians in addition to the EP. See Joschka Fischer, 'From Confederacy to Federation: Thoughts on the Finality of European Integration', Speech at the Humboldt University in Berlin, 12 May 2000 http://ec.europa.eu/dorie/fileDownload.do?docId=192161&cardId=192161 (last accessed 12 October 2016).

[79] Valéry Giscard d'Estaing, in his capacity as President of the Convention on the Future of Europe, continued to push for a 'Congress of the Peoples of Europe', but it failed to garner any support and was eventually dropped. Peter Norman, *The Accidental Constitution: The Making of Europe's Constitutional Treaty*, vol 2 (EuroComment 2005) 122–23.

[80] HL Paper 48, 7th Report of Session 2001–2002, 27 November 2001.

[81] See section 1.3. [82] See nn 11–17 and accompanying text.

[83] Ian Cooper, 'A "Virtual Third Chamber" for the European Union? National Parliaments after the Treaty of Lisbon' (2012) 35 WEP 441.

[84] Anand Menon and Stephen Weatherill, 'Legitimacy, Accountability, and Delegation in the European Union' in Anthony Arnull and Daniel Wincott (eds), *Accountability and Legitimacy in the European Union* (Oxford University Press 2002) 119.

[85] Protocol No 2 on the Application of the Principles of Subsidiarity and Proportionality ('Lisbon Subsidiarity Protocol'), 2008 OJ (C 115) 206, arts 2 and 5.

NPs should have a right to issue a 'red card'; that is, not merely to comment on but also to reject a draft legislative proposal outright.[86] In the muted words of the Convention Secretariat's summary of the plenary debate: 'Many Convention members were against this proposal, on the grounds that a "veto" mechanism would not be acceptable and would infringe the decision-making autonomy of European bodies'.[87] Echoing this sentiment directly, one member rejected the 'red card' for 'giving national parliaments the power of veto over the initiative of the Commission and that we should not do'.[88]

Manifest in these claims were typically functionalist understandings of the proper role of a delegating legislature vis-à-vis a more expert agent—in this case the Commission—which have been foundational to the post-war constitutional settlement of administrative governance. This negative attitude to the rights of NPs, even acting collectively, stood in contrast with the prerogatives of national executives. They continued to have the right to vote down legislative proposals in the Council, whether by a blocking minority under qualified majority voting or even a single vote under unanimity. In this way, mediated legitimacy through the EWM would continue to lean primarily on national executives and only secondarily on NPs (very much consistent with the balance of power under the post-war constitutional settlement of administrative governance at the national level). The compromise 'orange card' procedure that eventually emerged in the negotiations of the Treaty of Lisbon would not permit a national parliamentary veto outright. Instead, it provided that, if 55 per cent of the members of the Council or a majority of the EP conclude that a proposal challenged by one-third of NPs does not comply with the principle of subsidiarity, the draft legislation would fail.[89] In short, national parliamentary opposition could trigger an altered voting scheme in the supranational legislative process, thus slightly increasing the likelihood that the proposal might be defeated. The regulatory power, such as it was, still remained supranational, even as the democratic legitimacy in the most robust sense still flowed from NPs.

3. Concluding Reflections: Resilience, Resignation, and Beyond

The history of NPs as conduit of mediated legitimacy in EU governance certainly did not end with the adoption of the EWM. The tug-of-war pitting the functional and technocratic necessity of EU regulatory power and national democratic and constitutional legitimacy obviously continues. And in this process, the paradoxical combination of national parliamentary resilience and resignation is still very much on display.[90]

A degree of resilience can be seen, for example, in the blurry line between, on the one hand, the political dialogue between NPs and the Commission under the so-called Barroso Initiative and, on the other, the subsidiarity dialogue established under the EWM. The Barroso Initiative was announced in May 2006 in the interlude between the demise of the Constitutional Treaty and the adoption of the Treaty of Lisbon.[91] In

[86] Lindseth, *Power and Legitimacy* (n 1) 237–40.

[87] CONV 630/03, Summary report on the plenary session of 17 and 18 March 2003, 21 March 2003, http://register.consilium.europa.eu/pdf/en/03/cv00/cv00630.en03.pdf (last accessed 12 October 2016). See also Weatherill (n 37) 44.

[88] Norman (n 79) 170, quoting Lamberto Dini.

[89] Lisbon Subsidiarity Protocol, art 7(3)(b).

[90] See section 1.3.

[91] European Commission Communication, 'A Citizens' Agenda: Delivering Results for Europe', COM(2006) 211, 10 May 2006. For an assessment see Davor Jančić, 'The Barroso Initiative: Window Dressing or Democracy Boost?' (2012) 8 Utrecht L Rev 78.

it, the Commission committed to forwarding all legislative proposals and consultation documents to NPs, inviting their comments on any issue, not just subsidiarity, 'so as to improve the process of policy formulation' at the EU level. The initiative built on the Commission's 'Plan-D for Democracy, Dialogue and Debate' announced in October 2005, in the aftermath of the rejection of the Constitutional Treaty in the Dutch and French referenda. Plan-D involved a structured process of making individual commissioners and Commission representatives 'accessible and prepared to assist national Parliaments to explain Commission policies and provide an overview of recent EU developments'.[92]

As it has evolved, the political dialogue has moved well beyond questions of subsidiarity to which the EWM was restricted. And, as one observer later concluded: 'Since the entry into force of the Lisbon Treaty, the Barroso Initiative has blended with the early warning mechanism into one *hybrid procedure* with two purposes'.[93] Indeed, one might assert that the two purposes have themselves blurred into one: for example, in the first instance in which NPs successfully invoked the 'yellow card' under the EWM (regarding the draft Monti II Regulation in 2012), many of the national parliamentary objections did not in fact challenge subsidiarity.[94] Nonetheless, the strong manifestation of general political opposition, even though not restricted to subsidiarity, gave the Commission serious pause; looking ahead to likely difficulties in the Council, the Commission decided to withdraw the proposal.

But, as always, this measure of resilience must be weighed against the continuing manifestations of resignation by NPs in the face of integration's functional demands. Nowhere have these demands been more acutely felt than in the response to the Eurozone crisis. The adoption of the Six Pack, the Two Pack, and the Fiscal Compact have deeply curtailed the power of NPs in their core legislative prerogatives—taxing, spending, and borrowing—subjecting these powers to fiscal and macroeconomic surveillance enforced by supranational institutions, most importantly the Commission.[95] The traditional 'pre-commitment' method of European integration,[96] whereby supranational agents exercise delegated regulatory power to prevent 'principal drift',[97] now cuts ever closer to the rights of NPs in the mobilization of fiscal resources.[98]

The EU's powers in fiscal and macroeconomic surveillance have not, however, eliminated national parliamentary involvement in EU affairs; instead, they have arguably reinforced them in at least two ways. First, as Davor Jančić has recently shown, with the advent of heightened fiscal surveillance many NPs have demanded even more formal and informal 'tools to scrutinise EU decisions that impinge on their fiscal autonomy'.[99]

[92] The Commission's Contribution to the period of reflection and beyond: 'Plan-D for Democracy, Dialogue and Debate', COM(2005) 494, 13 October 2005, at 7.

[93] Jančić, 'The Barroso Initiative' (n 91) 83 (emphasis in original).

[94] For a critical assessment, see Federico Fabbrini and Katarzyna Granat, '"Yellow Card, but No Foul": The Role of the National Parliaments under the Subsidiarity Protocol and the Commission Proposal for an EU Regulation on the Right to Strike' (2013) 50 CML Rev 115.

[95] See generally Maurice Adams, Federico Fabbrini, and Pierre Larouche (eds), *The Constitutionalization of European Budgetary Constraints* (Hart Publishing 2014).

[96] See n 22 and accompanying text. [97] See n 84 and accompanying text.

[98] See n 5 and accompanying text.

[99] Davor Jančić, 'National Parliaments and EU Fiscal Integration' (2016) 22 ELJ 225, 230. The same may also eventually be true in the policing/Europol context. See art 51 of Regulation (EU) 2016/794 of the European Parliament and of the Council of 11 May 2016 on the European Union Agency for Law Enforcement Cooperation (Europol) and replacing and repealing Council Decisions 2009/371/JHA, 2009/934/JHA, 2009/935/JHA, 2009/936/JHA, and 2009/968/JHA. For an analysis see Miroslava Scholten, '[R]evolution in the EU System of Political Accountability: Joint Parliamentary Scrutiny Mechanism', RENFORCE Blog, 30 May 2016 http://blog.renforce.eu/index.

And secondly, in a way that demonstrates the EU's ultimate dependence on the robust democratic and constitutional legitimacy of NPs, the EU's own tools in fiscal and macroeconomic governance still do not involve any macroeconomically significant capacity to mobilize fiscal resources to address the crisis. In this crucial regard, the EU must either persuade or coerce the Member States, and most importantly their NPs, into acting. For the most part, the EU cannot act directly, despite all its 'pre-commitment' powers. The same is true in the policing and defence contexts in the face of the refugee and terrorism crises, because, aside from cooperation mechanisms through Frontex, Europol, and the EDA, the EU has essentially no autonomous capacity to mobilize human resources to confront these challenges.

As a consequence, in responding to both these crises, the EU has been forced to rely on a strategy whereby nearly all essential costs—political and economic—are borne internally by the individual states. Why? Because NPs remain the institutions where legitimate compulsory mobilization powers still reside. This is true even in Greece, where the perpetual drama over the last several years has been over whether the EU or the Troika can persuade or compel the Greek Parliament to take decisions that only a NP has the power and legitimacy ultimately to take. The supranational cannot displace the national in this regard; the EU must still 'borrow' the legitimacy of NPs, even in the atmosphere of crisis. The reason is that the ultimate management of each crisis (eg the Eurozone and Schengen crises) have required, at a micro level, autonomous capacities of legitimate compulsory mobilization of fiscal and human resources that only NPs possessed.[100]

Moreover, to the extent that transnational coordination has been necessary, decision-making has been primarily national and intergovernmental rather than supranational (ie via the Commission and the ECJ, the two 'pre-commitment' enforcement agents par excellence). The main exception has been the ECB.[101] But it is important to recognize that the ECB's sometimes 'heroic' role (eg in quantitative easing) has been primarily driven by the incapacity of the EU and the Member States to mobilize fiscal resources on a coordinated, supranational scale commensurate with the demands of the crisis.[102] This has been true even as supranational surveillance over national actors has also played an important, if ultimately suboptimal, role. This surveillance has been consistent with the function of EU bodies as 'pre-commitment' agents with regard to fiscal discipline in the Eurozone crisis, or in the enforcement of obligations under the Common European Asylum System in the refugee crisis.

Thus, in order to determine the status of NPs in European integration, we should also be analyzing EU institutions and EU public law more generally. The tug-of-war between EU regulatory power and national legitimacy continues. From this perspective, it should not surprise us that David Cameron, in his negotiations in the lead up to the June 2016 'Brexit' referendum, insisted on the establishment of a 'red card' procedure for NPs as part of a 'new settlement' between the UK and the EU.[103] Although

php/en/2016/05/30/revolution-in-the-eu-system-of-political-accountability-joint-parliamentary-scrutiny-mechanism/ (last accessed 12 October 2016).

[100] cf Christian Thimann, 'The Microeconomic Dimensions of the Eurozone Crisis and Why European Politics Cannot Solve Them' (2015) 29 J Econ Perspectives 141.

[101] See more in the chapter by Davor Jančić on the ECB in this volume.

[102] See generally Peter L Lindseth, 'Power and Legitimacy in the Eurozone: Can Integration and Democracy Be Reconciled?' in Maurice Adams, Federico Fabbrini, and Pierre Larouche (eds), *The Constitutionalization of European Budgetary Constraints* (Hart Publishing 2014).

[103] See Decision of the Heads of State or Government meeting within the European Council, Annex I to European Council Conclusions, 19 February 2016 http://data.consilium.europa.eu/doc/document/ST-1-2016-INIT/en/pdf (last accessed 15 November 2016). For an analysis

the deal lapsed with the victory of 'Leave', pressures for an increased role for NPs hardly ceased. With the prospect of Brexit shaping political reactions, the Commission was forced, for example, to recognize the EU-Canada Comprehensive Economic and Trade Agreement (CETA) as a 'mixed agreement' requiring approval by NPs in all the Member States. This may simply suggest that it is the EU that will need to be resigned in the face of the continued resilience of NPs as repositories of democratic and constitutional legitimacy, even as the functional demands of integration still constrain the rights of NPs in significant ways.

see Katarzyna Granat, 'The Draft Renegotiation Deal: A Genuine Red Card? Tusk's Proposal and National Parliaments' *EU Law Analysis*, 3 February 2016 http://eulawanalysis.blogspot.com/2016/02/the-draft-renegotiation-deal-genuine.html (last accessed 12 October 2016). See also Davor Jančić, 'Sovereignty Safeguards in the UK–EU Settlement' *Verfassungsblog*, 8 March 2016 http://verfassungsblog.de/sovereignty-safeguards-in-the-uk-eu-settlement/ (last accessed 12 October 2016).

4

Constitutional Review and the Powers of National Parliaments in EU Affairs

Erosion or Protection?

*Cristina Fasone and Nicola Lupo**

1. Introduction

The construction of the EU constitutional system has traditionally been a matter for courts, in particular for the Court of Justice of the EU (CJEU) and the national courts entitled to carry out constitutional review.[1] The prominent role of these courts in shaping European Union (EU) constitutionalism, among other things, has marginalized national parliaments (NPs) in the European integration process. The principle of primacy of EU law has weakened their legislative powers and prompted some of them to adopt a passive attitude towards the EU.[2]

This chapter first outlines the 'protagonism' of the CJEU and national constitutional courts in defining the main features of the EU legal order. Secondly, it considers whether domestic courts have challenged the distribution of legislative competences between the EU and national levels of government in the post-Lisbon Treaty judicial design of the EU constitutional architecture. Indeed, this has been the original function assigned to constitutional courts according to the Kelsenian model of constitutional review since the 1920s. The good functioning of a 'composite' EU constitution, which encompasses primary EU law and national constitutions and is shaped by the interplay between domestic and EU institutions,[3] requires adequate forms of constitutional review at all levels of government.

This chapter claims that, in addition to the role that constitutional courts have traditionally played in the EU as protectors of the national constitutional limits to European integration and often of democratic principles, 'constitutional review' of secondary EU law must also be *effectively* performed at the EU level. The CJEU is

* While the authors have jointly drafted the introduction and the conclusion, Cristina Fasone has written sections 2 and 5; Nicola Lupo authored sections 3 and 4.

[1] By 'constitutional review', we refer to the competence of constitutional and ordinary courts, depending on the country, to check the compliance of domestic legislation (even when implementing EU law) with the Constitution, which can result in such legislation being declared unconstitutional and void. See an overview of the different forms of constitutional review in the EU in Maartje De Visser, *Constitutional Review in Europe* (Hart Publishing 2014) 54–78.

[2] Paul Craig and Gráinne De Búrca, *EU Law: Texts, Cases, and Materials* (5th edn, Oxford University Press 2011) 256–96; Damian Chalmers, Gareth Davies, and Giorgio Monti, *European Union Law* (3rd edn, Cambridge University Press 2014) 235–42; Robert Schütze, *European Union Law* (Cambridge University Press 2015) 127–44.

[3] Leonard FM Besselink, *A Composite European Constitution* (Europa Law Publishing 2007) 15–20. See how parliaments cooperate within such a constitution in Nicola Lupo and Cristina Fasone (eds), *Interparliamentary Cooperation in the Composite European Constitution* (Hart Publishing 2016).

Constitutional Review and the Powers of National Parliaments in EU Affairs: Erosion or Protection?
First Edition. Cristina Fasone and Nicola Lupo.
Published 2017 by Oxford University Press.

tasked with checking the compliance of EU law with the 'basic constitutional charter, the Treaty',[4] particularly concerning the division of legislative competences between the EU and the Member States enshrined in the Treaties. However, this is lacking in practice. The low level of judicial protection of some NPs' prerogatives in EU affairs by domestic constitutional courts and weak constitutional review at the EU level put NPs at the margins of the European integration process.

The insufficiency and drawbacks of the CJEU's judicial control over the exercise of EU legislative competences, and especially over EU institutions' compliance with the principle of subsidiarity through the early warning system, have opened the door for NPs to become directly involved in EU decision-making processes. Yet the relationship between NPs and national and EU courts remains a 'troubled partnership'.[5] On the one hand, NPs have never made use of the Lisbon Treaty procedure that allows them to bring subsidiarity actions before the CJEU (Article 8, Protocol No 2). On the other hand, NPs' degree of involvement in EU affairs is largely determined by the level of protection of their prerogatives by national constitutional courts. This is shown, for instance, by constitutional case law in Germany and Poland on the ratification and implementation of the Lisbon Treaty.[6]

As a result, the attempt to strengthen judicial control of subsidiarity compliance has not been successful yet. Furthermore, where, as in Italy and Spain, NPs are less protected by constitutional courts, either because of the design of constitutional adjudication or because of judicial self-restraint, they tend to be less active in EU affairs, which may jeopardize citizens' political rights.[7] Although deemed a core element of EU democratic legitimacy (Article 10 TEU) alongside citizens' direct representation in the European Parliament (EP), citizens' rights to participate in EU affairs through NPs are enforced in asymmetrical ways, depending on the form of government of each Member State and on the extent to which each system of constitutional review protects its own NP's prerogatives.[8]

[4] Case 294/83 *Parti Écologiste 'Les Verts' v European Parliament* [1986] ECR-01339 para 23.

[5] See a European perspective in Koen Lenaerts, 'The Court's Outer and Inner Selves: Exploring the External and Internal Legitimacy of the European Court of Justice' in Maurice Adams and others (eds) *Judging Europe's Judges: The Legitimacy of the Case Law of the European Court of Justice* (Hart Publishing 2013) 13–60; and a national standpoint in Mattias Wendel, 'Exceeding Judicial Competence in the Name of Democracy: The German Federal Constitutional Court's OMT Reference' (2014) 10(2) EuConst 263–307. See more on the OMT decisions of the German Federal Constitutional Court in the chapter by Ingolf Pernice in this volume.

[6] See on Germany Davor Jančić, 'Caveats from Karlsruhe and Lisbon: Whither Democracy after Lisbon?' (2010) 16 Colum J Eur L 337, 337–85; and on the Czech Republic Rike U Krämer, 'Looking through Different Glasses at the Lisbon Treaty: The German Constitutional Court and the Czech Constitutional Court' in Andreas Fischer-Lescano, Christian Joerges, and Arndt Wonka (eds) 'The German Constitutional Court's Lisbon Ruling: Legal and Political-science Perspectives' (2010) ZERP Discussion Paper 1/2010, 14.

[7] See the Italian case and the limited margin of manoeuvre of the Constitutional Court in this field in Cristina Fasone, 'Qual è la fonte più idonea a recepire le novità del Trattato di Lisbona sui Parlamenti nazionali?' (2010) 3 Osservatorio sulle fonti online 3–13; and the Spanish case in Pablo Pérez Tremps, 'La jurisdicción constitucional y la integración europea' (2009) 29 Revista Española de Derecho Europeo 19, 19–48.

[8] Carlos Closa, 'National Higher Courts and the Ratification of EU Treaties' (2013) 36 W Eur Pol 97, 97–121; Cesare Pinelli, 'La giurisprudenza costituzionale tedesca e le nuove asimmetrie fra i poteri dei parlamenti nazionali dell'eurozona' (2014) 1 Costitutionalismo.it http://www.costituzionalismo.it/articoli/470/ (last accessed 2 November 2016), and Stefan Theil, 'What Red Lines, If Any, Do the Lisbon Judgments of European Constitutional Courts Draw for Future EU Integration?' (2014) 15 German LJ 601, 601–25.

2. The Judicial Construction of Europe and the Erosion of National Parliaments' Powers

It has been successfully argued that the EU would never have taken its current shape without the CJEU, 'the most effective supranational judicial body in the history of the world'.[9] Through a particular reading of the Treaties, this Court has devised some of the key structural principles of EU law, such as the principles of primacy and direct effect, which have shaped the European integration process.

The CJEU was not alone in this endeavour, as the role of national courts, in particular through preliminary reference proceedings, has been equally important.[10] Without them asking the CJEU to decide on the validity and interpretation of EU law, the latter court would never have rendered its landmark judgments on the relationship between EU law and national law, the nature of the EU Treaties, and the protection of fundamental rights.[11]

Among national courts, while lower courts have been by far the greatest activists in referring preliminary questions to the CJEU, supreme courts and constitutional courts have played a very significant—although complementary—role in the EU constitutional system. In particular, constitutional courts, often seen as the national institutions whose authority has been affected the most by the EU and in spite of their very cautious approach towards the CJEU,[12] have tried to rebalance the latter's activism. In a number of cases, national constitutional and supreme courts have tried directly or indirectly to signal to the CJEU the national constitutional limits to European integration. It is precisely the acknowledgement of those limits at the EU level that have led those courts gradually to accept the aforementioned structural principles of EU law. At the same time, they provided a sort of 'external' check on EU judicial authority, which does not face many other constraints on its own 'law-making'.[13] Thus, in spite of their reluctant approach to European integration, constitutional courts have contributed to the construction of the EU's composite constitution.[14]

Yet the activity of constitutional courts has not reinforced the CJEU's 'constitutional review' of the division of legislative competences between the EU and the Member States. The CJEU has usually supported the policy-making role of EU institutions against the Member States, thus endorsing a vertical expansion of EU competences by

[9] Alec Stone Sweet, *The Judicial Construction of Europe* (Oxford University Press 2004) 1.

[10] See Joseph HH Weiler, *The Transformation of Europe* (1991) 100 Yale LJ 2419 ff and Monica Claes, *The National Courts' Mandate in the European Constitution* (Hart Publishing 2006) 58–67.

[11] See eg Case 26/62 *Van Gend en Loos v Netherlands Inland Revenue Administration* [1963] ECR English Spec Ed 1; *Costa v Enel* [1964] ECR English Spec Ed 585; Case 11/70 *Internationale Handelsgesellschaft mbH v Einfuhr- und Vorratsstelle für Getreide und Futtermittel* [1970]; Case 4/73 *J Nold, Kohlen- und Baustoffgroßhandlung v Commission of the European Communities* [1974] ECR-I 491; Case 43/75 *Gabrielle Defrenne v Société anonyme belge de navigation aérienne Sabena* [1976] ECR-I 455; Case 8/74 *Procureur du Roi v Benoît and Gustave Dassonville* [1974] ECR-I 837; Case 120/78 *Rewe-Zentral AG v Bundesmonopolverwaltung für Branntwein (Cassis de Dijon)* [1979] ECR-I 649; *Andrea Francovich and Danila Bonifaci and Others v Italian Republic* [1991] ECR-I 5357; and the commentaries in Miguel Poiares Maduro and Loïc Azoulai, *The Past and Future of EU Law* (Hart Publishing 2010) 1–129, 433–73.

[12] See Jan Komárek, 'The Place of Constitutional Courts in the EU' (2013) 9 EuConst 420–50, quoting a declaration of the President of the Czech Constitutional Court shortly after the *Landtova* (Slovak pensions) case. See more on the relationship between constitutional courts and the CJEU in M De Visser, *Constitutional Review* (n 1) 403–27.

[13] See Thomas Horsley, 'Reflections on the Role of the Court of Justice as the "Motor" of European Integration: *Legal* Limits to Judicial Lawmaking' (2013) 50 CML Rev, 931, 931–64.

[14] Claes, *The National Courts' Mandate* (n 10) 39 ff.

means of Treaty interpretation.[15] Furthermore, the CJEU has not seen itself as a guardian of the horizontal separation of powers in the EU, because of its peculiar relationship with the EU legislature (the Council and the EP), the pursuit of the supranational interest and the fulfilment of EU objectives jointly with the Commission (Articles 17(1) and 19(1) TEU).[16]

On some occasions, national constitutional courts' positions had a clear effect on the CJEU's decisions;[17] on many others, however, they did not influence the final outcome of the CJEU's judgment. Yet, national constitutional case law was able to bring to the EU's attention a specific view on the role of NPs that would have otherwise remained out of the evolving EU constitutional dialogue.[18] What are the implications of this 'judicial construction of Europe'[19] on NPs?

It is undeniable that, by conferring legislative powers on EU institutions in a growing number of policy domains, EU treaties have simultaneously restricted NPs' ability to pass laws in those fields.[20] By the same token, until 1979 NPs were represented at the EU level within the EP, which at that time was merely consulted in the EU law-making process, often issuing non-binding opinions. In contrast, when the EP became directly elected, NPs were no longer represented at the EU level and were not able to intervene in the EU legislative process by issuing advisory opinions.[21] Strengthened parliamentary scrutiny over national executives was deemed the most appropriate response, since national ministers are members of one of the branches of EU legislature—the Council.[22] However, this kind of scrutiny, even when it permitted the parliament to

[15] See the debate in the UK about the 'repatriation' of some EU competences in House of Lords, EU Committee, HL Paper 140, *The Review of the Balance of Competences between the UK and the EU*, 12th Report of Session 2014–15, 25 March 2015.

[16] See Mark Dawson, 'Constitutional Dialogue between Courts and Legislatures in the European Union: Prospects and Limits' (2013) 19 (2) EPL 369, 369–96; and his 'The Political Face of Judicial Activism: Europe's Law–Politics Imbalance' in Mark Dawson, Bruno De Witte, and Elise Muir (eds), *Judicial Activism at the European Court of Justice* (Edward Elgar Publishing 2013) 11–31.

[17] See eg the German *Solange* saga in the 1970s and 1980s (Judgment of 29 May 1974, 37 BVerfGE 271 and Judgment of 22 October 1986, 73 BVerfGE 339 of the German Constitutional Court and Case 11/70 [1970] ECR 01125 *Internationale Handelsgesellschaft*, Case 4/73 [1974] ECR 491 *Nold* and Case 44/79 [1979] ECR 03727 *Hauer* of the CJEU) and, more recently, the case on the Data Retention Directive, Joined Cases C-293/12 and C-594/12 *Digital Rights Ireland Ltd v Minister for Communications, Marine and Natural Resources and Others and Kärntner Landesregierung and Others* [2014].

[18] See eg Case 107/77 *Amministrazione delle Finanze dello Stato v Simmenthal SpA* [1978] ECR-I 629; Joined Cases C-188/10 and C-189/10 *Aziz Melki* (C-188/10) and *Sélim Abdeli* (C-189/10) [2010] ECR-I 5667; Case 399/11 *Stefano Melloni v Ministerio Fiscal* [2013] ECR 0000; and, more recently, Case C-62/14 *Peter Gauweiler and Others v Deutscher Bundestag* [2015].

[19] Stone Sweet (n 9).

[20] Andreas Maurer, 'National Parliaments in the European Architecture: From Latecomers' Adaptation Towards Permanent Institutional Change?' in Andreas Maurer and Wolfgang Wessels (eds) *National Parliaments on their Ways to Europe: Losers or Latecomers?* (Nomos 2001) 28–30.

[21] Olivier Costa, *Le parlement européen, assemblée délibérante* (Institut d'Etudes Européennes 2001) 50–60; Berthold Rittberger, *Building Europe's Parliament: Democratic Representation Beyond the Nation-State* (Oxford University Press 2007) 73–142.

[22] See Maurer (n 20) 39–75; Tapio Raunio, 'Ensuring Democratic Control over National Governments in European Affairs', Leonard FM Besselink, 'Shifts in Governance: National Parliaments and Their Governments' Involvement in European Union Decision-making' in Gavin Barrett (ed), *National Parliaments and the European Union: The Constitutional Challenge for the Oireachtas and Other Member State Legislatures* (Clarus Press 2008), respectively 3–27 and 29–46; Philipp Kiiver, *The National Parliaments in the European Union: A Critical View on EU Constitution-Building* (Kluwer Law International 2006) 9–24.

issue a binding mandate to the executive,[23] was not enough to preserve NPs' control over the EU's exercise of the transferred domestic legislative powers. The government could easily be outvoted once unanimity was replaced with qualified majority voting in the Council.[24] Also, when a majority government is in office, the parliamentary opposition and minority parties lack a say in Council decision-making. Most importantly, the judicial creation of the principles of direct effect and primacy forced NPs passively to accept secondary EU law and give up what remained of their 'sovereignty'.

By asking national courts not to apply domestic legislation that is incompatible with EU law in order to promote the unity and uniformity of the EU legal system, the CJEU overturned the traditional constitutional role of NPs as original and autonomous legislatures. The competence of NPs as law-makers used to be *original*, because they implicitly accepted the limitation of their legislative powers by authorizing the ratification of the EU Treaties. Instead, the CJEU imposed the primacy of EU law on NPs through a creative interpretation of the Treaties. Moreover, the NPs' *autonomy* in passing legislation has been constrained and limited to that which the CJEU and national courts consider to be compatible with EU law without consulting NPs. Except for the UK and the Netherlands, where there is no constitutional review of legislation and where parliaments at least in theory have virtually limitless powers,[25] NPs must comply with domestic constitutions, which they may amend. According to the CJEU's interpretation of primacy as an absolute principle, however, EU law supersedes even national constitutional provisions that conflict with it.[26] In this regard, the NPs' law-making authority is seriously jeopardized and parliaments can find little assistance in the CJEU, because the latter has significantly contributed to their marginalization in the first place.

3. The Insufficiency of Judicial Control Over the Exercise of EU Legislative Competences

One way to contain the erosion of NPs' powers deriving from the expansion of EU policies was provided by the Treaty of Maastricht through the introduction of the principle of subsidiarity, which aimed to control the expansion of EU law-making in non-exclusive competences. This was consistent with the finalistic and functionalist mindset that has always inspired the process of European integration, based on the idea that the Member States should set the objectives first (eg the creation of the Coal and

[23] Mette Buskjær Christensen, 'The Danish Folketing and EU Affairs: Is the Danish Model of Parliamentary Scrutiny Still Best Practice?' in Claudia Hefftler and others (eds), *The Palgrave Handbook of National Parliaments and the European Union* (Palgrave 2015) 275–89.

[24] The most striking example of this happened in Austria in 1995 upon its EU accession, when the Lower House of Parliament, *Nationalrat*, issued the government with a binding mandate on how to vote on a directive on animal transport. Because the government was outvoted, Parliament never issued such a mandate again. See Martina Mayer, *Die Europafunktion der nationalen Parlamente in der Europäischen Union* (Mohr Siebeck 2012) 381.

[25] In the UK, for instance, the principle of parliamentary sovereignty has fundamentally changed after the *Factortame* saga. See Paul Craig, 'Sovereignty of the United Kingdom Parliament after *Factortame*' (1991) 11 YEL 221–55; Michael Gordon, *Parliamentary Sovereignty in the UK Constitution: Process, Politics and Democracy* (Hart Publishing 2015) 151–92.

[26] According to some scholars, the post-Lisbon Article 4(2) TEU on the EU's obligation to respect the Member States' national identity, challenges the idea of absolute primacy. See Armin von Bogdandy and Stephan Schill, 'Overcoming Absolute Primacy: Respect for National Identity Under the Lisbon Treaty' (2011) 48 CML Rev 1417–53.

Steel Community or the internal market), and then manage the means to achieve those objectives in a flexible way, so as to not go beyond what is sufficient and necessary.[27]

A degree of distrust towards the CJEU and courts in general also emerged from certain other provisions of the Treaty of Maastricht. It was then, three years after the fall of the Berlin Wall, that the European integration process attempted to overcome its functionalist origins and acquire a clearer political dimension. In order to avoid the risks associated with putting the regulation of new and sensitive policies in the hands of supranational institutions, which would expand their law-making powers thanks to the CJEU's weak 'constitutional review', two new intergovernmental pillars—Common Foreign and Security Policy ('second pillar') and Justice and Home Affairs ('third pillar')—were created. In these two pillars, governments could escape both the oversight of the EP and any effective form of collective scrutiny by NPs.[28]

Therefore, it was not by chance that the Treaty of Maastricht was the first EU treaty to address the role of NPs beyond the provisions of the Treaty of Rome on the composition of the EP. However, the Maastricht provisions on NPs were confined to two political declarations (Nos 13 and 14, concerning COSAC and the Assizes, respectively). The Treaty of Amsterdam eventually referred to NPs in an ad hoc Protocol, thus in primary EU law.

However, the shortcomings of the Treaty of Maastricht were twofold. First, the CJEU was unable to ensure that acts enacted by EU institutions were compliant with subsidiarity, mainly because of the difficulty of ascertaining the reach of this principle from a purely legal point of view as well as because of the limited number of subsidiarity actions brought before this court.[29] Secondly, the acts adopted under the second and third pillars remained excluded from any form of review by CJEU.[30] At the same time, some constitutional and supreme courts (eg in France, Ireland, and Spain) decided that constitutional amendments were needed to comply with the treaty. Those amendments restricted the NPs' margin of manoeuvre in implementing EU Treaty provisions on European citizenship and thus removed some constitutional limits to European integration. These constitutional amendments, as well as those enacted almost ten years later to implement the European Arrest Warrant,[31] additionally limited national parliamentary powers regarding policies traditionally falling within the remit of the Member States.

The problem of the marginalization of NPs was then gradually addressed by including domestic parliamentarians in the work of the Convention on the Future of Europe and by trying to restrain extensive interpretation of EU competences,[32] while bringing the EU closer to citizens through a form of direct involvement of domestic legislatures.

[27] This kind of mindset has also consistently informed the case law of the CJEU starting from its teleological (and meta-teleological) interpretation of the EU Treaties as a source of its legitimacy. See Mitchel de S-O-l'E Lasser, *Judicial Deliberations: A Comparative Analysis of Judicial Transparency and Legitimacy* (Oxford University Press 2004) 359; Miguel Poiares Maduro, 'Interpreting European Law: Judicial Adjudication in a Context of Constitutional Pluralism' (2007) 1(2) Eur J of L Stud 3–13.

[28] See more on interparliamentary cooperation in CFSP/CSDP and in EU external relations in the chapters by Ian Cooper and by Kolja Raube and Jan Wouters in this volume.

[29] See Robert Schütze, *From Dual to Cooperative Federalism: The Changing Structure of European Law* (Oxford University Press 2009) 241 ff. See *contra* Thomas Horsley, 'Subsidiarity and the European Court of Justice: Missing Pieces in the Subsidiarity Jigsaw?' (2012) 50 JCMS 270.

[30] Since the Treaty of Amsterdam and, even more so, the Treaty of Lisbon, the third pillar has been gradually 'Communitarised'. By contrast, the acts adopted under the second pillar remain non-legislative in nature and outside the jurisdiction of the CJEU (TEU, art 24).

[31] Council Framework Decision 2002/584/JHA of 13 June 2002 on the European Arrest warrant and the surrender procedures between Member States—Statements made by certain Member States on the adoption of the Framework Decision [2002] OJ L 190/1.

[32] See Stephen Weatherill, 'Competence Creep and Competence Control' (2004) 23 YEL 1, 1–55.

4. The Attempt to Involve National Parliaments as Guardians of the Subsidiarity Principle

The Laeken Declaration (2001) and the Convention on the Future of Europe (2002–2003) tried to address the shortcomings of the EU's post-Maastricht arrangements by involving NPs at an early stage of the EU legislative process as guardians of the subsidiarity principle. The objective was twofold: (a) to provide for a stricter political and judicial check on the observance of the subsidiarity principle; and (b) to increase the active involvement of NPs in EU affairs.[33] Consequently, through the 'constitutional moment' of the Convention, the drafters of the Lisbon Treaty sought to address the problem of the vertical division of competences between the EU and the Member States and the issue of the democratic legitimacy of EU decision-making.

NPs were thus called upon to issue reasoned opinions on the compliance of EU legislative acts that fall outside the domain of exclusive competences with the principle of subsidiarity. During the Convention, an attempt was made to give NPs the power to bring an action directly before the CJEU for infringements of the principle of subsidiarity unless the CJEU already had issued an opinion positively approving the same, which would preclude any further actions.[34] The proposal was rejected essentially for two reasons: first, to distinguish between the political check exercised by NPs and the legal check exercised by the CJEU; and, secondly, because NPs have no standing before the CJEU, even in case of subsidiarity actions.[35]

However, with the Treaty of Lisbon, the first objective of subsidiarity guardianship—that of ensuring stricter control over EU institutions' compliance with the principle of subsidiarity—was not properly fulfilled. Yet the same Treaty has indeed fulfilled the second objective of it—namely, a more active involvement of NPs in the EU. The early warning system and the 'political dialogue' have increased NPs' degree of Europeanization.[36]

This chapter argues that the failure to achieve the first objective derives from an unresolved ambiguity about the respective roles of the CJEU and NPs as gatekeepers of the exercise of legislative competence in the EU and subsidiarity in particular.[37] Although the CJEU has been compared to a constitutional court for its legal reasoning,[38] it has usually not acted as such. It has not played the role of an impartial arbiter

[33] Peter L Lindseth, *Power and Legitimacy: Reconciling Europe and the Nation-State* (Oxford University Press 2010) 225–50.

[34] See Convention on the Future of Europe, Working Group I on the principle of subsidiarity, CONV 286/02, Point II.

[35] Only the German *Bundestag*, the Czech, and Romanian parliaments enjoy rights to self-representation before the CJEU under national law. A constraint to the *locus standi* of NPs before the CJEU also derives from the Statute of the CJEU, which forces each Member State's parliament and government to agree on an agent to represent the state before the CJEU. Katarzyna Granat, 'National Parliaments and the Policing of the Subsidiarity Principle' (2014) PhD thesis, European University Institute 187.

[36] The political dialogue was introduced after the referendums in France and the Netherlands on the Constitutional Treaty. See Davor Jančić, 'The Barroso Initiative: Window Dressing or Democracy Boost?' (2012) 8 Utrecht L Rev 78, 78–91.

[37] See Gareth Davies, 'Subsidiarity: The Wrong Idea, in the Wrong Place, at the Wrong Time' (2006) 43 CML Rev, 63–84. See also Davor Jančić, 'The Game of Cards: National Parliaments in the EU and the Future of the Early Warning Mechanism and the Political Dialogue' (2015) 52 CML Rev 939–76, who convincingly proposes to shift the focus of the parliamentary scrutiny from the principle of subsidiarity to the principle of conferral and to the substance of legislative proposals.

[38] See Giulio Itzcovich, 'The European Court of Justice as a Constitutional Court: Legal Reasoning in a Comparative Perspective' Stals Research Paper 4/2014.

of the vertical separation of powers in the EU constitutional system, but has rather created a sort of alliance with the EU legislature and refrained from exercising effective judicial scrutiny over the exercise of EU competences.[39] The CJEU has been generally considered a policy-maker.[40] At the opposite end stand NPs, which are by nature political actors. Based on the Lisbon Treaty provisions on the early warning system, some scholars have argued that NPs could collectively exercise *ex ante* review of draft EU legislation on the grounds of subsidiarity, as if they were a Council of State.[41] This confusion between the judicial and political roles of the CJEU and NPs in the Treaty provisions and in practice undermined the potential of subsidiarity scrutiny to reduce the EU democratic deficit.

Other weaknesses of the early warning system include the fact that the Commission's impact assessment reports on draft EU legislative acts, which are the basis for parliamentary scrutiny of subsidiarity alongside national government reports, fall short of fulfilling the requirement enshrined in Protocol No 2 annexed to the Treaty of Lisbon. In particular, in order to ascertain compliance with subsidiarity, Article 5 of this Protocol requests the Commission to provide a detailed statement with an assessment of the proposal's financial impact, 'qualitative and, wherever possible, quantitative indicators' and a description of 'any burden, whether financial or administrative, falling upon the Union, national governments, regional or local authorities, economic operators and citizens, to be minimised and commensurate with the objective to be achieved'. Such a comprehensive statement is mostly lacking when an EU legislative proposal is presented, thus depriving the CJEU of a crucial standard for assessing subsidiarity.

By the same token, the Commission tends to delay significantly in replying to NPs' reasoned opinions and there is a lack of follow up on the effectiveness of these opinions in the following stages of the EU legislative process, in which NPs are not directly involved. Furthermore, many national legislatures lack the human and financial resources to carry out subsidiarity scrutiny and are forced to act under tight time constraints (eight weeks) as well as balance EU affairs with domestic activities.

Such a unidirectional expansion of EU action on the grounds of subsidiarity and implied powers of the EU (Article 352 TFEU)—ie only in favour of the supranational level of government—should give way to a more balanced and appropriate implementation of subsidiarity as a bidirectional 'move' of the non-exclusive competences—ie both from the Member States to the EU and vice versa—wherever the Member States' action is deemed necessary and sufficient to achieve the Union's objectives (Article 5(3) TEU). The need to ease this tension between the expansion of EU competences and the contraction of the domestic ones is even more compelling given that the reduction of the Union's competences by means of Treaty revision is politically highly unlikely. However, the number of draft legislative acts put forward by the Commission has indeed substantially decreased since the new Commission was appointed in 2014.[42]

[39] This approach does not share the view of those who have adopted a very minimal definition of what a constitutional court is, based on the mere fact that there is a 'constitution' and 'a court defending and interpreting this basic charter', although we concur that the EU should have a proper Constitutional Court (see Bo Vesterdof, 'A Constitutional Court for the EU?' (2006) 4 Intl J of Const L-CON 607–617).

[40] See Karen J Alter, 'Judicial Politics in the European Community: European Integration and the Pathbreaking *Cassis de Dijon* Decision' (1994) 26 Comparative Political Studies 535 ff.

[41] See Philipp Kiiver, *The Early Warning System for the Principle of Subsidiarity: Constitutional Theory and Empirical Reality* (Routledge 2012) 126–32.

[42] European Commission, 'Commission Work Programme 2015—A New Start' COM(2014) 910 of 16 December 2014; 'Commission Work Programme 2016—No Time for Business as Usual' COM(2015) 610 of 27 October 2015 'Commission Work Programme 2016— Delivering a Europe

It nonetheless seems that the legal response to the euro crisis and the need for a common European reaction has prompted EU institutions to increase their competences or exercise them in a way that stretches their legal bases,[43] although some NPs have strongly reacted to the new post-crisis measures.[44] Yet, the CJEU does not appear to provide an effective 'check and balance' to the de facto expansion of the EU's powers.

5. The 'Troubled Partnership' Between National Parliaments and Courts in the EU

5.1 The Road Not Taken: National Parliaments Seeking a Judicial Remedy Before the CJEU Against Violations of Subsidiarity

In spite of the general dissatisfaction of NPs regarding the implementation of the early warning system[45] and the three yellow cards that have been issued,[46] since the entry into force of the Treaty of Lisbon no parliament, or chamber thereof, has used the tool of *ex post* subsidiarity review before the CJEU (Article 8 of Protocol No 2).

This is surprising given the high number of reasoned opinions adopted by some parliaments (UK House of Commons and House of Lords, the Swedish Parliament, the Czech Senate, and the French Senate).[47] Also, Protocol No 2 has strengthened the most procedural dimension of subsidiarity, the requirements to be fulfilled by the Commission when presenting legislative proposals,[48] which, according to NPs' opinions in the early warning system and political dialogue, this EU institution often fails to comply. Moreover, as Stephen Weatherill has argued, NPs have an incentive to challenge the validity of EU legislative acts before the CJEU, because their

that protects, empowers and defends' COM(2016) 710 of 25 October 2016. See more on this in Davor Jančić, 'The Juncker Commission's Better Regulation Agenda and Its Impact on National Parliaments' in Cristina Fasone, Diane Fromage, and Zoe Lefkofridi (eds), 'Parliaments, Public Opinion and Parliamentary Elections in Europe' (EUI Working Papers MWP 2015/18) 48.

[43] See Thomas Beukers, 'Legal Writing(s) on the Eurozone Crisis' (EUI Working Papers Law 2015/11) 5–10.

[44] See Davor Jančić, 'National Parliaments and EU Fiscal Integration' (2016) 22(2) ELJ 225–49.

[45] This is visible from the latest COSAC contributions. See Contribution of the LI COSAC plenary meeting (Athens, 15–17 June 2014, at 4) and of the LII COSAC plenary meeting (Rome, 30 November–2 December 2014, at 3–4); COSAC 22nd Bi-annual Report of 4 November 2014, at 20–24.

[46] The first one was on the Draft Regulation on the Right to Take Collective Action in the Field on the Freedom of Establishment and to Provide Services, the second one was on the Draft Regulation Establishing the European Public Prosecutor's Office; the third one was on the Draft Directive concerning the posting of workers in the framework of the provision of services. See different accounts in Federico Fabbrini and Katarzyna Granat, '"Yellow Card, but No Foul": The Role of the National Parliaments under the Subsidiarity Protocol and the Commission Proposal for an EU Regulation on the Right to Strike' (2013) 50 CML Rev 115–43; Nicola Lupo, 'National and Regional Parliaments in the EU Decision-making Process, after the Treaty of Lisbon and the Euro-crisis' in (2013) 5(2) Perspectives on Federalism 15–19; Marco Goldoni, 'The Early Warning System and the Monti II Regulation: The Case for a Political Interpretation' (2014) 10 EuConst 90–108; Diane Fromage, 'The Second Yellow Card on the EPPO Proposal: An Encouraging Development for Member State Parliaments' (2015) YEL (early view) 1–23; Davor Jančić, 'The Game of Cards' (n 37) 939–76.

[47] See European Commission's annual reports on the application of the principles of subsidiarity and proportionality in the EU and on the Commission's relations with NPs.

[48] See Alberto Alemanno, 'A Meeting of Minds on Impact Assessment when Ex Ante Evaluation Meets Ex Post Judicial Control' (2011) 17 EPL 485–505; P Craig, 'Subsidiarity: a Political and Legal Analysis' (2012) 50 JCMS 72; Werner Vandenbruwaene, 'The Ambivalent Methods of Subsidiarity Review' in Marta Cartabia, Nicola Lupo, and Andrea Simoncini (eds), *Democracy and Subsidiarity in the EU. National Parliaments, Regions and Civil Society in the Decision-making Process* (Il Mulino 2013) 371–98.

positions—especially those of the parliamentary opposition and minority parties—may not be adequately represented *ex ante* in the intergovernmental bargaining within the Council during the EU legislative process.[49]

There are, however, quite evident reasons that can explain the lack of *ex post* subsidiarity review by NPs. First of all, as the CJEU is not so willing to curb EU legislative action, in practice NPs might not have an incentive to seek judicial protection from a court that has so far contributed to limiting their legislative powers. Secondly, not only have general actions for annulment brought against a violation of subsidiarity never succeeded,[50] but actions for annulment brought by non-privileged applicants, such as natural and legal persons, have usually proved difficult to pass the admissibility test.[51]

Although NPs are better placed than non-privileged applicants to initiate such actions, the relationship between NPs and the CJEU is still mediated through national governments. In the pre-Lisbon Treaty regime this already happened in the Netherlands, where the Government acted on Parliament's request and brought an action for annulment against a directive on the legal protection of biotechnological inventions on grounds of subsidiarity.[52] The Court of Justice dismissed the action by applying the tests of national insufficiency and comparative efficiency,[53] but the government explicitly linked its pleas to Parliament's request. At that time, there were no doubts that the Dutch Government was not bound by EU law to bring the action for annulment on behalf of the States General—hence, the action was an entirely discretionary choice. This is no longer the case under the Treaty of Lisbon, although there are no remedies at the EU level for a NP to force its government to act. Only if and where national proceedings exist to enable parliament to challenge the inaction of the government, usually before the Constitutional Court, can parliament enforce its new European prerogative. However, this depends on purely domestic constitutional arrangements. It appears that there must be an agreement between the NP and government on whether an action for annulment based on Protocol No 2 can be used.

Nevertheless, it is apparent that the positions of NPs and governments towards subsidiarity actions are asymmetrical. Governments are entitled to ask for the annulment of an EU measure on their own initiative and on any grounds, if the conditions set by Article 263 TFEU are fulfilled. After the Treaty of Lisbon, subsidiarity actions can also be notified by governments 'in accordance with their legal order on behalf of their national parliament or a chamber thereof' (Article 8 of Protocol No 2). The domestic implementation of this provision always triggers a more or less active role for the

[49] See Stephen R Weatherill, 'Better Competence Monitoring' (2005) 30 EL Rev 23; Granat, *National Parliaments* (n 35) 189.

[50] See Case 84/94 *United Kingdom v Council* [1996] ECR I-5755; Case 233/94 *Germany v Parliament and Council* [1997] ECR I-2405; and C-491/01 *British American Tobacco* [2002] ECR I-11453; Case C-358/14 *Republic of Poland v European Parliament and Council of the European Union* [2016] nyr; Case C-477/14 *Pillbox 38 (UK) Ltd v The Secretary of State for Health* [2016] nyr and Case C-574/14 *Philip Morris Brands SARL and Others v Secretary of State for Health* [2016] nyr. See also Gráinne De Búrca, 'The Principle of Subsidiarity and the Court of Justice as an Institutional Actor' (1998) 36 JCMS 214.

[51] Craig and De Búrca, *EU Law* (n 2) 490 ff; Chalmers, Davies, and Monti, *European Union Law* (n 2) 425 ff; Schütze, *European Union Law* (n 2) 347–59.

[52] Directive 98/44/EC of the European Parliament and of the Council of 6 July 1998 on the legal protection of biotechnological inventions [1998] OJ L 213/13. See Leonard FM Besselink, 'The Netherlands—The Role of the States General within the European Union' in GC Rodriguez Iglesias and L Ortiz Blanco (eds), *The Role of National Parliaments in the European Union*, Proceedings of the FIDE XXIV Congress, vol 1 (Madrid, Facultad de Derecho Universidad Complutense 2010) 516.

[53] Case C-377/98 *Kingdom of the Netherlands v European Parliament and Council of the European Union* [2001] ECR I-07079. See Granat, *National Parliaments* (n 35) 179.

national executive.[54] However, regardless of the threshold required by domestic legislation for such actions to be brought,[55] the presence of the executive in the proceedings is an essential condition for the application of Article 8 in practice. Hence, NPs have been described as 'indirect semi-privileged applicants'[56] and as *amici curiae* of the CJEU in *ex post* subsidiarity review.

5.2 Advantages and Disadvantages of Constitutional Courts' Protection of National Parliaments' Powers in EU Affairs

Absent an effective EU judicial safeguard for NPs, the protection of NPs' EU prerogatives is left to domestic courts,[57] which may only review the domestic dimension of the exercise of EU powers. There primarily refer to the fulfilment of information duties by national executives, the effectiveness of parliamentary scrutiny, and the ability of NPs to use their new powers, such as the right for them to participate in Treaty revision procedures.

The engagement of a constitutional or supreme court in this type of constitutional review depends on the model of adjudication in place and on its attitude towards Parliament. This is demonstrated below in turn with the examples of the Italian, Spanish, German, French, Polish, and Czech constitutional courts.

5.2.1 Italy

In Italy, the way in which constitutional review is designed prevents such an outcome, first of all because of the very limited rights of access to the Constitutional Court, which cannot carry out *ex ante* review of the constitutionality of EU Treaties, Treaty amendments, and laws authorizing their ratification. Moreover, neither actions brought by parliamentary minority parties nor direct individual complaints are envisaged in the Italian legal system. On the contrary, it is extremely unlikely that a constitutional challenge brought by one of the Italian regions, or a preliminary reference of constitutionality issued by an ordinary court, which are the only two ways to access the Court, would trigger a decision on the parliamentary powers in EU affairs. Unlike in Germany and France,[58] in Italy there was no court to prompt the strengthening of the NP's powers in the EU through a constitutional amendment. This helps explain, besides other reasons, why Italy adopted legislation implementing Lisbon Treaty provisions on NPs with a three-year delay, namely at the end of 2012.

54 See a detailed comparison of the subsidiarity action provisions in Granat, *National Parliaments* (n 35) 185–86.

55 In Germany, for example, the threshold is one-fourth of Members of the *Bundestag*. See Basic Law (*Grundgesetz*) art 23(1a); art 12(1) (of the *Bundestag*) and art 12(2) (of the *Bundesrat*) of Act on the Exercise by the Bundestag and by the Bundesrat of their Responsibility for Integration in Matters Concerning the European Union (Responsibility for Integration Act—IntVG); art 93(2d) of the Rules of Procedure of the *Bundestag*.

56 Granat, *National Parliaments* (n 35) 188.

57 This does not imply, however, that NPs' prerogatives in EU affairs are unprotected in countries where courts may not review the constitutionality of legislation—as in the UK or Finland. In the latter case, this issue is primarily dealt with by the Constitutional Law Committee of the Finnish Parliament, *Eduskunta*, through a strong system of political *ex ante* review of parliamentary acts and treaties. See Kaarlo Tuori and Klaus Tuori, *The Eurozone Crisis: A Constitutional Analysis* (Cambridge University Press 2014) 198.

58 See German Constitutional Court, Second Senate, Order of 30 June 2009—2 BvE 2/08; French *Conseil Constitutionnel*, Decision 2007–560 DC, Treaty of Lisbon amending the Treaty on European Union and the Treaty establishing the European Community.

5.2.2 Spain

The Spanish Parliament's EU prerogatives have also not been particularly protected by the *Tribunal Constitucional*, albeit for different reasons. This is mainly due to the type of questions that the Court has been asked to decide on and the very limited use of tools like the direct individual complaint (*recurso de amparo*) or the parliamentary minority's action in EU affairs. As for the type of questions that the *Tribunal Constitucional* addressed when it reviewed the constitutionality of the Constitutional Treaty, the Attorney General only raised concerns regarding the Charter of Fundamental Rights and the codification of the principle of primacy into primary EU law.[59] No reference was made to NPs except in the dissenting opinion (*voto particular*) of Justice Ramón Rodríguez Arribas, who considered the Treaty to be in breach of the Constitution. He argued that the Treaty provisions on the early warning system and on the participation of NPs and the CJEU in subsidiarity monitoring were highly likely to conflict with the Constitution. The lack of national parliamentary and governmental control over such conflicts has similarly led the French *Conseil Constitutionnel* to require a constitutional amendment before ratification of the Constitutional Treaty could be carried out.[60]

The second missed opportunity for the Spanish *Tribunal Constitucional* to make a pronouncement on the protection of parliamentary powers in EU-related issues was the *recurso de amparo* brought by Members of Parliament (MPs) from the political group *Esquerra Republicana-Izquierda Unida-Iniciativa Per Catalunya Verds* against the constitutional amendment passed to constitutionalize the balanced budget clause in response to the Euro Plus Pact (Order No 9/2012). They sought the annulment of the parliamentary resolutions and agreements that had led to the constitutional reform through the urgency procedure and in a single legislative reading in both parliamentary chambers.[61] They also contested the use of the ordinary, and least complex, procedure to amend the Constitution despite the fact that the constitutional bill was likely to impair the protection of citizens' fundamental rights and limit the prerogatives of MPs.[62] The *Tribunal Constitucional* declared the individual complaint (*amparo*) inadmissible because Parliament's governing bodies had simply applied the Standing Orders. Hence, the Court rendered no decision on the merits. The dissenting opinions of Justices Pablo Pérez Tremps and Luis Ignacio Ortega Álvarez emphasized that the issue at stake was of such complexity and institutional significance that it deserved a much more careful consideration. The Court's self-restraint[63] therefore caused it to

[59] Declaración del Pleno del Tribunal Constitucional 1/2004 de 13 de diciembre de 2004 (BOE núm 3, de 4 de enero de 2005).

[60] *Conseil constitutionnel*, Décision n° 2004–505 DC du 19 novembre 2004, p 173, para 41.

[61] On 23 August 2011, the government initiated a bill to amend Article 135 of the Constitution, which was jointly presented in the Lower House *Congreso* on 26 August by the two major parliamentary forces—the Socialists and the People's Party—and finally approved by the Upper House *Senado* on 7 September 2011 and published on the Official Bulletin on 27 September. Thus, the whole parliamentary procedure lasted less than one month. See Mirela Estrada-Cañamares, Germán Gomez Ventura, and Leticia Díez Sánchez, *Constitutional Change Through Euro Crisis Law: Spain* (2014) EUI Law Department Research Project, section VI.2 http://eurocrisislaw.eui.eu/country/spain/topic/euro-plus-pact/ (last accessed 2 November 2016).

[62] The procedure under art 167 was used instead of that under art 168 of the Spanish Constitution, which must be applied when constitutional provisions on fundamental rights and liberties are to be changed. The argument raised by the minority group contesting the use of art 167 was that, although the constitutional text's provisions on fundamental rights were not formally altered, they were nonetheless deeply affected by the new balanced budget clause.

[63] See on the traditional self-restraint of the Spanish Constitutional Court Victor Ferreres Comella, *The Constitution of Spain: A Contextual Analysis* (Hart Publishing 2013) 227–32.

overlook the democratic implications of its declaration of inadmissibility, namely the disrespect for Parliament's role in the constitutional amendment process that was tied to the European Council's response to the Eurozone crisis.

5.2.3 Germany

By contrast, other constitutional courts, especially in their judgments on the Treaty of Lisbon, took into account the strengthened role of NPs, although none of them developed clearly articulated reasoning comparable to that of the German Constitutional Court in the *Lissabon-Urteil*.[64] Since this judgment, the judicial protection of the *Bundestag* has been built by interpreting Article 38(1) of the Basic Law (*Grundgesetz* (GG)) on the right to vote in federal parliamentary elections as a 'right to democracy', a right that would be irremediably impaired if the powers and autonomy of this chamber, where German citizens are represented, were severely limited. The Court construed this right in conjunction with Article 20(2) GG, which lays down that state authority derives from the people and parliamentary elections; and Article 79(3) GG (the so-called 'eternity clause'), which makes the democratic principle unamendable due to it being a part of the German constitutional identity.[65]

5.2.4 France

The French *Conseil Constitutionnel*, furthermore, considered that the Lisbon Treaty prerogatives of NPs—in particular the power to veto the EU's use of the *passerelle* clauses (Articles 48(7) TEU and 81(3) TFEU) and Parliament's *ex ante* and *ex post* subsidiarity monitoring—needed to be implemented through a constitutional amendment, because they granted to the two parliamentary chambers autonomous prerogatives that were not foreseen in the Constitution.[66] Thus, a further constitutionalization of the French Parliament's powers in EU affairs was necessary and this was subsequently effected in line with the *Conseil*'s previous case law on the Treaty of Maastricht and the Constitutional Treaty. The precise effects of such a constitutionalization are dubious, however. Even if this may protect Parliament from the executive's arbitrary use of powers in EU matters, these 'new' constitutional provisions substantively duplicate what EU Treaties and Protocols already prescribe.[67]

[64] See 'The Federal Constitutional Court's Lisbon Case' (2009) 10(8) Special Section German LJ 1201–308; Philipp Kiiver, 'The Early-warning System for the Principle of Subsidiarity: The National Parliament as a *Conseil d'Etat* for Europe' (2011) 1 EL Rev 98–108; Jacques Ziller, 'The German Constitutional Court's Friendliness towards European Law: On the Judgment of Bundesverfassungsgericht over the Ratification of the Treaty of Lisbon' (2010) 16(1) EPL 53–73; Mattias Wendel, 'Lisbon Before the Courts: Comparative Perspectives' (2011) 7 EuConst 96–136; Theil, 'What Red Lines?' (n 8) 616–25; Tatjana Evas and Ulrike Liebert, 'Enhancing Democratic Legitimacy Through Constitutional Pluralism? The Czech, German and Latvian Lisbon Rulings in Dialogue' in Tatjana Evas, Ulrike Liebert, and Christopher Lord (eds), *Multilayered Representation in the European Union. Parliaments, Courts and the Public Sphere* (Nomos Verlag 2012) 107–27.

[65] The reasoning of the Court had partially been developed in its *Maastricht-Urteil* of 12 October 1993 (BVerfGE 89, 155).

[66] *Conseil Constitutionnel*, Decision 2007–560 DC, paras 28–32. The decision was issued after referral from the President of the Republic, pursuant to art 54 of the Constitution.

[67] See especially arts 88-6 and 88-7 of the French Constitution.

5.2.5 Poland

The Polish Constitutional Tribunal was even more concerned than the French *Conseil Constitutionnel* about the role of NPs after the Lisbon Treaty.[68] A group of Polish senators invoked 'the lack of legislative participation of competent constitutional state organs [the parliament] as a preliminary requirement' for Treaty amendments (Article 48 TEU), for the division of legislative competences between the EU and the Member States, and for the use of the implied powers clause (Article 352 TFEU). The case was dismissed on procedural grounds, because the President of the Republic had not asked for an *ex ante* review of constitutionality of the Treaty of Lisbon (Article 133 of the Constitution). This Treaty had meanwhile been ratified by a two-thirds majority in both parliamentary chambers,[69] which is higher than that necessary for amending the Constitution. The senators' petition was indeed filed after the ratification had successfully been completed, which made it difficult for the Court to decide otherwise.[70] Thus, the majority of the Court based its decision on the 'presumption of constitutional conformity'[71] of the Treaty of Lisbon with the Constitution and held that the strengthening of parliamentary powers in EU affairs at the domestic level is a matter for the national legislature to implement through the Act of Cooperation of the Council of Ministers with the *Sejm* and the Senate (para 4.2.14).

5.2.6 The Czech Republic

The Czech Constitutional Court, finally, in its two rulings on the Treaty of Lisbon, delivered before the Treaty's ratification was completed,[72] took a more balanced position compared to other courts. Namely, the Czech Court considered the EP and NPs as complementary bodies in ensuring democratic legitimacy of the EU constitutional system. In other words, reserving democratic legitimacy only for the EP or only for NPs is no longer satisfactory. The Court therefore supported stronger national parliamentary involvement, even though this was not seen as the only condition for upholding the constitutionality of the Treaty of Lisbon.[73]

5.2.7 Comparative Analysis

This overview of the recent national constitutional case law on the powers of NPs in the EU highlights that, while no relationship has been established in practice between the CJEU and NPs, there is a long-standing relationship between most NPs and their constitutional or supreme courts regarding the use of EU powers. However, the extent to which courts protect the role of NPs in the EU depends solely on the national

[68] See eg the judgment of the Polish Constitutional Tribunal on the Constitutional Treaty, K 18/04.

[69] Polish Constitution, art 90.2.

[70] Polish Constitutional Tribunal, K32/09, 24 November 2010, especially 4.2.

[71] The issue of the 'presumption of constitutional conformity' of the Treaty remained highly ambiguous and was the major point of controversy in the dissenting opinion of Justice Mirosław Granat.

[72] See Czech Constitutional Court, Judgments Pl.US 19/08 of 26 November 2008 and Pl.US 29/09 of 3 November 2009. The Czech Republic was the last Member State to ratify the Treaty of Lisbon because of the then-President of the Republic Václav Klaus's critical position on it.

[73] See Jiří Zemánek, 'The Two Lisbon Judgments of the Czech Constitutional Court' in José María Beneyto and Ingolf Pernice (eds), *Europe's Constitutional Challenges in the Light of the Recent Case Law of National Constitutional Courts—Lisbon and Beyond* (Nomos 2011) 57; and Theil, 'What Red Lines?' (n 8) 624–25.

constitutional system, particularly on the country's model of constitutional adjudication, the Court's self-restraint, and the concrete circumstances of the case. The national judicial protection of the German, French, Polish, and Czech parliaments appears stronger than that afforded to the Italian and Spanish parliaments by their constitutional courts. In fact, the Italian and Spanish constitutional courts have never taken a stance in favour of protecting parliamentary prerogatives in EU affairs, not even after the Treaty of Lisbon. This is not problematic per se, although a NP's weakness or inability to react to EU decisions can undermine the effective representation of the EU citizens who are part of that domestic polity.

Usually, the easier it is to access a court in a given country the more likely it is that its parliament will benefit from judicial safeguards of its powers as a representative institution, as in Germany.[74] It does not follow, however, that NPs' powers are automatically more protected when MPs or citizens can easily access the constitutional or supreme court to challenge the violation of parliamentary prerogatives and political rights caused by a given Member State's EU membership. The experience of Ireland is a case in point here.[75] There, parliamentary business is considered a matter of parliamentary privilege and is hence excluded from judicial review. At the same time, the Irish Supreme Court has offered a narrow reading of the *Oireachtas*' constitutional powers in EU affairs.[76] Even when the appellant was an MP, like Thomas Pringle in the *Pringle* decision,[77] the case did not focus on the role of the Irish Parliament in amending Article 136 TFEU and in adopting the Treaty establishing the European Stability Mechanism (TESM), but on the compliance of the European Council Decision 2011/199/EU (amending Article 136 TFEU) and the TESM with EU law.[78]

Furthermore, national constitutional case law gives parliaments varying powers in EU affairs and thus creates asymmetries among NPs.[79] Similarly, the rights of citizens to participate in EU affairs through their parliaments is ensured asymmetrically across the Member States. An important paradox emerges here. On the one hand, the existence of domestic avenues for the judicial protection of NPs' EU-related powers is seen as reinforcing citizens' participation in EU decision-making. On the other hand, because of NPs' various degrees of involvement in EU affairs, which is based on different levels of national judicial protection of parliamentary prerogatives, the domestic rights of EU citizens to shape EU policies substantially diverge and offer uneven opportunities for political participation.

[74] See on this point Philipp Kiiver, 'The Lisbon Judgment of the German Constitutional Court: A Court-ordered Strengthening of the National Legislature in the EU' (2010) 16(5) ELJ 578–88.

[75] Moreover, after the Irish Supreme Court's decision of 1987 in *Crotty v An Taoiseach* [1987] IR 713, any EU treaty amendment implies ipso facto a constitutional amendment and, thus, a referendum following the parliamentary approval of the constitutional bill, without mandatory *ex ante* involvement of the Supreme Court. See T Lang, 'The Irish Case Which Delayed the Single European Act: *Crotty v An Taoiseach*' (1987) 24 CML Rev 709.

[76] According to Elaine Fahey, 'Reflections on the Legal Role of the Irish Parliament (*Oireachtas*) in EU Affairs after Lisbon' (EUI Working Papers MWP 2010/20) 13 ('A largely conservative Supreme Court has in the last decade favoured a purist and Executive-centred Separation of Powers').

[77] *Pringle v Government of Ireland and Others* [2012] IESC 47.

[78] In particular with TFEU, arts 3, 119, 122, 123, 125, 126, and 127 and TEU, arts 4, 13, and 48.

[79] These asymmetries are even stronger within the framework of EU economic governance. See Cristina Fasone, 'Eurozone, Non-Eurozone, and "Troubled Asymmetries" Among National Parliaments in the EU: Why and To What Extent This Is of Concern' in Roberto Castaldi and Giuseppe Martinico (eds), 'The Never-ending Reform of the EU: Another Chain in the Semi Permanent Treaty Revision Process?' (2014) Special Issue 6(2) *Perspectives on Federalism* 1–41.

There is no easy way out of this paradoxical situation, because the EU could not remove these asymmetries by imposing a model of constitutional review that would be common to all the Member States, such as one that would mirror the German system. The choice of specific procedural and institutional arrangements for the constitutional review of legislation, as well as each NP's main features, are necessarily and legitimately left to national legal systems as 'inherent to their fundamental structure, political and constitutional' (Article 4(2) TEU).[80] Because of their high constitutional importance, these choices do not tolerate any direct EU interference. National autonomy in deciding the constitutional organization of the legislature is well illustrated by the Slovenian example. In this Member State, the exclusion of the National Council, the Upper House of the Slovenian Parliament, from being counted towards the votes for reasoned opinions within the early warning system was enacted by domestic legislation. Challenged before the Slovenian Constitutional Court, this exclusion was upheld because, according to the Court, EU Treaty provisions do not determine how each parliamentary chamber's participation in EU affairs is organized domestically; hence, this decision is a national prerogative.[81]

6. Conclusion

The process of European integration has eroded the legislative powers of NPs by increasingly conferring competences on the EU at every Treaty revision, while the CJEU has gradually but consistently validated the exercise of an expanded catalogue of competences by EU institutions. This chapter demonstrates that, beyond the general framework that the Treaty of Lisbon provides for all NPs, it is impossible to guarantee equivalent domestic judicial protection of national parliamentary prerogatives in EU affairs—and thus citizens' political rights—across the Member States. This is not just because of the many national models of constitutional adjudication and the different outcomes thereof, but also because of the asymmetries arising from different forms of government, that is from the relationship between parliament and government as designed by the national constitution.

NPs have indeed enjoyed various degrees of protection of their EU-related prerogatives by constitutional courts. The erosion of parliamentary powers has been more evident in some Member States, such as Italy, and Spain, than in others, such as Germany. The present analysis shows that the level of the erosion depends: (a) on the extent to which constitutional case law has conceived the protection of parliamentary prerogatives in EU affairs as a non-negotiable condition to ensure the effectiveness of citizens' political rights; and (b) on rules on access to the courts.

However, the trend of a spontaneous and gradual convergence among the national systems of constitutional adjudication in Europe, particularly in Eastern Europe, can be detected on matters such as individual complaints, parliamentary minority actions, and the predominance of *ex post* and concrete review. This sort of Europeanization is a positive sign of cross-fertilization, which brings about a more symmetric level

[80] See more on this in the introductory chapter by Davor Jančić in this volume.

[81] Maria Romaniello, 'Upper Chambers in EU Parliamentary Democracies' (2014) PhD Dissertation 97. However, Member States may ask for a sort of official 'clarification' of this at the EU level. This has been the case with the many Belgian parliaments, to which Declaration No 51 annexed to the Treaty of Lisbon is devoted. See Maria Romaniello, 'Beyond the Constitutional "Bicameral Blueprint": Europeanisation and National Identities in Belgium' (n 48) 285–316.

of protection of both parliamentary prerogatives in EU affairs and citizens' political rights.[82]

The CJEU could indirectly bolster NPs if it gradually embraced the role of a constitutional court and relinquished its traditional position as the engine of the EU integration, adjudicating mostly in favour of EU institutions. To achieve this, it would need to become an impartial arbiter and guarantor of a balanced relationship between the EU and the Member States and strictly check the action of EU institutions against ultra vires action. A more balanced relationship along these lines would ensure a greater protection for NPs' powers as domestic legislatures and aid EU citizens in fully exercising their political rights at the national level as well.

[82] See more on these asymmetries in Richard Bellamy and Sandra Kröger, 'Europe Hits Home—The Domestic Deficits of Representative Democracy in EU Affairs' in Tatjana Evas, Ulrike Liebert, and Christopher Lord (eds), *Multilayered Representation in the European Union. Parliaments, Courts and the Public Sphere* (Nomos Verlag 2012) 41–57.

5

National Parliaments and the European Union—A View From Westminster

Julie Smith[1]

'It is national parliaments which are, and will remain, the true source of real democratic legitimacy and accountability in the EU.'[2]

David Cameron, Bloomberg speech

1. Introduction

National parliaments (NPs), often seen as the losers in European integration, were hailed as the beneficiaries of Lisbon.[3] Yet over half a decade after the Lisbon Treaty came into effect, many parliaments still found it hard to find their voice loudly, clearly, or effectively on European Union (EU) matters. Each takes a different approach, all with their own strengths and weaknesses. The differences in the ways two chambers even in the same country tackle European issues can be profound. The UK provides a particularly dramatic example of this phenomenon.[4] While the House of Commons can be characterized by largely sceptical, confrontational, high-profile plenary debates, the work of the House of Lords is typically seen as quieter, more focused, and expert, with much work going on in committee, reflecting in part the very different nature of the two chambers and their roles in twenty-first century British political life. The elected Commons is the bedrock of the eponymous Westminster model, based on bipartisan, conflictual politics so alien in much of the rest of Europe, where politics is characterized by consensus and coalition. The predominantly appointed House of

[1] This chapter builds on various lectures and keynote addresses given by the author in early 2015. It is based in part on research undertaken for the Open Research Area OPAL (Observatory of Parliaments after the Lisbon Treaty) project—ESRC Grant No ES/1014853/1. She is grateful to the ESRC for its support and to colleagues and students who attended the lectures at the University of Leuven, London School of Economics, and the *Université Libre de Bruxelles* for their insightful comments. Empirical insights draw in part on the author's experience leading for the Liberal Democrats in the House of Lords on the EU Referendum Act 2015. Thanks go to Geoffrey Edwards, William Wallace, and David Yates for comments on earlier drafts and to Davor Jančić for his editorial input. Any errors are, of course, her own.

[2] David Cameron, Bloomberg speech, quoted in House of Commons, European Scrutiny Committee, HC 109-I 'Reforming the European Scrutiny System in the House of Commons', 24th Report of Session 2013–14 of 28 November 2013, para 64, 103.

[3] See eg Foreign Secretary David Miliband MP in HC Deb 21 January 2008, col 1241; Davor Jančić, 'The Game of Cards: National Parliaments in the EU and the Future of the Early Warning Mechanism and the Political Dialogue' (2015) 52 CML Rev 939; and Olivier Rozenberg and Claudia Hefftler, 'Introduction' in Claudia Hefftler and others (eds), *The Palgrave Handbook of National Parliaments and the European Union* (Palgrave Macmillan 2015).

[4] Ariella Huff and Julie Smith, 'Westminster and the European Union: Ever-increasing Scepticism?' in Claudia Hefftler and others (eds), *The Palgrave Handbook of National Parliaments and the European Union* (Palgrave Macmillan 2015).

National Parliaments and the European Union: A View from Westminster. First Edition. Julie Smith.

Lords works on a more consensual basis, partly because of the nature of the powers it enjoys and partly as an essential response to the fact that the government of the day rarely enjoys a majority there.[5]

How then does Westminster deal with 'Europe' in practice? The aim of this chapter is to show how the roles and engagement of parliamentary chambers can differ even within a Member State. Analysing the powers and tools that the two chambers enjoy—including the duty to hold the government accountable (both chambers), scrutinize and revise legislation (both chambers but with the Lords playing a more substantive role), and questions and private members' bills—the chapter shows how Members of Parliament (MPs) and peers have played their respective parts in EU policy-making. It looks first at the period of 'normal' EU business during the 2010–15 Coalition Government, which took office shortly after the introduction of the Lisbon Treaty, before turning to their responses to the government's decision to renegotiate the UK's terms of membership of the EU and hold a referendum on the matter.

In fact, there is no single Westminster approach to the EU. The Lords and Commons perform very different functions and this applies to European integration at least as much as to other areas. There are two initially plausible starting assumptions: (1) that the views expressed in the two chambers would be broadly similar; after all, MPs and peers tend to come from the same parties and are grounded in the same national culture and discourse; and (2) that the work of the two chambers would be complementary as they are in domestic legislation, given their respective roles within the British legislature. In practice, as will be shown below, the first of these assumptions was very far off the mark before 2015, although the situation then shifted somewhat. The second is only partially correct: the roles of the two chambers are different without precisely being complementary. Meanwhile, the language and tone used in the two chambers could not be more different: the leitmotif in the House of Commons in the 2010–15 Parliament was one of Euroscepticism (broadly defined and interpreted it is true, but scepticism nonetheless), while the predominant views expressed in the Lords were more clearly pro-European, harking back to a long-gone and only transitory period when the UK's place seemed squarely in the EU as a constructive player.

The Conservatives were rather unexpectedly returned to office with an absolute majority in 2015, ensuring they had to deliver on their manifesto commitment to hold a referendum on the UK's membership of the EU. This led to a change in both the volume and nature of EU business in both chambers. The House of Commons, which had previously appeared resigned but frustrated about the EU, began to reassert itself. The Lords, which had seemed resilient showed itself rather more ambivalent than might have been expected, challenging the conventional assumptions about the pro-EU credentials of the Lords. The vote to leave the EU in June 2016 marked an abrupt change in parliamentary thinking on the EU and immediately precipitated a shift in the European activities of both chambers, pending what was expected to be a

[5] All bar 92 'hereditary' peers are appointed either by a political party (from the ranks of 'supporters', Commons retirees, or members of the Commons who have failed to be re-elected) or on a non-partisan basis to sit on the cross-benches. Historically, the Conservative Party had an in-built majority in this chamber. Moves to create life peers since the 1950s and Lords reform in the late 1990s ensured that the balance would shift such that no party or group enjoys a majority there. The 2010–15 Parliament was very much the exception as the Conservatives could secure a majority with the support of their Liberal Democrat colleagues in the Lords, although majorities could not be guaranteed on EU matters, where the two parties have long held quite divergent views. Thus, on EU matters, the Lords/Commons differences would persist through the Coalition period, reflecting their differing roles and composition.

prolonged period during which the UK's relationship with the EU would be uncertain, the role of Parliament vital but as yet untested.

2. Resilient or Resigned?

As a latecomer to the European Communities, the UK accepted an institutional framework already agreed by the six founding Member States. Some pooling of national sovereignty was a given, as was the supremacy of Community law.[6] MPs thus ceded some of their powers when they approved the European Communities Act (ECA) in October 1972. For some members on both sides of the House, the loss of sovereignty was too great a cost to make membership acceptable but a majority of MPs including sixty-nine Labour rebels were willing to accept the changes that would inevitably come about with membership in return for the opportunities they believed it offered. They could be reassured by the fundamental principle that 'no parliament can bind its successor' and, hence, by the thought that the ECA could always be repealed, as many Conservative parliamentary candidates, MPs, and grassroots members opined after the Lisbon Treaty had been ratified.[7] Moreover, procedures for parliamentary scrutiny were established before the UK acceded to the then European Economic Community precisely because 'by joining the EU the UK agreed to be legally bound by directly effective EU legislation'.[8] Over the years many parliamentarians, like their electors, began to espouse Eurosceptic rhetoric, often claiming that they had never understood the political implications of membership despite the referendum on membership that had been held in 1975. Yet, as veteran Conservative MP Kenneth Clarke noted at the second reading of the EU Referendum 2015 Bill in the House of Commons:

> There must have been some strange juxtapositions in the campaign held in the 1970s, in which I took a very active part. Most of the debates I took part in were about the pooling of sovereignty and the direct applicability of European legislation without parliamentary intervention, which was a very controversial subject, and, besides, ever-closer union was in the treaty to which we were acceding.[9]

In ratifying the Single European Act (SEA) of 1986, Westminster, in line with other NPs across the ever-widening European Union, accepted a number of reforms to the founding treaties that resulted in more powers shifting to the institutions of the EU and an associated loss of powers for Parliament itself. Resignation prevailed as few MPs paid much attention to their loss of sovereignty, even if some objected to the proposed treaties.[10] Years later, Michael Forsyth, who at the time of the SEA had been Parliamentary Private Secretary (PPS) to Foreign Secretary Geoffrey Howe, one of its key advocates, said that he had agonized over whether to support the Act,

[6] The doctrine of the supremacy of EU law had been promulgated by the European Court of Justice in its 1964 *Costa v ENEL* ([1964] ECR English Spec Ed 585) ruling, some eight years before the UK joined the then European Economic Community. See inter alia Gavin Drewry, 'The Jurisprudence of British Euroscepticism: A Strange Banquet of Fish and Vegetables' (2007) 3(2) Utrecht L Rev 101–115.

[7] For a discussion of sovereignty, see Graham Gee and Alison L Young, 'Regaining Sovereignty? Brexit, the UK Parliament and the Common Law' (2016) 22(1) EPL 131–48.

[8] House of Commons (n 2) 103.

[9] HC Deb 9 June 2015, col 1047.

[10] At the time, few apart from Conservative MP Bill (now Sir William) Cash had challenged it. He tabled an amendment to the Single European Act to the effect 'that nothing in the Act shall derogate from the sovereignty of the United Kingdom Parliament'. See more recently: HC Deb 23 March 2016, col 1703, where Cash reminded the House of this.

given its implications for sovereignty.[11] That he did support the Act is indicative of the strength of the payroll vote that characterizes the British system of parliamentary democracy: the fusion between the legislature and the executive, characterized by the large and growing number of MPs participating in government, weakens Parliament's ability to hold the government effectively to account. An issue, perhaps, in the mid-1980s; a more profound problem thirty years later given the increasing numbers of MPs who held ministerial office of some sort and thanks to the introduction by the Coalition Government of 2010–15 of fixed-term parliaments, which made it harder for the Prime Minister to hold backbenchers in check with the threat of an early election.

While the SEA ceded significant parliamentary sovereignty thanks to the introduction of qualified majority voting in the Council of Ministers, meaning that Member States could be outvoted, it was the subsequent Treaty on European Union (the Maastricht Treaty) that marked the start of more public soul-searching among British parliamentarians and was nearly defeated in the House of Commons.[12] At that time, calls began to emerge for a popular vote on matters European. MPs and peers who had been content to ratify both initial membership and the SEA by parliamentary means suddenly developed an appetite for direct democracy that would paradoxically ensure their own roles on constitutional issues were diminished.[13]

While Margaret Thatcher had rejected the use of referenda in the 1970s and had not considered one for the SEA, by the time of the Maastricht Treaty ratification she was actively encouraging backbench MPs to reject the treaty and wanted a referendum. Her change of heart on a device she had considered to be one for demagogues set a trend that continued in popular and political circles. The establishment in the 1990s of the Referendum Party and of the UK Independence Party (UKIP) provided vehicles for a campaign to press for a referendum on the newly created EU. The leaders of the three main parties—Conservative, Labour, and Liberal Democrat—gradually all succumbed to calls for such a vote. Over the course of the next decade all made promises of referenda on whether to enter the euro and on ratifying the Constitutional Treaty agreed in 2004.

No such referendum was ever held as the UK never came close to joining the common currency, while French and Dutch voters put paid to the Constitutional Treaty, thereby ensuring that the UK did not have a referendum on that matter either. While the Conservatives sought a referendum on ratifying the replacement Lisbon Treaty, the Liberal Democrats went a step further, arguing that it was time to offer voters a choice on whether or not to remain in the EU. Despite the views of Opposition MPs, the Lisbon Treaty was deemed by Prime Minister Gordon Brown to be sufficiently different from the Constitutional Treaty not to require ratification by referendum.[14]

The Treaty had been ratified by the time the Conservatives and Liberal Democrats took office in the first post-war British coalition government and both incoming

[11] Interview with the author, House of Lords, 13 April 2016.

[12] Anthony Forster, *Euroscepticism in Contemporary British Politics: Opposition to Europe in the Conservative and Labour Parties Since 1945* (Routledge 2002); David Baker, Andrew Gamble, and Steve Ludlam, 'Whips or Scorpions? The Maastricht Vote and the Conservative Party' (1993) 46 Parl Aff 151.

[13] For a discussion of the impact on parliamentary sovereignty of the choice to use the referendum device see Ben Wellings and Emma Vines, 'Populism and Sovereignty: The EU Act and the In-Out Referendum, 2010–15' (2016) 69 Parl Aff 309. See also Hugo Young, *This Blessed Plot—Britain and Europe from Churchill to Blair* (Macmillan 1998).

[14] See HC Deb 21 January 2008.

Conservative Prime Minister David Cameron and Foreign Secretary William Hague accepted that a referendum would not be possible, to the frustration of backbench MPs and grassroots Eurosceptics, who continued to make the case for one. Thus, as Hague's successor as Foreign Secretary, Philip Hammond, told the Commons in June 2015, 'Treaty after treaty—the Single European Act, Maastricht, Amsterdam, Nice and Lisbon—individually and collectively have added hugely to the European Union's powers, often in areas that would have been unthinkable in 1975, and that change has eroded the democratic mandate for our membership to the point where it is wafer-thin and demands to be renewed'.[15]

The EU Act 2011, enacted by the Coalition Government, was intended to ensure that no further powers could be transferred to the EU without a referendum: sovereignty would be returned from Parliament to the people; no further loss of sovereignty could be approved by Parliament alone. Yet, this did not go far enough for many Conservative parliamentarians, who continued to press for an in/out referendum as discussed below. Calls for such a poll were only met after the entry into office of a majority Conservative Government in May 2015, following a pledge made by David Cameron at Bloomberg in January 2013.

As the UK sought to renegotiate its membership of the EU in 2015/2016 ahead of the promised referendum, one of David Cameron's demands was increased powers for NPs. This was in line with calls from the House of Commons European Scrutiny Committee, which had recommended moves to a 'red card' system in its comprehensive review of scrutiny. Coming from a Committee chaired by veteran Eurosceptic Sir William (Bill) Cash, the proposals could be seen as meeting the demands of some of Cameron's sceptic backbenchers—whether it was a mere palliative to such people was unclear at the time. Moreover, this was also one of the few areas where there had seemed to be common cause with other EU leaders, and with both chambers of the UK Parliament. After all, the origin of the 'democratic deficit' was precisely that nation states were ceding powers to the EU and powers previously wielded by NPs were being taken over by executives.[16]

Bringing Europe closer to its citizens has been an oft-repeated theme, notably since the Laeken Declaration of 2001; yet the experience was of continued drifting away with little evidence either of parliamentary resilience in the face of deepening European integration. Parliaments were given a greater role in the EU under the Lisbon Treaty, which went so far as to assert that they 'contribute actively to the good functioning of the Union' (Article 12 TEU) and was widely heralded by academics as granting new powers to the NPs.[17] Some politicians asserted that these were not 'new' powers, but rather powers that already belonged to NPs, which rather belied the drift that had long taken place unacknowledged in the public domain.[18] Nor did NPs make much use of their Lisbon powers.[19] They had been granted authority but lacked the 'attitude' and in some cases the ability to use their new powers in practice.[20]

[15] HC Deb 9 June 2015, col 1048. [16] Toussaint Report of 1986.

[17] This was the foundational premise of the Open Research Area-funded OPAL project.

[18] Question by Michael Connarty MP to Dr Smith in House of Commons, European Scrutiny Committee, HC 711-iii 'Minutes of Evidence' of 1 March 2013 (transcript of oral evidence given on 12 December 2012) http://www.publications.parliament.uk/pa/cm201213/cmselect/cmeuleg/c711-iii/c71101.htm (last accessed 2 August 2016).

[19] See Claudia Hefftler and others (eds), *The Palgrave Handbook of National Parliaments and the European Union* (Palgrave Macmillan 2015).

[20] The ideas of parliaments' attitudes, authority and ability are explored in Ariella Huff, 'Executive Privilege Reaffirmed? Parliamentary Scrutiny of the CFSP and CSDP', Special Issue 'After Lisbon: National Parliaments in the European Union' (2015) 38 WEP 396.

3. National Parliaments After the Lisbon Treaty—Westminster in Context

So what powers were formally given to NPs under the Lisbon Treaty, and how have they been used? Protocol 1 on the Role of National Parliaments in the European Union, annexed to the Treaty, refers to Member States 'desiring to encourage greater involvement of NPs in the activities of the European Union and to enhance their ability to express their views on draft legislative acts of the Union'. NPs were granted one new power—the so-called 'yellow card'.[21] The cards are 'played' or 'shown' under the early warning system, and if enough NPs believe that the draft EU legislation breaches the principle of subsidiarity, they can request the Commission to review it.[22] The subsidiarity check was not embraced enthusiastically by NPs: by mid-2016 only three yellow cards had been played. In any case, the new arrangements gave NPs little formal right to affect legislative outcomes if the European Commission persisted with its proposals.[23] Nonetheless, the change did mark a first step in the return of NPs to the European arena against the previous tide of disempowerment.

NPs responded differently to the Lisbon Treaty.[24] Two 'active' chambers whose work is often taken as good practice take quite different approaches. On the one hand, the Danish *Folketing* focuses on mandating government ministers ahead of summit meetings in accordance with its long-standing practice. However, if such an approach works well in a country that traditionally has minority government, it is less suitable for the UK, which typically has single-party majority government where the scale of the payroll vote makes it harder for Parliament to control the executive. On the other hand, the Dutch lower chamber, the *Tweede Kamer*, began to 'mainstream' European affairs, moving from a single European committee to a situation where all committees take the EU into consideration. While this latter approach has worked well in the Netherlands, and during the Coalition some British government ministers called for EU matters to be mainstreamed in Westminster, the Dutch system is costly in terms of administration and requires a depth of engagement that most British politicians arguably would not have wished to devote to European affairs in the normal course of events, although they found renewed interest in EU affairs *after* the vote to leave the EU. As a House of Commons European Scrutiny Committee (ESC) report lamented, MPs did not appear especially interested in the EU, the passion demonstrated in certain plenary debates notwithstanding.[25]

This was not surprising given that politics in Europe appears to adhere to the dictum usually attributed to late US Congressional Speaker Tip O'Neill that 'all politics is local'. Local is what matters to politicians: the parish pump, the pot-hole, and the pork-barrel. The EU is thus rarely of major concern to elected UK politicians.

[21] See Jančić (n 3).

[22] See various chapters in Hefftler and others (n 19) for a discussion of how the system works country by country. See also Jančić (n 3).

[23] Ian Cooper, 'A Yellow Card for the Striker: National Parliaments and the Defeat of EU Legislation on the Right to Strike' (2015) 22 JEPP 1406.

[24] Christine Neuhold and Julie Smith, 'Conclusion: From "Latecomers" to "Policy Shapers"?—The Role of National Parliaments in the "Post-Lisbon" Union' in Claudia Hefftler and others (eds), *The Palgrave Handbook of National Parliaments and the European Union* (Palgrave Macmillan 2015).

[25] The ESC noted in its *Reforming the European Scrutiny System* report (n 2 at 10) that members' responses to an online survey which the Committee had conducted on scrutiny were 'disappointingly low—which is perhaps indicative of the lack of interest in the details of EU policy-making within the House'.

The House of Lords is, in many ways, the privileged exception as members are not required to compete for office to secure their seat in the Lords, even if some peers are elected to positions in local government and many actively campaign for their Commons colleagues. The lure of the local, the immediate, and even of the party can affect peers as well. Nonetheless, there are very clear differences from the Commons, seen in the rhetoric and discourse of the two chambers: the Commons often reflecting the perceived negative public opinion; the Lords taking a more dispassionate approach. Ostensibly, therefore, peers have the opportunity to take the long view, to follow a Burkean approach to representation, reflecting their objective judgment more than naked party interest or what they think voters want to hear.[26]

In the Commons, the 'usual suspects', those who can be relied upon to speak in any and every debate on EU matters, are predominantly entrenched Eurosceptics—including Bill Cash, Bernard Jenkin, and Jacob Rees-Mogg—with the addition on the other side of veteran pro-EU Kenneth Clarke after he left the Cabinet. In the Lords, the main contributors are often 'experts' who have been involved in the EU over many years, either as Members of the European Parliament (MEPs), including Labour's Baroness Morgan of Ely and Lord Cashman, and the Conservative Lords Callanan and Inglewood, or diplomats (Lords Kerr and Hannay being the most notable) or have developed expertise by dint of service on the highly respected European Union Committee (EUC) or one of its sub-committees. The House of Lords is unusual in having an extensive series of sub-committees, dating back to the 1970s when the UK joined the then European Community.[27]

These sub-committees enable peers to engage in in-depth analysis of proposed EU legislation, ensuring that their work receives international attention. Indeed, former Commission President José Manuel Barroso said that 'the House of Lords is one of the best in Europe in terms of analysis. Very, very competent analysis of the legislation'.[28] Reforms in the structure of Lords committees in 2015 caused some concern among peers, however. Partly in response to the growth in numbers of working peers seeking to play a role in committees, a new system of 'rotation' was introduced requiring peers to come off any committee or sub-committee after three years, thereby reducing peers' ability to immerse themselves in the work of committees and really master their briefs before being required to move on.[29] By contrast, members of the Commons ESC can serve for an unlimited period of time and some members of the Committee, including the chairman, Bill Cash, had served on the Committee or its predecessors for many years. Over the years, the ESC also became heavily dominated by Eurosceptic members, not wholly representative of MPs' views generally but a situation that would recur in the formation of the Exiting the European Union Committee created in the aftermath of the referendum to shadow the newly established Department for Exiting the European Union (DfEEU).

[26] Edmund Burke's conception of representation entailed that representatives should exercise their judgement to act in the best interests of the represented rather than as delegates doing what their electors wanted them to do.

[27] See the exchange between Lord Hannay and evidence-giver Dr Julie Smith in House of Lords, EU Committee, 'Unrevised Transcript of Evidence', Inquiry on the Role of National Parliaments in the EU, evidence session (No 2) held on 22 October 2013 http://www.parliament.uk/documents/lords-committees/eu-select/Role%20of%20national%20parliaments/ucEU221013ev2.pdf (last accessed 2 August 2016).

[28] José Manuel Barroso's speech at Chatham House, cited in House of Lords, EU Committee, HL Paper 11 'Report on 2014–15', 1st Report of Session 2014–15 of 3 July 2015, 7.

[29] This issue was referred to by several contributors to the Lords' debate on the EUC 'Report on 2014–15' (n 28). See Lords Hansard, Grand Committee, Deb 15 July 2015, col GC57.

4. Formal Scrutiny Rights

The formal duties of the two long-standing European committees and their actual practices differ markedly. The House of Commons European Scrutiny Committee is appointed pursuant to Standing Order 143 to examine EU documents. Under the scrutiny reserve, 'Ministers should not give agreement to EU proposals which have not been cleared by the ESC, or on which when they have been recommended by the Committee for debate, the House has not yet agreed a resolution'.[30] The House of Lords' European Union Committee is more focused on EU-level activities than on the work of the government, although the Committee does also seek to hold the British government to account. As with the Commons, there is a scrutiny reserve: the government is required to answer letters regarding the scrutiny reserve within two weeks and respond to reports within two months. The Lords' EUC also 'conducts inquiries and makes reports. The Government are required to respond in writing to a report's recommendations within two months of publication. If the report is for debate then there is a debate in the House of Lords, which a Minister attends and responds to'.[31] Competition for time means that reports may wait for months before they are finally debated in the chamber. The Committee's report on *National Parliaments in the European Union* published in March 2014 was not debated until December that year, while the 2014–15 annual Scrutiny Report was received in Grand Committee rather than in the main chamber owing to pressure of other business.

Nor can the government be relied upon to respond to either the Lords or the Commons in a timely fashion. The Commons ESC expressed frustration over the government's lack of response to its Scrutiny Report, while Baroness Scott of Needham Market, chairman of the Lords EU Energy and Environment Sub-committee, pointed out that:

> It is with some sadness that I say that the government response to our report [on *The North Sea Under Pressure: Is Regional Marine Co-operation the Answer?*] was very late indeed. Despite an extended deadline, it took three attempts and a letter from the chairman before we finally received the response this morning. I can only assume that, knowing that this would come up in debate today, they were aware that the Minister's wrath would be swift and terrible had they not replied by this morning.[32]

The debate was held on 15 July, while the report had been published on 17 March that year, meaning that the government had taken two months longer to reply than it was formally permitted.

Apart from scrutiny committees, there are several ways in which each chamber can deal with EU business and the EU–UK relationship, including Private Members' Bills (PMBs), oral and written questions, full debates and Questions for Short Debate (Lords) or Westminster Hall debates (Commons), as well as questions following the Prime Minister's European Council statements.

Much parliamentary time is devoted to government business and it is difficult for individual members to get parliamentary time. Thus, the House of Commons ESC complained about government reluctance to schedule a debate on its 2015 Scrutiny

[30] House of Commons, European Scrutiny Committee, HC 918 'Scrutiny Reform Follow-up and Legacy Report', 38th Report of Session 2014–15 of 25 March 2015.

[31] Covering note to the House of Lords, European Union Committee, HL Paper 151 'The Role of National Parliaments in the European Union', 9th Report of Session 2013–14 of 24 March 2014.

[32] Lords Hansard, Grand Committee, Deb 15 July 2015, col GC57 (n 29), col GC61.

Report, as well as about the difficulty of securing a hearing with the Foreign Secretary, Philip Hammond. The Coalition Government did empower a new Backbench Business Committee, which gave backbenchers more scope to have matters debated. Therefore, in October 2011, a backbench debate on holding a referendum on the UK's membership of the EU was held following a petition run by *The Daily Express*. The vast majority of those who contributed to the debate, particularly but not exclusively from the Conservative benches, stressed their 'Euroscepticism', almost as if any speech would have been incomplete without such remarks.[33]

Yet, if MPs were uncomfortable about the UK's membership of the EU, their leaders were determined at that time that there should be no referendum. David Cameron, Ed Miliband, and Nick Clegg all imposed three-line whips ordering their MPs to oppose the draft bill, which failed despite eighty-one rebel Conservatives voting for it—a clear reflection of the executive dominance of the UK system which disempowers Parliament.[34] Cameron would subsequently change his mind, committing his party to an in/out referendum in his now famous Bloomberg speech given in January 2013, reflecting the fraught and transient nature of Conservative Party thinking on the UK's relationship with the EU, as well as the ability of backbench parliamentarians to influence the party leadership and ultimately the government's agenda as Cameron's proposals would be enshrined in the Conservatives' 2015 general election manifesto.

In plenary debates in the Commons, Eurosceptic rhetoric has long been prevalent, especially on the Conservative benches, as seen most clearly in the 2011 referendum debate, but also furthered after the so-called 'veto' over the Fiscal Compact in 2012, and over the EU's 2014–2020 Multiannual Financial Framework, where opposition Labour MPs and Tory rebels jointly ensured a government defeat. The nature of the debate is typically party political, tribal, and often ill-informed.[35]

Meanwhile, there was a generally pro-EU attitude in the Lords, quite out of tune with contemporary discourse on the EU in the UK—whether in the Commons, the media, or among the general public. This enabled the present author to make her maiden speech in a debate on 'The case for British membership of the European Union' without falling foul of the requirement that maiden speeches should not be controversial. Such a debate could not have failed to be highly contested in the Commons, whereas in the Lords no more than a handful of peers actively opposed the UK's membership of the EU at that time and few even espoused Eurosceptic rhetoric. Yet, the aftermath of the 2015 general election would demonstrate that the Lords' Europhilia had been overestimated as gradually advocates of leaving the EU began to speak in debates.

Whereas debates on legislation follow a similar structure in both chambers, the content of the debate was typically markedly different, at least before 2015.[36] This could be seen in the progress of the Bill that led to the EU Act 2011, which made provision for a referendum when it was proposed to transfer significant powers to the EU. The Commons, led by veteran Eurosceptic Bill Cash, focused on parliamentary sovereignty, a perennial theme of EU debates in that chamber. Labour's Yvette Cooper tried to have the bill rejected at the second reading stage 'on the grounds that, while the principle

[33] HC Deb 24 October 2011.

[34] A three-line whip requires MPs or peers to attend and vote with their party. It is the strongest requirement to vote and failure to do so or rebelling against the party line can result in sanctions.

[35] Ariella Huff and Julie Smith, Interim Report on 'United Kingdom' in Wolfgang Wessels and others, Study for the European Parliament Constitutional Affairs Committee (AFCO), *Democratic Control in the Member States of the European Council and the Euro Zone Summits*, 2013.

[36] This section draws on material gathered by the Cambridge team in the framework of the Open Research Area OPAL project.

of referendums on significant constitutional and monetary changes is appropriate, the Bill is a flawed measure which would confuse the important issues at stake and make vital constitutional issues justiciable by the courts rather than resolved under the sovereignty of parliament', a comment that would prove prescient in light of the legal cases brought in the wake of the 2016 referendum.[37]

The concerns of Cash and other Conservative Eurosceptics clearly reflected long-held and deeply felt attitudes towards the EU. Cooper's position perhaps owed more to a desire to oppose the government than to any strong objection to the legislation per se, an approach previously adopted by Labour over the ratification of the Maastricht Treaty, although it also reflected growing parliamentary concern about the role of courts.[38] The Lords' focus was more technical but with emphasis on the role of referenda per se and comparisons with procedures in other Member States.[39]

Neither chamber has a strong record of holding the British government to account over EU matters. During the Labour Government (1997–2010) the Prime Minister would address the Commons ahead of European Council meetings; under the Coalition (2010–15) and then Conservative (2015–) governments, this practice was dropped. While the Danish approach to mandating ministers ahead of Council or European Council meetings is viewed by some as beneficial, it has generally been eschewed in the UK, since it could arguably bind a government too tightly, thereby limiting the flexibility required in negotiations at the EU level. However, in recognition of the fact that Parliament could usefully engage more fully with ministers before Council meetings, in 2014 the House of Lords EUC began to ask the Europe Minister to give evidence in advance of European Council meetings, 'giving the Committee an opportunity to examine publicly and influence the Government's negotiating position on key issues'.[40] A practice did thus emerge whereby the Minister of State for Europe, David Lidington throughout David Cameron's premiership, attended the two Committees ahead of European Council meetings.[41]

After the European Council meeting, the Prime Minister makes a statement to the House of Commons, after which MPs may quiz him/her, ensuring a degree of *ex post* scrutiny. Such statements are usually repeated in the House of Lords by the Leader of the Lords, who reads out verbatim the statement that has been made in the Commons, before responses are made by the opposition front benches and finally questions taken from backbenchers. A similar process is used for other statements and Urgent Questions that have been raised in the Commons. The decision to repeat them in the House of Lords, along with other decisions on the business of the House, is made by the 'usual channels'—ie the government whips alongside the Labour and Liberal Democrat whips. Thus, rebels from the government benches cannot necessarily challenge their ministers; nor can the Opposition if their front benches do not wish to do so. On various EU questions in the run-up to the 2016 referendum it proved extremely difficult for the Lords to hold the government to account as the three front benches in

[37] HC Deb 7 December 2010, col 205.

[38] Gee and Young (n 7).

[39] Drawing on work by Auel and Benz, Wendler argues that 'a polarisation of parliamentary debates between parties of the government majority and the parliamentary opposition appears as one of the most typical patterns of domestic parliamentary debates'. Frank Wendler, 'Challenging Domestic Politics? European Debates of National Parliaments in France, Germany, and the UK' (2013) 35 J Eur Integration 801, 805. This is far less clearly the case in the House of Lords, particularly on EU matters where the front benches tend to share broadly similar views.

[40] House of Lords (n 28) para 21, at 14.

[41] See a comparative overview of parliamentary scrutiny over the European Council in the chapter by Diane Fromage in this volume.

the Lords were committed to remaining in the EU and thus reluctant to provide oxygen to voices that might be critical of the government's approach to the referendum.

The tone of the debate was very different in the two chambers until 2015. While the most frequent contributors to Commons debates—on the Conservative side, Bill Cash, Christopher Chope, Jacob Rees-Mogg, Peter Bone, and Douglas Carswell (who defected to UKIP in 2014), and, on the Labour benches, Gisela Stuart and Kate Hoey—were strongly Eurosceptic, in the Lords the key players were generally pro-EU. Notably, contributions by the Minister of State for the Foreign and Commonwealth Office, Baroness Anelay of St Johns, were frequently far more Europhile than would have been expected of her Commons' colleagues, even Europe Minister David Lidington. This dichotomy was well shown, and indeed magnified, in responses to the final European Council statement of the 2010–15 parliament in March 2015. David Cameron seemed to use his statement more as a platform for his party's re-election campaign, focusing as he did on a record of Conservative government action on Europe over the previous five years rather than the outcome of the European Council. That his party had been in coalition with the pro-European Liberal Democrats for the previous five years appeared to matter little to his oration. Nor did the fact that the main focus of the Summit had been on the Eurozone.

The focus of the statement was clearly on the relationship between the UK and the EU. The dangers of a 'disorderly Greek exit from the euro' were flagged up because of the importance of Eurozone stability to the UK even as a non-Eurozone country, and because 'it could be very damaging to the British economy'.[42] Cameron then stressed his government's economic success and the strength of the UK economy compared with that of Greece to which it had been compared in 2010.[43] The focus was unquestionably on the British national interest: 'Just as we are acting in our national interest at home, so we have acted to protect our national interest in Europe, too: we have cut the EU budget for the first time in its history; we got Britain out of the bailout schemes; we vetoed a treaty that was not in our national interest'.[44] He then gave his prospectus for reform and the referendum that his party was promising in the forthcoming general election, issuing a challenge to those who rejected a referendum to explain themselves to the House.[45]

The leader of the Labour Party, Ed Miliband, who did not favour a referendum, chose not to take up Cameron's challenge, preferring to revert to the main theme of the European Council: 'On Greece, rather than recycling his failing election slogans, can the Prime Minister tell us what the prospects are for a long-term agreement with Greece?'[46] Bill Cash took the opportunity to ask the Prime Minister: 'In what specific respects will he repatriate the powers of the British people to govern themselves and return the powers of sovereignty to this Parliament so that we can govern this country as we wish?'[47] The Prime Minister's answer outlined a set of issues that would subsequently form the core of his demands in the renegotiations of 2015/16.

If the debate in the Commons centred on party politics and Eurosceptic demands, the response in the Lords was somewhat different, focused as it was rather more on the substance of the European Council conclusions, and certainly more pro-EU. Peers took

[42] HC Deb 23rd March 2015, col 1121.

[43] In the five days it took to form the Conservative–Liberal Democrat coalition in 2010, the spectre of the financial crisis loomed large. See eg David Laws, *22 Days in May: The Birth of the Lib Dem–Conservative Coalition* (Biteback Publishing 2010).

[44] HC Deb 23 March 2015, col 1121. [45] ibid col 1122. [46] ibid col 1122.

[47] ibid col 1125.

the opportunity to mock the campaigning tone of the statement. As Liberal Democrat peer Baroness Falkner of Margravine put it, 'that Statement, ... sounded rather like the Conservative election manifesto—but then so did Labour's response'.[48] For once in the Lords there was a clear party political dynamic in the debate. Former Europe Adviser to Tony Blair, Lord Liddle enquired of Baroness Stowell, the Leader of the House of Lords, 'Does the noble Baroness agree that the statement she has just read out exposes the contradiction at the heart of the Government's European policy?'. Differences of opinion were evident but the marked government-opposition dichotomy, so evident in the Commons, was missing. Divisions were seen within the Tory ranks, notably over energy and climate change. One Conservative former minister, Lord Deben (formerly John Selwyn Gummer), asked the Leader of the Lords to pass a message back to the Prime Minister to the effect that Britain could only be influential in the EU if it remained a member:

> [w]ill she take the message back that it is very often easier to get people to join with you if you occasionally say how good it is to be party to and member of the European Union? Would it not be much more helpful, in the perfectly proper desire to have reform in the European Union, if we just remarked on the huge importance to Britain of being in the European Union and to the European Union that Britain is in it?[49]

Deben's tone was in keeping with the vast majority of members of the Lords, who received his comments with approval, even if Tory colleagues down the corridor may not have done, nor indeed his climate-sceptic and Eurosceptic colleague Lord Lawson.

Of course, these debates prefigured a general election in which the EU, traditionally a low salience issue for voters, would matter for the first time and where there was clear blue water between the parties, as the Tories campaigned on Cameron's Bloomberg commitments to reform, renegotiate, and then hold a referendum on the UK's ongoing membership of the EU. They are thus not wholly reflective of plenary sessions in either House but they are indicative of the marked differences between the two chambers over EU matters and, to a lesser extent, of party divisions over Europe. Nonetheless, they did appear to show that on these matters, the Commons were from Mars, the Lords from Venus.[50]

5. Towards a Referendum

David Cameron's Bloomberg speech served its purpose of holding his fractious party together over the contentious issue of EU membership.[51] The offer ensured a truce within the party. Eurosceptics such as Bill Cash were satisfied by the offer of a referendum, praising the Prime Minister 'for stating unequivocally in his Bloomberg speech that it is our national Parliament that is the root of our democracy, for which people fought and died',[52] while those on the relatively smaller Europhile wing of the party were also broadly content with Cameron's tone, as he had outlined a broadly positive case for the UK's membership of the EU.

[48] HL Deb 23 March 2015, col 1265. [49] ibid col 1269.

[50] Julie Smith, 'MPs Are from Mars, Peers Are from Venus: Westminster and the EU', The UK in a Changing Europe blog, 11 September 2015.

[51] For a discussion of the internal Conservative Party divisions and the impact of the Coalition on European policy see Julie Smith, 'Europe: The Coalition's Poisoned Chalice' in Anthony Seldon and Mike Finn (eds), *The Coalition Effect 2010–2015* (Cambridge: Cambridge University Press 2015).

[52] HC Deb, 23 March 2015, col 1125.

The government and the Commons thus came together to try to set the agenda after the Bloomberg speech. When Conservative MP James Wharton won the 2013 ballot for PMBs, he introduced a Bill to hold an in/out referendum by the end of 2017—with the support of the Conservative leadership, in marked contrast to the situation in 2011, when the Prime Minister had sought to block proposals for a referendum.[53] With such government support, the draft legislation—unusually for a PMB—made its way through the House of Commons without difficulty. However, it was blocked in the House of Lords thanks to pro-EU peers, who tabled numerous amendments and effectively talked out the Bill, demonstrating the ability of the House of Lords to thwart proposals that did not come from any government manifesto. Wharton was seen as a hero in the Conservative Party, but the Lords had shown both their Europhilia and the fact that they could have a significant impact on British EU policy.

A year later, Tory MP Bob Neill introduced a similar PMB but it ran aground thanks to intra-Coalition wrangles and the Bill did not make it through second reading in the Commons. Thus, no legislation for an in/out referendum would be approved by the 2010–15 parliament, partly due to the House of Lords and partly due to the nature of coalition government, where decisions were subject to greater negotiation and compromise than is the case with single-party government. The failures of Wharton and Neill demonstrated the difficulties that backbench MPs face effecting legislation in the face of contrary views in the upper chamber, even if they have government support. Only when there is a clear manifesto commitment from the governing party can peers be relied upon not to resist the will of the executive, thanks to the Salisbury-Addison Convention.

6. The EU Referendum Act 2015

The return of a Conservative government committed to renegotiating the UK's membership of the EU before holding a referendum on the matter ensured that Europe would be at the forefront of business for much of the first session of the new Parliament. Having secured an absolute majority of just twelve in the general election, Prime Minister David Cameron swiftly moved to introduce the legislation necessary for the promised referendum. The EU Referendum Bill, flagged up in the Queen's Speech, was introduced into the House of Commons on 28 May 2015 and received Royal Assent on 17 December that year. Its passage through Parliament saw the Bill amended several times and the debates at each stage brought out a range of opinions on the question of membership of the EU in addition to discussion of the merits of the Bill. In the Commons, the results of the 2015 general election had an impact on how MPs articulated their concerns and on their voting behaviour. Differences rapidly re-emerged among the Conservatives, whose divisions over Europe had been papered over in the period after Cameron's 2013 Bloomberg speech. While the 2015 intake of Conservative MPs was somewhat less Eurosceptic than the 2010 cohort, the second reading debate on the EU Referendum Bill highlighted the depth of feeling among those seeking to leave the EU. Many on both sides of the argument harked back to the 1975 referendum, and the themes that emerged were also redolent of debates

[53] Individual MPs and peers can enter an annual ballot to bring forward a piece of legislation known as a Private Member's Bill. Few are ever enacted into law unless they have the benefit of government support.

of the 1960s and 1970s, with Bill Cash again raising concerns about parliamentary sovereignty.

The dynamics in the Commons altered considerably as a result of the general election. The strongly pro-EU leaders of both the Labour Party, Ed Miliband, and Liberal Democrats, Nick Clegg, resigned immediately after their parties' disastrous results at the polls. In the case of the Labour Party, this resulted in a prolonged interregnum as the leadership election ran until September 2015, during which time Harriet Harman served as acting leader. Unlike other Labour leaders, she refused to play politics over the EU. Labour thus abstained on the EU Referendum Bill at second reading in the Commons, despite the fact that the Party's Chief Whip, Rosie Winterton, had lined up the parliamentary party to vote against, as John Smith had done over Maastricht in 1992.

The surprise election of veteran left-winger and serial party rebel Jeremy Corbyn, a traditional Eurosceptic, as Labour leader in September 2015 led to concerns that the Labour Party might drift to an anti-EU stance, reflecting a 'Lexit' narrative that the EU and its austerity measures since the Eurozone crisis were bad for workers, not least since there were rumours that David Cameron's renegotiation would seek to reduce workers' rights. In practice, however, the strongly pro-EU majority in the Parliamentary Labour Party held sway and Corbyn espoused the line that the UK was better off in the EU, where it could influence policy and where it would be able to reverse any malign effects of the renegotiations should they occur. However, he lost no opportunity to criticize Cameron's perceived failures of European policy, whether in terms of Conservative Party cohesion or the renegotiation.

Proceedings in the House of Commons also changed after May 2015 thanks to the arrival of a large and highly disciplined group of Scottish National Party (SNP) MPs and to the loss of all but eight Liberal Democrat MPs, who had previously been the junior coalition partner for five years. Both parties were strongly pro-European, but their approaches to the EU referendum differed considerably. Liberal Democrats in Coalition had been strong advocates of the EU, but while their rhetoric focused on reform, they saw little need for the government's renegotiation. Nonetheless, the rump Liberal Democrat group was reluctant to criticize the government's approach lest it undermine the case for remaining in the EU. The highly disciplined group of fifty-six SNP MPs felt no such compunction to avoid criticizing the government's plans. Nor did they feel the need to support government proposals for a referendum, becoming the only party to vote against the EU Referendum Bill at second reading.

The SNP, along with Labour, whose official position was also strongly in favour of remaining in the EU, and Tory rebels, managed to amend the EU Bill in the House of Commons to remove the government's proposals on 'purdah'. Under the Political Parties, Elections and Referendums Act (PPERA) of 2000, the government would have been subject to a period during which it would not be able to advocate European policy. The precise effect of this provision for a national referendum was somewhat unclear, since the only previous referendum to be fought under the PPERA rules was the 2011 poll on whether to change the electoral system, which was not a matter of the government's core day-to-day business in the way that EU policy is.

Foreign Secretary Philip Hammond initially sought to disapply the purdah provisions on the grounds that the government's day-to-day engagement with the EU could be compromised and, more contentiously, because the government would want to campaign on the issue.[54] MPs were not persuaded by this argument and successfully

[54] HC Deb 9 June 2015.

amended the draft legislation to the effect that the government would be subject to purdah. Neither the government nor pro-EU peers sought to reintroduce this issue when the bill arrived in the House of Lords in October 2015, accepting the will of the Commons, which for once was able to overcome the will of the executive.

Since it had been a firm Conservative Party manifesto commitment, peers made clear that they would not seek to block the government's proposals for a referendum, unlike the previous Wharton PMB, which they had successfully killed off in 2014. They were nonetheless determined to scrutinize the draft legislation thoroughly. Over the summer of 2015, the Electoral Commission, whose job inter alia is to ensure the fairness of referendums as well as elections, produced recommendations on the wording of the referendum question. Rather than the government's initial wording of 'Should the UK remain a member of the European Union?', the Commission advised the longer alternative question, 'Should the UK remain a member of the European Union or leave the European Union?', which it asserted to be the fairest formulation following extensive research. The vast majority of peers endorsed the Commission's view, as had the Prime Minister, and the proposed wording was thus accepted.

The Lords proved to be rather more divided on EU membership than had been apparent from their activity in the 2010–15 Parliament. Nor were all members as expert on the EU as previous analyses of the Lords might have led one to expect.[55] A hard core of former Conservative cabinet ministers led by former Chancellor of the Exchequer Lord (Nigel) Lawson and Thatcherite Michael Forsyth (Lord Forsyth of Drumlean) raised an array of concerns about the legislation. Eurosceptic peers were especially determined to ensure that the referendum should be 'fair'. The experience of the 1975 referendum, when the question clearly favoured the status quo of staying in the European Community and where the rules were somewhat lax, meant peers on both sides of the debate were anxious to avoid similar allegations in 2016/2017. The minister, Baroness Anelay, repeatedly stated that the government sought a level playing field for the two sides in the referendum. The issue of fairness thus featured in debates on the three major themes on which the Lords focused their scrutiny of the Referendum Bill: the franchise; the rules of engagement including funding for the campaigns; and requests for reports. Each is examined in turn below.

With respect to the *franchise*, Labour and the Liberal Democrats, supported by many cross-benchers and a handful of Tories, led the charge for votes for sixteen and seventeen-year-olds, which had been granted in the 2014 referendum on Scottish independence. Amendments were also proposed to enfranchise EU nationals resident in the UK and UK citizens resident in the EU, even if they had been abroad for more than fifteen years. That the Conservative Party's own 2015 manifesto had promised 'votes for life', ie the extension of the franchise to UK nationals regardless of how long they had lived abroad, cut no ice. On each of these points the government's position was that changes to the franchise should be tackled as part of a wholesale review of the Representation of the People Act 1983. Meanwhile, sceptics such as Lords Forsyth and Hamilton argued that these were just attempts by those seeking to remain to increase the numbers likely to support their cause.[56]

While the House of Lords passed an amendment at report stage to enfranchise sixteen and seventeen-year-olds, their amendment was overturned in the Commons. When the issue came back to the Lords, the Commons had asserted financial privilege, thereby reducing the Lords' room for manoeuvre, since peers formally have no right

[55] See eg Huff and Smith (n 4) and Neuhold and Smith (n 24).

[56] Forsyth on *The Week in Westminster*, BBC Radio 4, 7 November 2015.

to vote on financial matters. Coming just weeks after a highly controversial government defeat on tax credits in the Lords, peers were reluctant to challenge the will of the elected chamber again.[57] After a lengthy debate, the amendment was defeated and the franchise remained as proposed by the government—namely, the parliamentary franchise, which includes UK, Irish, and Commonwealth citizens resident in the UK and UK citizens resident overseas for less than fifteen years, with the addition for the purposes of the referendum of the House of Lords and residents of Gibraltar.

On the issue of the *rules of engagement*, there was again much discussion about the PPERA rules on expenditure, with Eurosceptics especially unhappy with what they felt was an unfair funding arrangement. The intricacies of PPERA meant that there would be a fixed expenditure cap of £7 million, as well as limited state funding (£600,000) and other benefits, such as TV broadcasts for two designated umbrella campaign groups, one for 'remain' and one for 'leave'. However, political parties were also entitled to spend up to certain thresholds set in accordance with the percentage vote each party had won in the preceding general election. Since the official Conservative position was to remain neutral, this meant that there would be a funding asymmetry as the Labour, Liberal Democrat, Scottish National, and Green parties, jointly entitled to spend up to £9.7 million, would all be campaigning to remain in the EU, while only UKIP, entitled to spend up to £3 million, would be supporting the leave side.

In the event, the Lords did not vote to alter the broad framework of expenditure, although the government did accept an amendment from cross-bencher Lord Hannay to the effect that if one side did not seek designation for an umbrella organization, the other side would not be precluded from having a designated umbrella group. The sceptics had made entirely clear to anyone who had chosen to listen to them that they would cry foul at any hint of unfairness. That the government chose not to listen was quite clear when a publicly funded brochure was distributed to 27 million households.[58]

Concerning *requests for reports*, peers successfully persuaded the government, represented by Baroness Anelay, to agree to produce a suite of documents intended to provide objective information. These included a White Paper on the outcome of the renegotiation, called for by Lord Forsyth, and reports on the consequences of withdrawal and alternatives to membership, called for by a cross-party group of peers, including the present author. The government initially argued that it was for those who sought to leave the EU to argue the case for what 'leave' would mean, but the pro-EU peers expressed their concerns in a series of private meetings that this was an unwise course of action: in the absence of objective information it would be possible for 'leavers' to make any case they wanted, regardless of its plausibility or viability.

The minister seemed to have been persuaded as she brought forward amendments committing the government to produce a White Paper on the renegotiation and one or more reports on the consequences of leaving and the alternatives. Peers were content with the changes, while MPs expressed some scepticism, querying where the amendments had come from. The answer, formally, was that they were government amendments because that was the government's preferred way of making changes to draft

[57] The government's defeat by the Lords on the matter of tax credits had provoked a review of the role of the House of Lords led by former Leader of the Lords, Lord Strathclyde.

[58] An amendment from Lords Liddle and Davies calling for such a taxpayer-funded publication was not carried but peers failed to amend the legislation to the effect that the government must *not* produce such literature.

legislation. Yet in reality the answer was that the amendments had arisen because of parliamentary pressure in the Lords, reflecting that chamber's role as a revising chamber.

7. The Renegotiation, White Papers, Objectivity, and Spin

The first of the government reports—the White Paper on the outcomes of the renegotiation, papers on the Article 50 TEU withdrawal process, and on the alternatives to membership—appeared almost as soon as the ink was dry on the renegotiated deal.[59] However, the speed with which these documents were produced was rather offset by the quality of papers, which seemed to owe more to the work of special advisers versed in the arts of 'spin' and a desire to make the government's case rather than to provide the objective information that peers had requested. MPs were not impressed: Bill Cash's reaction in the Commons was dismissive:

> The Government have just presented three White Papers to Parliament under their self-imposed legal duty to provide information under the European Union Referendum Act 2015. The Minister for Europe, during proceedings between the two Houses, gave me an undertaking that the Government information under that Act would certainly, as he put it, be accurate and impartial. The three recent White Papers are not. My right hon. Friend the Prime Minister is the enforcer of the ministerial code, which demands that Ministers give accurate information to Parliament. Will he issue instructions to Foreign Office Ministers to review and correct those White Papers?[60]

Meanwhile, in the Lords, Lord Forsyth quizzed the minister on whether she did not know 'the difference between information and propaganda'.[61] From the Liberal Democrat frontbench, the minister was merely thanked for producing the reports, although regret was expressed, somewhat tongue in cheek, that Lord Forsyth did not appreciate the White Paper of which he had been the instigator.[62] It was, however, hard not to agree with the sceptics on this point that the papers the government had produced lacked the objectivity and impartiality that those seeking them had expected. Indeed, the importance of not appearing to undermine the government's stance in the referendum was all that prevented this member of the Liberal Democrat benches from simply endorsing the points made by Lord Forsyth. It was clear that when the frontbenches converge on a common position, it is even harder for Parliament to thwart the will of the government.

The lines of engagement for the post-renegotiation debate in the Lords were, as the EU Referendum Act had been: the Labour and Liberal Democrat frontbenches in the

[59] See also the following policy papers published by the Cabinet Office of the UK Government: 'The Best of Both Worlds: The United Kingdom's Special Status in a Reformed European Union' of 22 February 2016 https://www.gov.uk/government/uploads/system/uploads/attachment_data/file/502291/54284_EU_Series_No1_Web_Accessible.pdf; 'Alternatives to Membership: Possible Models for the United Kingdom Outside the European Union' of 4 March 2016 https://www.gov.uk/government/uploads/system/uploads/attachment_data/file/504661/Alternatives_to_membership_possible_models_for_the_UK_outside_the_EU_Accessible.pdf; 'The Process for Withdrawing from the European Union' of 29 February 2016 https://www.gov.uk/government/uploads/system/uploads/attachment_data/file/503908/54538_EU_Series_No2_Accessible.pdf (all last accessed 2 August 2016).

[60] HC Deb 9 March 2016, col 275.

[61] HL Deb 2 March 2016, col 834; see also HL Deb 23 May 2016, col 148.

[62] HL Deb 2 March 2016, col 839.

Lords gave the government their (almost) full support, while the real challenges came from the Tory Privy Council bench—as well as Tory and, to a lesser extent, Labour backbenchers—reflecting the parties' established positions on membership of the EU. There was no serious challenge to the Prime Minister's preferred referendum date of 23 June 2016, although the SNP and Plaid Cymru were unhappy with the overlap with Scottish Parliament and Welsh Assembly elections on 5 May. With the Statutory Instrument setting the date for the referendum agreed, everything was in place for the UK's second referendum on membership of the EU.

8. Concluding the EU Referendum Tale: The Exit Door

The dynamics of parliamentary engagement with the EU changed with the prospect of a referendum on EU membership on the horizon. Departmental select committees, which had paid little attention to the EU for decades, leaving EU affairs to the ESC, began to commission reports on the UK's relationship with the EU. That the Coalition Government had completed an extensive review of the balance of competences between the EU and the UK just months earlier did nothing to weaken a new-found enthusiasm for exploring the UK's relations with the EU, whether by the Treasury, Defence, or Foreign Affairs Committees.[63] As was to have been expected, the House of Lords EUC also produced a series of reports on the issues of the referendum and the reform process in the EU.[64] Parliamentarians who had previously appeared resigned to European integration had never seemed so engrossed by EU matters as in the run-up to the referendum as the plethora of reports made clear. Yet, the divisions among parliamentarians ensured that the select committees found it difficult to reach agreements on conclusions for their reports.

Those advocating that the UK should leave the European Union argued vigorously that this would allow the UK to 'take control', including control over national laws, reducing the role of courts. The expectation might have been that the EU would henceforth play little role in Parliament. The reality could not have been more different. The June 2016 decision to leave the EU precipitated a host of new committee enquiries by both Commons' select committees and the Lords' EUC and its sub-committees and even a new select committee in the House of Commons. MPs and peers immediately pressed the government for answers to questions about how the process of disengaging from the EU would work in practice—questions that government ministers were ill-prepared to give since neither the 'Vote Leave' campaign nor the Cameron Government had paid much attention to planning for the reality of a leave vote. Parliamentarians thus appeared to up their attempts to hold the government to account,[65] albeit to little avail in the immediate aftermath of the referendum, when the default answer of ministers was: 'That will be a matter for the next Prime Minister'.[66]

The arrival of Theresa May to replace David Cameron as Prime Minister just three weeks after the referendum heralded some restructuring of government to include a new Department for Exiting the European Union, led by David Davis. The outcome

[63] See more on the Review of the Balance of Competences in Jančić (n 3) 939, 956.

[64] See House of Lords, EU Committee, HL 122 'The EU Referendum and EU Reform', 9th Report of Session 2015–16 of 30 March 2016.

[65] See House of Commons, European Scrutiny Committee, HC 458 'UK Government's Renegotiation of EU Membership: Parliamentary Sovereignty and Scrutiny', 14th Report of Session 2015–16 of 15 December 2015.

[66] See eg HL Debs 29 June 2016 and 4 July 2016.

of the referendum and the establishment of a new department ensured that over the summer of 2016 both chambers of the UK Parliament would review their roles vis-à-vis the government. There were immediate demands for Parliament to play a role in triggering Article 50 TEU, the device by which a Member State can begin the process of leaving the EU, suggesting that Parliament would indeed begin to reclaim some control and prove resilient, even resurgent as the UK contemplated the prospect of life outside the EU. The Government was reluctant to allow Parliament to take the decision on triggering Article 50 but on 3 November 2016 the High Court ruled in *R (Miller) v Secretary of State for Exiting the European Union*[67] that Parliament should indeed take the decision on whether to trigger Article 50. While the Government immediately stated its intention to appeal the decision, the ruling was a first indication of the changing relations between the three branches of government arising from the decision to leave the EU. Quite how Parliament would respond to the challenge of leaving rather than working within the EU only time will tell.

[67] [2016] EWHC 2768.

6

Mind the Gap! The Implications of Comitology and the Open Method of Coordination for National Parliaments

Gavin Barrett

1. Introduction

The European Coal and Steel Community and the European Economic Community, the progenitor organizations of today's European Union (EU), were created by treaties agreed as far back as 1951 and 1957 respectively. Yet it took many years—and in some cases, decades—before national parliaments (NPs) in all Member States adjusted their behaviour to EU membership: Germany's *Bundesrat* was the leader, setting up a European Affairs Committee (EAC) in 1957. Italy's *Senato* followed only in 1968 with the next such committee. It was as late as 1989 that the Parliament of Luxembourg—a founding member of all three of the original Communities—set up an EAC, no less than *thirty-eight years* after the creation of the Coal and Steel Community. But the trend of conferring a European role on NPs had by then been well set. In a parallel and agonizingly slow development, NPs increasingly gained express recognition at the EU level, beginning with the non-legally binding declaration annexed to the Maastricht Treaty and culminating with the far more extensive recognition afforded by the Lisbon Treaty—most prominently through that Treaty's remodelling of Articles 10 and 12 of the Treaty on European Union and the Lisbon Protocols on National Parliaments and on Subsidiarity.

Given the scarcity of resources and the number of tasks that tend to compete for the legislature's attention, NPs have had to make choices concerning the objectives they wish to prioritize. Several attempts have been made to classify both the nature of NPs' activities in EU affairs and the effectiveness of their interventions. As regards the *nature of their activities*, Auel, Rozenberg, and Tacea have usefully categorized NPs according to the functions performed (scrutiny, debate or policy influence) and according to the addressee of scrutiny (national government or EU institutions).[1] As regards NPs' *effectiveness*, some writers, such as Raunio, and Maurer and Wessels, have focused on a variety of criteria, such as access to documents, the timeliness of supply of information, and the existence of a mechanism enabling the filtering out of EU measures unlikely to prove of interest to national parliamentarians.[2] Others, including Winzen

[1] Katrin Auel, Olivier Rozenberg, and Angela Tacea, 'Fighting Back? And, If So, How? Measuring Parliamentary Strength and Activity in EU Affairs' in Claudia Hefftler and others (eds), *The Palgrave Handbook of National Parliaments and the European Union* (Palgrave 2015).

[2] See Tapio Raunio, 'Hesitant Voters, Committed Elite: Explaining the Lack of Eurosceptic Parties in Finland' (2005) 27 J Eur Integration 381; Andreas Maurer and Wolfgang Wessels (eds), *National Parliaments on Their Ways to Europe: Losers or Latecomers?* (Nomos 2001).

and Bergman, have concentrated on the roles played by committees and the plenary.[3] Other oft-cited criteria include parliamentary infrastructure and the presence or absence of mandates and scrutiny reserves. This topic is returned to in Section 2 below.

Importantly, an additional and sometimes forgotten layer of complexity regarding NPs' intervention in EU decision-making has crept in through developments such as (a) the extensive adoption of delegated legislation at the EU level and the use of comitology to this end; and (b) the widespread use of non-legislative means to cooperate at the EU level via the Open Method of Coordination (OMC). This chapter examines the ways in which decision-making in these 'non-standard' fields differ from decision-making in the traditional 'Community' system and the implications that this has for the NPs' approach to accountability.

Two hypotheses are advanced in this chapter. The first is the high probability of strong similarities emerging between the Member States' efforts to cope with the non-standard fields of integration, on the one hand, and the development in the approach of many NPs towards the traditional 'Community' system, on the other. This means that one may expect an initial lack of any response on the part of the Member States to the need for parliamentary control, followed by a gradual increase in involvement by many states with considerable variation in their respective approaches.[4] Secondly, it is hypothesized that earlier Member States' choices regarding their European vocation ought logically to be reviewed and, if necessary, adapted in the light of these developments, if the risk of circumvention is to be avoided.

A brief review of how Member States have coped with the task of reviewing 'Community' decision-making is appropriate before comparing and contrasting this with their approach to non-standard fields of integration.

2. The Awakening of National Parliaments and the Traditional 'Community' System

NPs found no mention of significance in the original Community Treaties. Indeed, they were excellent candidates for the title of the most neglected institutions in the new dispensation—the 'institutional Cinderellas of European integration', as Desmond Dinan memorably termed them.[5] Through the transfer of competences to the EU level, NPs were deprived of their most fundamental right in domestic legal systems—the right to say 'yes' or 'no' to legislation before its adoption. They therefore needed to react and obtain compensating rights at an early stage in the EU decision-making process.

After the delayed start adverted to in the first paragraph of this chapter, such rights were secured at national level in the form of modified institutional arrangements, committee structures, and legal rules—varying from constitutional provisions to parliamentary

[3] See Thomas Winzen, 'European Integration and National Parliamentary Oversight Institutions', (2013) 14 Eur Union Pol 297; Torbjörn Bergman, 'National Parliaments and EU Affairs Committees: Notes on Empirical Variation and Competing Explanations' (1997) 4 JEPP 373.

[4] A series of studies have indicated that in terms of institutional capacity, Germany, Austria, the Netherlands, and the Nordic Member States are strong; the Central and Eastern European Member States rather strong; the United Kingdom, France, and Italy are in-between; and the remaining, mostly Southern European Member States, weak. See the summary of the relevant literature in Katrin Auel and Thomas Christiansen, 'After Lisbon: National Parliaments in the European Union' (2015) 38 WEP 261, 268.

[5] D Dinan, 'Governance and Institutions: Impact of the Escalating Crisis' (2012) 50 JCMS 85, 85.

standing orders. As Auel, Rozenberg, and Tacea put it,[6] continuing the fairy-tale analogy, by now NPs are 'clearly no longer the sleeping beauties of EU affairs: they have been kissed and are wide awake'.[7] There is, moreover, very considerable evidence of the extent of that awakened state. In the three-year period from 2010 to 2012, NPs issued over 4,000 mandates or resolutions on EU documents and decisions, sent over 1,500 opinions to the European Commission, and spent thousands of hours both discussing EU affairs in plenary sessions and scrutinizing them in EACs.[8] NPs' investment in EU policy issues has therefore been considerable.[9]

Arriving at the present state of intensified national parliamentary involvement in EU matters did not happen all at once, however. Rather, it increased over time. As Winzen puts it,[10] there is thus a little-studied 'longitudinal' aspect to NPs' EU-related activities. The structuring of NPs' involvement arguably never seemed likely to remain capable of being carried out in one fell swoop without there ever being any need to revisit the matter. The history of the EU has been characterized by rapid, dramatic, and complex institutional developments and it followed that, if NPs were going to keep pace with the rapidly developing Union, an appropriate degree of adaptation on their part would be needed too. This is a theme returned to in section 3 of this chapter.

There has also been a very significant variation in how NPs have reacted to European integration. All NPs have developed an EU-related role over time. However, not all have developed in the same way. Important cross-national differences exist both insofar as concerns the *extent* of the activities of NPs and as concerns the *categories* of such activity. Factors that explain such heterogeneity include national path dependencies, the domestic institutional strength of NPs (or lack thereof), and the presence or absence of a strong degree of Eurosceptical opinion at the national level.

Attempts have been made from time to time to categorize the range of national approaches. A recent and useful categorization is Rozenberg and Hefftler's list of idealized and non-mutually exclusive models for parliamentary involvement in EU matters:[11] (i) *policy shapers* (which seek to influence government positions); (ii) *government watchdogs* (which seek to hold the government accountable); (iii) *public fora* (which seek to communicate with the public); (iv) *EU experts* (which aim at producing expert knowledge about EU initiatives); and (v) *European players* (which seek to act directly at the EU level). Others uncharitably—but not inaccurately—throw in the extra category of (vi) *scrutiny laggards* to cover national parliamentary chambers with an extremely low level of overall activity.

The extent of such differences should not be exaggerated, however: the limited number of categories identified by the foregoing writers draws our attention to the fact

[6] See Note 1. For a contrary view, according to which NPs are seen as remaining somewhat transfixed by national matters notwithstanding the burgeoning influence of EU law on national legal systems and thus still 'asleep', see eg Piotr Maciej Kaczynski, 'Paper Tigers or Sleeping Beauties? National Parliaments in the Post-Lisbon European Political System', CEPS Special Report, February 2011; Hussein Kassim, 'Europeanization and Member State Institutions' in Simon Bulmer and Christian Lequesne (eds), *The Member States of the European Union* (2nd edn, Oxford University Press 2012). See further Olivier Rozenberg and Claudia Hefftler, 'Introduction' in Claudia Hefftler and others (eds), *The Palgrave Handbook of National Parliaments and the European Union* (Palgrave 2015) 1, 16–17.

[7] See an analysis focusing on the positive effect of the euro crisis in Davor Jančić, 'National Parliaments and EU Fiscal Integration' (2016) 22 ELJ 225.

[8] Auel, Rozenberg, and Tacea (n 1) 75.

[9] Note the considerable variety of 'types' of NPs' involvement in EU affairs, dealt with in the text at Note 12.

[10] See generally Thomas Winzen, 'National Parliamentary Control of European Union Affairs: A Cross-national and Longitudinal Comparison' (2012) 35 WEP 657.

[11] Rozenberg and Hefftler (n 6) 28.

that there also seems to be a limited number of choices open to NPs as to how they approach EU affairs. As Auel, Rozenberg, and Tacea put it, perhaps 'there is nothing like a single type of parliament in EU affairs, but nor are there 27—or 40'.[12] A further qualification regarding the above noted variations is that there are major commonalities between *all* of the national approaches. For example, every single one of the twenty-eight NPs has established an EAC, even if there is considerable variety both in what such committees do and in the status accorded to membership thereof within national parliamentary systems.

How are we to measure the relative strengths of the various national approaches? Winzen has identified three dimensions of parliamentary control in EU affairs: (i) access to information; (ii) processing of information; and (iii) the enforcement of parliamentary preferences for EU level negotiations.[13] Perhaps more penetratingly, Auel has enumerated the 'scope, timing, management and impact of parliamentary scrutiny' as factors to be taken into account in measuring the strengths and weaknesses of NPs in EU affairs.[14]

However, there seems little point in focusing on constitutional provisions and formal rules alone. This is because the formal legal rights and institutional capacities of NPs in EU affairs will not necessarily be automatically translated into any actual parliamentary behaviour or activity. This is a point best illustrated by the case of the Austrian *Nationalrat*, which has perhaps the strongest mandating powers of any parliament in the EU—with its rights guaranteed in the text of the Austrian Constitution itself—and yet, in contrast to, for example, the Danish *Folketing*, it makes hardly any use of these.[15]

Institutional strength appears to provide no inevitable guarantees either as to the extent to which a NP engages in plenary debates or as to the time it spends debating EU affairs in committee meetings.[16] Hence, institutional strength alone cannot be used as a proxy test of the strength of individual NPs in EU matters. The motivation of parliamentarians must also be taken into account.[17] Whatever way we judge the strength of national parliamentary involvement in EU affairs, two factors therefore seem key—parliamentary capacity *and* motivation for action. Recent research has nonetheless asserted a strong correlation between the institutional strength of NPs and

[12] Auel, Rozenberg, and Tacea (n 1) 89. These being respectively the number of parliaments and chambers then in the EU. With the accession of Croatia, the numbers would now be 28 and 41.

[13] Winzen, 'National Parliamentary Control of European Union Affairs' (n 10) 660.

[14] Katrin Auel, 'Democratic Accountability and National Parliaments: Redefining the Impact of Parliamentary Scrutiny in EU Affairs' (2007) 13 ELJ 487, 487.

[15] See on Austria Eric Miklin, 'The Austrian Parliament and EU Affairs: Gradually Living Up to its Legal Potential' in Claudia Hefftler and others (eds), *The Palgrave Handbook of National Parliaments and the European Union* (Palgrave 2015); and Barbara Blümel and Christine Neuhold, 'The Parliament of Austria: A Large Potential with Little Implications' in Andreas Maurer and Wolfgang Wessels (eds), *National Parliaments on Their Ways to Europe: Losers or Latecomers?* (Nomos 2001). See on Denmark Mette Buskjaer Christensen, 'The Danish Folketing and EU Affairs: Is the Danish Model of Parliamentary Scrutiny Still Best Practice?' in Claudia Hefftler and others (eds), *The Palgrave Handbook of National Parliaments and the European Union* (Palgrave 2015); Finn Laursen, 'The Danish Folketing and its European Affairs Committee: Strong Players in the National Policy Cycle' in Andreas Maurer and Wolfgang Wessels (eds), *National Parliaments on Their Ways to Europe: Losers or Latecomers?* (Nomos 2001).

[16] The previously argued view that the general strength of a NP (ie including in relation to non-EU matters) or the degree of Euroscepticism of the population as a whole were in turn the most important factors at play in determining the amount of time which a parliament dedicates to EU matters has been challenged in Katrin Auel and Arthur Benz, *The Europeanisation of Parliamentary Democracy* (Routledge 2006).

[17] Auel and Christiansen (n 4) 261.

both the degree and kind of activity that they engage in, with some writers going so far as to assert that, leaving aside political dialogue opinions, a parliament's institutional strength has a decisive impact on all types of EU-related activities, whether aimed at exerting influence or merely communicating.[18]

The fact that institutional capacity matters so much results to a great extent from the exercise of rational choices by busy parliamentarians, who will only be interested in spending time on activities which have a chance of making some difference. A strong case can be made for the argument that in order to be effective, NPs first of all need to be able to wield the power of veto. More exactly:

> in order to influence European policy making effectively national parliaments need institutional veto power that can be translated strategically into power to influence. The more a national parliament can credibly threaten to veto the government's position, the more it is in the interest of the government to engage in informal cooperation with the legislature or its parliamentary majority. Effective cooperation with the executive needs the shadow of veto power of the parliament.[19]

A second factor, above and beyond institutional veto power, is arguably also required. This is 'public parliamentary deliberation and scrutiny of governmental action' and only when this takes place 'can parliaments truly serve as an intermediary between the government and the citizen'.[20]

3. The Growth of Non-standard Approaches to Integration and the Challenges for National Parliaments

Although the identities of the institutions involved in the EU legislative process have not fundamentally changed, the nature of European integration has certainly evolved. The formerly standard approach (in many states, now politically unacceptable) of transferring powers to supranational institutions has lost much of its pre-eminence within the EU. A less visible and therefore less politically controversial option of integrating has now come to the fore in the form of intensified policy coordination. The workings of the European Council, which became a formal EU institution only in 2009, are arguably the example of this phenomenon par excellence.[21] Overall, hallmarks of the approach of recent years have included the consolidation of consensus as a decision-making method, diversification from the traditional supranational approach towards integration, a perceptible reluctance to transfer additional competences to the EU, and a penchant for transferring powers to newly created bodies rather than to EU institutions.[22]

[18] Katrin Auel, Olivier Rozenberg, and Angela Tacea, 'To Scrutinise or Not to Scrutinise? Explaining Variation in EU-related Activities in National Parliaments' (2015) 38 WEP 282, 298.

[19] Auel and Benz (n 16) 87. [20] ibid.

[21] Christopher Bickerton, Dermot Hodson, and Uwe Puetter, 'The New Intergovernmentalism: European Integration in the Post-Maastricht Era' (2015) 53 JCMS 703, 704.

[22] See one prominent recognition of this change in the speech by the German Chancellor Angela Merkel at the opening ceremony of the 61st academic year of the College of Europe (Bruges, 2 November 2010), in which she observed: '[a]s Herman Van Rompuy, our Council President, recently commented, "often the choice is not between the Community method and the intergovernmental method, but between a coordinated European position and nothing at all". In other words, a coordinated European position can be arrived at not just by applying the Community method; sometimes a coordinated European position can be arrived at by applying the intergovernmental method. The crucial thing is that on important issues we have common positions'. See https://www.coleurope.

Where intensified policy coordination occurs, the level at which it does so varies, ranging from experts in committees to heads of state or government at the European Council level. So does the level of formality and institutionalization involved. Compare, for example, the informal so-called 'Frankfurt Group'[23] with the Treaty-authorized actions of the Economic and Financial Committee.[24] Even within the classic system of Community-style legislation, the trilogue system of informal interinstitutional negotiations has to a considerable extent undermined the legislative process as originally designed, with the result that the vast bulk of legislation is nowadays adopted at first reading.[25]

The evolution of the means of European integration should probably not be oversimplified. Craig and de Búrca submit that the core of new governance is typified by moves away from hierarchical forms of governing.[26] Yet not all are persuaded that in practice the expansion in the palette of options by which European integration can be furthered is as revolutionary as this analysis would maintain.[27]

Why any such evolution in the nature of integration should have come about is debatable. One important contributory factor is the realization that, although inherent in the EU legislative process, a one-size-fits-all approach is not necessarily desirable in fields such as the economy, in which strong differences exist from one Member State to another. Another factor may be the growth of a more Eurosceptical attitude on the part of national electorates and a decline in the permissive consensus regarding Union activities—making the transfer of decision-making power to the EU level more difficult at exactly the time when a cooperative approach between the Member States is needed. The result of this combination of circumstances is that Member States are led to 'pursue more integration but stubbornly resist further supranationalism'.[28] It may be that a move to more informal and 'secluded' modes of decision-making also chimes well at a time of domestic disillusionment with representative politics and increasing contestation about the legitimacy of various organized interests.[29]

Regardless of the generality or the permanence of such changes, however, there can be no doubt that the years since the entry into force of the Treaty of Maastricht, in particular, have seen the EU become active in a range of policy areas without any associated involvement of the 'Community method' of decision-making. The most prominent examples of processes or policy fields involving this shift include comitology and the OMC.[30]

eu/content/news/Speeches/Europakolleg%20Brugge%20Mitschrift%20englisch.pdf (last accessed 13 October 2016).

[23] Criticized in Larry Elliott, 'The Emergence of the Frankfurt Group Has Turned Back the Democratic Clock' *Guardian*, 8 November 2011.

[24] See Article 134 TFEU and the Council Decision 2003/476/EC of 18 June 2003 on a revision of the Statutes of the Economic and Financial Committee (OJ L 158/58 of 27 June 2003). See more generally Bickerton, Hodson, and Puetter (n 21) 704.

[25] It has been estimated that some 90% of EU legislation is adopted in trilogues. See Christilla Roederer-Rynning and Justin Greenwood, 'The Culture of Trilogues' (2015) 22 JEPP 1148, 1148.

[26] Paul Craig and Gráinne de Búrca, *EU Law: Text, Cases and Materials* (6th edn, Oxford University Press 2015) 163 and see generally ch 6 thereof.

[27] See Burkard Eberlein and Abraham L Newman, 'Escaping the International Governance Dilemma? Incorporated Transgovernmental Networks in the European Union' (2000) 21 Governance 25.

[28] Bickerton, Hodson, and Puetter (n 21) 705.

[29] ibid 710.

[30] There are of course other candidates, such as the Social Dialogue and the effects of the 'pillarisation' of the Union under the Treaty of Maastricht in 1992 (which is still visible in the organization of the EU's CFSP), but space precludes further examination of them in this chapter. The budgetary aspect of the Economic and Monetary Union would be another candidate for inclusion under this rubric, but is analyzed elsewhere in this book.

3.1 Comitology

Every day thousands of civil servants travel to Brussels from EU Member States to discuss issues in 'comitology committees'. Comitology is multilevel governance in action. Its participants are deeply involved in implementing policy by discussing norms, standards, funding schemes etc. – and they are having a real say over it.[31]

Brandsma's above quoted description of the operation in practice of what is known as 'comitology' involves no exaggeration in terms of the numbers of officials involved. By 2014, no less than 287 comitology committees were active.[32] Such committees deal with issues that may appear detailed, technical, perhaps even boring to non-experts. There is a committee for everything from aromatized wine-based drinks, to the placing on the market of pyrotechnic articles to the implementation of the Directive on sulphur content in marine fuels.[33] The subject matter of comitology is frequently so technical that it might be felt questionable at times whether there is a need for accountability at all—but complacency here would arguably be a mistake for at least three reasons. First, the devil is well capable of residing in the detail: thus, for example, a European Parliament (EP) temporary committee of inquiry could legitimately conclude that some of the responsibility for the BSE ('mad cow' disease) crisis, which caused havoc in the European beef industry in the 1990s, rested with failings on the part of the relevant comitology committee.[34] Secondly, the impact of these committees on EU legislation has become very considerable.[35] Thirdly, the sheer amount of such legislation also generates accountability concerns since, judged by volume, about half of EU rules are now not decided upon by politicians but rather by civil servants in committees.[36]

In such circumstances, the question of accountability cannot easily be left to one side. Ironically for a system of policy-making the accountability of which is often questioned, comitology *itself* began life as an accountability mechanism—a supposedly intergovernmental check on the supranational Commission:[37] as Commission

[31] Gijs-Jan Brandsma, 'Accounting for Input in Comitology Committees: An Uncomfortable Silence' (2010) 17 JEPP 487, 487.

[32] The year 2014 is the latest year in respect of which such statistics are available. See European Commission, 'Report on the Working of Committees During 2014', COM (2015) 418, 3 September 2015, at 4. The most up-to-date information about comitology is available at http://ec.europa.eu/transparency/regcomitology/index.cfm?clx=en (last accessed 13 October 2016). See further reflections, on comitology in Davor Jančić, 'National Parliaments and European Constitutionalism: Accountability Beyond Borders' (PhD Dissertation, Utrecht University, 2011) 160.

[33] See a fuller list in European Commission (n 32).

[34] See Report of the temporary committee of inquiry into BSE on alleged contraventions or maladministration in the implementation of Community law in relation to BSE, without prejudice to the jurisdiction of the Community and national courts (A4-0020/97, 7 February 1997), especially Part 3 thereof. See also Laurie Buonanno, 'The European Food Safety Authority' in Christopher Ansell and David Vogel (eds), *What's the Beef? The Contested Governance of European Food Safety* (MIT Press 2006) 259, 262.

[35] Brandsma, 'Accounting for Input in Comitology Committees' (n 31) 489. See also Claudio Radaelli, 'The Public Policy of the European Union: Whither Politics of Expertise?' (1999) 6 JEPP 757.

[36] See further Gijs-Jan Brandsma, *Controlling Comitology: Accountability in a Multi-Level System* (Palgrave 2013). Indeed, 'throughout history 60 to 90 per cent of European directives, decisions and regulations have been executive acts adopted by the Commission' fleshing out and applying other European legislation. See Gijs-Jan Brandsma and Jens Blom-Hansen, 'The Post-Lisbon Battle over Comitology: Another Round of the Politics of Structural Choice' (EUI Working Paper SPS 2011/03).

[37] Gijs-Jan Brandsma, 'Accountability Deficits in European "Comitology" Decision-making' (2007) 11 European Integration Online Papers 3. Eriksen and Fossum note assertions that comitology can help 'repair' the democratic deficit at the EU level and argue themselves that it can be seen as

implementation of common policies took off in the early 1960s, the Council sought a means of keeping the Commission under control. It became the norm that when the Council entrusted the implementation of legislation to the Commission, it simultaneously set up a committee of national policy experts, which was chaired by a *chef de dossier* from the Commission, but otherwise represented the Member States. These experts voted on draft implementation measures proposed by the Commission.[38] Over time, however, many such committees acquired such a degree of autonomy and importance, that the question of their *own* accountability reared its head,[39] all the more so given that the intergovernmental nature of committees in practice is more supposed than real.[40] (This is because the topics dealt with *via* such committees are of such a nature that experts are required to populate them, and experts do not necessarily bargain on the basis of national preferences, but rather on the need to ensure epistemically good results.[41]) Comitology, unburdened by its own system of accountability, can in reality just end up being one supranational entity tracking the work of another.

Analysis of accountability has tended in the main to be focused on the roles of EU institutions,[42] with the EP and the Council well capable, should they choose to do so, of using direct and indirect influence to exert accountability in the comitology area.[43] The EP, under the new regime of comitology introduced by the Lisbon Treaty in 2009,[44]

contributing to good governance, since 'expert-based decision-making is not on its own illegitimate and antithetical to democracy—it is conducive to democratic legitimacy under certain modern conditions'. Erik Oddvar Eriksen and John Erik Fossum, 'Democracy Through Strong Publics in the European Union' (2002) 40 JCMS 401, 407 and 410.

[38] Brandsma, 'Accounting for Input in Comitology Committees' (n 31) 488.

[39] Hence the title of an early examination of comitology, Renaud Dehousse, 'Comitology: Who Watches the Watchmen?' (2003) 10 JEPP 798.

[40] It has been noted that 'the deliberative interaction style of the committee participants … gives a supranational twist to a committee system that was designed to safeguard intergovernmentalism'. See Brandsma, 'Accounting for Input in Comitology Committees' (n 31) 490.

[41] ibid 491. See also Gijs-Jan Brandsma, Deirdre Curtin, and Albert Meijer, 'How Transparent are EU "Comitology" Committees in Practice?' (2008) 14 ELJ 819, 826.

[42] Brandsma, 'Accounting for Input in Comitology Committees' (n 31) 488.

[43] Both institutions have Treaty and sub-Treaty powers in the field of comitology. See Articles 291 TFEU and Regulation (EU) No 182/2011 of the European Parliament and of the Council of 16 February 2011 laying down the rules and general principles concerning mechanisms for control by Member States of the Commission's exercise of implementing powers. But the EP can and has used its budgetary powers to freeze funding for comitology committees so as to obtain what it wants and the Council can use its own veto powers to help secure its wishes. See Brandsma and Blom-Hansen (n 36) 6.

[44] Under TFEU, art 291(2), wherever uniform conditions for implementing legally binding Union acts are needed, such Union acts are required to confer implementing powers—normally on the Commission—or, in duly justified specific cases and in the cases provided for in TEU, arts 24 and 26 (both of which relate to the common foreign and security policy) on the Council. Where this is not the case, Member States are required to adopt all measures of national law necessary to implement legally binding acts (TFEU, art 291(1)). For these purposes, the EP and the Council, acting by means of regulations in accordance with the ordinary legislative procedure, are required to lay down in advance the rules and general principles concerning mechanisms for control by Member States of the Commission's exercise of implementing powers (TFEU, art 291(3)). This was duly done with the adoption of Regulation No 182/2011, which lays down the rules and general principles concerning mechanisms for control by Member States of the Commission's exercise of implementing powers (in force since 1 March 2011). See analyses of comitology in the wake of these Lisbon Treaty rules in Herwig Hofmann, 'Legislation, Delegation and Implementation under the Treaty of Lisbon: Typology Meets Reality' (2009) 15 ELJ 482; Paul Craig, 'Delegated Acts, Implementing Acts and the New Comitology Regulation' (2011) 36 EL Rev 671; Michael Kaeding and Alan Hardacre, 'The European Parliament and the Future of Comitology after Lisbon' (2013) 19 ELJ 382; Steve Peers and Marios Costa, 'Accountability for Delegated and Implementing Acts after the Treaty of Lisbon'

has leveraged itself to a position of increased significance over time from an initially very weak footing.[45]

The challenge of establishing such accountability is no small one, however, and overall, even if the EP has strengthened its controlling role on comitology, 'the arrangements to hold it to account are still rather weak at the European level'.[46] The question thus arises of what role can be played at the national level in this regard, in particular by NPs.

3.2 The Open Method of Coordination

The Open Method of Coordination emerged most prominently as a policy-implementation strategy in the 2000 Lisbon Agenda adopted by the European Council,[47] although it could be seen in an earlier form in the shape of the broad economic policy guidelines introduced by the 1992 Maastricht Treaty and additionally in the 1997 Amsterdam Treaty's European Employment Strategy.[48] Already by 2007, there were thirteen different OMCs covering a broad spectrum of policy areas, ranging from the above two (both of which had a basis in the Treaties) to other areas such as social inclusion, pensions and healthcare, education, research and development, immigration, modernization of social protection, innovation, the information society, environment, and enterprise.[49]

The Open Method of Coordination involves fixing guidelines and timetables for achieving goals of various kinds, be they short, medium, or long-term. Hence, for example, the Open Method on Employment has targeted inclusive labour markets, full employment, and combining security in employment with flexibility. The OMC on pensions has targeted pension provision which is both sustainable and adequate. The OMC on social inclusion has focused on the elimination of social exclusion both through employment market participation and through guaranteed access to needed services and resources. The OMC on education has several aims: reducing the numbers of early school leavers and low-achieving pupils on literacy indicators, increasing the

(2012) 18 ELJ 427; Thomas Christiansen and Mathias Dobbels, 'Non-legislative Rule Making After the Lisbon Treaty: Implementing the New System of Comitology and Delegated Acts' (2013) 19 ELJ 382; Adrienne Héritier and others, *Changing Rules of Delegation: A Contest for Power in Comitology* (Oxford University Press 2013) ch 3.

[45] See for a view from within the EP: Kieran St C Bradley, 'The GMO Committee on Transgenic Maize: Alien Corn, or the Transgenic Procedural Maze' in MPCM van Schendelen (ed), *EU Committees as Influential Policy-makers* (Ashgate 1998).

[46] Brandsma (n 31) 503.

[47] There is a vast literature on the OMC. See eg Sabrina Regent, 'The Open Method of Coordination: A New Supranational Form of Governance?' (2003) 9 ELJ 190; Milena Büchs, *New Governance in European Social Policy: The Open Method of Coordination* (Palgrave 2007); Carolina de la Porte, 'Is the Open Method of Coordination Appropriate for Organising Activities at European Level in Sensitive Policy Areas?' (2002) 8 ELJ 38; Erika Szyszczak, 'Experimental Governance: The Open Method of Coordination' (2006) 12 ELJ 486; Dermot Hodson and Imelda Maher, 'The Open Method as a New Mode of Governance: The Case of Soft Economic Policy Coordination' (2001) 39 JCMS 719.

[48] See on the employment law field: Büchs (n 47); Jonathan Zeitlin and Philippe Pochet (eds), *The Open Method of Co-ordination in Action: The European Employment and Social Inclusion Strategies* (Peter Lang 2005); Martin Heidenreich and Jonathan Zeitlin (eds), *Changing European Employment and Welfare Regimes: The Influence of the Open Method of Coordination on National Reforms* (Routledge 2009).

[49] See in this regard Vassilis Hatzopoulos, 'Why the Open Method of Coordination Is Bad for You: A Letter to the EU' (2007) 13 ELJ 309. See also European Parliamentary Research Service (EPRS), 'The Open Method of Coordination', 5 November 2014, available at https://epthinktank.eu/2014/11/05/the-open-method-of-coordination/ (last accessed 13 October 2016).

number of graduates in science, mathematics, and technology, as well as the proportion of the adult population in life-long learning programmes.[50]

However, the OMC goes beyond merely setting targets: it involves quantitative indicators and benchmarks regarding the achievement of those goals, setting policy aims and adopting measures in the light of such guidelines, and then finally periodically monitoring, evaluating, and peer-reviewing the outcomes. National action plans play a key role, outlining the plans that each Member State intends to put in place. De Ruiter has summarized matters accurately and pithily in observing that 'the complete infrastructure of the OMC consists of guidelines or objectives, indicators and benchmarks, reporting via National Action Plans (NAPs), and peer review'.[51] Such an 'infrastructure', in some measure a strength, is simultaneously also weakness, and of a kind that has made the OMC a relatively controversial policy-making method. No EU legislation is used in the OMC. No legal sanctions exist to be wielded against non-compliant states. In consequence, the courts are effectively excluded and there is an absence of hierarchy between the participants in the coordination process. Furthermore, the OMC has been criticized even by its institutional supporters as 'ineffective and invisible at the national level' and 'not sufficiently [involving] the social partners and other civil society organisations'.[52] Highly relevantly for the purposes of the present chapter, the EP has termed the OMC as 'legally dubious, as it operates without sufficient parliamentary participation and judicial review'—and has been sufficiently concerned in this regard to express its belief that the OMC 'should therefore be employed only in exceptional cases'.[53]

Although doubts have been expressed about the OMC's long-term future,[54] so far it shows little sign of being abandoned as a policy-making tool, making it a phenomenon which parliaments at both EU and national levels will have to deal with for some time to come.

4. How Have National Parliaments Adapted to Such 'Non-standard' Methods of EU Decision-making?

4.1 Comitology

The overall picture regarding the political accountability of decisions made through comitology has not been a particularly encouraging one. Although it is true that the EP has a greater role now in relation to comitology than ever before, the controls imposed by this institution are nonetheless weak.[55]

It might therefore have been expected that attempting to ensure accountability at the national level instead of at the EU level would be felt worthwhile. This would be all the more so, given the observed tendency of experts attending comitology meetings to use their expertise and delivery to find technically optimal solutions rather than to

[50] See further Rik de Ruiter, 'The National Parliamentary Arena and Methods of Open Coordination: Explaining the Frequency of OMC-related Executive-legislative Interactions' (2011) 7 JCER 101, 103.

[51] ibid 102.

[52] See European Economic and Social Committee Opinion, 'The Open Method of Coordination and the Social Clause in the Context of Europe 2020', 2011/C 44/04, (OJ C 44/23 of 11 February 2011).

[53] European Parliament, Resolution of 4 September 2007 on Institutional and Legal Implications of the Use of 'Soft Law' Instruments (OJ C 187E/75 of 24 July 2008), point 4.

[54] EPRS (n 49).

[55] Brandsma, 'Accounting for Input in Comitology Committees' (n 31) 491.

negotiate on the basis of national preferences. Indeed, nationally imposed accountability would allow governments 'to control the wheeling and dealing of their representatives and also secure the intergovernmental aspect of comitology'.[56]

A distinction can be drawn in this regard between the collective accountability of comitology committees and the individual accountability of individual committee members. For a variety of reasons, it is notoriously difficult to impose accountability on the committees. These include secrecy, the fact that different committees meet together, the fact that committees formally set up may not meet at all in practice, the fact that they may have responsibilities under various acts, the fact that they can set up sub-groups, the fact that they may change their nature, and indeed the fact that they only actually function as groups when they vote.[57] The alternative—the imposition of accountability on individual delegates to the committees—itself involves major challenges, however, given that comitology committees are dominated by technocratic experts and it is hard for bodies or persons without such specialized knowledge to hold them to account.[58] The more expert knowledge an issue requires, the more difficult to hold the actors to account and the higher the likelihood of an accountability deficit.[59]

Evidence of NPs' systematically asserting accountability over comitology is difficult to find. Certainly, some parliaments have examined comitology, but this often tends to be more a case of studying the phenomenon and seeking to understand it than a concerted effort to impose accountability in respect of particular comitology activities. Thus, for example, the House of Lords EU Committee examined then-pending comitology reforms in an extensive report in 2003 and the Irish Joint *Oireachtas* Committee on European Affairs considered comitology the following year.[60] There is, however, no constancy in national parliamentary scrutiny of particular accountability gaps that comitology potentially involves.[61] Brandsma has argued in this respect that national arrangements do not make up for weakness in EP powers over comitology procedures and that 'the debate on the legitimacy of comitology, thus, is far from over'.[62]

Difficulties regarding the effectuation of governments' accountability to parliaments for comitology decisions appear to be enduring. They are nonetheless unlikely to cause an end to be brought to comitology itself. As Demmke puts it, 'criticising this reality would mean offering an alternative', but absent the political will, the expertise and the structure on the part of the Council and the EP to decide on detailed implementation of EU legislation, the question poses itself of what this alternative could possibly be.[63]

4.2 The Open Method of Coordination

Why parliaments should play a role in relation to the OMC seems clear.[64] Participation within OMC processes has been described as based upon an input-legitimacy model

[56] ibid.

[57] See Christoph Demmke, 'The Secret Life of Comitology or the Role of Public Officials in EC Environmental Policy' (1998) 3 EIPASCOPE 14, 17–18.

[58] Radaelli, 'The Public Policy of the European Union' (n 35) 758; Brandsma, 'Accountability Deficits in European "Comitology" Decision-making' (n 37).

[59] Brandsma, 'Accountability Deficits in European "Comitology" Decision-making' (n 37).

[60] House of Lords, EU Committee, HL 135 'Reforming Comitology', 31st Report of Session 2002–03, 1 July 2003; Presentation on comitology by Katherine Meenan to Joint *Oireachtas* Committee on European Affairs, 16 June 2004, available at https://www.oireachtas.ie/viewdoc.asp?DocID=2955&CatID=12&StartDate=01%20January%202004&OrderAscending=0 (last accessed 13 October 2016).

[61] Presentation on comitology by Katherine Meenan to Joint *Oireachtas* Committee on European Affairs (n 60).

[62] See Brandsma, 'Accounting for Input in Comitology Committees' (n 31) 503.

[63] See Demmke (n 57) 21.

[64] See generally De Ruiter (n 50) 103.

of stakeholder participation rather than a 'representative-parliamentarian' model.[65] Nonetheless, the OMC has been criticized as being 'far from meeting the criteria of participatory or deliberative democracy', with established social actors tending to dominate the process, rather than wider openness being encouraged. It has also been assessed as undermining the role of institutions to which executives are accountable—a situation argued not merely to be caused by the OMC being poorly executed but rather to be inherent in such a mechanism of deliberative coordination.[66] A national parliamentary function, in contrast, has several potential advantages. It is a route through which the supposed openness of the 'Open' Method of Coordination can really operate. The information gleaned from the OMC can also assist parliaments by providing a valuable comparative view on the performance of national policies. The involvement of parliaments is also a means through which accountability can be imposed on executives in relation to sub-optimal policy performances.

However, *what* parliaments should do in relation to the OMC requires reflection. Arguably, as much *ex ante* parliamentary scrutiny of government action as possible should be carried out. At present, however, putting the matter at its mildest, the opportunities for this to be done do not always translate into action.[67] Radaelli notes that 'although there is some preliminary evidence of limited technocratic-political learning, the potential in terms of participation, openness, real transparency, increasing visibility in the domestic media and parliaments—in a word, the democratic aspects of the process—has not been fulfilled'.[68] Duina and Raunio, for their part, have noted three marginalizing aspects of the OMC as far as national parliamentarians are concerned. First, the intergovernmental nature of the process—in which civil servants have primary responsibility for drafting national programmes and for subsequently presenting them in Brussels—seems to have failed to spark interest among parliamentarians. To them, the process may well seem dry, distant from the concrete interests of their constituents, and technically demanding—and in a context in which NPs are in any case often badly resourced in terms of expertise. Secondly, OMC processes, with their lack of fixed deadlines and rules, seem to be harder for parliamentarians to follow than the comparatively rule-bound and time-limited procedures of adopting legislation. Thirdly, the relatively modest impact of the OMC has given parliamentarians little incentive to take it as seriously as lawmaking activities to which they are more used.[69]

A range of imaginative suggestions for enhancing the role of NPs has been made.[70] Among the more compelling of these has been the idea of requiring national governments to consult with their parliaments before OMC objectives and guidelines are adopted at the EU level. Another has been that of providing the EP with a right of codecision on OMC objectives (even if these remain non-binding) and then to involve both the European and national parliaments in joint parliamentary sessions, thus giving both parliamentary levels an input concerning these objectives. Yet another is that of requiring national parliamentary discussions of the linkage between national and

[65] Milena Büchs, 'How Legitimate is the Open Method of Co-ordination?' (2008) 46 JCMS 765, 777.

[66] See Arthur Benz, 'Accountable Multilevel Governance by the Open Method of Coordination?' (2007) ELJ 505, 514.

[67] Note in this regard Tapio Raunio, 'Does OMC Really Benefit National Parliaments?' (2006) 12 ELJ 130, 131.

[68] Claudio Radaelli, 'The Open Method of Coordination: A New Governance Architecture for the European Union?', SIEPS (Swedish Institute for European Policy Studies) Report No 2003 1, at 50.

[69] Francesco Duina and Tapio Raunio, 'The Open Method of Coordination and National Parliaments: Further Marginalization or New Opportunities?' (2007) 14 JEPP 489, 498–99.

[70] See generally Büchs, 'How Legitimate is the Open Method of Co-ordination?' (n 65) 781–82.

EU OMC objectives. Regardless of the approach taken, given the strong concerns that have arisen about the present primary reliance on stakeholder involvement in providing input legitimacy for the OMC,[71] it is strongly arguable that it is necessary to find solutions to strengthen the representative-parliamentarian channel of OMC legitimacy and thereby also strengthen domestic parliamentary democracy.[72] Pending the emergence of any such solutions, however, it remains the case in relation to the OMC (as in the case of comitology) that, to use Jančić's memorable phrase, 'the absence of scrutiny is a chronic diagnosis'.[73]

5. Concluding Remarks: Can We Expect National Parliaments to Scrutinize the 'Gap' Policy Areas in the Future?

In analyzing the dynamics that shape accountability in the 'non-standard' areas of EU decision-making and assessing the capacity of NPs to adjust to their development, there are considerations pointing in different directions.

On the one hand, in favour of the idea that NPs will succeed in carving out a role for themselves in securing accountability in these fields, there is the fact that the entire history of national parliamentary involvement in the EU has been one of adaptation. They have 'fought back' and undergone a profound process of Europeanization.[74] There seems no reason to believe that this process has finished. In addition, every Treaty since the Treaty of Maastricht has resulted in some form of provision in favour of NPs. Most recently, commitments given to the UK prior to the 23 June 2016 referendum on 'Brexit' focused in part on strengthening the role played by NPs in EU policy-making: a red card mechanism was to be created to accompany the existing orange and yellow card procedures introduced by the Treaty of Lisbon to police subsidiarity.[75] As is well known, the United Kingdom electorate voted against the UK remaining an EU member, so that the creation of such a mechanism will not (at least for now) be brought about by new Treaty-level provisions. Nevertheless, empowerment-by-Treaty seems likely to continue, for example, by expanding NPs' information rights so as to cover some of the policy-making processes dealt with above.[76]

[71] ibid 779–780. See also Benz (n 66) 514 ff.

[72] Büchs, 'How Legitimate is the Open Method of Co-ordination?' (n 65) 782.

[73] Davor Jančić, *National Parliaments and European Constitutionalism* (n 32) 161.

[74] Tapio Raunio and Simon Hix, 'Backbenchers Learn to Fight Back: European Integration and Parliamentary Government' (2000) 23 WEP 142. See regarding Europeanization in the field of budgetary policy Jančić, 'National Parliaments and EU Fiscal Integration' (n 7).

[75] See section C para 3 of the Decision of the Heads of State or Government, meeting within the European Council, Concerning a New Settlement for the United Kingdom within the European Union (Annex 1 to Conclusions to European Council meeting of 18–19 February 2016 – EUCO 1/16 Brussels, 19 February 2016). For an analysis predicting that this new mechanism would have a limited impact see Sara Hagemann, Chris Hanretty, and Simon Hix, 'Introducing Cameron's EU Red Card Will Have Limited Impact' *Guardian*, 10 February 2016. See more generally on the UK–EU agreement Davor Jančić, 'Sovereignty Safeguards in the UK–EU Settlement' *Verfassungsblog*, 8 March 2016 http://verfassungsblog.de/sovereignty-safeguards-in-the-uk-eu-settlement/ (last accessed 13 October 2016).

[76] This is not to claim that the provision of additional information constitutes a panacea to any difficulties NPs are experiencing in exerting accountability in EU affairs. Indeed, in the wake of the Lisbon reforms, NPs can legitimately complain of an information overload. Proper filtering resources, in order to separate and discard less important EU measures, and the power to *do* something with information once obtained, are thus both important in ensuring the usefulness of national parliamentary interventions. Nonetheless, the *lack* of information provided to NPs about policy decisions

On the other hand, a number of factors also militate towards the view that NPs have only limited capacity to play a useful role in the 'gap' policy fields discussed. Most parliaments or chambers in engaging in EU matters—especially the active ones such as the Danish *Folketing*, the Finnish *Eduskunta* or the British House of Lords—largely focus on a very limited range of activities.[77] Such a tendency does not bode well for the prospects of combining the wide range of approaches necessary in order to cope with the non-standard policy-making methods analyzed in this chapter (for example, combining the involvement of plenary and committee sessions). Furthermore, considerable variation exists concerning the effectiveness of existing national parliamentary interventions. Effective scrutiny requires the conferring of institutional veto power, public parliamentary deliberation and scrutiny of governmental action. It is through these three types of action that NPs best serve as intermediaries between governments and the citizen.[78] Yet this is not universally provided for.

Even in relation to the ordinary EU lawmaking process, the bulk of the literature has tended to regard NPs as having been the losers or victims of integration.[79] It would be surprising if they fared better in relation to 'non-standard' EU decision-making procedures, which are, if anything, even more challenging in terms of the flexibility and the willingness to depart from established modes of procedure that they demand of NPs seeking to exercise control over them.

Rational choice theory has occasionally been deployed as a behaviour-explaining device in the field of parliamentary studies. It indicates that if we confer on NPs adequate powers in an EU policy field, this may give their members necessary incentives in order to get involved since they will have the prospect of exercising some influence. Certainly, this seems to be a lesson to be learned from scrutiny systems concerning

involving the use of comitology, social partnership, and the OMC can only be described as a hindrance to NPs playing any useful role here.

[77] Auel, Rozenberg, and Tacea observe that 'most chambers, and especially the most active ones, do focus on one type of activity. The Czech Senate and the German Bundestag, for example, give preference to the plenary, whereas the German Bundesrat or the Swedish Riksdag mainly issue resolutions or mandates. The only chamber that is fairly active in both categories is the Finnish Eduskunta, which again suggests that individual chambers develop their specific mode of dealing with EU affairs' (n 1, at 84). Note also that the much-lauded Danish and Finnish parliaments hardly involve themselves in the Commission's political dialogue process. For example, in 2015, the *Folketing* produced only two opinions within the political dialogue, while the *Eduskunta* produced just one. See European Commission, 'Annual Report 2015 on Relations between the European Commission and National Parliaments', COM(2016) 471 final, 15 July 2016, Annexes 1–3.

[78] Auel and others have noted a 'strong correlation' between strong institutional rights and the general level of a NP's activity in EU affairs. Indeed, a kind of virtuous circle seems to exist in that 'strong institutional rights are a precondition for becoming a policy shaper, and … in turn, strong chambers also make more active use of their rights to issue mandates/resolutions'. (n 1, at 83–84.)

[79] Tapio Raunio, 'National Parliaments and European Integration: What We Know and Agenda for Future Research' (2009) 15 J Legis Stud 317, 327. The reasons asserted for this vary: some claim that NPs struggle to control their governments in a satisfactory manner because the former have lost out through the transfer of legislative powers to EU level and because 'European integration has tilted the balance of powers at the domestic level decisively in favour of national executives, leading to a major shift in executive-legislative relations'. See eg Klaus H Goetz and Jan-Hinrik Meyer-Sahling, 'The Europeanisation of National Political Systems: Parliaments and Executives' (2008) 3 Living Rev Eur Gov 2, 6. Others focus on the lack of incentives for politicians and political parties to become involved in EU affairs. For instance, Raunio has commented that 'the ability of an individual legislator to influence politics at the European level is probably close to zero, even when the Council decides by unanimity. And … political parties have good reasons not to focus on European matters' (at 328).

general EU matters. It may be therefore that the conferring by national systems of strengthened institutional powers on NPs where these are lacking—up to and including veto powers on the various processes discussed above—would be helpful and perhaps might even constitute a *sine qua non* in stimulating interest on the part of NPs.

However, rational choice is a double-edged sword: it is not just an opportunity, but a challenge as well. Even given institutional incentives for action, there may simply be a limit on what busy national parliamentarians concerned with their own re-election can do within the EU policy field. As Raunio has put the matter:

> MPs normally have their hands full even without engaging in EU questions. Hence when legislators and political parties choose what issues to focus on, they make a rational calculus, weighing the costs and benefits of various parliamentary activities. Considering that re-election and policy influence are probably the primary goals of most MPs and political parties, focusing on EU matters is not a very attractive option for most deputies.[80]

It may well be that in attempting to create parliamentary accountability for the 'gap' areas, an ongoing challenge will be presented by collisions with this uncomfortable reality. It is becoming increasingly banal to assert that NPs have a vital role to play in closing accountability and communications deficits in EU policy-making. For some NPs at least and in some 'gap' areas at least, the challenge of generating sufficient will on the part of national political parties and national parliamentarians to take on this role may prove insurmountable.

It is sometimes forgotten that the whole process of European integration has been capable of coming to pass only because NPs gave their consent to it. However, the needs of providing accountability for an increasingly diverse integration process require that the role of NPs develop beyond this initial provision of approval (however indispensable this might have been) and, furthermore, develop beyond its current state. Such a process will require the assistance of national governments and the EU alike. It might well be that, as in other EU policy areas, the channels of democratic legitimacy and accountability for comitology and OMC processes will involve interparliamentary cooperation between the EU and national levels.

The challenge of determining how the role of NPs should best be given expression is one that arises each time a new form of EU decision-making emerges. In the case of some decision-making processes considered in this book, much has been achieved. In all cases, however—and certainly in the cases of comitology and the OMC—much more remains to be done.

[80] Raunio (n 79) 328.

PART II

NATIONAL PARLIAMENTS AND THE EURO CRISIS

7

Financial Crisis, National Parliaments, and the Reform of the Economic and Monetary Union

*Ingolf Pernice**

Introduction

Contrary to the expectations of many observers, the Treaty of Lisbon was not the end of the reform process of the European Union (EU)—it was not even sufficient to hold off any such reform for the following ten years.[1] Almost simultaneously with its ratification process, transatlantic shocks originating from the bankruptcy of Lehman Brothers not only hit the European financial markets and banking sector, but also made clear that the architecture of the Economic and Monetary Union (EMU) was not made for difficult political circumstances. In brief, the test of the original asymmetric approach—centralized monetary policy and a common currency based on the coordination of autonomous economic and financial policies of the Member States and, in particular, on budgetary autonomy of their parliaments—was not passed. This asymmetry, however, was not a mistake in itself. Although the authors of the Treaty of Maastricht agreed with all the economists that the euro must be sustained by a convergence of national economies, it was in the light of the principle of subsidiarity that they decided not to centralize powers concerning economic and financial policies, including redistributive policies and social security systems. The 'Masters of the Treaties' believed that legal commitments to coordination, the provisions on the independence of national central banks and budgetary discipline, the prohibitions of monetary financing and of privileged access of public authorities to financial institutions, and the bail-out clause, would suffice to ensure the needed economic convergence of national economies. They did not.

Coordination of economic, fiscal, and social policies of the Member States proved not to be effective as an instrument for ensuring the functioning of the EMU. The problem here is not one of politics or economics, but it seems to be of a conceptual nature for two reasons.

First, there is a contradiction between the political autonomy and the desired economic convergence. Autonomy means that national governments and parliaments are

* The author is most grateful to Davor Jančić for a critical review of the draft and for substantial advice and assistance provided by his WHI team and, in particular, Lars Otto and Martin Wapenhans, in finalizing this contribution. This contribution was finalized before the CJEU handed down its *OMT* judgment of 16 June 2015 (Case C-62/14). Where necessary, brief remarks have been made to evaluate the CJEU's 'answer' to the questions posed by the German Federal Constitutional Court in its request for a preliminary ruling.

[1] See, however, the then Secretary of State in the German Ministry of Economy, Joachim Wuermeling, 'Der Reformvertrag—das Ende der Verfassungsvision?' in Ingolf Pernice (ed), *Der Vertrag von Lissabon: Reform der EU ohne Verfassung?—Kolloquium zum 10. Geburtstag des WHI* (Nomos 2008).

free to decide on their respective policies, and freedom means diversity and mutual respect for political preferences that one or the other is opting for. Economic convergence, in contrast, means common principles and orientation, constraint, discipline, and surveillance. Article 5(1) TFEU states that 'the Member States shall coordinate *their* economic policies *within* the Union', whereas according to Article 119(1) TFEU 'the activities of the Member States and the Union shall include, as provided in the Treaties, the adoption of *an economic policy*'.[2] To make this clear, there is a plurality of national economic policies within the Union, on the one side, and there is one EU economic policy, on the other. Articles 121 to 126 TFEU indicate what is left of national autonomy and stress the responsibility of each Member State and their budgetary authorities both for the achievement of the objectives of the treaties and for their economic policies to be regarded 'as a matter of common concern' (Article 121(1) TFEU). If these obligations as well as the role given to EU institutions are taken seriously, there should not be any question for the functioning of the EMU. If not, as we have experienced, there is a problem.

Secondly, autonomy and cooperation are a matter for sunshine and calm waters, while legally binding rules and institutions are needed for times of economic and political turbulence. Both are based upon mutual trust, while the latter give trust particular support or insurance. Under the terms of the Westphalian system of 1648, it was believed that peace could be preserved by intergovernmental cooperation among sovereign states. More than three centuries of war among sovereign states in Europe showed that it could not. International law of cooperation does not serve the purpose. Jean Monet and Robert Schuman understood that only the creation of a supranational setting could possibly do the job. This means: common institutions vested with powers to take legally binding decisions, powers of adjudication, and—though very limited—powers of enforcement.

Recent history seems to confirm that their new approach is working. With the establishment of the EU, war among its Member States became unthinkable. Hence, why should the intergovernmental approach, which is limited to cooperation, be effective regarding economic policies and convergence, if it was not effective in general politics? In a policy field that is rightly considered fundamental for the achievement of the objectives of the Treaties, how can political leaders continue to believe, even after the experience of the financial crisis in Europe, that cooperation can do the job? To overcome the crisis, they simply opted for more of the same: cooperation instead of a meaningful institutional reform. What is the reason to believe that Member States will take their meanwhile enhanced commitments more seriously now than they did in the past?

Member States and their governments had no choice to limiting their action to striving at economic convergence by an enhanced cooperation and to some legislative measures allowed under the existing Treaties, coupled with supplementary international agreements like the European Stability Mechanism (ESM) and the Treaty on Stability, Coordination and Governance in the Economic and Monetary Union (Fiscal Compact). An attempt at a very limited revision of the EU Treaties was finally resisted by the British and Czech governments and does not seem to be on the political agenda, at least in a medium-term perspective.

One of the most relevant concerns for such resistance seems to be the idea of national sovereignty, or, in more concrete terms, that of self-rule of the peoples of the

[2] Emphasis added.

Member States as expressed by their parliaments; a core issue being to preserve meaningful political autonomy particularly in the fields of budgetary and redistributive policies. These concerns are shared by national governments and by the people in most of the Member States.[3] They are particularly prominent in the jurisprudence of the German Federal Constitutional Court (GFCC) regarding the Treaties of Maastricht and Lisbon, and the measures taken to preserve the functioning of the euro and the EU, such as the Euro Plus Pact, the ESM, and the Outright Monetary Transactions (OMT) programme of the European Central Bank (ECB).[4]

Of course, these concerns must be taken seriously. But there seem to be good reasons also to scrutinize the options available: are the measures taken or planned for rescuing the euro effective and in conformity with the principles of transparency and democracy? What are their implications on national parliamentary autonomy? How can democratic legitimacy and control be enhanced within the scope of the Treaties or by a revision of the Treaties' provisions on the EMU? Are there constitutional limits to further integration, and what are they in the light of the jurisprudence of the GFCC and other constitutional courts?

To answer these questions, this chapter first discusses some essential propositions developed by the GFCC regarding the protection of the German Parliament (*Bundestag*) and the principle of democracy in general against challenges from the developments in the EMU (section 1). The analysis then depicts some of the most important implications of the EMU reform for the autonomy of the NPs (section 2). With a view to remedying the existing or possible shortcomings in terms of transparency and democratic legitimacy, finally, some reform ideas to be implemented within the framework of the Treaties or requiring a revision of the Treaties will be developed (section 3).

1. The *Bundestag* and the Democratic Rights of the German People

At least since its 1993 judgment on the Treaty of Maastricht, the German Federal Constitutional Court has developed a particular concern for the democratic rights of the citizens, the powers, and the responsibilities of the *Bundestag*. It is a particular feature of the German constitutional system, and a result of Germany's experience with totalitarian regimes in the recent history, that the judiciary has the power to review the compatibility of legislative acts not only upon applications of other constitutional organs or in federal disputes, or on references made by ordinary courts in cases of doubt, but also upon 'constitutional complaints' brought by individuals directly to the GFCC if they consider their fundamental rights directly and individually to be affected by the public authority.

[3] See a new medium-term attempt in the 'Five Presidents' Report' on 'Completing Europe's Economic and Monetary Union', authored by Jean-Claude Juncker in close cooperation with Donald Tusk, Jeroen Dijsselbloem, Mario Draghi, and Martin Schulz, 22 June 2015. This designs three stages of development from a genuine economic union towards a financial union, a fiscal union and, finally, a political union http://ec.europa.eu/priorities/economic-monetary-union/docs/5-presidents-report_en.pdf (last accessed 13 October 2016).

[4] GFCC, Judgment of 21 June 2016, 2 BvR 2728/13 (*OMT programme*), not yet published. See also Press release 34/2016 of 21 June 2016, 'Constitutional Complaints and Organstreit Proceedings Against the OMT Programme of the European Central Bank Unsuccessful'. See more on the accountability of the ECB and this programme in the chapter by Davor Jančić in this volume.

Step by step, the GFCC has developed, on that basis, a jurisprudence interpreting the right to vote laid down in Article 38(1) of the Basic Law (BL) as a fundamental right to democracy. The judicial protection of the *individual* against the legislature was thus turned into a protection of the *legislature* against itself. Thereby, the GFCC has used individual constitutional complaints to prevent excessive self-restraint of the *Bundestag* where the latter gives consent under Article 23(1): to treaties conferring new powers on the EU; to supplementary international agreements in European matters, such as the ESM and the Fiscal Compact; to decisions of the executive acting within the framework of the ESM; or to financial guarantees given for loans accorded to Greece and other Member States within the framework of the euro rescue measures taken since May 2010.

The GFCC's preliminary ruling reference to the Court of Justice of the European Union (CJEU) in the case of the OMT programme seeks to extend this protection of parliamentary powers even to acts—or announcements—of the ECB. Had these legal demands been accepted by the CJEU (which in the end did not happen),[5] the result could have been that any German citizen, through a minority of members within the *Bundestag* or through an *actio popularis*, could bring a case before the GFCC for constitutional review possibly of every act not only of the *Bundestag* but also of any EU institution.[6] The GFCC's *OMT* reference suggests that even an alleged omission of certain acts—or a thorough debate—of the German Parliament could become the subject of consideration of the Constitutional Court. The GFCC has affirmed this view in its final judgment on the case. It accepted the admissibility of the constitutional complaint based on an alleged breach of the constitutional 'responsibility with respect to European integration (*Integrationsverantwortung*)' by Parliament's and the government's omission to take appropriate measures to protect Parliament's budgetary rights.[7] It states that this responsibility is rooted in the voters' rights enshrined in Article 38(1) BL, noting further that:

> This right requires the constitutional organs to ensure that the drop in influence (Einflussknick) and the restrictions on the voters' 'right to democracy' that come with the implementation of the European integration agenda do not extend further than is justified by the transfer of sovereign powers to the European Union.[8]

Some brief examples illustrate how the GFCC developed these positions in an attempt to safeguard—through the empowerment and encouragement of the *Bundestag*—the citizen's 'right to democracy' as a fundamental right aimed at providing a safeguard against excessive European constraints.

[5] Formally, the CJEU *has* accepted these demands in its judgment of 16 June 2015, C-62/14 (*OMT programme*), paras 24–31. It is noteworthy, however, that the guiding principle was that: 'it is solely for the national court before which the dispute has been brought, and which must assume responsibility for the subsequent judicial decision, to determine in the light of the particular circumstances of the case, both the need for a preliminary ruling in order to enable it to deliver judgment and the relevance of the questions which it submits to the Court'. So, despite several arguments regarding the admissibility, the CJEU followed its usual strand not to assess the background of the case and thus did not address the concerns raised above.

[6] See an extensive discussion of this preliminary ruling reference in: Special Issue 'The OMT Decision of the German Federal Constitutional Court' (2014) 15 German LJ 107; Mattias Wendel, 'Exceeding Judicial Competence in the Name of Democracy: The German Federal Constitutional Court's OMT Reference' (2014) 10 EuConst 263.

[7] GFCC, *OMT* judgment (n 4) para 94.

[8] GFCC, *OMT* press release (n 4) 2.d.

1.1 Powers of the *Bundestag* and the Individual Right to Democracy

The basis of the relevant strand of jurisprudence is Article 38(1) BL. This provision states that: 'Members of the German *Bundestag* shall be elected in general, direct, free, equal and secret elections'. With the judgment on the Treaty of Maastricht,[9] this provision became the anchor for a general control over EU-related agreements, as well as over acts of the EU. This provision was interpreted in light of Article 20(1) BL, which defines Germany as 'a democratic and social federal state'; and Article 79(3) BL, which prohibits constitutional amendments that affect in particular the principles laid down in Articles 1 and 20 BL, including human dignity and the principle of democracy.

In the judgment of 18 March 2014 on the ESM/Fiscal Compact, the GFCC confirmed its jurisprudence by stating that Article 38(1) BL is equal to a fundamental right and guarantees the self-determination of the citizens and, in particular, free and equal participation in the exercise of public power in Germany as a requirement of democracy within the meaning of Articles 20 and 79(3) BL. With a reference to a citizen's right to democracy rooted in the guarantee of human dignity, the GFCC understands these principles as belonging to the identity of the Constitution, which is to be protected even against interference by the constitution-amending legislature, and holds that the legislature must take sufficient measures to be able to meet its responsibility permanently with respect to European integration. In particular, the legislature may not relinquish its right to decide on the budget.[10]

The right to vote can thus be invoked by any German citizen whenever she alleges that her right to 'self-determination' or her right to 'free and equal and secret participation in the exercise of public power in Germany' has been affected.[11] This guarantee is not only extremely vague and broad, but also—being based on the principle of democracy and, consequently, being an element of Germany's constitutional identity—it is given an extraordinary and absolute value and protection. The Court thus strives to protect the powers of the *Bundestag*: first, with regard to the preservation of substantial political responsibilities, so that federal elections remain meaningful (this is what the responsibility with respect to integration is about); and, secondly, regarding in particular the protection of the budgetary autonomy of the *Bundestag*. Both aspects imply a considerable degree of control over Parliament's policies by the GFCC, with the explicit aim of preserving democracy and limiting EU constraints on the powers of the *Bundestag*.

It is in the final judgment on the OMT programme that the GFCC defines more concretely what it calls the 'right to democracy' as the subjective counterpart of the responsibility with respect to integration. Namely, national authorities have a constitutional obligation to observe and—in case of EU institutions acting ultra vires manifestly and in a structurally significant way, or acting in violation of national constitutional identity—to take any measure within their power to avoid or redress such violations.

[9] GFCC, Judgment of 12 October 1993, 2 BvR 2134, 2159/92 (*Maastricht Treaty*), paras 61–63, http://www.servat.unibe.ch/dfr/bv089155.html (last accessed 8 August 2016).

[10] GFCC, Judgment of 18 March 2014, 2 BvR 1390/12, 1421/12, 1438/12, 1439/12, 1440/12, 1824/12 and 2 BvE 6/12 (*ESM/Fiskalpakt*), paras 159 and 161–75.

[11] See a discussion of the concept concerning the criticism in the literature in GFCC, Judgment of 7 September 2011, 2 BvR 1099/10 (*Euro Rescue Package*), paras 101–2, where the GFCC limits the right based on Article 38 Basic Law to cases of an evident risk that the competences of the present or future *Bundestag* are eroded to an extent that parliamentary representation of the will of the people, aimed at implementing the political will of the citizens, is made legally or practically impossible.

Diverse political and legal measures are considered appropriate in this respect, including referring the case to the CJEU. If there is no individual right to a specific measure of this kind because of a large margin of political appreciation, the GFCC stresses that the *Bundestag* has at least an obligation to consider appropriate measures in a plenary session, particularly if the Constitutional Court has itself already stated that an EU act is manifestly ultra vires or a serious breach of national constitutional identity.[12]

This approach clearly strives to reconcile the respect for the constitutional powers and legitimacy of Parliament with the concern to preserve the sovereign self-determination of the German people against threats from Europe—a concern that the GFCC seems to share with the UK government. In an unprecedented way, however, it thus gives each individual a subjective right to judicial review, and itself the so far unknown power to pronounce on them in the name of democracy. Such an approach reminds one of that taken by the CJEU concerning the doctrine of direct effect in *Van Gend en Loos*, where it stated that 'the vigilance of the individuals concerned to protect their rights amounts to an effective supervision' of the application of the provisions of the Treaty, which the CJEU accepted in the interest of European integration, in addition to the 'supervision entrusted ... to the diligence of the Commission and the Member States'.[13] The constitutional responsibilities and constraints thus established are particularly relevant with regard to the measures taken or planned with respect to the financial crisis in Europe.

1.2 Obligations of the *Bundestag*: Responsibility with Respect to Integration

The concept of 'responsibility with respect to integration'—*Integrationsverantwortung*—developed by the GFCC already in the judgment on the Treaty of Lisbon of 2009, aims at encouraging the *Bundestag* and other institutions to be aware of and maintain control over the limits of EU powers as defined by the Treaties according to the principle of conferred competences. With regard to the measures undertaken to rescue the euro and to safeguard the stability of the EMU, the GFCC is going so far as to deduce from Article 38(1) BL two important obligations of German constitutional organs. First, they ought to refrain from participating in decision-making on ultra vires EU acts, as well as from implementing them. Secondly, they are obliged to take action, as far as possible, against excessive use or transgression of the powers conferred on the EU.

With regard to the OMT programme, which it finds clearly ultra vires, the GFCC states that German institutions have a constitutional obligation actively to oppose and not participate in any 'manifest and structurally significant transgressions of powers by the European organs', to refrain from their implementation, and to 'actively pursue the goal to reach compliance with the integration programme'. This could be reached, the GFCC stresses, by an amendment of the Treaties or, insofar as this is not feasible or wanted, by pursuing the reversal of acts that are not covered by the integration programme through legal or political means.[14]

In addition, the GFCC highlights a procedural component of right to vote by holding itself competent to admit constitutional complaints 'if the right to vote is in danger of being rendered ineffective in an area that is essential for the political self-determination of the people'. The Court thus takes the right to intervene, upon

[12] GFCC, *OMT* judgment (n 4) paras 166–73.

[13] ECJ, Judgment of 5 February 1963, Case 26/62 (*Van Gend en Loos*) [1963] ECR 1.

[14] GFCC, Order of 14 January 2014, 2 BvR 2728/13 (*OMT programme*), para 49.

the constitutional complaint of any citizen, if the 'democratic self-government of the people—embodied in particular in the German *Bundestag*—is permanently restricted in such a way that vital political decisions can no longer be made independently'.[15]

While excluding a general 'right that reaches beyond safeguarding the above-mentioned rights and that would let citizens have the legality of decisions taken by a democratic majority reviewed by the Federal Constitutional Court',[16] the GFCC nevertheless entitles the citizens to supervise their Parliament and reserves for itself the power to review what measures the *Bundestag* is taking in a given case with a view to remedying ultra vires acts of EU institutions. The GFCC understands this as a 'safeguard against an erosion of the legislature's substantial scope of action', implying that the citizen becomes a guardian of democracy, defending it against ultra vires acts of the EU: through the constitutional complaint, citizens can 'demand that the *Bundestag* and the Federal Government actively deal with the question of how the distribution of powers entailed in the treaties can be restored, and that they decide which options they want to use to pursue this goal'.[17]

Further explanations given in the preliminary ruling reference make very clear that the GFCC sees the OMT as such a 'unilateral usurpation of powers', for it understands it as a matter of economic policy and a violation of the prohibition of monetary financing of the budget enshrined in Article 123 TFEU.[18] One may ask whether this audacious construction was motivated by the wish to give the CJEU an opportunity to decide on the compatibility of the ECB's OMT programme with the EU Treaties, thus establishing a new path for individual action against acts of the EU institutions in circumvention of the restrictions posed by Article 263 TFEU,[19] more than by its preoccupation for the democratic powers of the *Bundestag*. What does it exactly mean for the *Bundestag* 'to deal with the question', if the result is not precisely defined? As Judge Lübbe-Wolff rightly emphasizes in her dissenting vote, the constitutional review of an omission to act is already precarious and limited to very exceptional cases of clearly defined obligations to act, and it seems even more difficult for a court to define the contents of any policy that the Parliament would be bound to undertake.[20]

What remains is the clear concern of the GFCC to compel the *Bundestag* to defend its sovereign rights in the name of the people, and the citizens' right to democracy rooted in the guarantee of human dignity, against any acts abandoning key elements of political self-determination and thus depriving the citizens of their possibilities of political participation.[21] It should be noted, however, that this judicial policy, if implemented generously, would be at the cost of the autonomy and independence of Parliament vis-à-vis

[15] ibid para 52. [16] ibid. [17] ibid para 53. [18] ibid, paras 55–98.

[19] See Ingolf Pernice, 'Guest Editorial: A Difficult Partnership Between Courts: The First Preliminary Reference by the German Federal Constitutional Court to the CJEU' (2014) 21 Maastricht J Eur & Comp L 3, 4. See also the dissenting opinion of Judge Gerhardt in GFCC, *OMT* order (n 14) para 7 of the dissenting opinion (each dissenting opinion has its own paragraph numbering).

[20] Dissenting opinion of Judge Lübbe-Wolff, ibid paras 12–23 of the dissenting opinion.

[21] See the wording in the GFCC's *Euro Rescue Package* judgment (n 11) para 169: 'Der letztlich in der Würde des Menschen wurzelnde Anspruch des Bürgers auf Demokratie'. In the aftermath of the CJEU's OMT judgment, it was noted that the CJEU delivered a very 'calm' decision. Its rather short decision was not only evaluated with respect to its content (a programme such as the OMT is compatible with Articles 119, 123(1), 127(1)–(2) TFEU, and Articles 17–24 of Protocol (No 4) on the Statute of the European System of Central Banks and of the European Central Bank), but also with respect to the judicial 'dialogue'. So, while the CJEU did not detect any ultra vires action contrary to what the GFCC seems to believe, it also does not address the GFCC's rhetoric regarding the principles of democracy and human dignity. Rather, the CJEU delivers a very 'technical' decision, thus designed perhaps to allow the GFCC to construct a subsequent decision without losing its face. This is what the GFCC eventually did.

the Court itself, and at the cost of the balance of powers among the institutions established by the BL. This might be one of the reasons why the GFCC has finally accepted the CJEU's preliminary ruling on the OMT, and stated that 'the policy decision on the OMT programme does not "manifestly" exceed the competences attributed to the European Central Bank'. Moreover, it confirms, that: 'if interpreted in accordance with the Court of Justice's judgment, the OMT programme does not present a constitutionally relevant threat to the German *Bundestag*'s right to decide on the budget'.[22]

1.3 Constraints on National Fiscal Policies and Budgetary Autonomy

This conclusion is a clear expression of the spirit of cooperation that the GFCC has adopted vis-à-vis the CJEU. Notwithstanding some doubts about the interpretation of certain conditions applicable to the implementation of the OMT programme,[23] the GFCC's final judgment is not in contradiction with the general limits that it had imposed on the *Bundestag* in earlier judgments regarding the preservation of national budgetary autonomy. This autonomy is what the Constitutional Court sees to be the heart of democracy. The principles are summarized as follows:

> Art. 38 sec. 1 GG [*Grundgesetz*–Basic Law] is violated in particular if the German *Bundestag* relinquishes its budgetary responsibility with the effect that it or a future *Bundestag* can no longer exercise the right to decide on the budget on its own. Deciding on public revenue and public expenditure is a fundamental part of the ability of a constitutional state to democratically shape itself. The German *Bundestag* must therefore make decisions on revenue and expenditure with responsibility to the people. In this context, the right to decide on the budget is a central element for shaping opinions in a democratic society, which must also be adhered to in a system of intergovernmental governing.[24]

The GFCC emphasizes that the budgetary autonomy has to be preserved and defended not only against threats from EU institutions, but is to be respected 'even in a system of intergovernmental governing', such as the first Euro Rescue Package for Greece,[25] the European Financial Stability Facility, or the ESM.[26] It does not exclude, however, agreements at the European or international levels restricting the discretion of German institutions in fiscal policies or a commitment of the budget-setting legislature to a particular budgetary and fiscal policy made under European or international law.[27] What is required, is that 'the legislature makes its decisions on revenue and expenditure independent of Union institutions and of other Member States of the European Union', so that the 'German *Bundestag* remains the place in which autonomous decisions on revenue and expenditure are made, including those with regard to international and European liabilities'.[28]

[22] GFCC, *OMT* press release (n 4).

[23] One might argue that at least one of the requirements that the GFCC set in its reference to the CJEU, asking for restrictive interpretation and application of the OMT programme—namely that the volume of any purchase of sovereign bonds be 'limited from the outset'—was not met by the CJEU's preliminary ruling. While the GFCC understands it in a quantitative sense, the CJEU seems to have understood it in a more general, factual sense (CJEU, *OMT* judgment (n 5) paras 87 and 116 (namely: 'the ECB has, de facto, restricted the volume of government bonds eligible to be purchased in the framework of the programme and, accordingly, has limited the scale of the programme's impact on the financing conditions of the States of the euro area'), clarifying that a prior quantitative limitation would weaken the effectiveness of the programme (para 88)).

[24] GFCC, *ESM/Fiskalpakt* judgment (n 10) para 161 (references omitted).

[25] See GFCC, *Euro Rescue Package* judgment (n 11) headnote 2.b) and para 124.

[26] GFCC, *ESM/Fiskalpakt* judgment (n 10) para 162.

[27] ibid paras 168 and 170–3.

[28] ibid paras 162 and 164.

These statements need explanation. The GFCC had already stated in its Lisbon Treaty judgment that the principle of democracy would be violated 'if the determination of the type and amount of the levies imposed on the citizen were supranationalised to a considerable extent'.[29] So, a limited supranational power of taxation would be acceptable. The concern here is a general loss of control through a liability for debts arising from policies of other Member States. Accordingly, the Constitutional Court stresses in the judgment of March 2014 on the EMS that 'the German *Bundestag* may not transfer its budgetary responsibility to other entities through imprecise budgetary authorisations'. It concludes that the *Bundestag* is constitutionally bound not to 'submit itself to financially significant mechanisms which … can result in incalculable burdens on the budget, be they expenses or losses of revenue, without first having given its constitutive consent'.[30]

Indirectly, these statements seem to exclude any kind of Eurobonds that might imply liabilities or guarantees? the amount of which are not determined and predictable, but automatic or in any other respect beyond control or influence of the *Bundestag*.[31] While the GFCC hence lays down strict principles regarding any European or international restriction of Parliament's budgetary autonomy, the Court nevertheless allows political institutions a broad margin of appreciation accepting that the 'ultimate limit following directly from the principle of democracy could only be exceeded if payment obligations and liability commitments took effect in such a way that the budget autonomy was not merely restricted, but suspended for at least a considerable period of time'. This could only happen 'in case of a manifest overstepping of ultimate limits'.[32]

This overstepping has clearly not happened in the case of the ESM,[33] nor does the GFCC consider the Fiscal Compact to 'affect the overall budgetary responsibility of the German *Bundestag* and … force the Federal Republic of Germany to make a permanent commitment regarding its economic policy that can no longer be reversed'.[34] The main instruments for rescuing Member States in trouble and for better coordination of national economic and fiscal policies have therefore been found to leave the *Bundestag* sufficient budgetary autonomy and political discretion as to comply with the constitutional requirements in Germany.

In turn, in respect of the requirements and principles developed by the jurisprudence of the GFCC, the role and practical control over the government by the *Bundestag* was considerably strengthened in the following respects:[35]

- First, the budgetary rights of the *Bundestag* extend to systems of intergovernmental governing with the effect that commitments of the government at the European or international levels cannot be undertaken without the constitutive

[29] GFCC, Judgment of 30 September 2009, 2 BvE 2/08 and 5/08, and 2 BvR 1010/08, 1022/08, 1259/08, 182/09 (*Lisbon Treaty*), para 256.

[30] GFCC, *ESM/Fiskalpakt* judgment (n 10) para 163.

[31] ibid para 164, where Eurobonds are not mentioned, however: 'it follows from the democratic basis of budget autonomy that the *Bundestag* may not consent to an intergovernmentally or supranationally agreed automatic guarantee or performance which is not subject to strict requirements and whose effects are not limited, and which—once it has been set in motion—is removed from the *Bundestag*'s control and influence'.

[32] ibid para 174. [33] ibid paras 183–222. [34] ibid para 244.

[35] See Katrin Auel, 'The Europeanization of National Parliaments' in José M Magone (ed), *Routledge Handbook of European Politics* (Routledge 2015) 366, 378–80; Oliver Höing, 'Differentiation of Parliamentary Powers. The German Constitutional Court and the German *Bundestag* within the Financial Crisis' in Marta Cartabia, Nicola Lupo, and Andrea Simoncini (eds), *Democracy and Subsidiarity in the EU: National Parliaments, Regions and Civil Society in the Decision-making Process* (Il Mulino 2013).

parliamentary consent including the authorization of each individual tranche of financial assistance of relevant size accorded to other countries.[36]

- Secondly, the German government has to inform Parliament promptly and comprehensively on all EU matters, and before participating in the adoption of EU legislative acts the Federal Government has to give the *Bundestag* an opportunity to state its position and take account of its position in the negotiations. Assuming that the ESM and the Fiscal Compact are 'matters concerning the European Union', the GFCC has extended these requirements to international treaties that do not amend but simply supplement the EU Treaties.[37]
- Thirdly, with a view to allowing the *Bundestag* properly to meet its budgetary responsibilities the GFCC has strengthened and extended the right of information of the *Bundestag* with regard to all European and international measures having an effect upon the national budget. This is particularly important with regard to international agreements such as the ESM. Usually, in an international framework Parliament is limited to allowing or not allowing the ratification of an agreement negotiated by the government. With respect to the ESM, however, operational decisions with financial implications to be taken under the agreement also cannot be agreed to by the German representative without prior parliamentary authorization.

2. The Financial Crisis: New Constraints on National Parliamentary Autonomy?

With the financial crisis, it is said that parliaments have lost much of their power through a new kind of 'Europeanization': governments have taken over and what they decide leaves little room for parliaments to shape policies. The result seems to be 'crisis management "by summit"'.[38] In addition, the European Commission is said to have gained considerable new power, namely concerning its supervisory functions in both the preventive and corrective arms of the economic and fiscal policy coordination process.

To adequately assess the political influence of NPs in this process at all levels, three areas need to be distinguished: measures adopted to rescue Member States that are or risk becoming insolvent (1); procedures and provisions aimed at closer coordination in order to ensure the convergence of the economies of the Member States (2); and policies striving to secure the functioning of the financial markets and the effectiveness of the monetary policy of the ECB (3).

2.1 The European Stability Mechanism: Rescuing the Economic and Monetary Union

With the outbreak of the euro crisis in 2010, the first concern of the European Commission and the governments was to avoid the insolvency of Greece and some

[36] GFCC, *Euro Rescue Package* judgment (n 11), para 128.

[37] GFCC, *ESM/Fiskalpakt* judgment (n 10) para 232.

[38] See Auel (n 35) 381.

other Member States. Beginning with the first Euro Rescue Package of May 2010, followed by the establishment of a 'permanent crisis mechanism to safeguard the financial stability of the euro area as a whole' in October 2010, which was replaced in 2012 with the ESM Treaty—the Eurogroup took action. These actions aimed to 'mobilise funding and provide stability support under strict conditionality', as Article 3 of the ESM Treaty points out, for 'Members which are experiencing, or are threatened by, severe financial problems if indispensable to safeguard the financial stability of the euro area as a whole and of its Member States'.

The 'if' is of utmost relevance, since the inclusion of this condition was the only way to envisage the assistance without infringing the bail-out clause laid down in Article 125 TFEU.[39] As was made clear in the new provision of Article 136(3) TFEU, introduced following the simplified revision of the TFEU pursuant to Article 48(6) TEU—it is not for the sake of the Member State in question, but to ensure the financial stability of the euro area as a whole, that the ESM may be mobilized. Therefore, the mechanism was established and should be managed in the spirit of solidarity of all contracting parties, including the countries with difficulties.[40]

Given the imminent threats of the crisis for the EMU as a whole, in spite of the financial and democratic implications of the ESM, including the financial volume and conditionality, NPs of the states acceding to the ESM had no choice but to agree to its establishment. Some of them were forced to undertake important financial commitments because of the risk that the EMU would otherwise break down, with unpredictable consequences for the economies of all Member States and beyond. The others had no choice but to accept assistance with strict conditionality, given the possibly catastrophic consequences that insolvency would have for their own economy and people. These measures could only be taken as a common effort towards a common goal and only the stabilization of the euro area as a whole can possibly justify any constraints that consenting to the system carried for NPs. But can it really?

The constraints—which are thrashed out in a memorandum of understanding negotiated between the Commission, the ECB, and the International Monetary Fund in collaboration with the government in question, for each given case[41]—are considerable. Moreover, the control powers exercised by the Troika seem to reach deeply into internal politics and administrative structures. The case of Greece is a telling example. It is true that these constraints would not be applicable without the consent of the Member State concerned in conformity with its constitutional requirements. However, the restrictions for NPs and thus on democratic self-determination—despite some opportunity for discussion or economic dialogue with the Commission and the European Parliament (EP)[42]—go certainly far beyond what the GFCC could ever admit as compatible with the principles, outlined above, of democracy understood as an expression of human dignity in Germany. The German *Bundestag*, in view of the principles developed by this jurisprudence, could never agree to such restrictions. Could it agree to such restrictions to be imposed on another democratic country in the

[39] See CJEU, Judgment of 27 November 2012, Case C-370/12 (*Pringle*).

[40] See more on the concept of solidarity in Ingolf Pernice, 'Solidarität in Europa. Eine Ortsbestimmung im Verhältnis zwischen Bürger, Staat und Europäischer Union' in Christian Calliess (ed), *Europäische Solidarität und nationale Identität—Überlegungen im Kontext der Krise im Euroraum* (Mohr Siebeck 2013), also available as WHI-Paper 01/2013.

[41] ESM Treaty, art 13(3).

[42] Regulation 472/2013 of the European Parliament and the Council of 21 May 2013 on the strengthening of economic and budgetary surveillance of Member States in the euro area experiencing

EU? Do the emergency situation and the common goal—rescuing the euro area as a whole—suffice to justify such an extraordinary instrument? This is difficult to believe! But the question is whether there is an alternative.

2.2 Enhancing Economic Governance in the European Union

Compared to the constraints on national parliamentary autonomy of the countries in crisis, constraints resulting from the Euro Plus Pact and the new legislative measures taken by the EU seem to be less important. They are said to already constitute a European 'economic government'[43] and to leave little room for autonomous budgetary policies of NPs.

Both hypotheses entail serious problems, for two reasons. If secondary legislation really establishes an economic government with meaningful powers in areas of national competence including economic and fiscal policies, the question arises of their compatibility with the Treaties, which leave these policies within the ambit of national competence. However, if autonomous budgetary policies and parliamentary discretion at the national level are indeed considerably constrained, there is a legitimacy problem at least insofar as there is no compensation through an effective parliamentary participation and control at the EU level.[44]

2.2.1 The Euro Plus Pact

The first step towards enhanced cooperation at least within the Eurozone has taken the form of the Euro Plus Pact. It paved the way for subsequent legislative measures aimed at strengthening the Stability and Growth Pact of 1997, while also containing some of the leading ideas agreed upon in the Fiscal Compact of 2012.

The Euro Plus Pact was agreed among the members of the Eurogroup and several other Member States. It lays down their common priorities for closer cooperation. It was published as an annex to the Conclusions of the European Council of April 2011,[45] so NPs were not involved directly in its adoption. Its introduction specifies that: 'This Pact focuses primarily on areas that fall under national competence and are key for increasing competitiveness and avoiding harmful imbalances'. This makes clear that significant competences of the Union are not involved. Nevertheless, reference is made to the EP in the first of the Pact's 'four guiding rules': 'it will play its full role in line with its competences'. The guiding rules include the goal of competitiveness and convergence, objectives to be agreed among the heads of government, commitments to be undertaken by each of them, and their implementation to be monitored on the basis of a report of the Commission. Member States also commit 'to consult their partners on each major economic reform having potential spillover effects before its adoption'. If there is no mention of the NPs,[46] the question of their involvement seems to be left to the individual Member States. They are free to provide for adequate involvement of their respective parliaments before any commitment is undertaken,

or threatened with serious difficulties with respect to their financial stability, arts 3(8)–(9) and 7(11) [2013] OJ L 140/1.

[43] See Carlino Antpöhler, 'Emergenz der europäischen Wirtschaftsregierung. Das Six Pack als Zeichen supranationaler Leistungsfähigkeit' (2012) 72 ZaoRV 353, 362–8.

[44] Cristina Fasone, 'European Economic Governance and Parliamentary Representation. What Place for the European Parliament?' (2014) 20 ELJ 164.

[45] European Council, Conclusions of 20 April 2011, EUCO 10/1/11 Rev. 1, Annex 1.

[46] See, however, para I.5 of the Conclusions (n 45): 'In implementing these policies, and in order to ensure wide ownership, close cooperation will be maintained with the European Parliament and

but it is difficult to see to what extent parliaments effectively participate in the process. As the Euro Plus Pact includes politically sensitive issues—including wages, ensuring 'costs developments in line with productivity', labour market reforms to promote 'flexicurity', tax reforms, aligning the pension systems, and limiting early retirement schemes, as well as the idea of a 'debt brake'—the lack of even mentioning NPs is even more striking.

Depending on the respective constitutional or legal arrangements in the Member States, their parliaments participate more or less decisively. Commitments of the German government have to be understood in terms of Article 23(2)–(3) BL as 'matters concerning the European Union'. The effect of this is that, according to the provisions of the Act on the Cooperation between the Government and the *Bundestag* in Matters Concerning the European Union, the government is bound to inform the *Bundestag* before making any commitment and to take Parliament's comments as a basis for its position.[47]

2.2.2 *The Six Pack and the Two Pack*

The need for parliamentary involvement has been made more explicit in the provisions of the Six Pack[48] and the Two Pack.[49] The Six Pack was adopted in 2011 primarily to strengthen the Stability and Growth Pact and EU economic governance by including provisions on the European Semester on economic policy coordination, while the Two Pack was adopted in 2013 with a view to gradually strengthening surveillance and coordination in the euro area and completing the European Semester. Two new instruments deserve special mention. The first establishes a timeline for synchronizing the key steps in the preparation of national budgets.[50] The second provides for enhanced surveillance and, if necessary, for 'enhanced economic policy coordination' through the requirement of 'macroeconomic adjustment programmes' for euro area Member States that are 'experiencing or threatened with serious difficulties with respect to their financial stability, likely to have adverse spill-over effects on other Member States in the

other EU institutions and advisory bodies (ESC, CoR), with the full involvement of national parliaments, social partners, regions and other stakeholders'.

[47] See n 37 and arts 7(1) and (11) and 8 of the Act.

[48] Regulation (EU) No 1173/2011 of the European Parliament and of the Council of 16 November 2011 on the effective enforcement of budgetary surveillance in the euro area, [2011] OJ L 306/1; Regulation (EU) No 1174/2011 of the European Parliament and of the Council of 16 November 2011 on enforcement measures to correct excessive macroeconomic imbalances in the euro area, [2011] OJ L 306/8; Regulation (EU) No 1175/2011 of the European Parliament and of the Council of 16 November 2011 amending Council Regulation (EC) No 1466/97 on the strengthening of the surveillance and coordination of economic policies, [2011] OJ L 306/12; Regulation (EU) No 1176/2011 of the European Parliament and of the Council of 16 November 2011 on the prevention and correction of macroeconomic imbalances, [2011] OJ L 306/25; Council Regulation (EU) No 1177/2011 of 8 November 2011 amending Regulation (EC) No 1467/97 on speeding up and clarifying the implementation of the excessive deficit procedure, [2011] OJ L 306/33; Council Directive 2011/85/EU of 8 November 2011 on requirements for budgetary frameworks of the Member States, [2011] OJ L306/41.

[49] Regulation (EU) No 472/2013 of the European Parliament and of the Council of 21 May 2011 on the strengthening of economic and budgetary surveillance of Member States in the euro area experiencing or threatened with serious difficulties with respect to their financial stability, [2013] OJ L140/1; Regulation (EU) No 473/2013 of the European Parliament and of the Council of 21 May 2013 on common provisions for monitoring and assessing draft budgetary plans and ensuring the correction of excessive deficit of the Member States in the euro area, [2013] OJ L 140/11.

[50] Regulation 473/2013, art 4.

euro area',[51] or which have requested financial assistance from the ESM or others.[52] As recital (9) of Regulation 1177/2011 points out, 'the strengthening of economic governance should include a closer and more timely involvement of the European Parliament and the national parliaments', and recital (16) of the same Regulation promises that:

> [i]n line with the legal and political arrangements of each Member State, national parliaments should be duly involved in the European Semester, and in the preparation of stability programmes, convergence programmes and national reform programmes in order to increase the transparency and ownership of, and accountability for the decisions taken.

Yet, Article 2-a of Regulation 1466/97 as amended by Regulation 1177/2011 only provides for the involvement of the EP, 'in particular by means of the economic dialogue'. According to Article 2-ab thereof, the economic dialogue, introduced throughout the Six Pack on the EP's request, only includes EU institutions and it allows the invitation of 'a Member State which is the subject of a Council recommendation under Article 6(2) or 10(2) to participate in an exchange of views'.[53] But NPs are not mentioned in the relevant provisions. As the obligations regarding the European Semester are addressed to the Member States, it is left to them to organise how their NPs shall be involved. The European Semester is understood as a specific tool giving effect to the provisions of Article 121 TFEU on the coordination and multilateral surveillance of the economic policies of the Member States.

In practice, NPs indeed used their opportunity to significantly improve their position in budgetary processes compared to the situation before the euro crisis either through national legislation or with the help of constitutional courts.[54]

2.2.3 *National Parliaments Under Enhanced Surveillance: the Revised European Semester*

Yet, the Two Pack Regulation 473/2013 goes a step further. It is based on the understanding that particularly within the euro area spill-overs of economic and fiscal policy from one Member State to another may create tensions. This is why, when communicating their draft budgetary plans to the Commission, Eurozone Member States are requested under Article 6(3) of this Regulation to pay '[p]articular and explicit attention … to major fiscal policy reform plans with potential spill-over effects for other Member States whose currency is the euro'. What was a political commitment in the Euro Plus Pact thus became a legally binding obligation. Recital (19) explains this by extending the obligation a step further:

> Member States whose currency is the euro are particularly subject to spill-over effects from each other's budgetary policies. Member States whose currency is the euro should consult the Commission and each other before adopting any major fiscal policy reform plans with potential spill-over effects, so as to allow an assessment of the possible impact for the euro area as a whole. They should also consider their budgetary plans to be of common concern and submit them to the Commission for monitoring purposes in advance of their becoming binding. The Commission, in cooperation with the Member States, should propose guidelines in the form of a harmonised framework for the specification of the content of draft budgetary plans.

[51] ibid art 2. [52] ibid art 7. [53] ibid art 15.

[54] See Davor Jančić, 'Parliamentary Involvement in the Economic and Monetary Union after the Euro Crisis' in Nicola Lupo and Cristina Fasone (eds), *Interparliamentary Cooperation in the Composite European Constitution* (Hart Publishing 2016) 183, 188; Davor Jančić, 'National Parliaments and EU Fiscal Integration' (2016) 22 ELJ 225.

Among the numerous criteria to be observed by the Member States when establishing and making public their medium-term fiscal plans under Article 4 are that such plans 'shall be presented together with their national reform programmes and the stability programmes'. These obligations seem to put in binding form what is explained in the recital. The more detailed the guidance and recommendations of the Council issued at the beginning of the cycle are, the more restrictive the corresponding constraints on national budgetary policies become.

In turn, Article 6 of Regulation 473/2013 provides, among the rules governing the assessment of draft budgetary plans of the Member States, that 'at the request of the parliament of the Member State concerned or of the European Parliament, the Commission shall present its opinion to the parliament making the request'. The importance of this direct dialogue between the Commission and NPs cannot be overestimated. It is not only a matter of mutual respect and understanding. While an *ex ante* consultation with each NP concerned would have been the more adequate and more democratic solution,[55] it may help the Commission's opinion to be well understood and eventually followed by the budgetary authorities of the Member State concerned. This applies in particular in cases where the Commission identifies problems such as non-compliance with budgetary policy obligations laid down in the Stability and Growth Pact or any other obligations and requests a revised draft budgetary plan according to Article 7(2) of the Regulation. Surprisingly, Regulation 1176/2011 on the prevention and correction of macroeconomic imbalances only allows, within the framework of the economic dialogue, the competent committee of the EP to 'offer the opportunity to participate in an exchange of views to the Member State which is the subject of a Council recommendation or decision under Article 7(2) or Article 10(4)'. NPs are not involved, although recital (5) of Regulation 1176/2011 clearly and rightly refers to them: 'The strengthening of economic governance should include a closer and more timely involvement of the European Parliament and the national parliaments'.

2.2.4 *Dialogue with National Parliaments as Part of Surveillance and Coordination Schemes*

This dialogue including NPs should become a regular part of the processes of surveillance and coordination of the economic and fiscal policies of the Member States. It is not sufficient to make it part of the European Semester and of the regime governing the specific situation of a Member State with serious financial difficulties or one receiving financial assistance. It is necessary to raise the awareness of national parliamentarians of any possible spill-over effects of their decisions on other Member States. Similar provisions on an 'exchange of views' or an 'economic dialogue' can be found in Article 3(7)–(8) of Regulation 472/2013 on enhanced surveillance and macroeconomic adjustment programmes in cases where, following the conclusions of the Commission that the financial and economic situation of a Member State 'has significant adverse effects on the financial stability of the euro area of its Member States', the Council recommends the adoption of precautionary corrective measures or the preparation of a draft macroeconomic adjustment programme; and in Article 3(9) of this Regulation 'during the course of the enhanced surveillance process' in general.

[55] See Jančić, 'Parliamentary Involvement in the Economic and Monetary Union After the Euro Crisis' (n 54) 183, 198.

Similar provisions also apply in the case of a Member State requesting or receiving financial assistance and subject, therefore, to a macroeconomic adjustment programme, which is aimed at discussing 'the progress made in the implementation of its macroeconomic adjustment programme'. The dialogue does not alleviate the constraints and pressures put on the NP in question, but it facilitates clarification and mutual understanding of the decision-making process and may lay bare the fact that national financial policies—within the internal market or at least within the euro area—can no longer be seen as a matter of self-determination of the people in one Member State in isolation from those of the other Member States.[56]

2.3 The Fiscal Compact and the Debt Brake

The Fiscal Compact is an attempt to make legally binding many of the commitments undertaken by the Member States of the euro area and some other Member States with a view to enhancing economic policy coordination. One of the most important provisions is Article 3 on the balanced budget or the so-called 'debt brake'. As paragraph 2 thereof states, contracting parties are bound to incorporate this rule through 'provisions of binding force and permanent character, preferably constitutional, or otherwise guaranteed to be fully respected and adhered to throughout the national budgetary processes'. There must be a correction mechanism as well as independent national institutions responsible for monitoring compliance with these rules.

The obligation to incorporate the debt brake supports and somewhat strengthens the provisions of Articles 2a, 5, 6, and 9 of Regulation 1466/97, as amended by Regulation 1175/2011 regarding the 'differentiated medium-term objective' for the Member States' budgetary position, also referred to in Article 5 of Regulation 473/2013 on the monitoring of compliance of the national budgetary plans with fiscal rules within the framework of the European Semester. Indeed, Article 2a(1) of Regulation 1466/97 allows 'country-specific medium-term budgetary objectives' to diverge from the requirement of a close to balance or in surplus position, while providing a safety margin with respect to the 3% of GDP government deficit ratio. But the principle of a balance or in surplus position seems to be accepted as a requirement of EU secondary legislation.

Although the last phrase of Article 3(2) of the Fiscal Compact asserts that 'such correction mechanism shall fully respect the prerogatives of national Parliaments', the provisions on the debt brake diminish NPs' options: instead of autonomous fiscal decisions their role is defined as executors of determined strict principles of austerity. In turn, such policy may result in recession rather than in growth, with adverse effects on employment and social conditions. It is difficult to see how, in periods of economic depression, national budgetary authorities would accept this strict rule without losing the support of the electorate.

If Article 16 of the Fiscal Compact envisages the incorporation of its provisions into the EU Treaties 'within five years, at most, of the date of entry into force of this Treaty', it does not seem likely that the debt brake will be part of the package, not least for the democratic problems it carries.

[56] Mark Dawson and Floris de Witte, 'Self-determination in the Constitutional Future of the EU' (2015) 21 ELJ 371.

3. Enhancing Democratic Legitimacy in a Functioning EMU

Given the interdependence of the national economies within the internal market with a common currency and the above-mentioned spill-over effects, preserving budgetary autonomy and individual responsibility of each Member State for its own debt cannot be the answer to the crisis. A common approach is required, so as to ensure that NPs include a European perspective in all decisions taken at the national level. The European Semester can be seen as a first step towards greater awareness of the European dimension of national economic and financial policies, and it paves the way for more intensive mechanisms of interaction and coherence between the EU and national levels. This may include new steps of integration, as far as needed in the light of the principle of subsidiarity, in order to create an effective political instrument to deal with problems that individual Member States are unable to solve. Consequently, common economic, fiscal, and perhaps even social, policies have to be developed on the basis of competences to be conferred on the Union to the extent needed to sustain the common currency.

This might not be compatible with the idea that democratic legitimacy for EU policies must primarily be founded on NPs. But is this assumption correct? Yes, it might be politically difficult, at present, to achieve the revision of the Treaties required to realize this objective. In this case, interim solutions allowing a more substantive cooperation among NPs are needed. The June 2016 'Brexit' referendum, if implemented through Article 50 TEU, could provide an opportunity to adapt the Treaties and, for the members of the Eurogroup to negotiate limited institutional reforms with a view to remedying the problems of the euro. What are the principles and model to be followed and what are the necessary steps to overcome the asymmetry between the economic and the monetary components of the EMU and to set up the conditions required for a well functioning EMU?

3.1 Democratic Legitimacy of the European Policies

Many observers state that strengthening democratic legitimacy would mean strengthening the role of NPs in the EU. Fifteen years ago, Joschka Fischer, the then German Foreign Affairs Minister, called in his well-known Humboldt speech of May 2000 for members of NPs to have a seat in the EP in order to bridge the gap between the national and European political elites. There are considerable arguments in favour of this proposition, because it is based on the understanding that EU policies are part of our daily life, that the EU is part of the political system we live in, and that members of our NPs carry a particular responsibility for the political decisions made at the EU level. The GFCC is even going so far as to repeat at any occasion that the democratic legitimacy of the EU is rooted primarily in NPs and that consequently the EP can only play a supplementary and subsidiary role.[57] In short: as long as there is no European people, as long as there is no equality in the voting rights of the citizens of the Union and, as a consequence, as long as the EU is not a state, substituting the sovereign

[57] Davor Jančić, 'Caveats from Karlsruhe and Berlin: Whither Democracy After Lisbon?' (2010) 16 Colum J Eur L 337.

statehood of the Member States—a change that is excluded under the German BL[58]—the democratic legitimacy of the EU basically rests upon NPs.[59]

This dogmatic approach of the GFCC is questionable, and nothing in the text of the BL supports it. The preamble and Article 23(3) BL, in contrast, suggest a clear departure from the classical concept of sovereign national statehood for Germany. According to the preamble, the German people have adopted the BL 'inspired by the determination to promote world peace as an equal partner in a united Europe'. And Article 23(1) BL specifies that 'with a view to establishing a united Europe, the Federal Republic of Germany shall participate in the development of the European Union'. It remains to be determined what the words 'united Europe' mean, but the term is open enough not to exclude even federal statehood.

The idea of European integration, however, does not necessarily follow the model of statehood. Jean Monnet and Robert Schuman rather envisioned a new kind of political organization, not national but supranational, based upon nations and states without itself becoming a nation state. Walter Hallstein rightly qualified the European Community as a Community based upon the rule of law, or as the CJEU now says, a Union of law. The new approach is the answer to the failure of the Westphalian system of sovereign states that has been unable to preserve peace among the peoples of Europe. If the preamble of the TEU emphasizes that the heads of state and government were 'resolved to continue the process of creating an ever closer union among the peoples of Europe in which decisions are taken as closely as possible to the citizen in accordance with the principle of subsidiarity', nothing in the Treaties can be understood to mean that the *finalité* of the EU means federal statehood. Those who only want to copy the nation state at the EU level show a deplorable lack of imagination.

What the GFCC seems to ignore, thus, is the original openness of the BL to a new model of political organization beyond the state, unifying the peoples of those states in order to preserve peace in Europe and beyond. Article 23(1) BL specifies that Germany shall cooperate in establishing a European Union 'that is committed to democratic, social and federal principles, to the rule of law, and to the principle of subsidiarity, and that guarantees a level of protection of basic rights essentially comparable to that afforded by this Basic Law'. The German Constitution rightly leaves open what these principles exactly mean in a supranational context. One has to ask whether, as long as the EU is not a state, the concrete meaning of these principles should be constructed as being identical to their meaning in the national context. The answer is: they should not.

The Treaty of Lisbon emphasizes the principle of subsidiarity and confers specific rights and responsibilities to NPs, as summarized in Article 12 TEU. Article 10(2) TEU specifically refers to the heads of state and the governments of the Member States being 'themselves democratically accountable either to their NPs, or to their citizens' as one of the two pillars of representative democracy on which that the EU is founded, the other pillar thereof being the 'citizens directly represented at Union level in the European Parliament'.

These two approaches—that of a dual basis of the democratic legitimacy of EU policies and that of the GFCC—are not necessarily incompatible in practice. The Treaties

[58] GFCC, *Lisbon Treaty* judgment (n 29) paras 228 and 232–34. See the role of Article 50 TEU in this context in paras 329–30.

[59] ibid paras 262, 277, and 297. See the limited application in the EU of state-based democratic principles in paras 271–2.

can be understood to establish a composite constitutional system.[60] In this system, transparency, public discourse on key political questions, popular participation, and democratic legitimacy and control, not only occur at both EU and domestic levels,[61] but the discourses and political processes developing at these two levels cannot be separated from each other. Thus, NPs and the EP should exercise their democratic function in the EU by acting in close cooperation: they have a common mission.

The question is one of the extent to which EU democratic legitimacy is effectively provided by NPs. After the experience of more than five decades, in how many cases has each of them (plenary, not only a committee) had a substantial public debate on specific policies or legislative proposals of the Commission, such as on the Framework Directive on Data Protection or on the Six Pack or the Two Pack? And, if so, have parliamentary debates and resolutions had a real impact on the legislative measure in question? In how many, and which, cases did a NP debate and decide a political initiative to be undertaken by the government on an issue of national interest at the EU level? The numbers are probably not overwhelming.[62]

Although the answer might be different for each of the twenty-eight NPs of the EU, there is an increasing need for them to exercise their responsibilities more extensively. Article 12 TEU gives them a constitutional role at the EU level, although the Treaty provisions implementing this role do not confer substantial powers on them. This is understandable, since their constituency is focused primarily on issues that can be dealt with by national institutions and, in particular, the governments. But the governments have an active role to play in the Council. As Article 10(2) TEU stipulates, they are accountable to their respective parliaments. And they can take a proactive role too: the more they become aware of the potential of EU institutions to deal effectively with issues beyond the national reach, the more they may actively stimulate EU institutions to take appropriate action at the EU level. It is crucial for democracy in Europe that NPs discuss and consider spill-over effects of their policies, enter into a dialogue with the other NPs, and make proactive use of the opportunities offered by the EU for more effective and democratically legitimate action at the EU level, where appropriate. Coordinated economic and fiscal policies, to the extent that national policies impact the economies of other Member States, may become more and more such a matter of common concern and interest.

3.2 Enhancing Democratic Legitimacy Within the Framework of the Existing Treaties

Enhancing the democratic legitimacy of EU policies and, in particular, of EU coordination of the economic, fiscal, and social policies of the Member States must include

[60] See more on this concept in Ingolf Pernice, 'Multilevel Constitutionalism and the Treaty of Amsterdam: European Constitution-making Revisited' (1999) 36 CML Rev 703; Ingolf Pernice, 'The EU—A Citizens' Joint Venture. Multilevel Constitutionalism and Open Democracy in Europe' in José M. Magone (ed), *Routledge Handbook of European Politics* (Routledge 2015).

[61] TEU, art 10.

[62] See more on parliamentary debates on the euro crisis in the chapters by Frank Wendler and Aleksandra Maatsch in this volume. See also analyses in Katrin Auel and Oliver Höing, 'Parliaments in the Euro Crisis: Can Losers of Integration Still Fight Back?' (2014) 52 JCMS 1184; Katrin Auel, Olivier Rozenberg, and Angela Tacea, 'To Scrutinise or Not to Scrutinise? Explaining Variation in EU-related Activities in National Parliaments' (2015) 38 WEP 282; Katrin Auel, Olivier Rozenberg, and Angela Tacea, 'Fighting Back? And, If So, How? Measuring Parliamentary Strength and Activity in EU Affairs' in Claudia Hefftler and others (eds), *The Palgrave Handbook of National Parliaments and the European Union* (Palgrave 2015).

both the EP and NPs. Accordingly, the economic dialogue not only needs to be strengthened, but also give representatives of the budget committees of the NPs concerned a say in order to make their positions and problems heard and to have them seriously taken into account. As long as these policy areas are recognized, as the Euro Plus Pact rightly does, as being within the ambit of national competence, it is not acceptable that discussing and setting the broad guidelines of the economic policies of the Member States and of the Union, as the basis for coordination and surveillance, is a matter, according to Article 121(2) TFEU, for the Commission and the governments only. Given its implications for the budgetary autonomy of NPs, they too must have a say in this process.

So far, this parliamentary involvement is organized at the EU level with the EP through the economic dialogue,[63] at the national level by each Member State in accordance with the constitutional arrangements regulating the interaction of their respective government and parliament. The participation and control by NPs of Council decisions, however, will remain weak and insignificant, as long as Council meetings are not public, and as long as national parliamentarians are not familiar with EU procedures and the situation in the other Member States. In a report of 17 September 2012, the 'Future of Europe Group'—composed of the foreign ministers of Austria, Belgium, Denmark, France, Italy, Germany, Luxembourg, the Netherlands, Poland, Portugal, and Spain—suggested the creation of a 'permanent joint committee' composed of the members of the EP and of NPs.[64] This could be a first step towards stimulating mutual information, understanding, and cooperation. In this vein, the Commission's 'Blueprint' of 30 November 2012 also emphasizes the role of NPs in a 'deep and genuine EMU':

> Whatever the final design of EMU, the role of national parliaments will always remain crucial in ensuring legitimacy of Member States' action in the European Council and the Council but especially of the conduct of national budgetary and economic policies even if more closely coordinated by the EU. Cooperation between the European Parliament and national parliaments is also valuable: it builds up mutual understanding and common ownership for EMU as a multilevel governance system.[65]

A new Interparliamentary Conference on Economic and Financial Governance was established on 23 April 2013 under Article 13 of the Fiscal Compact.[66] It has been criticized as a 'missed opportunity', because there is no clear membership, it has no decision-making powers, and it meets only twice a year.[67] As a mere forum for occasional discussion, it will not attract relevant members of NPs and the impact of its conclusions will, therefore, remain poor. Interparliamentary cooperation thus needs to be further developed through more substantial institutional ties among NPs and with the EP, for instance by giving the Interparliamentary Conference greater responsibility and powers,[68] although with due respect for the limits of the capacity of national

[63] See Jančić, 'Parliamentary Involvement in the Economic and Monetary Union After the Euro Crisis' (n 54) 198.

[64] See http://www.cer.org.uk/sites/default/files/westerwelle_report_sept12.pdf (last accessed 4 August 2016).

[65] European Commission, Communication 'A Blueprint for a Deep and Genuine Economic and Monetary Union: Launching a European Debate', COM(2012) 777, 35 (para 4.1. (2)).

[66] See more in the chapter by Ian Cooper in this volume.

[67] See Valentin Kreilinger, 'The New Inter-parliamentary Conference for Economic and Financial Governance' (2013) Notre Europe Policy Paper No 100, 17–19. See also Jančić, 'Parliamentary Involvement in the Economic and Monetary Union after the Euro Crisis' (n 54) 199.

[68] See, however, the doubts expressed by the EP in its Resolution of 12 December 2013 on constitutional problems of a multi-tier governance in the European Union (2012/2078(INI)), where it

parliamentarians to take their European responsibilities seriously in addition to their tasks in domestic politics.

At this stage, the question is to what extent it is a task and the competence of the Union to organize such an interparliamentary dialogue. As the Commission points out in its Blueprint, 'one fails to see how parliamentary accountability could be organised for an intergovernmental European level seeking to influence economic policies of individual euro area Member States'.[69] As far as intergovernmental governing is concerned, democratic accountability seems thus to be primarily a matter for national constitutional arrangements, notwithstanding the participation of the EP in ensuring that the European perspective is not left out of sight. In turn, cooperation with NPs is important for the EP when exercising its control over the Commission's shaping of recommendations on national budgetary policies and the latter's monitoring and surveillance action in EU economic governance.

3.3 Towards a Democratic Economic and Financial Policy of the EU

As long as the Member States remain the masters of their budgets and economic, financial, and social policies are regarded as their genuine competence, national autonomy will equate with diversity and imbalance not convergence. The more effective the mechanisms and procedures for ensuring convergence within the common currency become, the less room for the autonomy of the Member States there will be and the less political room for manoeuvre their parliaments will have. The complexity of the system of coordination and surveillance—consisting of common guidelines and principles, reporting, monitoring, recommendations, financial sanctions—a system established by primary law and further developed by secondary law, political agreements, and international treaties, has reached a point at which people in general, but also political leaders, have problems understanding it.

The influence of parliaments on fundamental political decisions, including the budget and redistribution, is becoming more and more marginal in spite of certain attempts to allow more discussion. Instead, power is shared among the executives acting, with the support of the European Commission, in a mode of what the GFCC calls 'intergovernmental governing'. The democratic deficit of the EMU is tangible and the gap between political decision-makers and EU citizens is reaching unsustainable levels. The attempt to remedy the situation by including parliaments in the debate and interparliamentary cooperation does not seem to be sufficient to bring about the democratic legitimacy needed.

Instead of further fine-tuning the existing system and adding certain channels for information and dialogue with NPs, the time has come to consider more or less radical alternatives. To better assist the Member States in financial difficulties, one solution proposed was the mutualization of debt through the issuance of Eurobonds. Its interest rates would be moderate and allow these states to recover more easily. Apart from the German veto and the consideration of the GFCC that no automatism may be

stresses that 'this cooperation should not be seen as establishing a new joint parliamentary body, which would be both ineffective and illegitimate from a democratic and constitutional point of view, and reaffirms that there is no substitute for a formal strengthening of the full legitimacy of the European Parliament, as a parliamentary body at Union level, with a view to reinforcing the democratic governance of the EMU' (para 32).

[69] European Commission, Blueprint (n 65) 36.

established regarding the liability of Germany for foreign sovereign debt beyond the *Bundestag*'s control, a very simple principle is relevant: no common liability without common policy.[70] The Commission's Blueprint gives a more detailed explanation of this principle:

> [s]pecial challenges to ensure appropriate democratic accountability would arise in case the Treaty is changed to permit the mutualisation of the issuance of sovereign debt underpinned by a joint and several guarantee of all euro area Member States. The underlying accountability problem is that such a joint and several guarantee, if claimed by creditors, may result in considerable financial burden for one individual Member State's finances, for which that Member State's parliament is accountable, although the burden is the result of policy decisions that have been made over time by one or several other Member States under the responsibility of their parliaments. As long as the EU level is not granted very far-reaching powers to determine economic policy in the euro area and the European Parliament is not responsible for deciding on the resources of a substantial central budget either, this fundamental accountability problem cannot be overcome simply by entrusting the management of mutualised sovereign debt to an EU executive even if it is accountable to the European Parliament.[71]

The Commission also frames a possible solution: new provisions on a common economic and financial policy following the 'Community method' and thereby establishing conditions where the system of dual legitimacy and accountability—to NPs and the EP—would be put in place. It suggests that the 'problem would no longer arise in a full fiscal and economic union'. This union would 'itself dispose of a substantial central budget'; it would have a 'targeted, autonomous power of taxation', as well as the possibility to issue its 'own sovereign debt, concomitant with a large-scale pooling of sovereignty over the conduct of economic policy at EU level'. Member States would not be jointly and severally liable for each other's sovereign debt but at most for that of the EU. Regarding democratic legitimacy, the Commission envisages the EP to 'have reinforced powers to co-legislate on such autonomous taxation and provide the necessary democratic scrutiny for all decisions taken by the EU's executive'.[72]

The open question remains of the role of NPs in such a new context. Two aspects need to be considered. First, does a full fiscal and economic union exceed the constitutional limits set by the budgetary autonomy of NPs (1)? Secondly, how can we design an appropriate participation of NPs in EU decision-making (2)?

3.3.1 A Full Fiscal and Economic Union and National Budgetary Autonomy

Would the Member States lose their key responsibility for the budget in a fully-fledged fiscal and economic union and be deprived of their 'overall budgetary responsibility', contrary to the constitutional limits established by the GFCC?[73] The answer to this question, as far as limits set by German constitutional law are concerned, can be found in the Lisbon Treaty judgment. The GFCC clearly draws the red line. The constitutional limits regarding the protection of the budgetary autonomy would be exceeded only 'if the determination of the type and amount of the levies imposed on the citizen were supranationalized to a considerable extent'.[74]

[70] Ingolf Pernice, 'Währungsunion—Zuerst kommt die europäische Disziplin', WHI Paper 04/2011 http://www.whi-berlin.eu/tl_files/documents/whi-paper0411.pdf (last accessed 4 August 2016).

[71] European Commission, Blueprint (n 65) 40.

[72] ibid.

[73] See the text accompanying nn 28–34.

[74] GFCC, *Lisbon Treaty* judgment (n 29) para 256.

An increased financial capacity of the EU, based upon targeted and limited powers of taxation at the EU level, would thus not be contrary to this constitutional requirement. Indeed, the GFCC had already clarified in the Maastricht Treaty judgment that the asymmetry of the EMU may need to be corrected. It expressly envisaged new steps towards a full-blown EMU if needed to safeguard its functioning as a stability union. This was confirmed in the *ESM* judgment, where the Court held that 'a continuous further development of the monetary union may be necessary if otherwise the conception of the monetary union, which had been designed as a stability union, would be departed from'. So, it leaves the door open for proceeding beyond the original structure of the EMU with a view to counteracting 'possible weaknesses of the monetary union' by amending EU law.[75]

This is not the place for a comprehensive consideration of possible amendments to the EU Treaties that might be in conformity with the limits set by the GFCC[76] and a number of other national constitutional courts.[77] Legally binding legislative provisions on and requirements for national budgets, adopted under the ordinary legislative procedure under Article 294 TFEU, could be drafted so as to leave sufficient leeway to NPs for autonomous budgetary policies in accordance with the respective political priorities of each of the Member States. The measures could be restricted to the key parameters necessary to ensure economic convergence and prevent excessive macroeconomic imbalances, but also be more specific and impose clear obligations and quantitative limits on national budgetary authorities. Such restrictive measures could be supported by financial flows through a revised system of structural funds and a drastically increased capacity of the cohesion fund. Other measures could be considered, including an enhanced European regional policy setting out a common unemployment insurance scheme so as to develop comparable living conditions throughout the Union.

Giving up the principle of exclusive national competence within the fields of economic, fiscal, and social policies and replacing it with a shared responsibility with limited EU powers in these fields following the Community method would considerably simplify the mechanisms established so far. The application of the ordinary legislative procedure would entail the involvement of the European Parliament and, as national provisions on the oversight over the governments taking fiscal and economic decisions in the Council evolve, NPs. This would ensure more transparent decision-making, including the usual channels for public participation and debate at the national and EU levels.

3.3.2 Enhanced Participation of National Parliaments in EU Decision-making

Are there ways to enhance the participation of NPs in EU decision-making on economic and fiscal policy-making in a fully-fledged economic and fiscal Union? The existing Treaties contain diverse tools for that, including a veto for NPs in matters of

[75] GFCC, Order of 12 September 2012, 2 BvR 1390/12, 1421/12, 1438/12, 1439/12, 1440/12, and 2 BvE 6/12 (*ESM interim*), para 118.

[76] See further Ingolf Pernice, 'Domestic Courts, Constitutional Constraints and European Democracy: What Solution for the Crisis?' in Maurice Adams, Federico Fabbrini, and Pierre Larouche (eds), *The Constitutionalization of European Budgetary Constraints* (Hart Publishing 2014) 297, 306–18.

[77] See a comprehensive analysis of the jurisprudence of national constitutional courts regarding 'the new constitution of EMU' in Federico Fabbrini, 'The Euro Crisis and the Courts: Judicial Review and the Political Process in Comparative Perspective' (2014) 32 Berkeley J Int'l L 64, 74–103 and 106.

particular political sensitivity, and they serve as a model for an appropriate control of NPs over Council decisions. Examples can be found in the involvement of NPs under Article 311(2) TFEU on the own resources of the EU, in the veto for NPs in Article 48(7)(3) TEU regarding the general *passerelle* clause with regard to Treaty revision, or the right of NPs to oppose measures envisaged by the Council in the area of family law under Article 81(3) TFEU. The 'emergency break' under Article 82(3) and 83(3) TFEU regarding measures to be taken under the ordinary legislative procedure in the area of judicial cooperation in criminal matters can also be understood as giving each NP a degree of control over the legislative activities of the Council, although this in a more indirect manner because of the need for the parliament concerned to convince its own government to request referral of the draft to the European Council.

Such instruments, however, are rather defensive and negative. They do not enable NPs to participate positively in and contribute to EU decision-making processes. More promising seem to be mechanisms of 'legitimate and accountable joint decision-making',[78] which reflects autonomous budgetary decisions made at the national level and the economic and distributional policies made at the EU level concerning the common responsibilities for stability, growth, and convergence and for the proper functioning of the EMU based upon the economic and social cohesion of the Union. Because of the need to reconcile the democratic responsibilities of the individual Member States and their parliaments with the common EU interest of achieving the objectives laid down in Article 3 TEU—in particular the well-being of the people (para 1), sustainable development based on balanced economic growth and price stability (para 3) and a functioning EMU (para 4 and Article 119 TFEU)—special provision for joint decision-making giving NPs a real stake is needed.

The German 'Glienicker Gruppe' proposed a new 'Euro Treaty for the Euro Union', establishing a 'Euro Parliament' that consists either of members of the EP or of NPs, to choose and scrutinize a 'Euro Government'.[79] The French 'Groupe Eiffel' has made a similar proposal with a manifesto advocating a 'Euro Community', although their 'Assembly' would consist of members directly elected by the peoples of the participating states on the same day and according to the same rules.[80] It is questionable, however, whether the Eurogroup should create its own constitutional framework, given that the Treaties view the EMU with the common currency as an element of the EU as a whole, provide for diverse obligations regarding economic and fiscal policies for all the Member States, and thus take account of the fact that special policies of the Eurozone have a strong impact on the Member States outside the Eurozone. A separation does not seem to comply with the principles of the Treaties setting a common objective for the Union as a whole and requiring all the Member States, including those that do not (yet) have the euro, to cooperate in order to achieve this objective.

The second problem of these proposals is the institutional separation of the Euro-Parliament, whatever its composition, from NPs. Joint decision-making would require a 'Joint Assembly', encompassing the budgetary committees of the EP and NPs meeting in plenary where decisions of a general character are taken, but also meeting in

[78] ibid 121.

[79] Glienicker Group, 'Towards a Euro Union', October 2013 http://glienickergruppe.eu/en/towards-a-euro-union (last accessed 4 August 2016).

[80] Groupe Eiffel, 'For a Euro Community', February 2014 http://bruegel.org/2014/08/for-a-euro-community (last accessed 4 August 2016). A recent announcement by the French President Hollande indicates a similar direction. See 'Hollande fordert Parlament für Eurozone' *Zeit Online*, 14 July 2015 http://www.zeit.de/politik/ausland/2015-07/griechenland-francois-hollande-euro-zone-parlament (last accessed 4 August 2016).

country-specific compositions where country-specific decisions are at stake. This assembly should have the power of codecision with the European Council on general guidelines and with the Council on any specific decisions related to the economic and fiscal policies of the Union having an impact on national budgetary, economic, and redistributive policies.

It is true that the EP should be the primary source of democratic legitimacy for EU policies, just as NPs play this role with respect to domestic policies. However, given the interdependence and spill-over of economic and fiscal policies in a multi-level polity like the EU—with an internal market and, for most of the Member States, a common currency—and given the increasing restrictive effects of the coordination and discipline of national policies required for the functioning of the EMU, special arrangements for the inclusion of NPs in the control over EU decisions on the common framework of these policies need to be established.

4. Conclusions

What do all these findings and ideas tell us with regard to the general title of this volume—resilience or resignation of NPs in the EU? Resignation could seem to be the most likely attitude in situations where Member States are under the threat of bankruptcy and negotiate a memorandum of understanding under the ESM in order to receive assistance. Not much is left of the budgetary or political autonomy of NPs also in cases where, under the enhanced coordination and surveillance mechanisms introduced by the Six Pack and the Two Pack, the heads of state and government in the European Council, the ministers in the Council, and the Commission establish principles and guidelines regarding national economic and redistributive policies, to be followed by national authorities without direct participation or effective control by NPs in these decision-making processes.

Remedies to such increasing executive federalism exist, however, both at the national and EU levels. This is the time of resilience. NPs may correct the situation by increasing their political control over, and the accountability of, their respective governments through appropriate constitutional or legislative mechanisms of consultation and reporting. Regarding the EU level, they may initiate amendments of the relevant provisions of secondary law and, if required, of the EU Treaties with a view to establishing a system of joint decision-making through a 'Joint Assembly', which would control the executives' action in coordinating and guiding the economic, fiscal, and social policies of the Member States. With such mechanisms in place, the resilience of NPs will replace resignation and the EMU will be prepared to tackle the challenges of the financial markets more effectively and more democratically.

8

Accountability of the European Central Bank in a Deepening Economic Monetary Union

Davor Jančić

1. Two Crises, Five Presidents, One Idea: Completing the Economic and Monetary Union

The financial crisis, which to a great extent originated from the unfettered issuance of subprime mortgages in the US, spilt over to the European continent after the bankruptcy of the Lehman Brothers in autumn 2008. This created an unfavourable financial climate in Europe and worldwide.[1] Plummeting confidence and trust in the ability of credit institutions, primarily banks, to make good on their financial obligations practically ground regular money circulation to a halt. Cross-border interbank lending, which is crucial for a normal functioning of the EU economy by ensuring adequate money supply through the provision of credit to enterprises, was severely restricted.[2] As a result, access to money, needed by states to pay off their public debt and invest, was no longer easily available.

This crisis exacerbated the predicaments caused by Greece's decade-long concealment of genuine public debt levels soon after adopting the euro in 2001, which it did by entering into complex financial deals with large US investment banks, primarily Goldman Sachs, through the use of derivatives and, above all, cross-currency swaps.[3] Since these were not treated as loans but as currency trades, such deals were kept away from the public eye and off the state's balance sheets. This, together with other 'creative' accounting practices, enabled Greece to misreport its deficit statistics to the EU, thus meeting the latter's prescribed targets while at the same time spending beyond its means.[4] These machinations were revealed in October 2009. Fearful that Greece had become unable to pay its sovereign debt due to overwhelming financing difficulties, global capital markets reacted negatively. The price of Greek government bonds plunged and their yield soared, making it ever more expensive for Greece to borrow

[1] Caroline Bradley, 'From Global Financial Crisis to Sovereign Debt Crisis and Beyond: What Lies Ahead for the European Monetary Union?' (2013) 22 Transnat'l L & Contemp Probs 9.

[2] Juan Carlos Frutos and others, 'Stressed Inter-bank Markets: Evidence from the European Financial and Sovereign Debt Crisis', ECB Working Paper No 1925, June 2016.

[3] This type of deal allowed Greece to swap government debt issued in US dollars and Japanese yen for euro-denominated debt for an agreed period of time according to a fictional, more favourable exchange rate, which effectively amounted to a loan. On paper, therefore, Greece had more euros to pay its bills and less debt on its accounting books. Beat Balzli, 'Greek Debt Crisis: How Goldman Sachs Helped Greece to Mask Its True Debt' *Der Spiegel (Online International)*, 8 February 2010 http://www.spiegel.de/international/europe/greek-debt-crisis-how-goldman-sachs-helped-greece-to-mask-its-true-debt-a-676634.html (last accessed 21 July 2016).

[4] Louise Story, Landon Thomas Jr, and Nelson D Schwartz, 'Wall St. Helped to Mask Debt Fueling Europe's Crisis' *New York Times*, 13 February 2010 http://www.nytimes.com/2010/02/14/business/global/14debt.html?pagewanted=all&_r=0# (last accessed 21 July 2016).

and repay its lenders.[5] This posed a serious 'contagion' risk, which eventually materialized. In different forms, solvency and liquidity problems befell a number of other Member States apart from Greece, thereby precipitating a wholesale sovereign debt crisis in the Eurozone, known as the euro crisis. In the event, not only Greece, but also Portugal, Ireland, and Spain received taxpayer-funded bail-outs, while Cyprus profited from a combination of a bail-out and a bail-in. Following the turmoil caused by the UK's referendum in favour of 'Brexit', Italy, the Union's oft-touted weak link, considered requesting a waiver from the EU's state aid prohibitions and bank bail-in rules in order to support its banking sector.[6]

The overarching EU plan for eliminating the Member States' financial woes that threaten the stability of the euro area as a whole was presented in the so-called 'Five Presidents' Report' of 22 June 2015.[7] This cross-institutional blueprint for a sustainable future of the Economic and Monetary Union (EMU) is based on personal discussions of these presidents, with the aim of achieving four 'Unions' by 2025. These are a 'genuine' Economic Union, a Financial Union, a Fiscal Union, and a Political Union. These are to be achieved inter alia by: creating a set of national competitiveness authorities and reinforcing the European Semester; completing the Banking Union through a Deposit Insurance Scheme[8] and launching the Capital Markets Union; and establishing an advisory European Fiscal Board and the possibility of setting up a euro area treasury in the future.[9] For all of them, it is acknowledged that public risk sharing has to be accompanied by 'stronger democratic participation and accountability both at national and European levels'.[10] However, the proposals to this end are rather minor and have rightly been assessed as the 'weakest' element of the Five Presidents' Report.[11] Namely, to secure legitimacy for the completion of the EMU, the report only envisages an enhancement of the economic dialogue between the European Parliament (EP) and the Commission, the Council and the Eurogroup through dedicated time-slots during the course of the European Semester, above all before and after the publication of the Annual Growth Survey and upon the presentation of country-specific recommendations. It also foresees efforts to make interaction with national parliaments (NPs) more efficient. The UK House of Lords correctly observed that the report's proposals on democratic accountability are 'largely exhortatory' and that organizing debates and hearings

[5] Roberto A de Santis, 'The Euro Area Sovereign Debt Crisis: Identifying Flight-to-Liquidity and the Spillover Mechanisms' (2014) 26 J Empirical Finance 150.

[6] Alex Barker and Rachel Sanderson, 'Renzi Seeks Help for Italy's Banks after Brexit Wobble' *Financial Times*, 27 June 2016. See particularly art 43 ff of Directive 2014/59/EU of the European Parliament and of the Council of 15 May 2014 establishing a framework for the recovery and resolution of credit institutions and investment firms and amending Council Directive 82/891/EEC, and Directives 2001/24/EC, 2002/47/EC, 2004/25/EC, 2005/56/EC, 2007/36/EC, 2011/35/EU, 2012/30/EU, and 2013/36/EU, and Regulations (EU) No 1093/2010 and (EU) No 648/2012 of the European Parliament and of the Council (Bank Recovery and Resolution Directive) [2014] OJ L 173/190. See also Karl Philipp Wojcik, 'Bail-in in the Banking Union' (2016) 53 CML Rev 91.

[7] The document entitled 'Completing Europe's Economic and Monetary Union' was adopted by the following five presidents: Jean-Claude Juncker (European Commission), Donald Tusk (European Council), Jeroen Dijsselbloem (Eurogroup), Mario Draghi (ECB), and Martin Schulz (European Parliament).

[8] European Commission, Proposal for a Regulation of the European Parliament and of the Council amending Regulation (EU) No 806/2014 in order to establish a European Deposit Insurance Scheme, COM(2015) 586.

[9] See Nazaré da Costa Cabral, 'Which Budgetary Union for the E(M)U?' (2016) 54 JCMS 1280.

[10] Five Presidents' Report (n 7) 5. See also Koen Lenaerts, 'EMU and the EU's Constitutional Framework' (2014) 39 EL Rev 753, 768–69.

[11] Dermot Hodson, 'Eurozone Governance: From the Greek Drama of 2015 to the Five Presidents' Report' (2016) 54 JCMS 162.

with Commissioners in the EP and NPs is 'not the same as ... exercising control over the process'.[12]

This chapter examines the democratic dimension of the burgeoning competence of the European Central Bank (ECB or the Bank) in the functioning of the EMU in the aftermath of the euro crisis.[13] It begins by laying out the EU's general monetary policy framework and the position of the ECB within it (section 2). On this basis, the next section analyses the variety of legal and policy measures that were taken in the aftermath of the crisis to contain the erosion of the Eurozone (section 3). The inquiry then turns to the existing mechanisms for the ECB's accountability to parliaments, including both the EP and NPs. The chapter first focuses on the accountability practices with respect to the ECB's monetary policy (section 4) and then on those concerning the Bank's role in prudential supervision under the rules of Banking Union (section 5). The concluding section outlines both the pitfalls and the advantages that these arrangements carry and highlights how the ECB and the EU's parliaments, particularly NPs, have adapted to the changed circumstances (section 6).

2. General Framework for EU Monetary Policy: Prohibition-based Stability

The primary goal of the EU's Monetary Union (the 'M' in the EMU) is price stability and the secondary goal is to 'support the general economic policies in the Union'.[14] Central to maintaining stable prices is ensuring that inflation is kept at a healthy level—usually below but close to 2 per cent over the medium term. Ensuring this is the core task of monetary policy. This is conducted by the Eurosystem, which consists of the ECB and the national central banks (NCBs) of the euro area Member States.[15] The ECB has four bodies: the Executive Board (President, Vice-President, and four other members), the Governing Council (Executive Board and euro area NCB governors), a transitional General Council in charge of administering derogations from the euro (President, Vice-President, and all NCB governors),[16] and a newly created Supervisory Board, examined further below.[17] It is the Governing Council that decides monetary policy and does so chiefly by setting a series of interest rates and by granting credit facilities, but also by determining intermediate monetary objectives and reserve supply levels.[18] The Executive Board then implements these in accordance with the Governing Council's guidelines and decisions.

Fiscal stability in the EMU is ensured by four prohibitions, which are necessary because the EU's Economic Union is not a single policy like the Monetary Union but

[12] House of Lords, EU Committee, HL Paper 143 '"Whatever it Takes": The Five Presidents' Report on Completing Economic and Monetary Union', 13th Report of Session 2015–16 of 12 May 2016, para 186, p. 51.

[13] Renaud Dehousse, 'Why Has EU Macroeconomic Governance Become More Supranational?' (2016) 38 J Eur Integration 617, 618; Rachel A Epstein and Martin Rhodes, 'The Political Dynamics Behind Europe's New Banking Union' (2016) 39 WEP 415; Zdenek Kudrna, 'Financial Market Regulation: Crisis-induced Supranationalization' (2016) 38 J Eur Integration 251; Thomas Beukers, 'The New ECB and Its Relationship With the Eurozone Member States: Between Central Bank Independence and Central Bank Intervention' (2013) 50 CML Rev 1579.

[14] TFEU, art 119(2)–(3). [15] ibid art 282(1). [16] ibid art 283.

[17] While the first three ECB bodies are the 'decision-making bodies' foreseen in the Treaties, the Supervisory Board is the only one created by secondary law.

[18] Protocol (No 4) on the Statute of the European System of Central Banks and of the European Central Bank, art 12.

a collection of coordinated national policies. In addition to the prohibition of excessive deficits and of privileged access by EU and national bodies to financial institutions, two further prohibitions are crucial for the present discussion.[19]

The first one is the *prohibition of bail-outs*, which means that neither the Union nor any Member State is liable for or may assume the commitments and liabilities of any central, regional, or local government or authority existing within the EU.[20] The second is the *prohibition of monetary financing*, which rules out both agreeing any credit or overdraft facility with the ECB or a NCB and direct purchase by these two types of banks of debt instruments (eg bonds) from the said governments or public authorities.[21] These prohibitions aim to ensure that the Member States remain subject to market discipline when they borrow in capital markets, which is only viable if their fiscal situation is sound. The said prohibitions therefore seek to ensure the Member States' budgetary diligence as required by the rules of EU economic governance, which could be frustrated if the Union or one or more Member States were allowed to act as guarantors for another Member State's debt.

3. Post-euro Crisis Reshaping of the Economic and Monetary Union: Tighter Economics, Looser Finance

The shape of the EMU has dramatically changed after the euro crisis, with considerable repercussions for democratic participation.[22] To avert the crisis spreading across the Eurozone, the EU took extensive action. For years, the Union has been adopting measures to reinstate financial stability, restore market confidence in the resilience of the euro area economies, and stem the spiralling indebtedness of some, mostly 'peripheral', Member States in Southern Europe. These measures can be divided into four strands: economic governance, lending, the Banking Union, and unconventional monetary policy.[23]

3.1 Economic Governance Reform's Fiscal Inroads

First, the EU overhauled the system of *economic governance*. As explained in the introductory chapter to this volume, the Six Pack, the Two Pack, and the Fiscal Compact resulted in the strengthening of the preventive and corrective components of the Member States' fiscal commitments. These concern the Union's economic policy

[19] Rosa M Lastra and Jean-Victor Louis, 'European Economic and Monetary Union: History, Trends, and Prospects' (2013) 32 YEL 57, 98.

[20] TFEU, art 125. This prohibition proved to be a misnomer in light of the *Pringle* case: Case C-370/12, *Thomas Pringle v Government of Ireland*, judgment of 27 November 2012, ECLI:EU:C:2012:756.

[21] TFEU, art 123(1).

[22] David Howarth and Lucia Quaglia, 'Banking Union as Holy Grail: Rebuilding the Single Market in Financial Services, Stabilizing Europe's Banks and "Completing" Economic and Monetary Union' (2013) 51 (Annual Review) JCMS 103, 119. See also John E Fossum and Agustin J Menéndez (eds), *The European Union in Crises or the European Union as Crises?*, ARENA Report No 2/14; Bruno de Witte, Adrienne Héritier, and Alexander H Trechsel (eds), *The Euro Crisis and the State of European Democracy* (European University Institute 2013).

[23] Most recently, options for debt relief or the so-called 'haircut' involving public creditors have been examined, including the possibility of extending the maturity of loans, reducing interest rates, transforming loans into interest-free bonds, and debt cuts on nominal values. See Armin Steinbach, 'The "Haircut" of Public Creditors under EU Law' (2016) 12 EuConst 223, 225.

coordination, oversight over national budgets through the European Semester, the maintenance of balanced budgets, and the avoidance of macroeconomic imbalances.

In the reformed framework of EU economic governance, the EP's competence has only been marginally strengthened and it thus remains rather limited.[24] By the same token, while NPs have acquired certain new rights of approval, scrutiny, and debate in the domestic budgetary process,[25] their competences are left constrained by more vigorous overarching EU fiscal parameters.[26] The latter are proposed and monitored by the Commission and set by the Council during the European Semester process, with both of them acting based on priorities decided by the European Council. However, it has been submitted that the effects of EU economic policy centralization on national sovereignty have been 'widely exaggerated'.[27]

The EP and NPs have moreover formalized their fiscal policy cooperation through a new interparliamentary conference. This is based on Article 13 of the Fiscal Compact.[28]

3.2 Lending Away the Crisis

Secondly, the Union engaged in *lending*. In these exceptional circumstances, the Union and the Member States stepped out of the boundaries of EU law and concluded the European Stability Mechanism (ESM) Treaty, which laid down arrangements for assisting governments in financial distress in order to improve their creditworthiness and thus reduce pressure on their domestic fiscal policies. This resulted in the creation of the ESM on 27 September 2012 as a fund financed by the euro area states and entitled to grant loans to such governments. The ESM then replaced two earlier temporary funds—the European Financial Stabilisation Mechanism (EFSM, created on 10 May 2010) and the European Financial Stability Facility (EFSF, created on 7 June 2010).

To receive a loan, the Member State must conclude a Memorandum of Understanding with the European Commission, the ECB, and the International Monetary Fund (IMF), which imposes strict conditions. These conditions require the recipient state to enact wide-ranging restrictive reforms in areas of law-making where the Union typically does not have competence to act or where it may only support, coordinate, or supplement otherwise national action. These areas encompass taxation, public spending, social welfare, employment, privatization, and healthcare. These are traditionally core areas of national sovereignty. This is salient because such austerity policies, pursued with a view to filling the Member States' budgets with ESM-loaned money to enable them to pay their international creditors, caused unemployment to rise and economic growth to slow down.

The *Pringle* jurisprudence,[29] initiated by an independent Irish left-wing MP Thomas Pringle and relayed to the Court of Justice of the European Union (CJEU) by the Irish Supreme Court by means of a preliminary ruling, epitomizes the tensions surrounding

[24] Cristina Fasone, 'European Economic Governance and Parliamentary Representation. What Place for the European Parliament?' (2014) 20 ELJ 164.

[25] Davor Jančić, 'National Parliaments and EU Fiscal Integration' (2016) 22 ELJ 225.

[26] Mark Dawson, 'The Legal and Political Accountability Structure of "Post-Crisis" EU Economic Governance' (2016) 53 JCMS 976, 988.

[27] Dariusz Adamski, 'Economic Policy Coordination as a Game Involving Economic Stability and National Sovereignty' (2016) 22 ELJ 180.

[28] See more in the chapter by Ian Cooper in this volume.

[29] Case C-370/12, *Thomas Pringle v Government of Ireland* (n 20). See the German Federal Constitutional Court's stance on the ESM in Special Section 'The ESM before the Court' (2013) 14 German LJ 1.

the lending dimension of the euro crisis. Among other things, this case challenged the creation of the ESM and the EU's compliance with the 'no bail-out' clause. Unsurprisingly, albeit dubiously, the CJEU relied on a highly formalistic, and for that matter problematic, interpretation of the EU rules to decide that the clause had not been breached. This conclusion was reached because Member States continue to be responsible for their debt, because loans may only be provided where that is necessary to safeguard the stability of the euro area as a whole, and because the disbursement of funds is subject to the fulfilment of strict conditions.[30] The case has important further consequences for the ECB's participation in ESM lending. The CJEU clarified that the ESM Treaty, including conditionality compliance monitoring, does not alter the essential character of the powers that the Treaties confer on the ECB.[31] However, ECB members could 'face conflicts of interests and threats to their independence' if they were to perform tasks within competing institutions.[32] This then negatively impacts both the EP's and NPs' ability to have a grip over the developments oriented at preserving financial stability through inter se agreements.[33]

3.3 The Banking Union's Promotion of the European Central Bank

Thirdly, in an act of 'unprecedented transfer of sovereignty',[34] the EU created the so-called *Banking Union*, aiming to decouple the banking sector from the state, thus preventing the use of taxpayers' money to rescue failing banks.[35] This was performed by establishing single EU mechanisms for the prudential supervision and resolution of banks. The third element, the Deposit Insurance Scheme, is currently undergoing legislative procedure.[36]

The Single Supervisory Mechanism (SSM),[37] composed of the ECB and the competent national supervisory authorities, is key for the present analysis because it has significantly empowered the ECB—conferring on it a far-reaching competence to carry out prudential supervision over all euro area credit institutions, predominantly banks (about 6,000 of them). Direct supervision over the largest and systemically most important banks is carried out by the ECB itself (123 of them), while the other ones are supervised by national supervisors. However, the ECB is also entitled to grant or withdraw authorization of all euro area banks, assess acquisition of qualifying holdings, carry out reviews and investigations which include stress tests and on-site inspections, and impose administrative penalties of up to 10 per cent of the total annual turnover.

[30] Case C-370/12, *Thomas Pringle v Government of Ireland* (n 20) para 138. See a positive assessment in Bruno de Witte and Thomas Beukers, 'The Court of Justice Approves the Creation of the European Stability Mechanism: Pringle' (2013) 50 CML Rev 805.

[31] Case C-370/12, *Thomas Pringle v Government of Ireland* (n 20) para 162.

[32] Steve Peers, 'Towards a New Form of EU Law? The Use of EU Institutions Outside the EU Legal Framework' (2013) 9 EuConst 37, 70.

[33] Angelos Dimopoulos, 'Taming the Conclusion of *Inter Se* Agreements between EU Member States: The Role of the Duty of Loyalty' (2015) 34 YEL 286, 294.

[34] Kern Alexander, 'European Banking Union: A Legal and Institutional Analysis of the Single Supervisory Mechanism and the Single Resolution Mechanism' (2015) 40 EL Rev 154, 158.

[35] See Jens-Hinrich Binder and Stefan Grundmann (eds), Special Issue 'The Banking Union and the Creation of Duties' (2015) 16 EBOL Rev 353.

[36] See n 8.

[37] See Gianni Lo Schiavo, 'Single Supervisory Mechanism: Building the New Top-down Cooperative Supervisory Governance in Europe' in Federico Fabbrini, Ernst H Ballin, and Han Somsen (eds), *What Form of Government for the European Union and the Eurozone?* (Hart Publishing 2015).

3.4 Unconventional or Non-standard Monetary Policy's Economic Effects

Fourthly, the ECB moved towards *unconventional or non-standard tools of monetary policy* in order to ensure its effectiveness in occasioning economic growth. These are last-resort measures when standard interest-rate policies have been exhausted, which is when the ECB's main lending rate is zero or goes into the negative territory. Such policies, it has been argued, have led to an institutional conversion of the EMU away from its pre-crisis constitutional blueprint.[38] Two non-standard monetary policy tools are central here, and both are asset purchase programmes effected by the creation of new money by the ECB. They are the Outright Monetary Transactions programme (OMT) and Quantitative Easing (QE), which are examined in turn.

Announced on 6 September 2012,[39] OMT enables the ECB to buy an unlimited amount of sovereign bonds of troubled Eurozone Member States in secondary capital markets, with a focus on short-term bonds with maturities of between one and three years.[40] While unlimited in volume, this programme is conditional on the country's participation in the EFSF/ESM and on full respect for and implementation of the agreed macroeconomic adjustment or precautionary programmes, failing which OMT could be suspended. The intermediate goal of OMT is thus to help reduce the Member States' borrowing costs in capital markets. This, however, serves the overall objective of restoring both the transmission mechanism of monetary policy and the belief in the irreversibility of the euro, which became necessary to deflate the so-called 'dissolution' or 'convertibility' risk. The incumbent President of the ECB, Mario Draghi, defended this programme in the Spanish Parliament, arguing that: 'OMTs are a backstop against destructive speculation. They are not a subsidy for government financing. OMTs should remove only the part of the interest rate at which governments borrow that is due to unfounded expectations of destructive scenarios for the euro area'.[41] Although OMT has hitherto not been activated, it replaced its predecessor—the Securities Markets Programme (2010–2012)—which was both limited in quantitative terms and unconditional.

QE relates to a number of asset purchase programmes involving both private and public sector issuers. This complemented the ECB's non-standard liquidity-providing measures: long-term refinancing operations (LTROs, maturity up to three years), targeted longer-term refinancing operations (TLTROs, maturity up to four years), and emergency lending assistance. The ECB began its QE operations in October 2014 through the purchase of covered bonds, which it continued doing with asset-backed securities the following month. The 'shopping list' was extended from these two types of corporate bond-buying programmes to public sector debt in the form of sovereign bonds in March 2015. In a further boost, in June 2016 the ECB expanded the two

[38] Arie Krampf, 'From Transparency to Ambiguity: The Impact of the ECB's Unconventional Policies on the EMU' (2016) 38 J Eur Integration 455, 467.

[39] European Central Bank press release, 'Technical Features of Outright Monetary Transactions' http://www.ecb.europa.eu/press/pr/date/2012/html/pr120906_1.en.html (last accessed 23 July 2016).

[40] See more on the conception and design of the OMT in Domenico Lombardi and Manuela Moschella, 'The Government Bond Buying Programmes of the European Central Bank: An Analysis of Their Policy Settings' (2016) 23 JEPP 851.

[41] European Central Bank, 'Introductory Statement at the Congreso de los Diputados de España', Madrid, 12 February 2013 http://www.ecb.europa.eu/press/key/date/2013/html/sp130212_1.en.html (last accessed 28 August 2016).

existing categories of corporate bond-buying and undertook new private sector debt purchases. While similar, QE differs from OMT in its nature, breadth, and objective. It is not tied to public policy conditionality within the ESM framework; rather, it is aimed at all Member States and companies, and it seeks not to shore up countries in financial difficulties but to stimulate economic activity and incentivize inflation by injecting the banking system with the necessary liquidity.[42]

Of the two types of non-standard monetary policy programmes, the legality of OMT was strongly questioned by the German Federal Constitutional Court (*BVerfG*) in its first ever preliminary ruling reference to the CJEU. This was prompted by an action brought by Peter Gauweiler, a former *Bundestag* member for the German Christian Social Union, and a number of other applicants.[43] One of the *BVerfG*'s key concerns was that the ECB was transgressing the powers conferred on it by the Treaties and that it was seeking to conduct economic rather than monetary policy, thus encroaching on the legislative and budgetary competences of the *Bundestag*.[44] Democracy was hence of critical importance.[45] When the ECJ replied validating OMT,[46] the *BVerfG* bowed but not before making further democracy caveats.[47] While accepting that OMT does not violate the *Bundestag*'s budgetary authority as long as the conditions prescribed by the ECJ with a view to restricting the scope and use of OMT are met, German constitutional judges warned that the principles of democracy, popular sovereignty, and constitutional identity are indeed affected.[48] Therefore, both the Federal Government and the *Bundestag* are obliged closely to monitor any possible implementation of OMT. This is required in order to ascertain that the ECB fulfils the said conditions and that no threat to the federal budget arises from the volume of, and risks associated with, the purchased bonds.[49] Unconventional monetary policies of the ECB thus carry a potential for agency and democracy slippages.[50]

[42] See the economic operation of QE measures in John Driffill, 'Unconventional Monetary Policy in the Euro Zone' (2016) 27 Open Econ Rev 387; Klaus-Jürgen Gern and others, 'Quantitative Easing in the Euro Area: Transmission Channels and Risks' (2015) 50 Intereconomics 206; Nuno Cassola and José Jorge, 'The ECB's OMTs: A Tale of Governments, Investors, and the Central Bank' (2016) 65 J Int'l Money & Finance 94.

[43] *BVerfG*, 2 BvR 2728/13, Order of the Second Senate of 14 January 2014. See more on this in the chapter by Ingolf Pernice in this volume. See also Special Issue 'The OMT Decision of the German Federal Constitutional Court' (2014) 15 German LJ 107.

[44] ibid para 78.

[45] Mattias Wendel, 'Exceeding Judicial Competence in the Name of Democracy: The German Federal Constitutional Court's OMT Reference' (2014) 10 EuConst 263. See more broadly Russell A Miller, 'Germany vs. Europe: The Principle of Democracy in German Constitutional Law and the Troubled Future of European Integration' (2014) 54 Virginia J Int'l L 579.

[46] Case C-62/14, *Peter Gauweiler and Others v Deutscher Bundestag*, judgment of 16 June 2015, ECLI:EU:C:2015:400. See various accounts thereon in Paul Craig and Menelaos Markakis, 'Gauweiler and the Legality of Outright Monetary Transactions' (2016) 41 EL Rev 4; Dariusz Adamski, 'Economic Constitution of the Euro Area After the Gauweiler Preliminary Ruling' (2015) 52 CML Rev 1451; Alicia Hinarejos, 'Gauweiler and the Outright Monetary Transactions Programme: The Mandate of the European Central Bank and the Changing Nature of Economic and Monetary Union' (2015) 11 EuConst 563.

[47] *BVerfG*, 2 BvR 2728/13, judgment of the Second Senate of 21 June 2016.

[48] ibid para 188. [49] ibid para 174.

[50] Anna-Lena Högenauer and David Howarth, 'Unconventional Monetary Policies and the ECB's Problematic Democratic Legitimacy' (2016), manuscript on file with the author.

4. Accountability of the European Central Bank for Monetary Policy

4.1 Accountability to the European Parliament

The Treaties require that all EU institutions, including the ECB, shall aim to promote the Union's values, one of which is democracy.[51] However, in the case of the ECB, this is watered down by endowing the Bank with legal personality and by 'constitutionalizing' its independence in fulfilling its Treaty mandate.[52] Thus, neither the European nor the national central banks may seek or take instructions from any EU institution, Member State, or any other external body.[53]

Consequently, the Treaty framework for the ECB's accountability is rather thin,[54] geared principally towards an exchange of information and reporting.[55] The ECB shall send an annual report on the activities of the European System of Central Banks (ESCB)[56] and on the monetary policy to the EP, the Commission, the Council, and the European Council. The President of the ECB shall present this report to the Council and the EP. The EP's supervisory function is limited to: (a) holding an optional 'general debate' on this report, which in practice results in the adoption of a resolution; and (b) to organizing a hearing with the President and Executive Board members of the ECB in the EP's Committee on Economic and Monetary Affairs (ECON) at their or the EP's request. These hearings are in practice often followed up by written questions to the ECB, to which it regularly replies.[57] There has indeed been a significant surge in the number of written questions sent by EP members (MEPs): 179 in 2015, compared to fifty-five each in 2014 and 2013, thirty-seven in 2012, twenty-eight in 2011, seventeen in 2010, and ten in 2009. This means that the ECB received more question letters from MEPs in a single year of the 8th legislative term (2015) than in the five years of the 7th term (2009–2014).[58]

Further, unless decided otherwise, the proceedings of Governing Council meetings are confidential and the documents produced by this ECB body are not freely available for thirty years.[59] The outcome of the deliberations may be made public and the ECB does so, albeit not in the form of minutes but rather through press conferences and a monthly bulletin. In January 2015, the ECB began publishing additional data, including notably accounts of deliberations of their monetary policy meetings and decisions on emergency liquidity assistance—all in order to increase the transparency of

[51] TEU, art 13(1) in conjunction with TEU, art 2(1).

[52] See the legal and practical aspects of this in René Smits, 'The European Central Bank's Independence and Its Relations with Economic Policy Makers' (2007) 31 Fordham Int'l LJ 1614. See generally on central bank independence Jakob de Haan, Donato Masciandaro, and Marc Quintyn (eds), Special Issue 'Does Central Bank Independence Still Matter?' (2008) 24 Eur J Pol Econ 717.

[53] TFEU, arts 130 and 282(3).

[54] Fabian Amtenbrink, *The Democratic Accountability of Central Banks: A Comparative Study of the European Central Bank* (Hart Publishing 1999).

[55] TFEU, art 284.

[56] The ECB, the NCBs of the euro area Member States and the NCBs of the non-euro area Member States come together to form the European System of Central Banks (ESCB). This collection of central banks, which is thus larger than the Eurosystem, has price stability as its key objective (TFEU, art 282(2)), but, logically, is not the monetary authority of the Eurozone.

[57] European Central Bank, 'The Accountability of the ECB' *Monthly Bulletin*, November 2002, 54.

[58] European Central Bank, 'Annual Report 2015', April 2016, 91.

[59] See Decision of the European Central Bank of 17 June 2004 adopting the Rules of Procedure of the General Council of the European Central Bank, art 10 (ECB/2004/12) (2004/526/EC), OJ L 230/61.

monetary governance.[60] The ECB, additionally, publishes quarterly reports on ESCB activities and weekly consolidated financial statements.[61]

The relationship of political control between the EP and the ECB, rooted in the so-called monetary dialogue, has evolved over time and has begun encompassing discussions of economic policy, albeit that the effectiveness of EP monitoring as a mechanism for reviewing ECB performance has been questioned.[62] Yet one early study shows that, in the first five years of its existence, the ECB exhibited a 'high degree of responsiveness to criticism' within the monetary dialogue, which translated into 71 per cent (five out of seven) of the clearly defined requests of the ECON Committee being heeded by the ECB.[63] Furthermore, while the dialogue has had little effect, or perhaps even a negative one, on the financial markets' stability during the euro crisis, it has contributed to greater democratic legitimacy of ECB policies.[64] The monetary dialogue has therefore given rise to what has been dubbed 'accountable independence' of the ECB, which has 'considerably widened in scope' and become 'especially productive' during the financial and sovereign debt crises.[65] This stems from the symbiotic convergence of the ECB's interest in acquiring legitimacy and the EP's interest in exerting influence on EMU decision-making.

4.2 Accountability to National Parliaments

The ECB defines its accountability as the 'legal and political obligation of an independent central bank to justify and explain its decisions to the citizens and their elected representatives'.[66] It argues that its *input legitimacy* stems from the NPs' approval of the transfer of monetary policy competences to the Union and from the Member States' involvement in the appointment of the ECB's Executive Board and Governing Council. Its *output legitimacy* is derived from the success in its performance of the tasks entrusted to it. Instrumental to this is the Bank's insulation from the vagaries of the political process. Although formally based on the principal–agent relationship,[67] the ECB's accountability is not premised on a possibility to remove central bankers from office.[68] This is precluded by the very nature of monetary policy, which requires policy-makers to concentrate on medium-term economic projections in order for changes in interest rates or other measures to be 'transmitted' to the real economy and thus affect price levels.

For this reason, the accountability of the Union's central bank is deemed more appropriate if effected *ex post* through 'constant scrutiny of the central bank's actions by the parliament and the public at large'.[69] The main goal of this is to verify that the ECB keeps within the margins of the principle of conferral and only exercises

[60] European Central Bank, 'Annual Report 2015' (n 58) 5.

[61] Protocol (No 4) on the Statute of the European System of Central Banks and of the European Central Bank, art 15(1)–(2).

[62] Fabian Amtenbrink and Kees P S van Duin, 'The European Central Bank Before the European Parliament: Theory and Practice After Ten Years of Monetary Dialogue' (2009) 34 EL Rev 561.

[63] Sylvester C W Eijffinger and Edin Mujagić, 'An Assessment of the Effectiveness of the Monetary Dialogue on the ECB's Accountability and Transparency: A Qualitative Approach' (2004) 39 Intereconomics 190, 202–203.

[64] Stefan Collignon and Sebastian Diessner, 'The ECB's Monetary Dialogue with the European Parliament: Efficiency and Accountability during the Euro Crisis?' (2016) 54 JCMS 1296.

[65] Francisco Torres, 'The EMU's Legitimacy and the ECB as a Strategic Political Player in the Crisis Context' (2013) 35 J Eur Integration 287, 295 and 297.

[66] European Central Bank, 'The Accountability of the ECB' (n 57) 46.

[67] Robert Elgie, 'The Politics of the European Central Bank: Principal–Agent Theory and the Democratic Deficit' (2002) 9 JEPP 186.

[68] See Amtenbrink (n 54). [69] ibid 47.

those powers that have been transferred to it by the Treaties. However, there is marginal space for *ex ante* scrutiny too. Namely, the ECB's proposals for EU legislation ('recommendations') have to comply with subsidiarity, since they are considered 'draft legislative acts' for the purposes of the early warning mechanism.[70] The Council shall forward them to NPs and the ECB shall review them where they are challenged by a 'yellow card', deciding whether to maintain, amend, or withdraw them and justifying its decision.[71] Conversely, the ECB wields significant *ex ante* influence over national authorities, which have a legal duty to consult it on draft domestic legislation that falls within the Bank's scope of competence.[72] In this case, it is the ECB that exercises a form of oversight. Therefore, for this advisory function of the ECB, there are no specific accountability arrangements.

Furthermore, the ECB argues that there is an important limitation for both the EP and NPs to hold individual NCB governors to account for its decisions. At the EU level, this is because no EU institution participates in the governors' appointment, and, at the national level, because NPs 'lack the legitimacy to judge' the governors' European duties given that in the performance thereof they are prohibited from defending their Member State's national interest.[73] But the euro crisis has revealed the outbreak of individual rifts within the Governing Council, which demonstrates that any difference in the views held by NCBs is likely to be significantly influenced by the national preferences of their Member State. This is evident from the strong opposition of the German central bank (*Bundesbank*) to the second round of LTROs to euro area banks, which the ECB carried out on 29 February 2012.[74]

After the resignations of an influential member of the ECB Executive Board, Jürgen Stark, and the former *Bundesbank* President, Axel Webber, over the ECB's previous purchase of Greek and Portuguese sovereign bonds, the incumbent *Bundesbank* President, Jens Weidmann, protested this course of action explicitly by sending a letter to the ECB President Draghi. In this letter, Weidmann stressed that the cumulative ECB loan of €529.5 billion to 800 euro area banks, at the low interest rate of 1 per cent for three years, was dangerous because it discouraged structural and capital consolidation of these banks and because the ECB was accepting lower-grade collateral to secure these loans. For Weidmann, this posed a concrete and serious risk for the *Bundesbank* because, if the euro area were to disintegrate, the *Bundesbank* would be left with hundreds of billions of bad debt owed by Southern European banks.

This episode shows that although ECB decision-making is formally focused on price stability, in essence it carries important implications for domestic economic and fiscal policy-making. A further consequence is that, in political terms, EU monetary policy is not completely independent of the national economic and financial interests. In fact, despite being an exclusive competence of the Union, monetary policy is subject to

[70] Protocol (No 2) on the Application of the Principles of Subsidiarity and Proportionality, art 3.

[71] Protocol (No 2) on the Application of the Principles of Subsidiarity and Proportionality, arts 4(3) and 7(a), second sentence.

[72] TFEU, art 127(4) in conjunction with Council Decision 98/415/EC of 29 June 1998 on the consultation of the European Central Bank by national authorities regarding draft legislative provisions, [1998] OJ L 189/42. See also the ECB's guide on this at https://www.ecb.europa.eu/pub/pdf/other/consultationguide201510.en.pdf?cff7d83dc6c3962c3a89bb0c9873739a (last accessed 28 August 2016).

[73] European Central Bank, 'The Accountability of the ECB' (n 57) 49.

[74] Sven Böll and others, 'Euro Crisis Crucible: Rift Grows Between Germany's Bundesbank and ECB' *Der Spiegel (Online International)*, 6 March 2012 http://spon.de/adBhX (last accessed 28 August 2016); Mary Watkins, 'Banks Deposit Record €821 bn at ECB' *Financial Times*, 5 March 2012 https://next.ft.com/content/29e5c006-66a4-11e1-863c-00144feabdc0 (last accessed 28 August 2016).

domestic political pressures striving to protect national identity *qua* monetary policy identity.[75] This, in turn, suggests that the ever-expanding competences of the ECB should not remain entirely unchecked by parliamentary actors.

Addressing this kind of preoccupation, Mario Draghi has since 2012 started appearing in NPs, which his predecessor Jean-Claude Trichet did much less proactively, if at all.[76] Such an approach stems from Draghi's understanding that 'because you are independent, you have to be twice as transparent as anyone else'.[77] Up to now, there have been five such visits, which are examined in turn below.

Following the ECB's announcement of the OMT programme in September 2012, the next month saw Draghi pay a visit to the German *Bundestag*. The two-hour discussion was held behind closed doors with over 100 parliamentarians, including members of the Budget Committee, the Finance Committee, and the European Affairs Committee, as well as the leaders of all parliamentary groups.[78] Recognizing that it was 'rare for the ECB President to speak in a national parliament', Draghi pointed out that the purpose of the gathering was not only ECB accountability but also democratic participation through direct input by parliamentarians. Referring to the OMT programme, Draghi stated:

> I am here today not only to explain the ECB's policies. I am also here to listen. I am here to listen to your views on the ECB, on the euro area economy and on the longer-term vision for Europe ... I would like to explain our view of the current situation and the rationale for our recent monetary policy decisions ... I am aware that some observers in this country remain concerned about the potential impact of this policy. I would therefore like to use this opportunity to go through those concerns – one by one ...[79]

In particular, Draghi offered four assurances: (a) that OMTs would not lead to the monetary financing of governments, because government bonds are purchased from investors in secondary markets and not directly from governments and because focus is on shorter maturities (up to three years), which would help ensure the effectiveness of market discipline; (b) that OMTs would not affect the ECB's independence, because the Bank's action would continue to be based on the evaluation of the monetary policy transmission mechanism and the objective of price stability; (c) that excessive risks for taxpayers would be avoided because OMTs are fully dependent on the implementation of macroeconomic reforms required under the Memorandums of Understanding imposed under the ESM; and (d) that OMTs would not cause inflation because so-called 'sterilization' measures are foreseen whereby 'for every euro we inject, we will

[75] See more on national identity in the introductory chapter by Davor Jančić in this volume.

[76] Former ECB President Trichet took part in a French parliamentary inquiry on tax avoidance in 2010, but declined an invitation by the Irish Parliament (*Oireachtas*) to attend an inquiry on the banking crisis invoking the absence of a duty to render account to institutions at the national level. Mark Bovens and Deirdre Curtin, 'An Unholy Trinity of EU Presidents? Political Accountability of EU Executive Power' in Damian Chalmers, Markus Jachtenfuchs and Christian Joerges (eds), *The End of the Eurocrats' Dream: Adjusting to European Diversity* (Cambridge University Press 2016) 190–217, 210.

[77] Andreas Framke, Eva Kuehnen, and Sakari Suoninen, 'Special Report: How Mario Draghi is Reshaping Europe's Central Bank' *Reuters*, 9 January 2013 http://reut.rs/VdstBn (last accessed 28 August 2016).

[78] Deutscher Bundestag, 'Interventionen der EZB führen nicht zu Inflation', 24 October 2012 https://www.bundestag.de/dokumente/textarchiv/2012/41171041_kw43_draghi/209770 (last accessed 28 August 2016).

[79] European Central Bank, 'Opening Statement at Deutscher Bundestag', Berlin, 24 October 2012 http://www.ecb.europa.eu/press/key/date/2012/html/sp121024.en.html (last accessed 28 August 2016).

withdraw a euro'. This *Bundestag* session was mostly positively assessed as contributing to the easing of German concerns. The Governor of the Finnish Central Bank (*Finlands Bank*), Erkki Liikanen, claimed: 'it went down very well … he should visit other parliaments, too'.[80] So, he did.

In his speech in the Spanish Lower House of Parliament (*Congreso de los Diputados*) in February 2013, Draghi similarly sought to explain the major ECB policies taken in response to the euro crisis. But in addressing the specifics of ECB plans, he made several other important points. In search of a 'good mutual understanding' between the Bank and parliaments, he clarified that NPs are crucial to sustaining the stability and credibility of the EMU because economic interdependence spills over into legislative interdependence:

> As the democratically elected representatives of the Spanish people, you are responsible for domestic economic policy. Yet in the exercise of those duties, just like all national parliaments in the euro area, you influence the functioning of our economic and monetary union as a whole. As the President of the European Council Herman van Rompuy has said, national parliaments have become European institutions. It is important that we all recognise these mutual interests … all national parliaments in the euro area influence the functioning of our economic and monetary union.[81]

This reasoning sheds light on the EMU dimension of the NPs' contribution to the good functioning of the Union.[82] As Draghi underlined, NPs are 'key contributors' to the correction of misalignments of national fiscal policies that is necessary to increase Union-wide economic growth and jobs creation. Alongside the ECB, national governments and the private sector, 'resolute action' by parliaments had a 'pivotal role' in the reduction of credit spreads on sovereign and corporate bonds, the recovery of equity prices and banks' greater access to financial markets. Critical importance, moreover, is attached to the discursive function of parliaments in providing for 'effective communication to the public of the ultimate goals' as part of 'consensus-building efforts within domestic constituencies'.[83] Ironically, however, the Speaker of the Spanish *Congreso* had prevented live broadcast of the debate by ordering the use of inhibitors of wifi and 3G connections, which caused outrage especially among the Socialist parliamentarians.[84]

Over four months later, in June 2013 the ECB President was hosted by the French Lower House of Parliament (*Assemblée nationale*). The meeting was held in a joint session of the European Affairs Committee, the Foreign Affairs Committee, and the Finance Committee. This time, however, Draghi was accompanied by a member of the Executive Board, Benoît Cœure, and the Governor of the French Central Bank (*Banque de France*), Christian Noyer. Draghi carried on with his 'present, listen, and learn' approach, emphasizing that any further pooling of powers at the EU level needs to be 'matched by greater democratic legitimacy'.[85] Dominating the dialogue were topics related to the ECB's legitimacy, the operation of the OMT programme, banking

[80] Framke, Kuehnen, and Suoninen (n 77).

[81] European Central Bank, 'Introductory Statement at the Congreso de los Diputados de España' (n 41).

[82] See more on the good functioning of the Union in the introductory chapter by Davor Jančić in this volume.

[83] European Central Bank (n 41).

[84] Gonzalo Cortizo, 'El día que Draghi apagó el Congreso' *El Diario*, 12 February 2013 http://www.eldiario.es/_5fc99dd (last accessed 28 August 2016).

[85] European Central Bank, 'Introductory Remarks at the French Assemblée Nationale', Paris, 26 June 2013 http://www.ecb.europa.eu/press/key/date/2013/html/sp130626.en.html (last accessed 28 August 2016).

supervision, and the orientation of monetary policy (eg towards growth). Answering the questions on the extent of the ECB's Treaty mandate, Draghi stated that:

> Central banks are powerful institutions, non-elected and, in the case of the ECB, they fiercely defend their independence. These three characteristics are not necessarily compatible. The only way to achieve that is for the ECB to act within the mandate that you, legislators, have established. That is why we are so concerned and so proud to respect our mandate. That said, the discussion on the breadth of this mandate is primarily in your hands, not in ours.[86]

The ECB's *tour des capitales* went on with a visit to the Finnish Parliament (*Eduskunta*) in November 2014.[87] The meeting was attended by Governor Liikanen, chairpersons of the Parliamentary Supervisory Council, the Finance Committee, and the Grand Committee (which is in charge of European affairs), and other parliamentarians.[88] Draghi took this opportunity to advise that these visits are 'ad hoc interactions' and that NPs' key role is to exercise political control over the national central bank to the extent envisaged under domestic law.

The last such visit was to the parliament of Draghi's country of nationality—the Italian Chamber of Deputies (*Camera dei Deputati*) in March 2015.[89] Unlike in Spain, this meeting, which lasted slightly less than two hours, was televised and is publicly available *in toto*.[90] It was jointly organized by the Budget Committee, the Finance Committee, and the European Affairs Committee.[91]

This incipient tradition of the ECB's informal visits to NPs resembles those that Commission representatives conduct within the framework of the political dialogue between the Commission and NPs called the 'Barroso Initiative', during which they explain EU policies and answer questions of particular concern to the inviting parliament. Through these practices, the ECB is increasing the awareness, publicity and understanding of EU monetary policy. This is significant because it establishes a direct communication link between the EU's monetary authority and domestic lawmakers, who are in charge of adopting fiscal laws that have a bearing on the success and direction of monetary policy. However, the nature of the dialogue between the ECB and NPs is essentially one of exchange of information and not of full-blown political control of the sort maintained between parliaments and governments.[92]

[86] Assemblée nationale, Commission des affaires européennes, Compte rendu no 73 'Audition conjointe sur la politique monétaire, la situation économique de la zone euro et le développement de l'Union économique et monétaire', 26 juin 2013, 23 http://www.assemblee-nationale.fr/14/europe/c-rendus/c0073.asp (last accessed 28 August 2016).

[87] European Central Bank, 'Introductory Remarks at the Finnish Parliament', Helsinki, 27 November 2014 http://www.ecb.europa.eu/press/key/date/2014/html/sp141127.en.html (last accessed 28 August 2016).

[88] Eduskunta, 'Euroopan keskuspankin pääjohtaja Mario Draghi vieraili eduskunnassa' [European Central Bank President Mario Draghi visited Parliament], 27 November 2014 https://www.eduskunta.fi/FI/tiedotteet/Sivut/Euroopan%20keskuspankin%20paajohtaja%20Mario%20Draghi%20vieraili%20eduskunnassa.aspx (last accessed 28 August 2016).

[89] European Central Bank, 'Introductory Statement at the Italian Parliament', Rome, 26 March 2015 https://www.ecb.europa.eu/press/key/date/2015/html/sp150326.en.html (last accessed 28 August 2016).

[90] See http://webtv.camera.it/evento/7695 (last accessed 28 August 2016).

[91] Camera dei Deputati, Commissioni reunite Bilancio, Tesoro e Programmazione (V), Finanze (VI) e Politiche dell'Unione Europea, Audizione seduta di giovedì 26 marzo 2015, Resoconto stenografico http://documenti.camera.it/leg17/resoconti/commissioni/stenografici/pdf/050614/audiz2/audizione/2015/03/26/leg.17.stencomm.data20150326.U1.com050614.audiz2.audizione.0001.pdf (last accessed 28 August 2016).

[92] Bovens and Curtin (n 76) 214.

5. Accountability of the European Central Bank for Prudential Supervision

In performing its new role, which is separate from the conduct of monetary policy, the ECB owes a duty of accountability both to the EP and, to a lesser extent, to NPs.[93]

5.1 Accountability to the European Parliament

A first element of the ECB's accountability refers to its leadership in *macro-prudential* oversight of the EU financial system as a whole. The ECB does this through the European Systemic Risks Board (ESRB), which is chaired by the President of the ECB. Regarding its activities, the ESRB shall send a report to the EP and the Council annually or more frequently where warranted by widespread financial distress.[94] The ESRB Chair (ECB President) presents this report in a hearing in the EP, which is distinct and separate from the ECB-EP dialogue on monetary policy. The EP may invite the ESRB to examine other specific issues and to attend a hearing in a competent EP committee. These are complemented by 'confidential oral discussions ... behind closed doors' with the Chair and Vice-Chairs of the EP's ECON Committee, which focus on the ESRB's 'ongoing activity' twice a year or more frequently, where necessary.

A second element of the ECB's accountability concerns *micro-prudential supervision*. To begin with, the EP has the right to approve the appointment and removal of the Chair and the Vice-Chair of the ECB Supervisory Board. Importantly, in case any of these Board officials commit 'serious misconduct' or suffer circumstances bringing their standing into question, the EP may inform the ECB that, in its view, the conditions for their removal have been met.[95]

With respect to accountability, the ECB shall submit an annual report to the EP, the Commission, the Council, and the Eurogroup on the execution of its supervisory tasks and the Chair of the Supervisory Board must present it in public to the EP and to the Eurogroup. Upon the EP's request, the said Chair must appear before the competent EP committee for a hearing and the ECB shall reply orally or in writing to any questions from the EP or from the Eurogroup.

Another channel for the ECB–EP dialogue is the closed-door confidential discussions of the sort held with the ESRB, whereby the ECB Supervisory Board Chair meets the Chair and Vice-Chairs of the competent EP committees upon the latter's request. In all of these instances, the ECB is obliged to 'cooperate sincerely' with EP 'investigations', which may be carried out in the form of committees of inquiry. The objective of these arrangements is to facilitate the 'exercise of democratic accountability and oversight' over the ECB's supervisory powers.[96]

Detailed arrangements for the ECB's accountability to the EP for its prudential supervisory functions are foreseen in an interinstitutional agreement concluded

[93] Council Regulation (EU) No 1024/2013 of 15 October 2013 conferring specific tasks on the European Central Bank concerning policies relating to the prudential supervision of credit institutions (SSM Regulation), arts 20 and 21 [2013] OJ L 287/63. See also Luis M Hinojosa-Martínez, 'The Role of the ECB in the Supervision of Credit Institutions' in Luis M Hinojosa Martínez and José María Beneyto, *European Banking Union: The New Regime* (Kluwer Law International 2015) 47–68, 62.

[94] Regulation No 1092/2010 of the European Parliament and of the Council of 24 November 2010 on European Union macro-prudential oversight of the financial system and establishing a European Systemic Risk Board (ESRB Regulation), art 19 [2010] OJ L 331/1.

[95] SSM Regulation, art 26(3)–(4). [96] ibid art 20(9).

between these two institutions in November 2013.[97] There have thus far been numerous exchanges between MEPs and Danièle Nouy, the incumbent Chair of the ECB Supervisory Board. From the establishment of this Board on 1 January 2014 until mid-July 2016, the ECB sent a total of fifty-six letters to European parliamentarians: one 'inaugural' letter in 2013, ten in 2014, twenty-six in 2015, and nineteen in the first half of 2016.[98]

5.2 Accountability to National Parliaments

When it comes to domestic legislatures, the same annual report that the ECB sends to the EP should also be directly submitted to NPs of the euro area Member States. In reaction, these NPs may issue 'reasoned observations' and request the ECB to reply in writing. Furthermore, any participating NP may invite the Chair or a member of the ECB Supervisory Board and a representative of the competent national authority for an exchange of views on the supervision of credit institutions in that Member State. The inclusion of NPs in the ECB's accountability regime has been viewed as 'a good example of the mixed administration that has been created within the SSM', whereby the ECB justifies its action not only at the EU level but also at the national level, where the impact of its work is most felt.[99] However, this multiplicity of parliamentary institutions to which the ECB shall give account may create a tension between upholding the Union's interest and appeasing differing domestic interests.[100]

This, however, is remedied by the fact that the outcome of these accountability practices stays in the realm of political pressure, as neither the EP nor NPs may sanction the ECB for any failures in its supervisory activities. Despite this, the ECB's accountability for prudential supervision has been evaluated as 'robust' and 'more intrusive' than its general accountability duty under the Treaties described above.[101] This is appropriate given the potentially formidable impact that supervisory measures may have 'on public finances, credit institutions, their customers and their employees, and the markets in the participating Members States'.[102] This is also why extensive independence of the ECB in monetary policy sits uneasily with the breadth and incisiveness of its supervisory powers.[103] A group of Dutch Central Bank lawyers nonetheless argue that the ECB's accountability has been adequately designed because 'these processes will put pressure on the ECB to properly explain "what it has been doing" and why it considers this the right way to fulfil its supervisory tasks. It leads towards a dialogue, which assures accountability'.[104]

[97] Annex XXI to the EP Rules of Procedure—Interinstitutional Agreement on the practical modalities of the exercise of democratic accountability and oversight over the exercise of the tasks conferred on the ECB within the framework of the Single Supervisory Mechanism, [2013] OJ L 320/1.

[98] Own calculation based on the data taken from the ECB's website at https://www.bankingsupervision.europa.eu/press/publications/date/2016/html/index.en.html (last accessed 22 July 2016).

[99] Gijsbert Ter Kuile, Laura Wissink, and Willem Bovenschen, 'Tailor-Made Accountability Within the Single Supervisory Mechanism' (2015) 52 CML Rev 155, 170–71.

[100] Chiara Zilioli, 'The Independence of the European Central Bank and Its New Banking Supervisory Competences' in Dominique Ritleng (ed), *Independence and Legitimacy in the Institutional System of the European Union* (Oxford University Press 2016) 125–79, 178.

[101] Niamh Moloney, 'European Banking Union: Assessing Its Risks and Resilience' (2014) 51 CML Rev 1609, 1636.

[102] SSM Regulation, recital (56).

[103] Alexander (n 34) 171.

[104] Ter Kuile, Wissink, and Bovenschen (n 99) 169.

6. Concluding Remarks

This chapter has queried what could be called the 'democratic sustainability of the EMU',[105] as envisioned by the Five Presidents' Report and as shaped by the relations between the EP and NPs and the ECB. The latter has proven to be the pivotal EU actor in providing a swift policy response to reassure the markets about the economic resilience and agility of the euro area and the aggregate EU economy. The need for a citizen-oriented democratic embedding of economic and monetary policy-making in the EU has led to calls for an increased involvement of parliaments at both EU and domestic levels.[106]

Control over the national government and NCB governors, scrutiny over the ECB's monetary policy and supervisory measures, and inter-parliamentary liaison—contribute to bringing this to fruition. No illusion, however, should be had that legislatures can and ought to become prime policy-makers supplanting expertise-rich executive and non-majoritarian bodies.[107] On the contrary, their role is one of monitoring and political mediation. Even if the ECB may prima facie appear a highly technocratic institution, merely applying economic postulates to achieve the desired monetary policy ends, the euro crisis has shown that even such action is inextricable from the systemic, interdependent and spillover-conducive nature of the EMU evolution that pulls it into the domain of fiscal policy. In addition to monetary policy stewardship, the Banking Union's investiture of the ECB as the ultimate supervisor of the Eurozone's credit institutions makes it, in the words of the UK House of Lords, an 'exceptionally powerful' institution.[108] For prudential supervision, the ECB's accountability arrangements, their Lordships' argument goes, are 'patently weak'—which makes an 'overwhelming' case for a 'strong accountability mechanism' to the EP and NPs alike.[109] These factors draw the ECB into the space of politicization.[110]

In this regard, elected representatives have a role to play by debating the ECB's policies and interventions and by holding its President to account. This helps to augment the level of transparency of monetary policy decisions, which is crucial for their adequate transmission into the real economy. On this note, the ECB President's political accountability has been appraised as 'the most developed' within the EU executive branch.[111] This is usefully explained by Draghi's aforesaid observation that the ECB's independence ought to be counterbalanced by reinforced efforts to justify its action. This has given rise to heightened contestation of the ECB and its policies.[112]

The nature of parliamentary oversight over the ECB is determined by its institutional independence, which shields its members from any attempts at capricious,

[105] Iain Begg and others, 'EMU and Sustainable Integration' (2015) 37 J Eur Integration 803, 810.

[106] Richard Bellamy and Albert Weale, 'Political Legitimacy and European Monetary Union: Contracts, Constitutionalism and the Normative Logic of Two-level Games' (2015) 22 JEPP 257, 270.

[107] See to this end Federico Fabbrini, *Economic Governance in Europe: Comparative Paradoxes and Constitutional Challenges* (Oxford University Press 2016) 192.

[108] House of Lords, EU Committee, HL Paper 88 'European Banking Union: Key Issues and Challenges', 7th Report of Session 2012–13 of 12 December 2012, para 56, p. 22.

[109] ibid para 57, p. 22.

[110] Hanspeter Kriesi and Edgar Grande, 'The Euro Crisis: A Boost to the Politicization of European Integration?' in Swen Hutter, Edgar Grande, and Hanspeter Kriesi (eds), *Politicizing Europe: Integration and Mass Politics* (Cambridge University Press 2016) 240–75, 246, and 262; Mark Dawson and Floris de Witte, 'From Balance to Conflict: A New Constitution for the EU' (2016) 22 ELJ 204, 215.

[111] Bovens and Curtin (n 76) 212.

[112] Nicole Scicluna, *European Union Constitutionalism in Crisis* (Routledge 2015) 135.

party-political ouster. However, formal and informal dialogues between the ECB and national and European parliamentarians serve as important information-sharing forums, giving publicity to ECB decisions and requiring justification for their adoption. Consequently, democratic oversight over the ECB is above all *ex post*. There is no requirement for the ECB to consult the EP or NPs before it makes policy.

Nevertheless, the combination of the debt crisis, the sluggish Eurozone economy, strong fiscal implications of the ECB's monetary measures, and the Bank's overall pre-eminence in tackling these problems—have prompted its President, Mario Draghi, to embark on a reform of the institution's democratic accountability. He has done so by means of ad hoc appearances in an increasing number of plenary and committee sessions of NPs as well as through greater commitment to monetary and supervisory dialogues with the EP. This may improve the transparency dimension of the ECB's accountability by explaining the data based on which it acts.[113]

The ECB's accountability furthermore differs from that of independent central banks elsewhere in an important foundational aspect. The examples of the US and Japan illustrate the importance of the institution of parliament. In the US, monetary authority is vested in the Federal Reserve System (the Federal Reserve or simply the Fed) by virtue of an act of Congress—the Federal Reserve Act of 1913. In Japan, such authority rests with the Bank of Japan, also thanks to a statute—the Bank of Japan Act (establishment in 1882, reorganization in 1942). Conversely, the ECB is the creation of a Treaty—the TFEU. The US Congress and the Japanese National Diet (*Kokkai*) can legislate to alter the prerogatives of their respective central banks and thereby indirectly exercise significant oversight powers. The EP may not do so with respect to the ECB because this would require a Treaty change, which is the domain of the Member States.

Moreover, parliamentarians have been active in utilizing judicial channels to challenge decisions that imply a significant or exclusive involvement of the ECB. This was the case with Mr Pringle regarding the ESM and with Mr Gauweiler regarding OMT.

The euro crisis has therefore brought about a transformation, albeit not a radical one, in the functioning of the democratic control over the ECB. The Bank has become more responsive to parliamentary sensitivities, while retaining its status as an independent monetary and supervisory authority for the Eurozone.[114] This is the core of the notion of the ECB's 'accountable independence', whose fulfilment hinges on continuing oversight over its operation.[115] A persisting challenge for legislators will be to adjust their scrutiny to these different roles of the ECB and address the redistributive implications of a developing EMU. However, for this to be effective, the EU will need to devise further political ways to 'accommodate citizen concerns while opening up decision-making processes to EU and national parliamentary representation'.[116]

[113] This problem has been diagnosed in Christopher Gandrud and Mark Hallerberg, 'Does Banking Union Worsen the EU's Democratic Deficit? The Need for Greater Supervisory Data Transparency' (2015) 53 JCMS 769; Francesco Giavazzi and Charles Wyplosz, 'EMU: Old Flaws Revisited' (2015) 37 J Eur Integration 723, 731.

[114] There are economists' views that the ECB's role of lender of last resort should be fortified and that this can only be done by making the ECB 'subordinate to the political power of elected officials'. See Paul de Grauwe and Yuemei Ji, 'Correcting for the Eurozone Design Failures: The Role of the ECB' (2015) 37 J Eur Integration 739, 749.

[115] Rosa M Lastra, 'The Evolution of the European Central Bank' (2012) Fordham Int'l LJ 1260, 1279–80.

[116] Vivien A Schmidt, 'The Forgotten Problem of Democratic Legitimacy: "Governing by the Rules" and "Ruling by the Numbers"' in Matthias Matthijs and Mark Blyth (eds), *The Future of the Euro* (Oxford University Press 2015) 90, 112.

9

Executive Accountability to National Parliaments in Post-crisis EU Affairs

The Persistent Shortcomings in the Council and European Council Oversight

*Diane Fromage**

1. Introduction

The Lisbon Treaty established for the first time that national parliaments (NPs) 'contribute actively to the good functioning of the Union'[1] and granted them certain rights of information and participation to this end.[2] In defining NPs as 'guardians of subsidiarity'[3] and in foreseeing the direct transmission of European Union (EU) documents to them—inter alia annual legislative programmes, legislative proposals, green papers, and white papers[4]—the Lisbon Treaty modified the balance between the executive and legislative powers at the national level: NPs have more information at their disposal to hold their governments to account and this could contribute to more thorough scrutiny than in the past.[5]

Nonetheless, since the documents transmitted to NPs pursuant to Protocol No 1 mainly include draft EU legislative acts and planning documents, asymmetries remain at the national level where governments do not sufficiently inform parliaments of their position in the EU institutional game, most importantly in meetings of the Council of the EU (Council) and the European Council. The need for parliaments to have access to and to scrutinize the positions that their governments defend in these two EU institutions has become even more salient in recent years, owing to the empowerment of the

* I would like to thank the participants at the conference 'Resilience or Resignation? National Parliaments and the EU' organized at the London School of Economics on 10 April 2015, and in particular Katarzyna Granat and the editor, for their useful comments. Research for this chapter was supported by the Spanish Ministry of Economy and Competitiveness (Grant DER2014-57116P).

1 TEU, art 12. See more on this in the introductory chapter by Davor Jančić in this volume.

2 The most important provisions in this sense are those laid down in art 12 TEU. However, arts 48(7) TEU and 81(3) TFEU also grant certain rights to NPs.

3 TEU, art 12 and Protocol No 2 annexed to the Treaties. See on subsidiarity checks Anna Jonsson Cornell and Marco Goldoni (eds), *National and Regional Parliaments in the EU-Legislative Procedure Post-Lisbon: The Impact of the Early Warning Mechanism* (Hart Publishing 2016).

4 A full list is contained in Protocol No 1, art 1. This formalizes an institutional practice initiated in 2006 by the former European Commission President, José Barroso, in the framework of the political dialogue between the Commission and NPs. See more in Davor Jančić, 'The Game of Cards: National Parliaments, Subsidiarity and the Future of the Early Warning System and the Political Dialogue' (2015) 52 CML Rev 939, 940–41.

5 The link between low scrutiny and lack of information in the pre-Lisbon era has been underlined by Adam Cygan, who has also observed that parliamentary scrutiny typically has a national rather than a European focus. Adam Cygan, 'National Parliaments within the EU Polity—No Longer Losers But Hardly Victorious' (2011) 12 ERA Forum 517, 519–20.

Executive Accountability to National Parliaments in Post-Crisis EU Affairs: The Persistent Shortcomings in the Council and European Council Oversight. First Edition. Diane Fromage.
Published 2017 by Oxford University Press.

European Council both through the Treaty of Lisbon[6] and through the management of the euro crisis.[7] NPs, which have traditionally focused their scrutiny on EU documents rather than on their executives' action in the Council and the European Council,[8] now have to adapt to this new reality.[9] Portugal, for instance, reformed its parliamentary scrutiny system to this effect in 2012,[10] and so did Italy, as described below.

Article 10(2) of the Treaty on European Union (TEU) further defines two channels for democratic legitimacy. The European Parliament (EP) represents the citizens, whereas the Member States' representation is ensured through the Council and the European Council.[11] Therefore, in order to bolster democracy in the Union, NPs are expected to hold their governments or heads of states accountable when the latter participate in Council and European Council meetings. This is particularly necessary because neither of these two institutions is democratically accountable as a body at the EU level,[12] despite their important role in the EU. Furthermore, when national ministers act in the Council or when the heads of state and government participate in European Council meetings, the guarantees of parliamentary involvement and accountability that exist in national legislative processes are de facto absent: NPs cannot debate and try to impose their will as they would be able to in the course of adopting national legislation. Instead, they are only left with the possibility to withdraw their confidence in the government if their voice is gravely disregarded.[13]

Against this background, the issue of executive accountability to NPs in EU affairs, ie accountability for 'how they behave and what they decide in the EU',[14] is crucial. Accountability is defined here as being bi-dimensional: 'as a control function … present both ex ante in the sense that a minister's policy position should be cleared prior to negotiation and ex post in that ministers can be called to explain negotiated policy

[6] TEU, art 15(1) provides that the European Council has to 'provide the Union with the necessary impetus for its development and define the general political directions and priorities thereof'. See further in Wolfgang Wessels, *The European Council* (Palgrave Macmillan 2015).

[7] Wolfgang Wessels and others, 'Democratic Control in the Member States of the European Council and the Euro Zone Summit' (European Parliament study 2013) 14 ff. See more on NPs' response to the euro crisis in Davor Jančić, 'National Parliaments and EU Fiscal Integration' (2016) 22 ELJ 225; and Davor Jančić, 'Parliamentary Involvement in the Economic and Monetary Union after the Euro Crisis' in Cristina Fasone and Nicola Lupo (eds), *Interparliamentary Cooperation in the Composite European Constitution* (Hart Publishing 2016).

[8] Wessels and others (n 7) 17.

[9] Claudia Hefftler and others, 'National Parliaments: Their Emerging Control Over the European Council' (2013) Notre Europe Policy Paper No 89, available at http://www.institutdelors.eu/media/parliamentarycontrol-hefftlerkreilingerrozenbergwessels-ne-jdi-mar13.pdf?pdf=ok (last accessed 14 October 2016).

[10] Davor Jančić, 'The Portuguese Parliament and EU Affairs: From Inert to Agile Democratic Control' in Claudia Hefftler and others (eds), *The Palgrave Handbook of National Parliaments and the European Union* (Palgrave Macmillan 2015) 369 ff.

[11] NPs are in fact sometimes seen as the primary guarantors of legitimacy in the EU. See David Cameron's Bloomberg speech of 23 January 2013, available at https://www.gov.uk/government/speeches/eu-speech-at-bloomberg (last accessed 14 October 2016). See also Adam Cygan, *Accountability, Parliamentarism and Transparency in the EU: The Role of National Parliaments* (Edward Elgar Publishing 2013) 40.

[12] Wessels and others illustrate this lack of democratic control over the European Council but their findings apply equally to the Council. See Wessels and others (n 7) 16.

[13] In some systems, such as the UK and the German ones, in certain cases they can show their disagreement by refusing to approve a law. These possibilities, however, are limited to particular cases such as the use of TFEU, art 352 or an agreement to use a *passerelle* clause.

[14] Carina Sprungk, 'A New Type of Representative Democracy? Reconsidering the Role of National Parliaments in the European Union' (2013) 35 J Eur Integration 547, 552.

outcomes'.[15] This issue is particularly important as NPs' primary role still lies at the national level, as it did in the pre-Lisbon era,[16] primarily because they cannot avoid implementing EU legislation once it has been adopted. Hence, in order to have a say in EU affairs, parliaments ought to influence their governments during EU legislative negotiations[17] and have to perform various tasks, including scrutinizing EU legislative proposals and consultation documents, monitoring their governments' activities in the Council and the European Council, engaging in vertical and horizontal interparliamentary cooperation, and maintaining direct political dialogue with the European Commission. All of these tasks have to be performed in addition to their 'ordinary' domestic duties of adopting legislation, controlling the government, and ensuring the publicity of parliamentary work. This duplication of their national and European tasks represents a challenge for their sometimes scarce resources, while also requiring very broad expertise.[18]

This chapter analyzes the ability, or inability, of five NPs—the British, French, German, Italian, and Spanish ones—to influence and hold their governments to account for their action in the Council and the European Council. These five Member States were chosen on the basis of several criteria: their size and influence, given that they are the largest Member States in the EU by population; their institutional systems accounting for both parliamentary and semi-presidential ones; and the strength of their parliaments in EU scrutiny, which has been assessed as traditionally 'strong' in the cases of Germany and the UK, and 'weak' in the case of the other three Member States.[19]

The present analysis suggests that a mandating system in all parliamentary chambers is not desirable as it would eventually impair negotiations in Council and European Council meetings. Yet it does show that even after the Lisbon Treaty and the euro crisis, the existing scrutiny mechanisms are still not sufficient for all parliaments to exert substantial influence on EU affairs. Most importantly, this chapter underlines that sometimes these mechanisms are not even fully used, although some progress can be observed in recent years.

This study first examines what accountability mechanisms NPs have at their disposal (section 2) and how they have been used in recent years (section 3). These findings will serve as basis for a more general reflection on the possibilities and desirability of tight parliamentary scrutiny of Council and European Council members. Finally, this chapter proposes a way forward in enhancing national parliamentary control over their government's EU policy (section 4).

[15] Caitríona A Carter, 'The Parliament of the United Kingdom: From Supportive Scrutiny to Unleashed Control?' in Andreas Maurer and Wolfgang Wessels (eds), *National Parliaments on Their Ways to Europe: Losers or Latecomers?* (Nomos 2002) 401–402. See generally on accountability in the EU: Deirdre Curtin, *Executive Power of the European Union: Law, Practices, and the Living Constitution* (Oxford University Press 2009) 249 ff.

[16] Cygan (n 5) 519.

[17] Thomas Winzen, 'National Parliamentary Control of European Union Affairs: A Cross-national and Longitudinal Comparison' (2012) 35 WEP 657, 658.

[18] As noted, NPs act at different levels in EU affairs and the distribution of their resources among these different tasks is an important issue. See on their participation in the early warning system: Pieter de Wilde and Tapio Raunio, 'Redirecting National Parliaments: Setting Priorities for Involvement in EU Affairs' (2015) Comparative European Politics, available at http://link.springer.com/article/10.1057/cep.2015.28 (last accessed 16 November 2016).

[19] See on this classification and on the NPs' role in EU affairs before the Lisbon Treaty Andreas Maurer and Wolfgang Wessels, 'National Parliaments After Amsterdam: From Slow Adapters to National Players?' in Andreas Maurer and Wolfgang Wessels (eds), *National Parliaments on Their Ways to Europe: Losers or Latecomers?* (Nomos 2001).

2. Parliaments' Growing Capacities and Information Rights

Different legal sources—notably constitutions, statutes, and regulations—contain provisions that guarantee NPs' access to information and allow them to hold their governments to account and try to influence them in EU matters. However, the information flows and control mechanisms necessary for adequate parliamentary scrutiny may also result from informal practices. The choice for a specific legal instrument or for informal practice depends on each Member State's institutional and political tradition and culture, as illustrated below. As the House of Lords put it, '[n]ational scrutiny systems will inevitably vary according to the national context'.[20]

NPs have the possibility to intervene mainly in three ways. First, they can scrutinize EU legislative proposals, which are as a rule subsequently adopted by the EP and the Council. Secondly, they can try to influence their government's position on proposals before Council meetings and hold the government to account for the position taken in these meetings, especially where the government did not follow parliamentary recommendations. In exceptional circumstances, such as the use of the flexibility clause[21] or certain *passerelle* clauses, government may have to obtain parliamentary consent by means of a statute or a motion. Thirdly, NPs may interact with their governments before and after European Council meetings. However, owing to the information gap from which most NPs suffer, this task often proves particularly difficult.[22]

Following the classification proposed by the Conference of Parliamentary Committees for Union Affairs of Parliaments of the European Union (COSAC),[23] three different scrutiny models can be defined: (a) the *document-based* system, which focuses on the scrutiny of documents emanating from EU institutions; (b) the *procedural* system concentrating on the 'scrutiny of the EU decision-making process, often concentrating on [the] government's position in the Council'; and (c) the *mandating* system, which differs from the procedural system in that the parliament, or its European Affairs Committee (EAC), is or may be required to give a mandate to the government on what policy position to defend at the EU level.[24] These three systems of scrutiny are not mutually exclusive and, in fact, most parliaments have opted for a hybrid system. This is demonstrated below with examples from the five Member States selected.

[20] House of Lords, EU Committee, HL 151 'The Role of National Parliaments in the European Union' 9th Report of Session 2013–14, 24 March 2014, 11.

[21] TFEU, art 352.

[22] Wessels and others (n 7) 52–53. However, the situation of the *Bundestag* improved since the publication of this study, following the decision of the Federal Constitutional Court on the ESM/Euro Plus Pact (*BVerfG*, 2 BvE 4/11 of 19 June 2012). This decision prompted the revision of the Act on Cooperation in 2013. This does not mean, however, that parliaments generally lack information. In fact, since the entry into force of the Lisbon Treaty quite the opposite is true. What many parliaments still do not have is strategic information on their own and other governments' positions. See on the overwhelming quantity of documents received Institute for Government, *Parliamentary Scrutiny of European Legislation. Lessons from Other European Countries* (2016) 17, available at http://www.instituteforgovernment.org.uk/publications/parliamentary-scrutiny-european-legislation (last accessed 14 October 2016).

[23] See on this interparliamentary conference: 'Part IV: Debating the role of COSAC' in Fasone and Lupo (n 7).

[24] COSAC, 8th Bi-annual Report, October 2007, 7.

2.1 Germany

In Germany, the relationship between Parliament and government in the EU legislative procedure is the most formalized and detailed. As is well known, the Federal Constitutional Court has been particularly protective of Parliament's prerogatives and this has resulted in a comprehensive and formal legal framework.[25] Since the adoption of the Maastricht Treaty, Article 23(2) of the Basic Law has required that 'the Federal Government shall keep the *Bundestag* and the *Bundesrat* informed, comprehensively and at the earliest possible time'. This general obligation was developed, together with other government's reporting obligations, in the 1993 Act on Cooperation between the Federal Government and the German *Bundestag* in Matters Concerning the European Union. This Act was amended in 2009 following the entry into force of the Lisbon Treaty and in 2013 to ensure that the *Bundestag* is adequately informed on EU matters in all circumstances.

Since the adoption of these two acts, the government's duty of information towards the *Bundestag* has been comprehensive. It now encompasses discussions held in: EU preparatory bodies and working groups; informal meetings such as Euro summits and Eurogroup meetings, after the Federal Constitutional Court confirmed this right of the *Bundestag*;[26] and discussions of 'comparable institutions that are held on the basis of international agreements and other arrangements which complement or are otherwise particularly closely related to the law of the European Union'.[27]

The *Bundestag*'s influence was also reinforced since the Act on Cooperation, after its second amendment post-Lisbon in 2013, better defines how Parliament's involvement is to take place in practice.[28] The *Bundestag* has the right to express its opinion on EU legislative proposals before they are examined in the Council and the government must take this opinion into account.[29]

As regards Council and European Council meetings, the *Bundestag* has to be informed both in writing and orally before each of these meetings.[30] The government must invoke the so-called parliamentary reserve, which makes it necessary for the government to obtain 'prior parliamentary approval in the negotiations if the main interests expressed in the decision of the *Bundestag* cannot be asserted'.[31] When the government proved unable to assert the *Bundestag*'s opinion, the latter should be informed and the reasons for this deviation have to be provided. In any event, the *Bundestag* has to be informed in writing as soon as a decision is made in the Council. Furthermore, since 2013, a parliamentary minority of one-quarter of Members of Parliament (MPs) may request the government to justify its deviation from the parliamentary opinion previously expressed during a plenary debate.[32] The *Bundestag* shall then receive information on the most important elements of the discussions at the EU

[25] See on this framework and its recent reinforcement: Alex Schäfer and Fabian Schulz, 'Der Bundestag wird europäisch—zur Reform des Beteilingungsgesetzes EUZBBG' (2013) 3 Integration 199; Cristina Fasone, 'The Transformation Effects of the Eurozone Crisis on National Parliaments' (2015) 2 Revista del postgrado en derecho de la UNAM 141, 150 ff.

[26] *BVerfG*, 2 BvE 4/11 of 19 June 2012.

[27] Act on Cooperation of 2013, art 3(3).

[28] ibid art 1.

[29] Basic Law, art 22(3).

[30] Before 2013, however, the government's obligations did not encompass Eurozone summits, which the government considered as not being a matter of EU law but that they were 'of a purely intergovernmental nature'. See Claudia Hefftler and Oliver Höing, 'Report on Germany' in Wessels and others (n 7) Annex 1, 53. Before the Lisbon Treaty, the government taking part in European Council meetings was not bound by the *Bundestag*'s will in any manner.

[31] Act on Cooperation of 2013, art 8(4).

[32] ibid art 8(5). See Christian Calliess and Timm Beichelt, *Die Europäisierung des Parlaments: Die europapolitische Rolle von Bundestag und Bundesrat* (Bertelsmann Stiftung 2015) 337.

level, on the state of the negotiations, and on the position the government has taken during them. Following these meetings, the government must inform the *Bundestag* orally and in writing of their outcome.[33]

The 'Federal Government is to reach agreement with the *Bundestag*' before any final decision in the Council or European Council is made, among other things on the opening of EU accession negotiations or on Treaty amendments. In certain cases, such as the use of the *passerelle* clause in the field of Common Foreign and Security Policy,[34] the approval of a motion is required; whereas in other cases, parliamentary consent has to take the form of a statute, for instance if the flexibility clause (Article 352 TFEU) is used to adopt EU legislation.[35] However, these provisions are scarcely used and remain 'Sunday questions'.[36]

In economic matters too, the *Bundestag*'s prerogatives were recently expanded. Its Budget Committee must approve rescue packages to other Member States, it keeps the budgetary authority, and controls the budgetary procedure.[37]

This means that the *Bundestag*'s rights were strongly reinforced after the entry into force of the Lisbon Treaty. As a consequence of the euro crisis, they are now comprehensively protected by the Basic Law and ordinary statutes.

2.2 Italy

In Italy, too, the prerogatives of Parliament—the *Camera dei Deputati* and the *Senato*—have become protected more comprehensively as a consequence of the Treaty of Lisbon and the euro crisis, which prompted the adoption of a statute on Italy's participation in EU affairs (Law Moavero Milanesi) of 2012.[38] This statute foresees the transmission of legislative proposals and other EU preparatory documents to both chambers, accompanied by a note containing the government's evaluation.[39] The government also has to transmit a more detailed report on these draft legislative acts to Parliament.[40] In specific and exceptional cases, such as the creation of a common Union defence policy based on Article 42(2) TEU,[41] the government has to seek parliamentary approval by statute or deliberation of both chambers, depending on the decision at stake.[42]

The government must inform Parliament of its negotiating position in the plenary before European Council meetings as well, and must—since the approval of the 2012 statute only—take the parliamentary position into account.[43] The same process of information and consultation applies to Council meetings if competent bodies of either parliamentary chamber demand it: therefore, this does not happen automatically.[44] The government is furthermore requested to ensure, in the Council and other EU institutions and bodies, that the Italian position is consistent with the opinions and the resolutions adopted by the Italian Parliament.[45] Whenever the government is unable to uphold parliamentary recommendations during negotiations in Brussels, the

[33] Act on Cooperation of 2013, art 4(4). [34] TEU, art 31(3).

[35] See on these procedures Davor Jančić, 'Caveats from Karlsruhe and Berlin: Whither Democracy After Lisbon?' (2010) 16 Colum J Eur L 337, 362 ff.

[36] *Sonntagsfragen*. Simon Neumann in Andreas von Arnauld and Ulrich Hufeld (eds), *Systematischer Kommentar zu den Lissabon-Begleitgesetzen* (Nomos 2011) 306.

[37] Jančić, 'National Parliaments and EU Fiscal Integration' (n 7) 245. See further on the *Bundestag*'s prerogatives in this domain Cristina Fasone, 'Taking Budgetary Powers Away From National Parliaments? On Parliamentary Prerogatives in the Eurozone Crisis' (2015) EUI Working Paper No 2015/37, 10 ff and 16 ff.

[38] Statute 234/2012. [39] ibid art 6(1). [40] ibid art 6(4).

[41] ibid art 11(2). [42] ibid art 11. [43] ibid art 4(1). [44] ibid art 4(1).

[45] ibid art 7(1).

President of the Italian Council of Ministers (typically the competent minister) has to inform Parliament promptly and provide reasons why the deviation has occurred.[46] The government shall in any case inform the relevant parliamentary committees of the results of Council and European Council meetings within fifteen days.[47] In addition, the Italian government also has to transmit to Parliament two yearly reports (prospective and conclusive ones), which address Council and European Council meetings.[48] A scrutiny reserve may also be invoked.[49] Although the reserve does not in itself necessarily allow Parliament to have influence, it guarantees that parliamentarians have enough time to perform their scrutiny and give their views on an EU proposal if they consider this to be necessary. By contrast, in Member States where no scrutiny reserve exists, such as in Spain, Parliament only has the eight-week period guaranteed by the Treaties to scrutinize draft legislative acts.[50]

Compared to the four other Member States analyzed in this chapter, the Italian case is specific in that the statute effecting parliamentary adaptation to the post-Lisbon legal framework was adopted only at the end of 2012, ie after much of the euro-crisis law had already been adopted.[51] This belated adaptation has permitted the inclusion of much of the novelties introduced in euro-crisis law and explains why the chambers have to be consulted on the agreements in the financial or monetary domains.[52]

It follows therefore that parliamentary control over the government in EU affairs has been strongly reinforced both as a consequence of the Lisbon Treaty and of the economic crisis and thanks to the delay in the adaptation of the Italian institutional framework after the new Treaty entered into force.

2.3 Spain

In Spain, the arrangements for parliamentary participation in EU affairs are also peculiar compared to the other four parliaments analyzed here. Indeed, although Parliament, *Cortes Generales*, is bicameral as well—being composed of the lower chamber *Congreso de los diputados* and the upper chamber *Senado*—EU affairs are mainly dealt with by the Joint Committee on EU Affairs, which is composed of both MPs and Senators. The government's obligations towards Parliament are contained in the statute that regulates this Joint Committee, which was reformed in 2009 and 2010 following the entry into force of the Lisbon Treaty but which has not been modified to include the novelties introduced by euro-crisis law.[53] This statute obliges the government to transmit to Parliament a 'brief report' on the 'substantial content' of the 'legislative proposals that have an impact on Spain',[54] but this provision has been reformed neither in 2009 nor in 2010 despite the large room for decision that it arguably leaves the government. The Joint Committee may organize a debate on a specific EU legislative proposal or request that one be held in the plenary of one of the two chambers. Once the proposal has been approved by the Council, the Joint Committee may organize a hearing in order for the government to give account of EU negotiations and their outcome.[55]

[46] ibid art 7(2). [47] ibid art 4(1). [48] ibid art 13. [49] ibid art 10.

[50] Protocol No 1, art 4.

[51] Note that previously the Law Buttiglione of 2005 had been reformed to allow for a partial adaptation to the post-Lisbon situation but that these attempts were insufficient. See Diane Fromage, *Les parlements dans l'Union Européenne après le Traité de Lisbonne. La participation des parlements allemands, britanniques, espagnols, français et italiens* (L'Harmattan 2015) 95 ff and 220 ff.

[52] Statute 234/2012. [53] Statute 8/1994. [54] ibid art 3(b).

[55] ibid art 3(c).

The Joint Committee has the right to be informed by the government of the main lines that inspire its EU policy as well as of the decisions made by the Council.[56] Since 2010, it may also decide which members of the government or other high-ranked civil servants should appear before it in anticipation of Council meetings to discuss the position that the government plans to adopt in relation to the items placed on the Council's agenda.[57]

As regards European Council meetings, the government must appear in the plenary of the Congress of Deputies after these meetings have taken place, to inform MPs of the decisions made and to engage in a debate on them.[58] It is also formally foreseen that, before European Council meetings take place, the government has to provide Parliament with a written report on the achievements of the outgoing Council Presidency.[59] This report, however, is commonly replaced by an oral statement, which allows *ex ante* control as well.[60]

Whereas the Lisbon Treaty has clearly given the impetus for the empowerment of Parliament towards the government, the euro crisis has not led to a major change in this regard: before and after the crisis neither the Spanish Constitution nor the Statute on Budgetary Stability and Financial Sustainability[61] guarantee any formal right of information to Parliament.[62]

2.4 The United Kingdom

In the UK, although European Union (Amendment) Acts were adopted in 2008 and 2011, neither these acts nor the standing orders of the House of Commons and the House of Lords guarantee any specific rights of parliamentary oversight over Council and European Council meetings.[63] Like in France, as highlighted below, in Britain political practice has supplemented the formal rules with additional informal scrutiny arrangements, which exist in both Houses of Parliament with respect to the preparatory phase of European Council meetings. Both chambers receive a letter from the government on the main issues on the European Council's agenda and the government's position on them.[64] However, despite this unilateral flow of written information from the government to Parliament, the latter cannot influence the government's position at that point because there are no exchanges of views. In contrast to the *ex ante* situation, *ex post* control is much tighter: it often takes place orally in the plenary and is led by the prime minister.[65] The same statement is read on the same day in both chambers: by

[56] ibid art 3(d). [57] ibid art 8. [58] ibid art 4. [59] ibid art 3(e).

[60] Manuel Sánchez de Dios, 'Report on Spain' in Wessels and others (n 7) Annex 1, 134; Diane Fromage, 'National Parliaments and Governmental Accountability in the Crisis: Theory and Practice' (2014) 6 Perspectives on Federalism 149, 161.

[61] Statute 2/2012.

[62] Fasone, 'Taking Budgetary Powers away from National Parliaments?' (n 37) 21.

[63] Note that the House of Commons is also concerned with the negotiations taking place at the COREPER level and their scrutiny. House of Commons, European Scrutiny Committee, HC 918 'Scrutiny Reform Follow-Up and Legacy Report', 38th Report of Session 2014–15, 25 March 2015, paras 95 ff, available at http://www.publications.parliament.uk/pa/cm201415/cmselect/cmeuleg/918/918.pdf (last accessed 14 October 2016). See more on the UK Parliament in the chapter by Julie Smith in this volume.

[64] Ariella Huff and Julie Smith, 'Report on the United Kingdom' in Wessels and others (n 7) Annex 1, 143. The same authors remark that 'under the Labour Government statements were sometimes made prior to European Council meetings; the practice has not been used by the Coalition Government that took office in May 2010'.

[65] The lack of organization of such hearings has recently given rise to criticisms from the members of the Commons' European Scrutiny Committee. House of Commons (n 63) para 24. Given the fact

the prime minister in the House of Commons and by a minister of state in the House of Lords. This is followed by a short debate.[66]

With regard to scrutiny over the Council, the tradition of ministerial responsibility to Parliament was simply extended to EU business.[67] The House of Commons European Scrutiny Committee introduced a procedure for pre- and post-Council involvement, which is deemed applicable to the House of Lords.[68] According to this procedure,[69] the government has to provide written information on its negotiating position to the competent parliamentary committees no later than three weeks before the scheduled Council meeting. The minister in charge may be called to give evidence. In any case, a written ministerial statement is provided to both Houses shortly, and no later than one day, before each formal Council meeting, setting out why the items are on the agenda and what the government's general position on these items is. After the Council meeting, ministers must inform the chambers within five days, in the form of a written statement, of the outcomes reached at the EU level and the position taken by the government during the negotiations. Further written information or oral evidence from the relevant minister may be requested.[70] Hence, these procedures mostly take place in writing.

Exchanges between the government and Parliament also take place on the basis of EU documents. Once the government has deposited an EU document in Parliament, it submits an explanatory memorandum in which it states its position.[71] Any such document may be subject to a scrutiny reserve until the House invoking it has completed scrutiny of the items concerned.[72] The government may not give the UK's agreement to the measure negotiated in the Council or in the European Council until the reserve has been lifted, unless there are compelling reasons of urgency that would afterwards have to be duly justified to Parliament. Hence, whereas *ex ante* control is permitted under the scrutiny reserve procedure, *ex post* scrutiny normally takes place in writing.[73]

Therefore, the British parliamentary chambers are fully informed about European Council and Council matters, but their possibilities of *ex ante* influence are rather limited beyond the scrutiny reserve. The euro crisis has not prompted the formalization of these procedures in a statute. Yet, despite its derogation from the Economic and Monetary Union (EMU), the UK Parliament has succeeded in establishing political and legal channels to influence fiscal decision-making.[74] In addition to certain prerogatives at the national level, both parliamentary chambers have indeed scrutinized EU fiscal affairs particularly actively.

that the minutes of the Commons' European Scrutiny Committee are not public, it is impossible to know whether any debate took place there as well.

[66] Ariella Huff and Julie Smith, 'Westminster and the European Union: Ever-increasing Scepticism?' in Claudia Hefftler and others (eds), *The Palgrave Handbook of National Parliaments and the European Union* (Palgrave Macmillan 2015) 319.

[67] Carter, 'The Parliament of the United Kingdom: From Supportive Scrutiny to Unleashed Control?' (n 15) 397.

[68] Cabinet Office, *Parliamentary Scrutiny of European Union Documents: Guidance for Departments* (HMSO 2013) 58.

[69] ibid Annex N.

[70] Huff and Smith, 'Westminster and the European Union: Ever-increasing Scepticism?' (n 66) 319.

[71] ibid 315 ff.

[72] House of Commons, Scrutiny Reserve Resolution of 17 November 1998; and House of Lords, Scrutiny Reserve Resolution of 30 March 2010.

[73] Huff and Smith, 'Report on the United Kingdom' (n 64) 144.

[74] Jančić, 'National Parliaments and EU Fiscal Integration' (n 7) 244.

2.5 France

In France, the rights of Parliament—the *Assemblée nationale* and the *Sénat*—to receive information on EU matters and to adopt so-called European resolutions are anchored in Article 88(4) of the Constitution and developed in the chambers' Standing Orders, a governmental ordinance (*ordonnance*), and a circular letter (*circulaire*).[75] While resolutions express the view of the entire chamber, the EAC may also adopt conclusions to give their views on a specific EU legislative proposal or another EU matter.[76]

In contrast, no formal possibility exists for the chambers to hold the government to account in the framework of Council and European Council meetings. Yet, in practice, since the failure of the Constitutional Treaty, Parliament has been involved both before and after European Council meetings.[77] Beforehand, the competent secretary of state or minister makes a statement in the plenary, which is followed by a debate.[78] After the European Council meeting has taken place, a debate is organized in the EACs of both chambers, which sometimes organize a joint session for that purpose. The President of the Republic never appears in Parliament in person because the Constitution forbids him or her to enter both parliamentary chambers.[79]

Parliamentary control over Council meetings is equally informal, though far more recent and incomplete: since October 2014, the EAC of the National Assembly has organized, sometimes with other sectoral committees, *ex ante* hearings behind closed doors.[80] The Senate is considering introducing a similar practice but has not implemented this yet. *Ex post* control is much rarer: until 2016, no such type of control existed. However, a hearing after a Council meeting was organized in March 2016,[81] and it remains to be seen whether this practice will be developed in the future. In fact, the only possibility for *ex post* control has thus far resided in the scrutiny of the reports that the government has produced since 2013 as follow-up to parliamentary resolutions.[82]

Even this procedure is not fully satisfactory, however, because it only applies to resolutions adopted on an EU legislative proposal (thus not to resolutions that do not address an EU legislative proposal but more general issues of EU policy) and the corresponding government report is transmitted after the Council has already agreed on the proposal, thus preventing the chambers from having any influence. Hence, whereas procedures of control over European Council meetings are well developed and well established, the mechanisms for monitoring Council meetings are significantly less comprehensive and more recent.

[75] *Ordonnances* are government acts in the legal domain, whereas *circulaires* are administrative orders of the government.

[76] Resolutions represent the respective chamber's position, whereas conclusions are approved by the EACs alone.

[77] Valentin Kreilinger, Kateryna Perepechay, and Olivier Rozenberg, 'Report on France' in Wessels and others (n 7) Annex 1, 47.

[78] Fromage, 'National Parliaments and Governmental Accountability in the Crisis' (n 60) 168.

[79] Constitution, art 18. A proposal to reform the Constitution to allow the President to appear in Parliament was made by MP Philip Cordery in November 2015. *Assemblée nationale, Rapport d'information no 3195 'L'Assemblée nationale et l'Union européenne: quel bilan? Quelles perspectives?'* (2015) 42. Note, however, that the President may give a statement to both chambers sitting together as Congress.

[80] *Assemblée nationale* (n 79) 24–25.

[81] Transcript of the meeting of the EAC of the National Assembly, No 263, 15 March 2016 http://www.assemblee-nationale.fr/14/europe/c-rendus/c0263.asp (last accessed 14 October 2016).

[82] See on this topic *Sénat, Rapport d'information no 441 fait au nom de la Commission des affaires européennes sur le suivi des résolutions européennes, des avis motivés et des avis politiques*, 4 March 2016.

As in the UK, the euro crisis has not prompted the formalization of Parliament's rights in the framework of these EU meetings. This does not mean, however, that it has not been empowered at all: for instance, the government now has to submit the yearly stability programme to Parliament and this represents an important change in the government's position of superiority in budgetary matters.[83]

2.6 Comparative Analysis

Of the five Member States analyzed, only Germany has well defined and formally anchored norms for the systematic parliamentary scrutiny of Council and European Council meetings. In Italy, instruments exist but for Council meetings MPs have to make a request for *ex ante* control to take place. In Spain, in practice the government appears in Parliament both before and after European Council meetings, whereas, as in Italy, the Joint Committee has to request the organization of a hearing for it to take place before or after Council meetings. In the UK, the exchange of information on Council meetings takes place in writing, unless the government is called to give evidence beforehand. Information on European Council meetings is also transmitted in the form of letters beforehand, and during a debate afterwards. Finally, the French system, like the British one, is solely based on practice and it is largely asymmetric: whereas debates have regularly been organized around European Council meetings in recent years, hearings around Council meetings are far more recent. They are in fact only held in the National Assembly and, until very recently, only *ex ante*.

Consequently, the Lisbon Treaty and the euro crisis have indeed prompted an increase in government accountability towards Parliament, but only in some of these five Member States and in different manners. For instance, the provision of information on European Council meetings was expanded in Germany, whereas concerning Council meetings the situation improved in Germany and Italy. The possibility for holding hearings with the government is now broader: in Germany on European Council meetings; and in Germany, Spain, and Italy on Council meetings. Finally, Parliament's potential for influence has increased in both frameworks in Germany and Italy.

In the following section, the practical use of these control instruments and their evolution over the years is examined in order to determine whether any variations are visible.

3. Political Practice of Executive Accountability and Its Evolution

While formal and informal procedures have been put in place for parliamentary control over their governments when they take part in Council and European Council meetings, assessing the extent to which these governments are accountable in practice is complicated by the fact that parliaments may prefer exerting influence through informal contacts where a link of confidence exists between a given parliamentary chamber and government: in this way, when divergences of views occur between the parliament and its government they are not visible to the public.[84] Additionally, information

[83] Jančić, 'National Parliaments and EU Fiscal Integration' (n 7) 243.

[84] Katrin Auel, 'The Europeanisation of the German Bundestag: Institutional Change and Informal Adaptation' (2006) 15 German Politics 249, 259 ff.

regarding written reports prepared by governments or even regarding the discussions held at the committee level may not always be available to the public, because transcripts are not always published. Nonetheless, the organization of plenary and committee debates *ex ante* and *ex post* may indicate the actual level of scrutiny exercised.

The aim of this section is therefore to analyze the evolution of this practice and determine whether the frequency of parliamentary control over the government has varied over time, especially where no formal rules exist. This will allow us to determine whether parliaments' interest for these European meetings was only ephemeral and due to the salience of the issues discussed; or whether, in contrast, these scrutiny procedures have become part of the parliamentary routine.

3.1 Germany

In Germany, numerous hearings have been organized before and after European Council meetings since the introduction of this obligation in 2009. Chancellor Merkel regularly appeared in the *Bundestag*'s plenary sessions during the period in which the European Council agreed on important measures in the economic domain,[85] although MPs adopted no legally binding mandates.[86] This practice has since continued and the Chancellor normally appears shortly before the European Council meeting takes place, when most information is available.[87] In contrast, very few *ex post* debates take place in the plenary.[88] Between 2009 and 2013, this happened on two occasions only: in relation to the European Council meeting of 8–9 December 2011, which decided on the Fiscal Compact;[89] and in relation to the European Council meeting of 7–8 February 2013, which concerned the approval of the EU multiannual financial framework. Since then—ie during the current, 18th legislature, which began in 2014—only two *ex post* hearings have taken place: after the informal meeting of 23 September 2015 on the refugee crisis, and after the informal dinner of 27 May 2014 on Ukraine and the new priorities for the EU. Otherwise, these hearings take place before the EAC.

As regards Council meetings, an analysis of the protocols of the meetings of this committee shows frequent parliamentary involvement both *ex ante* and *ex post*. Nevertheless, no transcripts of these meetings are available, so their content is unknown.

3.2 Italy

The Italian Parliament has long been 'fairly systematically' informed of the items on the European Council agenda and of the intended position of the Italian government, because the corresponding legal requirement was laid down in the so-called 'Law

[85] *Ex ante* debates: ordinary meetings of the European Council of 24–25 March 2011; informal meeting of the European Council and meeting of the Heads of State or Government of the Euro Area of 26 October 2011; ordinary meetings of the European Council of 8–9 December 2011 and of 1–2 March 2012. *Ex post* debate: ordinary meeting of the European Council of 8–9 December 2011. Claudia Hefftler and Oliver Höing, 'Report on Germany' in Wessels and others (n 7) Annex 1, 56.

[86] Oliver Höing, 'With a Little Help of the Constitutional Court: The Bundestag on Its Way to an Active Policy Shaper' in Claudia Hefftler and others (eds), *The Palgrave Handbook on National Parliaments and the European Union* (Palgrave Macmillan 2015) 198.

[87] *Europapolitische Debatten in der 18. Wahlperiode des Deutschen Bundestages—Auswahl* https://www.bundestag.de/bundestag/ausschuesse18/a21/-/272886 (last accessed 14 October 2016).

[88] *Datenhandbuch des Bundestags, Kap. 6.11*, 17th legislative period (2009–2013) 26–29.

[89] Treaty on Stability, Coordination and Governance in the Economic and Monetary Union of 2 March 2012.

Buttiglione' of 2005.[90] Since 2013, when the aforesaid new statute was adopted to adapt the Italian system to the Lisbon Treaty started to be applied, *ex ante* information on European Council meetings has been provided in plenary sessions. However, these exchanges with the government in the plenary are not very efficient because government statements are rather general, vague, and more of a political nature than of a technical one.[91] This was particularly problematic when the euro crisis was hitting hardest and MPs would have required to be informed in detail of the decisions taken by the European Council. Despite this, the crisis and the importance of European Council decisions did manage to trigger more parliamentary interest,[92] and MPs' closer involvement in enforcing executive accountability.[93] *Ex post* hearings take place at the committee level, usually before the Foreign Affairs and the EACs of both chambers convening in a joint session.[94]

With regard to Council meetings, the effectiveness of the existing procedures is still quite limited, not least because sectoral committees do not frequently request government officials to appear in hearings.[95] Only recently have the committees begun using their right to hold *ex post* hearings and they do not adopt resolutions beforehand. Therefore, there is still room for improvement in the involvement of the Italian parliamentary chambers, especially in the scrutiny of Council meetings.

3.3 Spain

In Spain, parliamentary control over European Council meetings—which precedes the Lisbon Treaty—is regularly conducted both *ex ante* and *ex post*.[96] However, since no timeframe is specified in the law, the prime minister as a rule informs the Congress of Deputies a long time after the European Council meeting has taken place.[97] The two Spanish parliamentary chambers are also not involved in the same way. *Ex ante* control takes place in the Joint Committee on EU Affairs. In contrast, *ex post* hearings take place before the Congress of Deputies only, which means that the Senate is not involved at all. This can be explained by the fact that no confidence relationship exists between the Senate and the Spanish government and that the Senate is weaker than the Chamber of Deputies also in domestic matters in many respects, for instance regarding the approval of organic laws or constitutional reforms.[98]

90 Sabrina Cavatorto, 'Italy: Still Looking for a New Era in the Making of EU Policy?' in Claudia Hefftler and others (eds), *The Palgrave Handbook of National Parliaments and the European Union* (Palgrave Macmillan 2015) 216.

91 Michele Comelli, 'Report on Italy' in Wessels and others (n 7) Annex 2, 41.

92 ibid.

93 Empirical data extracted from: Cristina Fasone and Diane Fromage, 'The Agenda-Setting Role of National Parliaments in the EU: Still Marginal?', Paper presented during the ECPR Research Sessions, Nijmegen, 1–2 July 2015.

94 Antonio Esposito, 'La legge 24 dicembre 2012, n 234, sulla partecipazione dell'Italia alla formazione e all'attuazione della normativa e delle politiche dell'Unione europea: Parte I—Prime riflessioni sul ruolo delle Camere' (2013) 2 Federalismi.it (Rivista di diritto pubblico italiano, comparato, europeo) 1, 22 and 36–39.

95 ibid 22.

96 Ariadna Salazar Quiñonez, *La participación de los parlamentos nacionales en la Unión Europea* (Congreso de los diputados 2015) 160 ff.

97 Fromage, '*Les parlements dans l'Union Européenne après le Traité de Lisbonne*' (n 51) 234.

98 For instance, the Congress of Deputies has the final say on the approval of organic laws (art 81 Spanish Constitution) and it can ignore the Senate's opposition to a reform of the Constitution (art 167).

When it comes to scrutinizing Council action, the Secretary of State still rarely appears to discuss a specific EU legislative proposal.[99] Hence, hearings largely focus on European Council meetings.

3.4 The United Kingdom

In the House of Commons, for a plenary debate to be organized the government must accept to put it on the agenda or schedule it on its own initiative.[100] As a result, not all parliamentary requests for debate are accepted.[101]

In this House, debates on European Council meetings still mostly take place *ex post*, while *ex ante* hearings with government representatives that existed in the past have not yet been restored, despite the fact that a recommendation in this regard has recently been made.[102] The frequency of government statements has not decreased.[103] Most recently, the EU referendum of 23 June 2016 and the possibility of a 'Brexit' have been at the top of the EU agenda in the last few months and this explains a higher interest for European Council meetings. In the House of Lords, a ministerial statement is simply read out in the plenary. This serves to fulfil the obligation to inform peers of EU affairs, but it does not allow for any kind of debate with the government.[104] As in other NPs, this has led the House of Lords to advocate a shift from *ex post to ex ante* scrutiny.[105] However, this was not welcomed by the government, which replied that 'in practice a pre-European Council session would be of limited value given that the Minister would be unable to disclose the details of UK negotiating aims publicly and that the agendas, and certainly the details, of such meetings are often finalized at the last minute'.[106] The existence of divergent views on this point was also visible from the government's refusal to organize a pre-European Council hearing in October 2014. This showed the government's reticence in divulging information on forthcoming European Council activities in spite of the Lords' disapproval, although the government was willing to organize two evidence sessions ahead of European Council meetings at the end of 2014 and at the beginning of 2015.[107]

With regard to the Council, although a formal scrutiny procedure exists, the Lords are dissatisfied with the manner in which it is implemented in relation to EU legislative documents. For instance, Lord Davies of Stamford (Lab) recently proposed lifting the scrutiny reserve only after a hearing with the responsible minister, instead of on

99 Quiñonez (n 96) 151–52.

100 This has been criticized in Christopher Howarth, 'What Does Putting Parliament Back in Control Entail?' in *Measured or Makeshift? Parliamentary Scrutiny of the European Union* (Hansard Society) 37, 40.

101 For instance, the EAC asked the government to organize a debate on the free movement of persons in January 2014 and one year later, but this initiative was not successful. House of Commons (n 63) paras 13 ff.

102 House of Lords (n 20) paras 179–80.

103 House of Commons Hansard.

104 For instance, on 21 July 2014 (Lords Hansard, col 980 ff), 23 February 2015 (col 1446 ff), and 23 March 2015 (col 1261 ff).

105 House of Lords (n 20) 11. In debating the role of NPs in the EU, Lord Teverson (LibDem) in fact recently advocated the publicity of pre-Council scrutiny sessions (Lords Hansard 15 December 2014, col 64).

106 UK Government, 'Government Response to the House of Lords European Union Committee Report HL 151 of Session 2013–14: The Role of National Parliaments in the European Union' (2014) 4.

107 House of Lords, EU Committee, 'Correspondence with Ministers—June-December 2014', 22–23.

the basis of the government's explanatory memorandums, as is currently the case.[108] The merely declaratory and informative nature of the written statements submitted to Parliament before Council meetings made by the responsible ministers supports, at least partially, the thesis that parliamentary scrutiny of Council meetings is unsatisfactory. However, given their different constitutional role and composition, the two UK parliamentary chambers have assigned different levels of importance to scrutinizing Council meetings. Whereas the House of Commons focuses almost entirely on influencing and monitoring EU ministers, the House of Lords also seeks to exchange views with, and exert influence on, EU institutions directly.[109] Beyond this, a positive aspect of the British system concerns transparency, in particular towards the citizens: all government statements are made public and put online.[110] This is not necessarily the case with documents exchanged between governments and parliaments in France or Spain. Yet, even in Britain, the government does transmit written information to the chambers, but it is not systematically called to give account of its actions orally.

3.5 France

As stated above, hearings before and after Council and European Council meetings take place informally in the French Parliament.

As regards European Council meetings, the Senate—which is not linked to the government by a relationship of confidence—has been much more strongly inclined to organize *ex ante* plenary debates than the National Assembly: twenty-one versus eight from 2010 to 2014.[111] However, the frequency of *ex ante* debates in the Senate has recently increased: in 2015 and 2016, all European Council meetings were systematically preceded by a debate.[112] Despite this increase, in the opinion of two MPs, the interest for the *ex ante* hearings in the National Assembly has decreased over time.[113] They propose that, in order to make them more attractive, resolutions should be adopted and debates on the most important European Council meetings should be followed by a vote.[114] Until recently, *ex post* debates were organized much more frequently by the EAC of the National Assembly than by the counterpart committee of the Senate: fifteen versus seven from 2010 to 2014. In the last two years, both committees have indeed organized systematic debates.[115]

Hearings before Council meetings in the National Assembly have only been organized since October 2014 and are still held rather infrequently: only seven such meetings took place between October 2014 and November 2015.[116] Nevertheless, this new practice is a positive development because it allows MPs to express their opinion to the government representative, especially since these pre-Council meetings take place

[108] Lords Hansard (15 December 2014, col 71). A similar statement was also made by Lord Inglewood (Con) (col 84).

[109] Huff and Smith, 'Westminster and the European Union: Ever-increasing Scepticism?' (n 66) 314.

[110] See http://europeanmemoranda.cabinetoffice.gov.uk/ (last accessed 14 October 2016).

[111] Fromage, 'National Parliaments and Governmental Accountability in the Crisis' (n 60) 168.

[112] *'L'Europe en séance publique'* http://www.senat.fr/europe/debats.html (last accessed 14 October 2016).

[113] *Assemblée nationale* (n 79) 42.

[114] ibid 42–43.

[115] Minutes of the meetings of the EACs are available at http://www2.assemblee-nationale.fr/14/autres-commissions/commission-des-affaires-europeennes/(block)/ComptesRendusCommission/(init)/0 (last accessed 14 October 2016) and http://www.senat.fr/europe/reunions.html (last accessed 14 October 2016).

[116] *Assemblée nationale* (n 79) 25.

behind closed doors. This procedure is very different from any mandating system, such as the Danish one,[117] but it is more efficient and it intervenes at a more appropriate moment than the approval of resolutions or conclusions does. Another novelty, witnessed in 2016, is the organization of a hearing after Council meetings.

3.6 Comparative Analysis

The analysis of the use of accountability mechanisms on the occasion of Council and European Council meetings in the five parliaments studied reveals a tendency in recent years towards tighter parliamentary scrutiny in France and Italy, although the practice shows that Council meetings in particular could still be more closely scrutinized in these two Member States. In Spain, too, the scrutiny of Council meetings could be tighter. In the UK and Germany, in contrast, the information flow works properly, although Germany has the most comprehensive accountability procedures that comprise both written and oral information.

The Lisbon Treaty and to some extent the euro crisis have led to the reinforcement of the rules that govern government accountability to parliament in the framework of Council and European Council meetings—especially in Germany, Italy, and Spain. In France, new informal procedures, not linked directly to the aforementioned developments, have produced similar effects. The practice shows that governments could still be more systematically held to account by their parliaments when they participate in Council or European Council meetings, but this situation surely marks an improvement with regard to the pre-Lisbon situation, when fewer formal rules existed and when the governments were hence even less accountable. More robust accountability is all the more important and necessary given that both the Lisbon Treaty and the euro crisis have contributed to the European Council becoming more powerful, as highlighted in the introduction.

4. Concluding Remarks

Although the Lisbon Treaty and the euro crisis have led to the empowerment of national governments by increasing the importance especially of the European Council, these same developments have also positively affected executive accountability to parliaments. The five case studies analyzed here show that the legal reforms carried out by these Member States to adapt to the new EU and fiscal framework have generally allowed for better information, more frequent hearings, and increased parliamentary influence. Practice has also been instrumental in allowing parliaments to better scrutinize and hold governments to account. This reveals that the changes made when particularly salient economic issues were dealt with by the European Council are long-lasting, whereas the control over Council meetings is, at least in some cases, still only beginning.

Furthermore, as noted by Ariella Huff and Julie Smith about European Council meetings, 'in the UK, as in many other states there has been a tradition of Prime Ministers appearing to say one thing on leaving a summit and another when inside the room'.[118] This is highly problematic because it allows neither citizens nor their

[117] See on the Danish system Mette Buskjaer Christensen, 'The Danish Folketing and EU Affairs: Is the Danish Model of Parliamentary Scrutiny Still Best Practice?' in Claudia Hefftler and others (eds), *The Palgrave Handbook on National Parliaments and the European Union* (Palgrave Macmillan 2015).

[118] Ariella Huff and Julie Smith, 'Report on the United Kingdom' (n 64) 67.

elected representatives to exercise effective scrutiny and sanction their representatives in a future election if they remain unsatisfied with the government's actions. However, an additional increase in transparency might lead to decisions being taken outside the formal arenas,[119] owing to the fear that there may be political consequences for the national representatives if it becomes openly clear that they have adopted a position which is not in line with parliament's views or with what they had committed to in their electoral programmes.

Some secrecy in the work of sectoral and European affairs committees of NPs is required to enable the government to disclose its positions on EU dossiers more freely, but also to justify their choices in relation to other Member States' positions, which they may be reluctant to do in a public session. Nevertheless, although the situation is less problematic with respect to the Council than it is with respect to the more opaque European Council,[120] a balance needs to be struck between, on the one hand, the need to ensure transparency and to enable the citizens to understand and be fully informed about the original position of their government, and, on the other hand, the secrecy required within these two EU institutions.[121] Because the Council and the European Council mostly function on the basis of consensus even where qualified majority voting applies,[122] secrecy is particularly important for government representatives to be able to negotiate freely and reach a consensus.

The preceding analysis of five EU Member States demonstrates that much room for improvement exists and that this would jeopardize neither the governments' negotiating capacities nor the possibility for them to reach a consensus. While parliamentary mandates are not necessary, it would be desirable for government officials to inform their parliaments more systematically and in good time before meetings at the EU level take place. Exchange of information a few days in advance would allow for transmitted information to be accurate and it would allow MPs better opportunities to give their opinion on EU affairs than up to now. It would therefore be desirable for EU-related information to be made available only to parliaments and not to the general public too. Furthermore, it is advised for these *ex ante* meetings to be organized before the competent sectoral and European affairs committees jointly and behind closed doors. In this way, government representatives, MPs, peers, and senators could have a more open and honest debate. In contrast, *ex post* scrutiny should be as open as possible and organized before the plenary, so that EU affairs do not remain a matter for a few interested MPs. The level of detail of the German system of scrutiny, which is extremely protective of parliamentary prerogatives, may be perceived as a model that all parliaments should consider adopting, whereas the Spanish system could be followed concerning the balance that it strikes between the involvement of the plenary and the EAC.

[119] House of Commons, European Scrutiny Committee, HC 86 'The Conclusions of the European Council and the Council of Ministers: Follow up Report', 10th Report of Session 2007–08, 4 February 2008, 6.

[120] See on the evolution of Council transparency Maarten Zbigniew Hillebrandt, Deirdre Curtin, and Albert Meijer, 'Transparency in the EU Council of Ministers: An Institutional Analysis' (2014) 20 ELJ 1.

[121] The necessity to preserve the confidentiality of the negotiating documents was underlined for instance by the French National Assembly. See *Assemblée nationale* (n 79) 43.

[122] TEU, art 15(4) states that 'except where the Treaties provide otherwise, decisions of the European Council shall be taken by consensus' and, in practice, the President of the European Council does everything in its power to reach a consensus. Jacques Ziller, *Diritto delle politiche e delle istituzioni dell'Unione europea* (Il Mulino 2013) 368. The 1966 Luxembourg Compromise, according to which even decisions that have to be taken by qualified majority voting should be taken on the basis of consensus, was never revoked (ibid 374) and consensus is usually sought.

The scrutiny of Council meetings is less problematic in the sense that NPs already scrutinize EU legislative proposals from the moment that they are published and in most cases promptly transmit their views to the government. However, it is the issues discussed *during* Council meetings that are the most contentious given that they could not be agreed upon within the Council's preparatory bodies. Scrutiny of Council meetings thus appears to be essential, especially because 'for EU legislation, the parliamentary majority does not have the power to amend decisions according to its preferences, and even its veto power is reduced in scope'.[123] Whereas in the national legislative process MPs normally have the possibility to propose amendments and vote against bills, in EU affairs they can only impose limited sanctions against the government when the latter does not follow parliamentary recommendations or does not defend the position it had announced it would. The only remaining option for a parliament to exert influence is to remove its confidence in the government. Even when it has to transpose EU measures with which it disagrees, the legislature only has a limited margin of manoeuvre since EU directives set the substantive framework of its actions.[124] Any attempt by a national parliament to use transposition as a means to exert influence in EU matters, a strategy that the French Parliament followed during the early years of the European integration process because it was not sufficiently consulted *ex ante*,[125] exposes the Member State to EU sanctions for not respecting EU norms.

In conclusion, even if the only risk the government faces is political blame, since this is usually the only tool parliaments have at their disposal, NPs should continue to control their governments' action in the Council and the European Council. This chapter shows that NPs have tended to be more active over the past years and this evolution is a particularly welcome development. Parliaments have therefore been resilient in their quest for greater governmental accountability rather than resigned. These efforts need to be pursued further in some parliamentary chambers, such as those in France and Italy. Only in this way will MPs, senators, and peers eventually truly contribute to the reduction of the EU democratic deficit.

[123] Sprungk (n 14) 554.

[124] See on parliaments' involvement in transposition procedures: Carina Sprungk, 'Legislative Transposition of Directives: Exploring the Other Role of National Parliaments in the European Union' (2013) 51 JCMS 298.

[125] Jean-Luc Sauron, 'Le contrôle parlementaire de l'activité gouvernementale en matière communautaire en France' (1999) 35 Revue Trimestrielle de Droit Européen 171, 196.

10

Parliaments as Arenas of Representation and Public Contestation

Insights from the Eurozone Crisis

Frank Wendler

1. The Eurozone Crisis—Endangering or Changing Parliamentary Representation?

An important concern arising from the Eurozone crisis is that it may have diminished the influence of parliaments in EU decision-making. Some observers have pointed out that at the supranational level, the decision-making role of the European Parliament has been challenged by the increased crisis-management role of technocratic institutions such as the European Central Bank, and by intergovernmental bodies such as the European Council, the Council of Ministers, and the Eurogroup.[1] At the level of domestic politics, concerns were raised that the role of national parliaments (NPs) has been affected through the often non-transparent and fast-paced intergovernmental negotiations of bail-out programmes and Eurozone governance arrangements.[2] These observations seem to suggest that the management of the Eurozone crisis has led to a crisis of parliamentary representation and democracy in Europe.[3]

This chapter seeks to challenge this view. Its main argument is that the involvement of NPs in Eurozone governance has not simply decreased, but that it has expanded and transformed through events related to the management of the Eurozone crisis. While the government-related involvement of parliaments as scrutinizers and policy-making actors may have come under pressure, NPs have assumed a stronger citizen-related role as institutions representing political actors with dissenting views on the resolution of the crisis, and as arenas of public deliberation between these actors. The key reason for this change is the increased political salience of EU decision-making: measures aimed at immediate crisis management in the form of bail-out programmes as well

[1] Berthold Rittberger, 'Integration without Representation? The European Parliament and the Reform of Economic Governance in the EU' (2014) 52(6) JCMS 1174; Cristina Fasone, 'European Economic Governance and Parliamentary Representation. What Place for the European Parliament?' (2014) 20(2) ELJ 164; Sergio Fabbrini, 'Intergovernmentalism and Its Limits: Assessing the European Union's Answer to the Euro Crisis' (2013) 46(9) Comp Pol Stud 1003.

[2] Arthur Benz, 'An Asymmetric Two-level Game: Parliaments in the Euro Crisis' in Ben Crum and John Erik Fossum (eds), *Practices of Inter-parliamentary Coordination in International Politics: The European Union and Beyond* (ECPR Press 2013); Sonja Puntscher Riekmann and Doris Wydra, 'Representation in the European State of Emergency: Parliaments against Governments?' (2013) 35(5) J Eur Integration 565.

[3] Jürgen Habermas, *The Crisis of the European Union: A Response* (Polity Press 2012); Ben Crum, 'Saving the Euro at the Cost of Democracy?' (2013) 51(4) JCMS 614; Fritz Scharpf, 'After the Crash: A Perspective on Multilevel European Democracy' (2014) MPIfG Discussion Paper 14/21 http://www.mpifg.de/pu/mpifg_dp/dp14-21.pdf (last accessed 22 May 2016).

Parliaments as Arenas of Representation and Public Contestation: Insights from the Eurozone Crisis. First Edition. Frank Wendler. Published 2017 by Oxford University Press.

as institutional innovations in Eurozone governance, such as the European Stability Mechanism (ESM), become politicized as issues that reach into the core of fiscal and economic competences.[4] This chapter seeks to show that, as a consequence, in NPs these issues can no longer be debated behind closed doors at the committee level. As the amount and visibility of domestic plenary debates on Eurozone decisions have grown, public communication and debate about EU issues have moved to the foreground, demonstrating a more openly political and democratic involvement of NPs in the making of decisions on the resolution of the Eurozone crisis.[5]

Against this background, the objective of this chapter is to provide insight into the manner in which NPs have performed their roles of representation and communication in the context of the Eurozone crisis. This is carried out by investigating two forms of involvement: (a) the authorization of bail-out measures and the ratification of institutional innovations through measures such as the Treaty on Stability, Coordination and Governance in the Economic and Monetary Union (Fiscal Compact); and (b) public communication through plenary debates addressing these decisions and the governance of the Eurozone generally.

The analysis adopts a comparative perspective by examining three parliaments of Eurozone Member States that establish very different institutional and party political contexts for public debate: the Austrian *Nationalrat*, the French *Assemblée nationale*, and the German *Bundestag*. The aim is to show that in addition to differences in the overall activity of legislatures in ratifying and debating Eurozone crisis decisions, the three parliaments set different conditions for the public interaction between three sets of political actors with different roles in the justification of the management of the Eurozone crisis: representatives of national executives, members of parliamentary majority groups, and groups in the parliamentary opposition. Starting with a survey of votes taken on the authorization of bail-out measures and the ratification of the institutional reforms in the governance of the Eurozone (such as the ESM), the main part of this chapter compares the interaction of these three actor groups with regard to their relative presence and form of interaction in parliamentary debates.

This comparison demonstrates that, while all the three parliaments compared have engaged in a substantial amount of public debate about the resolution of the Eurozone crisis, substantial differences are identifiable concerning the form of their involvement as debating and authorizing institutions. Depending on the format of parliamentary debate on EU decision-making (such as declarations by the government, thematic debates, or inquiries by the opposition), parliaments foster three different types of communication on the management of the Eurozone crisis: first, top-down discourse

[4] Hanspeter Kriesi and Edgar Grande, 'The Euro Crisis: A Boost to the Politicisation of European Integration?' in Swen Hutter, Edgar Grande, and Hanspeter Kriesi (eds), *Politicising Europe: Integration and Mass Politics* (Cambridge University Press 2016); Pieter de Wilde, Anna Leupold, and Henning Schmidtke, 'Introduction: The Differentiated Politicisation of European Governance' (2015) 39(1) WEP 3.

[5] Katrin Auel and Tapio Raunio, 'Introduction: Connecting with the Electorate? Parliamentary Communication in EU Affairs' (2014) 20(1) J Legis Stud 1; Katrin Auel and Tapio Raunio, 'Debating the State of the Union? Comparing Parliamentary Debates on EU Issues in Finland, France, Germany and the United Kingdom' (2014) 20(1) J Legis Stud 13; Pieter de Wilde, 'The Operating Logics of National Parliaments and Mass Media in the Politicisation of Europe' (2014) 20(1) J Legis Stud 46; Frank Wendler, 'End of Consensus? The European Leadership Discourse of the Second Merkel Government during the Eurozone Crisis and Its Contestation in Debates of the Bundestag (2009–13)' (2014) 23(4) German Politics 446; Arndt Wonka, 'The Party Politics of the Euro Crisis in the German Bundestag: Frames, Positions and Salience' (2016) 39(1) WEP 125; Christian Rauh, 'Communicating Supranational Governance? The Salience of EU Affairs in the German Bundestag, 1991–2013' (2013) 16(1) Eur Union Pol 116.

on the justification of EU decisions that is framed and dominated by the executive and that is most visible in the French National Assembly; secondly, critical contestation of government policies by parties in the parliamentary opposition, a form of debate most strongly found in the Austrian *Nationalrat*; and thirdly, horizontal deliberation between parliamentary party groups with proportionate amounts of participants and speaking time, a form of debate most clearly present in the case of the German *Bundestag*.

The chapter proceeds in four steps. The following section reviews the authorizing role of parliaments in the Eurozone crisis (section 2). The main part then presents a survey of plenary debates in the three parliaments selected (section 3). The findings are systematized in a comparative section (section 4) and summarized in the conclusion (section 5).

2. The Authorizing Role of National Parliaments in the Management of the Eurozone Crisis

Ratification and authorization votes required by Eurozone crisis decisions are among the key triggers for an increased communicative involvement of NPs. These votes are mostly taken in the plenary and in most cases they are preceded by a substantial amount of debate. The Eurozone crisis led to several institutional innovations that required ratification by NPs. The first was the creation of the European Financial Stabilization Facility (EFSF), established after approval votes were passed in the NPs of all the euro area Member States. Beyond this temporary mechanism, further novelties were the establishment of a permanent ESM, the conclusion of the Fiscal Compact, and the related revision of Article 136 TFEU. These institutional modifications required ratification not just within the Eurozone but across EU Member States, in some cases even requiring super-majorities to be passed into law. Therefore, except for the Member States that were not parties to these agreements (the United Kingdom and the Czech Republic), the NPs of all EU Member States passed ratification votes on the ESM and Fiscal Compact.[6]

Furthermore, some legislatures were also involved in the operation of financial assistance programmes through plenary votes. In this context, the German *Bundestag* stands out as very active in authorizing the enactment of crisis management measures, a development that was to a considerable degree prompted by rulings of the Federal Constitutional Court.[7] Until the authorization of a third bail-out programme for Greece, a total of thirteen votes were passed by the *Bundestag*, both to ratify European

[6] European Parliament, Note of DG for Internal Policies—Policy Department C on Citizens' Rights and Constitutional Affairs, 'Article 136 TFEU, ESM, Fiscal Stability Treaty—Ratification Requirements and Present Situation in the Member States', 11 June 2013; Aleksandra Maatsch, 'Limited and Asymmetrical: Approval of Anti-crisis Measures (EFSF, ESM, and TSCG) by National Parliaments in the Eurozone' in Cristina Fasone, Diane Fromage, and Zoe Lefkofridi (eds), *Parliaments, Public Opinion and Parliamentary Elections in Europe*, EUI Working Paper MWP 2015/18; Anna-Lena Kirch and Daniela Schwarzer, 'Die Ratifizierung des Fiskalpakts und des ESM in den Ländern der Eurozone—rechtliche und politische Rahmenbedingungen' (2012) Forschungsgruppe EU-Integration, SWP Berlin https://www.swp-berlin.org/fileadmin/contents/products/arbeitspapiere/Fiskalpakt_Ratifizierung_KS.pdf (last accessed 7 January 2016).

[7] Oliver Höing, 'With a Little Help of the Constitutional Court: The Bundestag on Its Way to an Active Policy Shaper' in Claudia Hefftler and others (eds), *The Palgrave Handbook of National Parliaments and the European Union* (Palgrave Macmillan 2015); Mattias Wendel, 'Judicial Restraint and the Return to Openness: The Decision of the German Federal Constitutional Court on the ESM and the Fiscal Treaty of 12 September 2012' (2013) 14(1) German LJ 21.

decisions needing parliamentary approval and to authorize political action taken for the management of the Eurozone crisis.[8] However, the *Bundestag* is not the only NP voting on them. For example, on the adoption of a third bail-out programme for Greece in August 2015, votes were also passed in the parliaments of Austria, Estonia, Finland, France, Lithuania, Latvia, the Netherlands, and Spain—in addition to that of Greece. On balance, the parliaments of nine out of eighteen Member States of the euro area passed a vote to authorize this bail-out.[9]

The significance of these authorization votes lies not so much in influencing the specific details of Eurozone crisis management policy as much in triggering public debate and party political contestation of it. In most cases, agreements between Eurozone Member States that need to be ratified are forwarded to parliament without the possibility of significant modification, especially in the case of institutional innovations such as the ESM or Fiscal Compact, which were negotiated beforehand and are not easily modified by a single legislature. In political reality, therefore, a positive outcome of authorization votes is almost certainly assured. However, such votes in the plenary matter insofar as they enable us to identify dissenting actors not just within the opposition but frequently also within the parliamentary majority groups as well as to provide a setting for them to articulate their arguments. In this sense, ratification votes matter less as an institutional check on the executive than as an indicator of the degree of consensus on European integration between political parties, and often also as a test for the cohesion of the parliamentary majority. Therefore, the political significance of ratification and authorization votes cannot properly be appraised without considering the voting results and, more specifically, the number and distribution of dissenting votes against the adoption of crisis management measures. A brief survey of the voting results in the three Eurozone legislatures selected—in Austria, France, and Germany—demonstrates that although parliamentary votes on these measures were generally passed by clear majorities, the results of votes nevertheless indicated the emergence of party political disagreement on Eurozone crisis management policies.

In the case of the *Bundestag*, the major source of disagreement stems from the voting behaviour of the Left Party (*Die Linke*), whose parliamentary caucus has consistently voted against all decisions taken in the management of the Eurozone crisis, except for the extension of the financial assistance programme for Greece in February 2015. Among the mainstream parties, the Social Democrats (SPD) shifted from abstention in the first bail-out for Greece and the EFSF to positive votes with relatively few dissenters. Within the ranks of the governing Christian Democrats (CDU/CSU), the number of abstentions and dissenting votes has grown over the course of the Eurozone crisis: from about a dozen to twenty-nine in the vote on the extension of the Greek bail-out programme; then sixty votes against the mandate for negotiations on a new bail-out programme in July 2015; and no less than sixty-three votes against the third

[8] In addition to the votes on the establishment of the EFSF (21 May 2010), the ESM and the Fiscal Compact (both on 29 June 2012), the *Bundestag* also passed votes on the three financial assistance programmes for Greece (7 May 2010, 27 February 2012, and 19 August 2015), the bail-out programme for Ireland (1 December 2010), Portugal (12 May 2011), Spain (19 July 2012), and Cyprus (18 April 2013), the extension of the operation of the EFSF (29 September 2011), and three decisions required for the prolongation of the existing assistance programme for Greece, and a mandate for negotiations on the third bail-out for Greece (18 December 2014, 27 February 2015, and 17 July 2015).

[9] EurActiv, 'France Accepts Greek Deal, Calls for Eurozone Government', 16 July 2015 http://www.euractiv.com/sections/euro-finance/france-accepts-greek-deal-calls-eurozone-government-316375 (last accessed 7 January 2016); EurActiv, 'Dutch Vote Gives Final Go-Ahead to Greek Bailout', 29 August 2015 http://www.euractiv.com/sections/euro-finance/dutch-vote-gives-final-go-ahead-greek-bailout-316940 (last accessed 7 January 2016).

Greek bail-out package. As this brief survey shows, authorization votes have exposed the limits of the party political consensus on EU decision-making in Germany.

Ratification and authorization votes in the Austrian *Nationalrat* show a clearer pattern of polarization between parties of the parliamentary majority and the opposition. In party political terms, this pattern highlights the contrasting positions between the pro-European consensus of the mainstream parties of the 'Grand Coalition'—the Social Democrats (SPÖ) and the centre-right People's Party (ÖVP)—and the Eurosceptic stance of the two populist right-wing parties—the Freedom Party (FPÖ) and the Alliance for the Future of Austria (BZÖ).[10] In the case of the French National Assembly, votes refusing the authorization of decisions for the management of the Eurozone crisis have been cast by a range of parliamentary groups. While the vote on the ratification of the Fiscal Compact on 9 October 2012 passed with a majority of 477 to 70, negative votes were cast by the governing Socialists (twenty votes) as well as the Greens (twelve votes), the Democratic Left (GDR) (thirteen votes), and the centre-right Union for a Popular Movement (UMP) (seventeen votes) of the former President of the Republic Nicolas Sarkozy.[11] The vote on the ratification of the third Greek bail-out on 15 July 2015 was passed by a majority of 412 to 69, with most negative votes cast by parliamentarians of the radical left and the Greens.[12]

This review of the authorization and ratification votes demonstrates that, while political disagreement with the management of the Eurozone crisis has remained limited to minority votes, it has grown enough to erode the consensus between the mainstream parties and to show the dissent of Eurosceptic challengers of both the far-right and the left sides of the political spectrum. Building on these insights on plenary *votes* cast on Eurozone measures, the following section investigates plenary *debates*, where disagreement between political parties emerges even more clearly.

3. Communicative Involvement: Plenary Debates in Three Eurozone Parliaments

It is only quite recently that public communication by parliaments through plenary debates has been discovered as a topic of research for scholars working on the Europeanization of legislatures. Throughout the initial stages of research in this field, a common assumption was that the involvement of parliaments in European governance would take place at the committee level and through informal exchanges behind closed doors. What is more, it was assumed that the most relevant political incentives encountered by parliamentary actors would work against the public communication of and debate on European issues, such as the indifference and sceptical attitudes of the public towards European integration, the often technical and complex content of EU decisions and intra-party disagreements.[13] The considerable increase in the public salience of European politics, caused not least by the Eurozone crisis, now provides more

[10] This pattern emerged in the authorization votes of the *Nationalrat* on the third bail-out programme for Greece (17 July 2015), a vote on the assistance programme for Cyprus (22 April 2013), and the votes on the ESM (3 July 2012) and the extension of the EFSF (30 September 2011).

[11] cp JO 2012/56, 10 October, at 3442.

[12] JO 2015/89, at 6725. See also Euractiv, 'France Accepts Greek Deal, Calls for Eurozone Government', 16 July 2015 http://www.euractiv.com/sections/euro-finance/france-accepts-greek-deal-calls-eurozone-government-316375 (last accessed 7 January 2016).

[13] Tapio Raunio, 'National Parliaments and European Integration: What We Know and Agenda for Future Research' (2009) 15(4) J Legis Stud 317.

solid empirical grounds to assume that public communication is an important part of parliamentary activity in the context of EU decision-making.[14]

Research about public parliamentary debate on the Eurozone crisis has so far been taken forward in two directions. On the one hand, comparative studies have sought to quantify the amount of time spent in the plenary on debates about the EU and Eurozone governance, both in absolute terms and in relation to other parliamentary business. The existing surveys indeed show an increase in the communicative activity of legislatures, but also a considerable variation among NPs in debating EU topics in the plenary.[15] On the other hand, several studies have investigated the content of parliamentary debates on the Eurozone crisis and the related questions of party political contestation and polarization, concluding mostly that these debates feed into the existing cleavages between the political parties on the left and the right.[16]

On this basis, this chapter seeks to establish a new perspective by examining the contextual conditions that determine political representation and communication in various legislatures of the Eurozone Member States. More specifically, the subsequent analysis compares three Eurozone legislatures with respect to the format of debate used to address the management of the crisis (such as government declarations, open debates or question time), the length of debates and number of speakers, and the style of interaction between the speakers. The aim is to investigate the effect that different settings of parliamentary debate have on the balance between three competing forms of public discourse: the positive justification of Eurozone crisis management by governmental actors and parliamentary majority, the critical contestation of these policies by the parliamentary opposition, and the interaction between opposition groups and parliamentary majority.

To elucidate these differences, the analysis compares three parliaments that differ with regard to their institutional position and status, and the party political setting in debates on topics of European integration. While both the German *Bundestag* and the Austrian *Nationalrat* are typically characterized as transformative legislatures (ie parliaments with a strong influence on the substance of policy) with relatively strong rights of involvement in EU affairs, they differ in party political terms because of the presence of two strongly Eurosceptic, populist-right challenger parties in the *Nationalrat*.[17] In comparison, the constellation of a small parliamentary opposition and an oversized parliamentary majority composed of a 'Grand Coalition' of the two mainstream parties is only partially present in the German case—namely, after the federal parliamentary

[14] Thomas Risse, 'European Public Spheres, the Politicization of EU Affairs, and Its Consequences' in Thomas Risse (ed) *European Public Spheres: Politics is Back* (Cambridge University Press 2015); Hutter, Grande, and Kriesi (n 4).

[15] Auel and Raunio (n 5) 13; Katrin Auel, Olivier Rozenberg, and Angela Tacea, 'Fighting Back? And If So, How? Measuring Parliamentary Strength and Activity in EU Affairs' in Claudia Hefftler and others (eds), *The Palgrave Handbook of National Parliaments and the European Union* (Palgrave Macmillan 2015).

[16] Aleksandra Maatsch, 'Are We All Austerians Now? An Analysis of National Parliamentary Parties' Positioning on Anti-Crisis Measures in the Eurozone' (2014) 21(1) JEPP 96; Eric Miklin, 'From "Sleeping Giant" to Left-Right Politicization? National Party Competition on the EU and the Euro Crisis' (2014) 52(6) JCMS 1199; Frank Wendler (n 5) 446–459; Frank Wendler, *Debating Europe in National Parliaments: Public Justification and Political Polarization* (Palgrave Macmillan 2016); Wonka (n 5).

[17] Eric Miklin, 'The Austrian Parliament and EU Affairs: Gradually Living Up to Its Legal Potential' in Claudia Hefftler and others (eds), *Palgrave Handbook of National Parliaments and the European Union* (Palgrave Macmillan 2015); Johannes Pollak and Peter Slominski, 'The Silence of the Shepherds: How the Austrian Parliament Informs Its Citizens on European Issues' (2014) 20(1) J Legis Stud 109.

election in 2013, which led to the return to power of a CDU/SPD coalition after the CDU/FDP minimum-winning coalition.

The French National Assembly, in turn, differs from both previous cases, because it has a weaker institutional position, a more reduced control over the government and over the President of the Republic as the head of the French executive; and because the parliamentary majority is either dominated by or even exclusively consists of one major political party.[18] Combining these institutional and party political factors, the contestation of European policy by the parliamentary opposition would be expected to be strongest in the case of the Austrian *Nationalrat*, whereas a more government-led parliamentary debate would be expected in the French National Assembly, with the German *Bundestag* remaining in-between.

The following empirical review generally confirms but also refines these assumptions. In all three cases, the analysis focuses on plenary debates on the Eurozone crisis since the year 2010, using online parliamentary archives and debate transcripts. The subsequent discussion seeks to demonstrate that differences in the communicative activity of NPs emerge not just with regard to the absolute amount of time spent by parliamentarians debating Eurozone decisions in the plenary,[19] but also with regard to other factors. Importantly, the analysis will show that parliamentarians use different formats of debate to assess decisions taken to resolve the Eurozone crisis and that this carries important implications for the questions of who sets the topic of debate, how time on the parliamentary floor is divided between competing political groups, and how deep and detailed discussions on Eurozone crisis management are.

3.1 German *Bundestag*: Balanced Party Political Debate on the Government's EU Policy

The existing research described above portrays the German *Bundestag* as one of the most active legislatures in the EU in terms of public communication and debate. The comparison presented here resonates with these findings, but tries to go beyond by asking how prevalent formats of debate affect the representation and mutual engagement of public claims made by the executive, the parliamentary majority, and opposition groups. The empirical analysis shows that debates in the *Bundestag* are almost always framed in the terms set by a statement by the Federal Government (usually the Federal Chancellor), but subsequently organized as an extended (usually over an hour) argumentative exchange between all parliamentary groups, with a proportionate number of participants and speaking time allocated to each party group commensurately to its parliamentary representation. In comparison with the two other cases, the *Bundestag* therefore stands out with its very regular, stable, and proportionate form of interaction in the plenary debates on the management of the Eurozone crisis.

Concerning the format of debate, the type of parliamentary session almost exclusively held on EU issues is that on the 'Declaration by the Government' (*Regierungserklärung*), followed by a discussion between all parliamentary groups. Between 2010 and 2015, parliamentary records reveal a total of twenty-nine such debates that are directly related

[18] Anja Thomas and Angela Tacea, 'The French Parliament and the European Union: "Shadow Control" through the Government Majority' in Claudia Hefftler and others (eds), *The Palgrave Handbook of National Parliaments and the European Union* (Palgrave Macmillan 2015); Julien Navarro and Sylvain Brouard, 'Who Cares about the EU? French MPs and the Europeanisation of Parliamentary Questions' (2014) 20(1) J Legis Stud 93.

[19] Katrin Auel, Olivier Rozenberg, and Angela Tacea (n 15) 60–93.

to EU policies, resulting in an average of some five or six debates a year. There is a relatively even spread of these debates over time: eighteen debates took place between 2010 and the end of the 17th legislative period in September 2013, and eleven since then. The topic of these debates is usually a forthcoming or a very recent meeting of the European Council, with a focus on the decisions advocated by the Federal Government at the EU level. While it is difficult to draw a clear line between debates exclusively or primarily addressing the Eurozone crisis and other EU issues, the Eurozone crisis is at the forefront of these debates and several Declarations by the German Government were made that explicitly address questions related to the crisis.[20]

Other types of debate on EU matters either take place less frequently or have less visibility in overall parliamentary business. Only one example of the '*Aktuelle Stunde*', which is an open parliamentary debate without an introductory statement by a government representative, was found with a clear thematic link to the Eurozone crisis. This was the debate on the implications of the Fiscal Compact on democracy and the social state initiated by the Left Party on 9 February 2012.[21] Debates on EU affairs during question time are frequent but less prominent because they are typically a part of extended explanations of the Federal Government's EU policies.

The duration and style of debates on *Regierungserklärungen* are very similar and show little variation among parliamentary sessions. In all but four of the twenty-nine cases reviewed here, the debate started with an opening speech by the Chancellor. After this statement of about 20–25 minutes, some 90–120 minutes are scheduled for debate by representatives of all parliamentary groups, which makes for a parliamentary session of usually two and two and a half hours. In most cases, about twelve speakers are each granted about ten minutes of speaking time to contribute to the debate, sometimes interrupted by questions from the floor. A review of the list of speakers in the debates on European Council meetings reveals that discussion is led by a politically senior but also relatively selective group of parliamentarians. In most cases, the leaders of parliamentary groups address the plenary in extended speeches, followed by relatively shorter statements of parliamentarians specialized in EU affairs, mostly the chairpersons or party spokespersons from committees in charge of EU or budgetary affairs. Through this succession of speakers, the beginning of debates is typically perceived as an exchange between the Federal Chancellor and the leader of the biggest opposition party, an encounter that shifted to a rhetorical duel between Chancellor Merkel and her Social Democratic challenger in the 2013 federal election, Peer Steinbrück.[22]

The later stages of the debate take the form of policy-specific exchanges between less well known specialist MPs, usually allowing speaking time to about four to five speakers from the governing Christian Democrats, two to three speakers from the Social Democratic Party, and one or two speakers from the smaller parties—FDP, B90 Greens, and the Left Party. When it comes to the division of speaking time between the parliamentary majority and the opposition, generally about 70 minutes is allocated to the majority and about 50 minutes to the opposition. This ratio has shifted towards 90/30 after the formation of the 'Grand Coalition' of CDU/CSU and SPD after 2013.

[20] Examples include a debate on 'Stability Assistance for Greece' on 19 August 2015 (BT Plenary Protocol (PlPr) no 18/118), on 'Progress in the Adjustment Program for Greece' on 30 November 2012 (PlPr no 17/212), the extended debate on 'the Creation of a Stability Union' on 29 June 2012 (PlPr no 17/188), and on a 'Declaration on the Measures Taken for the Stabilization of the Euro' on 19 May 2012 (PlPr no 17/42).

[21] cp BT Plenary Protocol 17/158.

[22] Examples of this are debates on 24 March 2011 (BT Plenary Protocol 17/99), 18 October 2012 (17/198), 21 February 2013 (17/222), and 27 June 2013 (17/250).

The only parliamentary group with a Eurosceptic tendency, the Left Party, receives about 15–20 minutes of speaking time in each debate.

In sum, debates in the *Bundestag* provide extensive space for debate on EU issues between all political parties represented in parliament. They are framed as an exchange on the government's policy. The fact that most debates begin with a statement by the Federal Chancellor and that they mostly concentrate on European Council meetings, privileges the decision-making role of the Federal Government. While debates are frequent and sufficiently long to provide adequate room for the expression of views of all parliamentary groups, the governing parties are in a dominant position through the combination of the opening speech and proportional time during debate. In addition, the formation of a 'Grand Coalition' between the two major parties after the 2013 federal election further restricts the relative amount of time allocated to the two remaining, much smaller parties in the parliamentary opposition.

3.2 Austrian *Nationalrat*: The Populist Right as a Driver of Critical Debate on Europe

In comparison to the German *Bundestag*, the Austrian *Nationalrat* provides a very different setting of public debate on the Eurozone crisis. Whereas the German and Austrian legislatures are rather similar in institutional terms (both with regard to their domestic institutional position and their rights of involvement in European governance), an important difference is the presence in Austria of a vocally Eurosceptic group of opposition parties, consisting mostly of the Freedom Party (FPÖ) and the Alliance for the Future of Austria (BZÖ). Active interventions by these parliamentary groups, and a more variegated combination of formats of parliamentary debate, cause public debate in the Austrian legislature to evolve mostly as opposition parties' contestation of the Austrian government's policy concerning the Eurozone. More than in the German case, therefore, the Austrian legislature provides a setting for the representation of critical positions and discourses directed against existing crisis management policies in the Eurozone.

Parliamentary records show that parliamentarians in the Austrian *Nationalrat* are generally as actively engaged in the public debate on EU affairs as their German counterparts. Some thirty plenary debates were identified in the period 2010–2015 that directly relate to EU policies and in most cases to the Eurozone crisis. A major difference between the German and Austrian parliaments, however, concerns the format and style of public debate on the EU. While 'Declarations of the Government' on EU topics are available just as in the German case, this type of debate is less common and is used in addition to two other formats of parliamentary discussion that give more room to opposition parties: thematic EU debates allowing equal input by all parliamentary parties (*Aktuelle Europastunde*); and urgent inquiries (*Dringliche Anfrage*), which consist of questions put to the government that are often framed in highly critical terms. These three types of debate are reviewed in turn below.

First, debates on the Eurozone crisis exhibit a considerable number of 'Declarations by the Chancellor' or by a senior minister (*Erklärung des Bundeskanzlers* or *Erklärung des Bundesministers der Finanzen*), which strongly resemble debates in the *Bundestag*. Six of these debates were identified during the 24th legislative period between April 2010 and October 2013. These debates were thematically focused on the government's policy positions and on decisions of immediate importance for the management of the Eurozone crisis, as in the German case.[23] One difference, however, is

[23] The topics of these debates were the stabilization of the euro and the assistance programme for Greece (19 May 2010, Plenary Protocol XXIV/66), the European Stability Mechanism (7 July

that debates in the Austrian *Nationalrat* are generally longer, include more speakers, and give less weight to the opening speech by the Chancellor. The parliamentary sessions listed above lasted 90–180 minutes, with most debates lasting about two hours. The number of speakers ranged between fourteen and twenty-five, which is higher than in most debates in the *Bundestag*. In addition, the opening speech by the Chancellor generally lasted only 10–15 minutes and this was hence only about half as long as Declarations by the Government in the German case, although in some *Nationalrat* debates the Chancellor and Vice Chancellor speak directly after each other.

The presence of opposition groups becomes even more prominent if one reviews the other types of EU debates in the *Nationalrat*. The first is the *Aktuelle Europastunde*, a thematic debate held four times a year without a necessary link to current events and with contributions from the speakers of all party groups. The most remarkable aspect of these debates is that they often reverse the sequence of speeches found in the previously discussed formats. Quite frequently, the topic of an *Aktuelle Europastunde* is set by a party group of the opposition and introduced by its leader. Only after that, a response is given by a senior representative of the government, in most cases the Chancellor, who needs to accept the framing of the debate by the initial speaker. Especially when the topic is set by one of the Eurosceptic parties of the populist right—the FPÖ or BZÖ—the debate is framed in much more critical or even polemical terms, as indicated by the aggressive and often derogatory terms used to describe actors, institutions, and policies of the Eurozone in the titles of these debates.[24] Other *Europastunden*, initiated by one of the government parties or the Greens, carry more moderate, but still potentially critical titles.[25] These debates often lead to rather adversarial and polarized exchanges on the parliamentary floor. Debates during *Europastunden* are quite extensive, usually lasting about 80–90 minutes and including twelve to fourteen speakers.

Finally, opposition parliamentarians also use so-called *Dringliche Anfragen* to force the parliamentary majority into debates that are often framed in highly critical terms. The titles of these urgent inquiries echo those mentioned above. Examples of this include inquiries concerning raises in taxes for 'barrels without a bottom' (a German expression for a bottomless pit used to refer to the Greek bail-out),[26] or questioning

2011, XXIV 113), the results of a European Council meeting (14 December 2011, XXIV/139), Europe's future and employment, growth, and stability in the Eurozone (4 July 2012, XXIV/164), the results of another European Council meeting (19 February 2012, XXIV/190), and the financial assistance programme for Cyprus (25 April 2013, XXIV/199). Three additional debates initiated through 'Declarations' in the 25th legislative period addressed another European Council meeting (4 May 2015, XXV/49), the situation after the referendum in Greece on the terms of the third bail-out programme (9 July 2015, XXV/86), and the agreement on this third bail-out (1 September 2015, XXV/89).

[24] Examples of these debates include the following (author's own translation): 'Stop transfers now—enough has been paid for rotten banks and bankrupt Euro-countries' (15 June 2011, Plenary Protocol XXIV/109); 'the Euro lie—we have paid enough for rotten banks and bankrupt Euro-countries' (18 May 2011, XXIV/107); 'No European liability mechanisms without a referendum, Mister Chancellor' (20 January 2011, XXIV/93); 'No Debt Union without a referendum, Mister Chancellor' (19 September 2012, XXIV/169), or 'Bad Bank ECB: This monetary policy destroys our prosperity' (19 November 2014, XXV/49).

[25] Examples are debates on the following topics (author's own translation): 'Europe with more growth, employment, fairness and sustainability' (30 January 2013, XXIV/187) and 'Sustainable investment instead of transforming Europe into a savings society' (15 May 2012, XXIV/155).

[26] Debate on 5 May 2010 (Protocol No XXIV/64).

the 'European Transfer Union' and its 'rescue mechanism for rotten banks and bankrupt Euro-countries'.[27]

Although these titles suggest an attempt at political polarization rather than at substantive policy analysis, the debates of this kind are very extensive, lasting about three hours and including more than twenty speakers in the case of the three stated examples. Populist right parties are prominent in these debates, featuring as many speakers and having as much speaking time as the two governing parties, the centre-left Social Democrats (SPÖ), and the centre-right People's Party (ÖVP). In the three examples, the two government parties were represented by eight to ten speakers covering 65–75 minutes, whereas the two populist right parties were represented by seven to ten speakers covering 70–73 minutes. These numbers reveal virtual parity between the speakers of the majority and the populist opposition, which is even more remarkable considering that the former belong to a 'Grand Coalition'.

Combining these observations, the main difference between the German and Austrian parliaments is less in the overall extent than in the style and format of public debates on European integration. Plenary sessions on the Eurozone crisis in Austria are used by the populist right as an instrument for criticizing government policies more than as a venue for the justification of the government's policy. This results in the Austrian government and parliamentary majority parties taking a more defensive stance and being challenged more than in the case of the *Bundestag*.

3.3 French National Assembly: The Government in the Spotlight

Debates about the Eurozone crisis in the French *Assemblée nationale* are almost the complete opposite of those in the Austrian legislature. While both the frequency and the format of debate are generally more mixed and volatile than in the German and Austrian cases, a general observation is that French parliamentary debates are also more asymmetrical, in the sense that the presence and share of speaking time of government actors and majority groups is much greater. Throughout the period of analysis, government representatives and parliamentary majority parties were dominant in the plenary debates, both in terms of the number of speakers and the amount of speaking time.

After the power switched from conservatives to the political left supporting President Hollande in 2012, the prevalent format of parliamentary debate on European issues changed towards question time, in which one or more government members appeared to answer short questions from a number of parliamentarians. Before the parliamentary elections of 2012, however, the primary format EU discussions in the National Assembly was debate on the so-called 'Declaration of the Government prior to the European Council' (*Déclaration du Gouvernement préalable au Conseil européen*). Between the outbreak of the Eurozone crisis in 2010 and the end of the 13th legislative period in 2012, eight such debates were identified from parliamentary records—a frequency of debate just below that in the *Bundestag*. In comparison, the debates in the National Assembly are considerably shorter, with an average duration of 60–100 minutes, and even stronger preference is given to speakers from the government and parliamentary majority groups.

In most debates, speakers belonging to the 'presidential majority' of the two centre-right party groups—UMP and *Nouveau Centre*—were given about twice as much speaking time as their counterparts from the opposition groups—Socialist, Republican

[27] Debates on 17 May 2011 (Protocol No XXIV/105) and on 28 October 2011 (Protocol No XXIV/128).

and Citizen (SRC), and GDR. The reason for this imbalance is that after the introductory speech by the prime minister or a senior government member, the floor is given to the chairmen of the parliamentary committees on European and foreign affairs, followed by the leaders of parliamentary party groups. The debate is closed by a concluding statement by a member of the government, usually the competent minister or state secretary for European affairs. An exception to this was the debate of 21 February 2012 on the ratification of the ESM and the revision of Article 136 TFEU, which involved twenty speakers and lasted close to three hours, with an almost balanced participation of the majority and opposition speakers. However, parliamentary debate on the Eurozone crisis in the 2010–2012 period was mostly framed as a debate on declarations by the government.

This style of debate considerably changed following the election of the current, 14th legislature in May 2012. Since then, only four government declarations on EU issues were debated in the National Assembly, including two recent debates on the situation in Greece and its implications for Europe,[28] and another session on the agreement between the Eurozone and the Greek government on a third bail-out programme.[29]

A notable change during this period is that in some cases, debates on a government declaration have been combined with question periods within the same parliamentary session. An example of such a combined format is the debate prior to the European Council of 13–14 December 2012. After the opening statements of the Minister for European Affairs and the Chairwoman of the European Affairs Committee, the floor was opened for shorter statements of about 2–3 minutes and questions from parliamentary groups, all answered by the minister.[30] On balance, the sequence of speakers shows that the debate is structured so that representatives of the government and of the parliamentary majority can use about twice as much speaking time (some 50 minutes) than speakers of the opposition (about 25 minutes).

Even more recently, the most frequent format for debating EU affairs is the question period specifically devoted to European issues (*Questions au Gouvernement sur des sujets européennes*), which lasts about 60–70 minutes and in which members of all parliamentary party groups pose questions to members of the government, often including the prime minister. Such question periods took place six times in 2015,[31] while only two question periods specifically dedicated to EU affairs were held in 2014.[32] This format has gradually replaced debates on declarations by the government as the most common form of parliamentary deliberation on topics related to the EU.

The predominant use of question periods influences the debate on European issues in two ways. First, the discussion is no longer focused on a particular matter or draft EU decision, but fragmented in very different thematic aspects. An example is the question period of 14 October 2015, in which questions were put on the situation in the Middle East, Air France, a forthcoming European Council meeting, Franco-German cooperation, the refugee crisis, the European Charter of regional languages, and many other issues. As in other debates of this kind, a total of fifteen questions were posed by parliamentarians and answered by the ministers of foreign affairs, finance, and the interior, the secretary of state for European affairs, and the prime minister—leaving on

[28] Debate on 8 July 2015, JO No XIV/87.

[29] Debate on 15 July 2015, JO No XIV/89.

[30] Debate on 13 December 2012, JO No XIV/94.

[31] See the sessions of the National Assembly on 16 December (JO 2015/146), 14 October (JO 2015/108), 24 June (JO 2015/79), 1 June (JO 2015/66), and 11 February (JO 2015/19).

[32] See the sessions on 17 December (JO 2014/137) and 22 October (JO 2014/102).

average about two minutes for each question and answer. It is apparent from such a structure of interactions that the main aim of debate is not an elaborate justification of specific decisions or policies, but the provision of information to questions by parliamentarians as a minimum standard of political accountability by government ministers towards parliament.

A second implication of the use of question periods to debate EU affairs is the centrality of executive actors. Whereas only a select number of members of the executive regularly appear in question periods and cover about half of all the speaking time, the questions from the floor come from a different set of speakers in each question period, which means that there is no constancy in the parliamentarians who pose questions and that they are not limited to those specializing in European, budgetary, or economic affairs.

This strongly contrasts with debates in the *Bundestag*, where debate is dominated by a relatively small circle of party group leaders and policy experts, and focused on the extended discussion of a single policy or draft EU decisions. Moreover, the dominance of speakers supporting the government in France is ensured through the fact that questions are put not just by opposition parties, but also by the majority parties. As a consequence, more than two-thirds of the speakers usually belong to the parliamentary majority or are government representatives, taking up about the same proportion of speaking time on the floor. Therefore, debates on EU affairs in the French National Assembly differ from those in Germany and Austria in two respects: the clear dominance of speakers from the parliamentary majority; and the preference for a fast-paced sequence of questions and answers on a wider range of issues rather than for extended deliberations on narrower, more specific issues.

4. Assessment of Parliamentary Communication and Democratic Representation

The above comparison has shown that it is not just the duration, but also the style of parliamentary communication during the Eurozone crisis that constitutes the key difference between the three legislatures under review. Three criteria can be used to summarize the differences between debates on the Eurozone crisis in the German, French, and Austrian parliaments and illustrate their relevance for democratic representation in the context of EU politics: the format, thematic scope, and structure of plenary debates.

First, the *format* of plenary debates reveals whose political demands or statements—whether those of the executive, parliamentary majority groups, or the opposition—are defined as the point of departure and thematic frame of parliamentary sessions. In this regard, major differences were found, on the one hand, between the German and French legislatures, where Eurozone crisis debates are almost exclusively framed by government statements; and the Austrian Parliament, where plenary sessions are more frequently based on the statements, inquiries, or thematic frames set by opposition groups. Thus, in terms of political representation, the choice of the format of debate determines whose political claims and arguments are used as the point of departure for public debate.

Secondly, the *scope* of plenary debates is a criterion used to capture their thematic focus and the amount of time available for public deliberation between the competing views and arguments. In this respect, debates in different parliamentary settings are either defined relatively narrowly, by focusing on a specific European Council meeting or particular EU decision; or aim at a broader, more openly defined discussion of policies used for the management of the Eurozone crisis. This has important implications for democratic representation, because debates can be restricted to those issues proposed and advocated by the government; or, conversely, expanded to encompass the discussion of wider interests, preferences, and perceptions. When it comes to the time devoted to debating Eurozone crisis management, the three legislatures compared differ considerably, varying from those permitting more extended (Germany and Austria) to more limited duration of debates (France).

Finally, the *structure* of plenary debates describes the form and balance of interaction between speakers from the executive, parliamentary majority groups, and the opposition. This aspect varies from a relatively strong dominance of the executive and parliamentary majority groups to a greater presence of opposition groups. Concerning democratic representation, parliaments therefore differ in their character as arenas for the communication and justification of government discourses or as forums for the contestation of Eurozone crisis management through criticism by opposition groups. The three criteria used for the comparison of the German, Austrian, and French legislatures reveal differences that are summarized in Table 10.1 below.

The empirical survey carried out above thus shows that the three legislatures have established very different framework conditions for the representation and communication of political claims. These range from a strong emphasis on the communication of government policy in the French case, to a more balanced debate between all parliamentary groups in the German case, to a much stronger articulation of claims by the Eurosceptic opposition in the Austrian case. While these findings resonate with expectations from a comparative politics perspective, they shed a new light on the difference of conditions in which different national debates on the Eurozone crisis evolve.

5. Conclusion: Towards a New Representative Role of Parliaments in the EU?

The analysis presented in this chapter leads to two main insights. First, a general conclusion is that the Eurozone crisis has extended and transformed the involvement of NPs in EU decision-making processes, leading to them assuming a stronger role in the public representation and communication of competing political actors and interests. This change is not exclusively caused by or limited to the Eurozone crisis but is a part of a broader trend towards an increased politicization of European integration, prompting NPs to be more actively involved in the public debate on EU institutions and EU policies. However, it is evident that the management of the Eurozone crisis has contributed to this trend both by requiring a considerable number of authorization and ratification votes to be cast by NPs, and by increasing the salience of supranational decision-making for domestic publics and competing political parties. While this chapter cannot present detailed longitudinal data on the activity of legislatures in the EU, the argument advanced here resonates with the findings of the existing literature that indicate an increased debating function of NPs in the last decade owing to several highly significant events.[33]

[33] Auel and Raunio (n 5) 13; Wendler, *Debating Europe in National Parliaments* (n 17).

Table 10.1 Plenary Debates on the Eurozone crisis in three national parliaments

	German Bundestag	Austrian Nationalrat	French Assemblée nationale
Format of debate	Framed by statements of the Federal Government	Mixed, framed by statements of the executive, thematic questions and inquiries by opposition groups	Mixed but centred on the communication of executive actors
Scope of debate	Extended debating time but limited thematic focus (focus on EC meetings)	Extended debating time and wide thematic focus (open thematic discussions)	Limited debating time and unstable thematic focus (EC meetings and thematic debate)
Structure of debate	Limited and stable set of speakers, prominent executive discourse combined with proportional assignment of participants and speaking time	Extended set of speakers, strong presence of opposition groups in terms of participants and speaking time through their use of inquiries and access to thematic debates	Unstable and asymmetric set of speakers, privileged speaking time for executive actors and majority groups

Source: author's own scheme

Regarding the representative role of NPs in the EU on a more general level, these insights have several important implications. One of them is that future research ought to go beyond the conceptualization of parliaments as entities interacting with the national executive (in terms of scrutiny, information, and oversight) or with EU institutions (in terms of the subsidiarity mechanism or interactions with the European Commission). Instead, an important remaining task is to open up the black box of parliament for a closer analysis of the interactions between parliamentary groups and actors representative of the diversity of political interests of the Member States. It follows from this that with respect to authorization and communication functions, parliaments emerge as legitimizing institutions in their own right rather than as delegating principals or veto players transferring decision-making authority to external political actors.

An increased amount of parliamentary communication and debate can be identified as the first major citizen-oriented activity of NPs in the context of EU politics, after a long trajectory of government-oriented forms of parliamentary involvement through scrutiny, control, and mandating functions. In this context, regular dedication of plenary time to debates on Eurozone policy-making may be an indication of a more fundamental change of political representation in the context of European governance.

Secondly, beyond these general findings, this chapter has presented comparative insights into the different settings that three Eurozone legislatures provide for interaction between the government, parliamentary majority, and the opposition. The main results of this analysis are twofold. On the one hand, parliaments differ with regard to the degree to which they privilege the public discourse of government actors, to which they allow critical challenges by the opposition, and to which they promote a balanced exchange between all parliamentary groups. On the other hand, the choice of the format of debate and the allocation of speaking time affects the nature and breadth of plenary debates—namely, whether they are limited to a specific events or policy, or whether they allow for a wider assessment of policies pursued to tackle the Eurozone crisis.

In conclusion, these findings call for a closer connection between research on the responses of political parties to European integration and the development of parliaments as institutional forums for their representation and public communication. Faced with the challenge of justifying increasingly important and contentious crisis-related policy-making, political parties start engaging in a public debate on the goals and future of European integration. In this context, NPs stand out as arenas for the organization and structuring of the interaction between government actors and political parties in their public communication towards the citizen. In conclusion, this chapter also demonstrates that members of parliament have not resigned their role as scrutinizers and critical commentators of government policy in the European Union, but have shown resilience in seeking a communicative connection to the public.

11

European Semester Compliance and National Political Party Ownership

Aleksandra Maatsch

1. Introduction

According to the European Commission (Commission) and various academic sources, compliance within the European Semester remains low and is decreasing.[1] The Commission observed that in 2015 only 10 per cent of country-specific recommendations were fully implemented by the Member States. As a consequence, identifying the causes of weak compliance has become an objective of both European and national decision-makers. Contemporary debates have focused predominantly on the issue of 'ownership' of the European Semester by national political parties.[2] There seems to be a widespread opinion that ownership, understood as commitment to given rules, constitutes a key factor in ensuring compliance with European Semester requirements. Along these lines, the Commission observed that 'ownership of the European Semester by Member States is overall still too weak at national level, but also at European level. This limits the quality of the discussion and subsequent implementation of the country-specific recommendations'.[3]

Policy-makers are concerned with a low degree of compliance not only because of economic reasons but also because of those of a political nature. They are particularly concerned about the legitimacy of the European Semester, because if national political parties are not willing to comply, they probably do not identify with the mechanism indicating that they do not recognize the recommendations as a legitimate and economically useful source of policy advice. As a consequence, recent attempts at reforming the European Semester, such as the Five Presidents' Report,[4] have devoted particular attention to the mechanism's legitimacy. The proposed measures aim to improve domestic ownership of the European Semester, particularly by national parliaments (NPs) and parliamentary parties.

This chapter contributes to the debate by examining the factors that account for the political parties' willingness, or lack thereof, to comply with the European Semester. Using Germany, Austria, Ireland, and France as case studies, the chapter investigates how parliamentary parties of these four Member States accommodated conflicting

[1] Zsolt Darvas and Alvaro Leandro, 'The Limitations of Policy Coordination in the Euro Area under the European Semester', Bruegel Policy Contribution No 2015/19, November 2015; Valentin Kreilinger, 'National Parliaments, Surveillance Mechanisms and Ownership in the Euro Area', Jacques Delors Institute, Studies and Reports No 110, March 2016.

[2] Kreilinger (n 1).

[3] European Commission, Explanatory Memorandum to 'Annual Growth Survey 2015', COM(2014) 902 of 28 November 2014.

[4] Jean-Claude Juncker, Donald Tusk, Jeroen Dijsselbloem, Mario Draghi, and Martin Schulz, 'The Five Presidents' Report: Completing Europe's Economic and Monetary Union', 22 June 2015. See more in the chapter on the European Central Bank by Davor Jančić in this volume.

pressures from the Commission and national constituencies and industries within the 2014 and 2015 cycles of the European Semester.

Compliance within the European Semester is a particularly challenging task for NPs, because their institutional design does not allow them to deal with the *negative externalities* of their national policies effectively. A negative externality implies that certain activity from a given actor imposes costs on third parties. The actor generating negative externalities may or may not be negatively affected.

Parliamentary parties are accountable to domestic constituencies, which are interested primarily in securing their own interests, not the interests of other states or geopolitical regions. Parties, as vote- and office-seeking institutions, depend on support from national voters. A party is very likely to be punished by voters if it fails to serve their vital interests.[5] National parliamentary parties therefore find it particularly difficult to eliminate negative externalities when a policy generating these externalities is profitable to their voters. By the same token, it is easier for parliamentary parties to counter negative externalities when costs also affect their states. In other words, national parties are likely to eliminate negative externalities as long as their response to them is not associated with high costs.

The European Semester counters negative policy externalities in both monetary and economic areas. A significant budgetary deficit is associated with negative consequences, both for the state generating the deficit as well as for the Eurozone. In particular, persistent budgetary instability in one Member State may undermine the international credibility of the euro. Furthermore, an excessive trade surplus in one Member State is likely to a have a negative impact on export industries in other Member States of the Eurozone. As a result, NPs are confronted with a difficult dilemma when responding to country-specific recommendations.

Compliance within the European Semester is likely to be influenced by institutional factors that traditionally guide parliamentary party behaviour. Drawing on the existing literature, the chapter tests the impact of the following factors on parliamentary party compliance within the European Semester: (a) the strength of parliaments' formal powers in budgetary and EU matters; (b) whether a party is in government or in opposition; and (c) coherence between country-specific recommendations and the economic preferences of a political party.

The chapter begins by reviewing the literature on the factors that shape parliamentary parties' compliance within the European Semester. In a second step, the chapter presents the study's research design and methodological approach, followed by a discussion of the empirical findings. The chapter demonstrates that the concept of *ownership* of the European Semester by national political parties is not particularly helpful in identifying the mechanisms that determine their willingness to comply with the European Semester. The findings suggest that compliance does not depend on their intrinsic *commitment* to EU economic coordination, as the Commission assumes, but rather on a variety of external, formal, and institutional factors that limit their decisions. Namely, strong formal powers in European and budgetary matters constitute an incentive for non-compliance. This means that national parliamentary parties are less likely to comply with the European Semester when they enjoy strong formal powers. Compliance within the European Semester also becomes problematic when there is no coherence between country-specific recommendations and the economic preferences

[5] Russell J Dalton, 'Political Parties and Political Representation: Party Supporters and Party Elites in Nine Nations' (1985) 18 Comp Pol Stud 267; Anthony Downs, *An Economic Theory of Democracy* (Harper & Row 1957).

of a political party. Cleavage over such compliance has therefore been structured along the ideological dimension (left–right conflict) rather than that of political power (government–opposition conflict).

2. The European Semester: Enhancing EU Economic Policy Coordination

The European Semester, in force since 2011, is an institutional instrument for preventive surveillance of economic and fiscal policies of the EU Member States.[6] The goal is to ensure 'closer coordination of economic policies and sustained convergence of the economic performance of the Member States'.[7] Since the entry into force of the Stability and Growth Pact and the European Semester, national budgets have become a *European* concern more than ever before. The reform of the Economic and Monetary Union (EMU) significantly extended the Commission's and the Council's competences and brought about two important innovations. First, national budgetary processes have become coordinated, so that the Commission has sufficient time to provide recommendations to the Member States before NPs approve their budgets. Secondly, EU-level control has been extended beyond public finances and now covers macroeconomic imbalances, as well as changes in the Member States' competitiveness.[8]

Various studies have demonstrated that *formally* the institutional set up of the European Semester does not limit the budgetary competences of NPs.[9] However, in the course of the reform of EU economic governance, the Commission's and the Council's de facto powers in budgetary matters increased substantially. Above all, the Commission reviews national budgets and provides recommendations that have to be implemented by NPs. If the latter fail to comply with the new budgetary standards or recommendations concerning economic policies, the Commission can impose financial sanctions. Furthermore, a new decision-making procedure has been established: the reverse qualified majority voting procedure (RQMV).[10] According to this procedure, a Commission recommendation to impose sanctions on a Member State is automatically adopted unless the Council rejects it. Unsurprisingly, the Commission has been heralded as the 'unexpected winner of the European financial crisis'.[11] As a result, the European Semester de facto disempowers NPs in their budgetary decision-making competence.[12]

[6] Davor Jančić, 'Parliamentary Involvement in the Economic and Monetary Union After the Euro Crisis' in Nicola Lupo and Cristina Fasone (eds), *Interparliamentary Cooperation in the Composite European Constitution* (Hart Publishing 2016).

[7] Regulation 1175/2011, art 2a. See more in the chapter by Ingolf Pernice in this volume.

[8] Niels Thygesen, 'Governance in the Euro Area: Approaching an Optimum Currency Area?' in Amy Verdun and Alfred Tovias (eds), *Mapping European Economic Integration* (Palgrave Macmillan 2013); Mark Hallerberg, Benedicta Marzinotto, and Guntram B Wolff, 'An Assessment of the European Semester' (2012), Study for the European Parliament, DG for Internal Policies, Policy Department A—Economic and Scientific Policy.

[9] Cristina Fasone, 'Eurozone, Non-Eurozone and "Troubled Asymmetries" Among National Parliaments in the EU. Why and to What Extent This Is of Concern' (2014) 6 Perspectives on Federalism 1.

[10] Council press release No 12/12/2011.

[11] Michael W Bauer and Stefan Becker, 'The Unexpected Winner of the Crisis: The European Commission's Strengthened Role in Economic Governance' (2014) 36 J Eur Integration 213.

[12] There are studies demonstrating that the European Semester created new avenues for NPs' involvement in the economic governance. The new rights have a potential to counterbalance the

The European Semester begins in November, when the Commission publishes the Annual Growth Survey in which it presents a list of policy priorities and objectives for the EU as a whole. The Commission also publishes an alert mechanism report (AMR), which 'aims to identify and address imbalances that hinder the smooth functioning of the economies of Member States, the economy of the EU, and may jeopardise the proper functioning of the economic and monetary union'.[13] The Commission uses the AMR to screen Member States and analyze those identified as being in need of policy action through an in-depth review. Finally, during May and June, the Commission proposes country-specific recommendations for budgetary, economic, and social policies and monitored compliance with previous recommendations. The recommendations are adopted by the Council and endorsed by the European Council. By 30 April, the Member States submit their Stability and Convergence Programmes and National Reform Programmes. By the end of December, Member States are expected to adopt their annual budgets taking into account the recommendations issued.

3. What Factors Account for Compliance Within the European Semester?

According to the literature, parliamentary activity to a significant extent depends on the strength of NPs' formal competences in a given policy area.[14] Formal powers, particularly those stipulated at the constitutional level, delineate the scope of policy activities available to NPs, and specify how much influence NPs can exercise over budgetary matters and which forms of oversight they must or may exercise.

Budgetary matters have always been one of the core responsibilities of NPs. However, over time, NPs have lost their exclusive powers and today it is the executive branch that usually leads the budgetary process.[15] As a consequence, if a parliament enjoys very weak formal powers in budgetary matters, the government encounters fewer difficulties in complying with country-specific recommendations. Weak NPs are usually not entitled to debate or vote on proposals concerning, for instance, the National Reform Programme. As a consequence, weak parliaments cannot effectively challenge the government or politicize a given issue. The stronger the parliament, particularly the opposition, the more constrained the government is in its activities. The first hypothesis tested in this chapter thus stipulates that the stronger the formal powers of NPs in budgetary and EU matters, the more likely it is that compliance with the European Semester will decrease.

dominance of the executive. For more details see Davor Jančić, 'National Parliaments and EU Fiscal Integration' (2016) 22 European Law Journal 225.

[13] European Commission, 'Alert Mechanism Report 2016' http://ec.europa.eu/europe2020/pdf/2016/ags2016_alert_mechanism_report.pdf (last accessed 17 August 2016).

[14] See for instance Berthold Rittberger and Thomas Winzen, 'Parlamentarismus nach der Krise: Die Vertiefung Parlamentarischer Asymmetrie in der Reformierten Wirtschafts- und Währungsunion', 56 Politische Vierteljahresschrift 430; Aleksandra Maatsch, *Parliaments and the Economic Governance of the European Union: Talking Shops or Deliberative Bodies?* (Routledge 2016); Thomas Christiansen, Anna-Lena Högenauer, and Christine Neuhold, 'The Europeanisation of National Parliaments Post-Lisbon: Bureaucratisation and Transnationalisation rather than More Democracy in the European Union?' (2014) 12 Comp Eur Pol 121.

[15] Violeta Ruiz Almendral, 'A Myopic Economic Constitution? Controlling the Debt and the Deficit without Fiscal Integration', EUI Law Working Paper no. 2015/12.

The literature on NPs and parliamentary parties has demonstrated that the major political conflict is not between government and parliament, but between government and opposition.[16] The role of the opposition is to challenge the government and propose alternative policy solutions. If a certain policy pursued by the government is socially contested, opposition parties are likely to respond by proposing policies that accommodate these preferences.[17] In contrast to governing parties, the opposition does not have to bear the immediate cost of their promises.

According to the second hypothesis of this study, governing parties are more likely than opposition parties to advocate compliance within the European Semester. According to Birch[18] and Mair,[19] governing-party responsibility implies prudence, consistency, and predictability in their actions over a longer period of time as well as a sense of duty in respecting international norms and commitments that have been made by previous governments. In other words, governing parties sometimes have to take an unpopular decision that their voters dislike. The literature notes that in a situation of conflict between the terms of an international agreement and the voters' preferences, governing parties are more likely than opposition parties to adhere to 'international responsibility'.[20] There is thus an expectation that democratic governments, as representatives of their states in the international arena, will respect the existing international agreements even if they are not entirely in favour of them.

However, political parties usually adhere to the preferences of their voters (constituencies), particularly in matters related to redistribution. According to classical theories, political parties attempt to accommodate the preferences of a median voter or those of specific constituencies.[21] As a consequence, a third factor that influences the willingness of parliamentary parties to comply with the requirements issued within the European Semester is the economic orientation of the political party. In particular, given the preference for pro-cyclical policies among right-wing parties, it is likely that they would support policies oriented towards budgetary consolidation. Hence, if the Commission recommends budgetary consolidation, right-wing parties are more likely to support these measures than left-wing parties. In contrast, if measures proposed by the Commission better correspond to the economic preferences of left-wing parties, they are more likely than right-wing parties to advocate compliance. For instance, if the Commission recommends fostering domestic demand by increasing the minimum wage, left-wing parties are likely to be in favour. Consequently, the third hypothesis focuses on the ideological orientation of a party and posits that the more coherent country-specific recommendations are with the economic preferences of a political party, the more likely the political party is to advocate compliance. By the same token, if these recommendations cannot be reconciled with the party's stance, parties may be

[16] Tapio Raunio, 'National Parliaments and European Integration: What We Know and Agenda for Future Research' (2009) 15 J Legis Stud 317.

[17] Lawrence Ezrow and others, 'Mean Voter Representation and Partisan Constituency Representation: Do Parties Respond to the Mean Voter Position or to Their Supporters?' (2010) 17 Party Pol 275.

[18] Anthony H Birch, *Representative and Responsible Government: An Essay on the British Constitution* (George Allen & Unwin 1964).

[19] Peter Mair, 'Bini Smaghi vs. the Parties: Representative Government and Institutional Constraints', EUI RSCAS Working Paper No 2011/22.

[20] Aleksandra Maatsch, 'Drivers of Political Parties' Voting Behaviour in European Economic Governance: The Ultimate Decline of the Economic Cleavage?' (2016) 39 WEP 648; Richard Rose, 'Responsible Party Government in a World of Interdependence' (2014) 37 WEP 253.

[21] Dalton (n 5); Downs (n 5).

more reluctant to advocate compliance out of the fear of losing the support of their constituencies.

4. Research Design, the Method, and the Explanatory Variables

The dependent variable of this study is defined as the willingness of a parliamentary party to comply with the European Semester and, more specifically, with country-specific recommendations. The dependent variable is operationalized in a binary manner as a discursive position of a parliamentary party advocating compliance or non-compliance. The scope of the analysis concerns two full budgetary cycles—those in 2014 and 2015.

The cases selected for analysis differ with respect to the explanatory variables. First, NPs in Austria and Germany enjoy strong formal powers in budgetary and EU matters, while those of France and Ireland have weak formal powers. Secondly, the country-specific recommendations issued to France and Germany required more radical short-term adjustments than those issued to Ireland and Austria.

The data on the dependent variable was established on the basis of information provided electronically by NPs in each of the selected Member States. The analysis concentrated on the following activities: plenary debates, question hours, official correspondence,[22] committee debates, and documents issued by committees (such as communiqués on national reform programmes or recommendations concerning parliamentary party resolutions).[23]

The data regarding the formal powers of NPs in EU and budgetary affairs (the first explanatory variable) was established on the basis of the constitutions in force in the Member States under study as well as on the basis of the literature. The classification of parliamentary parties along the government-opposition dimension (the second explanatory variable) drew on the web pages of NP, while the data on the left-right affiliation of parliamentary parties (the third variable) was based on the PIREDEU classification.[24] The method employed for the analysis of official documents was qualitative comparative content analysis.

According to Winzen,[25] German and Austrian parliaments enjoy the strongest powers in EU politics among the EU-15 Member States. At an aggregate level, ranking allowed identification of the following clusters of NPs: parliaments with strong control powers over EU matters (Germany: index value 2.17 and Austria: index value 1.67); a parliament with moderate powers (France: 1.00); and NPs with weak powers (Italy: 0.83 and Ireland: 0.50). The strength of national parliamentary powers to control EU matters has been operationalized and adjusted to the analysis of budgetary procedures drawing on three major indicators: access to information; processing of information; and the enforcement of parliamentary preferences in EU negotiations.[26] The first indicator measures the quality of national parliamentary access to information

[22] The study investigated parliamentary correspondence with the government and the EU.

[23] The empirical database has been completed with the support of two research assistants: Sarah Herbertz and Dennis Höfer.

[24] Collaborative Project on 'Providing an Infrastructure for Research on Electoral Democracy in the European Union' http://www.piredeu.eu (last accessed 17 August 2016).

[25] Thomas Winzen, 'National Parliamentary Control of European Union Affairs: A Cross-National and Longitudinal Comparison' (2012) 35 WEP 657.

[26] ibid.

in the EU legislative process. In particular, the indicator measures whether a given parliament has an incomplete access to information, access to legislative proposals, access to legislative planning documents, and access to governments' memoranda.

In order to assess the level of NPs' powers in budgetary matters, the analysis concentrated on two indicators: (a) the level of constitutional protection of national parliamentary powers in budgetary matters; and (b) the level of formal budgetary constraints on NPs and governments. The analysis of constitutional provisions clearly demonstrated that the NPs of Germany and Austria enjoy stronger formal budgetary powers than the parliaments of France and Ireland. The four parliaments' formal powers are described in turn.

Both chambers of the German Parliament, the *Bundestag* and the *Bundesrat*, are involved in approval of the national budget. The budget has to be approved by a vote in each chamber in order to enter into force (Article 110 of the Basic Law). Furthermore, members of the *Bundestag* are entitled to present motions aimed, for instance, at decreasing the revenues. If an extraordinary situation requires expenditure exceeding the constitutional limit of public debt, Parliament has to approve the bill by a vote.[27]

In Austria, the budgetary competences of Parliament are also protected at the constitutional level. Article 51 of the Austrian Constitution stipulates that the lower house, the National Council (*Nationalrat*), is entitled to vote on the federal Finance Act. As in Germany, the Austrian Constitution guarantees Parliament's right to be informed about all subsequent stages of the drafting process (Article 51). Article 51(7) of the Constitution stipulates that in cases of imminent danger, the government shall ask the competent committee of the National Council for consent to exceed the expenditure limit.

The French Parliament does not enjoy strong constitutional protection. Regarding EU matters, Article 88(4) stipulates that Parliament shall establish a specialized committee dealing with matters related to the European Union. The national parliament also approves accession of new EU members (Article 88(5)). In budgetary matters, only the government enjoys the right of initiative. If parliament (both chambers) fails to approve the Finance Bill within the time limit provided by the Constitution (seventy days), the government may bring the provisions into effect.

In the Irish Parliament (*Oireachtas*), the lower chamber, *Dáil Éireann*, is responsible for scrutinizing and authorizing the budget. The upper chamber, the *Seanad Éireann*, plays a more limited role. In general, it is the government that plays the dominant role in the budgetary process and EU affairs. Although the *Dáil* may table amendments to draft tax legislation, proposals concerning expenditure may not be adjusted by Parliament at all. Article 17(2) of the Irish Constitution stipulates that the *Dáil* has to be consulted on expenditure estimates. Nonetheless, the *Dáil* 'shall not pass any vote or resolution, and no vote shall be enacted, for the appropriation of revenue or other public money unless the purpose of the appropriation shall have been recommended to Dáil by a message from the government signed by the Taoiseach [Prime Minister]'. Furthermore, according to Article 42 of the Constitution, only the government can propose finance bills. If Parliament fails to table a finance bill, the government may adopt it as a matter of urgency.

Interestingly, while NPs in Austria and Germany enjoy strong constitutional protection of their budgetary powers, the level of constitutional budgetary constraints on national institutions is prominent too. In particular, the constitutions of Austria

[27] Christian Callies and Timm Beichelt, *Die Europäisierung des Parlaments: Die europapolitische Rolle von Bundestag und Bundesrat* (Verlag Bertelsmann Stiftung 2015).

(Article 51 of the Constitution) and Germany (Article 115 of the Basic Law) each contain a debt brake provision as well as a balanced budget clause. However, both constitutions also stipulate the conditions under which these rules can be violated. In these cases, decisions have to be approved by the NPs. In contrast, the French and Irish constitutions contain no debt brakes and balanced budget clauses. These matters are regulated by means of secondary legislation.

Therefore, while parliamentary powers in relation to domestic budgets are not directly linked to the EU level, they are particularly relevant for the European Semester. As the goal of the European Semester process is to coordinate and influence national budgetary and economic policies, parliamentary performance within the process is delineated by formal budgetary powers that each parliament enjoys.

5. Empirical Findings

The empirical findings of this study (see appendices) demonstrate that the willingness of parliamentary parties to comply with the requirements issued within the European Semester depends on a combination of two factors: the strength of NPs' formal powers in budgetary and EU matters and coherence between country-specific recommendations and the economic preferences of a political party. Contrary to the expectations, conflicts between government and opposition proved to be irrelevant in explaining parliamentary parties' compliance. In general, political parties represented in the parliaments of Austria and Ireland advocated compliance with their country-specific recommendations, while in France and Germany parliamentary parties were deeply divided on this issue.

5.1 Political Parties in Parliaments with Strong Formal Powers: Austria and Germany

Although the German and Austrian parliaments enjoy very similar constitutional protection in budgetary and EU matters, the patterns of parliamentary party engagement within the European Semester were entirely different. In Austria, all parliamentary parties expressed their willingness to comply with country-specific recommendations. In Germany, however, parliamentary parties were deeply divided on the issue. In particular, the governing parties (the CDU/CSU[28] and the SPD[29]) disapproved of these recommendations whereas the opposition parties (the Greens[30] and the Left[31]) advocated compliance.

5.1.1 Austria

The 2014 and 2015 country-specific recommendations for Austria were very 'soft' and had little potential to antagonize the parties. The Commission observed that the state should avoid potential deviations from their mid-term objectives. The Commission also recommended reforms of the pension and healthcare systems in order to ensure

[28] *Christlich Demokratische Union Deutschlands* [Christian Democratic Union of Germany] (CDU); and *Christlich-Soziale Union in Bayern* [Christian-Social Union in Bavaria] (CSU).

[29] *Sozialdemokratische Partei Deutschlands* [Social Democratic Party of Germany] (SPD).

[30] *Bündnis 90/Die Grünen* [Alliance 90/The Greens].

[31] *Die Linke* [The Left].

their long-term sustainability. According to the Commission, the Austrian government should introduce incentives to limit early retirement. The Commission also recommended improving participation within the labour market and reducing the tax burden on labour. In sum, the recommendations had a very long-term character and did not require any radical short-term reforms. All parties agreed on a long-term need to reform the pension system, owing to Austria's aging population. There was also general agreement that participation in the labour market could be improved.

The Austrian Parliament remained thoroughly informed about the progress of the budgetary process. Nonetheless, the vast majority of budget-related activity was carried out at the committee level. In particular, the government communicated intensively with the committees evaluating the Stability Programme and the National Reform Programme. The committees issued communiqués in which they summarized the content of the documents.

As the empirical analysis has demonstrated, the committees concentrated on matters related to the European Semester, whereas plenary activity revolved around the form of the national budget. However, budgetary discussions were not linked to the European Semester.

5.1.2 Germany

In Germany, the European Semester became rather controversial. In 2014 and 2015, Germany became subject to an in-depth review as a result of the excessive trade imbalance that reached 8 per cent. The Commission observed that the German surplus required 'decisive policy action and monitoring'.[32] As a result, in 2014 the Commission recommended that Germany 'improve conditions for further support of domestic demand'. According to the Commission, the imbalance could be effectively reduced if the German government undertook steps aimed at fostering domestic demand. The German government was particularly encouraged to increase public investment and reduce taxes on security contributions for low wage earners. The Commission advocated reducing fiscal disincentives to work, as well as facilitating a transition from the 'mini-job' sector to regular forms of employment. Finally, the Commission recommended further reforms aimed at securing the sustainability of public pensions and later retirement. The government was also urged to address shortages in childcare supply.

In 2015, the country-specific recommendations revolved around the same themes. In the in-depth review the Commission complained that:

> Germany has made limited progress in addressing the 2014 country-specific recommendations. As regards policies relevant to the Macroeconomic Imbalance Procedure, some steps were taken to increase public investment, but they appear insufficient to address the investment backlog in infrastructure, education and research. No measures were taken to improve the efficiency of the tax system or reduce high taxes and social contributions. The potential of the general minimum wage to foster private consumption may be limited ... Fiscal disincentives to work have not been tackled. No significant efforts have been made to stimulate competition in the railway and service sectors.[33]

[32] European Commission, 'European Economy—Macroeconomic Imbalances Germany 2014', Occasional Papers 174, March 2014 http://ec.europa.eu/economy_finance/publications/occasional_paper/2014/pdf/ocp174_en.pdf (last accessed 17 August 2016).

[33] European Commission, 'European Economy: Macroeconomic Imbalances Country Report—Germany 2015', Occasional Papers 214, June 2015 http://ec.europa.eu/economy_finance/publications/occasional_paper/2015/pdf/ocp214_en.pdf (last accessed 17 August 2016).

These country-specific recommendations polarized parliamentary parties in Germany along the left–right conflict. The centre-left SPD and the centre-right CDU/CSU positioned themselves against the country-specific recommendations, whereas the leftist Greens and the Left (radical left) became the advocates of compliance. Contrary to expectations, the governing parties did not prioritize international responsibility. If the governing coalition had decided to act upon their international responsibility, they would have fully endorsed the recommendations. Rather, both the governing and the opposition parties decided to uphold the interests of their constituencies.

In April 2014, the Green Party initiated a plenary debate on a draft resolution that it tabled under the title 'National Reform Programme 2014: Taking Seriously the Economic Coordination in the EU and Fostering Investment'.[34] In it, the party voiced concern about the persisting trade surplus in Germany and urged the government to implement the country-specific recommendations. It proposed tackling the problem by strengthening domestic consumption. According to the party, stronger domestic consumption—generated, for instance, by wage increases—would boost imports and thus reduce the trade imbalance. The Green Party's resolution was reviewed by the Committee for Economic Affairs and Energy. Following a formal recommendation by this Committee, the *Bundestag* rejected the resolution in a vote.

During the plenary debate, the Green Party also criticized the SPD and the CDU/CSU for not being truly committed to EU economic governance. The Greens noted that the government had done little to promote parliamentary discussion on the National Reform Programme. In their view, if it were not for the initiative of the Green Party, the *Bundestag* would have missed an opportunity to discuss this programme.

In 2015, the Left Party proposed a resolution entitled 'Diminishing Trade Surpluses and Changing the Wage Policy',[35] which was also debated and put to a vote in a plenary session. The Left predominantly concentrated on domestic economic consequences of the trade imbalance. The party observed very critically that wages had been suppressed for more than fifteen years. Furthermore, in many sectors of the German economy precarious work contracts had become dominant. The party urged the government to diminish the trade surplus by fostering domestic consumption. According to the party, the minimum wage should be increased and precarious work contracts restricted. Finally, the Left observed that the coalition sought to turn the European Semester into a mechanism to punish deficits. Eventually, the Left's resolution was also rejected.

The governing coalition maintained that the trade imbalance was small and hence not really dangerous. In their view, the imbalance emerged through increased exports to third countries and not to EU Member States. The coalition also noted that the German trade surplus contributed to the creation of new jobs abroad and thus should not be perceived so negatively. In the view of the coalition, the policies proposed by the Green Party should be 'handled with care'. According to the coalition, permanent contracts would limit the flexibility of the labour market. Furthermore, wage increases could have a negative impact on German exports and thereby reduce employment in domestic export industries. Nonetheless, the coalition stressed its commitment to

[34] Bundestag, Drucksache 18/978 of 2 February 2014, 'Antrag: Nationalesreformprogramm 2014 nützen, wirtschaftspolitische Steuerung in der EU ernst nehmen und Investitionen stärken' http://dip21.bundestag.de/dip21/btd/18/009/1800978.pdf (last accessed 17 August 2016).

[35] Bundestag, Drucksache 18/4837 of 6 May 2015, 'Antrag: Exportüberschüsse abbauen—Wende in der Lohnpolitik einleiten' http://dip21.bundestag.de/dip21/btd/18/048/1804837.pdf (last accessed 17 August 2016).

implement country-specific recommendations by increasing expenditure on research, education, and infrastructure.

During the plenary debate on the Left Party's resolution, the coalition clearly stated that deficits were economically more hazardous than trade surpluses. When the Left observed that trade imbalances had also contributed to the recent economic crisis in Europe, the coalition responded that 'in some EU states the crisis has been an effect of domestic factors'.[36] Furthermore, the coalition referred to a yearly expert report on the general economic condition of the state,[37] which urged the government not to introduce any measures aimed at decreasing the trade surplus. During the question hour held on 14 January 2015 on 'the German Budget 2014 without New Debt', the coalition argued that 'it would have been easy for Angela Merkel to give in to the international pressure and say: alright, let's spend some €20 billion on investment, and by the same token, increase the debt. She has not done that. She supports the policy of growth-oriented consolidation'.[38]

In a letter to Commissioner Jyrki Katainen, the German Minister of Finance, Wolfgang Schäuble, and the German Minister of Economic Affairs and Energy, Sigmar Gabriel, proposed reforming the European Semester.[39] The coalition defended the export-oriented growth model and attempted to downplay the negative effect of the German trade surplus. The major points raised in the letter were repeated later in a resolution drafted by the CDU/CSU and the SPD entitled 'Strengthening, Better Implementation and Further Development of the European Semester'.[40] In the letter, the ministers advocated closer cooperation between NPs, national social partners, and EU actors within the European Semester. In their opinion, the Commission should prepare country-specific recommendations in cooperation with national ministries, not the permanent representation in Brussels. The resolution from the coalition was approved by Parliament.

5.2 Political Parties in Parliaments With Weak Budgetary Powers: France and Ireland

National parliaments in France and Ireland enjoy rather weak constitutional protection in budgetary and EU matters. As a consequence, it is very difficult for the French and Irish parliaments to influence the budgetary process. However, formal powers cannot fully explain their engagement within the European Semester. Whereas in France the country-specific recommendations generated a very deep conflict among the parliamentary parties, in Ireland none of the parties challenged the content of the recommendations.

[36] Bundestag, Plenarprotokoll 18/106, 106. Sitzung of 21 May 2015 http://dipbt.bundestag.de/doc/btp/18/18106.pdf (last accessed 28 August 2016).

[37] ibid.

[38] Intervention by Norbert Barthle (CDU/CSU) in Bundestag, Plenarprotokoll 18/78, 78. Sitzung of 14 January 2015, at 7448 (author's translation).

[39] Letter No 2014/0750485 of 20 October 2014 http://www.bmwi.de/BMWi/Redaktion/PDF/B/brief-gabriel-schaeble-an-eu-kommission,property=pdf,bereich=bmwi2012,sprache=de,rwb=true.pdf (last accessed 17 August 2016).

[40] Bundestag, Drucksache 18/4426 of 24 March 2015, 'Das ES stärken, besser umsetzen und weiterentwickeln' http://dip21.bundestag.de/dip21/btd/18/044/1804426.pdf (last accessed 17 August 2016).

5.2.1 France

In March 2014, France became subject to the 'corrective arm' of the Stability and Growth Pact, which means that the Commission began an in-depth review of the state's economic performance. The key objective of the French government was to bring the deficit below 3 per cent. Although the Commission welcomed the government's programme of saving €50 billion from the budget, it concluded that such a fiscal effort remained below the recommended level.

The same year, the Commission recommended meeting the 3 per cent target by limiting social security spending, reducing administrative personnel, cutting the cost of labour, decreasing corporate tax, promoting competitiveness in services, and modernizing vocational training. In 2015, the French government managed to negotiate an extension until 2017 for correcting the deficit. The Commission observed that the slow pace of growth and low inflation in the EU made it particularly difficult for the French government to bring the deficit under the 3 per cent threshold. It therefore recommended correcting the excessive deficit by identifying savings opportunities across all sub-sectors, focusing predominantly on social security and local government, while reducing labour costs (by adjusting the development of wages to productivity), removing barriers preventing access to different professions, and broadening the tax base. Finally, the Commission encouraged investment and incentives for the unemployed to return to work, as well as a broader availability of open-ended contracts.

Responding to the Commission's pressure, the French President François Hollande adopted an economic approach combining harsh consolidation with growth-oriented policies.[41] However, the left wing of the governing Socialist Party severely contested his approach and opposed compliance with country-specific recommendations. In 2014, the internal division within the Socialist Party became so deep that forty-one party members abstained when Parliament voted on the Stability and Growth Programme.

As in Germany, the dominant conflict line in the French Parliament had ideological underpinnings. The centre-right parties, the UMP[42] and the UDI,[43] were in favour of compliance while the leftist and communist political group GDR[44] was against. As advocates of compliance, the UMP and the UDI were particularly careful not to legitimize the government's policy. They therefore argued that, while the general goal of the government was correct in terms of budgetary consolidation, the particularities of the policy were poorly designed.

In 2014, Prime Minister Manuel Valls announced that the key documents related to the European Semester should be debated in Parliament to foster dialogue and cooperation among all parliamentary parties. As a result, Parliament debated the Stability and Reform Programme, the National Reform Programme, the financial policy framework, and France's country-specific recommendations.

The ensuing debate revealed a very deep conflict in Parliament. The Finance Minister, Michel Sapin, announced that the government's primary goals were to restore the French economy and the country's international credibility in economic matters.[45] Parliamentary parties responded differently to the government's agenda. While the UMP and the UDI remained sceptical with respect to the *feasibility* of the

[41] Ben Clift, 'The Hollande Presidency, the Eurozone Crisis and the Politics of Fiscal Rectitude', SPERI Paper No 10, March 2014.

[42] *Union Pour un Mouvement Populaire* [Union for a Popular Movement].

[43] *L'Union des Démocrates et Independents* [Union of Democrats and Independents].

[44] *Gauche Démocrate et Républicaine* [Democratic and Republican Left].

[45] Committee for Finance, the Economy and Budgetary Control, meeting of 21 January 2014.

government's plan, the EELV[46] and the GDR criticized its *essence*. In particular, the UDI argued that France would be unlikely to bring the deficit level below 3 per cent in the short term. The GDR were highly critical of the government's approach combining budgetary consolidation with growth-oriented policies. According to the GDR, the approach would probably contribute to prolonged stagflation.

The polarization of the political scene manifested itself also during the adoption of the budget that took place in autumn 2014. The internal split within the Socialist Party surfaced again. Its left wing accused the Commission of interfering in France's sovereignty, specifically referring to the recommendation to reform the constitutional provisions on the minimum wage. The UDI supported the annual budget, but found the internal split within the Socialist Party unacceptable and irresponsible. The GDR criticized the governing party for abandoning its electoral commitment to growth-oriented policies.

In April 2015, the prime minister announced that neither the Stability Programme nor the National Reform Programme should be voted on in the plenary that year. As a consequence, Parliament became involved in the adoption of the budget for 2016, which, to a limited extent, addressed the Stability Programme.[47] At the committee level, there were a few discussions concerning the European Semester, which, however, remained technocratic. In the plenary and in the committees, many parliamentarians expressed their criticism of the prime minister's decision to exclude Parliament from the European Semester.

In March 2015, there was a brief discussion in the Committee for Finance, the Economy and Budgetary Control of the *Assemblée nationale* that was devoted to the extension of the deadline for the correction of the deficit by 2017. However, the discussion was merely aimed at information sharing. The following month, this Committee also reviewed the draft Stability Programme. The debate was attended by high-ranking politicians, Finance Minister Michel Sapin, and the Economy Minister Emmanuel Macron. In June, this Committee teamed up with the European Affairs Committee to host Pierre Moscovici, the incumbent European Commissioner for Economic and Financial Affairs, who elaborated on the reform of the European Semester. The meeting had a technocratic character.

In sum, the non-involvement of Parliament in the European Semester process in 2015 eliminated the political discussion on compliance. The few meetings that took place at the committee level did not allow for a broad and in-depth discussion among all parliamentary parties.

5.2.2 Ireland

During the financial crisis, the Irish economy had to be stabilized through a bail-out loan from the European Financial Stability Facility. However, in 2014 the economy was clearly on a recovery track. As a result, although the government had still not

46 *Europe Ecologie—Les Verts* [Europe Ecology—The Greens].

47 In this respect, the chairman of the Finance Committee of the National Assembly, Gilles Carrez, noted that: 'for their own reasons, the government will not organise a plenary debate on this programme this year. It is, of course, not obliged to do so, but it has since 2011 been a tradition to do so, and everyone knows how important traditions are in our country. It appears essential to us to convene the Committee once more on this issue' (author's translation). See Assemblée nationale, Commission des Finances, de l'économie générale et du contrôle budgétaire, Compte rendu no 78, 22 April 2015 http://www.assemblee-nationale.fr/14/pdf/cr-cfiab/14-15/c1415078.pdf (last accessed 28 August 2016).

met the deficit goal, the Commission evaluated the economic progress of the country very positively. The recommendations that the Commission issued in 2014 did not require any radical short-term measures. Rather, the Commission noted that the government concentrated on the gradual correction of the excessive deficit, fostering long-term employment and education, prevention of poverty among children, monitoring of banks' performance, as well as the reduction of the costs of legal proceedings. The Commission also advised for the government to improve cost-effectiveness in the healthcare system. In 2015, the recommendations stipulated that the government was to ensure durable correction of the excessive deficit and to broaden the tax base. The government was also recommended to foster employment, provide affordable childcare, and help to restructure mortgages. Finally, the Commission advocated improving the monitoring over the Irish Central Bank.

As the Irish Parliament enjoys very weak constitutional protection in budgetary and EU matters, the low level of activity in *Dáil* was not very surprising. In the plenary, parliamentary parties were involved in the approval of the Finance Bill. However, approval of the domestic budget was not linked to the European Semester: the two processes were treated separately. The European Semester was debated in committee only. Two committees led the process: the Joint Committee on European Union Affairs and the Committee on Finance, Public Expenditure and Reform.

In Ireland, there was widespread agreement that the country-specific recommendations were good for the country and the committees demonstrated their interest in the European Semester. The two committees were searching for a framework that would help them to engage systematically with the European Semester. Over the 2014 and 2015 cycles analyzed, both committees invited various experts in order to learn more about the functioning of the European Semester. Yet the activity was predominantly of a technocratic nature, whereby the committees were mainly interested in gaining greater knowledge of the functioning of the European Semester.

During the 2014 cycle, Irish parliamentarians posed a large number of written questions regarding the functioning of the European Semester. In January 2014, there was a plenary debate on the Commission's Annual Growth Survey. In spring 2014, the Joint Committee on EU Affairs debated the European Semester as well as the National Reform Programme. The Committee members observed that the timing of the Semester was too tight for NPs to contribute substantially to the process. The discussion was predominantly focused on clarifying details concerning compliance with particular country-specific recommendations. In June 2014, this Committee debated the country-specific recommendations. While there was no disagreement regarding these recommendations, it was observed that they were too general. Instead, the Committee expected more specific guidelines concerning, for instance, the creation of jobs. In autumn 2014, the committees and the plenary began working on the Finance Bill. The budget for 2015 was approved by both chambers of the *Oireachtas* in December, but the budgetary process was not linked to the European Semester.

In 2015, the European Semester remained salient for parliamentary committees. In January, the Committee on Finance, Public Expenditure, and Reform debated the Annual Growth Survey, concluding that it should be involved more closely in the European Semester. The National Reform Programme was discussed in the Joint Committee on EU Affairs, which concluded that the European Semester was very important for Europe. The chairman initiated a discussion on how NPs could be better involved in the process.

The country-specific recommendations were debated in the Committee on Finance, Public Expenditure, and Reform. The guest speaker, Commissioner Moscovici, noted that the Commission acknowledged the progress that Ireland had made and observed that Ireland's economic recovery had been impressive but that there were 'still legacies of the crisis that continue to create risks for the country'.[48] The Committee members specifically enquired whether the Commission expected Ireland to implement each and every recommendation. In reply, the Commissioner confirmed that the implementation of some of the recommendations was expected to take place over a period of few years and not necessarily within one budgetary cycle. The discussion on country-specific recommendations continued in the Joint Committee on EU Affairs and it revolved around their interpretation and implementation. In September, the Committee discussed the Five Presidents' Report. The guest speaker was José Leandro, the principal adviser on the EMU to the president of the European Commission, Jean-Claude Juncker, who was asked about the content of the proposed reforms. In October, the committees and both chambers of Parliament started working on the Finance Bill, which was approved in December.

6. Conclusions

This chapter has presented an analysis of national parliamentary participation in two budgetary cycles of the European Semester—those of 2014 and 2015—in Austria, France, Germany, and Ireland. The study's dependent variable was the willingness of a parliamentary party to comply with the requirements of the European Semester. Drawing on the literature, the analysis tested the impact of the following three factors: (a) the strength of parliaments' formal powers in budgetary and EU matters; (b) whether a party is in government or in opposition; and (c) coherence between the country-specific recommendations and the economic preferences of a party.

The empirical analysis established that compliance within the European Semester depends on the *combination* of the first and the third factors: formal powers and coherence between the country-specific recommendations and the economic preferences of a party. This means that non-compliance is more likely if national parliaments enjoy strong formal powers *and* if there is no coherence between the recommendations and the economic preferences of a party. Conversely, compliance is more likely the weaker the formal powers of national parliaments are *and* the more coherent the recommendations are with the economic preferences of a party.

In this context, strong formal powers in budgetary and EU matters constitute an important institutional *prerequisite*, allowing parliamentary parties to voice their contestation of EU recommendations. However, the willingness to comply depends most directly on whether the content of country-specific recommendations is coherent with the economic preferences of a political party and not on the government–opposition conflict.

The study further shows that the politics of the European Semester is extremely contentious in some Member States. The analysis demonstrates that parliamentary parties in Austria and Ireland advocated compliance, whereas parliamentary parties in France and Germany remained deeply divided on the issue. Against expectations, governing parties have not been more willing to comply with EU recommendations than opposition parties. It is also notable that governing parties, or their sub-groups, did not automatically act towards meeting the terms of international agreements. It is likely

[48] Dáil, Committee on Finance, Public Expenditure, and Reform, debate on 26 May 2015.

that the *perceived* pressure to comply has not been particularly strong among governing parties. After the establishment of the EMU, many governments have vaguely interpreted the rules of the Stability and Growth Pact and have not ruled out the possibility of temporarily violating them. Usually, governing parties assume their international responsibility for the agreements that they have negotiated and approved. Instead, they decided to represent the interests of their constituencies.

Furthermore, it is shown that German parliamentary parties made very effective use of their strong formal powers in order to initiate debates on the European Semester. In the case of France, although Parliament enjoys weak formal powers in budgetary and EU matters, the prime minister nonetheless invited it to participate in the European Semester process in 2014. During plenary discussions, a deep conflict over compliance emerged. In 2015, the prime minister excluded Parliament from the European Semester process, resulting in Parliament not being invited to pass a vote on the Stability Programme. As a consequence, the opponents of compliance could no longer challenge the government. The few activities related to the European Semester took place at the committee level and had a purely technocratic form. With Parliament excluded, the government could take steps towards compliance without particular difficulties.

The Austrian Parliament enjoys strong formal powers; however, given the fact that the recommendations did conflict with political parties' economic preferences, Parliament did not make use of its competences in order to jeopardize compliance. As expected, in Ireland there was a palpable willingness to comply with the European Semester. This is explained by the combination of weak formal parliamentary powers and recommendations that clearly reflected the Commission's recognition of the government's success in bringing the Irish economy back on track.

The findings suggest that the stronger involvement of NPs in the European Semester process may actually bring effects contrary to the Commission's and the Council's expectations of compliance with the recommendations. On the one hand, a stronger involvement of NPs in the European Semester enhances the democratic legitimacy of the process by strengthening the domestic control of decisions taken at the EU level. On the other hand, the intensive involvement of NPs may also diminish domestic compliance with the European Semester, because parliaments can use their enhanced powers to jeopardize the European Semester by challenging the recommended policy measures and proposing alternative ones.

The questions then emerge: how does the observed pattern of politicization affect the legitimacy of the European Semester? Is it likely to contribute to compliance with the mechanism? The findings of this chapter seem to suggest that the politicization of the European Semester is more likely to undermine its legitimacy: the higher the politicization, the more likely it is that compliance will reduce. As a consequence, the European Semester creates a situation in which democracy has to be sacrificed in order to achieve compliance.

The political conflict over the European Semester has not been organized along the government–opposition conflict but rather along political party positioning on redistribution. By the same token, parliamentary parties managed to represent their voters' interests. The literature notes that democratic representation is fostered if the parliamentary conflict is organized along the classical left–right conflict.[49] The assumption

[49] Sandra Kröger and Richard Bellamy, 'Beyond a Constraining Dissensus: The Role of National Parliaments in Domesticating and Normalising the Politicisation of European Integration' (2016) 14 Comp Eur Pol 131.

is that politics is about preferences and alternative choices that are communicated from voters to their parties. In these respects, parliamentary conflict within the European Semester met the basic requirement of representative democracy. That was not the case during the reform process of EU economic governance. As one recent study demonstrated, the left–right conflict was absent in the voting behaviour of parliamentary parties on anti-crisis measures related to the establishment of bail-out funds (above all the European Stability Mechanism) and the ratification of the Fiscal Compact.[50] During that period, parliamentary parties failed to vote according to their positions on redistribution. Their vote outcome was instead dominated by international responsibility.

Against that background, it is clearly a positive development from the normative perspective that parliamentary parties re-connected with their constituencies and began acting according to their preferences. However, as this study has demonstrated, the 'normalisation' of politics is likely to take place at the expense of compliance within the European Semester. In the absence of an immediate remedy to the problem, the dilemma is likely to remain unresolved in the near future.

Appendix 11.1: European Semester in Germany (2014–2015)

Bundestag 2014

Date	Activity	Content
30.01.2014	Regierungserklärung — Finanzen und Haushalt.	Question-hour in which the government outlines financial and budgetary priorities for 2014.
03.04.2014	Antrag: 'Nationalesreformprogramm 2014 nützen, wirtschaftspolitische Steuerung in der EU ernst nehmen und Investitionen stärken'.	Plenary debate devoted to the motion of the Green Party 'National Reform programme 2014: taking seriously economic coordination in the EU and fostering investment'.
08–11.04.2014, 24.06.2014, 27.06.2014	Gesetz über die Feststellung des Bundeshaushaltsplans für das Haushaltsjahr 2014 & Finanzplan des Bundes 2013–2017.	Plenary debates: determination of the budget for the year 2014 and the Stability Programme 2013–17.
09–13.09.2014, 25–28.11.2014	Gesetz über die Feststellung des Bundeshaushaltsplans für das Haushaltsjahr 2015 (Haushaltsgesetz 2015) & Finanzplan des Bundes 2014 bis 2018.	Plenary debates: budget 2015 and the Stability Programme 2014–18.
20.10.2014	A letter of the Minister of Finance (W Schäuble) and the Minister of Economy and Energy (S Gabriel) to the EU Commissioner Jyrki Katainen	The ministers advocate closer cooperation between national (national parliaments and social partners) and European actors in the European Semester.
13.11.2014	Antrag: 'Nationalesreformprogramm 2014 nützen, wirtschaftspolitische Steuerung in der EU ernst nehmen und Investitionen stärken'.	Motion of the Green Party: Plenary debate and vote (rejected) 'Making use of the NRP 2014, taking seriously the EU economic coordination and strengthening investment'

[50] Maatsch (n 19). See also the chapter by Frank Wendler in this volume.

Date	Activity	Content
11.07.2014	Unterrichtungdurch die Delegation des Deutschen Bundestages in der Konferenz gemäß Artikel 13 des Vertrags über Stabilität, Koordinierung und Steuerung in der Wirtschafts- und Währungsunion (Fiskalvertrag).	Report by the German delegation from the Bundestag to the Art.13 Conference, 3–4 February, Brussels.

Bundestag 2015

Date	Activity	Content
14.01.2015	Aktuelle Stunde auf Verlangen der Fraktionen der CDU/CSU und SPD: Bundeshaushalt 2014 ohne neue Schulden.	Question hour: German budget 2014 without new debts.
26.03.2015	Antrag (CDU/CSU, SPD) 'Das ES stärken, besser umsetzen und weiterentwickeln' Motion by the governing parties	Motion 'Strengthening the European Semester: better implementation and development'.
23.04.2015 & 21.05.2015	Gesetz über die Feststellung eines Nachtrags zum Bundeshaushaltsplan für das Haushaltsjahr 2015 (Nachtragshaushaltsgesetz 2015)	Plenary debates: revisions of the current budget (2015). 1st, 2nd, and 3rd reading. Approved.
21.05.2015	Antrag (DIE LINKE) 'Exportüberschüsse abbauen — Wende in der Lohnpolitik einleiten'	Motion: 'Diminishing Trade Surpluses and Changing the Wage Policy'. Plenary debate.
21.05.2015	'Das Europäische Semester stärken, besser umsetzen und weiterentwickeln'. The motion by the CDU/CSU and SPD	Motion 'Strengthening the European Semester, improving the implementation and further development', approved without a debate.
21.05.2015	Antrag (die Grünen) 'Nationales Reformprogramm 2015 — Wirtschaftspolitische Steuerung in der EU ernst nehmen und Investitionen stärken'.	Motion: 'National Reform programme 2015: taking seriously economic coordination in the EU and fostering investment'. Rejected.
18.06.2015	Rechnung des Bundesrechnungshofes für das Haushaltsjahr 2014.	Approval of the audit, vote in the plenary.
08.11.2015, 24.11.2015 & 26.11.2015 & 27.11.2015	Gesetz über die Feststellung des Bundeshaushaltsplans für das Haushaltsjahr 2016 (Haushaltsgesetz 2016). Finanzplan des Bundes 2015 bis 2019	1st reading in the plenary (budget law and the Stability Programme 2015–19)
10.10.2015 & 05.11.2015	Nachtragshaushaltsgesetz 2015	Revision of the current budget (2015). Approved.

Bundesrat 2014 and 2015

Date	Activity	Content
11.04.2014	Entwurf eines Gesetzes über die Feststellung des Bundeshaushaltsplans für das Haushaltsjahr 2014 (Haushaltsgesetz 2014).Entwurf eines Haushaltsbegleitgesetzes 2014.	Debate: Budget 2014.
19.09.2014 & 25.09.2014	Gesetzes über die Feststellung des Bundeshaushaltsplans für das Haushaltsjahr 2015 (Haushaltsgesetz 2015) & Finanzplan des Bundes 2014 bis 2018.	Budget 2015 and the Stability Plan 2014–18. Approved.
25.09.2015 & 18.12.2015	Gesetz über die Feststellung des Bundeshaushaltsplans für das Haushaltsjahr 2016 (Haushaltsgesetz 2016). Finanzplan des Bundes 2015 bis 2019 Budget Law 2016 and the Financial Federal Plan 2015–2019 (Haushaltgesetz 201 und Finanzplan des Bundes 2015–2019)	Budget 2016 and the Stability Plan 2015–19. Approved

Appendix 11.2: European Semester in Austria (2014–2015)

Nationalrat 2014

Date	Activity	Content
22.01.2014	Gesetzliches Budgetprovisorium 2014, das Bundesfinanzrahmengesetz 2014–2017	Budget Committee
29.01.2014	Gesetzliches Budgetprovisorium 2014, das Bundesfinanzrahmengesetz 2014–2017	Debated in the plenary
24.02.2014	Reports of the Audit Committee regarding the Reports of the Auditing Authority (Rechnungshof): Reihe Bund 2010/11 (III-4/37 dB), RB 2011/8 (III-5/38 d.B.), RB 2013/13 (III-33/40 dB)	Plenary
30.04.2014	Bundesfinanzgesetz 2014 — BFG 2014	Plenary
30.04.2014	Bundesfinanzgesetz 2015 — BFG 2015	Plenary
08.05.2014	Kommuniqués: Concerning the Austrian Stability Programme 2013–2018 (21/KOMM)	Budget Committee
08.05.2014	Kommuniqués: concerning the National Reform Programme for Austria 2014 (22/KOMM)	Budget Committee, debate and vote (approved) in the Committee only
08.05.2014	Budgetbegleitgesetz 2014	Committee
16.05.2014	BFG 2014 and 2015	Committee
20.05.2014	Budgetbegleitgesetz 2014	Plenary

Date	Activity	Content
21.05.2014	Bundesfinanzrahmengesetz 2014–17, 2015–18.	Plenary
22.05.2014		
23.05.2014		
26.11.2014	Report: Haushalt 2015	Budget Committee
11.12.2014	Report Haushalt 2015 (III-118/382 dB)	Plenary

Nationalrat 2015

Date	Activity	Content
19.02.2015	Structural zero-deficit in 2016 (circulated by the Ministry of Finance)	Parliamentary correspondence
22.04.2015	Bundesfinanzrahmengesetz (BFRG 2016–19)	Plenary, 1st reading: law authorizing the Federal Financial Framework Law 2016–19
07.05.2015	Bundesfinanzrahmengesetz (BFRG 2016–19)	Budget Committee
07.05.2015	Kommuniqués: Bundesfinanzrahmengesetz 2014–19 (21/KOMM)	Budget Committee
07.05.2015	Kommuniqués: National Reform Programme for Austria 2015 (135/KOMM)	Budget Committee, debate and vote (approved)
20.05.2015	Bundesfinanzrahmengesetz 2016–19 (BFRG 2016–19)	Plenary
16.10.2015	Bundesfinanzgesetz 2016 — BFG 2016	Plenary
29.10.2015	Kommuniqués: (Haushaltsplannung 2016), (191/KOMM)	Budget Committee
16.11.2015	Bundesrechnungsabschluss 2014	Budget Committee
20.11.2015	Bundesfinanzrahmengesetz 2015–18, 2016–19, Bundesfinanzgesetz 2015 2016	Budget Committee
24.11.2015	Bundeshaushaltgesetz 2013, Budgetbegleitgesetz 2016	Plenary
25.11.2015	Budgetbegleitgesetz 2016	Plenary
25.11.2015	Bundesfinanzgesetz 2016- BFG 2016	Plenary
26.11.2015	Bundesfinanzgesetz 2016 — BFG 2016	Plenary

Bundesrat 2014 and 2015

Date	Activity	Content
10.04.2014	EU yearly preview (2014) by the Ministry of Finance (III-516-BR/2014 dB, 9158/BR dB)	
28.05.2014	Budgetbegleitgesetz 2014 (53 dB, 130 dB, 9183/BR dB, 9184/BR dB)	
12.03.2015	EU yearly preview (2015) by the Ministry of Finance (III-550-BR/2015, 9329/BR dB)	
19.11.2015	European Audit Authority/ Yearly report concerning the budget year 2014 (83167/EU XXV.GP)	
03.12.2015	Budgetbegleitgesetz 2016 (821 bD, 882 dB, 9486/BR dB, 9487/BR dB)	

Appendix 11.3: European Semester in France (2014–2015)

Assemblée nationale 2014

Date	Activity	Content
21.01.2014	Examen annuel de croissance (Commission des finances, de l'économie générale et du contrôle budgétaire).	Question hour: Annual Growth Survey.
16.04.2014	A letter from the Socialist Party to the prime minister Manuel Valls concerning the NRP.	
29.04.2014	Programme de stabilité 2014–2017 (Commission des finances, de l'économie générale et du contrôle budgétaire).	The government presents the Stability Programme 2014–2017 in the Finance Committee.
28.05.2014	Déclaration du Gouvernement sur le projet de programme de stabilité 2014–2017.	Plenary debate and vote (approved).
	Certification des comptes de l'État — exercice 2013 — et rapport relatif aux résultats à la gestion budgétaire de l'exercice 2013 (Commission des finances, de l'économie générale et du contrôle budgétaire).	The President of the Court of Auditors outlines the development of the budget 2013.
03.06.2014	Projet de loi de règlement du budget et d'approbation des comptes de l'année 2013 (Commission des finances, de l'économie générale et du contrôle budgétaire).	Budget 2013, Finance Committee.
11.06.2014	Projet de loi de finances rectificative pour 2014 (Commission des finances, de l'économie générale et du contrôle budgétaire).	Budget 2014, Finance Committee
17.06.2014	Rapport sur la situation et les perspectives des finances publiques (Commission des finances, de l'économie générale et du contrôle budgétaire).	The report on the situation and perspectives of public finances, Finance Committee.
18.06 & 23.06.2014	Projet de loi de finances rectificative pour 2014 (Commission des finances, de l'économie générale et du contrôle budgétaire).	Finances 2014, Finance Committee.
24.06.2014	Recommandations par pays.	Country specific recommendations, vote (approved).
23–26.06.2014 & 01.07.2014	Projet de loi de finances rectificative pour 2014.	Plenary debates, 1st reading and vote (approved).
02.07.2014	Projet de loi de règlement du budget et d'approbation des comptes de l'année 2013 (Commission des finances, de l'économie générale et du contrôle budgétaire).	Review of the budget for the year 2013.
08.07.2014	Rapport d'information préalable au débat d'orientation des finances publiques (Commission des finances, de l'économie générale et du contrôle budgétaire).	Examination of the report on public finances, Finance Committee.

Date	Activity	Content
09.07.2014	Projet de loi de règlement du budget et approbation des comptes de l'année 2013.Débat d'orientation sur les finances publiques.	Plenary debate, revision of the budget 2013 (approved). Plenary debate about public finances.
10.07.2014	Projet de loi de finances rectificative pour 2014 (Commission mixte paritaire).	
10.07 & 15.07.2014	Projet de loi de finances rectificative pour 2014 (Commission des finances, de l'économie générale et du contrôle budgétaire).	
15–16.07.2014	Projet de loi de finances rectificative pour 2014.	Budget 2014 revisions, vote (approved).
17.07.2014	Projet de loi de règlement du budget et approbation des comptes de l'année 2013 (Commission des finances, de l'économie générale et du contrôle budgétaire). Projet de loi de règlement du budget et approbation des comptes de l'année 2013 (Commission mixte paritaire).	
21.07.2014	Projet de loi de règlement du budget et approbation des comptes de l'année 2013.	Vote (approved).
23.07.2014	Projet de loi de finances rectificative pour 2014 & Projet de loi de règlement du budget et approbation des comptes de l'année 2013 (Commission des finances, de l'économie générale et du contrôle budgétaire).	3rd reading.
16.09.2014	Projet de loi de finances rectificative pour 2014 & Projet de loi de règlement du budget et approbation des comptes de l'année 2013.	Vote (approved).
01.10.2014	Déclaration de politique générale du Gouvernement.	Plenary debate and vote about the general policy (approved).
07.10.2014	Projet de loi de programmation des finances publiques pour les années 2014 à 2019 & projet de loi de finances pour 2015 (Commission des finances, de l'économie générale et du contrôle budgétaire). Projet de loi de programmation des finances publiques pour les années 2014 à 2019 (Commission des finances, de l'économie générale et du contrôle budgétaire).	
08.10.2014	Projet de loi de finances pour 2015 (Commission des finances, de l'économie générale et du contrôle budgétaire).	
14.10.2014	Projet de loi de programmation des finances publiques pour les années 2014 à 2019 & projet de loi de finances pour 2015 (Commission des finances, de l'économie générale et du contrôle budgétaire).	
14.10 & 15.10.2014	Projet de loi de programmation des finances publiques pour les années 2014 à 2019 & Projet de loi de finances pour 2015.	Plenary debates

Date	Activity	Content
16–21.10.2014	Projet de loi de finances pour 2015.	Plenary debates
20.10 & 22–24.10 & 27–29.10 & 30.10 & 31.10 & 03–07.11.2014	Projet de loi de finances pour 2015 (Commission des finances, de l'économie générale et du contrôle budgétaire).	
21.10.2014	Projet de loi de programmation des finances publiques pour les années 2014 à 2019 & Projet de loi de finances pour 2015.	Plenary debate, vote
27.10.2014	Lettre du ministre des finances (Michel Sapin) à Jyrki Katainen.	
28–30.10.2014 & 3–7.11.2014	Projet de loi de finances pour 2015.	Plenary debates
12.11.2014	Projet de loi de finances rectificative pour 2014 (Commission des finances, de l'économie générale et du contrôle budgétaire).	
12–14.11.2014 & 18.11.2014	Projet de loi de finances pour 2015.	Plenary debates
01–03.12.2014 & 05.12 & 09.12.2014	Projet de loi de finances rectificative pour 2014.	
11.12.2014	Projet de loi de programmation des finances publiques pour les années 2014 à 2019 (Commission mixte paritaire).	
11 & 12.12.2014	Projet de loi de finances pour 2015 (Commission mixte paritaire).	
12.12.2014	Projet de loi de finances pour 2015 (Commission des finances, de l'économie générale et du contrôle budgétaire).	
15.12.2014	Projet de loi de finances pour 2015.	Plenary debate
	Projet de loi de finances rectificative pour 2014 (Commission mixte paritaire).	
16.12.2014	Projet de loi de finances pour 2015.	Plenary debate, 2nd reading and vote (approved).
	Projet de loi de finances rectificative pour 2014.	Plenary debate, 2nd reading and vote (approved).
	Projet de loi de programmation des finances publiques pour les années 2014 à 2019.	Plenary debate, 2nd reading and vote (approved).
18.12.2014	Projet de loi de finances pour 2015.	Plenary debate, 3rd reading and vote (approved).
	Projet de loi de finances rectificative pour 2014.	Plenary debate, 3rd reading and vote (approved).
	Projet de loi de programmation des finances publiques pour les années 2014 à 2019.	Plenary debate, 3rd reading and vote (approved).

Sénat 2014

Date	Activity	Content
29.04.2014	Projet de loi de programmation des finances publiques pour les années 2014 à 2019 (Commission des finances).	Government declaration and discussion about the Stability Programme.
04.06 & 10.06.2014	Projet de loi de règlement du budget et approbation des comptes de l'année 2013 (Commission des finances).	1st reading.
11.06.2014	Projet de loi de finances rectificative pour 2014 (Commission des finances).	1st reading.
18.06.2014	Situation et perspectives des finances publiques et avis du Haut Conseil relatif au projet de loi de finances rectificative pour 2014 et au projet de loi de financement rectificative de la sécurité sociale pour 2014 (Commission des finances).	
02.07.2014	Projet de loi de finances rectificative pour 2014 (Commission des finances).	1st reading.
07.07 & 08.07.2014	Projet de loi de finances rectificative pour 2014.Projet de loi de finances rectificative pour 2014 (Commission des finances).	Plenary debates
10.07.2014	Projet de loi de règlement du budget et approbation des comptes de l'année 2013 & Débat d'orientation des finances publiques pour 2015 (Commission des finances).	Examination of the report.
15.07.2014	Débat d'orientation sur les finances publiques & Projet de loi de règlement du budget et approbation des comptes de l'année 2013.	Plenary debate, 1st reading and vote (rejected).
17.07.2014	Projet de loi de finances rectificative pour 2014 (Commission des finances).	2nd reading.
21.07.2014	Projet de loi de finances rectificative pour 2014.Projet de loi de finances rectificative pour 2014 (Commission des finances).	Plenary debate, 2nd reading and vote (rejected).
		2nd reading.
22.07.2014	Projet de loi de règlement du budget et approbation des comptes de l'année 2013 (Commission des finances).	2nd reading.
	Projet de loi de règlement du budget et approbation des comptes de l'année 2013.	Plenary debate, 2nd reading and vote (rejected).
09.10 & 15.10 & 21.10 & 22.10 & 29.10 & 30.10 & 04.11 &	Loi de finances pour 2015 & Loi de programmation des finances publiques pour les années 2014 à 2019 (Commission des finances).	1st reading.
05.11.2014		
06.11.2014	Programmation des finances publiques pour les années 2014 à 2019.	Plenary debate, 1st reading and vote (modified).
12.11 & 13.11 & 18–20.11 &	Projet de loi de finances pour 2015 (Commission des finances).	1st reading.
25.11 & 26.11 & 02.12 & 06.12 & 08.12.2014		

Date	Activity	Content
20–22.11 & 24–26.11 & 28.11 & 29.11 & 1–06.12 & 08.12 & 09.12.2014	Projet de loi de finances pour 2015.	Plenary debates, 1st reading and vote (modified).
10.12 & 12.12.2014	Projet de loi de finances rectificative pour 2014 (Commission des finances).	1st reading.
11.12 & 12.12.2014	Projet de loi de finances rectificative pour 2014.	Plenary debates, 1st reading and vote (modified).
17.12.2014	Projet de loi de finances rectificative pour 2014.Projet de loi de finances pour 2015. Programmation des finances publiques pour les années 2014 à 2019.	Plenary debate, 2nd reading and vote (rejected). Plenary debate, 2nd reading and vote (rejected). Plenary debate, 2nd reading and vote (rejected).

Assemblée nationale 2015

Date	Activity	Content
11.02.2015	Résultats de l'exercice 2014 (Commission des finances, de l'économie générale et du contrôle budgétaire).	
04.03.2015	Recommandation de la Commission européenne au Conseil del'Union européenne relative au déficit budgétaire de la France (Commission des affaires européennes).	
18.03.2015	Recommandation du Conseil de l'Union européenne du 10 mars visant à ce qu'il soit mis fin à la situation de déficit public excessif en France (Commission des finances, de l'économie générale et du contrôle budgétaire).	
15.04.2015	Prévisions macroéconomiques - programme de stabilité pour les années 2015–2018 (Commission des finances, de l'économie générale et du contrôle budgétaire).	Discussions about the Stability Programme 2015–2018.
22.04.2015	Programme de stabilité pour les années 2015–2018 et programme national de réforme (Commission des finances, de l'économie générale et du contrôle budgétaire).	Examination of the report.

Date	Activity	Content
27.05.2015	Certification des comptes de l'État — exercice 2014 — et rapport relatif aux résultats à la gestion budgétaire de l'exercice 2014 (Commission des finances, de l'économie générale et du contrôle budgétaire).	The president of the Court of Auditors outlines the development of the budget 2014.
23.06 & 24.06 & 01.07.2015	Projet de loi de règlement du budget et d'approbation des comptes de l'année 2014: Cycle d'auditions de responsables de programmes sur l'exécution des crédits (Commission des finances, de l'économie générale et du contrôle budgétaire).	
24.06.2015	Recommandations par pays (Commission des affaires européennes).	Country-specific recommendations.
	Rapport sur la situation et les perspectives des finances publiques (Commission des finances, de l'économie générale et du contrôle budgétaire).	
01.07.2015	Projet de loi de règlement du budget et d'approbation des comptes de l'année 2014 & Rapport préalable au débat d'orientation des finances publiques 2015 (Commission des finances, de l'économie générale et du contrôle budgétaire).	
06.07.2015	Projet de loi de règlement du budget et approbation des comptes de l'année 2014.	Plenary debate
09.07.2015	Débat d'orientation des finances publiques.	Plenary debate about public finances.
15.07.2015	Projet de loi de règlement du budget et d'approbation des comptes de l'année 2014 (Commission mixte paritaire).	
	Projet de loi de règlement du budget et d'approbation des comptes de l'année 2014 (Commission des finances, de l'économie générale et du contrôle budgétaire).	
16.07.2015	Projet de loi de règlement du budget et d'approbation des comptes de l'année 2014.	
22.07.2015	Projet de loi de règlement du budget et d'approbation des comptes de l'année 2014 (Commission des finances, de l'économie générale et du contrôle budgétaire).	
	Projet de loi de règlement du budget et d'approbation des comptes de l'année 2014.	
30.09 & 07.10 & 13.10 & 15.10 & 19–22.10 & 26–30.10 & 2–5.11 & 9.11.2015	Projet de loi de finances pour 2016 (Commission des finances, de l'économie générale et du contrôle budgétaire).	1st reading Budget Law 2016

Date	Activity	Content
13–16.10 & 19.10 & 20.10 & 27–29.10.2015 & 02–6.11 & 9–13.11 & 17.11.2015	Projet de loi de finances pour 2016.	
13.11 & 25.11 & 30.11.2015	Projet de loi de finances rectificative pour 2015 (Commission des finances, de l'économie générale et du contrôle budgétaire).	
30.11. & 01.12. & 02.12. & 04.12. & 08.12.	Projet de loi de finances rectificative pour 2015.	
10.12.2015	Projet de loi de finances pour 2016 (Commission mixte paritaire).	
10.12 & 11.12.2015	Projet de loi de finances pour 2016 (Commission des finances, de l'économie générale et du contrôle budgétaire).	
11.12.2015	Projet de loi de finances pour 2016.	
14.12.2015	Projet de loi de finances rectificative pour 2015. (Commission mixte paritaire).	
15.12.2015	Projet de loi de finances rectificative pour 2015 (Commission des finances, de l'économie générale et du contrôle budgétaire).	
15.12.2015	Projet de loi de finances rectificative pour 2015.	
16.12.2015	Examen annuel de croissance pour 2016 et l'avis de la Commission européenne sur les projets de budgets nationaux pour 2016 (Commission des affaires européennes).	Communication about the Annual Growth Survey and the opinion of the European Commission on draft national budgets.
17.12.2015	Projet de loi de finances pour 2016 (Commission mixte paritaire).	3rd reading.
	Projet de loi de finances rectificative pour 2015 (Commission des finances, de l'économie générale et du contrôle budgétaire).	3rd reading.
	Projet de loi de finances rectificative pour 2015.	Plenary debate, 3rd reading and vote (approved).
	Projet de loi de finances pour 2016.	Plenary debate, 3rd reading and vote (approved).

Sénat 2015

Date	Activity	Content
15 & 16.04.2015	Programme de stabilité pour les années 2015 à 2018 et programme national de réforme (Commission des finances).	Discussion and communication on the Stability Programme.
03.06 & 10.06 & 17.06 & 24.06 & 01.07 & 08.07.2015	Projet de loi de règlement du budget et d'approbation des comptes de l'année 2014 (Commission des finances).	1st reading.
09.07.2015	Projet de loi de règlement du budget et d'approbation des comptes de l'année 2014.	Debate, 1st reading and vote (rejected).
21.07.2015	Projet de loi de règlement du budget et d'approbation des comptes de l'année 2014 (Commission des finances).	2nd reading.
	Projet de loi de règlement du budget et d'approbation des comptes de l'année 2014.	Debate, 2nd reading and vote (rejected).
30.09 & 05.10 & 14.10 & 20–21.10 & 28–29.10 & 04–05.11 & 10.11 & 12. 11 & 17–20.11 & 23–27.11 & 30.11–03.12 & 07.12.2015	Projet de loi de finances pour 2016 (Commission des finances).	1st reading.
19–21.11 & 23–18.11 & 1–4.12 & 7.12 & 8.12.2015	Projet de loi de finances pour 2016.	Debate, 1st reading and vote (modified).
09.12 & 11.12 & 16.12.2015	Projet de loi de finances rectificative pour 2015 (Commission des finances).	1st reading.
10 & 11.12.2015	Projet de loi de finances rectificative pour 2015.	Debate, 1st reading and vote (modified).
16.12.2015	Projet de loi de finances rectificative pour 2015 (Commission des finances).	2nd reading.
	Projet de loi de finances pour 2016 (Commission des finances).	2nd reading.
	Projet de loi de finances rectificative pour 2015. Projet de loi de finances pour 2016.	Debate, 2nd reading and vote (rejected). Debate, 2nd reading and vote (rejected).

Appendix 11.4: European Semester in Ireland (2014–2015)

Dáil 2014

Date	Activity
23.01.2014	Debate on the 'Role of National Parliaments in European Semester and Annual Growth Survey 2014: Secretary General of European Commission', Joint Committee on European Union Affairs.
01.04.2014	Debate on the 'European Semester Process: Committee of the Regions' and on the 'National Reform Programme for Ireland 2014: Minister of State at Department of Foreign Affairs and Trade', Joint Committee on European Union Affairs.
15.04.2014	Debate on the 'Irish Stability Programme Update: Minister for Finance'. Joint Committee on Finance, Public Expenditure and Reform (Vol 2 No 101)
12.06.2014	Debate on the 'European Commission Country Specific Recommendations for Ireland: Minister of State at Department of Foreign Affairs and Trade', Joint Committee on European Union Affairs.
19.06.2014	Debate on the 'Business of Joint Committee' and on the 'Fiscal Assessment Report 2014: Irish Fiscal Advisory Board', Joint Committee on Finance, Public Expenditure and Reform.
09.10.2014	Debate in Dáil: Priority Question No 4 about 'Budget Consultation Process'
14.10.2014	Debate in Dáil: Financial Resolutions 2015 — Budget Statement 2015
15.10.2014	Debate in Dáil: Financial Resolutions 2015 — Financial Resolution No 3: General (Resumed)
22.10.2014	Debate in Dáil: Financial Resolutions 2015 — Financial Resolution No 3: General (Resumed)
04.11.2014	Debate on the 'Response to 2014 Country Specific Recommendations for Ireland: Better Europe Alliance'. Joint Committee on European Union Affairs
04.11.2014 05.11.2014 & 06.11.2014	Debate in Dáil: Finance Bill 2014: Second Stage
18.11.2014 & 19.11.2014	Debate on 'Finance Bill 2014: Committee Stage'. Select Sub-Committee on Finance (Vol 2 No 55)
25.11.2014 & 26.11.2014	Debate in Dáil: Finance Bill 2014: (Order for) Report Stage and Final Stage
04.12.2014	Debate on the 'Annual Growth Survey 2015: European Commission Office Ireland'. Joint Committee on European Union Affairs

Seanad 2014

Date	Activity
14.10.2014	Plenary Debate in Seanad about 'Budget 2015: Statements'
04.12.2014	Plenary Debate in Seanad about 'Finance Bill 2014 (Certified Money Bill): Second Stage'
10.12.2014	Plenary Debate in Seanad about 'Finance Bill 2014 (Certified Money Bill): Committee Stage'
11.12.2014	Plenary Debate in Seanad about 'Finance Bill 2014 (Certified Money Bill): Report and Final Stages'

Dáil 2015

Date	Activity
21.01.2015	Debate on the Annual Growth Survey 2015. Joint meeting of the Committee on Finance, Public Expenditure and Reform.
23.04.2015 & 30.04.2015	European Semester — Draft National Reform Programme 2015 — Discussion in the Committee on European Union Affairs.
29.04.2015 & 30.04.2015	'Spring Economic Statement' (containing the Stability Programme as well). Plenary debate in the Dáil.
26.05.2015	Country Specific Recommendation (issued by the European Commission): debate in the Committee on Finance, Public Expenditure and Reform.
09.06.2015	Fiscal Responsibility (Amendment) Bill 2015. First stage. Plenary debate in the Dáil.
11.06.2015	Fiscal Assessment Report by the Irish Fiscal Advisory Council. Committee on Finance, Public Expenditure and Reform.
18.06.2015	'Country Specific Recommendations 2015'. Discussion in the Committee on European Union Affairs.
15.07.2015	'Latest European Developments and Future Implications for Euro Currency'. Discussion in the Committee on Finance, Public Expenditure and Reform.
24.09.2015	'European Economic and Monetary Union'. Discussion in the Committee on European Union Affairs, guest speaker: Mr Jose Leandro, Economic Adviser to the President of the European Council.
01.10.2015	'European Economic and Monetary Union'. Discussion in the Committee on European Union Affairs.
06.10.2015	'Macroeconomic Forecast for 2016 prepared by the Department of Finance'. Debate in the Committee on Finance, Public Expenditure and Reform.
07.10.2015	Finance Bill 2015. Discussion in the Sub-committee on Finance 2015.
13.10.2015 & 14.10.2015	'Financial Resolutions 2016'. Plenary debate in the Dáil.
21.10.2015	'Country Specific Recommendations of the European Semester: Better Europe Alliance'. Committee on European Union Affairs.
03.11.2015	'Finance Bill 2015: Message to Dáil'. Prepared by the Sub-committee on Finance.
04.11.2015	'European Economic and Monetary Union'. Discussion in the Committee on European Union Affairs.
17.11.2015 & 18.11.2016	Finance Bill 2015. Sub-Committee on Finance.
22.10, 04.11, 5.11, & 10.11, 12.11, 24.11, & 25.11	Finance Bill. Second Stage, plenary debate in the Dáil.
03.12.2015	'Fiscal Assessment Report' prepared by the Irish Financial Advisory Council. Debate in the Committee on Finance, Public Expenditure and Reform.

Seanad 2015

Date	Activity
13.10.2015	'Budget 2016: Statements'. Plenary debate.
12.11.2015	'Finance (Miscellaneous Provisions) Bill 2015'. Second Stage, debate in the plenary.
18.11.2015	'Finance Bill 2015'. Committee and Remaining Stages & Motion for Earlier Signature.
03.12.2015	'Finance Bill' Second Stage.
08.12.2015	'Finance Bill'. Order for Second Stage, Committee and Remaining Stages.
09.12.2015 & 10.12.2015	'Finance Bill' Committee Stage.
11.12.2015	'Finance Bill' Report and Final Stages.

PART III

INTERPARLIAMENTARY COOPERATION IN EU INTERNAL AND EXTERNAL AFFAIRS

12

The Emerging Order of Interparliamentary Cooperation in the Post-Lisbon EU

Ian Cooper

1. Introduction: Order or Disorder?

There has been significant upheaval in the world of interparliamentary cooperation in the years since the Treaty of Lisbon passed into law. Most significantly, two major new Interparliamentary Conferences (IPCs) have been launched: in 2012, the 'Interparliamentary Conference on the Common Foreign and Security Policy and the Common Security and Defence Policy of the EU' (the CFSP-CSDP Conference) was established;[1] and in 2013, the 'Interparliamentary Conference on Stability, Economic Coordination and Governance in the European Union' (the SECG Conference) was initiated.[2] However, in both cases the act of creation was marred by conflict, in particular between the European Parliament (EP) and national parliaments (NPs), over how these new IPCs should be established, organized, and run—leading them to be described with words such as 'contested'[3] and even 'battlefield'.[4] More generally, the number of interparliamentary meetings—both small and large, formal and informal—has continued to increase without, according to one observer, any overall sense of order or control.[5] Adding to the potential confusion, in addition to face to face meetings, more and more interparliamentary cooperation also takes place *virtually*, ie by correspondence, as is largely the case with the early warning mechanism for subsidiarity control.[6] It therefore seems reasonable to describe interparliamentary cooperation in the EU as being in a state of 'disorder'.[7]

[1] Jan Wouters and Kolja Raube, 'The Interparliamentary Conference on Common Foreign and Security Policy: A Quest for Democratic Accountability in EU Security Governance' in Nicola Lupo and Cristina Fasone (eds), *Interparliamentary Cooperation in the Composite European Constitution* (Hart Publishing 2016).

[2] Ian Cooper, 'The Interparliamentary Conference on Stability, Economic Coordination and Governance in the European Union (the "Article 13 Conference")' in Nicola Lupo and Cristina Fasone (eds), *Interparliamentary Cooperation in the Composite European Constitution* (Hart Publishing 2016). While this conference met previously under different names, it will be referred to as the 'SECG Conference' throughout this chapter.

[3] Ian Cooper, 'The Politicization of Interparliamentary Relations in the EU: Constructing and Contesting the "Article 13 Conference" on Economic Governance' (2016) 14 Comp Eur Pol 196.

[4] Anna Herranz-Surrallés, 'The EU's Multilevel Parliamentary (Battle)Field: Inter-Parliamentary Cooperation and Conflict in Foreign and Security Policy' (2014) 37 WEP 957.

[5] Diane Fromage, 'Increasing Interparliamentary Cooperation in the EU: Current Trends and Challenges' (2016) 22 EPL 749.

[6] Ian Cooper, 'A "Virtual Third Chamber" for the European Union? National Parliaments after the Treaty of Lisbon' (2012) 35 WEP 441.

[7] Cristina Fasone, 'Ruling the (Dis-)Order of Interparliamentary Cooperation? The EU Speakers' Conference' in Nicola Lupo and Cristina Fasone (eds), *Interparliamentary Cooperation in the Composite European Constitution* (Hart Publishing 2016).

The Emerging Order of Interparliamentary Cooperation in the Post-Lisbon EU. First Edition. Ian Cooper.

It will be argued here, on the contrary, that there is an emerging *order* of interparliamentary conferences in the EU after the Lisbon Treaty. This order stems from three major trends representing changing norms and practices in the field of interparliamentary cooperation. These three trends pertain not to 'virtual' cooperation but specifically to the structure and organization of face-to-face interparliamentary meetings. The first trend concerns *what kind of interparliamentary conferences* are being created: overwhelmingly, the new meetings being created are functionally specialized, focused on particular policy areas. The second trend concerns *how these new bodies should be constituted and how their ongoing development should be monitored*: increasingly, it is the EU Speakers Conference that has taken on the task not only of creating these new bodies, but also reviewing their continuing functioning after their creation.[8] The third trend concerns *how the logistical arrangements for interparliamentary conferences are organized*, in terms of their timing and location and which parliament acts as chair and sets the agenda. This task falls increasingly upon the rotating Presidency Parliament, which now has the responsibility for organizing the six-monthly series of events that has become known as the 'Parliamentary Dimension' of the Council Presidency. The argument here is that the collective effect of these three trends is to rationalize interparliamentary meetings within the EU, making them significantly more 'orderly'.

There are a few caveats to be inserted at this point. To claim that there is an emerging 'order' of interparliamentary cooperation is not to deny that there is conflict among its participants; rather, it helps to put such conflict into a broader context. Even years after the two new IPCs have been in operation, participating parliaments continue to disagree over their exact nature and purpose, a dispute sometimes framed as a debate over whether they ought to be 'discussion forums' or 'oversight bodies'.[9] Despite this persistent disagreement, these IPCs still serve as examples of the three trends to be highlighted in this chapter. On the other hand, they also demonstrate, in different ways, that there are limits to these trends. For example, while policy-specific IPCs have been established in the fields of foreign and security policy and economic governance, an interparliamentary mechanism foreseen in the field of justice and home affairs (JHA) has not yet been established. Similarly, while the EU Speakers Conference now has a commonly accepted role in establishing and supervising other IPCs, there is still debate within that body over the exact extent—and the concomitant limits—of its role. Thus, the purpose of this chapter is to show that these trends are emerging, but also to recognize that they have not fully taken hold. As a final caveat, the goal of the present analysis to draw attention to these trends as significant empirical developments in the world of interparliamentary cooperation, not necessarily to approve or disapprove of them from a normative point of view.

The chapter aims to explain these three post-Lisbon trends in interparliamentary cooperation. First (section 2), the chapter describes the development of functionally specific interparliamentary cooperation. The two new functionally specific IPCs, the CFSP-CDSP Conference and the SECG Conference, are described briefly, as their development is already well documented. Then, there is a more detailed discussion of the lesser-known case of interparliamentary cooperation in JHA. In this field, it is expected that a new interparliamentary oversight mechanism will be created in the near future—specifically for the political monitoring of Europol—but this has yet to happen. It is posited that these three policy fields—foreign and defence policy, economic

[8] ibid.

[9] Ian Cooper, 'The Interparliamentary Conference on Stability, Economic Coordination and Governance' (n 2).

governance, and JHA—share certain common attributes that set them apart from most other EU policies: (a) they were all partly developed outside the Community method, so that the oversight powers of the EP may be limited; (b) they involve EU action that is largely executive rather than legislative; and (c) they touch on sensitive issues of national sovereignty and identity, regarding which important powers rest with the Member States. These commonalities suggest a rationale for establishing specialized interparliamentary bodies in these specific policy areas, for NPs and the EP together to exercise joint oversight over the executive actions of the EU.

The next section (section 3) chronicles the emerging role of the EU Speakers Conference as the interparliamentary body with the authority to establish and supervise the development of other forms of interparliamentary cooperation. Both the CFSP-CSDP Conference and the SECG Conference recognized this authority insofar as both of them deferred entirely to the guidelines set down by the EU Speakers Conference in establishing and/or revising their own Rules of Procedure. Yet when the EU Speakers Conference reviewed the functioning of these two IPCs at its 2015 meeting in Rome, it also demonstrated self-restraint in exercising its supervisory authority, acknowledging that the IPCs are autonomous bodies and it could not simply impose its will on them.

The inquiry continues (section 4) with an examination of the third trend in order to demonstrate that the logistical demands of the interparliamentary calendar have heightened the role of the Presidency Parliament—the parliament of the Member State that holds the rotating Council Presidency and acts as the organizer and agenda-setter for interparliamentary meetings. Even as the Council Presidency has declined in importance, the role of the Presidency Parliament has gained greater prominence. The 'Parliamentary Dimension of the Council Presidency' is a new term coined to refer to the series of events, including not only the major IPCs but also smaller chairpersons' meetings, organized by the Presidency Parliament in a way that to some extent reflects its policy priorities. Finally, the chapter concludes (section 5) that on the whole these three trends, which to varying degrees developed as a consequence of the Treaty of Lisbon and the financial crisis, indicate the resilience of NPs.

2. Interparliamentary Cooperation in Functionally Specific Fields

Prior to the Treaty of Lisbon, there were just two long-standing interparliamentary conferences in the EU, both of which had a 'general' rather than functionally specific competence. These were COSAC (the Conference of Parliamentary Committees for Union Affairs of Parliaments of the European Union)[10] and the EU Speakers Conference. The Convention on the Future of Europe of 2002–2003 had discussed, and ultimately rejected, the idea of creating a parliamentary 'third chamber' for the EU with a general policy competence. Instead, the Convention devised the so-called early warning mechanism as a device that would give NPs a direct role in EU politics—as 'subsidiarity watchdogs'—without actually creating any new EU-level institutions.[11] This was

[10] Morten Knudsen and Yves Carl, 'COSAC—Its Role to Date and its Potential in the Future' in Gavin Barrett (ed), *National Parliaments and the European Union: The Constitutional Challenge for the Oireachtas and Other Member State Legislatures* (Clarus Press 2008).

[11] Ian Cooper, 'The Watchdogs of Subsidiarity: National Parliaments and the Logic of Arguing in the EU' (2006) 44 JCMS 281.

subsequently incorporated into the Treaty of Lisbon. As a consequence, this Treaty did not establish any new interparliamentary bodies, either of a general or a functionally specific character. It did, however, mention two specific policy fields as potential areas for enhanced interparliamentary cooperation—CFSP and JHA. Moreover, a later treaty, the Treaty on Stability, Coordination and Governance in the Economic and Monetary Union (TSCG or Fiscal Compact), introduced the idea of creating an interparliamentary conference to oversee the policy field of economic governance. Thus, in these three specific policy areas, EU treaties provided at least a minimal treaty basis for the specialized policy-specific interparliamentary cooperation that would be developed in the post-Lisbon EU. The following sub-sections examine these IPCs in turn.

2.1 The CFSP-CSDP Conference

The first policy-specific interparliamentary body was established in the field of CFSP-CSDP. This policy area is mentioned in Article 10 of Protocol No 1 on the Role of National Parliaments in the European Union, annexed to the Lisbon Treaty, which stated that COSAC may 'organise interparliamentary conferences on specific topics, in particular to debate matters of common foreign and security policy, including common security and defence policy'.[12] This can be read as giving COSAC a mandate to organize an IPC on CFSP-CSDP. However, in the event it was not COSAC but the EU Speakers Conference that set the guidelines for the CFSP-CSDP Conference, doing so at its meetings in Brussels (April 2011) and in Warsaw (April 2012).[13] The new conference was in part a replacement for the Parliamentary Assembly of the Western European Union (WEU), which was abolished in 2011. It also replaced and consolidated two smaller twice-yearly meetings, the Conference of Foreign Affairs Committee Chairpersons (COFACC) and the Conference of Defence Affairs Committee Chairpersons (CODACC). The CFSP-CSDP Conference itself met for the first time in Cyprus in September 2012, at which time it adopted its own Rules of Procedure and a set of Conclusions. Since then, it has met twice a year, each time in the Member State holding the Council Presidency. It is customary for each meeting of the CFSP-CSDP Conference to be addressed by the High Representative of the Union for Foreign Affairs and Security Policy as well as the Foreign Minister and the Defence Minister from the Member State holding the Council Presidency.[14]

2.2 The SECG Conference

The impetus for the second policy-specific interparliamentary body came not from the Treaty of Lisbon but from the TSCG. In early 2012, to address the ongoing financial crisis, twenty-five EU Member States signed the TSCG outside the framework of the EU Treaties. Article 13 thereof mandated the creation of an interparliamentary conference in the field of EU economic governance calling upon the EP and NPs to determine the organization and promotion of a conference of representatives of their relevant committees in order 'to discuss budgetary policies and other issues covered by this Treaty'.

[12] At art 10 thereof. [13] See section 3.

[14] Of the eight meetings that took place up to early 2016, seven were addressed by the High Representative (the one exception being The Hague in April 2016), and seven were addressed by both the foreign minister and the defence minister (the one exception being Luxembourg in September 2015).

Much as it had done with the CFSP-CSDP Conference, the EU Speakers Conference established the guidelines for the new IPC at its meeting in Nicosia in April 2013. According to these guidelines, this IPC consolidated and replaced previous meetings of the chairs of the budget and finance committees of the EP and NPs. Furthermore, whereas the meeting in the second half of the year would be hosted and chaired by the Presidency Parliament, as is usual for IPCs, the meeting in the first half of the year should take place on the EP premises in Brussels and be co-chaired by the Presidency Parliament and the EP.[15]

The first meeting of the new IPC, which met in Vilnius in October 2013 under the title of the 'Interparliamentary Conference on Economic and Financial Governance', was rancorous. In fact, the chief disagreement was not over economic policy—eg right versus left, pro- versus anti-austerity, ordo-liberalism versus Keynesianism—but rather over the conference's institutional arrangements. The parliament chairing the meeting, the Lithuanian *Seimas*, had proposed an ambitious agenda including the adoption of Rules of Procedure and Conclusions. This was supported by a number of parliaments, including the French, but opposed by the EP as well as some other parliaments, including the German. This dispute reflected a deeper disagreement about whether it should be a strong conference with a broad scope or a weak conference with a narrow scope.[16]

Subsequent meetings alternated between a conference at the EP in Brussels within the context of the 'European Parliamentary Week' in January or February, and a conference in the Presidency Parliament in the autumn. After much delay, and after having been issued further guidelines by the EU Speakers Conference in May 2015 (see section 3), the conference agreed its own Rules of Procedure at its fifth meeting in Luxembourg in November 2015. At that point, the conference, which had met under many different names, finally called itself the 'Interparliamentary Conference on Stability, Economic Coordination and Governance'—the SECG Conference.

2.3 The Prospective JHA Conference on Europol

Among these three policy areas, it is arguably in the field of JHA where the Treaty basis is strongest for the specialized involvement of NPs. The Treaty of Lisbon states that NPs have both a general role overseeing the whole policy field, and a specific oversight role in relation to two agencies—Europol and Eurojust. One of the ways NPs contribute to the 'good functioning of the Union' is in part by 'taking part, within the framework of the area of freedom, security and justice, in the evaluation mechanisms for the implementation of the Union policies in that area', and, more specifically, 'through being involved in the political monitoring of Europol and the evaluation of Eurojust's activities'.[17] More generally, the EU Treaty singles out JHA as a policy field subject to enhanced scrutiny under the early warning mechanism, requiring that NPs 'ensure' that new proposals in this area are compliant with subsidiarity,[18] and the

[15] See more on the national parliamentary participation in the European Semester in the chapter by Aleksandra Maatsch in this volume.

[16] Ian Cooper, 'The Politicization of Interparliamentary Relations in the EU' (n 3).

[17] TEU, art 12(c). Europol and Eurojust are the only two EU agencies with an explicit Treaty basis under the Treaty of Lisbon. Jorrit J Rijpma, 'Institutions and Agencies: Government and Governance after Lisbon' in Diego A Arcarazo and Cian C Murphy (eds), *EU Security and Justice Law: After Lisbon and Stockholm* (Hart Publishing 2014) 54–76, 64.

[18] Mendeltje van Keulen, 'New Parliamentary Practices in Justice and Home Affairs: Some Observations' in Ronald L Holzhacker and Paul Luif (eds), *Freedom, Security and Justice in the European Union* (Springer 2014) 13–28, 18–19.

voting threshold for a 'yellow card' is lowered from one-third to one quarter. Despite these Treaty provisions, no interparliamentary mechanism has yet been created in the field of JHA. It remains uncertain not only what form an interparliamentary mechanism should take, but also how it should be established—whether to do so through EU legislation or through interparliamentary negotiation.

The most significant movement in this direction has been in relation to Europol, the EU agency for police cooperation. Europol was established in 1999 as an international organization under the EU's 'Third Pillar', subject to very limited oversight from the EP and only indirect oversight from NPs, via their government ministers in the Council.[19] While the EP has long sought greater oversight powers vis-à-vis Europol, there have also been various proposals for some form of joint scrutiny involving NPs. For example, in 2002 the Commission suggested the creation of a joint supervisory committee in relation to Europol, to be made up of members of parliament (MPs) and members of the EP (MEPs).[20] Europol became an EU agency following a Council Decision of 2009, and the Treaty of Lisbon made it subject to regulation in accordance with the ordinary legislative procedure (ie co-decision): the EP and the Council 'shall determine Europol's structure, operation, field of action and tasks', including 'the procedures for scrutiny of Europol's activities by the European Parliament, together with national Parliaments'.[21]

In March 2013, the Commission proposed a Regulation that would finally bring Europol into line with the Treaty of Lisbon. The proposal stated that Europol's activities would be subject to 'parliamentary scrutiny by the European Parliament, together with national parliaments', but left it open as to what form this should take.[22] The EP, however, responded with very specific proposals of its own in February 2014. In its amendments to the draft Regulation, the EP proposed the creation of a specialized body to be called the Joint Parliamentary Scrutiny Group (JPSG), made up of all the MEPs in the EP's Justice and Home Affairs (LIBE) Committee in addition to two members of the relevant committee from each NP.[23] The JPSG would exercise something close to a traditional parliamentary oversight function with respect to Europol, in that executive officials would appear before it at its request, and key documents related to the agency's activities and performance would be presented and debated. It would review the appointment (and re-appointment) of the Executive Director of Europol, and hold hearings with the Chairperson of the Europol Management Board, Commission representatives, the European Data Protection Supervisor, and other relevant officials. If created, the JPSG would be the first institution of its kind, in that it would involve national parliamentarians in the direct and structured oversight over an EU agency.

This issue was discussed at the EU Speakers Conference in Vilnius in April 2014. The Italian Parliament, traditionally an ally of the EP, proposed that the EU Speakers Conference should endorse the 'prompt adoption' of the Europol Regulation, including

[19] Daniel R de Garibay, 'Coordination Practices in the Parliamentary Control of Justice and Home Affairs: The Case of Europol' in Ben Crum and John E Fossum (eds), *Practices of Inter-Parliamentary Coordination in International Politics: The European Union and Beyond* (ECPR Press 2013).

[20] ibid 89–90.

[21] TFEU, art 88.

[22] See art 53(2) of the Proposal for a Regulation of the European Parliament and of the Council on the European Union Agency for Law Enforcement Cooperation and Training (Europol) and repealing Decisions 2009/371/JHA and 2005/681/JHA, COM(2013) 173, 27 March 2013.

[23] Amendment 200 (art 53), European Parliament, Legislative Resolution of 25 February 2014 on the Proposal for a Regulation of the European Parliament and of the Council on the European Union Agency for Law Enforcement Cooperation and Training (Europol) and Repealing Decisions 2009/371/JHA and 2005/681/JHA, 25 February 2014.

its provisions with respect to parliamentary scrutiny. However, some participants resisted this proposal on procedural grounds, saying that any new mechanism should be established by parliaments themselves, rather than through the EU legislative process in which NPs are not directly involved.

A very different proposal was put forward by Eva Kopacz, Speaker of the Polish *Sejm* (who later became Polish Prime Minister), with the support of the Polish Senate, the Irish Senate, and the Hungarian Parliament. The speakers of these chambers proposed the creation of a full-blown interparliamentary conference for the whole policy field of JHA, including scrutiny of the activities of Europol and Eurojust. The new IPC would be modelled on the formula of the CFSP-CSDP and SECG Conferences, in that it would replace the existing meetings of chairpersons, meet twice a year, and be co-hosted and co-presided over by the EP and the Presidency Parliament. This new body, it was suggested, could also exercise oversight over the European Public Prosecutor's Office, if and when the latter comes into being.[24]

However, the idea of a new interparliamentary conference was rejected as unnecessary by the EP representative, Vice-President Miguel Angel Martinez Martinez. He remarked acerbically that one could envisage interparliamentary conferences for every policy area—sport, agriculture, transport—much like the multiple configurations in the Council: by that logic, there could be fifteen interparliamentary conferences.[25] He preferred instead the EP's approach of holding interparliamentary committee meetings on an ad hoc basis. He reminded his colleagues that this field is now largely covered by co-decision, and that NPs should focus their scrutiny on their own governments' positions in the Council. In the face of this disagreement, no decision was taken.

In late November 2015, the EP and the Council reached an agreement on the Europol Regulation. It was adopted in May 2016 and was set to enter into force on 1 May 2017. The Regulation endorsed the establishment of a JPSG, but it did not specify how it should be constituted. Instead, it merely stated that the JPSG, its organization and rules of procedure, shall be established together by the EP and NPs in accordance with Article 9 of Protocol No 1 annexed to the Lisbon Treaty. This Article states that the EP and NPs 'shall together determine the organization and promotion of effective and regular interparliamentary cooperation within the Union'. This means in practice that it will be the task of the EU Speakers Conference to make the decision regarding the practical arrangements for the JPSG.

At its May 2016 meeting in Luxembourg, the EU Speakers Conference recognized that while the Europol Regulation defined the 'objectives and missions' of the JPSG, the 'modalities of parliamentary scrutiny' must be defined by the parliaments themselves, 'while stressing that the European Parliament and national Parliaments are on equal footing'. To that end, it set up a Working Group to consider possible scrutiny mechanisms and, after consulting other parliaments, to present a draft proposal in

[24] The second 'yellow card' under the early warning mechanism was issued in response to the Commission's proposal to create the European Public Prosecutor's Office. Diane Fromage, 'The Second Yellow Card on the EPPO Proposal: An Encouraging Development for Member State Parliaments?' (2015) YEL (advance access).

[25] '*On peut envisager … de commencer à travailler comme travaille le Conseil. Avec les conférences … les conseils des ministres du sport, des ministres de l'agriculture, des ministres de transport. … Nous pourrions envisager de travailler sur la base d'une quinzaine de conférences. Et l'on serait tout le temps en conférence.*' Miguel Angel Martinez Martinez, 8 April 2014. Transcribed by the author from video archived on the Lithuanian Presidency website, available at http://www.lrs.lt/intl/presidency.show?theme=842&lang=4&p_eventguid=5149749b-73c7-45ec-a613-33517db95b83 (last accessed 19 July 2016).

autumn 2016. It was hoped that after further discussions a text setting out the organization of the JPSG could be adopted by the EU Speakers Conference in early 2017.[26]

2.4 Commonalities Between the Policy Fields Covered by Interparliamentary Cooperation

Is there a common thread that connects these three policy areas? Is there a discernible logic to having NPs exercise an enhanced oversight role with respect to EU policy in these three particular fields, but not all the others? Is there a rejoinder to Mr Martinez's comment that we might as well go ahead and have fifteen interparliamentary conferences? In response, we may begin by noting that the Council also treats these three specific policy areas differently: this is apparent in the division of labour between Coreper I and Coreper II—the two formations of the Committee of Permanent Representatives that do the preparatory work for Council meetings. Coreper II is the senior body, consisting of the Member States' ambassadors to the EU, whereas Coreper I is made up of their deputies. Whereas Coreper I deals with low-salience policy areas such as transport, education, employment, and the environment, Coreper II deals with policy areas of the highest political salience. In addition to 'general affairs', Coreper II prepares the work of three policy-specific Council formations: Economic and Financial Affairs, Foreign Affairs, and JHA. This gives some indication that these three policy areas share certain commonalities.

On a cautionary note, it should be acknowledged that all three of these policy fields have uncertain boundaries, in that each of them may be defined narrowly or broadly. In all three cases, there has been a debate over whether the interparliamentary body overseeing the policy field in question should have a narrow or broad field of concern. There was debate within the CFSP-CSDP Conference as to whether it should focus solely on CFSP-CSDP matters or also discuss related policy fields, such as development cooperation and humanitarian aid.[27] The field of economic governance is generally less well-defined as a policy field than CFSP-CSDP.[28] Within the SECG Conference, there was a debate over whether the discussions should be focused solely on the terms of the Fiscal Compact—ie fiscal consolidation and structural reform within the Member States—or whether it should also deal with broader financial concerns, such as the Banking Union.[29] That the EP was among the strongest advocates of a narrow scope of interparliamentary cooperation was demonstrated on two particular occasions: (a) when it objected to the original title—the 'Interparliamentary Conference on Economic and Financial Governance'—and pushed to change the word 'financial' to 'fiscal' to reflect a narrower sphere of concern;[30] and (b) when, at the 2014 EU Speakers Conference, it rejected the creation of a full-blown IPC that would have covered the whole policy field of JHA. Thus, in thinking about what these three policy fields have in common, we should bear in mind that how they should be defined is a politically contested question, the answer to which may have practical consequences for the organization of interparliamentary oversight bodies. This said, these

[26] Conclusions of the EU Speakers Conference, Luxembourg, 22–24 May 2016, paras 34 and 35.

[27] Jan Wouters and Kolja Raube, 'The Interparliamentary Conference on Common Foreign and Security Policy' (n 1) 239.

[28] I Cooper, 'The Interparliamentary Conference on Stability, Economic Coordination and Governance' (n 2) 252–55.

[29] See more on the accountability of the European Central Bank to parliaments in the chapter by Davor Jančić in this volume.

[30] I Cooper, 'The Politicization of Interparliamentary Relations in the EU' (n 3) 206–207.

three policy areas, broadly defined, share certain commonalities that separate them from other EU policy fields.

First, EU policy development in these three areas has, to varying degrees, been at least partly outside the traditional Community method: decision-making has been intergovernmental, with a limited role for the supranational institutions of the EU—the Commission, the EP, and the European Court of Justice. After the Treaty of Maastricht, two of these policy areas—CFSP-CSDP and JHA—were two separate intergovernmental 'pillars' of the EU, legally outside the first, Community Pillar. This was because they both involved sensitive questions of national sovereignty, concerning respectively the external and internal security of the Member States. Even today, after the Treaty of Lisbon has dissolved the pillar structure and the EU has become a single legal entity, the field of CFSP-CSDP remains largely intergovernmental, over which the supranational EU institutions, including the EP, have limited sway.[31] However, the field of JHA has now largely been brought within the realm of the Community method, and here the EP enjoys increased powers, including legislative co-decision, which it is anxious to preserve.

Compared to the other two, the policy field of EU economic and financial governance is relatively new. Of course, the groundwork for the Economic and Monetary Union, including many of its attendant rules, date back at least to the Maastricht Treaty. But the recent financial crisis gave rise to a new regime of EU economic governance that has also been largely developed outside the Community method, relying instead on the intergovernmental 'Union method'. Indeed, some of its legal instruments—including the TSCG, Article 13 of which gave the impetus for the SECG Conference—are outside of the framework of the EU treaties. While the Commission has in fact seen an increase in its powers of surveillance of national budgets, this process has adversely affected the EP, which is largely excluded from exercising oversight in this area.[32] Unlike CFSP-CSDP and JHA, EU economic governance does not concern security, but it does touch on sensitive issues of national sovereignty. Most notably, it encroaches on the power of Member States to make independent decisions about public finances, and this encroachment particularly affects NPs, the institutions that enact national budgets.

A second commonality is that the EU's activities in these three policy fields tend to emphasize executive action rather than legislation. As a rule, foreign and security policy, whether at the national or EU level, is the realm of executive action par excellence. The CFSP-CSDP Conference enables members of the foreign affairs and defence committees of the parliaments of the EU to exchange information and best practices to enhance their oversight of their respective governments in these matters. But the conference itself also to some extent directly oversees these EU policies—including the European External Action Service and its head, the High Representative, who customarily attends the CFSP-CSDP Conference to make a statement and answer questions from the assembled parliamentarians. Similarly, while the field of JHA does involve EU legislation, it is also notable in that it involves executive agencies exercising discretionary powers in sensitive fields such as police cooperation (Europol) and judicial cooperation (Eurojust).

Finally, while much of the EU economic governance regime was put in place by EU legislation—most notably the system of budgetary surveillance and economic

[31] Anna Herranz-Surrallés, 'The EU's Multilevel Parliamentary (Battle)Field' (n 4).

[32] Cristina Fasone, 'European Economic Governance and Parliamentary Representation. What Place for the European Parliament?' (2014) 20 ELJ 164.

coordination set out in the 'Six Pack' and the 'Two Pack'—it is largely implemented by the Commission. The Commission has considerable discretion in enforcing the rules of this regime, although in the background lies the threat of punitive sanctions imposed by the Council against a persistent rule-breaker.[33]

Since these three policy fields involve governance to some extent outside the Community method, and as a result fall less under the control of the EP, then an increased role for NPs could compensate for this deficiency. There is a case to be made that if the policy question touches on sensitive issues of national sovereignty, such as external or internal security of the individual Member States, then this too is a reason for greater involvement of NPs. Moreover, if the policy in question has an adverse impact on NPs—for example their budgetary autonomy—then this could provide an additional rationale for their involvement in scrutinizing it. The fact that EU activity in these policy areas favours executive action over legislation means that NPs have no power to intervene to object under the early warning mechanism, because this mechanism does not encompass executive acts. For all these reasons, there is a case for *joint oversight*, involving the EP and NPs acting together, rather than *centralized oversight*, concentrated in the EP, in these particular policy fields.[34]

3. The Supervisory Role of the EU Speakers Conference

A second important trend in the emerging order of interparliamentary cooperation is the 'quasi-constitutional' role of the EU Speakers Conference. This conference has assumed the role of supervising the establishment and development of other interparliamentary bodies in the EU. As we have already seen (section 2), it was the EU Speakers Conference that established both the CFSP-CSDP Conference in 2012 and the SECG Conference in 2013. Moreover, in 2016 it was commonly accepted that it would be the task of the EU Speakers Conference to establish the future JPSG for Europol. This foundational role is not altogether new: the impetus for the first meeting of COSAC, in 1989, came from an initiative put forward at the EU Speakers Conference. What is new, however, is that the EU Speakers Conference has also assumed an ongoing *supervisory* role: not only did it establish the two new interparliamentary conferences, but in doing so it pledged to review their arrangements at a later date, despite the fact that the new conferences were supposed to be autonomous, self-governing entities. Yet on the other hand, there appear to be limits to this supervisory role, as became apparent at the meeting of the EU Speakers Conference in Rome in April 2015.

It is perhaps surprising that the EU Speakers Conference has assumed the role of 'gatekeeper' of interparliamentary cooperation in the EU, given that it is not mentioned anywhere in the EU Treaties, and that throughout much of its history it was only loosely affiliated with the EU and its predecessor institutions, the European Communities. The EU Speakers Conference met for the first time in 1963, for the second time in 1973, and then more or less annually from 1975 onwards. Between 1980 and 1998, the annual meetings alternated between a small conference of the Speakers of the 'European Communities Parliaments' (NPs of the European Communities, plus the EP) and a large conference of the Speakers of the 'European Parliamentary Assemblies' (NPs of the Council of Europe, plus the EP and the Parliamentary Assembly of the Council of Europe). It is only since 1999 that the EU Speakers Conference 'has

[33] Davor Jančić, 'National Parliaments and EU Fiscal Integration' (2016) 22 ELJ 225.

[34] Ian Cooper, 'The Politicization of Interparliamentary Relations in the EU' (n 3).

become an autonomous forum of cooperation and has affirmed its general competence of coordination and supervision of the interparliamentary cooperation in the EU'.[35]

While it does not have 'standing orders' or 'rules of procedure',[36] in 2000 the EU Speakers Conference adopted its own 'Guidelines', which were amended in 2010. In addition, it adopted Guidelines of Interparliamentary Cooperation in 2004, which were amended in 2008. These two sets of guidelines are generally accepted as the documents that set out the basic rules of interparliamentary cooperation and establish the key role of the EU Speakers Conference in organizing it.

However, this leadership role of the EU Speakers Conference was contested, in particular regarding the establishment of the CFSP-CSDP Conference. It may be argued that the Treaty of Lisbon gave COSAC a mandate to establish the CFSP-CSDP Conference, but this was 'stolen' by the EU Speakers Conference.[37] Specifically, a debate arose as to whether the CFSP-CSDP Conference should be established by the EU Speakers Conference (based on Article 9 of Protocol No 1 annexed to the Lisbon Treaty) or by COSAC (based on Article 10 of the same Protocol).[38] Whereas some NPs favoured COSAC, the EU Speakers Conference was favoured in particular by the EP. In the end, after much delay, the EP position won the day, and this cemented the role of the EU Speakers Conference as the body that governs interparliamentary cooperation. The establishment of the CFSP-CSDP Conference by the EU Speakers Conference proved a powerful precedent, so that when the time came to establish the SECG Conference, few questioned the legitimacy of the EU Speakers Conference playing the same foundational role again.

Despite the general acceptance of the EU Speakers Conference in establishing new forms of interparliamentary cooperation, disagreement persists—not least within the conference itself—over the extent and limits of its supervisory role. Specifically, are the internal Rules of Procedure of the new interparliamentary conferences dependent on the approval of the EU Speakers Conference, and if so, what form should such approval take? This question arose because when the EU Speakers Conference established the other conferences it recommended 'conducting a review' of their 'arrangements' at a later date. With regard to the CFSP-CSDP Conference, the 2012 Presidency Conclusions requested such a review 'after two years from its first meeting'.[39] A similar recommendation was issued with regard to the Article 13 Conference. In both these cases, the role of the EU Speakers Conference was ambiguous. On the one hand, it laid the foundation for a new, and presumably autonomous, IPC; on the other hand, it asserted its own supervisory role regarding the review of the ongoing arrangements for the new body.

Even after it was generally acknowledged that it is the job of the EU Speakers Conference to 'establish' a new IPC, it remained uncertain whether it should make

[35] 'The History of the EU Speakers Conference' http://www.ipex.eu/IPEXL-WEB/dossier/files/download/082dbcc54af19e11014af1d1d7770017.do (last accessed 19 July 2016).

[36] Cristina Fasone, 'Ruling the (Dis-)Order of Interparliamentary Cooperation?' (n 7) 274.

[37] ibid 283.

[38] Antonio Esposito, 'The Role of COSAC in EU Interparliamentary Cooperation: An (Endless) Quest for an Identity' in Nicola Lupo and Cristina Fasone (eds), *Interparliamentary Cooperation in the Composite European Constitution* (Hart Publishing 2016); Pier G Casalena, Nicola Lupo, and Cristina Fasone, 'Commentary on the Protocol No 1 Annexed to the Treaty of Lisbon' in Hermann-Josef Blanke and Stelio Mangiamelli (eds), *The Treaty on European Union (TEU). A Commentary* (Springer 2013).

[39] Presidency Conclusions of the EU Speakers Conference, Warsaw, 20–21 April 2012, 5 http://www.ipex.eu/IPEXL-WEB/dossier/files/download/082dbcc5367c573a0136ded147ab331a.do (last accessed 19 July 2016).

all important decisions regarding the new body or simply set the parameters for it. Nowhere was this ambiguity in greater evidence than in relation to the Rules of Procedure for each of the new IPCs. In substantive terms, must the Rules for the new IPC remain within the guidelines set by the EU Speakers Conference, or could the new body, by an autonomous act, go beyond them? In procedural terms, does the new body autonomously establish its own Rules of Procedure, or is it up to the EU Speakers Conference to 'confirm' or 'ratify' them? Moreover, if an IPC is unable to agree on its Rules of Procedure—as was the case initially with the SECG Conference—can and should the EU Speakers Conference pre-emptively 'adopt' them on its behalf?

These questions were addressed in concrete, practical terms at the EU Speakers Conference in Rome in April 2015, which was tasked with reviewing the arrangements for the CFSP-CSDP and SECG Conferences, which were in very different states. Whereas the CFSP-CSDP Conference had a relatively smooth and consensual internal review process, the SECG Conference was still internally divided over basic questions concerning its structure and functioning. Even so, both cases showed how the EU Speakers Conference—or at least a number of its members—was reluctant to adopt Rules of Procedure on behalf of another IPC. Many of the speakers and/or representatives of NPs were ambivalent about the EU Speakers Conference imposing its will upon the other IPCs, which they regarded as autonomous. Despite this ambivalence, the EU Speakers Conference made all the important substantive decisions regarding the Rules of Procedure for the SECG Conference, even if it did not formally 'adopt' them.

Furthermore, rather than insisting on their 'self-determination', the two new IPCs were entirely deferential to the decisions of the EU Speakers Conference. Both the CFSP-CSDP Conference, when conducting an internal review of its workings between 2013 and early 2015, and the SECG Conference, when finalizing its Rules of Procedure in November 2015, acted entirely in conformity with the parameters set by the EU Speakers Conference. This was due in no small part to the EP's consistent promotion of the supervisory role of the EU Speakers Conference both within this Conference and within the policy-specific IPCs.

3.1 Review of the CFSP-CSDP Conference

The CFSP-CSDP Conference adopted its own Rules of Procedure at its first meeting in Cyprus in September 2012. This document recognized an ongoing supervisory role for the EU Speakers Conference in two specific ways: (a) it stipulated that any amendments to the Rules of Procedure must be decided by consensus and 'must be in accordance with the framework set by the Conference of Speakers of the EU Parliaments' (Article 8(2)); and (b) it foresaw that an Ad Hoc Review Committee reviewing the workings of the Conference would 'make recommendations thereon to be deliberated upon by the Conference of EU Speakers' (Article 9).

One year later, at the meeting in Vilnius in September 2013, the Ad Hoc Review Committee was convened and a Working Group—made up of representatives of the 'presidency trio' of Ireland, Lithuania, and Greece, with the addition of Cyprus, Italy, and the EP—compiled and categorized the proposed amendments, and made recommendations to the Ad Hoc Committee, which reported them to the Athens Conference in April 2014. The Ad Hoc Committee recommended a few minor changes to the Rules of Procedure, and the adoption of another document, called 'Best Practices', to serve as supplemental guidelines as to how the conference should be conducted. These changes were submitted for the approval of the EU Speakers Conference in Rome in April 2015.

It is notable that the internal process by which the CFSP-CSDP Conference reviewed its own procedures deferred *entirely* to the EU Speakers Conference. This is no exaggeration: the Ad Hoc Review Committee categorically denied consideration to any proposed amendment to the Rules of Procedure that was 'in contradiction with the Warsaw Conclusions'. This ruled out, for example, consideration of a proposal to change the voting rules to those in use at COSAC: both the German *Bundestag* and the Latvian *Saiema* separately proposed that the conference should not operate solely on a consensus basis, but rather should be able to adopt Conclusions by a qualified majority of 3/4 of votes cast in circumstances where consensus is unobtainable. This meant, in effect, that the review process did not permit any major revision of the Rules of Procedure, but was basically a modest housekeeping exercise.

Yet despite the deference shown to it, the EU Speakers Conference in Rome proved cautious in the manner in which it exerted its authority vis-à-vis the CFSP-CSDP Conference. The Italian Parliament hosting the meeting had originally proposed that the EU Speakers Conference should 'ratify' the result of the review, but this met with objections from a number of representatives, including from the UK, Sweden, and the Netherlands. The representative from the UK remarked: 'We are of the opinion that it is not the business of this conference to ratify or adopt Rules of Procedure for any other conference'. Similarly, the Swedish representative said: 'We should only limit ourselves to discussions, and not ratifications, in this setting'. The Speaker from the Netherlands rejected the use of 'ratify' or similar terms, such as 'adopt' or 'confirm', because they tend to usurp the authority of the conferences to adopt their own rules: 'The specific conferences draft their own Rules of Procedure and *they are the masters of those Rules of Procedure*'.[40] Many proposed that the EU Speakers Conference should merely 'take note of', rather than 'ratify' the CFSP-CSDP Conference's Best Practices and amended Rules of Procedure.

By contrast, EP President Martin Schulz insisted that it was the responsibility of the EU Speakers Conference to 'adopt' the documents. He even went as far as to quote directly to them the words of the 2008 Guidelines for Interparliamentary Cooperation, which said that the EU Speakers Conference 'shall oversee the coordination of inter-parliamentary EU activities'. Schulz took from this that the authority of the other conferences is entirely dependent on the EU Speakers Conference:

> Our role is to coordinate what all the sectorial assemblies do … What they have decided has to [be] coordinated here … They adopt Rules of Procedures for their sectorial body, but the frame in which they act is our conference … We adopt it … If we would not adopt it, it is not adopted, because they have no right to provide themselves with their own rules.[41]

While some parliamentarians thought that this was merely a semantic debate: 'We are splitting hairs here', said the Irish Speaker; others maintained that it was significant: 'I've got a legal background, and as a lawyer you know that the wording is important', said the Speaker from the Netherlands. The chair of the meeting, the Speaker of the Italian Senate, seemed puzzled by the controversy, and continually tried to bring the discussion back to what he saw as the salient point, that the CFSP-CSDP Conference had itself reached a consensus (unlike the SECG Conference), which only

[40] Emphasis added. These exchanges can be viewed courtesy of the Italian Parliament at https://www.youtube.com/watch?v=fQ4CZG3TpCk (last accessed 19 July 2016).

[41] ibid.

needed to be affirmed by the EU Speakers Conference. However, the debate over what word to use to describe that act of affirmation reflected differing views of the nature of the EU Speakers Conference's supervisory role and its implied relationship to the other conferences. In the end, the Presidency Conclusions referred to the 'Discussion and approval of the revision of the Rules of Procedure of the Conference for the CFSP-CSDP', noting also that the Speakers 'welcome' the conclusion of the review.

3.2 Review of the SECG Conference

The 2015 EU Speakers Conference in Rome also reviewed the functioning of the SECG Conference, which was in a state of uncertainty. Unlike the CFSP-CSDP Conference, the SECG Conference had not yet agreed upon its Rules of Procedure, despite having met four times between late 2013 and early 2015. The Italian Parliament chairing the meeting proposed that the EU Speakers Conference should impose a set of Rules of Procedure and this was supported *inter alia* by the representatives of the EP and the French and German parliaments.

However, as was the case with the review of the CFSP-CSDP Conference, a number of representatives from NPs were reluctant to adopt the rules for another, ostensibly autonomous, conference. So, the EU Speakers Conference instead adopted a further set of 'principles' for the SECG Conference that effectively settled most of the outstanding questions regarding its organization. These principles were then incorporated into a new draft of the Rules of Procedure, which was finally adopted by the SECG Conference itself in Luxembourg in November 2015. This outcome was almost derailed by a last-minute dispute over whether the Rules of Procedure should recognize a continuing supervisory role for the EU Speakers Conference, as outlined below.

When the EU Speakers Conference in Rome considered whether to impose Rules of Procedure on the SECG Conference, the rationale for this move was that the latter had 'failed' to debate and adopt them of its own accord. To set the record straight, it should be stated clearly that the SECG Conference had never had a chance to properly debate and subsequently adopt its own Rules of Procedure, because at all four meetings this item was either removed from the agenda at the last minute or kept off the agenda altogether. This was, in particular, a consequence of the actions of representatives of the EP and the Italian Parliament.

For the first meeting (Vilnius, October 2013) the host parliament, the Lithuanian *Seimas*, had produced a draft 'Rules of Procedure' and included on the agenda a session for the debate and adoption of this document; but after particularly vehement objections from the EP, this item was removed and replaced with a more general discussion of the purpose and vision of the conference. Many of the national parliamentarians in attendance, who had expected to swiftly debate and adopt the Rules of Procedure, criticized this last-minute change to the agenda. The second conference (Brussels, January 2014) was hosted and co-chaired (along with the Greek *Vouli*) by the EP, which saw to it that the item was left off the agenda entirely.

The original agenda for the third conference (Rome, September 2014) had included a session for the debate and possible adoption of the Rules of Procedure, and the ground was prepared for this debate given that many parliaments had submitted opinions on the Rules of Procedure and proposed amendments to the original draft produced by the *Seimas*. However, at the start of the third conference, the Speaker of the Italian *Camera dei Deputati*, Laura Boldrini, abruptly announced that the conference would not adopt the Rules of Procedure; rather, the decision would be left to the next EU Speakers Conference, which was to be held the following April in Rome, hosted by the Italian Parliament and co-chaired by herself. What this meant was that the third conference held its scheduled 'debate' on the Rules of Procedure but it was largely moot, as the parliament chairing the meeting had already ruled out the possibility that the Rules of Procedure would be adopted. Many of the attendees—including representatives from the French, German, Lithuanian, and Polish parliaments—objected to this move, with some arguing that consensus was achievable, and therefore the conference could and should go ahead and adopt its own Rules of Procedure rather than leaving the matter to the EU Speakers Conference. However, these objections went unheeded. After this, the Italian Parliament proceeded to collect and compile the proposed amendments to the Rules of Procedure in anticipation of their final adoption in Rome in April 2015.

No discussion of the Rules of Procedure took place at the fourth conference (Brussels, February 2015) because the Italian Parliament's review was still ongoing, and also because the EP, again the host and co-chair of the meeting, wanted to leave it off the agenda anyway. Thus, of the first four meetings of the Article 13 Conference, two (Vilnius and Rome) were prevented from holding a decisive debate on the Rules of Procedure, and two (both at the EP in Brussels) did not discuss it at all.

Notwithstanding the absence of debate on the Rules of Procedure within the SECG Conference itself, it was proposed by the representatives of the Italian Parliament, with the full support of those of the EP, that the EU Speakers Conference in Rome should 'adopt' the Rules of Procedure in its stead. However, this proposal faced the same backlash as that concerning the CFSP-CSDP Conference—that it was inappropriate for the EU Speakers Conference to be making such a decision on behalf of another IPC. Yet, unlike the CFSP-CSDP Conference, the SECG Conference had not reached an internal agreement regarding its ongoing arrangements that would make up the substantive content of the Rules of Procedure. Consequently, the EU Speakers Conference discussed and agreed a set of 'principles' which 'shall be transposed in detailed Rules of procedure' by the SECG Conference itself. These were in fact detailed guidelines which left very little discretion to the SECG Conference in deciding on its own Rules of Procedure. The EU Speakers Conference made specific decisions regarding a number of outstanding issues: the conference's name (hitherto the 'Interparliamentary Conference on Economic and Financial Governance of the EU'), its general scope, timing, language regime, EU officials who should be invited to attend, the establishment of a presidential *troika*, and the manner in which it should adopt conclusions.[42]

Hence, the EU Speakers Conference essentially dictated the terms of the Rules of Procedure for the SECG Conference, even though it did not formally 'adopt' them. The SECG Conference subsequently transposed the EU Speakers Conference's set of principles into its Rules of Procedure with strict fidelity, deferring, just as the CFSP-CSDP Conference did, *entirely* to the EU Speakers Conference in establishing its own rules.

There was, however, a final hitch, leading to a last-minute dispute at the SECG Conference in Luxembourg, which reveals how the EP went to great lengths to maintain the EU Speakers Conference in a superior position in relation to other IPCs. The Luxembourg Parliament drafted Rules of Procedure and circulated the document to the other parliaments prior to the meeting. However, when the heads of delegation (mostly the chairs of finance committees of the EP and NPs) met for the final *in camera* session to adopt the document, two further changes had been made to it. One change

[42] Ian Cooper, 'The Interparliamentary Conference on Stability, Economic Coordination and Governance' (n 2) 265–67.

was merely technical (clarifying the meaning of the term 'Presidency Parliament'), but the other involved a substantive change regarding how the Rules of Procedure would be amended. Whereas the original had only said: 'Any amendments shall be subject to a decision by consensus by the Interparliamentary Conference on SECG'; the new version had added: 'and must be in accordance with the framework set by the Conference of Speakers of the EU Parliaments'. This added text is identical to language in the CFSP-CSDP Conference's Rules of Procedure. In both cases, this implies that even after the new IPC has established its Rules of Procedure it is not really a self-governing entity: while it may amend the rules in future, any change must still conform to the framework established by the EU Speakers Conference.

Many representatives from NPs strongly objected to these eleventh-hour textual changes, and wondered where they had come from. It emerged that they had been inserted at the request of the EP delegation.[43] In the debate, the heads of delegation from NPs did not object on *substantive* grounds to the fact that the Rules of Procedure must conform to the framework established by the EU Speakers Conference; rather, they raised the *procedural* objection that they cannot agree to a document with last-minute changes, as they did not have sufficient time and opportunity to consult with their respective parliaments.

For the EP, on the other hand, the *substantive* point was non-negotiable. The head of the EP delegation, Roberto Gualtieri, indicated that he would veto any Rules of Procedure that did not contain this language, and he doggedly stuck to this position even when, at one point in the debate, he seemed utterly isolated. The other heads of delegation argued that the Luxembourg conference should simply adopt the Rules of Procedure document as originally circulated and adopt the amendments at the next conference. But to the growing exasperation of the national parliamentarians present, Gualtieri refused this suggestion too, saying that he could not agree without consulting EP President Schulz. It was then agreed to reconvene for one more unplanned session after breaking for lunch. During the break, Gualtieri consulted with colleagues in Brussels (though not with Schulz, who was travelling) and came back with a compromise: he would drop his insistence on the change regarding the definition of the 'Presidency Parliament', but he would not relent on the main point—that the Rules of Procedure must respect the framework established by the EU Speakers Conference. This small gesture broke the impasse and, with some reluctance, the other heads of delegation accepted the document under these conditions.

This episode is noteworthy because it had the effect of consolidating the position of the EU Speakers Conference as the pre-eminent interparliamentary body in the EU, with a role as the organizer and supervisor of other forms of interparliamentary cooperation. It also shows that the EP will devote tremendous effort to preserve such a status for the EU Speakers Conference. The prospect that COSAC should instead perform this function—as implied in the Treaty of Lisbon, and preferred by some NPs—has been decisively rejected, largely as a result of the EP's efforts.

Objectively, it makes some sense to assign decision-making authority over interparliamentary cooperation collectively to the Speakers/Presidents, who are, in formal terms, the highest officials in their respective parliaments, as opposed to the chairs of the European affairs committees, as represented in COSAC. But it is also advantageous

[43] It appears that the other members of the Presidency *Troika*—the Latvian and Dutch parliaments—had also been consulted. However, such a consultation is of uncertain legitimacy because, strictly speaking, the Troika did not yet exist because the Rules of Procedure had not yet been adopted.

for the EP to work through the forum of the EU Speakers Conference because it is a forum where all decisions are made by consensus, and therefore the EP may veto any unwanted decisions. Furthermore, the EP's position is enhanced by the fact that within the EP the position of the President enjoys greater prestige than the Speaker of a typical national parliament within the EU. Maintaining the EU Speakers Conference in its pre-eminent position is consistent with the EP's overall preference that direct parliamentary oversight of EU institutions should be exercised by the EP itself rather than by IPCs, and that the latter, if created, ought to be of marginal importance, with limited scope and no formal decision-making power.[44]

Whether one agrees that the emerging quasi-hierarchy among interparliamentary bodies is a positive development, there is no doubt that it makes interparliamentary cooperation more orderly.

4. The Parliamentary Dimension of the Council Presidency

The third trend in the emerging order of interparliamentary cooperation in the EU concerns the time and place of interparliamentary meetings. The Parliamentary Dimension of the Council Presidency (Parliamentary Dimension) contributes to this 'order' by providing an organizational framework for the overall sequence of parliamentary meetings. The aforesaid IPCs indeed do not take place in isolation but within the context of an increasingly elaborate biannual calendar of parliamentary events. These events constitute the 'Parliamentary Dimension' of the rotating six-month Council Presidency, as they are generally hosted and chaired by the parliament of the EU Member State holding the Council Presidency—hence, the 'Presidency Parliament'. This is a notable institutional development in interparliamentary cooperation that has received little academic attention.[45]

These meetings are not 'Council' events because they are chaired by the *parliament*, not the *government*, of the Member State holding the Council Presidency. The term 'Parliamentary Dimension' captures this ambiguity. It was coined in 2011 by the Polish Parliament, which wanted to differentiate its own series of events from those of the Polish Council Presidency, which took place in the second half of that year. Since then, whenever a new government has assumed the Council Presidency, its parliament has adopted the term Parliamentary Dimension to give a separate identity to its own parallel series of events. This effort has even extended to developing a separate 'brand identity': the Parliamentary Dimension will often have its own logo, of a design that is related to but different from that of the official logo of the Council Presidency, and its own website.

The Parliamentary Dimension refers specifically to the series of six to ten events under the Council Presidency that are: (a) organized and chaired by the Presidency Parliament, sometimes in cooperation with the EP; (b) attended by members from the parliaments of all EU Member States plus the EP; and (c) involve the discussion of EU policies. Most of these are chaired by the Presidency Parliament alone and held in the Member State holding the Council presidency, often in the parliamentary chamber itself. However, some Parliamentary Dimension events are held in the EP in Brussels

[44] I Cooper, 'The Politicization of Interparliamentary Relations in the EU' (n 3).

[45] Zbigniew Czachór, 'Parliamentary Dimension of the Polish Presidency' (2013) 3 *Środkowoeuropejskie Studia Polityczne* 7.

and co-organized and co-chaired by the EP and the Presidency Parliaments. These include the first-semester SECG Conference and the occasional Joint Committee Meeting (JCM) or Joint Parliamentary Meeting (JPM).

This definition excludes those meetings held in Brussels and solely chaired by the EP: for example, the EP typically hosts several Interparliamentary Committee Meetings (ICMs)[46] in a given year that are attended by national parliamentarians, but these are not Parliamentary Dimension events as the Presidency Parliament is not involved in their organization. The above definition would also exclude any parliamentary diplomacy event involving large numbers of parliaments from non-EU countries, even if it were hosted by the Presidency Parliament.[47] While Parliamentary Dimension events may also be attended by observers from parliaments outside the EU—such as candidate countries or special guests—they are primarily meetings of members of EU parliaments and their focus is on EU-related subjects.

Since the creation of the two new IPCs in 2012 and 2013, four of the events in the six-month Parliamentary Dimension calendar now have a set format. In addition to the CFSP-CSDP and SECG Conferences, there are two COSAC meetings: the COSAC Chairs meet near the beginning of the six-month semester, and the Plenary meets towards the end. Beyond these, a number of additional meetings—typically at least two, but sometimes more—are organized at the discretion of the Presidency Parliament, often reflecting its political priorities. Most such events are not large conferences but meetings of the chairpersons of other sectoral committees of NPs and the EP, depending on the subject of the meeting. Examples of such meetings include those focusing on 'Human Trafficking in the Digital Age' and 'Energy' (Netherlands, first semester 2016); 'Employment and Social Affairs' and 'Economic and Digital Affairs' (Latvia, first semester 2015); and 'Fundamental Rights', 'Agriculture, Industrial Development, and SMEs', and 'Employment, Research and Innovation' (Italy, second semester 2014).

Sometimes, the Presidency Parliament will co-chair a JCM at the EP in Brussels. Such was the case, for example, with the 'Joint Meeting of the Committees on Justice and Home Affairs' held under the Greek Parliamentary Dimension (first semester 2014). In addition, a Presidency Parliament will occasionally convene an ad hoc meeting on relatively short notice to discuss a current or salient subject. The Luxembourg Parliamentary Dimension (second semester 2015) did this when it held a 'COSAC Working Group Meeting' to discuss the enhanced political dialogue (the 'green card')[48] and how to improve the early warning mechanism (the 'yellow card').

Two additional yearly meetings are closely associated with, but not strictly part of, the Parliamentary Dimension. The EU Speakers Conference takes place annually in the Spring (normally April-May), but it is hosted and chaired by the parliament of the Member State that held the Council Presidency the previous autumn. Moreover, the Speakers Conference is preceded by a preparatory meeting of the Secretaries-General of the EU Parliaments, typically in February–March. The latter meeting is the only major interparliamentary meeting involving parliamentary staff rather than elected officials.[49]

[46] Katjana Gattermann, 'Brussels Calling!? Understanding National Parliamentarians' Participation in Inter-Parliamentary Committee Meetings', Paper presented at EUSA Conference, Baltimore MD, 9–11 May 2013.

[47] See more on parliamentary diplomacy in: Special Issue 'Parliamentary Diplomacy Uncovered: European and Global Perspectives', guest editors: Stelios Stavridis and Davor Jančić (2016) 11 Hague J Dipl 105.

[48] See on this the chapter by Karolina Borońska-Hryniewiecka in this volume.

[49] Cristina Fasone, 'Ruling the (Dis-)Order of Interparliamentary Cooperation?' (n 7) 276.

The introduction of the Parliamentary Dimension points to the fact that, while the takeover of European Council chairmanship by the President of the European Council has caused the importance of the rotating Council Presidency to decline, that of the Presidency Parliament has increased. Nowadays, some of the largest meetings that take place in the Member State holding the Council Presidency are the major IPCs—typically, gatherings of hundreds of elected and non-elected officials. The Parliamentary Dimension gives the Presidency Parliament the power to set the agenda for both the major IPCs and the smaller ad hoc meetings which it organizes, and thus an opportunity—albeit a modest one—to influence the debate concerning its own policy priorities.

One should not exaggerate the potential influence of the Presidency Parliament. To take one example, the Lithuanian Parliament (second semester 2013) made a concerted effort to raise the profile of smaller Parliamentary Dimension events, even pushing for the meetings of chairpersons to formally adopt Conclusions in the same manner as the major IPCs.[50] However, no subsequent Presidency Parliament has followed this example, so the smaller Parliamentary Dimension meetings have in general remained low-profile events. Even so, the Parliamentary Dimension framework is an important element of the emerging order of interparliamentary cooperation in the EU.

5. Conclusion

Interparliamentary cooperation in the EU has developed in dramatic and unexpected ways in recent years. Broad disagreement still persists—not only between the EP and NPs, but also among NPs themselves—over exactly what form interparliamentary cooperation should take. Nevertheless, while the field is still unsettled and contested, a new framework for interparliamentary cooperation has been evolving which in part builds upon, but also goes well beyond, that foreseen in the Treaty of Lisbon.

This chapter has highlighted three major trends in interparliamentary cooperation. First, two new major policy-specific interparliamentary conferences have been created—one in the field of foreign policy (the CFSP-CSDP Conference) and the other in the field of economic governance (the SECG Conference)—to complement the two long-standing conferences concerned with EU affairs in general (COSAC and the EU Speakers Conference). In addition, another policy-specific interparliamentary mechanism is foreseen in the field of JHA, although its exact form and scope have yet to be determined.

Second, the EU Speakers Conference has in recent years taken on a quasi-constitutional role as the interparliamentary body with the authority not only to establish other forms of interparliamentary cooperation—including the policy-specific bodies mentioned above—but also to supervise their ongoing development.

Third, the parliament of the Member State holding the Council Presidency now bears the considerable responsibility of hosting and chairing the most important interparliamentary meetings, under the auspices of the six-month 'Parliamentary Dimension' of the Council Presidency. These three features lend credence to the notion that there is an emerging order of interparliamentary cooperation in the post-Lisbon EU.

The Treaty of Lisbon and the financial crisis were instrumental to these developments to varying degrees. First, they provided the impetus for the growth in

[50] See more on this in 'Strengthening Political Dialogue', remarks by Loreta Graužinienė, Speaker of the Lithuanian *Seimas*, delivered at the EU Speakers Conference, Rome, 21 April 2015.

policy-specific interparliamentary cooperation, in that both the CFSP-CSDP Conference and the future oversight body for Europol are outgrowths of the Treaty of Lisbon, and the SECG Conference was an outgrowth of the TSCG, which was in turn a direct response to the financial crisis. Furthermore, when it became apparent that policy-specific cooperation would take the form of new IPCs, this raised the question of how these should be created and supervised—tasks which eventually fell to the EU Speakers Conference. Finally, the increase in interparliamentary activities raised the profile of the Presidency Parliament, whose enhanced organizational role was regularized in the institution of the 'Parliamentary Dimension'.

It would be inappropriate to exaggerate the importance of all this interparliamentary activity, as the newly created IPCs do not have any independent decision-making authority. However, they do provide a discussion forum for MPs and MEPs to debate pressing public policy questions, and they perform an oversight function vis-à-vis the executive authorities of the EU. For these reasons, the emerging order of interparliamentary cooperation is a sign of NPs' resilience, not resignation, as actors in the political system of the European Union.

13

From the Early Warning System to a 'Green Card' for National Parliaments

Hindering or Accelerating EU Policy-making?

Karolina Borońska-Hryniewiecka

1. Introduction

The issue of national parliamentary engagement in European Union (EU) affairs has recently travelled from the field of academic dispute to the world of high politics. The strengthening of national parliaments (NPs) in the EU was indeed one of the most important bargaining chips in the process of negotiation of a new settlement for the United Kingdom pursued by the British Prime Minister David Cameron.[1] While this was motivated by the British conviction that the EU enjoys excessive legislative powers, of which at least some should be returned to the national level,[2] it has also been widely acknowledged in the literature that EU governance suffers from a deficit of representative democracy.[3] The latter has partly been a consequence of the deparliamentarization of policy-making as a result of European integration.[4]

For a long time, one of the main reasons behind this assertion was the gradual increase in the executive power over EU decision-making—that of national ministers in the Council and unelected appointees in the Commission—to the detriment parliamentary control. The Lisbon Treaty was supposed to remedy this by strengthening the European Parliament (EP), by extending NPs' control over the principle of subsidiarity, as well as by boosting interparliamentary cooperation in EU affairs. Yet, six years on, the various 'representation deficits' in the EU's multilevel structure persist.[5]

[1] See David Cameron's letter to the President of the European Council, Donald Tusk, 'A New Settlement for the United Kingdom in a Reformed European Union', 10 November 2015 https://www.gov.uk/government/publications/eu-reform-pms-letter-to-president-of-the-european-council-donald-tusk (last accessed 27 April 2016).

[2] See a detailed analysis in Karolina Borońska-Hryniewiecka and others, 'Brexit just a Bugaboo: Unravelling the British EU "Wish List"' (2015) 10(73) PISM Strategic File.

[3] Joseph Weiler and others, 'European Democracy and its Critique' (1995) 18(3) WEP 4, 39; Andreas Follesdal and Simon Hix, 'Why There is a Democratic Deficit in the EU: A Response to Majone and Moravcsik' (2006) 44(3) JCMS 533–62; Richard Bellamy and Dario Castiglione, 'Three Models of Democracy, Political Community and Representation in the EU' (2013) 20(2) JEPP 206, 223.

[4] John O'Brennan and Tapio Raunio, 'Deparliamentarization and European Integration' in John O'Brennan and Tapio Raunio (eds), *National Parliaments Within the Enlarged European Union* (Routledge 2007) 1, 26; Claudia Hefftler and Christine Neuhold, 'Introduction' in Claudia Hefftler and others (eds), *The Palgrave Handbook of National Parliaments and the European Union* (Palgrave Macmillan 2015) 1, 39.

[5] Richard Bellamy and Sandra Kröger, 'Representation Surpluses and Deficits in EU Policy-Making' (2013) 35(5) JEI 477–497.

From the Early Warning System to a 'Green Card' for National Parliaments: Hindering or Accelerating EU Policy-making? First Edition. Karolina Borońska-Hryniewiecka.
Published 2017 by Oxford University Press.

The EP, though institutionally empowered, is still weak in terms of its democratic representativeness and political leverage.[6] Electoral turnout in the 2014 European elections was only 42.54 per cent—the lowest ever.[7] As regards NPs, the so-called early warning system (EWS) for subsidiarity monitoring introduced by the Lisbon Treaty has fallen short of expectations. In spite of producing positive spillover effects—such as restoring control over the EU-oriented action of national executives, increased inter-parliamentary deliberation, and accelerated Europeanization of national legislatures—it fails to ensure effective parliamentary engagement and input in EU policy-making.[8]

Although the number of reasoned opinions issued in the first three years of the operation of the EWS had gradually increased,[9] 2014 marked a rapid decline of no less than 76 per cent compared 2013.[10] This should only partially be explained by a decrease in the number of legislative proposals initiated towards the end of the Barroso II Commission's term. Another reason is the general disenchantment of NPs with the influence that they can exert through the EWS. Out of the three yellow cards issued thus far, only the 'Monti II' proposal on the right to take collective action was withdrawn by the Commission, yet not on subsidiarity grounds.[11] The second yellow card, raised with respect to the proposal to set up a European Public Prosecutor's Office was dismissed and the Commission maintained it.[12] The third yellow card, issued in May 2016 on the revised Posting of Workers Directive, is yet to receive a response from the Commission. More generally, the main weaknesses of the EWS pointed out by NPs include: too short scrutiny periods, too narrow scope due to the exclusion of the principle of proportionality; and insufficient Commission feedback on parliaments' reasoned opinions. With regard to the latter, the Commission's responses tend to come late, are inconclusive, and give little impression to parliaments that they have an influence on the EU legislative process.[13] In other words, contrary to some authors' optimism, the EWS does not amount to a 'virtual third chamber' collectively fulfilling the legislative, representative, and deliberative functions in the EU.[14]

Moreover, the shift to intergovernmental decision-making as a response to the sovereign debt crisis in the Eurozone has marginalized national legislatures to the benefit

[6] Maia de la Baume, 'The Parliament is Bored' *Politico*, 21 May 2015 http://www.politico.eu/article/parliament-bored-better-regulation (last accessed 1 May 2016).

[7] See data on the EP electoral turnout http://www.europarl.europa.eu/elections2014-results/en/turnout.html (last accessed 12 May 2016).

[8] Ian Cooper, 'A "Virtual Third Chamber" for the European Union? National Parliaments after the Treaty of Lisbon' (2012) 35(3) WEP 441, 465; Karolina Borońska-Hryniewiecka, 'Democratizing the European Multi-Level Polity? A (Re-)Assessment of the Early Warning System' (2013) 16 Yearbook of Polish European Studies (YPES) 167.

[9] Report from the Commission on Subsidiarity and Proportionality (19th Report on Better Lawmaking Covering the Year 2011), COM(2012) 373 of 10 July 2012; House of Lords, EU Committee, HL Paper 151, *The Role of National Parliaments in the European Union*, 9th Report of Session 2013–2014 of 24 March 2014.

[10] European Commission, Annual Report 2014 on Subsidiarity and Proportionality, COM(2015) 315 of 2 July 2015.

[11] Federico Fabbrini and Katarzyna Granat, 'Yellow Card, But No Foul: The Role of the National Parliaments Under the Subsidiarity Protocol and the Commission Proposal for an EU Regulation on the Right to Strike' (2013) 50(1) CML Rev 115, 143; Davor Jančić, 'The Game of Cards: National Parliaments in the EU and the Future of the Early Warning Mechanism and the Political Dialogue' (2015) 52(4) CML Rev, 939, 976.

[12] Diane Fromage, 'The Second Yellow Card on the EPPO Proposal: An Encouraging Development for Member State Parliaments?' (2016) 35 YEL, first published online 29 December 2015.

[13] Conclusions of the meeting of the Working Group on the yellow card held on 13 May 2015 in Warsaw; interview with representatives of the Polish *Sejm* and *Senat* (April 2015).

[14] Cooper, 'A "Virtual Third Chamber"' (n 8).

of the European Council. Since NPs can issue yellow or orange cards only on draft EU legislation, the whole spectrum of non-legislative but otherwise binding EU economic decisions remains beyond their control.[15] Institutional reforms, such as the Fiscal Compact and the European Stability Mechanism, adopted outside the EU legal framework and with superficial parliamentary scrutiny,[16] have challenged parliamentary leverage in fiscal governance.[17] They have also exacerbated distrust between domestic and EU institutions, which can be illustrated by the relations between NPs and the EP. In the field of economic governance, the latter is very active in promoting itself as the appropriate venue for evaluating the European Semester, which affects domestic budgetary policies, the making of which is a traditional prerogative of NPs.[18]

Such a state of affairs has encouraged some NPs to invest more resources in exploring new ways of participation at the EU level. The latest initiative endorsed by several national parliamentary chambers—including the British House of Lords, the Danish *Folketing*, and the Dutch Lower House *Tweede Kamer*—is the 'green card' procedure. This foresees a group of parliaments working together to suggest to the Commission new EU legislative initiatives or initiatives for reviewing or repealing existing EU legislation. The initiative to launch a green card deserves special attention not only in the context of the effort to strengthen the role of NPs in EU policy-making, but also because it reveals aspects of interparliamentary dynamics in EU affairs that would otherwise remain unaddressed.

This chapter analyzes the nature and scope of the green card proposal with a special emphasis on the potential repercussions for the domestic and EU-level interinstitutional relations. It argues that while the green card is in principle a positive and constructive project, its current design might challenge the established domestic and EU legal frameworks by granting NPs the right to take a proactive role in shaping EU policy which goes beyond national constitutional arrangements. It might also call into question the institutional balance between NPs and the EP by sidelining the latter.

The chapter is structured in the following way. The second section explains the green card procedure as envisaged by a group of NPs. Section 3 discusses the first green card, which was launched in 2015. The fourth section presents an overview of institutional actors' responses to the green card initiative, including NPs, the Commission, and the EP. Section 5 analyzes the legal status of the green card at the EU and domestic levels. Section 6 discusses the potential effect of the mechanism on the institutional balance in the EU. The chapter finishes with the conclusion that in order to achieve a genuine parliamentary acceleration in EU policy-making, the green card initiative should be modified by adopting an interparliamentary approach combining the EP's right of legislative initiative with NPs' representative leverage. In this way, the new card could

[15] Danuta Adamiec, 'The Position of National Parliaments within the New EU Economic Governance' (2013) 16 YPES 198.

[16] See Cristina Fasone, 'Taking Budgetary Powers Away from National Parliaments? On Parliamentary Prerogatives in the Eurozone Crisis' (2015) 37 EUI WP LAW. See more on national parliamentary debates on key euro crisis measures in the chapter by Frank Wendler in this volume.

[17] Since the national budgetary procedure is now more strictly controlled by EU institutions within the framework of the European Semester, the capacity of NPs to affect state spending is more constrained. See more on the party politics of compliance with EU recommendations issued within the European Semester in the chapter by Aleksandra Maatsch in this volume.

[18] Different authors point to national parliamentary adaptation to the crisis-induced EU fiscal measures resulting in the emergence of new channels of involvement in EU economic governance. See Davor Jančić, 'National Parliaments and EU Fiscal Integration' (2016) 22(2) ELJ 225–49.

contribute both to enhancing their respective legitimating capacities in the EU's 'multilevel parliamentary field'[19] and to reducing their institutional rivalry.

2. The Scope and Nature of the Green Card

The idea of a proactive parliamentary engagement in EU policy-making has been maturing among national legislatures for the last two years. This idea found one of its first formal expressions at the June 2013 COSAC plenary meeting in Dublin, which adopted the following contribution:

> COSAC considers that national parliaments should be more effectively involved in the legislative process of the EU not just as the guardians of the subsidiarity principle but also as active contributors to that process. This goes beyond the adoption of reasoned opinions on draft legislative acts which may block those acts and would involve a more positive, considered and holistic view under which Parliaments could invite the Commission to develop legislative proposals which they believe to be necessary or to review and adapt existing proposals for specific stated reasons.[20]

This proposal was labelled 'green card' procedure in a House of Lords report of March 2014.[21] The procedure was subsequently discussed in several other contributions of the Danish *Folketing* and the Dutch *Tweede Kamer*.[22] The appointment of a new European Commission on 1 November 2014 was marked by a pledge by its President, Jean-Claude Juncker, to forge a stronger partnership with NPs, which have indeed mobilized to enhance their involvement at the EU level.

On 19 January 2015, on the occasion of a meeting between 14 national parliamentary chambers and the EP in Brussels, the *Tweede Kamer* published a document laying out the scope and nature of the green card initiative.[23] In principle, the green card was conceived as a means for NPs to increase their influence on the development of EU policies and legislation through direct dialogue with the Commission. It was viewed as a way for a group of national parliamentary chambers to collaborate and make constructive suggestions for EU policy initiatives or for reviewing and repealing existing EU legislation, including delegated and implementing acts. The authors of the initiative envisaged the green card as building on mechanisms already in place, that is on the infrastructure of the existing political dialogue also known as the 'Barroso Initiative',[24] through which NPs and the Commission exchange views on the contents of EU policy proposals. According to them, such a solution would not require a Treaty change.

The Dutch document foresaw that any parliamentary chamber would be able to formulate a proposal for a green card, which would include the reasons, anticipated benefits, and preferred type of action on the part of the Commission. To qualify as a green card, a proposal would have to gain one quarter of the votes allocated to NPs

[19] Ben Crum and John Erik Fossum, 'The Multilevel Parliamentary Field: A Framework for Theorizing Representative Democracy in the EU' (2009) 1(2) EPSR 249, 271.

[20] Contribution of the XLIX COSAC, Dublin, 23–25 June 2013.

[21] House of Lords (n 9).

[22] The *Folketing*'s analysis is available at http://renginiai.lrs.lt/renginiai/EventDocument/6fa11f98-fc15-4443-8f3f-9a9b26d34c97/Folketing_Twenty-three%20recommendations_EN.pdf; The *Tweede Kamer*'s report is available at http://www.houseofrepresentatives.nl/sites/default/files/news_items/ahead_in_europe_tcm181-238660_0.pdf (both last accessed 1 May 2016).

[23] See the 'Green Card' Discussion Paper http://www.tweedekamer.nl/kamerstukken/detail?id=2015D00583&did=2015D00583 (last accessed 1 May 2016).

[24] Davor Jančić, 'The Barroso Initiative: Window Dressing or Democracy Boost?' (2012) 8(1) Utrecht L Rev 78, 91.

under the EWS,[25] and be delivered to the Commission within six months from the date of the proposing chamber circulating the draft. Ideally, similarly to the European Citizens' Initiative, the Commission should react to the green card by means of a formal response stating whether it intends to take the proposed action or not, and give reasons for its decision. The authors of the initiative also suggested that the competent Commissioner could go to the initiating chamber to respond to the green card in the presence of all the co-signatories.

3. Testing the Ground

In July 2014, the Commission proposed a Circular Economy Package, but later withdrew it as part of its political discontinuity plan, aimed at reducing the volume of legislation that the EU produces. At the same time, the Commission undertook to initiate a new proposal on this matter by the end of 2015. In order to test the feasibility of the green card project, the EU Committee of the House of Lords put forward a proposal for a trial green card on the issue of food waste. Consequently, the first green card was issued on 22 July 2015 in the form of a letter inviting the Commission, when it tables the new Circular Economy Package, to adopt a strategic approach to the reduction of food waste within the EU. The letter was co-signed by 16 out of the 41 national parliamentary chambers. The Commission formally responded to the green card on 17 November 2015.[26]

On 2 December 2015, it published its Circular Economy Package, which addressed majority of NPs' suggestions on food waste. In line with NPs' recommendations, the Commission undertook to: develop a common EU methodology to measure food waste; define relevant indicators for this purpose; establish a platform for Member States and stakeholders to share best practice on the management of food waste; create rules concerning the donation of food to food banks; and clarify relevant EU legislation related to food waste in order to facilitate food donation.[27]

In spite of the seemingly positive outcome of the first green card, one should be careful about being too enthusiastic about its impact for several reasons. First, the solutions proposed by NPs did not amount to a new legislative proposal but merely stressed the necessity of boosting the Commission's concrete action in this policy field. Secondly, this first parliamentary green card was not the only initiative on food waste. It acted in synergy with another initiative calling for support for an EU directive that would require all supermarkets in Europe to pass their unsold supplies on to charities instead of throwing them away.[28]

The green card also complemented the EP's resolution on circular economy of July 2015, calling upon the Commission to lay down targets, measures, and instruments to efficiently tackle food waste and to encourage the creation in the Member States of

[25] By way of comparison, the threshold under the EWS is one-third of the votes for the yellow card and a simple majority of the votes for the orange card.

[26] Letter C(2015) 7982 of 17 November 2015 https://www.parliament.uk/business/committees/committees-a-z/lords-select/eu-select-committee-/news-parliament-2015/food-waste-green-card-commission-response/ (last accessed 12 May 2016). See further Jančić, 'The Game of Cards' (n 11) 965.

[27] European Commission, Communication 'Closing the Loop—An EU Action Plan for the Circular Economy', COM(2015) 614; Proposal for a Directive of the European Parliament and of the Council amending Directive 2008/98/EC on waste, COM(2015) 595.

[28] See https://www.change.org/p/frans-timmermans-stop-food-waste-in-europe-stopfoodwaste (last accessed 1 May 2016).

rules enabling the food retail sector to distribute unsold products to charitable organizations.[29] While these are all positive efforts, they show the limited influence of the first green card and portray it rather as an additional 'encouraging factor' in an already existing legislative initiative of the Commission. Finally, in its response to NPs, the Commission referred to the green card as an 'opinion' not a 'proposal'.[30] This reveals that, while endorsing the sort of dialogue sought by NPs, the Commission does not treat it as a form of legislative initiative.

In 2015, two more green cards were initiated by NPs: one by the Latvian *Saeima* on the review of the Audio-visual Media Services Directive and the other by the French *Assemblée nationale* on corporate social responsibility. They have not been addressed by the Commission at the time of writing.

4. Institutional Actors' Reactions to the Green Card Initiative

4.1 National Parliaments

The idea of a green card was put to parliamentary appraisal for the first time between February and May 2015 and later also in November 2015 through COSAC questionnaires,[31] which revealed considerable variations in attitudes as to the shape of the initiative.

While the majority of NPs were enthusiastic about the green card, many of them expressed concern about its legal status and were dubious about its feasibility. In this regard, some of the parliaments pointed out that the procedure might be unnecessary or incompatible with the Treaties or their domestic constitutions.

Three parliamentary chambers have expressed clear opposition to the idea of a green card (the Finnish *Eduskunta*, the Italian *Camera dei Deputati* and the Romanian *Senate*) while several others remain sceptical (eg the Polish *Senat*, the Estonian *Riigikogu*, and the Belgian *Chambre des représentants*). The Finnish *Eduskunta* pointed out that the green card would require making institutional or quasi-institutional arrangements outside of the Treaty framework adding to the complexity of the present EU decision-making process without significant added value.[32] Similarly, the Italian *Camera dei Deputati* underlined the well-established practice of political dialogue, pointing out that entering into any kind of additional collective exchanges between the Commission and a group of parliaments is not necessary. While both the Romanian and Polish upper chambers dismissed the formalization of the green card procedure on grounds of it requiring a Treaty change, the latter chamber also invoked constitutional limitations for initiating EU policy. Finally, the Estonian Parliament preferred to concentrate on scrutinizing EU-related activities of the executive. Among other voices, the Belgian

[29] European Parliament, Resolution of 9 July 2015 on resource efficiency: moving towards a circular economy, P8_TA-PROV(2015)0266.

[30] See https://www.parliament.uk/business/committees/committees-a-z/lords-select/eu-select-committee-/news-parliament-2015/food-waste-green-card-commission-response/ (last accessed 1 May 2016).

[31] COSAC, 23rd Bi-annual Report http://www.cosac.eu/53-latvia-2015/plenary-meeting-of-the-liii-cosac-31-may-2-june-2015/ (last accessed 12 May 2016). The feedback provided by NPs in this report corresponds with that subsequently provided in the 24th Bi-annual Report of COSAC and with the opinions expressed by representatives of NPs during the November 2015 COSAC working group meeting http://www.eu2015parl.lu/en/reunions/?ID=10# (both last accessed 1 May 2016).

[32] COSAC, 23rd Bi-annual Report (n 31).

Chambre des représentants warned that the green card might impose additional administrative burdens on the parliament, while the German *Bundestag* did not adopt any formal position, emphasizing that the procedure should first gain approval of the EP.

This data shows that apprehensive national parliamentary chambers position themselves as firm guardians of the Treaties, while the supporters of the idea are more flexible in their approach to the green card. These differences might be explained by the heterogeneity of national parliamentary traditions and different perceptions of parliamentary roles in EU governance. For example, while the UK House of Lords and the Dutch *Tweede Kamer* strive to become active players in the EU legislative system, there is consensus between the Swedish *Riksdag*, the Finnish *Eduskunta* and the German *Bundestag* that parliaments should not have an independent role at the EU level, but that they should limit themselves to controlling their own governments.[33] Yet, the differences of opinion can be detected even between chambers of the same parliament. For example, contrary to the Dutch *Tweede Kamer*, the Upper House *Eerste Kamer* neither formally endorsed the green card nor supported the joint letter on food waste.

The COSAC questionnaire also revealed differences as regards the scope and technical details of the green card. While all NPs agreed that a green card might be issued by any chamber according to its own domestic procedures, a number of chambers opposed the proposed minimum threshold of 1/4 of all the votes allocated to NPs to launch the procedure (eg the Bulgarian, Latvian, and Lithuanian chambers).

Instead, they suggested to adopt a solution similar to that applicable in the EWS, where the threshold is 1/3 of the votes. Moreover, while the Slovenian *Državni zbor* and Polish *Sejm* suggested to shorten the time period for collecting the signatures from 16 to eight weeks, the Czech and the British upper chambers asked for its extension to six months. Finally, the French *Sénat* pointed out that in the absence of a specific EU legal basis for the green card, it would be delicate to create anything going beyond informal cooperation. In the same vein, the Italian *Camera dei Deputati* emphasized that the green card procedure should not alter the existing institutional balance.

4.2 EU institutions

The Commission's attitude towards the green card initiative has been cautious. While in June 2014 the former Commission President, José Barroso, expressed his readiness to consider NPs' input concerning possible EU legislation or reviews thereof; the new Commission First Vice-President, Frans Timmermans, clearly changed the tone. In his letter to the Latvian *Saeima* in February 2015, he stated that 'rather than entering into a potentially complex discussion on new institutional arrangements not foreseen by the treaty, the issue should be addressed in a more pragmatic and immediate way'.[34] Such a diplomatic response should be, however, viewed in the light of the abovementioned Commission's reaction to the first green card, which recognized parliaments' input as a 'valuable contribution to the policy debate at EU level'.[35]

The position of the EP on the green card is even less clear. In none of the two consecutive COSAC questionnaires conducted in 2015 did the EP answer the question

[33] Ellen Mastenbroek and others, *Report: Engaging with Europe: Evaluating National Parliamentary Control of EU Decision-making after the Lisbon Treaty* (Radboud University 2014) 24.

[34] Frans Timmermans, Letter to the COSAC Chairpersons Meeting in Riga of 1–2 February 2015 http://www.cosac.eu/53-latvia-2015/meeting-of-the-chairpersons-of-cosac-1-2-february-2015/ (last accessed 1 May 2016).

[35] See n 28.

whether it supports the initiative. While the Constitutional Affairs Committee of the EP (AFCO) did not take a formal position on the matter, it indicated that the initiative is positive in terms of enhancing the existing political dialogue with NPs as long as it does not amount to a right of legislative initiative not foreseen by the Treaties.[36]

Quite a different view, however, was expressed by an EP official responsible for interinstitutional relations with NPs.[37] In his opinion, the green card procedure, understood as a tool of legislative initiative, should be dismissed as incompatible with the Treaties. He did not envisage a scenario where NPs may propose EU legislation through a gentleman's agreement with the Commission. Instead, referring to the Report on relations between the EP and NPs published in March 2014,[38] he pointed out that the latter's role is to control their governments by scrutinizing EU legislation under the EWS and exchanging views with EU institutions under the political dialogue. In those areas, the Lisbon Treaty potential is still unexploited.

However, the EP has lately expressed some support for the green card. This can be seen in the latest opinion of the AFCO Committee, which encourages consideration of this mechanism as means of raising the participation and activity of NPs in the EU legislative process.[39]

The views expressed by institutional actors facilitate the analysis of the potential repercussions of the green card. As regards the democratic underpinning of this initiative, the most important aspects to be examined are its compatibility with the existing legal framework and its potential influence on the interinstitutional relations between parliaments as well as between parliaments and their executives. These two aspects should be considered in both EU and domestic contexts, because the proposed procedure, similarly to the EWS, is a tool that cuts across the two levels of governance.

5. The Legal Status of the Green Card

5.1 EU Level Considerations

The main concern regarding the operationalization of the green card mechanism relates to the fact that its ultimate purpose—enabling NPs to initiate legislation—goes beyond the scope of competences granted to them by the Treaties. According to Article 12 of the Treaty on European Union (TEU), the main task of NPs is to 'contribute actively to the good functioning of the Union'. Although this provision grants them a broader right of involvement at the EU level,[40] the Treaties do not lay down any right of direct or indirect initiation of EU legislation. The former is, as a rule, reserved for the European Commission (Article 17(2) TEU). While authors of the green card emphasize that the procedure would not infringe the Commission's right of legislative initiative, in light of the abovementioned *Tweede Kamer*'s document on the green card, it would constitute an indirect legislative initiative, whereby a group of parliaments

[36] Answer by AFCO to Question 37 of the Annex to 23rd Bi-Annual Report of COSAC (n 31).

[37] Interview with Haris Kountouros, Legislative Dialogue Unit in the European Parliament's Directorate for Relations with National Parliaments, 14 April 2015.

[38] European Parliament, AFCO Report 2013/2185 (INI) of 27 March 2014, rapporteur Carlo Casini.

[39] Opinion of AFCO on the Annual Report 2014 on Subsidiarity and Proportionality (2015/2283(INI)), approved on 20 April 2016, rapporteur Kazimierz Ujazdowski.

[40] Cooper, 'A "Virtual Third Chamber"' (n 8); Anna-Lena Högenauer and Christine Neuhold, 'National Parliaments after Lisbon: Administrations on the Rise?' (2015) 38(2) WEP 335–54.

would pressure the Commission to respond. Indirect legislative initiative mechanisms already exist in the EU.

Such a right is enjoyed by the two EU co-legislators—the EP (Article 225 TFEU) and the Council of the EU (Article 241 TFEU). Each of them can ask the Commission to submit an appropriate proposal on matters pertaining to EU competence. If the Commission does not submit such a proposal, it must inform them of the reasons. Moreover, the Treaty of Lisbon granted the right of legislative initiative also to EU citizens by introducing the so-called European Citizens' Initiative (ECI), whereby one million citizens coming from at least seven EU Member States can invite the Commission to propose legislation (Article 11 TEU). In other words, all the existing legislative initiatives have their legal basis in the Treaties.

Hypothetically, giving the same possibility to NPs would require the EU to consider three options: (a) amending the Treaties, which is highly unlikely in the current political context due to the reluctance of the most powerful EU Member States; (b) signing a formal interinstitutional agreement between the Commission and NPs, possibly including the EP, without amending the Treaties; and (c) proceeding in an informal way. Supporters of the green card tend to opt for the third solution, pointing out that the green card would not grant NPs the right of legislative initiative per se and that green cards should be treated as soft policy suggestions. Consequently, the green card procedure could be successfully incorporated into the framework of the existing political dialogue, which lacks a Treaty basis. Yet, treating the green card as a distinct part of the political dialogue raises several issues.

First, as in the case of the political dialogue, the decision to engage in the green card mechanism would have to be acknowledged and, ideally, endorsed by the European Commission President. Yet, while in the case of the Barroso Initiative no detailed, formal procedures were agreed (eg deadlines or thresholds), the green card proposal foresees a range of such requirements. While under the political dialogue the exchange of information between NPs and the Commission does not oblige the latter to formally respond to parliamentary comments, the green card proposal envisages such a possibility. The Dutch Parliament's proposal is that the Commission should publish a formal response to a green card within a specified deadline (eg 8 or 12 weeks), stating whether it intends to take the proposed action and giving reasons for its decision.

Another possibility would be for the relevant Commissioner to appear before the initiating parliamentary chamber for a hearing. Formalizing such a commitment does not seem likely because of the above-mentioned reserved approach of the First Commission Vice-President Timmermans towards initiating procedures not foreseen in the Treaties. Because of this, parliaments would have to carry on suggesting legislative solutions to the Commission counting on its good will and political commitment. In this way, the proposed green card would, in fact, constitute an enhancement of the political dialogue and not a separate institutional mechanism of indirect legislative initiative. This is why the EP's AFCO Committee suggested, in its reply to the 23rd COSAC questionnaire, that the initiative should be renamed 'Green Card exercise', pointing out that the word 'procedure' brings up the question of its legality under the Lisbon Treaty. The question remains whether not formalizing the green card would discourage NPs from devoting their resources to the process.

Secondly, the collective character of the green card—requiring the Commission's response only when an agreed number of parliaments co-sign the proposal—might give rise to further concerns. The scarcity of yellow and orange cards is usually blamed on insufficient coordination and communication among national parliamentary chambers, which makes it difficult to reach the thresholds foreseen within the EWS.

One might therefore be sceptical as to the capacity of NPs to agree a unified position on proposing new or amending the existing EU legislative acts.

While the EWS prescribes certain conditions regarding the scope of subsidiarity assessment, as well as guidelines on how to test the compliance of an EU legislative draft with subsidiarity, the green card would be based on pure parliamentary creativity. One can imagine that it might be rather challenging for nineteen parliamentary chambers, composed of different political forces, to agree on the shape of a proposal. While it might be easier when the initiative merely encourages the Commission to take action on a certain matter or for it to adopt a certain strategic approach (eg food waste), it might become more difficult when a proposal includes policy details that might affect national interests.

Finally, the requirement for green cards to be submitted jointly could paradoxically weaken the influence or leverage of individual parliaments within the political dialogue. This is because the Commission might feel obliged to respond only to those proposals that reach the prescribed threshold, while feeling within its right to ignore individual voices. One could, however, disagree with this argument, given that the political dialogue concerns draft legislative acts already proposed by the Commission, while the green card refers to new legislative ideas of NPs.

5.2 National Level Considerations

Regardless of whether the green card would be introduced through an interinstitutional agreement or as an informal political commitment, its operationalization might encounter domestic legal obstacles. The insight gained from the COSAC questionnaires shows that at least in two Member States, Poland and Sweden, this kind of parliamentary action could be incompatible with their constitutional frameworks.

According to the Polish Constitution, the competence over foreign policy belongs to the government (Article 146). Since according to the Polish legal doctrine, the field of EU affairs forms part of foreign policy because the Constitution does not have a separate chapter on the EU, there is no legal basis for a proactive action of the Parliament in EU policy-making.[41] Only the government has the right to act at the EU level, while Parliament performs controlling and scrutiny functions. Such interpretation does not deprive Parliament of the Treaty rights to parliamentary participation in the EWS and to issuing opinions on draft EU legislative acts.[42] However, the Treaties do not foresee the possibility for NPs to propose or amend EU policies, be it individually or collectively. In other words, within the current Polish legal framework, neither the *Sejm* nor the *Senat* possess the constitutional capacity to make use of the green card.

Similarly, in the Swedish constitutional framework, the government has the sole responsibility for representing Sweden in the EU. Parliament's EU-oriented action is aligned to that of the government to such an extent that even the political

[41] See more in Jan Barcz and Anna Pudło, 'The Polish Parliament and EU Affairs' in Claudia Hefftler and others (eds), *The Palgrave Handbook on National Parliaments and the European Union* (Palgrave Macmillan 2015) 594–612.

[42] Act of 8 October 2010 on the Cooperation of the Council of Ministers with the Sejm and the Senate in Matters Relating to the Republic of Poland's Membership of the European Union (Cooperation Act), *Dziennik Ustaw* 2010, No 213, item 1395.

dialogue with the Commission take places through the executive.[43] The latter is, however, accountable to the *Riksdag*.[44]

While these two countries are evident cases where the green card would be incompatible with domestic legal frameworks, it could be expected that such concerns might be present also in other states, because in most Member States the competence over foreign policy belongs to the executive. However, only a few NPs have conducted legal analyses of the potential implementation of the green card, let alone consulted their governments on the matter. But even if these concerns were valid only for some Member States, it would mean that some national parliamentary chambers would be excluded from participation in the procedure resulting in asymmetry of democratic representation. The implementation of the green card might then differ among NPs, as some of them would not be able to use it without changing domestic law.

6. The Impact of the Green Card on Interinstitutional Relations

Apart from the concerns related to the legal status of the green card, this initiative seems capable of challenging the established institutional balance in the EU. While the main dimension of this challenge refers to the role of the EP in the EU legislative process, the second refers to the domestic legitimating function of NPs. As regards the former function, the green card might be perceived by the EP as endangering its institutional position as it would de facto grant NPs an indirect right of legislative initiative thus bringing them closer to being on an equal footing with the EP.[45] The latter, however, dislikes the idea of becoming a *primus inter pares*. For this reason, the EP has long fought against the creation of any mechanism that could challenge its position as the sole parliamentary forum at the EU level. This is why the EP prefers for EU parliamentary democracy to be strengthened through supranational tools that it can control,[46] and the green card, in its current form, would not be one of them.

Although a number of national parliamentary chambers (eg the German *Bundestag*) emphasized in the above-mentioned 23rd and 24th COSAC questionnaires that the procedure should be in line with the competences of EU institutions and the position of the EP, the majority of parliaments reveal the tendency to sideline the EP in the green card mechanism. Only three parliamentary chambers stated that the EP should play a role in this mechanism (the Romanian *Senat*, the Hungarian *Országgyűlés*, and the Belgian *Sénat*). Some of the opposing chambers point out that the EP already enjoys the right of indirect legislative initiative, so there is no need for its participation in the additional procedure (the House of Lords). Several other chambers were of the opinion that the EP should only be informed about the initiated cards, but not actively involved in their development (eg the Lithuanian *Seimas*, the Polish *Sejm*, and the Czech *Senate*).

[43] That is one of the reasons for the relatively little activity of *Riksdag* under the political dialogue compared to its activity within the EWS.

[44] See more in Hans Hegeland, 'The Swedish Parliament and EU Affairs: From Reluctant Player to Europeanized Actor' in Claudia Hefftler and others (eds), *The Palgrave Handbook on National Parliaments and the European Union* (Palgrave Macmillan 2015) 425–41.

[45] The EP itself does not have a right to initiate EU legislation and can only request the Commission to submit an appropriate proposal (TFEU, art 225).

[46] Contribution of John Erik Fossum in the 9th Report of the House of Lords (n 9).

However, some of the respondents were not clear about the exact role of the EP in this undertaking. For example, according to the Polish *Sejm*, while the EP should not be involved in co-signing the green card, its support would lend greater strength to national parliamentary proposals. What is more, this chamber suggested that the EP could exercise legislative initiative in cases where the Commission did not show willingness to consider NPs' green cards.

Such an expectation does not, however, seem logical in the context of a collective attempt by NPs to bypass the EP. In fact, it is hard to imagine the green card's success without the EP's support. Moreover, since these two parliamentary arenas co-exist in the same political environment and, mostly, in front of the same electorate, an endorsement of the EP would surely lend green cards additional political weight. On the contrary, sidelining the EP could exacerbate mistrust and increase competition between the two. Yet even if the Commission pursues the green card, the proposal could later be heavily amended or even rejected by the EP.

Studies confirm that while the European and NPs are interconnected and stimulate each other's activities,[47] NPs are likely to be the drivers of this co-evolution. Moreover, political parties and parliamentarians at the national and EU levels take conscious positions as regards each other's empowerment.[48] As much as increasing the EP's powers has enhanced the pressure on NPs to strengthen their own EU-related competences, introducing the green card by bypassing the EP might pressure the EP to counteract this. In order to reduce such negative trade-offs between the empowerment at the EU and national levels, the green card should be designed so as to generate a new sense of complementarity between the two parliamentary levels and not one of conflict.

In this vein, the EP, acting in the capacity of its indirect legislative initiative (Article 225 TFEU), could perform the role of a leader in initiating or amending legislation, supported by a group of like-minded national parliamentary chambers. The process could be initiated, as in the case of the green card, by any parliament but developed jointly with the competent sectoral committees of the EP. Although, unlike in the case of the green card, the legislative proposal would be submitted to the Commission by the EP and not by NPs, it would include reference to all parliamentary chambers subscribing to the initiative, which would surely add political weight to it. In this way, the EC would have the formal obligation to respond not only to the EP, as is currently the case under Article 225 TFEU, but also to a number of national chambers presenting the same positions.[49]

Last, but not least, there is a question of the consent of national executives. Should these institutional actors be consulted or could the green card procedure be operationalized by circumventing the governments? So far, the opinions are divided. While some parliaments have already discussed such a possibility with their executives (eg Irish *Oireachtas*), others do not feel obliged to do this, stressing that if the procedure is implemented within the framework of the political dialogue, it is the parliament's right to pursue its EU-oriented activities without prior government approval.[50]

However, it looks like there is not much enthusiasm about the green card in the executive circles. As reported by the British Minister of State for Europe, David

[47] Crum and Fossum, 'The Multilevel Parliamentary Field' (n 19). See also the chapter by Ian Cooper in this volume.

[48] Thomas Winzen and others, 'Parliamentary Co-evolution: National Parliamentary Reactions to the Empowerment of the European Parliament' (2015) 22(1) JEPP 75, 93.

[49] Karolina Borońska-Hryniewiecka, 'The Best of Both Worlds: The Unexploited Potential of Inter-parliamentary Cooperation in the EU' (2015) 27(129) PISM Policy Paper.

[50] Interviews with representatives of the Polish *Sejm* (April 2015) and Latvian *Saeima* (May 2015).

Lidington, during a hearing organized by the House of Lords—representatives of national governments expressed 'outright opposition' to the idea of strengthening NPs through the green card, while 'some leaders think more automatically of the European Parliament as the place where they assume that public accountability should lie for Brussels decisions'.[51]

In spite of political commitments to make Europe more democratic, discussions with representatives of national governments about the possibility of reinforcing the role of NPs in EU affairs quite often come down to the conclusion that national MPs lack the necessary understanding required to effectively engage with the EU. In a similar vein, the former President of the European Council, Herman Van Rompuy, observed that while 'the provisions for democratic legitimacy and accountability should ensure that the common interest of the union is duly taken into account ... national parliaments are not in the best position to take it into account fully'.[52]

Strikingly, similar opinions can be heard from among the ranks of national parliamentary committees for EU affairs. In their views, most MPs have neither the time nor the willingness to learn more about the EU. While a handful of MPs from EU committees keep track of the EU agenda, the rest seem to focus merely on domestic politics, not paying attention to the stream of EU legislation.[53] Limited electoral salience of EU affairs causes MPs not to perceive their engagement in scrutinizing EU dossiers as particularly politically rewarding.[54] While it could be expected that a formalized green card procedure might encourage national parliamentarians to get involved and gain greater visibility at the EU level, it is debatable to what extent they would be able to rise above their national perspective and suggest compromise-yielding solutions for the whole EU.

7. Conclusions

NPs find themselves at a critical juncture. On the one hand, in light of the EU's deficit of democratic representation, there is a clear need to strengthen domestic parliamentary engagement in EU policy-making. Due to their proximity to the citizens, NPs have a crucial role in increasing the legitimacy of EU decisions by establishing links between the multiple national *demoi* and the EU legislative process.[55] Since genuine policy development upstream—if properly communicated—is much more appealing to citizens than the control of subsidiarity or proportionality, it seems that the green card might be more conducive to the idea of strengthening the European *demos*. On

[51] House of Lords, EU Committee, Inquiry on the Role of National Parliaments in the EU, Session 13, 14 January 2014 http://www.parliament.uk/documents/lords-committees/eu-select/Role%20of%20national%20parliaments/nat-parl-evidence-volume.pdf (last accessed 1 May 2016).

[52] Herman Van Rompuy and others, 'Towards a Genuine Economic and Monetary Union', 5 December 2012, 16, available at https://www.google.pl/url?sa=t&rct=j&q=&esrc=s&source=web&cd=1&cad=rja&uact=8&ved=0ahUKEwib5s251pTQAhWDBiwKHZvMCioQFggfMAA&url=http%3A%2F%2Fwww.consilium.europa.eu%2Fuedocs%2Fcms_Data%2Fdocs%2Fpressdata%2Fen%2Fec%2F134069.pdf&usg=AFQjCNHNEH7J_O31hPv_KwtlQ9UOZzKl0A (last accessed 5 November 2016).

[53] Interview with a representative of the Polish *Sejm* (April 2015).

[54] Karolina Borońska-Hryniewiecka, 'The "Green Card" Opportunity: Time to Rethink Parliamentary Engagement in European Affairs' (2015) 41(773) PISM Bulletin.

[55] Sonia Piedrafita, 'EU Democratic Legitimacy and National Parliaments' (2013) 7(25) CEPS Essay; Arthur Benz, 'Linking Multiple Demoi. Interparliamentary Relations in the EU' (2011) 1 IEV-Online.

the other hand, asserting that granting NPs the right to suggest legislative proposals would automatically increase the EU's democratic legitimacy is too simplistic and hardly convincing.

This is not only because national MPs still lack the necessary 'EU knowledge' to be able to 'contribute effectively to the good functioning of the Union'. Sceptics could go further and argue that, once formalized, the green card would not guarantee influence at the EU level. It could be expected that if the Commission does not respond constructively to the concerns raised by NPs under the EWS, or by the citizens under the ECI,[56] it will not treat green cards in a significantly different way either. More importantly, the current design and scope of the green card might become counterproductive to boosting the overall EU legitimacy as it tends to position one parliamentary level against the other. Genuine democratic legitimacy calls for combining the best of the two worlds.

As much as it may not be convincing to some NPs, the EP is the legitimate locus of legislative power in the EU and it can act as a power multiplier for NPs by adding its institutional weight to green card proposals. It is of course up to parliamentary chambers how they will organize their cooperation with the EP, but a systematic exchange of information between the two levels is an essential starting point. Already in June 2014 the President of the EP, Martin Schulz, issued a letter to NPs offering them a new form of cooperation, calling on them to share their positions with the EP and provide it with background knowledge on the domestic implementation of EU legislation that the Commission intends to amend. NPs could build on this proposal and agree a mutually satisfying arrangement that produces a more efficient and democratic legislative output at a time of executive dominance.

Instead of pushing for the green card in its current form, NPs could reframe the initiative in a more pragmatic way, by turning it into a joint amendment procedure. Thus, rather than proposing new legislation at the EU level, the green card could focus on improving or repealing the existing legislation with the support of the EP. Such cooperation would be based on a two-directional feedback loop between the EP and NPs implemented through a systematic sharing of information on the EU legislative process (on the part of the EP) and on the domestic implementation of EU legislation that is already in place (on the part of NPs).[57] There is much potential for this in line with the Commission's Better Regulation agenda.[58]

In this regard, there is still much unexploited potential for the sharing of information on the so-called trilogues,[59] which fail to ensure a satisfactory level of transparency.[60]

[56] Karolina Borońska-Hryniewiecka and Elisabeth Monaghan, The European Citizens' Initiative as Democratic Legitimacy Enhancing Tool: Towards a Broader Conceptualization' in Beatriz Perez de las Heras (ed), *Building a European Demos: Democratic Legitimacy in the Post-Lisbon European Union and Its Impact on Global Governance* (Palgrave Macmillan, forthcoming).

[57] Borońska-Hryniewiecka, 'The Best of Both Worlds' (n 49).

[58] Especially the Regulatory Fitness and Performance Programme (REFIT), which evaluates the existing stock of EU legislation. See on this Davor Jančić, 'The Juncker Commission's Better Regulation Agenda and Its Impact on National Parliaments' in Cristina Fasone, Diane Fromage, and Zoe Lefkofridi (eds), 'Parliaments, Public Opinion and Parliamentary Elections in Europe' (2015) Special Issue 18 EUI MWP 45.

[59] These are interinstitutional consultations between the Commission, the EP, and the Council, whose goal is to reach compromise on an EU legislative proposal at an early phase of the legislative process. It is estimated that after the Lisbon Treaty, around 80% of EU laws have been agreed before the first reading through trilogues http://www.ombudsman.europa.eu/en/press/release.faces/en/59975/html.bookmark (last accessed 21 May 2016).

[60] Karolina Borońska-Hryniewiecka, 'The Black Box of EU Legislation: The Motivation (or Lack of it) Behind Transparency in EU Policy-making' (2015) 4(106) PISM Strategic File.

As there is no mention of them in the Treaties and no safeguards exist to enable oversight over them, trilogue meetings are held behind closed doors with no public access. Only a handful of EU officials from the Council, the Commission, and the EP are involved in trilogues,[61] and the deals that emerge from them often bear little resemblance to the draft legislative acts scrutinized by NPs under the EWS. As the European Ombudsman, Emily O'Reilly, launched an inquiry aiming to improve the transparency of trilogues in May 2015, this is an opportune moment for NPs to re-arrange their cooperation with the EP on this matter.[62]

Cooperation with the EP on the green card might constitute the most effective mechanism for the Europeanization of NPs, which could enable MPs to channel their positions to the EU legislature more efficiently and increase the citizens' feeling of ownership of amended EU legislation. It could also play an essential role in driving European integration forward by fostering common examination and understanding of various policy issues as well as a smoother transposition of EU legislation into national law. If effective, such a joint exercise could gradually include the initiation of new legislative proposals. While the EP has so far rarely used its power to propose legislation, the decreased number of legislative proposals coming from the Commission has led the EP to take a more pro-active approach to legislating.[63] An interparliamentary approach to the green card might help the EP to enhance its own legitimacy vis-à-vis the European *demos*. This might also direct NPs to take a middle, more pragmatic, way between resilience and resignation: that of power sharing and synergy building with their EU counterpart.

[61] Owing to the ad hoc nature of trilogues, no standard format of their composition is foreseen, which means trilogue meetings gather representatives ranging from staff-level officials to national ministers and Commissioners.

[62] European Ombudsman, Press release No 9/2015 of 28 May 2015 http://www.ombudsman.europa.eu/press/release.faces/en/59975/html.bookmark (last accessed 12 May 2016).

[63] Interviews with representatives of the EP AFCO Committee and EP Legal Services, Brussels, July 2015.

14

National Parliaments as Political Safeguards of Federalism

Interparliamentary Cooperation in the EU, the US, and Switzerland

*Katarzyna Granat**

1. Introduction

This chapter studies the role of parliaments at non-central level in federal systems. To this end, it analyzes the function of US state legislatures, national parliaments (NPs) in the EU, and Swiss cantonal parliaments as 'political safeguards of federalism'. This notion, introduced by Herbert Wechsler in the US context, describes the mechanisms that offer states protection from federal overreach and focuses on the role of states in the appointment and composition of the central government.[1] The aim of the 'political safeguarding of federalism' is to maintain an optimal balance between the states and federal government rather than to advance state autonomy, thereby seeking to 'achieve a well-functioning *national* democracy'.[2]

The chapter adopts a comparative perspective in order to gain insights from the American and Swiss experiences that could inform the ongoing debate on the strengthening of NPs in EU affairs through interparliamentary cooperation.[3] The comparison is based upon the wider notion of a federal union, under which the EU can be classified. As Schütze explains, the EU stands on a federal 'middle ground', since it has a 'mixed or compound structure ... combining international and national elements'.[4] He does not follow the view that the EU's federal tradition of indivisible sovereignty implies a notion of a federation as a national state. Instead, he argues that the federal label can be applied beyond the state and that it encapsulates the idea of a 'Federation of States'. This chapter takes this broader approach and adopts the view that the subsidiarity principle, strengthened by the scrutiny of NPs, represents the EU's own political safeguard of federalism that allows for comparisons with similar safeguards in other federal systems.[5]

* Research for this chapter was carried out under EU grant agreement No 267209. This chapter has also benefited from discussions within the context of the Durham 'Neo-Federalism' Project (EU Framework Programme 2007.13: ERC Grant Agreement No 312304).

[1] H Wechsler, 'The Political Safeguards of Federalism: The Role of the States in the Composition and Selection of the National Government' (1954) 54 Colum L Rev 543.

[2] H Gerken and A Holtzblatt, 'The Political Safeguards of Horizontal Federalism' (2014) 113 Michigan L Rev 57, 68.

[3] See the currently discussed reforms in House of Lords, European Union Committee, *The Role of National Parliaments in the European Union*, 9th Report of Session 2013–14.

[4] R Schütze, *From Dual to Cooperative Federalism* (Oxford University Press 2009) 70.

[5] See in contrast Lindseth's argument that the 'increase in the national parliamentary role is a further reflection of the fundamentally administrative character of European integration'.

In the EU, concerns over a 'democratic deficit'[6] and the so-called 'competence creep'[7] led the drafters of the Lisbon Treaty to grant NPs an oversight function with respect to the compliance of EU draft legislative acts with the principle of subsidiarity.[8] More than this, as explained by Lindseth, the reinforcement of the role of NPs within the EU legislative process was grounded in a 'democratic disconnect' between EU institutions and EU citizens.[9] This disconnect arose from the assertion that, for cultural and historical reasons, it is the national level that ultimately enjoys the highest degree of democratic legitimacy, and without more involvement of NPs, the EU would remain disconnected from this source of legitimacy. This stands in contrast to the idea of the 'democratic deficit', which concentrates solely on the democratization of EU institutions independently of the national level. This chapter departs from this approach and argues that efforts towards greater democratization of the EU should focus on enhancing the linkages between EU institutions that produce legal norms and the national level that oversees these institutions.

The involvement of NPs was also partly inspired by disappointment with the jurisprudence of the Court of Justice of the European Union, and its fulfilment of the function of judicial guardian of subsidiarity.[10] Its jurisprudence on the subsidiarity principle[11] has been subject to strong criticism, especially the Court's reluctance to 'deal with subsidiarity frontally' and the Court's 'misleading application' of this principle by focusing on the procedural dimension of subsidiarity instead of conducting a cost/benefit test of the necessity of EU action.[12] Moreover, the Court's case law is labelled a 'drafting guide', meaning that as long as EU institutions use the Court's vague vocabulary and draft EU legislation accordingly, the Court will not annul such acts on the grounds of a violation of subsidiarity.[13] To address such concerns about democratic legitimacy and the insufficient contribution of the Court to address the challenges facing EU legislative action, the Lisbon Treaty introduced the so-called early warning system (EWS), granting NPs the role of 'watchdogs' of subsidiarity.[14] The EWS creates a link between EU institutions and NPs by involving the latter in the subsidiarity control of draft legislation put forward by the European Commission.

In contrast to the EU, no mechanism similar to the EWS exists in the US or Swiss constitutional systems. Nonetheless, state legislatures and cantonal parliaments have also taken an active role in safeguarding balanced relations between states and the

PL Lindseth, *Power and Legitimacy: Reconciling Europe and the Nation-State* (Oxford University Press 2010) 227.

[6] JHH Weiler, 'In the Face of Crisis: Input Legitimacy, Output Legitimacy and the Political Messianism of European Integration' (2012) 34 J Eur Integration 825, 837.

[7] S Weatherill, 'Competence Creep and Competence Control' (2004) 23 YEL 1.

[8] TEU, art 5(3).

[9] P Lindseth, 'Delegation is Dead, Long Live Delegation: Managing the Democratic Disconnect in the European Market-Polity' in C Joerges and R Dehousse (eds), *Good Governance in Europe's Integrated Market* (Oxford University Press 2002) 151. See also his chapter on mediated legitimacy in this volume.

[10] See G Martinico, 'Dating Cinderella: On Subsidiarity as a Political Safeguard of Federalism in the European Union' (2011) 17 EPL 649.

[11] See an analysis of this problematic case law in A Estella De Noriega, *The EU Principle of Subsidiarity and its Critique* (Oxford University Press 2002).

[12] Martinico, 'Dating Cinderella' (n 10) 655.

[13] S Weatherill, 'The Limits of Legislative Harmonization Ten Years after Tobacco Advertising: How the Court's Case Law has Become a Drafting Guide' (2011) 12 German LJ 827.

[14] I Cooper, 'The Watchdogs of Subsidiarity: National Parliaments and the Logic of Arguing in the EU' (2006) 44 JCMS 281.

federation and between cantons respectively. This chapter focuses on fiscal federalism in the US, horizontal federalism in Switzerland, and the contribution of interparliamentary cooperation to the safeguarding of the federal structure of government. Section 2 discusses Wechsler's notion of 'political safeguards of federalism'. With regard to the US, the focus will be on the question of the level of government that should bear the cost of implementing federal legislation.[15]

Specifically, section 3 studies the Unfunded Mandates Reform Act (UMRA) of 1995 that aims to limit the practice of imposing federal unfunded mandates on state and local governments. In general terms, an unfunded mandate is a compulsory federal law that requires a state or local government to perform certain actions without providing federal funding for it.[16] For instance, the 1990 Americans with Disabilities Act obliges state and local governments to make buildings accessible to disabled people and to finance it from their own budgets. This section also explores the role of the National Conference of State Legislatures (NCSL), an 'informal political safeguard of federalism', in the operation of the unfunded mandate in the US federal system, and draws parallels and highlights differences with the involvement of NPs in the EWS.[17]

Section 4 studies the involvement of the Swiss cantonal parliaments in issues related to federalism. Although sufficient political safeguards of federalism seem to be in force in Switzerland, when it comes to intercantonal treaties, intercantonal parliamentary cooperation is still developing. To respond to the dominance of cantonal executives in this aspect of horizontal federalism, cantonal parliaments have launched a number of regional conferences, while a national conference is underway. Finally, section 5 offers insights from the functioning of the NCSL and Swiss conferences for the involvement of NPs within the EU system. The key finding of the chapter is that, in all of the cases studied, interparliamentary cooperation was used by the legislatures to strengthen their position in the relations between the parliament and government in the system of vertical (the EU and the US) or horizontal (Switzerland) federalism.

2. Political Safeguards of Federalism

2.1 US Political Safeguards of Federalism

In Wechsler's view, the political safeguards of federalism serve to prevent or limit intrusions by the federal government on the realm of the states.[18] As a consequence, courts do not need to police federalism on behalf of states because the latter are adequately represented in Congress.[19]

First, according to Wechsler, the US federal tradition 'supports placing the burden of persuasion on those urging national action'.[20] Secondly, states play a central

[15] See the differences between the EU and the US in financing of federal policies in I Pernice, 'Framework Revisited: Constitutional, Federal and Subsidiarity Issues' (1995) 2 Colum J Eur L 403, 414.

[16] See RJ Dilger and RS Beth, 'Unfunded Mandates Reform Act: History, Impact, and Issues, Congressional Research Service' available at https://fas.org/sgp/crs/misc/R40957.pdf (last accessed 16 October 2016).

[17] See on the notion of informal safeguards of federalism JD Nugent, *Safeguarding Federalism. How States Protect Their Interests in National Policymaking* (University of Oklahoma Press 2009) 54 ff.

[18] Wechsler, 'The Political Safeguards of Federalism' (n 1) 558.

[19] ibid 559. See a contrasting view claiming that judicial review is necessary to maintain and reinforce the political safeguards of federalism in LA Baker, 'Putting the Safeguards Back into the Political Safeguards of Federalism' (2001) 46 Villanova L Rev 951.

[20] Wechsler, 'The Political Safeguards of Federalism' (n 1) 545.

role in the selection and composition of the federal parliament and government. Specifically, members of both houses of Congress are elected on the basis of electoral districts formed across the states and, as such, are politically accountable to the voters of their home state,[21] although the Senate only became directly elected after the 17th Amendment of the US Constitution adopted in 1913. Furthermore, the US president is elected by electors appointed by each individual state.[22] Thirdly, the equality of states in the Senate enables the blocking of legislation by a coalition of states whose population is just a fraction of the total number of citizens.[23]

In the same vein, states can influence the House of Representatives through state control over voters' qualifications (criteria by which people are eligible to vote) and districting (the redrawing of borders between electoral districts).[24] While the former means of state influence is arguably severely restricted by the prohibitions against the denial of franchise, especially by virtue of the 15th and 19th Amendments, the latter means remains prevalent today under the label of gerrymandering. Finally, Wechsler argues that although the US president is the 'repository of "national spirit" in the central government', due to his or her election by the Electoral College, he or she is also required to be 'responsive to local values that have large support within the [S]tates'.[25]

The political safeguards have been negatively assessed in the literature since state legislatures do not have any important powers in federal elections except for setting residence requirements, which is difficult to transform into an effective way to influence national policy.[26] At the same time, the US president's veto power over federal legislation is more a sign of his or her competition for power with the states rather than of responsiveness to local values.[27] Other critics point out that the political safeguards are 'ahistorical', since the Framers saw the Constitution as providing for judicial review of the balance of power between the national and state levels; while it is a historical fact, it is argued, that the political safeguards were not the only safeguards of federalism.[28]

Wechsler's notion of the political safeguards of federalism was relied on by the US Supreme Court in the *Garcia v San Antonio Metropolitan Transit Authority* case, which concerned the question of whether, under the Constitution's Commerce Clause, Congress could extend to state and local governments the Fair Labor Standards Act requiring minimum wage and overtime pay for employees.[29] The US Supreme Court decided that the political safeguards of federalism provided sufficient protection from federal commerce power that would excessively burden the states. However, the dissenting opinion of Justice Powell, which was joined by Chief Justice Rehnquist and Justice O'Connor, pointed out that Wechsler's view that the structure of the federal government sufficiently protects the states did not reflect the current state of affairs.[30]

Their opinion is echoed in the literature: the adoption of the 17th Amendment, although acknowledged by Wechsler, directs the attention of senators towards national

[21] US Constitution, art I s 2 and Clause 1 of 17th Amendment to the US Constitution.

[22] US Constitution, art II s 1.

[23] Wechsler, 'The Political Safeguards of Federalism' (n 1) 547.

[24] ibid 549 ff.

[25] ibid 558.

[26] J Pittenger, '*Garcia* and the Political Safeguards of Federalism: Is there a Better Solution to the Conundrum of the Tenth Amendment?' (1992) 22 Publius: The Journal of Federalism 1, 3.

[27] ibid.

[28] See JC Yoo, 'The Judicial Safeguards of Federalism' (1996) 70 S Cal L Rev 1311, 1357, and 1381.

[29] *Garcia v San Antonio Metropolitan Transit Authority*, 469 US 528 (1985). See n 11 of the judgment.

[30] See n 9 of the dissenting opinion.

rather than state issues.[31] Others argue that, despite this change, the Senate still protects federalism because senators participate in federal lawmaking procedures to the same extent as prior to this amendment.[32]

A number of US scholars understand the system of political parties as a political safeguard of federalism. Although they are focused on the election process of their members rather than on the political programme of those members and although they lack a strong centralized organization, political parties work together at all levels so that the party's candidate is elected.[33] They influence federalism by creating political frameworks where politicians at different levels of government depend upon each other to get elected and stay in office.[34] Specifically, political parties act as safeguards of federalism by focusing on long-term benefits and developing priorities of a national rather than local character.[35] Moreover, implementation of federal statutes is perceived as an important way for states to protect their powers. Specifically, major pieces of federal legislation, such as the Affordable Care Act of 2010, require implementation by the states and this empowers them to 'limit or shape the federalization of government functions'.[36]

Finally, the scholarship identifies 'informal political safeguards of federalism' and defines them as 'informal modes of intergovernmental representation through which state officials apprise federal policymakers of the interests of State governments'.[37] While sharing Wechsler's idea that representation is key to the preservation of the authority of state governments, Nugent argues that the best safeguards in this respect are state officials themselves rather than members of Congress or the US President.[38] This chapter focuses on NCLS, which gathers officials of state legislatures.

2.2 Swiss Political Safeguards of Federalism

The Swiss Constitution foresees that: '[t]he principle of subsidiarity must be observed in the allocation and performance of state tasks'.[39] However, in contrast to the EU, no safeguards similar to the EWS have been introduced in Switzerland. Instead, a number of other mechanisms are in force that might be seen as political safeguards of federalism.

First, the Council of States, the Upper House of the Swiss Federal Assembly, consists of representatives of cantons elected according to the rules set by each canton.[40] Currently, in almost all cantons members of the Council of States are elected through direct elections at the same time as members of the National Council, the Lower

31 Pittenger, '*Garcia* and the Political Safeguards of Federalism' (n 26) 2.

32 BR Clark, 'Separation of Powers as Safeguard of Federalism' (2001) 79 Texas L Rev 1328, 1371.

33 L Kramer, 'Putting the Politics Back into the Political Safeguards' (2000) 100 Colum L Rev 215, 278 ff.

34 ibid 282.

35 J Bednar, *The Robust Federation* (Cambridge University Press 2008) 116. On political parties as political safeguards see also S Jenkins and DD Roscoe, 'Parties as the Political Safeguards of Federalism: The Impact of Local Party Activity on National Elections' (2014) 44 Publius: The Journal of Federalism 519, 537.

36 AR Gluck, 'Federalism from Federal Statutes: Health Reform, Medicaid, and the Old-Fashioned Federalists' Gamble' (2013) 81 Fordham L Rev 1749, 1768.

37 JD Nugent, 'The Informal Political Safeguards of Federalism' (2002) at 3 https://www.academia.edu/801677/The_Informal_Political_Safeguards_of_Federalism (last accessed 16 October 2016) This notion is further elaborated on in Nugent, *Safeguarding Federalism* (n 17) 54 ff.

38 JD Nugent, 'The Informal Political Safeguards of Federalism' (n 37) 4.

39 Swiss Constitution, art 5a.

40 ibid, art 150.

House of the Federal Assembly.[41] As a consequence, members of the Council of States represent the citizens of their own canton, and not necessarily the canton as such.[42]

Secondly, in the realm of direct democracy, a referendum is necessary for the passage of amendments to the Federal Constitution, for the accession of Switzerland to international organizations, and for emergency federal acts that do not have a constitutional basis and that are valid for more than one year. Such a referendum requires a majority of votes of both 'the People and cantons'—thus, a double majority.[43]

In addition to the Council of States and the referendum procedures, cantons can directly participate in the shaping of federal legislation through the petition process. This allows a number of constitutional actors, including the cantons, to submit a legislative proposal to the Federal Assembly.[44] Moreover, eight cantons may start a referendum procedure against a federal law within 100 days of the official publication of the act.[45] In 2003, eleven cantons, in an effort coordinated by the Conference of Cantonal Governments, which is a political platform gathering cantonal executives, successfully triggered this mechanism against a tax reform that would have significantly decreased the tax revenues of cantons.[46] This case exemplifies the fact that cantons can be veto players in the federal legislative process if they coordinate their action.[47]

Finally, in contrast to the EU and US systems, the Swiss Constitution does not provide for judicial review of the constitutionality of federal laws, although some attempts were made to introduce such a procedure.[48] Specifically, the institution of referendum itself led to the rejection of such judicial safeguards of federalism.[49] In a 1939 referendum, the Swiss people rejected a constitutional amendment put forward by means of the popular initiative which sought 'protection of the constitutional rights of the citizens (expansion of the constitutional jurisdiction)' and which thus proposed the introduction of constitutional review of federal legislation.[50] In consequence, the Federal Supreme Court of Switzerland cannot review acts of the Federal Parliament for their compatibility with the Swiss Constitution, but enacted federal acts can be subject to referendum if at least 50,000 people or eight cantons request it.[51] Such referendums

[41] The only exception is canton Appenzell-Rhodes-Intérieures, where members of the Council of States are elected by *Landsgemeinde*.

[42] H Kriesi and AH Trechsel, *The Politics of Switzerland: Continuity and Change in a Consensus Democracy* (Cambridge University Press 2008) 39.

[43] Swiss Constitution, art 140(1). The 'double majority' means the majority of the voters and the majority of 12 out of 23 votes (there are 26 cantons, but six of them count as half-cantons and have half a vote).

[44] ibid art 160(1). However, bills initiated by cantons in the framework of the 'parliamentary initiative' constitute a very small portion of all bills. See Kriesi and Trechsel, *The Politics of Switzerland* (n 42) 39.

[45] Swiss Constitution, art 141.

[46] W Linder and I Steffen, 'Swiss Confederation' in K Le Roy and C Saunders (eds), *Legislative, Executive, and Judicial Governance in Federal Countries* (McGill-Queen's University Press 2006) 308.

[47] Kriesi and Trechsel, *The Politics of Switzerland* (n 42) 40.

[48] EC Ritaine and A-S Papeil, 'Federalism and Legal Unification in Switzerland' in D Halberstam and M Reimann (eds), *Federalism and Legal Unification* (Springer 2014) 453.

[49] D Halberstam, 'Comparative Federalism and the Role of the Judiciary' in GA Caldeira, RD Kelemen, and KE Whittington (eds), *The Oxford Handbook of Law and Politics* (Oxford University Press 2010) 147.

[50] *Eidgenössische Volksinitiative Wahrung der verfassungsmässigen Rechte der Bürger (Erweiterung der Verfassungsgerichtsbarkeit)* available at https://www.admin.ch/ch/d/pore/vi/vis40.html (last accessed 16 October 2016). See also T Fleiner, 'Constitutional Revision: The Case of Switzerland' in X Contiades (ed), *Engineering Constitutional Change* (Routledge 2013) 343.

[51] Swiss Constitution, art 141.

play an important role in preventing violations of cantonal powers guaranteed in the Constitution.[52]

2.3 EU Political Safeguards of Federalism

Within the EU, it is the principle of subsidiarity that acts as a political safeguard of federalism.[53] To this end, the Lisbon Treaty granted NPs a role in the enforcement of this principle through the EWS, anchored in Articles 6 and 7 of Protocol No 2.[54] Hence, in contrast to the US and Switzerland, NPs are tasked with the operationalization of the political safeguards of federalism in the EU legal order.

The EWS procedure allows NPs to submit, within eight weeks of the date of transmission of a draft EU legislative act, a reasoned opinion to the Commission explaining why the draft does not comply with subsidiarity. Depending on the number of reasoned opinions, which count as votes (each chamber of a bicameral parliament has one vote, while unicameral parliaments have two votes), NPs may trigger two procedures. First, in the procedure labelled the 'yellow card', if the number of reasoned opinions reaches at least one third of all the votes allocated to NPs, or one quarter of the votes for the proposals in the area of freedom, security, and justice, the Commission may decide to maintain, amend, or withdraw the draft, giving reasons for its decision.

Secondly, in the procedure commonly referred to as the 'orange card', if reasoned opinions represent at least the majority of votes assigned to NPs, the Commission may, again, decide to maintain, amend or withdraw the draft. If it maintains the draft, a majority of 55 per cent of the votes in the Council or a majority of the votes cast in the European Parliament (EP) is required to halt the legislative procedure. Furthermore, the so-called 'political dialogue' initiated in 2006 by the President of the Commission José Manuel Barroso, and hence often referred to as 'Barroso Initiative', complements the exchange between NPs and the Commission beyond the EWS.[55]

3. Interparliamentary Cooperation in the US

In the EU, subsidiarity monitoring was introduced to ensure democratic oversight over the exercise of non-exclusive EU competences. In the US, state legislatures did not develop such a mechanism because of the well-established review of competence exercised by the US Supreme Court, the existence of a set of political safeguards of federalism, and the lack of a similar democratic deficit problem. This does not mean, however, that there is no role for state legislatures in US federalism. The US case could actually provide useful insights for the EU debate on subsidiarity and this is examined below with the example of fiscal federalism, the introduction of UMRA, and the role of the NCSL.[56]

[52] T Fleiner, 'The Current Situation of Federalism in Switzerland' (2009) 9 Revista d'Estudis Autonòmics i Federals 51, 61.

[53] Schütze, *From Dual to Cooperative Federalism* (n 4) 243.

[54] ibid 257.

[55] D Jančić, 'The Game of Cards: National Parliaments in the EU and the Future of the Early Warning System and the Political Dialogue' (2015) 52 CML Rev 939, 948 ff.

[56] RW Adler, 'Unfunded Mandates and Fiscal Federalism: A Critique' (1997) 50 Vanderbilt L Rev 1137.

3.1 Unfunded Mandates: Rationale and Contents

The goal of UMRA was to limit the practice whereby a federal unfunded mandate is imposed upon state and local governments, and to raise awareness about the fiscal impact that federal legislation has on the states. Owing to a shift in its approach in the 1970s and 1980s, the federal government was introducing more intrusive compulsory programmes and regulations requiring compliance by states and smaller entities (localities).[57] UMRA was supposed to prevent federal legislation and regulation from imposing costly obligations on states and localities.[58] More specifically, the objective was to reduce the number of unfunded mandates and provide Congress with information on the costs of federal legislation leading to a more informed decision-making process in this institution.[59] Arguments against UMRA were that broad national issues—such as those in the fields of the environment, the economy, health, immigration, and education—demand national solutions, which necessitate the adoption of unfunded mandates.[60] Moreover, in order to avoid '[S]tate shopping', certain issues of an interstate nature need to be addressed at the federal level.[61] Finally, it was underlined that federal mandates dictate the necessary minimum requirements ('floors') in some regulatory areas, such as the environment or workplace conditions.[62]

By introducing several reforms, UMRA addressed the problems arising from the fact that the federal government may require a state government to take action without allocating funds for the latter to cover the costs associated with it. UMRA is thus supposed to make it harder to enact unfunded mandates.[63] The Act proposes specific tools to achieve this, such as information requirements and the point of order vote, which are discussed in turn below.

First, the information requirements demand for Congress to be better informed about the cost of mandates. UMRA requires from the Congressional Budget Office (CBO) to prepare information statements on the mandates and their costs.[64] This obligation should arguably make it easier to solve problems related to collective action and free-riding.[65]

Secondly, UMRA establishes a congressional point of order against legislation containing significant federal government mandates without providing funding for their implementation and on bills that lack a CBO assessment. If a point of order is raised and accepted, it will be debated for 20 minutes followed by a vote on whether to continue consideration of the legislation. Such a vote is seen as a 'speed bump', allowing members of Congress to initiate debate and a vote on unfunded mandates independently from the vote on the legislation itself.[66] In the extreme, a point of order may

[57] Dilger and Beth, 'Unfunded Mandates Reform Act' (n 16) 2. [58] ibid.

[59] S Anderson and R Constantine, 'Unfunded mandates' Briefing Paper No. 7, Harvard Law School, p 13, available at http://www.law.harvard.edu/faculty/hjackson/UnfundedMandates_7.pdf (last accessed 16 October 2016).

[60] Congressional Record, Senate, Senator Lautenberg, 12 January 1995, at 862.

[61] ibid. [62] ibid.

[63] TJ Conlan, JD Riggle, and DE Schwartz, 'Deregulating Federalism? The Politics of Mandate Reform in the 104th Congress' (1995) 25 Publius: The Journal of Federalism 23, 37. Unfunded mandates, however, are not forbidden by UMRA.

[64] Some parallels could be drawn here with the EU's impact assessments and a 'move towards proceduralisation' in subsidiarity monitoring. See X Groussot and S Bogojević, 'Subsidiarity as a Procedural Safeguard of Federalism' in L Azoulai (ed.), *The Question of Competence in the European Union* (Oxford University Press 2014).

[65] E Garrett, 'Enhancing the Political Safeguards of Federalism? The Unfunded Mandates Reform Act of 1995' (1997) 45 *U Kansas L Rev* 1113.

[66] PL Posner, 'The Politics of Coercive Federalism' in T Conlan and P L Posner (eds.), *Intergovernmental Management for the 21st Century* (Brookings Institution Press 2008) 297.

stop the legislation. In addition, the very possibility of a point of order being raised can lead to a change of the legislative proposal to ensure consistency with UMRA requirements.[67] Finally, UMRA altered the balance of power within Congress. It shifted decisions on unfunded mandates towards the plenary, giving members and party leaders greater influence if they can command the necessary majority, while taking power away from the committees, which might be much more willing to adopt unfunded mandates, even if their adoption would be inefficient or would happen at the cost of federalism.[68]

One of the weaknesses of UMRA is that points of order can be overridden by a simple majority of the Representatives in the House, and since 2006 by 60 senators in the Senate.[69] Another oft-mentioned weak point is the Act's narrowness, because the rights it affords do not apply to obligations that states must fulfil in order to receive federal assistance.[70] In addition, UMRA contains a list of situations where its application is excluded, for example in case of bills that enforce the constitutional rights of individuals.[71] Indeed, an empirical study has shown that UMRA did not substantively decrease the number of unfunded mandates imposed by the federal government.[72] Arguably, the reasons included 'information asymmetries, the difficulties of monitoring political agents; and the self-promoting behaviour of mandate-dispensing officers'.[73] Specifically, disorganized voters blame local authorities instead of the state or federal government for local tax rises caused by unfunded mandates. This contrasts with interest groups, which are well organized and capable of influencing federal legislators, thus benefiting from the mandated services.[74]

The assessment of UMRA is therefore not entirely positive. Congress adopted a number of new bills requiring that more attention be paid to state and local interests during the federal legislative process.[75] Yet, UMRA remains the key accomplishment in this respect.

3.2 The National Conference of State Legislatures

Although UMRA rules were supposed to limit the enactment of unfunded mandates, legislation containing such mandates was still pursued. Consequently, this situation demanded a degree of continuing oversight.[76] The state legislatures' control over this type of mandates is primarily exercised by the NCSL. This section analyzes the

[67] ibid.

[68] E Garrett, 'Framework Legislation and Federalism' (2008) 83 Notre Dame L Rev 1495, 1521 ff.

[69] Anderson and Constantine, 'Unfunded mandates' (n 59) 19. See also Garrett, 'Framework Legislation and Federalism' (n 68) 1502.

[70] Garrett, 'Framework Legislation and Federalism' (n 68) 1499 ff.

[71] 2 USC 658a. The issue of narrowness of scrutiny is also pertinent in the case of the EWS. See F Fabbrini and K Granat, 'Yellow Card, but No Foul': The Role of the National Parliaments under the Subsidiarity Protocol and the Commission Proposal for an EU Regulation on the Right to Strike' (2013) 50 *CML Rev* 115.

[72] S Nicholson-Crotty, 'National Election Cycles and the Intermittent Political Safeguards of Federalism' (2008) 38 Publius: The Journal of Federalism 295, 304.

[73] EA Zelinsky, 'The Unsolved Problem of the Unfunded Mandate' (1997) 23 Ohio N U L Rev 741, 744.

[74] ibid.

[75] See examples of such acts in J Dinan, 'Strengthening the Political Safeguards of Federalism: The Fate of Recent Federalism Legislation in the U.S. Congress' (2004) 34 Publius: The Journal of Federalism 55, 61.

[76] See examples in Anderson and Constantine, 'Unfunded Mandates' (n 59) 9.

involvement of state legislatures in scrutinizing unfunded mandates in order to draw insights for the EU from the experience of US interparliamentary cooperation.

One of the ways for state governments to influence federal policy making is through intergovernmental lobbying during the federal legislative process.[77] When it comes to parliaments, this is performed by the NCSL. The NCSL dates back to 1975 and aims to 'improve the quality and effectiveness of state legislatures; promote policy innovation and communication among state legislatures and ensure state legislatures a strong, cohesive voice in the federal system'.[78]

It has a bipartisan character, serving both Republicans and Democrats, and supports both legislators and legislative staff. The Executive Committee is the governing body of the NCSL, and is composed of legislators and legislative staff, who broadly represent the leadership and top staff of state legislatures. Each state has a liaison officer at the NCSL so that state legislators and their staff receive the necessary information. The NCSL meets twice a year, in autumn at the Forum and in summer at the Legislative Summit. Those two meetings gather the Standing Committees, which are the main institutional feature of the NCSL and which are composed of state legislators and legislative staff appointed by state legislatures. They put forward policy directives and approve resolutions on state-federal issues, except for when the question at stake is internal to the states concerned. Besides committee meetings, the Forum and the Legislative Summit also feature a Business Meeting. During those meetings, the legislators vote by jurisdiction on a policy directive at the Forum and, once adopted at the Legislative Summit, it evolves into an official policy directive. Those directives then become a basis for the NCSL's office in Washington DC to lobby Congress, the White House, and federal agencies.

3.3 The Involvement of the NCSL in Unfunded Mandates

The NCSL opposes the imposition of unfunded federal mandates and the unjustified pre-emption of state authority, and strives to provide state legislatures with some flexibility for innovation and responsiveness to their citizens' needs.[79] For this purpose, the NCSL monitors mandates in federal laws and lists them in the Catalogue of Cost Shifts to states.[80] Prepared within the NCSL Standing Committee on Budgets and Revenue, the Catalogue traces the costs that the federal government imposes on the states by means of proposed and adopted legislation in which the CBO has identified a federal mandate. In doing so, the NCSL adopts a definition of unfunded mandates that is broader than that provided by UMRA, because it includes any federal act that leads to the spending of state or local funds. In contrast, an unfunded mandate under UMRA is more narrowly defined as 'any provision in legislation, statute, or regulation that would impose an enforceable duty upon state, local, or tribal governments or that would reduce or eliminate the amount of authorization of appropriations' that would have covered the costs of existing mandates.[81] This excludes, for example, costs arising from non-mandatory entitlement programmes, such as Medicaid, which the NCSL sees as unfunded mandates.[82] In addition, UMRA does not officially declare a measure

[77] J Dinan, 'Relations between State and National Governments' in DP Haider-Markel, *The Oxford Handbook of State and Local Government* (Oxford University Press 2014) 16.

[78] See http://www.ncsl.org/aboutus.aspx (last accessed 16 October 2016).

[79] See http://www.ncsl.org/ncsl-in-dc.aspx (last accessed 16 October 2016).

[80] See http://www.ncsl.org/print/standcomm/scbudg/catalog.pdf (last accessed 16 October 2016).

[81] 2 USC 658, Sec 421 (5).

[82] See the discussion at http://www.ncsl.org/blog/2016/03/01/at-what-cost-ncsl-president-testifies-on-unfunded-mandates.aspx (last accessed 16 October 2016).

an unfunded mandate if the total annual cost to the states does not exceed a certain minimum threshold.[83]

The NCSL encourages Congress to avoid imposing new federal unfunded mandates on state and local governments. Specifically, the NCSL points out to Congress those cases where legislation should not be adopted because it will place a burden on the states. Two examples of this are presented below.

The first example is the NCSL's reaction to the federal Prison Rape Elimination Act (PREA), which was adopted in 2003. This Act dealt with the sexual assault of prisoners by setting standards for physical space for prisoners and training staff in detention facilities. If these standards were not fulfilled, prisons would lose 5 per cent of their funding from any federal grant used for 'prison purposes', including from funds unrelated to the operation of prisons, such as for the reintegration of prisoners. The NCSL supported an amendment proposed by Senator Cornyn in September 2014, which sought to restrict the scope of the penalty—and thereby reduce the cost to the states—to funds directly related to the administration and operation of the prison.[84] The amendment was supported by the chairman of the Senate Judiciary Committee, Patrick Leahy, making it the Leahy/Cornyn amendment. The amendment passed the Senate Judiciary Committee by a vote of thirteen to five, but Congress adjourned before the amendment could be voted on in the House, so it was not adopted.

The second example concerned the draft Digital Accountability and Transparency Act (DATA Act), which was passed by the House of Representatives in 2012. It required that recipients of federal funds, including state and local governments, submit quarterly reports to a newly created Federal Accountability and Spending Transparency Board on how they had used the funds awarded. The NCSL opposed the reporting requirement on the grounds that no funds for establishing such a procedure were allocated to the states and thus the act presented an unfunded federal mandate.[85] While the bill did not become law because the Congress adjourned, a new bill incorporating the essence of the failed DATA Bill was enacted in 2014. This law did not contain any unfunded mandates under UMRA, which suggests that the NCSL's action had been successful.[86] In sum, the NCSL took a leading role in protecting states from costly mandates imposed by federal legislation.

4. Interparliamentary Cooperation in Switzerland

Although Swiss cantonal parliaments do not act as guardians of the subsidiarity principle to the same extent as NPs in the EU do, they did develop interparliamentary cooperation as a means of strengthening their influence on cantonal executives. Hence, their cooperation does not concern vertical federalism as in the cases of the EU and the US. In Switzerland, cantonal parliaments cooperate on matters of horizontal federalism—those arising between the cantons. The core of the cooperation between cantonal parliaments takes place regarding intercantonal treaties, which

[83] This was US$50 million in 1996, adjusted annually for inflation.

[84] See http://www.ncsl.org/documents/Statefed/Cornyn_PREA_penalty_amendment_Ltr.pdf (last accessed 16 October 2016).

[85] See http://www.ncsl.org/press-room/digital-accountability-and-transparency-act.aspx (last accessed 16 October 2016).

[86] Congressional Budget Office, Cost Estimate, Section 994 DATA Act, Summary, 5 December 2013.

are traditionally dominated by cantonal executives.[87] Cantonal parliaments may only approve such treaties without the possibility to amend them.[88] In this context, cooperation between the cantonal parliaments of north-western Switzerland, western Switzerland, and the Intercantonal Legislative Conference show the possibilities of overcoming the dominance of the cantonal executives. The ongoing discussion on the creation of a National Conference of Cantonal Parliaments also indicates that further development of intercantonal parliamentary cooperation is needed. The following sections elaborate on the operation of these interparliamentary conferences.

4.1 The Interparliamentary Conference of North-western Switzerland

The Interparliamentary Conference of north-western Switzerland (*Interparlamentarische Konferenz der Nordwestschweiz*—IPK) consists of the representatives of five cantonal parliaments (Bern, Solothurn, Basel-Stadt, Basel-Landschaft, and Aargau). Each cantonal parliament has six representatives: the president and vice-president of the parliament, the former president, and three permanent members of the cantonal parliament.[89] The permanent members are part of the working committee.[90] As a rule, the conference meets once a year in October.[91]

The conference aims to foster the exchange of information between the cantonal parliaments of north-western Switzerland, in particular on regional issues and projects prior to their discussion in cantonal parliaments.[92] The Secretariat of the conference, the functions of which are performed by the Chancellery of Basel-Landschaft canton, facilitates the smooth exchange of information between this conference and the conference of the cantonal governments of the same region.[93]

The topics that the conference has dealt with in recent years concerned specific policies, such as energy, health, the economic conditions in north-western Switzerland, but also the more general questions of federalism, such as fiscal transfers and cross-subsidization between different cantons.[94] In 2010, the conference discussed the purpose of intercantonal cooperation.[95] It underlined that cooperation between cantonal parliaments seeks to strike a balance between efficiency and legitimacy. This is important because greater cooperation can facilitate efficiency at the cost of diminished legitimacy given that cantons only send a delegation (thus ensuring a lower level of legitimacy because not all members of the legislature are represented) and that representation of the voters is indirect.[96]

[87] M Strebel, *Exekutivföderalismus in der Schweiz? Einbezug der Parlamente bei interkantonalen Vereinbarungen* (Nomos 2014) 88.

[88] ibid 116.

[89] See § 2 of the Agreement on the Interparliamentary Conference of Northwestern Switzerland of 7 December 1978 (*Vereinbarung über die Interparlamentarische Konferenz der Nordwestschweiz vom* 7 December 1978).

[90] ibid § 3. [91] ibid § 5. [92] ibid § 1. [93] ibid § 6.

[94] See the recent topics of the yearly meetings at https://www.baselland.ch/ipk.315649.0.html.

[95] See https://www.baselland.ch/politik-und-behorden/landrat-parlament/diverses/interparlamentarische-konferenz-der (last accessed 16 October 2016).

[96] *Protokoll der IPK-Informationstagung 2010 'Interkantonale Zusammenarbeit in der Nordwestschweiz-mehr als Informationsaustausch?'*, 29 October 2010, at 11.

4.2 Cooperation of Cantonal Parliaments of Western Switzerland

The second example of intercantonal cooperation in Switzerland concerns the six French-speaking cantons of western Switzerland (Fribourg, Vaud, Valais, Neuchâtel, Genève, and Jura). Their cooperation, commonly referred to as *CoParl* or *ParlVer*, began in 2002 in the form of the '*Convention des conventions*',[97] which had the objective of improving the involvement of cantonal parliaments in intercantonal treaties beyond simply accepting or rejecting the final agreement.[98] Owing to the lack of impact in practice,[99] the *Convention* was replaced in 2011 with *ParlVer*, which obliges cantonal governments to inform parliaments on foreign policy at least once a year.[100] The main reform, however, is the establishment of the Office for Interparliamentary Coordination (*Interparlamentarische Koordinationsstelle*).

This Office consists of one member and one deputy from each cantonal parliament.[101] The Office assists and coordinates the exchange of information concerning intercantonal and international treaties that affect the six cantons.[102] It also provides and updates the documents on intercantonal cooperation and intercantonal treaties to which the cantons of this Swiss region become parties.[103] The Office also acts as a point of contact with the governmental conference of western Swiss cantons and with the relevant regional conferences,[104] which keep the Office informed of any relevant treaties.[105]

Another reform of *ParlVer* was the establishment of a clear scope of cooperation, which was missing in the *Convention des conventions.*[106] If a treaty affects at least two cantons of western Switzerland in a manner that requires parliamentary approval, the parliaments call an interparliamentary commission (*interparliamentarische Kommission*) consisting of seven representatives of each of the cantons.[107] The commission issues an opinion on the treaty, which is forwarded to the executives for consideration.[108] Before signing the intercantonal treaty, the executives report back to the commission on the effect of the latter's opinion.[109] If necessary, the commission can reply with additional requests.[110] Finally, after the executives sign the treaty, the relevant parliaments receive it for approval. At this point, they are also provided with the opinion prepared by the commission.[111]

[97] *Vereinbarung vom 9. März 2001 zwischen den Kantonen Freiburg, Waadt, Wallis, Neuenburg, Genf und Jura über die Aushandlung, Ratifikation, Ausführung und Änderung der interkantonalen Verträge und der Vereinbarungen der Kantone mit dem Ausland.* The name *Convention des conventions* is hence a shorthand for the name of this agreement: convention on treaty-making powers of the cantons.

[98] Strebel, *Exekutivföderalismus in der Schweiz?* (n 87) 380. [99] ibid 381.

[100] See art 3(1) of *Vertrag vom 5. März 2010 über die Mitwirkung der Kantonsparlamente bei der Ausarbeitung, der Ratifizierung, dem Vollzug und der Änderung von interkantonalen Verträgen und von Verträgen der Kantone mit dem Ausland (Vertrag über die Mitwirkung der Parlamente, ParlVer).*

[101] ibid art 4.

[102] ibid art 5(1). The work of the Coordination office is regulated in detail in the Regulation of Interparliamentary Office of Coordination.

[103] See art 5(2) of *Vertrag vom 5. März 2010 über die Mitwirkung der Kantonsparlamente bei der Ausarbeitung, der Ratifizierung, dem Vollzug und der Änderung von interkantonalen Verträgen und von Verträgen der Kantone mit dem Ausland (Vertrag über die Mitwirkung der Parlamente, ParlVer).*

[104] ibid art 5(3). [105] ibid art 6.

[106] See http://www.fr.ch/cha/de/pub/mobile/aussenbeziehungen/gesetzliche_grundlagen_.htm (last accessed 16 October 2016).

[107] *Vertrag vom 5. März 2010 über die Mitwirkung der Kantonsparlamente bei der Ausarbeitung, der Ratifizierung, dem Vollzug und der Änderung von interkantonalen Verträgen und von Verträgen der Kantone mit dem Ausland (Vertrag über die Mitwirkung der Parlamente, ParlVer)* art 9(1).

[108] ibid arts 9(3) and 10(6). [109] ibid art 11(1). [110] ibid art 11(2).

[111] ibid art 13(2).

4.3 The Intercantonal Legislative Conference

Following the example of the interparliamentary commission of the cantons of western Switzerland, the German-speaking cantons established the Intercantonal Legislative Conference (*Interkantonale Legislativkonferenz*—ILK) in 2011. This conference similarly aims to enhance the influence of cantonal parliaments on intercantonal treaties and is convened only when necessary. This is the case when at least two cantons request a discussion of an intercantonal treaty or whenever such a treaty involves endowing an institution with parliamentary tasks concerning voting, legislative or oversight functions.[112] The ILK consists of three members from each cantonal parliament.[113] Unlike western Switzerland's interparliamentary commission, the ILK has an informal character.[114] The ILK aims to formulate a common position by consensus, which is then communicated to the relevant executives and cantonal parliaments.[115]

The first cantonal treaty for which the ILK was convened concerned the agreement on higher education (*Hochschulkonkordat*) concluded in July 2012.[116] The ILK submitted an opinion requesting from cantonal executives to keep the legislatures informed on higher education policy as well as asking for the creation of an intercantonal supervisory body.[117] The first request succeeded in a number of cantons, while the second one was implemented in a couple of intercantonal agreements.[118]

4.4 The National Conference of Cantonal Parliaments

In addition to the three mechanisms discussed above, there was a debate in the past about the establishment of a national conference of cantonal parliaments (*Nationale Konferenz der Kantonsparlamente*—NKK) that would have included representatives of all cantonal parliaments.[119] The proposal envisaged that the conference would design and evaluate intercantonal treaties as well as represent the interests of the cantons within the Swiss federation and within international organizations.[120] The proposal for the NKK has not been realized to date.[121] While fourteen cantonal parliaments supported its creation, a quorum of eighteen parliaments was required for it to be formally established.[122]

One of the key differences between the *ParlVer* on the one hand and the ILK and NKK on the other, is the extent to which cooperation is formalized. While the *ParlVer* is anchored in public law and provides for binding involvement of cantonal parliaments, the ILK and NKK represent less formal modes of cooperation with little concrete added value for the legislatures in question.[123]

[112] Strebel, *Exekutivföderalismus in der Schweiz?* (n 87) 394. [113] ibid.

[114] *Grosser Rat, Medienmitteilung*, 2 December 2011 http://www.be.ch/portal/de/index/medicenter/medienmitteilungen.meldungNeu.html/portal/de/meldungen/mm/2011/12/20111208_1743_interkantonale_legislativkonferenzilk-diekantonalenparlamenteset (last accessed 16 October 2016).

[115] Strebel, *Exekutivföderalismus in der Schweiz?* (n 87) 394.

[116] *Bericht über die Ergebnisse der Vernehmlassung zum Entwurf des Hochschulkonkordats sowie zum Entwurf der Zusammenarbeitsvereinbarung*, 25 March 2013 http://www.edudoc.ch/static/web/aktuell/vernehmlassung/hsk_bericht_d.pdf (last accessed 16 October 2016).

[117] Strebel, *Exekutivföderalismus in der Schweiz?* (n 87) 401. [118] ibid.

[119] *Medienmitteilung, Grosser Rat Kanton Basel*, 23 September 2006 http://www.bs.ch/news/2006-09-23-mm-32253.html (last accessed 16 October 2016).

[120] *Mitteilungsblatt der Schweizerischen Gesellschaft für Parlamentsfragen* (2006) Vol 9, No 2, 19.

[121] D Schwarz, R Steiner, and J Fivaz, *Mitwirkungsmöglichkeiten des Urner Landrats* (Universität Bern Kompetenzzentrum für Public Management 2015) V.

[122] Strebel, *Exekutivföderalismus in der Schweiz?* (n 87) 403 ff.

[123] Schwarz, Steiner, and Fivaz, 'Mitwirkungsmöglichkeiten des Urner Landrats' (n 121) V.

In sum, in Switzerland, the participation of cantons in federal decision-making is safeguarded through the Council of States, double majority referendums, legislative initiative, and the possibility of initiating a referendum against a federal law. Still, interparliamentary cooperation between cantonal parliaments developed horizontally, namely with regard to intercantonal treaties. The rationale for the participation of legislatures is therefore different than in the EU and the US, because it does not concern vertical relations between the cantons and the federal government. Instead, it developed because of the dominance of cantonal executives in intercantonal treaty making. A parallel between the three polities studied in this chapter is thus that legislatures and their mutual cooperation represent useful institutional avenues for addressing issues related to federalism.

5. Insights for National Parliaments of the EU Member States

In order to draw lessons for the EU from the US and Swiss federal systems, the following section deals with: the issue of the plurality of forums of interparliamentary cooperation; the involvement of the EP, the US Congress, and the Swiss Parliament in such forums; the representation of the interests of NPs in the EU; and the use of personal liaisons between different institutions.

5.1 Plurality of Forums

While the sole forum for cooperation between state legislatures in the US is the NCSL, there are three interparliamentary conferences in the EU: one general (COSAC) and two specialized ones (CFSP/CSDP conference and 'Article 13 Conference' on economic governance).[124] Beyond unfunded mandates, the NCSL tackles a wide variety of issues ranging from education, health, and infrastructure to budgetary matters—without having any specialized sectoral bodies. COSAC could hence be seen as the EU's counterpart of the NCSL, because it discusses both specific policies, such as energy and trade, and more general issues, such as EU democratic legitimacy with a focus on the role of NPs in ensuring it. Nevertheless, the Lisbon Treaty enables the creation of other specialized interparliamentary conferences, whose launch involved disagreements related to their rules of procedure and membership.[125]

To some extent, Switzerland resembles the EU with respect to the number of interparliamentary forums, which however mostly specialize in the same subject matter—intercantonal treaties—and are spread regionally. One example of EU interparliamentary cooperation that has been constituted similarly to the Swiss model refers to the NPs of the Visegrád Group (Poland, the Czech Republic, Slovakia, and Hungary), which have since 2003 met once a year to discuss both EU policies and procedural aspects of their scrutiny, such as subsidiarity control.[126] They convene in different constellations, usually gathering the presidents of these parliaments or the

[124] See chapter by Ian Cooper in this volume.

[125] I Cooper, 'The Politicization of Interparliamentary Relations in the EU: Constructing and Contesting the "Article 13 Conference" on Economic Governance' (2016) 14 Comparative European Politics 196.

[126] See the overview of their mission and activities at http://oide.sejm.gov.pl/oide/en/index.php?option=com_content&view=article&id=14731&Itemid=754 (last accessed 16 October 2016).

chairpersons of their European affairs or sectoral committees. However, this interparliamentary dialogue remains on the periphery of the EU political process, enjoying only local significance and visibility. Hence, the existence of different types of interparliamentary forums seems to diminish the political visibility of NPs, because the lack of a single overarching parliamentary forum disperses the attention given to their pronouncements.

5.2 Cooperation with the European Parliament

Arguably, the role of NPs in the EU is best captured by the model of a 'Euro-national parliamentary system', which demands coordination between different institutional actors—for example, between the EP and NPs.[127] Under the EWS, NPs participate in a dialogue with the Commission, while in interparliamentary conferences, they involve members of the EP (MEPs). In contrast, the NCSL does not include members of Congress, which, together with the Administration, is the main interlocutor of the NCSL.[128] This is also not the case with Switzerland, because interparliamentary conferences there focus on intercantonal rather than canton-federation matters.

Cooperation between the EP and NPs has in the past led to conflicts, because the EP preferred the creation of weak conferences, where it was hard to take collective decisions.[129] Cooperation within the NCSL has a more vertical character, involving state legislators and legislative staff, which is visible in its committee structure. Moreover, while some exchange with members of Congress and the federal government takes place during two major meetings (the Forum and the Legislative Summit), these officials are not members of the NCSL.

Hence, organizing EU interparliamentary cooperation without the EP and without creating a new conference merits consideration. If, for example, the CFSP/CSDP and Article 13 conferences followed the US model, pertinent issues could be discussed in committees and later in plenary sessions with MEPs. Such a system could shield national parliamentarians from possible power struggles with the EP. However, the downside of the exclusion of MEPs would be the limitation of access to EU information directly from the EP as well as further antagonism between MPs and MEPs.

5.3 Aggregation of Interests

The NCSL seems to aggregate various US state interests and to speak with one voice on behalf of states. In Switzerland, although cooperation has a regional character, which does not necessarily mean that the cantonal parliaments are univocal, its aim is similarly to search for consensus and coordination in the oversight over cantonal executives in intercantonal treaty making. In the EU's EWS, however, each national parliament may prepare its own reasoned opinion, which often reflects the specific political, social, or geographical concerns of the given parliament. Moreover, NPs were not unanimous on the question of the role of COSAC in coordinating the submission of reasoned opinions to the Commission, and COSAC itself did not see that as a priority.

[127] See C Fasone and N Lupo, 'Interparliamentary Cooperation in the Framework of Euro-national Parliamentary System' in N Lupo and C Fasone (eds), *Interparliamentary Cooperation in the Composite European Constitution* (Hart Publishing 2016) 349.

[128] The representatives of the government, academia, and business may also participate in the Forum and Legislative Summit http://www.ncsl.org/ncsl-in-dc/standing-committees/budgets-and-revenue/budgets-and-revenue-committee-members.aspx (last accessed 16 October 2016).

[129] Cooper, 'The Politicization of Interparliamentary Relations in the EU' (n 125) 198.

Accordingly, the collection of reasoned opinions by COSAC for the purpose of the EWS stopped with the entry into force of the Lisbon Treaty.[130]

The difference between the roles of the NCSL, the Swiss and EU interparliamentary conferences seems to be related to the fact that in their reasoned opinions, or opinions under 'the political dialogue', NPs are much more motivated by the idiosyncratic interests of the given Member State. In comparison, the NCSL coordinates the position of state legislatures on issues that concern all states, at least when it comes to unfunded mandates, given that the lack of federal funding affects them all equally. Similarly, the regional character of Swiss interparliamentary forums might reduce the divergences between cantonal interests and the unwillingness to create a national conference. These insights show one of the possible obstacles for interparliamentary cooperation in the EU.

5.4 Parliamentary Liaison Officers

The engagement of liaison officers enables the exchange of information between different participants in interparliamentary cooperation. In the US, staff members of the NCSL are assigned to a specific state and ensure communication between the NCSL and state legislatures.[131] In Switzerland, one of the functions of the administrative bodies of the conferences (eg the IPK Secretariat or the Office for Interparliamentary Coordination) is to communicate with cantonal executives or the conference of cantonal executives. In the EU, national parliamentary representatives in Brussels (NPRs) have become an important link between NPs and EU institutions.[132] The difference lies in the forums that these liaison officers link: in the US, it is the conference and state legislatures; in the EU, the link is between the EP and NPs; and in Switzerland, it is between the conferences and cantonal governments. These differences stem from the different tasks of each of these interparliamentary conferences.

Establishing a liaison between a national parliament and the COSAC Secretariat or any other EU interparliamentary conference would be superfluous, because members of NPs constitute the bulk of members of these forums. In addition, NPRs already transmit information on EU affairs from and to NPs. No extra liaison seems necessary to ensure ongoing exchange with interparliamentary conferences. In contrast, the concept of a network of NPRs sharing information from Brussels might be useful for the US, since only some state legislatures have an office in Washington DC.[133] To some extent, the DC Office of the NCSL, as well as the offices and secretariats of the Swiss interparliamentary conferences, might be seen as fulfilling such a role on behalf of state and cantonal legislatures collectively.

[130] 14th Bi-annual Report on EU Practices and Procedures (October 2010), 30. See also Conclusions of the XLIII COSAC, Madrid, 31 May–1 June 2010.

[131] See liaisons by state at http://www.ncsl.org/aboutus/ncslservice/ncsl-state-liaisons-map.aspx (last accessed 16 October 2016).

[132] See their positive role in I Cooper, 'A Yellow Card for the Striker: How National Parliaments Defeated EU Strikes Regulation' (2015) 22 JEPP 1406; and A-L Högenauer and C Neuhold, 'National Parliaments After Lisbon: Administrations on the Rise?' (2015) 38 WEP 335.

[133] Dinan, 'Relations Between State and National Governments' (n 77) 16.

6. Conclusion

The objective of this chapter was to draw insights from the American and Swiss practices for the functions that parliaments perform at non-central level in federal systems. Wechsler originally described the political safeguards of federalism in the US as being anchored in the role of states in determining the composition of federal institutions. The NCSL developed as an informal political safeguard of federalism with an active role in the control of unfunded mandates as an important aspect of fiscal federalism. On the other side of the Atlantic, the Swiss constitutional system provides for a number of in-built political safeguards of federalism: the Council of States, whose members are directly elected in the cantons; 'double majority' referendums; legislative initiative of the cantons; and the possibility to initiate a referendum against a federal law.

However, cantonal parliaments created additional forms of interparliamentary cooperation within the horizontal dimension of federalism in form of regional conferences in order to strengthen their powers in intercantonal treaty making, which is usually controlled by cantonal executives. In the case of the EU, the subsidiarity principle and its watchdogs, NPs, became a formal political safeguard of federalism under the Lisbon Treaty. Therefore, all of these polities' legislatures assumed roles in developing interparliamentary cooperation, with variations that depended on the problems associated with federalism in each case.

Although state and cantonal legislatures and NPs within the EU deal with different issues of federalism, this chapter has shown that they have adopted a resilient approach towards the federal level, be it as watchdogs of the subsidiarity principle, scrutinizers of federal legislation that places a financial burden on the states, or towards cantonal executives in order to counterbalance the power of governments in the making of intercantonal treaties.

This chapter indicates several conclusions. When it comes to the aggregation of legislatures' interests, NPs in the EU may clearly follow the solutions developed by their US and Swiss counterparts. In the case of liaisons between interparliamentary conferences and parliaments, the structural and institutional dissimilarities between the Swiss, American, and EU conferences discourage the application of solutions adopted in Switzerland and the US for the EU, while the EU's NPRs could be a useful model for the NCSL. With regard to the plurality of forums and cooperation with the EP, following the US example in the EU would bring some benefits and some disadvantages. On the one hand, parliamentary cooperation would benefit from increased visibility and lack of conflicts between the EP and NPs. On the other hand, it could lead to a reduction of policy-specific expertise among EU interparliamentary forums, while the absence of MEPs could cut NPs off from an important source of information and support in the EU legislative process. Finally, the effectiveness and impact of interparliamentary cooperation in federal systems remains an issue for further research.

15

The Many Facets of Parliamentary Involvement and Interaction in EU External Relations

A Multilevel Tale

*Kolja Raube and Jan Wouters**

'Let us not be deluded into believing that the strictly institutional limitations on its powers can prevent a Parliament such as ours from speaking out at all times, and in every field of Community action, with the political authority conferred on it by its election.'[1]

Simone Veil, President of the European Parliament

1. Introduction

The Treaty of Lisbon has reinforced the role of the European Parliament (EP), strengthening both the supranational and parliamentary elements of the European Union (EU or Union). At the same time, the EU's Common Foreign and Security Policy (CFSP) and the Common Security and Defence Policy (CSDP) remain of a predominantly intergovernmental nature[2]—dominated by the European Council, the Council, and national governments, and scrutinized by national parliaments (NPs). Against this background, the question arises whether the post-Lisbon environment has seen a stronger role for parliaments in EU external action emerging. Have parliaments become more resilient actors in EU external affairs? Or have parliaments become resigned, unable to exercise their functions in this area? Last but not least, how does stronger individual and collective parliamentary involvement at the national level impact action taken at the EU level and vice versa? When tackling these questions, we cannot deal with parliamentary resilience or resignation in general. Rather, we need to

* The authors are grateful to Diane Fromage and Davor Jančić for valuable comments on an earlier version of this chapter, which was presented at the London School of Economics and Political Science in April 2015. The authors are also thankful for the feedback received at conferences, seminars, and summer schools at the University of Amsterdam (May 2015), the PADEMIA conference in Brussels (June 2015), and LUISS Guido Carli School of Government (July 2015). Research for this chapter has received financial support from the European Commission in the framework of the Jean Monnet Network PACO ('Interparliamentary Cooperation in the EU External Action—Parliamentary Scrutiny and Diplomacy in the EU and Beyond').

[1] Simone Veil, President of the European Parliament, Speech at the first session of the EP elected by direct universal suffrage, 18 September 1979.

[2] Sergio Fabbrini, *Which European Union? The European Union after the Crisis* (Cambridge University Press 2015) 41 ff.

examine the EP and NPs as distinct yet interrelated actors. They control and scrutinize EU external action at different levels and their actions may mutually reinforce each other. We build upon the notion of a 'multilevel parliamentary field',[3] which conceptualizes parliamentary action, interaction, and cooperation in EU multilevel governance.

Such an approach is optimal because EU external action is fragmented and made up of a variety of policy fields (CFSP, trade policy, development cooperation, humanitarian aid, etc.). Each of these fields is subject to a distinct set of institutional arrangements, decision-making modes and instruments. We take issue with the argument that EU foreign policy is wholly intergovernmental[4] and that it can only be understood by zooming in on CFSP/CSDP. For this reason, this chapter takes a broader perspective and aims to identify potential variations of parliamentary involvement, not only in CFSP, but also in other areas of EU external action, such as trade policy and human rights. We have chosen these areas so as to provide a sample of politics encompassing those that are of an intergovernmental (CFSP/CSDP), exclusive (trade) and transversal (human rights) nature.

The chapter proceeds as follows. It first outlines the idea of a multilevel parliamentary field, which encompasses parliamentary action, interaction, and cooperation. Subsequently, we show the various forms of involvement of the EP and NPs as 'constitutive units' of this field[5] in three different segments of EU external action: CFSP/CSDP, trade policy, and human rights. Following the approach by Born and Hänggi,[6] we assess the 'abilities' (resources) and 'attitude' (actions) of the EP and NPs in each policy field. Furthermore, we assess whether interparliamentary interactions and cooperation have been established in the multilevel field. The aim is to identify the many facets of parliamentary involvement and interaction in EU external action and draw conclusions on whether parliaments can be characterized as resilient or resigned in the respective policy domains.

2. Parliaments in the Multilevel Parliamentary Field of EU External Relations: Resilient or Resigned Actors?

Introduced by Crum and Fossum, the concept of a *'multi-level parliamentary field'* builds on Di Maggio and Powell[7] and recalls what sociologists characterize as an 'organizational field', which encompasses 'those institutions that, in the aggregate, constitute a recognized area of institutional life, with some element of connectedness and structural equivalence'.[8] Crum and Fossum submit that 'the EU's Multilevel Parliamentary Field is not foremost a (professional) sector; what keeps its components together is a shared function and the role perception that comes with it: that of representing people's interests in EU decision-making'.[9] Hence, they focus on the interaction between national parliamentarians and the EP. Their overarching idea is that the web of relations between parliamentarians in the multilevel EU can be seen as an emerging 'parliamentary field'. In their view, a 'parliamentary field' can be observed and explained by analyzing the 'constitutive units'[10] as well as 'interparliamentary interactions'[11] that develop within it.

Until recently, the role of parliaments in the external relations of the Union was understudied. Scholars were primarily interested in the intergovernmental and

[3] Ben Crum and John E Fossum, 'The Multilevel Parliamentary Field: A Framework for Theorizing Representative Democracy in the EU' (2009) 1 Eur Pol Sci Rev 249.

[4] Fabbrini (n 2) 41 ff. [5] Crum and Fossum (n 3) 263.

[6] ibid. See also Ariella Huff, 'Executive Privilege Reaffirmed? Parliamentary Scrutiny of the CFSP and CSDP' (2015) 38 West European Politics 396.

[7] Paul J DiMaggio and Walter W Powell, 'The Iron Cage Revisited: Institutional Isomorphism and Collective Rationality in Organizational Fields' (1983) 48 Am Sociolog Rev 147.

[8] Crum and Fossum (n 3) 261. [9] ibid 261. [10] ibid 262. [11] ibid 263.

transgovernmental nature of this policy domain and in the related questions of the EU's competences, institutional set-up, and international representation.[12] A 'parliamentary turn' and the potential 'parliamentarisation' of EU external relations have only begun being explored after the entry into force of the Treaty of Lisbon.[13]

Traditionally, foreign policy is seen as a domain reserved for executives rather than legislatures. Especially war powers and treaty-making powers are historically a prerogative of the executive and beyond the reach of popular sovereignty.[14] From this perspective, the role of parliaments stands in sharp contrast to the functions that constitutions otherwise assign to parliaments in domestic policy making regarding control over the executive and legislative power. It is often argued that such 'deficits' of parliamentary involvement in foreign policy are justified by the need for discretion and secrecy during international negotiations and diplomacy, as well as the need for an efficient implementation of foreign policy decisions.[15] In parallel and to varying degrees, parliaments have been able to claim, receive, and exercise an appropriate role with regard to foreign policy, be it by approving military budgets and international agreements or by holding governments accountable for their external action. In fact, not all parliaments have the same 'limited' role to play in foreign policy. The US Congress is often viewed as an example of how the executive can be held to account for its international action, which it does by means of 'congressional-executive agreements'.[16] However, in reality, the fact that the US President is Commander-in-Chief, and concludes so-called 'presidential agreements', undermines the influence of the US Congress to control war and treaty powers of the executive.[17] The US hence serves as a critical reminder of the difference between the 'resources', 'abilities', and the actual exercise of power by parliaments. Applying such a perspective to the EU, the question emerges as to whether the provisions of national constitutions and EU Treaties foresee the involvement of parliaments in international relations and whether empirical realities suggest a limited ('resigned') or rather expanded ('resilient') role for parliaments in this arena.

In the EU, the involvement of the EP and NPs varies from policy field to policy field. Before the Treaty of Lisbon, the dominance of the executive in EU external relations was emphatic, regardless of whether this referred to policies in the first (supranational) pillar or the second (intergovernmental) pillar.[18] Since its entry into force, the

[12] Marise Cremona, 'The European Union as a Global Actor: Roles, Models and Identity' (2005) 41 CML Rev 553; Ian Manners, 'Normative Power Europe: Contradiction in Terms?' (2002) 40 JCMS 235; Michael E Smith, *Europe's Foreign and Security Policy: The Institutionalization of Cooperation* (Cambridge University Press 2003); Helen Wallace and Christine Reh, 'An Institutional Anatomy and Five Policy Modes' in Helen Wallace, William Wallace, and Mark Pollack (eds), *Policy-making in the European Union* (7th edn, Oxford University Press 2014).

[13] Anna Herranz-Surralés, 'The EU's Multilevel Parliamentary (Battle)Field: Explaining Interparliamentary Cooperation and Conflict in the Area of Foreign and Security Policy' (2014) 37 West European Politics 957; Davor Jančić, 'World Diplomacy of the European Parliament' (2016) 11 *The Hague Journal of Diplomacy* 121; Davor Jančić, 'Globalizing Representative Democracy: The Emergence of Multilayered International Parliamentalism' (2015) 38 Hastings Int'l & Comp L Rev 197; Kolja Raube, 'Democratic Accountability and EU Diplomacy: The EEAS and the Role of the European Parliament' in Jozef Bátora and David Spence (eds), *The European External Action Service: European Diplomacy Post Westphalia* (Palgrave Macmillan 2015); Kolja Raube, 'Parliamentarisation Approaches: Parliamentary Control in EU Foreign Policy' in Marciej Wilga and IP Karolewski (eds), *New Approaches to EU Foreign Policy* (Routledge 2014); Kolja Raube, 'The European External Action Service and the European Parliament' (2012) 7 *The Hague Journal of Diplomacy* 65; Guri Rosén, 'EU Confidential: The European Parliament's Involvement in EU Security and Defence Policy' (2015) 53 JCMS 383; Robert Schütze, *Foreign Affairs and the European Constitution: Selected Essays* (Cambridge University Press 2014); Wolfgang Wagner, *Die demokratische Kontrolle internationalisierter Sicherheitspolitik* (Nomos 2015).

[14] Schütze (n 13) 359.

[15] Stephan Keukeleire and Tom Delreux, *The Foreign Policy of the European Union* (2nd edn, Palgrave Macmillan 2014).

[16] Schütze (n 13) 403. [17] ibid 403.

[18] Stephan Stetter, 'Cross-pillar Politics: Functional Unity and Institutional Fragmentation of EU Foreign Policies' (2004) 11 JEPP 720.

EU has been made up of different 'unions', led by different actors acting in accordance with different decision-making procedures.[19] Even within particular policy areas of EU external relations, decision-making procedures vary across specific sub-areas.[20] These differentiated settings for EU action in foreign affairs have an impact on the way parliaments exercise their legislative and control functions.

As *'constitutive units'* of the multilevel parliamentary field, the EP and NPs differ in terms of their *'ability'* (resources and competences) to exercise core parliamentary functions—those of adopting legislation and holding the executive accountable at the EU and national levels.[21] Such abilities refer to both formal and informal parliamentary powers: while parliaments may gain these powers thanks to interest-driven or norm-driven institutional and constitutional changes, they may also evolve.[22] Furthermore, the *attitude* (actions) of specific parliaments in particular policy fields may also vary.[23] For example, attitude is well illustrated with the example of 'incomplete' treaty-making, whereby parliaments seek to expand their powers where treaties have been unspecific about them or where they otherwise leave room for this kind of parliamentary empowerment.[24] In particular, the EP tries to increase its influence on EU policies through informal rule-making, which gradually evolves into formal rules.[25] However, while informal and formal changes in the role of the EP may explain its 'ability' and 'attitude' in EU external relations,[26] they may not entirely explain why NPs are enabled to take action in the Union's external relations. To do so, one has to take into account the institutional changes at the level of the Member States, often linked to so-called 'external shocks' and 'critical junctures', such as the 9/11 terrorist attacks in 2001 or the Iraq War in 2003. Furthermore, the relationship between national governments and their parliaments, and the individual behaviour of NPs, may only be explained if one also considers the normative quest for legitimate action in international relations as well as the politicization and salience of EU policy issues in the public realm of the Member States. In any event, the 'abilities' and 'attitudes' of parliamentary actors can show whether they have become 'resilient' or 'resigned' after the Lisbon Treaty.

Apart from analyzing constitutive units, we also assess *interparliamentary interactions*. These include the formal and informal settings of interparliamentary exchanges,[27] such as interparliamentary cooperation forums dealing with EU external relations that were established after the entry into force of the Treaty of Lisbon.[28] That said, initial studies have identified the interparliamentary conference (IPC) in CFSP/CSDP as an 'interparliamentary battlefield' more than as a forum for mutually understood roles and norms.[29] While such interparliamentary cooperation shows the resilience of

[19] Fabbrini (n 2); Benjamin Leruth and Christopher Lord, 'Differentiated Integration in the European Union: A Concept, a Process, a System or a Theory?' (2015) 22 JEPP 754.

[20] Raube, 'Democratic Accountability' (n 13) 147 ff.

[21] Crum and Fossum (n 3) 264.

[22] Raube, 'Parliamentarisation Approaches' (n 13) 129; Rosén (n 13) 394.

[23] Huff (n 6) 398; Hans Born and Heiner Hänggi, 'Governing the Use of Force under International Auspices: Deficits in Parliamentary Accountability' in *SIPRI Yearbook: Armaments, Disarmament and International Security* (Oxford University Press 2005).

[24] Walter Mattli and Alec Stone Sweet, 'Regional Integration and the Evolution of the European Polity: On the Fiftieth Anniversary of the Journal of Common Market Studies' (2013) 50(S1) JCMS 1; Raube, 'Parliamentarisation Approaches' (n 13).

[25] Berthold Rittberger, 'The Creation and Empowerment of the European Parliament' (2003) 41 JCMS 203.

[26] Huff (n 6) 397.

[27] Crum and Fossum (n 3) 262.

[28] See more broadly on EU interparliamentary cooperation in the chapter by Ian Cooper in this volume.

[29] Herranz-Surrallés (n 13) 10 ff.

parliaments after Lisbon, the lack of coordination within and among them points to their resignation.

Finally, we examine the overarching *field dynamics*, such as the 'Europeanisation' of the mechanisms available to parliaments for the exercise of their core functions.[30] This can yield valuable insights not only into the reasons why parliaments should be seen as either resilient or resigned actors across levels and policy fields, but also into the consequences that this has for the overall democratic accountability of EU external relations.

3. Parliamentary Resources and Action

In this section, we analyze 'ability' (resources) and 'attitude' (action) at various parliamentary levels and across a variety of different policy fields of EU external relations. These two elements relate to the abovementioned core functions of parliaments, which are dissected below in turn with respect to CFSP/CSDP, trade policy, and human rights.

3.1 Common Foreign and Security Policy/Common Security and Defence Policy

Studies on CFSP/CSDP have highlighted the intergovernmental nature of the decision-making arrangements in this field—notably unanimity voting and the limited roles of the Commission, the Court of Justice, and the EP—as the key elements of the 'specific' nature of CFSP/CSDP.[31] The literature shows that the EP has 'gained weight' after the Treaty of Lisbon, especially with the establishment of the European External Action Service (EEAS) and accountability of the High Representative of the Union for Foreign Affairs and Security Policy (HR/VP) and EEAS personnel.[32] Whereas the double democratic deficit in the area of CFSP/CSDP is hardly going to be overcome by such developments,[33] the EP's and NPs' abilities and attitudes point to new developments.

3.1.1 European Parliament: Claiming Access to Intergovernmental 'Territory'

As shown elsewhere, the making of the EEAS in the aftermath of the Treaty of Lisbon has enabled the EP to enhance its relationship with the HR and to widen its sphere of influence in CFSP/CSDP.[34] Before Lisbon, the role of the EP remained very limited in this field. It was to be informed on CFSP issues by the rotating Presidency. Even after Lisbon, the EP's role in CFSP/CSDP remains rather limited, although it can now hold

[30] Crum and Fossum (n 3) 265.

[31] Alan Dashwood, 'Mixity in the Era of the Treaty of Lisbon' in Christophe Hillion and Panos Koutrakos (eds), *Mixed Agreements Revisited: The EU and its Member States in the World* (Hart Publishing 2010).

[32] Raube, 'EEAS and EP' (n 13) 75.

[33] Born and Hänggi (n 23); Dirk Peters and Wolfgang Wagner, 'Between Military Efficiency and Democratic Legitimacy: Mapping Parliamentary War Powers in Contemporary Democracies, 1989–2004' (2010) 64 Parl Aff 175; Wagner, *Kontrolle internationalisierter Sicherheitspolitik* (n 13); Wolfgang Wagner, 'The Democratic Control of Military Power Europe' (2006) 13 JEPP 200.

[34] Raube, 'EEAS and EP' (n 13); Elisabeth Wisniewski, 'The Influence of the European Parliament on the European External Action Service' (2013) 18 EFA Rev 81.

the HR indirectly accountable through the latter's function as Vice President (VP) of the Commission. Article 36 of the Treaty on European Union (TEU) only guarantees that the HR informs the EP on all matters of CFSP/CSDP and that the EP's views thereon must be taken into account. Furthermore, Article 36 foresees that 'twice a year [the European Parliament] shall hold a debate on progress in implementing the common foreign and security policy, including the common security and defence policy'.[35]

However, during the negotiations on the establishment of the EEAS, the EP was able to expand its role by: (a) invoking its veto power over the budget of the EEAS and the latter's future institutional changes; (b) requiring the HR to be replaced by Commissioners or Council members if she could not appear in the EP; (c) demanding that nominees for EU ambassadorial posts appear in the EP Committee for Foreign Affairs (AFET) before taking up their posts; and (d) accessing classified CSDP documents beyond the scope of the 2002 Interinstitutional Agreement.[36] Accordingly, in the aftermath of the Lisbon Treaty, the HR/VP is replaced by Commission or Council members when the former cannot be present in the EP. Future heads of EU Delegations are interviewed *in camera*. These informal changes correspond with the active role of the AFET Committee and of its Sub-committees on Security and Defence (SEDE) and on Human Rights (DROI). For example, the AFET Committee chairperson takes part in informal, so-called 'Gymnich' meetings of EU foreign ministers, receiving first-hand information on CFSP/CSDP activities and agenda setting. This Committee has also developed resources and expertise to complement EU action in CFSP/CSDP. This is exemplified not only by the large number of reports and resolutions produced by the AFET Committee in the shadow of intergovernmental decision-making, but also by the increasing number of hearings organized with officials from the CSDP decision-making machinery and with external experts in this field.

Overall, while the EP's role in CFSP/CSDP is formally limited and falls short of enabling it to control and sanction the Council, this institution has gained considerable informal powers to scrutinize this policy area. This 'attitude' is motivated by the EP's self-assertive attempt to 'normalise' CFSP/CSDP—that is, for the EP to acquire an 'eye-level' position towards the Council, thus gradually overcoming the 'special' status of CFSP/CSDP.

3.1.2 National Parliaments: Variable Exercise of Parliamentary Functions in an Intergovernmental Area

In the context of CFSP/CSDP, many NPs are said to have hardly any *ex ante* control functions, which means that they cannot influence the executive before CFSP/CSDP decisions are taken in the Policy and Security Committee (PSC) and the Council. Yet, some Member States provide for parliamentary involvement regarding international military interventions and require parliamentary consent before troops may be committed. However, in Member States such as Belgium, Greece, Poland, Portugal, Slovenia, and the United Kingdom, there is no formal control over international military missions.[37] Only a few parliaments have *ex ante* decision-making powers and can theoretically control whether troops are sent on CSDP missions or not (eg Austria,

[35] See also Raube, 'EEAS and EP' (n 13) 68–69; Jančić, 'World Diplomacy of the European Parliament' (n 13).

[36] Raube, 'EEAS and EP' (n 13) 70.

[37] Wagner, *Kontrolle internationalisierter Sicherheitspolitik* (n 13) 124.

Germany, Finland, Ireland, Lithuania, and Sweden). When, however, *ex ante* powers exist, parliamentary majorities generally back government decisions made in the Council of the EU.[38]

Wagner and Peters have shown that the influence of NPs is far from static and that both in the context of accessions to NATO and after the 2003 Iraq War, a number of EU Member States have altered their parliaments' rights of control over international military missions.[39] After the Iraq War, Spain and France enhanced parliamentary powers: in both cases, under certain circumstances, the executive can no longer decide on international military missions on its own and needs the approval of parliament.[40] Conversely, some other Member States—like Bulgaria, Hungary, Slovakia, and the Czech Republic—reduced the role of their NPs in the wake of their accession to NATO.[41] Wagner speaks of a 'trend towards a de-parliamentarisation' in EU external affairs in Central and Eastern European democracies.[42]

However, the formal 'inability' and theoretical disengagement of parliaments need not always match the actual 'attitude' of parliaments in practice. Parliaments may have a say on the legitimization of international missions, thus exercising parliamentary functions, even though they may not formally be in charge. Therefore, while a de-parliamentarization may suggest a 'resignation' of NPs, they may factually be more resilient than expected. A good example thereof is the seemingly growing tendency of governments asking their parliaments to give their consent to military missions, even where they are not formally obliged to do so. For instance, the House of Commons voted against a possible UK intervention in Syria in 2013 after being asked by the government authorize the intervention. After the vote, Prime Minister David Cameron stated: 'I strongly believe in the need for a tough response to the use of chemical weapons, but I also believe in respecting the will of this House of Commons … the British parliament, reflecting the views of the British people, does not want to see British military action. I get that, and the government will act accordingly'.[43]

Despite such informal enabling of parliaments and their arguable 'resilience', most CSDP missions are in fact civilian missions and they do not involve the deployment of military but rather of administrative and police capacities.[44] Accordingly, parliamentary consent may often not be necessary. At the same time, NPs remain important actors when it comes to approving defence and development cooperation budgets and holding the executive accountable.

Therefore, the roles of NPs vary from one national context to another and must be assessed against the background of national institutional changes, critical junctures, and external shocks. It can be observed that governments often seek to bolster and legitimize their international action through parliamentary votes, especially in the domain of security policy. This gives extra *de facto* powers to NPs in those cases where formal powers did not exist in the first place. While the governments' ultimate *ratio* for soliciting parliamentary backing in these circumstances requires further research, we observe

[38] Wagner, 'Democratic Control of Military' (n 33).

[39] Wagner, *Kontrolle internationalisierter Sicherheitspolitik* (n 13); Peters and Wagner (n 33).

[40] Wagner, *Kontrolle internationalisierter Sicherheitspolitik* (n 13) 124.

[41] Peters and Wagner (n 33); Wagner, *Kontrolle internationalisierter Sicherheitspolitik* (n 13) 121.

[42] Wagner, *Kontrolle internationalisierter Sicherheitspolitik* (n 13) 186.

[43] 'Blow to Cameron's Authority as MPs Rule Out British Assault on Syria' *Guardian*, 30 August 2013 http://www.theguardian.com/politics/2013/aug/30/cameron-mps-syria (last accessed 4 January 2017).

[44] Stephan Keukeleire and Kolja Raube, 'Common Security and Defence Policy: Development, Added Value, and Challenges' in Federiga Bindi (ed), *The Foreign Policy of the European Union: Assessing Europe's Role in the World* (2nd edn, Brookings Institution Press 2012) 62–84, 76.

that NPs' limited 'ability' does not always match the actual dynamics and influence on the ground: NPs do in such circumstances exercise greater powers than originally foreseen.

3.1.3 Interparliamentary Cooperation: From Competition and Coexistence to Mutual Parliamentary Exchanges

Article 10 of Protocol No 1 annexed to the Treaty of Lisbon on the role of NPs in the European Union introduces interparliamentary cooperation in the field of CFSP/CSDP in the form of a 'Conference of Parliamentary Committees for Union Affairs' to nurture 'the exchange of information and best practice between NPs and the EP, including their special committees'. The Protocol was adopted not only to strengthen the role of NPs in the EU, but also to make up for the dissolution of the Western European Union (WEU) Assembly in June 2011. Indeed, the statement of the WEU Member States dismantling the WEU provides that this Protocol 'may provide a basis' for continuing the work of the WEU Assembly.

The Treaty of Lisbon and the dissolution of the WEU Assembly put parliaments in a difficult situation of having to reconcile often competing interests and decide the organization and goals of the interparliamentary conference. They also had to bring together the EP and NPs, which until then had not exchanged their views on CFSP/CSDP in the context of the WEU, because members of the EP (MEPs) were not part of the WEU Assembly. Moreover, the establishment of a new conference happened in parallel with the financial crisis, which constrained public budgets and forced the new conference to be cost-effective.

After a well-documented conflict to find a final compromise on questions of delegation sizes, the role of the secretariat and the scope of competences,[45] the Interparliamentary Conference on CFSP/CSDP was finally established in 2012.[46] Its bi-annual sessions have so far shown that the conference is primarily focused on exchanging information among parliamentarians and their interaction with the HR/VP and national executives. Both HR/VPs Ashton and Mogherini have appeared at every single Conference. Moreover, this Conference is seen as strengthening a 'European security culture', creating an awareness among parliamentarians of the added value of European cooperation in this domain.[47] The lack of a permanent secretariat and the establishment of a rotating Council Presidency meant that the EP and NPs now coordinate the agenda setting for each Conference. As a result, the themes covered often reflect the interests of the specific Presidency, while the EP serves as a counterweight emphasizing the EU perspective. Despite the formal exchanges and hearings with the HR/VP, most parliaments have so far never been represented at the Conference by the maximum number of delegates that they were entitled to. Delegations are often composed of bureaucratic staff who often join the MPs on the delegations. Moreover, the fear of some NPs that the Conference would address external relations themes beyond CFSP/CSDP and be dominated by the EP does not seem to have materialized. However, rather than

[45] Jan Wouters and Kolja Raube, 'Towards an Interparliamentary Scrutiny of CSDP' (2012) 47 International Spectator 149; Herranz-Surrallés (n 13).

[46] See further on this interparliamentary conference the chapter by Ian Cooper in this volume.

[47] Jan Wouters and Kolja Raube, 'The Interparliamentary Conference on Common Foreign and Security Policy: A Quest for Democratic Accountability in EU Security Governance' in Nicola Lupo and Cristina Fasone (eds), *Interparliamentary Cooperation in the Composite European Constitution* (Hart Publishing 2015).

strengthening democratic legitimacy in this area of EU external action, the Conference has become a channel of communication between MPs and MEPs. Importantly, this has given rise to further informal channels, whereby the AFET Committee in particular invites national parliamentarians to ad hoc meetings in Brussels. These meetings are normally convened before specific decisions are taken at the EU level, for example the establishment of the EEAS in 2010 or the EU's policy towards the Western Balkans in 2014.

3.2 Trade Policy

3.2.1 European Parliament: A Foot in the Door and Asking for More

Before the Treaty of Lisbon, the role of the EP in the conclusion of EU international agreements was limited.[48] After its entry into force, Article 218 TFEU 'extends the conditions requiring EP consent' to agreements that cover those policy fields in which the ordinary legislative procedure applies.[49] The introduction of the consent procedure for a larger number of international agreements and, more specifically, for trade agreements, brings the EP closer to the heart of EU decision-making.[50] The EP can now veto international trade agreements negotiated by the EU.[51]

Over time, the EP's limited role regarding EU international agreements has been strengthened through arrangements such as the Luns–Westerterp Procedure,[52] the Stuttgart Declaration,[53] and the 2005 and 2010 inter institutional agreements (IIAs) between the EP and the European Commission. The 2005 IIA guaranteed that the EP would be consulted during international treaty negotiations, while it formally continued to lack the right of consent to such agreements. This was seen as insufficient to cure the democratic deficit in trade.[54] That the EP is willing to use its veto in international agreements after the Lisbon Treaty and that it is also willing to veto a concluded agreement was exemplified with its rejection of the SWIFT Agreement on 11 February 2010.[55]

Yet, despite its consent power, the EP still cannot influence the contents of the EU's negotiating mandate. Nevertheless, using the 'shadow of the future', it can pressure the

[48] Piet Eeckhout, *External Relations of the European Union: Legal and Constitutional Foundations* (Oxford University Press 2004) 177.

[49] Stephen Woolcock, *European Union Economic Diplomacy: The Role of the EU in External Relations* (Ashgate 2012) 60.

[50] TFEU, art 207.

[51] Woolcock (n 49); Ariadna Ripoll Servent, 'The Role of the European Parliament in International Negotiations after Lisbon' (2014) 21 JEPP 568.

[52] The procedure introduced in 1964 informally foresaw that the European Commission would keep the EP informed on the ongoing negotiations in the context of international agreements. See Timothy Teasdale and Timothy Bainbridge, *Penguin Companion to the European Union* http://penguincompaniontoeu.com/additional_entries/luns-westerterp-procedure (last accessed 20 June 2016).

[53] According to the Stuttgart Declaration, 'the Opinion of the European Parliament will be sought before ... the conclusions of other significant international agreements by the Community'. Moreover, it foresees that 'the existing procedures for providing the European Parliament with confidential and unofficial information on progress in negotiations will be extended, taking into account the requirements of urgency, to all significant international agreements concluded by the Communities' (see the Solemn Declaration on the European Union, European Council, Stuttgart, 19 June 1983, Bulletin of the European Communities No 6/1983).

[54] Ricardo Passos, 'Mixed Agreements from the Perspective of the European Parliament' in Christophe Hillion and Panos Koutrakos (eds), *Mixed Agreements Revisited: The EU and Its Member States in the World* (Hart Publishing 2010).

[55] Jörg Monar, 'The Rejection of the EU–US Swift Agreement by the European Parliament: A Historic Vote and Its Implications' (2010) 15 EFA Rev 143.

Commission and require information on all stages of the negotiations. To this end, the 2010 IIA was signed between the Commission and the EP, underlining *inter alia* that 'the Commission shall inform Parliament about its intention to propose the start of negotiations at the same time as it informs the Council' and that 'the Commission shall take due account of Parliament's comments throughout the negotiations'.[56] The EP's actions have thus had an essentially twofold purpose: (a) to achieve an institutionally balanced relationship with the Council and the Commission, which has now been partially achieved; and (b) to add a layer of democratic legitimacy to EU external action.[57]

3.2.2 National Parliaments: Asking for a Role in EU Trade Policy-making

In the area of trade policy, an exclusive competence of the EU, NPs are not directly involved. As mentioned by the COSAC report of November 2008, 'national parliaments' influence is limited to scrutiny of their Government's position in the Council'.[58] However, they can get involved in cases of mixed agreements if a range of different conditions are met.[59] As illustrated by the same COSAC Report, NPs are 'usually not involved in the phase when the Council authorizes the Commission to open the necessary negotiations'.[60] Typically, parliaments get involved at a later stage, when mixed agreements undergo 'the standard procedure for parliamentary ratification of international agreements'.[61]

Given the salience and contestation of free trade agreements (FTAs) like the Transatlantic Trade and Investment Partnership (TTIP), several NPs—including the French *Sénat*, the UK House of Lords, the Irish *Oireachtas*, the Croatian *Sabor*, the Portuguese *Assembleia da República*, the Luxembourg *Chambre des Députés*—expressed in a 2014 COSAC report that they were following EU trade negotiations, and specifically TTIP negotiations, with great interest.[62] Twelve parliaments underlined 'that they had developed specific tools or procedures regarding the involvement of parliaments in trade agreement negotiations'.[63] Other expressions of such an 'attitude' are the House of Lords' 'Report on the Transatlantic Trade and Investment Partnership' in May 2014[64] and expert hearings, plenary sessions, and parliamentary questions (*Kleine Anfrage*) by parliamentary groups in the German *Bundestag* in 2014.

The 'ability' of NPs to give consent to EU international agreements was also actively advocated in 2014, when parliaments of the sixteen Member States signed a letter drafted by the Dutch *Tweede Kamer* and sent it to the then EU Trade Commissioner, Karel De Gucht, urging him 'to consider comprehensive trade agreements such as TTIP and CETA as mixed agreements'. Their reason was that these agreements:

> [c]ontain provisions that concern policy areas which are within the competences of the member states. For CETA, as well as TTIP … this is the case for certain elements of policy areas such

[56] Annex III, Points 1 and 3 thereof.

[57] Lore van den Putte, Ferdi de Ville, and Jan Orbie, 'The European Parliament's New Role in Trade Policy: Turning Power into Impact', CEPS Special Reports, May 2014.

[58] COSAC, 10th Bi-annual Report, Paris, 3–4 November 2008, 40.

[59] Passos (n 54); Ivo van der Steen, 'Mixity in Practice: A View from the Netherlands' in Christophe Hillion and Panos Koutrakos (eds), *Mixed Agreements Revisited: The EU and its Member States in the World* (Hart Publishing 2010).

[60] COSAC, 10th Bi-annual Report (n 58) 40.

[61] ibid.

[62] COSAC, 22nd Bi-annual Report, Rome, 30 November–2 December 2014, 29.

[63] ibid.

[64] House of Lords, HL Paper 179, 'The Transatlantic Trade and Investment Partnership', 14th Report of Session 2013–14, 6 May 2014.

as services, transport and investor protection. In the case of a mixed status, all Member States, namely through their national parliaments, have to ratify the agreement. In view of the important role national parliaments have in the democratic decision-making process of the EU, we feel that it is of great importance that trade agreements such as CETA and TTIP are ratified by the national parliaments.[65]

In its response, the Commission stated that it was 'a recurring issue whether FTAs should be concluded by the Union alone, following a decision by the Council further to the consent of the EP, or whether they should be concluded as "mixed" agreements by the Union and the Member States, according to their respective national procedures'.[66] Furthermore, the Commission argued that, during the negotiation rounds and after the signature of the agreement, both the Council and the EP were fully informed about the state of play, so that at the EU level there were 'numerous occasions for national authorities of the Member States to be involved in the negotiation and approval of trade agreements. NPs therefore have several opportunities throughout this process to exercise their oversight over such negotiations'.[67]

Finally, the Commission noted that the nature of the agreement can only be determined at the end of the negotiations and pointed out that the FTA with South Korea had already been concluded as a mixed agreement and ratified accordingly, while other FTAs, such as that with Peru/Colombia, were originally considered by the Commission as non-mixed, while the Council decided to sign it as mixed.[68] On a related note, Commissioner Malmström's current positioning on the matter suggests making negotiations and decision-making on future FTAs, such as TTIP and those with Japan and Vietnam, as transparent and inclusive as possible. This also includes a more informed and decisive role for NPs.[69] Part of her strategy is to engage in dialogues with as many NPs as possible.[70]

Being asked in a questionnaire conducted by COSAC how NPs actually performed on matters like TTIP, twenty-three out of thirty-four parliamentary chambers mentioned that they do establish a 'policy for defining their country's priorities for EU trade and investment negotiations with third countries'.[71] A majority of the responding twenty-eight parliamentary chambers mentioned 'that they had been engaged in recent years in the debate on the impact that the EU trade and investment policy may have on the EU and/or their country'.[72] However, the report also reveals large differences among parliaments on the way they scrutinize the initial negotiation mandate and ongoing negotiations. Only eight parliamentary chambers report to have scrutinized EU trade and investment negotiations by what they referred to as 'the normal scrutiny process'.[73]

[65] *Tweede Kamer*, Letter to Karel De Gucht (the then European Commissioner for Trade), The Hague, 25 June 2016 http://www.ttip2014.eu/files/content/docs/Full%20documents/Letter_to_Mr_De_Gucht_-_role_of_national_parliaments_in_free_trade_agree..._181-238913.pdf (last accessed 20 June 2016).

[66] European Commission, Letter to 17 Presidents and Chairmen of National Parliaments, Brussels, 16 October 2014, C(2014) 7557.

[67] ibid. [68] ibid.

[69] European Commission, Statement by EU Trade Commissioner Cecilia Malmström on the European Parliament's vote on the TTIP resolution, Brussels, 8 July 2015 http://europa.eu/rapid/press-release_STATEMENT-15-5327_en.htm (last accessed 20 June 2016).

[70] European Commission, Speech by EU Trade Commissioner Cecilia Malmström, 'National Parliaments: Vital for Trade and TTIP', Riga, 53rd COSAC Plenary Meeting, 1 June 2015 http://trade.ec.europa.eu/doclib/docs/2015/june/tradoc_153508.pdf (last accessed 20 June 2016).

[71] COSAC, 24th Bi-annual Report, Riga, 31 May–2 June 2015, 51 ff. [72] ibid.

[73] ibid.

The above-mentioned letter underlines the NPs' awareness of and 'attitude' (Huff 2015: 398) towards the strengthening of the democratic dimension of the EU's trade policy. NPs' actions can be explained by their concern to protect the competences of the Member States and enhance the overall democratic legitimacy of EU trade agreements.

3.2.3 Interparliamentary Cooperation: Bringing the Multiple Levels Together?

There is no explicit forum for interparliamentary cooperation in the framework of EU trade policy. It has been suggested that COSAC would be the ideal forum for interparliamentary cooperation in this field.[74] However, trade issues have so far not been extensively discussed in the framework of COSAC. One remarkable exception is the COSAC bi-annual report of November-December 2014, prepared for the COSAC meeting in Rome in November 2014. This report reveals the positive stance of the EP's Committee for International Trade (INTA) towards the 'parliamentarisation' of trade policy at the EU level. However, this Committee also acknowledges the NPs' interest in scrutinizing draft trade agreements and suggests the organization of 'bilateral meetings with parliamentarians interested in trade issues'.[75] Here, the INTA Committee shows not only its recognition of the importance of NPs in EU trade policy, but also its disposition towards interparliamentary cooperation.

In view of the possible engagement of NPs in the case of mixed trade agreements, this further means that the EP is willing to understand trade as a shared parliamentary domain rather than one that the EP should scrutinize on its own. However, questions related to the format and objectives of potential interparliamentary meetings remain open. Moreover, the aforementioned letter to the Commission can be seen as an effort by NPs to assert their independence vis-à-vis the EP. In this regard, it is astonishing that the letter was issued by sixteen NPs rather than by the collective body gathering both MPs and MEPs—COSAC. INTA Committee's proposal also points to an informal coordination effort in the context of EU trade policy. However, it remains to be seen whether NPs and the EP will further formalize their interparliamentary exchanges in this field.

3.3 Human Rights

3.3.1 European Parliament: Human Rights Promotion in a Transversal Policy Field

Human rights can be seen as a transversal policy field because it implies the application of different institutional and procedural arrangements in CFSP/CSDP and because it has close linkages with other segments of EU external action. In this area, the involvement of the EP varies according to the specific policy contexts concerned. With the Treaty of Lisbon, the EP has gained considerable powers in controlling EU external action that is relevant, from a human rights point of view, in the realm of the common commercial policy. As mentioned by Sicurelli, 'by providing the Parliament with the right to approve or reject international agreements and by establishing the High

[74] Passos (n 54) 291. [75] COSAC, 22nd Bi-annual Report (n 62) 29.

Representative ... the treaty has formally increased the access of human rights promoters into trade policy-making'.[76]

The EP has obviously strengthened human rights oversight when it refused to give consent to international agreements, such as the SWIFT Agreement and the Anti-Counterfeiting Trade Agreement (ACTA).[77] In one of its latest resolution drafts, the EP required the Commission 'to step up its efforts towards policy coherence between EU trade, development and environmental policies in all the treaties in ways consistent with international commitments to HR'.[78] Following the EP's Resolution of 25 November 2010,[79] the Commission inserted human rights impact assessments in the negotiations with Georgia, Moldova, Armenia, Tunisia, and Morocco.[80] Recently, in trade negotiations with Vietnam, the EP promoted 'human rights clauses and labour standards'.[81] At the same time, CFSP/CSDP measures regarding human rights policies escape the EP's scrutiny.

The EP oversees the EU's budget and, with it, the EU's financial instruments, including the European Instrument for Democracy and Human Rights (EIDHR). These have enabled the EP to directly impact human rights promotion and decide on the allocation of EU financial resources to these ends. On the EP's instigation, for example, the European Initiative for Democracy and Human Rights was introduced in 1994 as a separate heading in the EU budget. This later evolved into a fully fledged financial instrument and its financial envelope has expanded over the past two decades. Institutionally, the EP scrutinizes EU human rights policy primarily through the DROI Sub-Committee, whose work is complemented by that of the Committee on Civil Liberties, Justice and Home Affairs (LIBE).

Taken together, the EP has been described as 'a champion of human rights and democracy promotion'.[82] Its actions can be best explained by its drive to contribute to the EU's 'normative power'[83] and a coherent, credible, and proactive EU engagement in global human rights advocacy. In other words, despite mixed abilities to control EU human rights policies, the EP has invested its resources in this policy field, demonstrating a positive 'attitude' and institutional resilience.

3.3.2 National Parliaments: Guarantors of Human Rights?

NPs have claimed to be the 'guarantors of human rights'. In this respect, the Council of Europe has listed four functions of NPs as being crucial in the field of human rights: (a) legislating, including the ratification and domestic implementation of human rights and other treaties; (b) approving the budget and setting national policy priorities, thus ensuring the availability and appropriate use of funds for human rights

[76] Daniela Sicurelli, 'The EU as a Promoter of Human Rights in Bilateral Trade Agreements: The Case of the Negotiations with Vietnam' (2015) 11 J Contemp Eur Res 230–45, 235.

[77] Jörg Monar (n 55); Ripoll Servent (n 51).

[78] European Parliament, Committee on International Trade, Draft Report on Implementation of the 2010 Recommendations of Parliament on Social and Environmental Standards, Human Rights and Corporate Responsibility [2015/2038(INI)], 3 February 2016.

[79] European Parliament, Resolution of 25 November 2010 on Human Rights and Social and Environmental Standards in International Trade Agreements [2009/2219(INI)], 25 November 2010.

[80] Sicurelli (n 76) 235.

[81] ibid.

[82] Jan Wouters and others, Study for the European Parliament, DG for External Policies of the Union, 'Enhancing Cooperation between the European Parliament and EU National Parliaments on EU Human Rights Policy', March 2014, 23 http://www.europarl.europa.eu/RegData/etudes/etudes/join/2014/433789/EXPO-DROI_ET(2014)433789_EN.pdf (last accessed 19 July 2016).

[83] Manners (n 12).

protection; (c) overseeing the action of the executive to ensure human rights obligations are complied with; and (d) contributing to the creation of a human rights culture in their respective countries.[84]

The involvement of NPs in the EU's human rights policy depends on the instruments through which this policy is pursued. While the financial instruments of the Union escape the direct influence of NPs, association agreements and CSDP military missions do, at least partly, fall within the competence of NPs. For example, while CSDP military missions primarily serve the EU's security and other external interests, their underlying objective is also often the preservation of human security and human rights enforcement on the ground.

Despite these overarching functions, NPs operate in very different institutional setups.[85] With regard to the internal parliamentary dimension of human rights, the committees that are most involved are those on justice, constitutional affairs, and legal affairs. Moreover, committees for foreign affairs are involved in scrutinizing the external dimension of human rights promotion (eg in Belgium, Denmark, Estonia, Finland, Luxembourg, Malta, the Netherlands, Spain, and Sweden). Furthermore, parliaments have created specialized human rights committees or sub-committees (eg in Austria, Bulgaria, Croatia, Cyprus, the Czech Republic, France, Germany, Greece, Hungary, Ireland, Italy, Latvia, Lithuania, Poland, Portugal, Romania, Slovakia, Slovenia, and the United Kingdom). In practice, NPs in the EU do largely impact human rights policies by means of scrutiny over the human rights policies within their own states as well human rights promotion by the EU.[86] Here, specialized parliamentary committees of inquiry, such as those in Germany, need to be mentioned, because they can investigate executive mismanagement and its impact on human rights.[87] Furthermore, the cooperation between National Human Rights Institutions (NHRI) and NPs is meaningful for informing parliaments on pending human rights questions which can then be picked up by parliamentary scrutiny. In the case of Germany, the *Bundestag* scrutinizes and drafts a resolution on the government's annual report on human rights in Germany, the EU, and the world.[88] Regarding the EU, it is useful to mention that NPs, such as the German *Bundestag*, discuss the EU's Annual Human Rights Report in their respective plenary settings.[89]

3.3.3 Interparliamentary Cooperation: Exchanging Information on Human Rights

As in trade policy, there is no specific forum for interparliamentary cooperation in the field of human rights in the EU. While the Parliamentary Assembly of the Council of Europe (CoE) is indeed occupied with the human rights scrutiny of the CoE Member States and other international actors such as the EU,[90] in the EU context, cooperation

[84] Parliamentary Assembly of the Council of Europe, Committee on Legal Affairs and Human Rights, 'National Parliaments: Guarantors of Human Rights in Europe' (Doc 12636), 6 June 2011, 6.

[85] Wouters and others (n 81). [86] ibid.

[87] *Bundestag*, Committee of Inquiry http://www.bundestag.de/bundestag/ausschuesse18/ua (last accessed 20 June 2016).

[88] *Bundestag, Beschlussempfehlung und Bericht des Ausschusses für Menschenrechte und humanitäre Hilfe (17. Ausschuss), Elfter Bericht der Bundesregierung über ihre Menschenrechtspolitik, Drucksache 18/6183*, 29 September 2015 http://dip21.bundestag.de/dip21/btd/18/061/1806183.pdf (last accessed 26 June 2016).

[89] *Bundestag, Bundestag erörtert EU-Menschenrechtsbericht* https://www.bundestag.de/dokumente/textarchiv/2016/kw07-ak-menschenrechte/405892 (last accessed 20 June 2016).

[90] See eg the Parliamentary Assembly of the Council of Europe.

is carried out within various other institutional formats.[91] From time to time, the EU Speakers Conference and COSAC focus on matters such as the 'role of EU national parliaments and the EP in enhancing democracy and human rights in third countries'[92] and the 'role of the EU in Defending Democracy and Human Rights in the World'.[93] The Speakers Conference concluded that the EU's 'international action should be guided by the principles of democracy, the rule of law, universality and indivisibility of human rights and fundamental freedom' and that 'Parliaments can play an important role in helping build democratic systems and good governance, while they can also prove to be important agents of stability in cases of transition'.[94]

Furthermore, the Conference encouraged NPs and the EP 'to pursue their activities in this domain, including technical assistance, exchange and twinning programmes, the support of human rights and democracy defenders and the adoption of pertinent resolutions and ratification of treaties and conventions'.[95] Similarly, in 2009 COSAC reiterated 'the importance of EU parliaments cooperating with bodies such as the Council of Europe in promoting human rights and democracy in the world'. And more specifically, COSAC 'welcomes the insertion of "human rights and democracy suspension clauses" in treaties the EC agrees with third countries. These clauses are an effective tool allowing for better parliamentary control of human rights and protection of democracy'.[96]

In the framework of CFSP/CSDP, NPs may also table human rights issues as part of interparliamentary cooperation. IPC on CFSP/CSDP has dealt with human rights on a number of occasions and has become a forum 'through which the EU's human rights policies have been scrutinized and contributed to'.[97] This IPC has explicitly addressed human rights policies and their implementation in most of its meetings since 2012 (Cyprus 2012, Vilnius 2013, Rome 2014, Luxembourg 2015, The Hague 2016). Whereas the Cyprus meeting touched upon the effective implementation of the EU's Strategic Framework on Human Rights, the Vilnius meeting addressed human rights with respect to the political situation in the European Neighbourhood.[98] The Rome, Luxembourg, and The Hague meetings focused on further human rights efforts towards 'strengthening the international trend for the abolition of the death penalty', 'a coherent and strict implementation of the EU Common Position on arms exports especially with regard to non-democratic countries', 'the new Action Plan on Human Rights and Democracy for the period 2015–2019', and the 'use [of] every available political and diplomatic opportunity to uphold the respect of human rights as a priority objective of external relations'.[99]

Next to COSAC and the IPC on CFSP/CSDP, human rights issues have also been on the agenda of a number of ad hoc interparliamentary committee meetings. Thus, the DROI Sub-Committee has hosted such meetings since 2007, for example focusing on 'human rights conditionality in development and poverty eradication' (October 2011) and 'internal and external coherence of human rights at the national and EU

[91] Wouters and others (n 82).

[92] Speakers Conference, Presidency Conclusions, Nicosia, 21–23 April 2013.

[93] COSAC, Minutes of the XLI Meeting, Prague, 11–12 May 2009.

[94] Speakers Conference (n 92). [95] ibid.

[96] COSAC, Contribution of the XLI Meeting, Prague, 10–12 May 2009, http://www.cosac.eu/documents/contributions-and-conclusions-of-cosac/ (last accessed 20 June 2016).

[97] Wouters and others (n 82). [98] ibid.

[99] See COSAC Contributions from Rome (2014), Luxembourg (2015), and The Hague (2016), http://www.cosac.eu/documents/contributions-and-conclusions-of-cosac/ (last accessed 20 June 2016).

levels' (September 2013). The analysis also reveals poor attendance across NPs at various interparliamentary meetings. Their absence does not necessarily follow a certain pattern. Rather, parliaments are present or absent from one session to another (only France and Estonia have been absent in all meetings), which speaks about time constraints due to overlapping parliamentary schedules. Furthermore, the multilevel field of interparliamentary cooperation on human rights is led by the EP insofar as it has been able to set the agendas of three out of four interparliamentary committee meetings in the 2009–2013 period.[100] This can be explained by the decentralized system of parliamentary cooperation on human rights.

4. Conclusion: Parliamentary Field Dynamics in EU External Action

In EU external action, the dynamics of the EU's multilevel parliamentary field are mostly visible from the involvement of the EP in policies that have been transferred to the EU level and from that of NPs concerning EU policies decided at the EU or international levels and that need to be ratified and implemented in the domestic legal order. However, these dynamics are also present in the channels of interparliamentary cooperation between the EP and NPs. These three dimensions of parliamentary participation—the EP, NPs, and interparliamentary cooperation—are schematically presented in Table 15.1 for the three fields analyzed in this chapter—CFSP/CSDP, trade, and human rights.

In the previous sections, we have shown that different dynamics are at play in EU external relations, both with regard to the resources and the actual commitment and attitude at all three levels of parliamentary involvement outlined in Table 15.1. In most of the cases observed, the multilevel parliamentary field shows the occurrence of 'Europeanisation' effects,[101] which can be understood as 'parliamentarisation' in the sense of a gradual increase of institutional resources, influence, and activity of parliaments in EU external relations.[102] In the three areas of EU external action examined, the EP and NPs have responded to institutional change, external shocks, and critical junctures by reinforcing their individual and collective scrutiny of EU external relations.

Albeit to varying degrees, this is true for the EP's action in all three areas analyzed. However, we cannot speak of full parliamentarization in the fields of CFSP/CSDP, trade, and human rights, because the EP's input lags behind that of other institutional actors, above all the Commission and the Council. This asymmetry in EU institutional participation in external affairs can be explained by the following factors: (a) the special nature of CFSP/CSDP;[103] (b) the reluctance to treat EU trade policy as any other single market policy; and (c) the mixed and transversal nature of the EU human rights policy.

For their part, not all NPs have stepped onto the path of parliamentarization. One can indeed expect 'substantial cross-national variations within the EU parliamentary field to persist'.[104] Especially in the field of CFSP/CSDP, we detected elements of deparliamentarization in some Member States going hand in hand with parliamentarization in other Member States. This implies a partial vertical asymmetry of the EP vis-à-vis NPs and a horizontal asymmetry across the latter. In the area of trade, we also

[100] Wouters and others (n 82). [101] Crum and Fossum (n 3) 263.
[102] Raube, 'Democratic Accountability' (n 13). [103] Dashwood (n 31).
[104] Crum and Fossum (n 3) 265.

Table 15.1 EU External Action—Parliamentary dynamics

	CFSP/CSDP	Trade Policy	Human Rights
European Parliament	Limited ability, informal institutionalization and assertive, pro-active attitude, partial vertical asymmetry vis-à-vis NPs	Very strong ability after Lisbon, institutionalization and assertive attitude, vertical asymmetry vis-à-vis NPs	Varying abilities, self-proclaimed role and promotional attitude, vertical asymmetry vis-à-vis NPs
National Parliaments	Varying degrees of abilities, (de) parliamentarization, varying assertive attitudes, horizontal asymmetry across NPs	Increasing assertiveness of NPs (mixity), horizontal symmetry	Varying degrees of institutionalization, varying assertive attitudes, horizontal asymmetry across NPs
Interparliamentary Cooperation	IPC on CFSP/CSDP, formal and informal cooperation forums	Potential cooperation, COSAC	Various formal and informal cooperation forums

Source: Own Research

noted a vertical asymmetry of the EP vis-à-vis NPs and a horizontal symmetry across NPs (see Table 15.1). The activities of NPs further depended on the salience and contestation of FTAs. A number of NPs seem willing to use their powers ('ability') to act *ex ante*—in the run-up to the conclusion of such agreements. Regarding human rights, parliaments are able and willing to live up to their label as 'human rights protectors', both in their respective Member States, their Member States' foreign policy, and the EU's internal and external policies. As with trade, in human rights we also observe a vertical asymmetry of the EP vis-à-vis NPs and a horizontal asymmetry across NPs (see Table 15.1). However, the general observation remains valid that parliamentarization can be seen as a converging dynamic, despite differences and diversities across the various areas and levels of EU external action.

This converging dynamic is also noticeable in interparliamentary cooperation. We showed that interparliamentary cooperation can have different forms and functions, ranging from informal arrangements to networks and more specialized and formal forms of cooperation with well-defined functions. This chapter has identified the dynamics of interparliamentary cooperation in the areas of CFSP/CSDP, trade policy, and human rights, demonstrating that cooperation has developed to varying degrees.

Among them, the CFSP/CSDP setting, although still rather new and not yet fully consolidated, can be seen as the most formalized channel of interparliamentary cooperation, because it is based on an institutionalized rotating Conference in which parliamentarians exchange their views and information on a bi-annual basis. The system is accompanied by softer, informal mechanisms of joint committee meetings arranged by the AFET Committee and its SEDE and DROI Sub-Committees. This relatively advanced system of interparliamentary cooperation stems from the EP's strive to gain influence by liaising with NPs where it has limited formal powers. The same holds true for the field of human rights, in which the EP lacks information on how NPs and governments are conducting and implementing policies. In trade policy, although there is no established system of interparliamentary cooperation, NPs have shown their interest in FTAs, especially mixed agreements. This has prompted the INTA Committee to offer cooperation in a domain where the EP has been given substantial new powers after the Lisbon Treaty.

However, these rather positive findings for EU interparliamentary cooperation should be seen in context. Our analysis also emphasized that interparliamentary cooperation does at times lack the support of parliamentarians themselves, who do not regularly attend meetings or do not use the possibility to be represented by larger delegations. Moreover, interparliamentary cooperation in EU external relations currently does not go beyond networking and information exchange, which underlines its still rather informal character.

Despite these shortcomings, which are common 'behavioural' characteristics of parliamentary action both in domestic and international settings, our analysis demonstrates that there is an incremental general trend of parliamentarization in the three policy areas of EU external relations examined. The chapter also shows that the individual activities of the EP and NPs, as 'constitutive units' of the parliamentary field, are complemented by the emergence of interparliamentary cooperation in different areas.

Overall then, while the EP and NPs could be deemed 'resigned' in view of their formal competences in CSDP/CSDP, human rights, and trade, they have been—with variations among parliaments—active in the respective fields and do actually show signs of resilience.

16

EU Law's Grand Scheme on National Parliaments

The Third Yellow Card on Posted Workers and the Way Forward

Davor Jančić

1. One's Resilience is Another's Resignation

This volume has sought to unearth how the Lisbon Treaty and the euro crisis have influenced the development of the European role of national parliaments (NPs). This was viewed from the lens of a dichotomous inquiry of whether these domestic sources of EU democratic legitimacy exhibit resilience or resignation given the economic and financial challenges facing European integration.

The verdict presented by the contributors is split. The prevalent general diagnosis is that NPs have encountered new obstacles for participation in EU decision-making due to constraints imposed to ensure the stability and sustainability of the Member States' fiscal policies, but that they nonetheless remain salient actors within the Union's constitutional construct.

When it comes to the concepts of *European constitutionalism and democratic legitimacy* examined in Part I, NPs are expected to contribute to the good functioning of the EU and to the accountability of EU institutions in order to strengthen the notion of limited government in the Union. Yet with rising popular scepticism and ineffective communication between EU policy-makers and domestic electorates, the locus of politics has partly turned to a more direct involvement of the citizens. This is evident from calls for referenda to be organized on European matters and the spread and influence of social media on the shaping of political attitudes and preferences. While referenda are rightly judged as an inadequate legitimating tool because they do not guarantee an ongoing scrutiny of EU business (Besselink), they may—as the UK's 'Brexit' referendum of 23 June 2016 has shown—incentivize parliamentary engagement in a broader discussion of the benefits of European integration (Smith).

In a similar fashion, the fragmentation of the political sphere caused by what can be seen as the digitalization of politics through social media also offers additional avenues for democratic participation, insofar as many parliamentary chambers, parliamentarians, political parties, and their regional and local branches, committees, and political groups, maintain a strong online presence. This can be illustrated by the fact that the House of Lords EU Committee, one of the most revered and most influential chambers in EU affairs, has recently positively evaluated the effectiveness of its Twitter account.[1] Such strategies have proven to engender new liaisons between public officials

[1] House of Lords, EU Committee, HL Paper 35 'Report on 2015–16', 3rd Report of Session 2016–17 of 28 July 2016, paras 105–109, pp. 26–28.

and the electorate, thereby providing supplementary platforms for an exchange of views on EU matters.

The crisis has furthermore led to the situation in which the Union must 'persuade or coerce' the Member States to achieve its policies. However, the fact that EU institutions remain reliant on the legitimacy supplied by NPs accentuates their 'continued resilience … as repositories of democratic and constitutional legitimacy' (Lindseth). However, whether and how this materializes is neither only a matter of EU law nor only a matter of domestic legislative enactment, but also of constitutional adjudication. Both national courts and the European Court of Justice (ECJ) influence the level of protection of parliamentary prerogatives in EU affairs to a considerable, albeit variable, extent given that both judicial levels are constitutionally designed to provide a check against ultra vires action of EU institutions (Fasone and Lupo). It is indeed the question of conferred powers that should drive the future development of national parliamentary involvement in EU affairs.[2] This would address the democratically problematic fact that the EU's competence has been shaped and interpreted as one seeking to achieve a pre-determined, unquestionably desirable ultimate goal.[3] This goal needs to be opened up for contestation and NPs must be made part of that if they are to contribute to the good functioning of the EU. The nascent but still very limited capacity of NPs to scrutinize non-legislative areas of EU decision-making, such as comitology and open methods of cooperation, further confirms the need for stronger 'institutional incentives for action' (Barrett). While challenged, the constitutional and legitimating roles of NPs have therefore proven resilient.

Concerning the *impact of the financial and sovereign debt crises* on domestic and EU democracy analysed in Part II, the evolution has gone in the direction of extending the Union's executive federalism at the expense of the budgetary autonomy of NPs, which has provoked vocal opposition by the German Federal Constitutional Court (Pernice). The leading role of the European Central Bank in containing the crisis, through conditional loans and unconventional monetary policy, has prompted a self-imposed commitment of its President to account to NPs for its decisions (Jančić). Domestically, the crisis has also benefited legislatures.[4] This took the form of enhanced procedures for the accountability of the government for decisions taken in the European Council and the Council.[5] But although this resulted in 'better information, more frequent hearings and increased parliamentary influence', the overarching problem remains that parliamentarians' main tool for sanctioning the executive is not more than 'political blame' (Fromage). Although a degree of secrecy in the European Council and the Council remains necessary to enable a frank government–parliament dialogue, the limited scope for national parliamentarians to leave a concrete imprint on EU policy-making warrants a bolder reform of the EU settlement to rectify this.

[2] Davor Jančić, 'The Game of Cards: National Parliaments in the EU and the Future of the Early Warning Mechanism and the Political Dialogue' (2015) 52 CML Rev 939, 953.

[3] Gareth Davies, 'Democracy and Legitimacy in the Shadow of Purposive Competence' (2015) 21 ELJ 2.

[4] Davor Jančić, 'National Parliaments and EU Fiscal Integration' (2016) 22 ELJ 225.

[5] See the role of these two EU institutions in this context in Sergio Fabbrini and Uwe Puetter, 'Integration without Supranationalisation: Studying the Lead Roles of the European Council and the Council in Post-Lisbon EU Politics' (2016) 38 J Eur Integration 481; Andrew Glencross, 'The European Council and the Legitimacy Paradox of New Intergovernmentalism: Constitutional Agency Meets Politicisation' (2016) 38 J Eur Integration 497.

Redistributive effects of the euro crisis management have also generated higher levels of politicization than before.[6] Thanks to the salience of parliamentary debates on the approval of EU decisions to establish and utilize financial rescue funds, parliaments' communicative activity has become more pronounced and, rather than concentrating merely on executive control,[7] it has begun focusing more emphatically on upholding the interests of the citizens and of the respective constituencies (Wendler). At the same time, the European Semester process of economic policy coordination constitutes another avenue requiring parliamentary adaptation. The empirics of party politics of compliance with European Semester requirements, which demand domestic pursuit of budgetary and fiscal targets prescribed by the EU, has shown how essential the existence of formal parliamentary powers is for successful political contestation of EU economic governance (Maatsch).

These insights expose the resilience of NPs in adjusting their role to the post-crisis context of reduced fiscal autonomy, while concomitantly suggesting the underlying resignation of both EU and national actors in safeguarding domestic legislative institutions through 'harder' mechanisms. Sensitive Union-wide issues of wealth redistribution, which are the bread-and-butter of electoral bargaining in domestic politics, have been catapulted to the very centre of parliamentary affairs in many a Member State. This requires parliaments to view and understand their national interest in light of the overarching European interest. However, the disparities between the national interests of the Member States are both an advantage and a disadvantage. The advantage is that domestic sensitivities are better articulated and represented, while the disadvantage is that they might be difficult to reconcile, thus stymieing EU progress and fostering a fall-back to populism if strict national blueprints are not followed at the EU level. To avoid this risk, a further Europeanization of NPs is requisite in a more binding fashion than hitherto. The crisis-induced domestication of European politics must hence be counterbalanced by the Europeanization of domestic politics.

Interparliamentary dynamics, studied in Part III, paint a picture of an emerging collective awareness of parliaments of the added value of cooperation in the process of evaluating EU policy and overseeing executive action. In internal EU affairs, both the Lisbon Treaty and the euro crisis have been 'instrumental' to what can be seen as a stratification of parliamentary forums at the EU level (Cooper). This has evolved according to different policy fields (foreign and security policy, economic and financial governance, and justice and home affairs) and according to the level of authority that the various forums enjoy (the Speakers Conference and the Parliamentary Dimension of the EU Presidency). In this respect, the 'green card' initiative—seeking to enable NPs to take part in proposing, amending, or repealing EU legislation—demonstrates that any antagonisms between the European Parliament (EP) and NPs can be harmful for their respective functions and that their shared commitment to the betterment of the lives of EU citizens requires their relations to be transformed into a more overt partnership towards 'power sharing and synergy building' (Borońska-Hryniewiecka).

In external EU affairs, too, the elimination of conflict between the EP and NPs is a lesson that the EU could learn from the manner in which the US and Switzerland

[6] See also on this Katrin Auel and Oliver Höing, 'National Parliaments and the Eurozone Crisis: Taking Ownership in Difficult Times?' (2015) 38 WEP 375.

[7] See, however, that government membership plays an important role in the processes of parliamentary approval of international fiscal aid measures in Hanno Degner and Dirk Leuffen, 'Keynes, Friedman, or Monnet? Explaining Parliamentary Voting Behaviour on Fiscal Aid for Euro Area Member States' (2016) 39 WEP 1139.

have organized their parliamentary safeguards of federalism at their respective State and cantonal levels (Granat). Finally, although asymmetries and variations persist, parliaments mainly exhibit convergence in terms of increased resources and ability to scrutinize the EU's foreign, security, and defence policies, trade policy, and human rights protection (Raube and Wouters). These endeavours, however, continue to take the shape of informal networking, characterized by the absence of entitlement to issue binding pronouncements. These assessments highlight a palpable measure of resilience in interinstitutional relations of parliamentary participation at the EU level.

Put together, the findings of this book point to the conclusion that, while the idea of NPs as carriers of a portion of democratic legitimacy of the EU has been resilient, the means to achieve this were resigned to 'old-style' parliamentary involvement through gradual, evolutionary, and predominantly domestically driven attempts to exact unofficial increments to their existing Treaty portfolio of competences. If this has been the model on which national parliamentary involvement could be built before the crisis, the latter's compelling inroads into national sovereignty makes it obsolete.

A viable answer to a 'revolution' cannot be an 'evolution'; tough times require tough measures. What is required is not only an inward-looking importation and nationalization of 'Europe', but also, and crucially so, the exportation and Europeanization of 'the Member State'. This means that the EU's input legitimacy cannot rest on NPs in a constitutionally significant way if their powers, which are tangibly affected by the crisis, do not acquire a more binding nature. Parliaments' function of identity building and contestation need to be made constitutionally relevant not only at the national level but also at the EU level, lest their resilience be overcome by integrative forces of European integration. These forces need to be politically challenged and appraised in a fundamental manner, which, as the following section outlines, subsidiarity policing does not afford.

2. Grand Schemes With Little Bite: The Third Yellow Card and the False Promise of Subsidiarity

2.1 Reasons for EU Action: Social Dumping Riddance

The principle of subsidiarity,[8] policed through an early warning mechanism, is the key EU-level instrument for NPs to have a say in EU law-making.[9] Parliaments, it transpires, have seriously taken their role to issue reasoned opinions opposing draft EU legislation in non-exclusive areas of competence where this is deemed better achievable at the national level. Following the first yellow card on the proposal for a Council regulation on the right to collective action[10] and the second yellow card on the creation of the European Public Prosecutor's Office,[11] the NPs' last concerted objection

[8] This section builds on the author's presentation given at the European Institute, Leiden Law School on 25 May 2016.

[9] Anna J Cornell and Marco Goldoni (eds), *National and Regional Parliaments in the EU-Legislative Procedure Post-Lisbon: The Impact of the Early Warning Mechanism* (Hart Publishing 2017).

[10] Federico Fabbrini and Katarzyna Granat, '"Yellow Card, but No Foul": The Role of the National Parliaments under the Subsidiarity Protocol and the Commission Proposal for an EU Regulation on the Right to Strike' (2013) 50 CML Rev 115; Ian Cooper, 'A Yellow Card for the Striker: National Parliaments and the Defeat of EU Legislation on the Right to Strike' (2015) 22 JEPP 1406.

[11] Diane Fromage, 'The Second Yellow Card on the EPPO Proposal: An Encouraging Development for Member State Parliaments?' (2016) 35 YEL 5; Irene Wieczorek, 'The EPPO Draft Regulation

was directed at the Commission's proposal to amend the Directive on the Posting of Workers.[12]

Observing the rise in the number of posted workers of close to 45 per cent in the 2010–2014 period in an otherwise small market accounting for no more than 0.7 per cent of total EU employment, the Commission sought to improve the conditions of work for posted workers in the host Member States.[13] The goal is to avoid distortion of the single market and ensure a level playing field, which is jeopardized by growing wage differences between the Member States. This is to be accomplished primarily by imposing the applicability of the same remuneration rules (thus not only the minimum wage but also other types of compensation that may make up a worker's pay such as bonuses) to both posted and local workers and by extending to posted workers and to all economic sectors the rights laid down in universally applicable collective agreements (thus not only in the construction sector). This is aimed at preventing social dumping, whereby posted workers may be 'cheaper' and subject to laxer employment rules, thus causing a downward pressure in the host Member State to lower social and labour law standards.[14] This in turn favours the posting service provider by making it more competitive than the local one, which leads to unfair competition prohibited under EU law. However, the *Viking* and *Laval* cases have shown the readiness of the ECJ to defend the freedom of establishment and the freedom of movement of services in the internal market, while recognizing collective action as a fundamental right.[15]

2.2 Absence of Subsidiarity Appraisal

Strikingly, the proposal only contains one single sentence on subsidiarity compliance: 'An amendment to an existing Directive can only be achieved by adopting a new Directive'. The proposals leading to the first two yellow cards were not comprehensive either, but they at least extended to several paragraphs.

This kind of approach merits a twofold criticism. Firstly, this obviously short statement is more a unilateral dismissal of a duty of justify adherence to subsidiarity than a thorough analysis of all the options available to achieve the goals of the action sought. Secondly, this has nothing to do with subsidiarity whatsoever. Instead of providing a substantive policy analysis of subsidiarity, backed up by comparative data, the Commission takes a purely technical stance based on the form of the legal act at hand. Admittedly, the Commission's Directorate-General for Employment, Social Affairs

Passes the First Subsidiarity Test: An Analysis and Interpretation of the European Commission's Hasty Approach to National Parliaments' Subsidiarity Arguments' (2015) 16 German LJ 1247.

[12] European Commission, Proposal for a Directive of the European Parliament and the Council amending Directive 96/71/EC of the European Parliament and of the Council of 16 December 1996 concerning the posting of workers in the framework of the provision of services, COM(2016) 128 of 8 March 2016.

[13] See detailed background in Marco Rocca, *Posting of Workers and Collective Labour Law: There and Back Again—Between Internal Market and Fundamental Rights* (Intersentia 2015).

[14] See for instance Jan Cremers, Jon E Dølvik, and Gerhard Bosch, 'Posting of Workers in the Single Market: Attempts to Prevent Social Dumping and Regime Competition in the EU' (2007) 38 Industrial Relations J 524.

[15] Case C-438/05, *International Transport Workers' Federation and Finnish Seamen's Union v Viking Line ABP and OÜ Viking Line Eesti*, judgment of 11 December 2007; Case C-341/05, *Laval un Partneri Ltd v Svenska Byggnadsarbetareförbundet and Others*, judgment of 18 December 2007. See an analysis of relevance to NPs in Dorte S Martinsen, *An Ever More Powerful Court? The Political Constraints of Legal Integration in the European Union* (Oxford University Press 2015) ch 6.

and Inclusion did commission an expert study on wage-setting systems and minimum rates of pay, but this did not address the question of subsidiarity in any way.[16]

The Commission thereby failed to meet the requirements foreseen under the Subsidiarity Protocol, which obliges it to produce a detailed statement assessing the financial impact of the proposed action accompanied by qualitative and quantitative indicators that EU action is more efficient and that domestic action is insufficient. The Commission did not fulfil the duty of 'making it possible to appraise compliance with the principles of subsidiarity and proportionality'.[17]

In my view, this provides sufficient ground for any national parliamentary chamber to take the matter before the ECJ for violation of subsidiarity,[18] which to this date remains unused. In a more informal fashion, the failure adequately to consider the principle of subsidiarity is at odds with the 'electoral' vow made by the Commission's President, Jean-Claude Juncker, and its First Vice-President, Frans Timmermans, towards a deeper dialogue with NPs, especially on subsidiarity matters.[19] With this attitude, the Commission jettisoned its own promise to treat yellow cards as red cards. Yet this did not go unnoticed.

2.3 Parliamentary Reasoned Opinions

On 10 May 2016, fourteen parliamentary chambers from eleven Member States flagged the third yellow card against this EU legislative proposal.[20] Apart from Denmark, the other ten parliaments were from Central and Eastern Europe: Bulgaria, Croatia, the Czech Republic (both the Chamber of Deputies and the Senate), Estonia, Hungary, Latvia, Lithuania, Poland (both the *Sejm* and the Senate), Romania (both the Chamber of Deputies and the Senate), and Slovakia. This regional clusterization showcases the ability of parliaments to coalesce around a common interest, which is a corollary of successful cooperation on the previous two yellow cards. Conversely, parliaments in another six Member States submitted positive reactions within the framework of the political dialogue known as the Barroso Initiative: Spain (both the Congress of Deputies and the Senate by means of a joint statement), Italy (both the Chamber of Deputies and the Senate), the Portuguese Assembly, the UK House of Commons, and the French Senate.

A qualitative analysis of the reasoned opinions shows that the key reasons why NPs protested were sevenfold: (a) the lack of subsidiarity justification; (b) the perceived decrease in the competitiveness of lower-wage Member States with negative repercussions for their service providers' access to higher-wage markets; (c) intrusion in domestic collective bargaining schemes; (d) overregulation and legal uncertainty given that the deadline for the transposition of the Posting of Workers Enforcement Directive had

[16] European Commission, 'Study on wage setting systems and minimum rates of pay applicable to posted workers in accordance with Directive 96/71/EC in a selected number of Member States and sectors', January 2016.

[17] See Protocol (No 2) on the application of the principles of subsidiarity and proportionality, art 5.

[18] See Protocol (No 2) on the application of the principles of subsidiarity and proportionality, art 8. See also Carlo Panara, 'The Enforceability of Subsidiarity in the EU and the Ethos of Cooperative Federalism: A Comparative Law Perspective' (2016) 22 EPL 305 and the chapter by Cristina Fasone and Nicola Lupo in this volume.

[19] Jančić (n 2) 967.

[20] Interparliamentary EU Information Exchange (IPEX—an online database documenting NPs' scrutiny activities) http://www.ipex.eu/IPEXL-WEB/dossier/document.do?code=COM&year=2016&number=128&extension=null (last accessed 20 August 2016).

Table 16.1 Reasoned opinions on the Revised Posting of Workers Directive

Grounds	Parliamentary Chamber	No. of chambers
Lack of justification of subsidiarity and added value	Bulgaria, Croatia, the Czech Republic (both the Chamber of Deputies and the Senate), Hungary, Latvia, Lithuania, Polish Sejm, Romania (both the Chamber of Deputies and the Senate), Slovakia	11
Competitiveness decrease	Bulgaria, Croatia, the Czech Chamber of Deputies, Estonia, Hungary, Latvia, Lithuania, the Polish Senate, the Romanian Chamber of Deputies, Slovakia	10
Overregulation and legal certainty	Croatia, the Czech Senate, Estonia, Latvia, Lithuania, the Polish Senate, Romania (both the Chamber of Deputies and the Senate), Slovakia	9
Proportionality and necessity	Bulgaria, the Czech Republic (both the Chamber of Deputies and the Senate), Hungary, Latvia, the Polish Senate, Slovakia	7
Intrusion in collective bargaining	Bulgaria, Croatia, the Czech Senate, Slovakia	4
Legal basis	Romania (both the Chamber of Deputies and the Senate), Slovakia	3
Conferral	Denmark (minority view)	1

Source: own analysis based on the Commission's data[57]

not expired;[21] (e) the principle of proportionality; (f) legal basis; and (g) the principle of conferral. These considerations are presented above in Table 16.1.

The most important insights from the NPs' reasoned opinions are as follows. The most frequent objection put forward by the issuing chambers was of a procedural nature and challenged the lack of subsidiarity analysis and the lack of a wide enough prior consultation.[22] Of the same nature was the criticism that the said Enforcement Directive was still being transposed and that this fell foul of the Commission's Better Regulation agenda, which seeks to increase mutual coherence and quality of EU legislation. Yet this agenda does not foresee any substantial improvement in the relations between the Commission and NPs.[23]

The most important commonality among the reasoned opinions is that, to a certain extent, virtually all chambers carried out a substantive analysis of the proposal. The Latvian *Saeima* expressly noted that the content of the proposal is 'essential in assessing its compliance with the subsidiarity principle'.[24] In relation

[21] Directive 2014/67/EU of the European Parliament and of the Council of 15 May 2014 on the enforcement of Directive 96/71/EC concerning the posting of workers in the framework of the provision of services and amending Regulation (EU) No 1024/2012 on administrative cooperation through the Internal Market Information System ('the IMI Regulation') [2014] OJ L 159/11.

[22] See on the 'proceduralisation' of subsidiarity Xavier Groussot and Sanja Bogojević, 'Subsidiarity as a Procedural Safeguard of Federalism' in Loïc Azoulai (ed), *The Question of Competence in the European Union* (Oxford University Press 2014).

[23] See a critique of this in Davor Jančić, 'The Juncker Commission's Better Regulation Agenda and Its Impact on National Parliaments' in Cristina Fasone, Diane Fromage, and Zoe Lefkofridi (eds), 'Parliaments, Public Opinion and Parliamentary Elections in Europe' (2015) 18 EUI MWP 45.

[24] Latvian *Saeima*, Opinion of the European Affairs Committee of 5 May 2016 http://ec.europa.eu/dgs/secretariat_general/relations/relations_other/npo/docs/latvia/2016/com20160128/com20160128_saeima_opinion_en.pdf (last accessed 20 August 2016).

to this, most parliaments assessed that the equalization of pay regimes applicable to posted and local workers would extinguish the competitive advantage that they enjoy thanks to lower labour costs. Therefore, in their view, the proposal is liable to distort competition and restrict the freedom of movement of services and establishment. Instead, any convergence between the pay levels must be a consequence of economic development and not of EU action. The only exception was the majority view of the Danish *Folketing*, which supported the fight against social dumping, but was concerned that certain inconsistencies between the legal provisions of the existing Directive and those envisaged in the proposal provided insufficient clarity as to the scope of national competence for regulating pay and terms and conditions of employment.

A further important observation is that, as with the first two yellow cards, NPs extended their scrutiny beyond subsidiarity and appraised proportionality, legal basis, as well as conferral.[25] Although explicitly invoked only by a minority of the Danish *Folketing*, this last concern is salient because it pays attention to the existence of EU competence and not only to the way in which the Union exercises it.[26] Members of the Danish Liberal Party, Liberal Alliance, the Social Liberal Party, and the Conservative People's Party argued that:

> [i]t is not within the EU's competence to regulate pay. What is important is thus not whether the provision is in compliance with the subsidiarity principle or not, but *whether the EU has competence to regulate at all.* The minority does not find it necessary to submit a reasoned opinion according to the protocol on subsidiarity, but finds instead that there is reason to submit a *policy statement* to the effect that the competence to regulate is questioned and that an explicit passage to this effect should be included in the current Directive.[27]

This clearly reveals what it is that attracts parliamentary attention and what the genuine target of parliamentary monitoring should be. Indirectly, the division of competences also underlay the Polish *Sejm*'s response. Based on a thorough evaluation of the proposal's substance and the Commission's impact assessment, this chamber made the case that the Commission had violated the principle of sincere cooperation, according to which the Union and the Member States 'shall, in full mutual respect, assist each other in carrying out tasks which flow from the Treaties'.[28] Hence, at hand are only those tasks that fall within the boundaries of the EU constitutional settlement written down in the Treaties, which is a matter of conferral. What belies some of these assertions is the simmering political will for parliaments to engage in real politics. The Czech senators, for instance, suggested policy directions that they deemed appropriate for the Union to take. Charging highly majoritarian institutions with executing a largely technical task of subsidiarity monitoring therefore neglects and undervalues the political and legitimating potential that NPs can proffer to the Union.

[25] See in this respect Eric Miklin, 'Beyond Subsidiarity: The Indirect Effect of the Early Warning System on National Parliamentary Scrutiny in European Union Affairs' JEPP (forthcoming).

[26] See an analysis hereof in Robert Schütze, 'EU Competences: Existence and Exercise' in Anthony Arnull and Damian Chalmers (eds), *Oxford Handbook on European Union Law* (Oxford University Press 2015).

[27] Danish *Folketing*, 'Reasoned Opinion' of 6 May 2016 (emphases added) http://ec.europa.eu/dgs/secretariat_general/relations/relations_other/npo/docs/denmark/2016/com20160128/com20160128_folketing_opinion_en.pdf (last accessed 20 August 2016).

[28] TEU, art 4(3).

2.4 The Commission's Unwavering Response

As with the second yellow card, the Commission issued a formal collective response concluding that it had not infringed subsidiarity, that neither amendment nor withdrawal were required, and that it was maintaining the proposal as it was.[29] This it defended by reference to its Political Guidelines and the 2016 Work Programme, which foresee the legislative amendment proposed.

However, in its reply and on several occasions, the Commission attempted to narrow the scope of assessment that it owes to NPs by interpreting it as encompassing only the comparative efficiency test. It thereby omitted the second element of the subsidiarity test, which refers to domestic sufficiency and requires that evidence be adduced that policy objectives cannot be sufficiently achieved at the national level.[30] In support of this approach, the Commission relied on the latest *Philip Morris* case, where the ECJ held that it had to determine 'whether the EU legislature was entitled to consider, on the basis of a detailed statement, that the objective of the proposed action could be better achieved at EU level'.[31] Yet it is astonishing that the Court should question the EU legislature's right to verify subsidiarity compliance, given that the Subsidiarity Protocol explicitly mandates that 'each institution shall ensure constant respect for the principles of subsidiarity and proportionality'.[32] The Court, moreover, was concerned with the EP's and the Council's relationship with subsidiarity not with that of NPs, whose role in it is constitutionally stronger and more emphatic. This line of reasoning of the Commission is hence unconvincing.

A further pitfall is the Commission's claim that when the EU legislature adopted the 1996 and 2014 Directives the latter had 'already … decided' that the policy goal of facilitating cross-border services provision through a broader level playing field 'was better achieved' at the EU level.[33] The subsidiarity query is, hence, practically an *acte éclairé* in the eyes of the Commission. But this is erroneous because it short-circuits the process whose purpose is to enable NPs to fulfil their Treaty duty of supervising the manner in which the Union uses and executes competence in areas where Member States may act too.

The final 'line of defence' that the Commission invoked was that subsidiarity had been justified in its Impact Assessment Report. However, the relevant passage of this report immediately enables one to discard it as a credible piece of evaluation, because it begins by stating that a regulatory framework for the posting of workers 'can only be established at EU level'.[34] This immediately pre-empts any role for NPs, given that the key question that requires explanation is outright answered in the positive, followed merely by a statement of *what* aims are sought but not *why* these aims can only be achieved through EU action. The European Commissioner for Employment, Social Affairs, Skills and Labour Mobility, Marianne Thyssen, publically admits this: 'We take it for granted that the objectives of the proposed directive on posted workers will

[29] European Commission, Communication to the European Parliament, the Council, and National Parliaments on the proposal for a Directive amending the Posting of Workers Directive, with regard to the principle of subsidiarity, in accordance with Protocol No 2, COM(2016) 505 of 20 July 2016.

[30] See the Commission's remark that its review is 'limited to determining whether the objective of the proposed amending Directive can be better achieved at Union level', thus omitting the second element of the test which refers to domestic sufficiency requiring evidence that policy objective cannot be sufficiently achieved at the national level (at 5).

[31] Case C-547/14, *Philip Morris Brands SARL and Others v the Secretary of State for Health*, judgment of 4 May 2016, para 218. See European Commission (n 29) 6.

[32] See Protocol (No 2) on the application of the principles of subsidiarity and proportionality, art 1.

[33] European Commission (n 29) 7.

[34] ibid 9.

be better accomplished at a European level'.[35] To use the academic vernacular, the Commission could be said to be both the author and the peer reviewer and that does not bode well for EU legitimacy.

A positive evolution, which follows on from the second yellow card, is that the Commission addressed NPs' concerns transcending subsidiarity by means of letters sent to the individual issuing chambers within the Barroso Initiative. This means that subsidiarity is by and large merely a pretext for a more comprehensive cross-border discussion of EU policy-making between the EU's legislative initiator and domestic parliamentarians.

3. Analysis and the Way Forward: A Need for a Rethink of the National Parliaments' Place in the EU

Both the findings of this book and the third yellow card expose the current deficiencies of EU law's 'grand scheme' on NPs. Parliaments' legislative powers have been replaced by a mechanism that steers their members away from politics and into the domain of technocracy, in which the Commission's dominance has proven virtually untouchable. This is complemented by a series of merely informal interparliamentary developments in search of a stronger voice in EU decision-making. The success of both channels, however, is subject to the discretion of EU institutions. This means that resilience in procedural terms has been overshadowed by resignation cast by the impotence of NPs to bring influence directly to bear on EU policies. Despite the Lisbon Treaty and mostly thanks to the euro crisis, domestic parliamentarians remain in limbo: empowered but constrained regarding both the use and effects of their powers. Compensation for the loss of power thus continues to be wanting even after these two events.

Consequently, the potential for democratic legitimation expected of NPs remains underwhelming. The problem is that the peremptory dimension of the early warning mechanism is not only hard to trigger, but, even more importantly, it is primarily a procedural device which is ill-suited to full-blown policy deliberation to which parliaments are excellently tailored. Instead, parliaments are forced to 'smuggle' substantive concerns to the EU level. Only a mechanism that does justice to the nature of parliaments as legislative institutions can provoke polarization and give rise to political conflict that may lead to politicization and, ultimately, democratization. Subsidiarity has therefore failed to bring about a European Union 'in which decisions are taken as openly as possible and as closely as possible to the citizen'.[36]

It should be recalled, however, that EU founding fathers never saw domestic parliamentarians as a stand-alone force in the Union.[37] Even while the latter acted as members of the unelected EP before 1979, this was a provisional solution only. The default position of NPs has rather been that of curtailment. Absenteeism demonstrated in these early stages of European integration discourages permanent involvement of parliamentarians at the EU level, but periodic involvement might be both practically feasible and democratically advantageous.

[35] Cécile Barbière, 'Brussels Prepares to Overrule Eastern Europe on Posted Workers Directive' *EurActiv* (14 July 2016) http://eurac.tv/2TEX (last accessed 21 August 2016).

[36] TEU, art 1(2). For a more optimistic view of subsidiarity monitoring see Özlem Ülgen, 'Strengthening European Union Democratic Accountability Through National and Treaty-based Prelegislative Controls' (2015) 16 German LJ 741.

[37] See the introductory chapter to this volume by Davor Jančić.

At a time of unprecedented economic, fiscal, socio-political, and identity crises,[38] can EU law afford to keep parliaments at bay? If the Union is truly to be brought closer to EU citizens, their languishing on the sidelines of the EU institutional setup is untenable. The multiplication of crises in the EU requires a serious rethinking of the value that NPs have for the democratization of European politics and law-making. If NPs are considered a constitutionally worthy source of democratic legitimacy, they need to be given greater legal prominence through a more far-reaching formalization of their European role. This ought to be done by turning them into platforms that will address issues that match the foundational legitimacy which they are ultimately called upon to provide to the EU. These EU parliamentary platforms, populated by national parliamentarians, should deal with cornerstone questions of future European integration such as European identity, European values, European solidarity, and European powers.[39]

Normative political and public debate which can affect outcomes at the EU level is what can revive the institutional utility of NPs in a changing Europe. Expecting non-expert members of parliament to be savvy about the nitty-gritty of a vast variety of sectoral issues that require specialist knowledge is neither realistic nor desirable. Knowledge accumulation and sharing are indeed important as a basis for discussion, but it is the larger political questions of vision, direction, and method of achieving welfare in the Union that divide the electorate. This is why NPs should be viewed and treated as internal rather than external to the Union.

Before assuming office, Commission President Juncker set out a plan for a new start for Europe, which—apart from jobs, growth, and fairness—focuses on democratic change. 'We must take care of the big issues', he advises, because time is not one for hesitation. This is why, delivering his pre-vote candidacy presentation, he warned the EP that:

> [e]ither we will succeed in bringing our citizens closer to Europe, or we will fail. Either we will succeed in making Europe a political whole that deals with the big issues and leaves the small ones alone, or we will fail. Either we will succeed, hand in hand with the Member States, with their governments, with their parliaments, with the social partners, in reducing the level of unemployment drastically, or we will fail.[40]

Declaratory though they may be, these instructions for developing a 'European Union that is bigger and more ambitious on big things, and smaller and more modest on small things' are implausible if those institutions that are invited to approve the process of European unification are not consulted on those same big issues and if their role in European integration is not constitutionally meaningful, perceptible to their electorates, and truly contributory to the EU's good functioning. The EU cannot function well if its component institutions, including NPs, are not truly integral to its structure.

This new executive dynamism hence needs to encompass parliaments too and they are calling for this themselves. On 30 June 2014, while still President-elect, Juncker

[38] See the determinants of European identity in Theresa Kuhn, *Experiencing European Integration: Transnational Lives and European Identity* (Oxford University Press 2015).

[39] See a programmatic example of this in Declaration 'Greater European Integration: The Way Forward', Rome, 14 September 2015, which was signed by the Presidents of the Italian *Camera dei Deputati*, the French *Assemblée nationale*, the German *Bundestag*, and the Luxembourgish *Chambre des Députés*.

[40] The documents from which this is drawn bundle together Jean-Claude Juncker's political guidelines for the next European Commission, his opening statement to the EP of 15 July 2014, and the main messages from his speech to the EP ahead of the vote on the College in the plenary session of

received a letter signed by twenty-nine chairpersons of the European Affairs Committees of NPs demanding the establishment of a working group composed of both national parliamentarians and representatives of EU institutions in order to examine ways for NPs to engage in EU decision-making beyond subsidiarity and governmental accountability.[41] Since a response was not forthcoming, the House of Commons renewed the call.[42] While the impetus of this initiative has dissipated, it exhibits the parliamentarians' awareness both of the limitations of their current European functions and of the necessity for this to change. A 'red card' procedure, an upgraded version of the 'yellow card' offered to the former UK Prime Minister David Cameron as a concession to try and keep Britain in the EU, was flawed at birth as it merely sought to make the early warning mechanism more efficient. Some commentators rightly note the feebleness of the early warning mechanism and advocate enabling NPs to veto or disapply existing EU legislation by means of a 'collective facultative waiver',[43] or even by an act of an individual parliament.[44]

Yet both of these options are reactionary and negative, as they only allow parliaments to say 'no'. Neither spells a positive, constructive role of parliamentarians that would refocus the mechanism on Juncker's big issues. Most recently, in reaction to the Commission's dismissal of the third yellow card, the Visegrad countries (Poland, the Czech Republic, Hungary, and Slovakia) undertook jointly to discuss avenues for limiting the Commission's autonomy and enhancing national participation in EU affairs.[45] These are all signs of resilience, demonstrating that parliaments actively endeavour to expand their influence and scope of scrutiny within their means in an effort to contribute to the good functioning of the Union. This expansion is presently underway in both substantive and institutional terms.

Firstly, seeking to reinforce the Union's capacity to thwart a rising number of terrorist attacks on EU territory, the 2016 Europol Regulation implements the Lisbon Treaty provisions on the 'political monitoring' of Europol by NPs.[46] A new interparliamentary forum is established under the name of Joint Parliamentary Scrutiny Group (JPSG), composed of members of both NPs and the EP. This body is to scrutinize the law enforcement activities of Europol, which are aimed at combating serious crimes across the Union. However, parliamentary tasks go beyond this and include assessing the 'impact of those activities on the fundamental rights and freedoms of natural persons'.[47] For that purpose, not only shall the Chairperson of Europol's Management Board, the agency's Executive Director or their deputies appear before the JPSG, the European Data Protection Supervisor shall too for a discussion of matters related to data protection. This vindicates the thesis, affirmed in this book (Raube and Wouters), that parliaments merit the epithet of human rights protectors.

22 October 2014. See https://ec.europa.eu/priorities/sites/beta-political/files/juncker-political-guidelines_en.pdf (last accessed 21 August 2016).

[41] Jančić (n 2) 969.

[42] House of Commons, European Scrutiny Committee, HC 342-iii 'Third Report of Session 2015–16' of 23 September 2015, para 4.8, p. 24.

[43] Thorsten Hüller, 'Out of Time? The Democratic Limits of EU Demoicracy' (2016) 23 JEPP 1407.

[44] Damian Chalmers, 'Democratic Self-government in Europe: Domestic Solutions to the EU Legitimacy Crisis', Policy Network Paper, May 2013, 3.

[45] Aleksandra Eriksson, 'EU Failed to Learn Lesson from Brexit, Poland Says' *EUobserver*, 22 July 2016 https://euobserver.com/economic/134458 (last accessed 21 August 2016).

[46] TEU, art 12(c) and TFEU, art 88(2).

[47] See art 51(2) of Regulation (EU) No 2016/794 of the European Parliament and of the Council of 11 May 2016 on the European Union Agency for Law Enforcement Cooperation (Europol) and

The importance of the human rights dimension of national parliamentary work also resonates within the Council of Europe.[48]

Secondly, NPs have also expressed concern over the state of the rule of law in the Union and the tensions between the Commission on the one hand, and the governments in Poland (led by Prime Minister Beata Szydło of the Law and Justice Party) and Hungary (led by Prime Minister Viktor Orbán of the Fidesz Party) on the other.[49] The reason why parliaments are competent to act in this context is because they are the Union's 'enabling' institutions.[50] This is conveniently encapsulated by this passage:

> [t]he Union derives its legitimacy not from being a continent-wide democracy … rather, it can claim legitimacy, because national parliaments have freely voted to bind themselves and follow European rules—and, most importantly, they have freely established certain sanctions for those not following said rules, with Article 7 Treaty on European Union (TEU) being the clearest example.[51]

Thirdly, the aspirations of NPs extend beyond the boundaries of the Union, which is visible from their increasing interest in parliamentary diplomacy,[52] as well as their strong insistence on being granted the right to approve mega-regional EU international agreements, notably the Transatlantic Trade and Investment Partnership (TTIP) with the US and the Comprehensive Economic and Trade Agreement (CETA) with Canada.[53]

In conclusion, it has rightly been argued that the EU's legitimacy is 'limping' and that 'a more fundamental remedy would be to buy in legitimacy from national parliaments'.[54] The spiralling multiplication of crises in the Union—spanning at least the euro, terrorism, refugees, the rule of law, and tax evasion—push NPs deeper into the realm of emergency EU policy-making. This invites two responses: on the one side, a swift response, to which executive institutions are attuned; and on the other, a reflection on the longer-term policy routes to be paved for the future, where parliaments can significantly contribute. Constraints concerning the parliamentarians' lack of time and low level of interest in EU affairs are well known.[55]

replacing and repealing Council Decisions 2009/371/JHA, 2009/934/JHA, 2009/935/JHA, 2009/936/JHA, and 2009/968/JHA [2016] OJ L 135/53.

[48] Parliamentary Assembly of the Council of Europe, Committee on Legal Affairs and Human Rights, Report 'National Parliaments: Guarantors of Human Rights in Europe', Doc 12636 of 6 June 2011.

[49] COSAC, 25th Bi-annual Report, 18 May 2016 (55th Meeting, The Hague, 12–14 June 2016) ch 2.

[50] See the EP's proactive role in the rule of law debate in Judith Sargentini and Aleksejs Dimitrovs, 'The European Parliament's Role: Towards New Copenhagen Criteria for Existing Member States?' in Dimitry Kochenov, Amichai Magen, and Laurent Pech (eds), 'Symposium: The Great Rule of Law Debate in the EU' (2016) 54 JCMS 1085.

[51] Jan-Werner Müller, 'Should the EU Protect Democracy and the Rule of Law Inside Member States?' (2015) 21 ELJ 141, 144.

[52] ibid. See more on this in Stelios Stavridis and Davor Jančić (eds), Special Issue 'Parliamentary Diplomacy Uncovered: European and Global Perspectives' (2016) 11 Hague J Dipl 105.

[53] Davor Jančić, 'TTIP and Legislative-executive Relations in EU Trade Policy' (2017) 40 WEP 202; Davor Jančić, 'EU-Canada Strategic Partnership, CETA and the Role of Parliaments in Foreign and Trade Policy', Paper presented at the PACO Conference on 'Parliamentary Cooperation and Diplomacy in Europe and Beyond: Theories, Practices and Comparisons', Brussels, 18–19 February 2016.

[54] Carol Harlow, 'The Limping Legitimacy of EU Lawmaking: A Barrier to Integration' (2016) 1 Eur Papers 29, 53.

[55] See analyses in Mads Dagnis Jensen and Dorte Martinsen, 'Out of Time? National Parliaments and Early Decision-making in the European Union' (2015) 50 Government and Opposition 240;

But the euro crisis and other pressing challenges have raised the stakes: the Union is increasingly making law and policy on core issues of national sovereignty. This may alter the political resignation of some parliamentarians and galvanize them into action. Similarly, while the citizens' trust in NPs may even be slightly lower than their trust in EU institutions,[56] the 'Brexit' referendum has shown that the institution of Parliament does stand for democratic participation, self-rule, and identity formation. Therein lie opportunities for reforming the European prerogatives of NPs. Upgrading the status of interparliamentary cooperation seems the most expedient and most widely acceptable way to achieve this.

Merging the many parliamentary forums operating in parallel at the EU level into a single body could be one model. This body would have working groups organized according to a given policy field and, in the first period, it would exercise a formal consultative role similar to that of the Committee of the Regions. Another model would be that of a parliamentary 'Council of Elders', which would periodically meet to give broad-brush but binding recommendations on the core problems of European integration in the form of 'action plans'. These would address the principle of conferral and the management of crises. This book has merely begun disentangling the ideas and practices that inform this kind of exploration, which is bound to remain in the spotlight of EU policy-makers for years to come.

Katjana Gattermann and Claudia Hefftler, 'Beyond Institutional Capacity: Political Motivation and Parliamentary Behaviour in the Early Warning System' (2015) 38 WEP 305.

[56] Some 33% of Europeans claim to trust the EU, while only 28% of them trust their national parliament and 27% their national government. Standard Eurobarometer 85, 'Public Opinion in the European Union—First Results', July 2016, 14. See further Daniela Braun and Markus Tausendpfund, 'The Impact of the Euro Crisis on Citizens' Support for the European Union' (2014) 36 J Eur Integration 231.

[57] Data extracted from http://ec.europa.eu/dgs/secretariat_general/relations/relations_other/npo/index_en.htm (last accessed 20 August 2016).

Index

Note: please see under the main headings for entries relating to particular countries
NPs = National Parliaments